HOW THE SWANS CAME TO THE LAKE

HOW THE SWANS CAME TO THE LAKE

A NARRATIVE HISTORY OF BUDDHISM IN AMERICA

Third Edition, Revised and Updated

Rick Fields

SHAMBHALA
BOSTON & LONDON
1992

Shambhala Publications, Inc.
Horticultural Hall
300 Massachusetts Avenue
Boston, Massachusetts 02115
http://www.shambhala.com

9 8 7 6 5 4

Printed in the United States of America
♾ This edition is printed on acid-free paper that meets the American National Standards Institute Z39.48 Standard.
Distributed in the United States by Random House, Inc., and in Canada by Random House of Canada Ltd

Library of Congress Cataloging-in-Publication Data
Fields, Rick.
How the swans came to the lake: a narrative history of Buddhism in America / Rick Fields.—3rd ed., updated.
p. cm.
Includes bibliographical references and index.
ISBN 0-87773-631-6 (pbk.)
1. Buddhism—United States—History. I. Title.
BQ732.F52 1992 90-53681
294.3'0973—dc20 CIP

CONTENTS

ILLUSTRATIONS

Gary Snyder, Berkeley, Summer 1955 (*Photograph by Allen Ginsberg, courtesy of the Ginsberg Archives*)

Jack Kerouac, 1957 (*Photograph by William Eichel for* Mademoiselle)

Philip Whalen and Allen Ginsberg, San Francisco, August 1971 (*Photograph by Gordan Ball, courtesy of the Ginsberg Archives*)

Shunryu Suzuki-roshi

Hakuun Yasutani-roshi (*Courtesy of the Zen Center of Los Angeles*)

Philip Kapleau-roshi (*Photograph by Casey Frank*)

Joshu Sasaki-roshi

Eido Shimano-roshi (*Photograph by Peggy Crawford*)

Gyoun Aitken-roshi (*Courtesy of the Zen Center of Los Angeles*)

Zentatsu Baker-roshi (*Courtesy of the San Francisco Zen Center*)

Jakusho Kwong-sensei (*Photograph by Vikki Kinmont*)

Kobun Chino-sensei (*Photograph courtesy of Ellen Richter*)

Katagiri-roshi

Taizan Maezumi-roshi and his two senior disciples, Bernard Tetsugen Glassman-sensei (on roshi's left) and Dennis Genpo Merzel-sensei (*Photograph courtesy of the Zen Center of Los Angeles*)

BETWEEN PAGES 338-339:

His Holiness the Dalai Lama

The Translator and the Editor: Lama Kazi Dawa-Samdup and W.Y. Evans-Wentz taken in Gangtok, Sikkim, 1919 (*Photograph reproduced from* The Tibetan Book of the Dead, *compiled and edited by W.Y. Evans-Wentz, courtesy of Oxford University Press*)

Geshe Wangyal

Thomas Merton, early 1960s, at Abbey of Gethsemani (*Courtesy of the Abbey of Gethsemani Archives*)

Tarthang Tulku (*Photograph courtesy of the* San Francisco Chronicle)

His Holiness Dudjom Rinpoche

Joseph Goldstein and Jack Kornfield, Barre, Mass., July 1981 (© *Lionel J-M. Delevingne 1981*)

Anagarika Munindra, Barre, Mass., July 1981 (© *Lionel J-M. Delevingne 1981*)

His Holiness the Gyalwa Karmapa (*Photograph by Peter Barry Chowka*)

Kalu Rinpoche (*Photograph by Emily Wasserman*)

His Holiness Dilgo Khyentse Rinpoche and Chögyam Trungpa, Rinpoche (*Photograph by Blair Hansen*)

Tripitaka Master Hsuan Hua (*Photograph courtesy of Gold Mountain Monastery*)

Soen-sa-nim [Seung Sahn] (*Photograph courtesy of the Providence Zen Center*)

Ku San Sunim, Los Angeles, 1981 (*Photograph by Sarah Sadowsky*)

D.T. Suzuki (*Photograph by Boris Erwitt*)

Alan Watts (*Photograph by Pirkle Jones*)

The Venerable Thich Thien-an (*Photograph by Don Farber*)

CREDITS

Various excerpts: *The Asian Journal* of Thomas Merton. Copyright 1968, 1970, 1973 by the Trustees of the Merton Legacy Trust. Reprinted by permission of New Directions.

A selection from *The Dharma Bums* by Jack Kerouac. Copyright 1958 by Jack Kerouac. Reprinted by permission of Viking Penguin, Inc.

Excerpts from *The Eastern Buddhist*, New Series, Vol. II, No. 1, August 1967. Copyright The Eastern Buddhist Society, Tokyo, Japan.

Selection from *Dropping Ashes on the Buddha* by Zen Master Seung Sahn. Compiled and edited by Stephen Mitchell. Copyright 1976 Providence Zen Center and Grove Press.

Gary Snyder: Poem, "He blazed out the new path for all of us. . . ." Reprinted by permission of the author.

Selections from *Like A Dream, Like A Fantasy: The Zen Writings and Translations of Nyogen Senzaki*. Edited and With an Introduction by Eido Shimano Roshi. Copyright 1978 in Japan by the Zen Studies Society Inc.

Selections from *Namu Dai Bosa: A Transmission of Zen Buddhism to America* by Nyogen Senzaki, Soen Nakagawa and Eido Shimano. Edited by Louis Nordstrom. Copyright 1976 by The Zen Studies Society, Inc. Published in the Bhaisajaguru Series by Theatre Arts Books, New York, and used with permission of the publisher.

Excerpts from Gary Snyder, *The Real Work: Interviews and Talks 1964–1979*. Copyright 1969, 1972, 1974, 1978, 1979, 1980 by Gary Snyder. Reprinted by permission of New Directions.

Excerpt from *The Tibetan Book of the Dead or the After-Death Experiences on the Bardo Plane according to Lama Dawa-Samdup's English Rendering* by W.Y. Evans-Wentz. Copyright 1960 by W.Y. Evans-Wentz. Reprinted by permission of Oxford University Press, Inc.

Selections from *Three Steps, One Bow* by Bhikshu Heng Ju and Bhikshu Heng Yo. Copyright 1977 by The Buddhist Text Translation Society. Reprinted by permission of the publisher.

Excerpt from *Beat Zen, Square Zen, and Zen* by Alan Watts. Copyright 1959 by City Lights Books.

Selections from *Zen Notes*, Mary Farkas, editor. Copyright by the First Zen Institute of America, Inc. By permission of the publisher.

Selections from *Wind Bell*. Copyright by Zen Center, San Francisco. By permission of the publisher.

TO AL AND REVA, MY PARENTS,
FOR THEIR LOVE, PATIENCE AND SENSE OF HUMOR.

2,500 years after I have passed away into Nirvana, the Highest Doctrine will become spread in the country of the red-faced people.

—Shakyamuni Buddha to the goddess Vimala,
as given in Bu-ston's *History of Buddhism*

. . . there is an orientalism in the most restless pioneer, and the farthest west is but the farthest east.

—Henry David Thoreau,
A Week on the Concord and Merrimack Rivers

The Karmapa told an interviewer this week that he came to the United States because the teachings of the Lord Buddha had preceded him. "If there is a lake, the swans would go there," he said, speaking through an interpreter.

—The Boston Globe, Dec. 10, 1976

AUTHOR'S NOTE

During the five years spent researching and writing this book, I have often found myself feeling, like Fitzgerald's Gatsby, "borne back ceaselessly into the past," as what had begun as a short introductory chapter to a book about American Buddhism grew, seemingly against all my efforts, into a full-length examination of the history of American Buddhism.

The World Parliament of Religions, which took place in Chicago in 1893, is usually considered the beginning of the introduction of Buddhism—and Eastern religion in general—to America. But the Parliament could also, I found, just as easily be seen as the culmination of a movement that had begun much earlier. Arthur Christy's 1932 study, *The Orient in American Transcendentalism*, opened my eyes to the extent that Emerson and Thoreau had been moved and informed by the East. Thoreau's enthusiastic raptures over the work of Sir William Jones, whom I had never heard of, drew me to the pioneer orientalists of the British Raj, and when I held the original folio volumes of Jones's *Asiatick Researches* in my hands, I felt myself carried even further back. Finally I dug in at the point from which Buddhist historians have traditionally begun—with the life of Siddhartha Gautama, the Buddha of our time.

Buddhist history is the record of lineage—of who gave what to whom—not as dead doctrine but as living truth; it is more a matter of the freshly baked bread than of the recipe. Though lineage is chronological and linear, or seems to be, and the story has gone on for twenty-five hundred years, Buddhism insists on the primacy of the present. Zen masters sometimes talk about locking eyebrows with the ancient patriarchs, and it is in this sense that history—or at least Buddhist history—is never out of date.

Professor Nagatomi of the Harvard-Yenching Institute was possibly right when he told me at the beginning of this journey that there were not yet enough documents (I suspect he meant that not enough time had passed) to tell what shape American Buddhism will or has taken. Scholars like to point out that it has usually taken at least three hundred years for Buddhism to become fully at home in a new land. But time seems to have accelerated in our technological age, and news travels fast. Perhaps we cannot yet talk of an American Buddhism in the same way that we might talk about, say, Chinese or Tibetan Buddhism, and yet we can certainly talk about an American Buddhist lineage—one that is woven of lineages from all over the Buddhist world, as well as from certain strands that are characteristically American. This is the lineage I have attempted to trace.

ACKNOWLEDGMENTS

My research has taken me to libraries and archives across the country. It has also taken me to many American Buddhist centers and communities—particularly those that represent the contemplative or meditation tradition of Buddhism. This book, then, is the result of many people's efforts and interests, those of the past, who committed themselves to paper, and those of the present who answered my often clumsy questions cheerfully, on the spot, as well as those who allowed me to sit quietly with them. It is a book that expresses, I hope, the richness and diversity of the new American sangha—the community of practitioners—and what may be of value in it comes from those who have been brave and foolhardy enough to set out on the same journey that Shakyamuni began when he left his palace twenty-five hundred years ago.

For the particular shape and emphasis of the narrative, however, and for the inevitable errors and distortions which may have crept in, the author must take full responsibility.

I would like to offer, then, my deepest gratitude and acknowledgment to all those who gave so much of their time and energy to help bring this project to completion.

Specifically to: Professor Nagatomi, who warned me; and Chogyam Trungpa, Rinpoche, who told me to go ahead; to Bill Stracahan, who got it started; Stewart Brand, who commissioned "Beginning Buddhism," my first writing on the subject for the first issue of *CoEvolution Quarterly*; and Sara Vogeler, for early love and enthusiasm.

To all the dharma teachers who made time in their demanding schedules for interviews: Robert Aitken-roshi, Zentatsu Baker-roshi, Deshung Rinpoche, Dhiravamsa, H.H. Dudjom Rinpoche, Dennis Genpo-sensei, Joseph Goldstein, Philip Kapleau-roshi, Katagiri-roshi, Sonam Kazi, Jack Kornfield, Jakusho Kwong-roshi, Taizan Maezumi-roshi, Anagarika Munindra, Rev. Nakajima, Mahathera Piyananda, H.H. Sakya Tridzin,

Ku San Sunim, Joshu Sasaki-roshi, Mahasi Sayadaw, Rev. Seki, Eido Shimano-roshi, Soen-sa-nim, Osel Tendzin, Bernard Tetsugen-sensei, the late Dr. Thich Thien-an, Chogyam Trungpa, Rinpoche, and Geshe Wangyal. Without their generosity this book could never have been written.

To the staff and librarians of the New York Public Library, particularly the Frederick Lewis Allen Room (and my fellow writers there) and especially Mr. Francis W. Paar of the Oriental Department, who brought me three books for every one I asked for; Richard Gard and Hannah Robinson of the Institute for the Advanced Study of World Religions at Stony Brook; the staff of the Athenaeum, Boston, where I first came across *The Buddhist Ray*; the Houghton Library; the Massachusetts Historical Society Library; the Paul Carus collection of the Morris Library/Special Collections at the University of Southern Illinois, Carbondale; Rita Bottoms of the Special Collections, University of California, Santa Cruz; the Oriental Library at UC Berkeley, where Professor Lewis Lancaster allowed me to lose myself in Nyogen Senzaki's papers; the California Historical Society Library; the Philosophical Research Library in Los Angeles; the Huntington Hartford Library; the Japanese-American Research Projects Archives at UCLA; and the libraries of The First Zen Institute of New York, The Zen Studies Society, Naropa Institute, San Francisco Zen Center and especially the Zen Center of Los Angeles.

To Gary Snyder, who read early portions of the MS, made his library at Kitkitizzie available, and showed, by example, how to work without being "nickel and dimed to death;" Mary Farkas, American Zen historian emerita, who gave invaluable advice and generously allowed the use of material gathered over twenty-five years of *Zen Notes;* Robert Aitken who provided inspiration to keep going by his openness in sharing his long experience on the path; and Maezumi-roshi, who provided a place to work and practice at the Zen Center of Los Angeles.

For interviews and conversations that added greatly to the narrative: Albert Saijo, Philip Whalen, Allen Ginsberg, Rev. Boris Erwitt, Bob Jackson of the Marysville Buddhist Church, Sarah Harding, Richard Gard, Charlotte Joko Beck, C.T. Shen, Robert Thurman, Brian Cutillo, Harold Talbott, Lobsang Lhalungpa, Gary Snyder, Elsie Mitchell, David Farrelly, Stephen Mitchell, Joanne Kyger, Dr. Holmes Welch, Ellen Conant, George Bowman, David Chadwick, Dr. James Green, Jane Warner, David Schneider, Keith Scherr.

To Lou Nordstrom, Robert Thurman, and Ed Leites, who provided the opportunity at conferences they organized for the presentation of the work-in-progress.

To John Steinbeck IV, who came up with the title one night in Le Bar, Boulderado Hotel, and who read portions of the proofs; John Giorno, who said "the book is finished," before I thought it could be; Peggy Taylor, Eric Utne and Sandy MacDonald of *New Age*, who published early takes; Karl Ray; Eric Lerner, who edited, published and encouraged the work-in-progress in *Zero*; Andy Taido Cooper, who edited and published portions in *Ten Directions*; Eve Wallace who began typing the first version from a sea of notes, and Denmark Groover, who continued; Elsa First who listened to it all before it got down on paper—as did Caron Smith, Jeffrey Steingarten, Terry Clifford, Jean Ransick, George and Susan Quasha and Chuck Stein; and John Daishin Buksbazen, beyond the call of duty.

To the Greens, for refuge at the end—Ellen Green for doubleproofing and typing, and Jonathan Green for last minute library work; and Wendy Lou Egyoku Nakao who researched, bibliographed, kept me going, typed and gave special assistance on Japanese American Hawaiian history.

To all those who gave shelter and support and aid in ways too numerous to mention: Sidney Goldfarb and Peter Warshall, over the long distance; Paul and Sachiko Williams for crosscultural inspiration; Jim Nolmann, Aram Saroyan, Carole Gale, Don Farber, Barbara Meier and John Barkin, Ilka Hartmann, Jose Arguelles, Mark Barasch, Peter Kakuzan Gregory, Marty Nakell, Josefina Gordh, Joanna and Dr. Fred Bogin, Sara Hammond, Elizabeth Tuomy, Phoebe MacAdams, Lewis MacAdams, Buzz Erikson, Peter Barry Chowka, Barbara Stewart, John Welwood, Bobbie Louise Hawkins, Katy Butler, Steven Levine, Bill LaFleur, Michael Attie, Steve and Holly Baer, Tim Buckley, Rudy Wurlitzer, Lawrence Shainberg, the late Joel Wiley, Roger Ricco, Allen and Roberta Ehrlich, Ann Buchanan, Barry Miles, Nancy Bacal, Rita Cooper, Bob Rosenthal, Stanley Weiser, Ethel Himmelstein, Laura and Bob Jawitz, Jed and Susie Rasula, Bob Del Tredici, Brother Patrick Hart.

For special financial and moral support: Eric Weiss and Stu and Sonia Sapadin of W.J. Stuart Management Consultants; PEN; Gary Dainin Galsworthy and Leslie Jokaku Daniels, Zen plumbers; Su Il, and Jun Soon Kim.

To the Shambhala Publications staff, especially Sam Bercholz, who waited; Larry Mermelstein, who cut with accuracy, kept an eye on the details, and also kept his sense of humor; Bea Ferrigno-Lee, for weekend doubleproofing; and Julia Runk, who designed and got it out.

Finally this book could not have been finished without the dedicated assistance of Mary Goodell, typist, editor, friend, and amanuensis extraordinaire; and the solitude, just at the right time, of an artist-in-residence fellowship provided by the Briarcombe Foundation, and its director, Kate Marsh.

EDITOR'S NOTE

Chapter 15 of this third edition of *How the Swans Came to the Lake* has been supplemented with new information on Vietnamese Buddhism in America, and a new chapter 16, which consists of entirely new material, has been added.

ATTENTION: PREFACE TO THE ASSEMBLY

The sesshin began like every other *sesshin*—with the deep hollow sound of the bell—and it continued for seven days like every other sesshin, with alternating periods of sitting and walking, eating formally in the zendo, working for short periods at manual labor, *sanzen* with the roshi, and a few hours of sleep. But instead of one roshi, like most sesshins, this one had more than twenty roshis and dharma teachers in attendance.

Concluding on July 4, 1976, this session has been held to mark the opening of Dai Bosatsu, the first traditional Japanese-style Zen monastery in America. Richard Baker-roshi had come from San Francisco for the opening ceremony, Sasaki-roshi and Maezumi-roshi from Los Angeles, Takeda-roshi from Mexico City, and Philip Kapleau-roshi from Rochester. Seung Sahn, not a Japanese or American Zen master, but a Korean Zen master, had come up from Providence, and then there was a large contingent of visiting roshis from Japan. There was even a Tibetan, who had incorporated certain aspects of Zen into his teaching, Chogyam

Trungpa, Rinpoche, the Eleventh Trungpa Tulku, not wearing his best robes like the roshis, but a dark suit of English cut.

The monastery had cost its principal donor more than three million dollars and was modeled on an ancient monastery in Japan that was now a National Treasure. A contingent of Shinto priests wearing pointed wizard hats chanted and made offerings, and somebody rang the big, brass bell on the hill for the first time, with a log wrapped in red, white, and blue bunting for the occasion. There was a speech in Japanese and then Baker-roshi said a very few words in English, and Eido-roshi mentioned someone who should have been there, but wasn't. Though he didn't use his name nearly everyone there knew he meant Nakagawa Soen-roshi, who was considered eccentric even for a Zen master and who always did what he pleased without worrying about social niceties. Soen-roshi was one of the pioneer Zen masters; his dharma connections through his close friend Nyogen Senzaki went way back to the first Zen master to come to America, Soyen Shaku, who had spoken at the World Parliament of Religion in Chicago in 1893, giving a speech *his* student, D.T. Suzuki, had translated for him in Japan. In any case, Nakagawa Soen-roshi was perhaps all the more present by his absence.

The ceremony was broken by thunderstorms, and went on into the night around a raging bonfire where the water of wisdom, otherwise known as saké, flowed freely. Meanwhile, in New York City, a fleet of schooners sailed up the East River to celebrate the Bicentennial, and Dudjom Rinpoche, the head of the Nyingma School of Tibetan Buddhism, who had just arrived in the country, addressed the FM radio audience on a WBAI program, *In the Spirit*, that claimed more than 78,900 listeners, while another wing of Buddhism, the Sokagakkai, two thousand strong, paraded down Fifth Avenue with their marching band. Nobody was sure what all this Buddhist activity meant on the Fourth of July Bicentennial, a mere two hundred years after the United States of America had been founded, but it was clear to all the buddhas, bodhisattvas, arhats, lay people, and Japanese tourists who had gathered together to inaugurate Dai Bosatsu Zendo in the Catskills that this was only the beginning.

BOOK ONE

CHAPTER ONE

TURNING THE WHEEL

I

Siddhartha Gautama was born around 567 B.C., in a small kingdom just below the Himalayan foothills. His father was a chief of the Shakya clan. It is said that twelve years before his birth the brahmins prophesied that he would become either a universal monarch or a great sage. To prevent him from becoming an ascetic, his father kept him within the confines of the palace. Gautama grew up in princely luxury, shielded from the outside world, entertained by dancing girls, instructed by Brahmins, and trained in archery, swordsmanship, wrestling, swimming and running. When he came of age he married Gopa, who gave birth to a son. He had, as we might say today, everything.

And yet, it was not enough. Something—something as persistent as his own shadow—drew him into the world beyond the castle walls. There, in the streets of Kapilavastu, he encountered three simple things: a sick man, an old man, and a corpse being carried to the burning grounds. Nothing in his life of ease had prepared him for this experience, and when his charioteer told him that all beings are subject to sickness, old age, and death, he could not rest. As he returned to the palace, he passed a wandering ascetic walking peacefully along the road, wearing the robe and carrying the single bowl of a sadhu, and he resolved to leave the palace in search of the answer to the problem of suffering. He bade his wife and child a silent farewell without waking them, rode to the edge of the forest where he cut his long hair with his sword and exchanged his fine clothes for the simple robes of an ascetic.

With these actions Siddhartha Gautama joined a whole class of men who had dropped out of Indian society to find liberation. As long as anyone could remember there had always been wandering rishis, homeless wanderers devoted to meditation, yoga, and ascetic practices. But during the time of Shakyamuni, with India torn by wars between rival kingdoms, and the rites and rules of the brahmin priests suddenly open to question, the number of seekers had increased. There were a variety of methods and teachers, and Gautama investigated many—atheists, materialists, idealists and dialecticians. The deep forest and the teeming marketplace were alive with the sounds of thousands of arguments and opinions, and in this it was a time not unlike our own.

Gautama finally settled down to work with two teachers. From Arada Kalama, who had three hundred disciples, he learned how to discipline his mind to enter the sphere of nothingness; but even though Arada Kalama asked him to remain and teach as an equal, he recognized that this was not liberation, and left. Next Siddhartha learned how to enter the concentration of mind which is neither consciousness nor unconsciousness from Udraka Ramaputra, who had seven hundred students, and who also asked Siddartha to teach with him. But neither was this liberation and Siddhartha left his second teacher.

For six years Siddhartha along with five companions practiced austerities and concentration. He drove himself mercilessly, eating only a single grain of rice a day, pitting mind against body. His ribs stuck through his wasted flesh and he seemed more dead than alive. His five companions left him after he made the decision to take more substantial food and abandon asceticism. Then, Siddhartha entered a village in search of food. There, a woman named Sujata offered him a dish of milk and rice and a separate vessel of honey. His strength returned, Siddhartha washed himself in the Nairanjana River, and then set off to the Bodhi tree. He spread a mat of kusha grass underneath, crossed his legs and sat.

He sat, having listened to all the teachers, studied all the sacred texts and tried all the methods. Now there was nothing to rely on, no one to turn to, nowhere to go. He sat solid and unmoving and determined as a mountain, until finally, after six days, his eye opened on the rising morning star, so it is said, and he realized that what he had been looking for had never been lost, neither to him nor to anyone else. Therefore there was nothing to attain, and no longer any struggle to attain it.

"Wonder of wonders," he is reported to have said, "this very enlightenment is the nature of all beings, and yet they are unhappy for lack of it." So it was that Siddhartha Gautama woke up at the age of thirty-five, six years after leaving the palace, and became the Buddha, the Awakened One, known as Shakyamuni, the sage of the Shakyas.

It has been said that in the first watch of that last night Siddhartha saw all his former births. In the second watch he gained the divine eye that sees that the death and rebirth of beings depends on the nature of their actions. He saw clearly that there is no security in the cycle of becoming, which is without substance. In the third watch, in the space of time it takes to beat a drum, he realized the twelve links of conditioned co-origination, which beginning with ignorance lead to old age and death, and which, beginning with the cessation of ignorance, lead to the end of birth, old age, and death. And at the same time, just before dawn, he saw the Four Noble Truths: the truth of suffering, the origin of suffering, the cessation of suffering, and the Noble Eightfold Path—consisting of right view, right thought, right speech, right action, right means of livelihood, right effort, right mindfulness, and right meditation. This is the Fourth Noble Truth that leads to the realization of the first three.

While this formulation is a traditional one it is important to remember that in the 2,500 years since that morning the content of Shakyamuni's enlightenment has been interpreted differently by various schools. But all those who now call themselves "Buddhist" agree that this samyaksambodhi, this true, complete enlightenment, is not something the Buddha realized for himself, as his own, but is the very nature, the birthright, of every human being.

It was the earth—"the support of all living things, equal and impartial to all that moves and does not move"—that the Buddha touched with his right hand as witness to his enlightenment. Other than that, he sought no confirmation. For seven weeks he enjoyed the freedom and tranquility of liberation. At first he had no inclination to speak about his realization, which he felt would be too difficult for most people to understand. But when, according to legend, Brahma, chief of the three thousand worlds, requested that the Awakened One teach, since there were those "whose eyes were only a little clouded over," the Buddha agreed.

Shakyamuni's two former teachers, Udraka and Arada Kalama, had both died only a few days earlier, and so he sought the five ascetics who had left him. When they saw him approaching the Deer Park in Benares they decided to ignore him, since he had broken his vows. Yet they found something so radiant about his presence that they rose, prepared a seat, bathed his feet and listened as the Buddha turned the wheel of the dharma, the teachings, for the first time.

The First Noble Truth of the Buddha stated that all life, all existence, is characterized by *duhkha*—a Sanskrit word meaning suffering, pain, unsatisfactoriness. Even moments of happiness have a way of turning into pain when we hold onto them, or, once they have passed into memory, they twist the present as the mind makes an inevitable, hopeless attempt to recreate the past. The teaching of the Buddha is based on direct insight into the nature of existence and is a radical critique of wishful thinking and the myriad tactics of escapism—whether through political utopianism, psychological therapeutics, simple hedonism, or (and it is this which primarily distinguishes Buddhism from most of the world's religions) the theistic salvation of mysticism. Duhkha is Noble, and it is true. It is a foundation, a stepping stone, to be comprehended fully, not to be escaped from or explained. The experience of duhkha, of the working of one's mind, leads to the Second Noble Truth, the origin of suffering, traditionally described as craving, thirsting for pleasure, but also and more fundamentally a thirst for continued existence, as well as nonexistence. Examination of the nature of this thirst leads to the heart of the Second Noble Truth, the idea of the "self," or "I," with all its desires, hopes, and fears, and it is only when this self is comprehended and seen to be insubstantial that the Third Noble Truth, the cessation of suffering, is realized.

The five ascetics who listened to the Buddha's first discourse in the deer park became the nucleus of a community, a *sangha*, of men (women were to enter later) who followed the way the Buddha had described in his Fourth Noble Truth, the Noble Eightfold Path. These *bhikshus*, or monks, lived simply, owning a bowl, a robe, a needle, a water strainer, and a razor, since they shaved their heads as a sign of having left home. They traveled around northeastern India, practicing meditation alone or in small groups, begging for their meals.

The Buddha's teaching, however, was not only for the monastic community. Shakyamuni had instructed them to bring it to all: "Go ye, O bhikshus, for the gain of the many, the welfare of the many, in compassion for the world, for the good, for the gain, for the welfare of gods and men."

For the next forty-nine years Shakyamuni walked through the villages and towns of India, speaking in the vernacular, using common figures of speech that everyone could understand. He taught a villager to practice mindfulness while drawing water from a well, and when a distraught mother begged him to heal the dead child she carried in her arms, he did not perform a miracle, but instead instructed her to bring him a mustard seed from a house where no one had ever died. She returned from her search without the seed, but with the knowledge that death is universal, and began to practice the Noble Eightfold Path. During the rainy season, when travel was impossible, the Buddha and the sangha practiced meditation. The sites of these first retreats were no more than camps, but they gradually became more permanent. As the Buddha's fame spread, kings and other wealthy patrons donated parks and gardens for retreats. The Buddha accepted these, but he continued to live as he had ever since his twenty-ninth year: as a wandering sadhu, begging his own meal, spending his days in meditation. Only now there was one difference. Almost every day, after his noon meal, the Buddha taught.

None of these discourses, or the questions and answers that followed, were recorded during the Buddha's lifetime. According to the tradition followed by Bu-ston, the twelfth-century Tibetan author of the *History of Buddhism in India and Tibet*, the Buddha's teachings can be divided into three periods, or turnings of the wheel. The first turning announced the Four Noble Truths and the teaching of *anatman* (no self, no-atman), the nonexistence of a permanent soul or self. The second turning, the prajnaparamita (perfection of wisdom), exposed the nonsubstantiality of not only self, but all the elements (*dharmas* as they were called) of existence. Central to this period is the teaching of *shunyata*, or emptiness, which might also be rendered as "fullness," since it suggests an experience that is empty of concepts, and therefore vivid and dynamic.

The third and last turning of the wheel, said Bu-ston, "demonstrated Absolute Reality." It is here that the Tibetans generally locate the source of the *vajrayana*, or "diamond vehicle" teachings.

The Buddha died in the town of Kushinagara, at the age of eighty, having eaten a meal of either pork or mushrooms. Some of the assembled monks were despondent, but the Buddha, lying on his side, with his head resting on his right hand, reminded them that everything is impermanent, and advised them to take refuge in themselves and the dharma—

the teaching. He asked for questions a last time. There were none. Then he spoke his final words: "Now then, bhikshus, I address you: all compound things are subject to decay; strive diligently."

II

The first rainy season after the Buddha's *parinirvana*, it is said that five hundred elders gathered at a mountain cave near Rajagriha, where they held the First Council. Ananda, who had been the Buddha's attendant, repeated all the discourses, or *sutras*, he had heard, and Upali recited the two hundred fifty monastic rules, the *Vinaya*, while Mahakashyapa recited the *Abhidharma*, the compendium of Buddhist psychology and metaphysics. These three collections, which were written on palm leaves a few centuries later and known as the Tripitaka (literally "three baskets"), became the basis for all subsequent versions of the Buddhist canon.

The First Council unified the sangha. The complex of events surrounding what has been called by the Buddhist tradition, the Second Council, began to divide it. These events, which began about one hundred years after the Buddha's parinirvana, involved the accusation that some monks had strayed from certain of the Vinaya rules. Some monks, for example, were said to have accepted money as alms in the interest of amassing wealth. Behind that charge, however, lay a deeper dispute. According to one story, just before his parinirvana the Buddha had told Ananda that the sangha could modify the minor rules of the Vinaya. Ananda had conveyed this message to the elders of the First Council, but when they asked him which rules the Buddha had considered minor and which major, Ananda admitted that he had forgotten to ask, and the elders decided that it would be safer to simply keep all the rules as they had been given. During the events surrounding the Second Council, however, a group of monks put forth the argument that the Vinaya rules, which had been formed in response to specific circumstances, should be changed in response to new conditions.

According to the *Chronicle of the Elders* the ten thousand bhikshus who did not adhere to the orthodox Vinaya were expelled from the Council. This group formed a school called the Mahasanghika which spread throughout northern India, while the school of the elders, the Sthaviras, established itself in the south. (By the third century A.D. there would be four major schools, which were further divided into eighteen schools, all with varying philosophical and doctrinal views.)

It is probable that the differences of opinion expressed in the Second Council reflected in part the development of a strong lay movement within Buddhism. The Mahasanghikas and other similar schools contributed to the evolution of the *mahayana* ("great vehicle"), which was open to everyone, while the Sthavira's type of Buddhism survived into the present as the Theravadins, the School of the Elders, in Southeast Asia.

The Mahayanists taught that lay people as well as monks could attain nirvana. In place of the *arahant*, who achieved liberation through his own effort, they strove to be *bodhisattvas*, who took vows to remain in samsara until all sentient beings attained liberation. At the same time, the mahayanists further developed the early idea of buddhahood as a transcendent principle. The Buddha of mahayana sutras taught and lived in one of the higher realms, surrounded by retinues of bodhisattvas and arahants, speaking from the depths of immeasurable space and time. While this gave Buddhism a devotional dimension, it also emphasized that it was not essentially something that had happened in the past, and which had to be preserved, but rather is something which is eternal, continuous, and always being created.

III

From its home in Magadha, Buddhism traveled northwest to the Iranian border, Pakistan, and Central Asia, and then to China along the Silk Route, carried not only by bhikshus but by merchants, caravaners, and foreigners—worldly, cosmopolitan men attracted to Buddhism by its practicality (traders could understand the ethical accountability of karma) and its transcendence of caste, race, and nation.

In the third century B.C. the Mauryan Emperor Ashoka sent Buddhist missionaries as far west as Greece (where they had little, if any, success), and south across the Indian ocean to Sri Lanka. Sri Lanka, followed by Burma, Siam, and Cambodia became the home of the Theravadins, the one surviving school of the elders of the Second Council.

Buddhism entered China during the first century A.D. Both mahayana and hinayana scriptures were translated into Chinese, and the monastic sangha established. The Chinese intelligentsia were fascinated by the new Buddhist literature, but many Confucians felt that the monastic life (i.e., leaving home) subverted filial piety and loyalty to the emperor, and branded Buddhism an unwholesome, parasitic, foreign religion. The early Taoists and some neo-Confucians, on the other hand, who already had a tradition of contemplation and withdrawal from worldly life, took up the study and translation of Buddhist meditation manuals with enthusiasm.

As the Chinese obtained translations of different Indian sutras, they became perplexed at the contradictions in the different versions, all of which claimed to be the Buddha's word. In an attempt to unify the various schools of Indian Buddhism, the Chinese formed a major synthesis: the T'ien-t'ai school, based on the *Lotus Sutra*, and the Hua-yen, based on the *Avatamsaka Sutra*. Both schools, however, were grand intellectual structures requiring so much study and learning that there was little time for actual practice.

The Pure Land and Ch'an schools, on the other hand, emphasized practice and realization. The Pure Land school, imported from India, depended on the faithful recitation of Amitabha's name to insure rebirth in the Pure Land, where, it was said, enlightenment could easily be won. All that was necessary was faith. The Pure Land was popular among the illiterate villagers, but it also spread quickly through all levels of society.

The Ch'an school taught a direct way of seeing one's buddha nature, without recourse to scriptures. Ch'an is the Chinese pronunciation of the Sanskrit *dhyana*, or meditation, and it naturally was taken up by the Chinese who had been influenced by Taoist meditation techniques. It achieved its quintessential Chinese form when the Ch'an master Pai-chang (whose rule was, "One day no work, one day no food") made manual labor and farming integral parts of the training in Ch'an monasteries. While the Pure Land and Ch'an approaches might seem mutually exclusive, the Chinese eventually brought the two together, and Pure Land recitation sessions were held in most Ch'an temples.

From China, Buddhism traveled to Korea and Vietnam. In both countries Ch'an (which became "Son" in Korean and "Thien" in Vietnamese) attracted intellectuals while the Pure Land school predominated among farmers and villagers.

Buddhism first reached Japan in 550 A.D., when a Korean king sent Buddhist images and sutras as gifts to the Japanese imperial court. In the seventh and eighth centuries a number of schools were brought from China to Japan. The Tendai (Chinese T'ien-t'ai) along with Shingon (esoteric Buddhism) entered in the ninth century, a period when Shinto deities were absorbed into the Buddhist pantheon. In the twelfth century both Ch'an (pronounced "Zen" in Japanese), and Pure Land took on Japanese forms.

Buddhism entered Tibet from India and Central Asia around the seventh century. There was also some Chinese influence. Padmasambhava, the great tantric guru, entered Tibet from Afghanistan in the eighth century, and subdued the native shamanistic Bon religion by subjugating demons and deities and then making them protectors of the buddhadharma, the teachings of the Buddha. In the eleventh century a number of Tibetans, among them the translator Marpa, made the perilous journey to India, returning with many new texts.

As Buddhism took root in the Asian countries surrounding India, it eventually was destroyed in its homeland by the Muslim invasions that culminated in the invasion of Mohammed Al Ghauri in 1192, in which he swept across India and, in time, destroyed the great Buddhist centers of learning: Nalanda, Vikramashila, Odantapura and others. By the end of the twelfth century, Buddhism had ceased to exist, except for a few isolated instances, in the home of its birth.

CHAPTER TWO

EAST AND WEST: THE CENTRAL REGION

I

Buddhism is commonly thought of as an "Eastern" religion, but neither it nor the country it rose from can be so easily characterized. East and West are, after all, little more than shifting designations on a round earth, depending more on where one stands than on any absolute point through which the sun sets or rises. Though it may be east of the Mediterranean, India is west of China, and it is worth remembering that the same people who invaded Europe from the northern steppes around 1700 B.C. also swept through India during the same millenium. These Aryas, as they called themselves, were tall, light-skinned nomads who possessed fast chariots, worshipped a pantheon of sky-gods, and practiced patrilineal descent. The hymns they brought with them to India developed into the *Rig Veda* and other sacred songs. These were all composed in a language whose similarity to a possible Proto-Indo-European tongue would one day profoundly alter the way Westerners thought about Asia. Today, it seems more reasonable to follow the cultural anthropologist Tadeo Umesao who suggests that India, along with the area stretching to the Mediterranean, might best be seen as a kind of Central Region in the earth's cultural geography.

Aside from the Aryas, the earliest "western" civilization to affect India was that of the Persian Empire. Darius I, third of the Achaemenid emperors, claimed possession of Gandhara and Hindukush, and Indian troops fought with Persians against Greeks at Thermopylae. By the time Alexander the Great defeated Darius III in 333 B.C., Persian architecture and court manners had left an enduring impression on Indian life—even the Buddhist architecture of Ashoka, with its pillars and winged lions, owed much to the Persians.

Alexander's army advanced into India accompanied by Greek scientists, artists and historians, all of whom influenced Indian thought to some extent, especially in the fields of mathematics and astronomy. At the same time, the Greeks made use of Indian science: finding nothing pertaining to cobra bites in their pharmacopoeia, for example, the Greeks relied on the advice of Hindu Ayurvedic physicians.

At the Indus, Alexander's troops refused to go further. They were battle-weary, far from home, and in no mood to penetrate an unknown country said to harbor strange creatures like the *anthropophagi*, whose heads were sunk into their chests. They had reached the limits of the old Persian empire. That was far enough.

Alexander died of a fever in Babylon in 323 B.C. In the confusion that followed, the garrison trading towns he had left behind were cut off from the homeland. Some of these towns would become centers of a new hybrid Graeco-Buddhist civilization, "one of the loveliest," as Rene Grousset has written, "that the world has ever known."

Alexander's death, however, had a more immediate effect on Indian, and Buddhist, history. Taking advantage of the disarray in the Greek camp, the Indian Chandragupta, who may have once acted as Alexander's guide, consolidated the Mauryan Dynasty, the first of the great Indian Empires. Whatever his real relationship to Alexander may have been, Chandragupta had learned his lessons well—well enough to defeat Seleukus Nikator in 305 B.C., who tried to re-establish Alexander's empire. In the treaty that followed the battle, Chandragupta gave Seleukus five hundred elephants, receiving in return a fair portion of what is now Afghanistan, and a Greek or perhaps Scythian princess. More significantly, Seleukus and Chandragupta established diplomatic relations, and, in a way, it could be said that it was Alexander's defeat rather than his celebrated and short-lived victory that brought Greece and India together.

The Greek Megasthanes was dispatched as an ambassador to Chandragupta's court at the end of the fourth century B.C., and it was from his *History of India* that the Mediterranean first learned about India in a systematic way. Megasthanes described the seven-level bureaucracy of Mauryan society in great detail. Of the religious realm he had less to say, though he did mention both Brahmins and *shramanas*. Some scholars identify these shramanas as Buddhists; others feel it is more likely that Megasthanes used the term to refer to Jains, Buddhists, and forest-dwelling rishis or sages. He had, at any rate, more to say of the Brahmins, whose beliefs he compared to those of Plato or Pythagoras, saying that they believed in a deity which permeated the world. Megasthanes exhibited a characteristic Greek openness to what we now call comparative religion, comparing Indra with Zeus, and the Shakti orgies with the Bacchic rites. The scarcity of Megasthanes' information about the Buddhists may have reflected the still small number of Buddhists in India, the Greek's lack of interest, or he may have found that, as the Greek philosopher Mandanis put it, trying to "explain philosophical doctrines through the medium of interpreters who know nothing of the subject . . . is like asking water to flow pure through mud."

At first Ashoka, grandson of Chandragupta, was as fierce and ruthless as his predecessors, but after viewing the dead left by a particularly difficult battle, he became a Buddhist. In a series of rock-edicts, Ashoka set forth the principles of Buddhist government: religious tolerance, pacifism, and nonviolence, and these set a pattern which was followed as Buddhism spread beyond India. Rather than armies, Ashoka sent missionaries—as far west as Greece and Egypt. At home he established rest houses for travelers, built hospitals not only for people, but also for animals, and provided caves for the ajivakas, the naked ascetics.

Although we know from inscriptions on Ashoka's rock-edicts that he sent missionaries to Greece, we have no hint of how they were received. We do know, however, that many of the Greeks who remained behind after Alexander's retreat became Buddhists, especially in the northwest border kingdoms of Bactria and Gandhara. The conversion of one of the most powerful of the Bactrian kings, Menander, is chronicled in a Pali text known as *The Questions of King Milinda*. While many of the Greeks were, perhaps, attracted to Buddhism because they were casteless foreigners, the *Questions* show that at least some of them were led to Buddhism by logical argument. The dialogue between Menander and the Indian monk Nagasena is conducted in a cool, rational, Socratic fashion, eminently suitable for Nagasena's orthodox hinayana arguments. The doctrine of anatman, or no-self, is explained by the analogy of a chariot which Menander is forced to admit has no existence distinct from the sum of its parts. The idea of a self is therefore "a mere empty sound," as Nagasena says. A Siamese version of the *Questions* adds that Menander attained the liberation of an arhat, and Pliny writes that all the states Menander had subjected claimed his ashes after his death in order to distribute them in stupas. If we accept this legend, Menander may be considered the first Westerner (if a Greek ruler born in northwest India can be called a Westerner) to successfully complete the Buddhist path.

Though the *Questions of King Milinda* is still to this day an important text in Southeast Asia, it is in the realm of art, not philosophy, that the Graeco-Buddhist kingdoms are most memorable. Before the flowering of arts in Gandhara, the Indians had represented the Buddha solely by his absence—as a mat, a tree, footprints, or a parasol. The Greeks and Romans, however, were accustomed to portraying their gods and heroes in human form, and with the emergence of a new devotional Buddhism during the reign of the Kushan monarch and Buddhist patron Kanishka, it was natural for them to take the revolutionary step of portraying the Buddha as a human being.

The school of Gandharan art came to its fullest flowering from the first to the fifth century of our era, at a time when the Roman Empire reached to within six hundred miles of the Kushan border, and Indian merchants and emissaries were given senator's seats at Roman theatres. During this era the Kushans employed the Greek and Roman sculptors from Asia Minor who were most probably responsible for giving the Buddha human form and western features—"profiles of Appolonian purity," in Rene Grousset's phrase, "framed by their waving locks and faultless draperies, so pleasing often in their fluid treatment."

For a time Kushan became a great center of Buddhist culture, as well as a major way-station for the Chinese monks making the perilous overland journey to India in search of authentic texts and teachings. In imagining these monks, men like Fa-hsien and Hsuan-tsang, Rene Grousset calls the Ghandharan figures, now exiled in museums, back to life: "Could the Chinese pilgrims," he wonders, "who must have seen them there still in their places, suspect that they had before their eyes the first images produced by the hands of man of the apostle of their religion? Did they know that formerly, six centuries earlier, without doubt, at a time when as yet no one dared represent the Buddha, except by difficult symbols, one of these Yavana artists, as the Indians called them, a man from far off Ta-ch'in, as they said in China, had dared for the first time to represent in human form the images of the Blessed One? And all the Buddhist images had sprung from this one, from those that were worshipped in the shrines of Ceylon to statues of China and Japan themselves. . . ."

II

How far west Buddhism penetrated in pre-industrial times is still a matter of scholarly conjecture and controversy. Trade between Asia and the Mediterranean countries can be traced back to pre-history—a white jade ax of Chinese design found in the second city of Troy, and Indian teak from Nebuchadnezzar's palace being two examples. Certainly it was not until mariners discovered the monsoon winds during the reign of Claudius, thus cutting sailing time between Alexandria and the south Indian coast from thirty months to two, that Indian merchants became familiar figures in Rome, while philosophers, sages and poets gathered in the polyglot streets and parks of Alexandria.

Dion Chrystomas mentions Bactrians, Scythians and Indians among the citizens of Alexandria who listened to his discourses, and H.G. Rawlinson, in his *Intercourse Between India and the Western World*, tells us that the "philosophical and religious writers of the time . . . often exhibit an unexpectedly intimate knowledge of Indian philosophy, religion, and social observances." Clement of Alexandria, for example, whose source was his teacher Pantaenus, an early Christian missionary to India, speaks of "Indians who follow the precept of Boutta, venerate him as a god, and worship a kind of pyramid beneath which they imagine that the bones of a divinity of some kind lie buried."

Some scholars have suggested that Gnostic ideas owe more than a little to Buddhism. J. Kennedy, writing in the *Journal of the Royal Asiatic Society* in 1902 argued that the "negative theology" of Basilides, the great Gnostic systematizer, who lived in Alexandria, was "Buddhist Gnosticism." More recent research, however, tends to discount this view. Father de Lubac, whose *La Rencontre du Buddhisme et de l'Occident* is the most authoritative work on the subject, says that, "Although there is an undeniable analogy between the way he [Basilides] spoke about the First Principle, as neither comprehensible nor incomprehensible, and the ways in which the Buddhist authors spoke, that does not prove that there was the slightest influence of Buddhism on him." Nevertheless, the question remains open. As Guy Welborn remarks in *The Buddhist Nirvana and Its Western Interpreters*, "Lamentably, no historian of Gnosticism has been at the same time either an Indologist or a student of Buddhist thought."

The work of the neo-Platonist Bardesanes the Babylonian provides evidence of a link between neo-Platonism and Buddhism. Bardesanes' book on the Indian Gymnosophists clearly distinguishes the Brahmins, who lived a life of solitary meditation in the mountains, from the Sarmanes [shramanas], who lived in a monastery supported by the king. The Sarmanes, said Bardesanes, might come from any of the castes, and upon taking the robe registered with the village magistrate, a Sarmane disposed of his goods, returned his wife to her parents, and entrusted his children to the care of the state. "Both the Brahmins and Buddhist monks," said Bardesanes, "are held in such high esteem that the king himself will come and ask for their prayers and their counsel in times of emergency and danger."

The belief that Buddhism influenced Christianity has been a persistent one, at least in some circles. In a recent book Daisaku Ikeda, president of the four-million-member lay Buddhist organization, Sokagakkai, quotes Origen's third-century commentary on the Book of Ezekiel: "In that island [Britain], the Druid priests and Buddhists spread teachings concerning the oneness of God, and for that reason the inhabitants are already inclined toward it [Christianity]." It has also been suggested that the Essene community to which Christ is believed to have belonged owed more to Buddhist monastic forms than to its own Jewish heritage. Another popular theory is that Christ spent his "lost years" wandering through India. Perhaps more respectable are the theories that propose that mahayana teachings might owe something to Christian influence, or vice versa. The *Lotus Sutra*, in particular, contains a striking parallel to the Biblical tale of the prodigal son, and the doctrines of the three *kayas*, or "bodies," of the transcendent Buddha have seemed to some highly suggestive of some kind of Christian-Buddhist cross-fertilization. Similar correspondences between Indian forms of spirituality and Christian ones—the common use of rosaries, the custom of relic worship, a belief in transmigration (not yet condemned as heresy in the early Church), and the similarity between the life led by the desert fathers of Egypt and Syria and the Indian forest-dwelling rishis and Buddhist monks—all lend further support to the cross-fertilization theory. Still, no historical evidence yet exists to clarify whether these, and other similar examples, are instances of true cultural interaction or parallel development.

Curiously enough one of the unlikeliest cases of Buddhist influence on Christianity is also one of the best documented. This is the legend of Barlaam and Josaphat which resulted in the unwitting canonization of the Buddha as a Christian saint in 1585.

The story of Barlaam and Josaphat, as it was narrated by St. John of Damascus in the eighth century, tells of a son born to an Indian king with the prophecy, delivered by Chaldean oracles, that the prince would one day leave home and embrace the true religion. Josaphat's father, like Shakyamuni's before him, tried to prevent this by surrounding the prince with luxury, but the Christian hermit Barlaam (alias the Buddha) revealed the true nature of the world to Josaphat, who followed him to the desert where they both led the lives of Christian hermits. The legend traveled a twisting route, passing from a Sanskrit original into Pahlevi, Greek and Latin, and then into French, German and Swedish. The name Josaphat was derived from Bodhisattva, which the Arabs rendered Bodasaph, the Greeks read as Ioasaph, and the Europeans as the more familiar Josaphat, and it was under this name, all traces of the original Bodhisattva forgotten, that Cardinal Baronius included "The Holy Saints Barlaam and Josaphat, of India, on the borders of Persia, whose wonderful acts St. John of Damascus has described . . ." in the standardized Martyrologium of 1585.

III

Whatever tentative, indirect communication may have existed between Europe and India was further weakened by barbarian invasions of Europe and the fall of Rome to the Goths in 410—an event echoed in Kushan a hundred years later when the White Huns utterly destroyed the flourishing Gandharan monasteries Fa-hsien had visited on his way to India. The West did not reach out to Asia again until the middle of the thirteenth century, when Pope Innocent IV, hearing rumors that there were Christians among the Mongols, sent the Franciscan William of Rubuck to convince the khan to join Christendom in the war against Islam. Rubuck found Christians at the khan's court, but they were Nestorians. He also found Moslems, Tibetan lamas and probably Confucians. There were so many priests of so many various religions around the khan that Rubuck complained that they were "*sicut muscae mel*," that is, like flies after honey. The Mongols seemed to be inclined towards Buddhism, but they were a nomadic people with no set culture of their own, willing to pick up what they could from the cultures they conquered, and the khan encouraged friendly religious debates. Rubuck described one in which a Nestorian priest addressed a Uigur priest and a group of Saracens. "They all listened without contradiction," he wrote in his *Iternarium*, "but none said: 'I believe. I wish to become a Christian.' Then the Nestorians and Saracens sang together in a loud voice, but the Buddhists kept silent. And afterwards they all drank deeply."

Rubuck learned enough of Buddhism to make a Latin transliteration of the mantra *om mani padme hum: Ou man haetavi* or *Ou man baccam*, but the doctrines of Buddhism remained closed to him. He left after six months, having made half a dozen converts in that time.

Marco Polo, who also visited the court of the khan, came closer to discovering the true spirit of Buddhism. The priests of Sagamoni Borcan (as he called Buddha, following the Mongolian pronunciation) seemed more like miracle workers and shamans than religious men, at least around the khan's court. But in Sri Lanka Marco Polo heard the story of Shakyamuni's life. He tells his readers that Shakyamuni was the son of a king, encountered old age and death, and then abandoned the palace to spend "the rest of his days most virtuously and chastely and in great austerity." Though Marco Polo routinely addressed Buddhists as idolators, along with all other Westerners at this time, the character of Sagamoni Borcan impressed him enough to write: "For a certainty, if he had been baptized a Christian he would have been a great saint before God."

IV

Unfortunately (from the Christian point of view) Shakyamuni had not been baptized, which meant that his followers, no matter how pure and ethical their lives, were idolaters and heathens. They were damned.

During the colonization that followed Vasco da Gama's voyage to India in 1497, European traders and military men, along with priests and missionaries, reached China, Japan, Sri Lanka, India, Indochina and Tibet. A few of these men sent information about Buddhism back to Europe. The Jesuits, who took the trouble to learn the languages, were especially energetic in this regard, but for the most part the missionaries had nothing but contempt for the idolators. Father de Lubac gives us a collection of the epithets used to describe Buddhism up to the eighteenth century. It is variously a "monstrous religion," an "abominable sect," a "plague," and a "gangrene" founded by a "very wicked man."

Even those rare missionaries who did happen to discover something of the inner teachings of Buddhism considered it nihilism at best. "The secret doctrine of the ministers of the god Fo [Buddha]," wrote Noel Alexander in his *Apology of the Dominican Missionaries of China* in 1700, "is unalloyed atheism. The void which they consider to be the principle of all things is, they say, completely perfect and tranquil, without beginning or end, unmoving, without knowledge, and without desire." The Buddhist teaching, Father Alexander concluded, in a charge that was to be frequently repeated, "reduces everything to a confused void with a simple nothing as its beginning and end; and . . . considers that perfection consists in perfect indifference, apathy, and an undisturbed quietude."

So much for the rhetoric. The actions were far worse. When the Portuguese soldiers, accompanied by Roman Catholic friars, landed on the south coast of Sri Lanka (Ceylon) in 1501, their instructions were "to begin by preaching, but, that failing, to proceed to the decision of the sword." The friars must not have been very effective, for the Portuguese immediately set about slaughtering the Sinhalese. "There is no page in the story of European colonisation," writes the English historian Sir Emerson Tennent, "more gloomy and repulsive than that which recounts the proceedings of the Portuguese in Ceylon." A Sinhalese historian, drawing from the records of the Portuguese, furnished the particulars: children were murdered on the soldier's pikes, while their mothers were forced to watch. As for the men, they "were thrown over bridges for the amusement of the troops to feed the crocodiles in the river, which eventually grew so tame that at a whistle they would raise their heads above the water in anticipation of a feast." In addition to this slaughter, the Portuguese zealously carried out the orders of the king of Portugal to his viceroy: "We charge you to discover all idols by means of diligent officers, to reduce them to fragments and utterly consume them." Buddhist books were burned, and the Portuguese proclaimed "rigourous penalties against . . . those who shall celebrate in public or private any festivities which have any gentile taint." In the end, the only parts of Buddhist temples the Portuguese did not carry off or destroy were the stones. These they used to build churches.

Having thoroughly terrorized the population, the Portuguese turned to trickery and intrigue. To impress the Sinhalese they pretended to be Brahmins of a superior caste from the Western world, affecting orange colored robes, hanging tiger's skins from their shoulders, and smearing sandlewood on their foreheads. They even went so far as to forge a document "in ancient characters," which proved that "the Brahmins of Rome were of a much older date than the Brahmins of India, and descended in an equally direct line from the Brahma himself."

The culmination of their efforts came when the Sinhalese King found himself so divided from his people that he had to appeal to the Portuguese to guarantee the succession of his grandson, Dharmapala. The Portuguese agreed on the condition that Dharmapala and his queen take Christian names and become baptized. Dharmapala (the name means "protector of the Dharma") accepted the Portuguese terms and transferred the funds traditionally used to support the monasteries to the Roman Catholic Church.

Only the powerful presence of the king of Kandy in the north saved Sinhalese Buddhism from complete obliteration. He provided a place of refuge for Buddhists and astutely allied himself with the Dutch Calvinists who were engaged in a colonial war with the Portuguese.

The Dutch had seized the most important trading posts by 1644. Although they had promised the Sinhalese that they wanted only trading privileges, it soon became apparent that they were actually replacing the Portuguese as colonial masters. At first the Dutch were more interested in destroying Roman Catholicism than Buddhism. In 1658 they made it a crime, punishable by death, for any person to harbor or give protection to a Roman Catholic priest. (The king of Kandy, in an act of religious tolerance worthy of Ashoka, now granted asylum to Catholics.) But the Dutch soon followed the Portuguese example. They made it unlawful for any Sinhalese not baptized in the Dutch Reformed Church to hold office or farm land. Buddhists had to forfeit a third of their property to the government, and the Church became the sole legal means for registering births, marriages and deaths. Nevertheless, due to the strength of the king of Kandy and to the resilience of the Sinhalese Buddhists, the Dutch finally admitted that most of their "converts" were still "incorrigible Buddhists." "They make offerings to the idol at Kataragama," complained one official report, "They bestow gifts on the mendicant servants of the temple, and, in short, the highest benediction they can pronounce on their friends is, *May you become a Buddha*."

V

The Portuguese atrocities in Ceylon were the darkest side of the coin. In other countries, primarily China, Japan and Tibet, Jesuit missionaries followed the example of St. Francis Xavier, who realized that in order to convert the Japanese ruling class he would first have to learn something of their philosophy. Xavier arrived in Japan in 1549. He met Buddhists from a number of schools, but became most friendly with a Zen priest named Nanjio, who seems to have matched the Jesuit in wit and urbanity. When, for example, Xavier visited the abbot's monastery, he observed the monks sitting zazen and asked what they were thinking. The abbot answered with the candid irony of one seasoned ecclesiastic to another. "Some," he said, "are counting up how much they took from the faithful last month; some are considering where they can get better clothing and treatment for themselves; others are thinking of their recreations and pastimes. In short, none of them is thinking of anything that has any sense whatever." Despite the abbot's friendliness and openness, the Jesuits had no success among the Zen school. As one Jesuit put it, the Zen priests believed there was nothing beyond birth and death, no afterlife, no punishment for good and evil, and, to make matters worse, no Creator. Furthermore, the Jesuits found that the Zen masters they spoke with asked penetrating questions (known today as *koans*) which, the Jesuits complained, could only be answered with the help of Divine Grace.

Xavier had better luck with the adherents of Shingon (Esoteric) Buddhism, who told him that the Christian God sounded like the esoteric meaning of Dainichi (Vairocana). For a time, Xavier thought he had found an ally, and he took to the streets exhorting the people to have faith in Dainichi. Upon further questioning, however, he found that some of the Shingon monks laughed at the idea of a man dying on a cross to save mankind. This time Xavier had his interpreter denounce not only the Shingon, but all the Buddhist schools as inventions of the Devil, while Shakyamuni and Amida (Amitabha, the buddha of the western paradise) were "those two demons."

The Jesuits had considerable success in Japan, partly because they came under the protection of feudal lords who were political opponents of the Buddhists, and partly because Christianity had become something of a fashion among the Japanese aristocracy. By 1582, according to an estimate of the visiting general of the Jesuits, there were 150,000 Christians in Japan.

Five years later, however, the political climate changed abruptly, and the Jesuits' protector, General Hideyoshi, ordered the banishment of foreign missionaries. Although his decree was not enforced, probably due to the wish to maintain trade, subsequent decrees expelled the Spanish, Portuguese and Dutch. This first period of Christian influence in Japan ended by 1637 with the Shimabara Rebellion. About 20,000 remaining Christian converts joined a peasant revolt and took over Hara Castle. During the battle, every single man in the castle died except one.

VI

It would be misleading to give the impression that the missionaries, paramount though they were, were the only ones to encounter Buddhism at the beginning of the colonial period. For example La Loubere, Louis the XIV's envoy to the court of the king of Siam during the years 1678-9, may well have been the first European to mention Pali or use the term *nirvana*. In his *Description du royaume de Siam*, La Loubere wrote, "Nireupan is not a place, but a way of being . . . Nireupan, they say—that is, this soul has disappeared. It will not return again to any world. And it is this word which the Portuguese have translated as follows: *it is annihilated*, and also as: *it has become God*; even though according to the Siamese, it is neither true annihilation nor the acquisition of any divine nature." As Guy Welbon remarks, this is "an amazingly modern evaluation of the term."

Finally, there is Englebert Kaempfer's *History of Japan Together with a Description of the Kingdom of Siam*, which, when it was published in London in 1727, became the first book in English to describe Zen Buddhism. Kaempfer was physician to a Dutch trading party which the Japanese, having learned caution from their earlier experiences with Jesuits and Franciscans, had confined to a small island. "I should rather say 'prison'," wrote Kaempfer, who nevertheless found ways to gather accurate information. He did this by winning the confidence of his interpreters and a young servant with information on medicine, astronomy, mathematics, "and with a cordial and plentiful supply of European liquors."

Kaempfer's description of one of the priests who accompanied Ingen, the founder of the Obaku line of Zen, from China to Japan in 1653, introduced the English speaking world to *zazen* and *satori* for the first time. This priest, wrote Kaempfer, was considered by the Japanese to be

> a person blessed with a divine and most accurate understanding whom they suppose to be able to find out by his *Satori*, or *Enthusiastic Speculations*, such mysterious truths as are far beyond the reach of common knowledge . . . He holds a small staff in his hand, with some horse-hair ty'd to the end, as a particular mark of his mysterious manner of thinking, it being customery among all Sasen Priests, to carry something of this nature about them. *Sasen* is a profound meditation of divine mysterious and holy things; which so entirely takes up a man's mind, that his body lies, as it were, destitute of all sense and life, unmov'd by any external object whatsoever.

These last accounts may seem to be accurate, and to even demonstrate a moving breadth of sympathy, but we must conclude that they are merely the exceptions that prove the rule. Until the later nineteenth century, some twenty-four hundred years after Shakyamuni's enlightenment under the bodhi tree, we can find virtually no real exchange between the European mind and Buddhism. That we have gleaned a fair number of references to Shakyamuni and his teachings scattered among the Greeks, Romans and later Europeans should not surprise us so much as the fact that, at the beginning of the nineteenth century, scarcely anyone had even begun to imagine that the religion that had shaped the great civilizations of India, China, Japan and Southeast Asia might have anything to offer the West.

VII

Strangely enough, perhaps the most suggestive and well-documented case for an early and profound Buddhist influence outside of Asia leads us not to Europe, but to North America.

In 1761 the French sinologist M. De Guignes electrified the Academy of Inscriptions and Belles Lettres with the publication of a paper describing a document he had found in the Chinese Imperial Archives. According to M. De Guignes a Chinese bhikshu named Hwui [Hui] Shan ("Universal Compassion") had presented the Chinese emperor with an account of a voyage taken by himself and five other monks to a country called Fu-sang in A.D. 458. This country, Fu-sang, M. De Guignes identified as Mexico, which he believed the Chinese to have reached by a route leading through the Aleutian islands to Alaska and then down the west coast of North America. The theory won acceptance among nearly all of M. De Guignes' learned colleagues, both sinologists and Americanists.

Fifty years later, however, the Prussian sinologist Julius H. Klaproth attacked. Most scholars of the controversy now admit that while Klaproth may have been right, his specific arguments were specious. Klaproth denied, for example, that the Chinese (who had invented the compass) had sufficient navigational skills for the voyage. He also asserted that the grapevine, mentioned in the Chinese account, was unknown in America. Despite these blunders Klaproth's reputation was so high, and his argument so vehement, that his opposition effectively destroyed the Fu-sang theory as a subject for respectable scholarly research.

The theory was not revived until Dr. Karl Friedrich Neumann of Munich published a paper defending De Guignes. Then in 1875 Neumann's student, the pioneer American folklorist, Charles G. Leland, published *Fu-sang or the Discovery of America by Chinese Buddhist Priests in the Fifth Century*. Leland also supported De Guignes's theory, including expert testimony from an American naval officer proving that the Chinese could easily have arrived by the route De Guignes had suggested. Then in 1885 another American, Edward Payson Vining, published what will probably be the lengthiest account of the controversy, the eight-hundred-page tome, *An Inglorious Columbus; or, Evidence that Hwui Shan and A Party of Buddhist Monks from Afghanistan Discovered America in the Fifth Century A.D.* Beneath this imposing title, Vining threw down his challenge with a quote from Charles G. Leland: "If Buddhist priests were really the first men who, within the scope of written history and authentic annals, went from the Old World to the New, it will sooner or later be proved. Nothing can escape history that belongs to it."

The Chinese account (Vining published it in the original, along with eight, variant, character-by-character translations) begins by telling us that, "During the reign of the dynasty Tsi, in the first year of the year-naming 'Ever-lasting Origin,' (A.D. 499) came a Buddhist priest from this kingdom, who bore the cloister-name Hoie-Shin [Hui Shan], Universal Compassion . . . who narrated that Fusang is about twenty thousand Chinese miles in an easterly direction from Tahan, and east of the Middle Kingdom." The country, said the document, was named for the Fusang tree, whose leaves "are the color of the oak. In its early stages the leaves look like the bamboo shoots. It has an edible fruit which is pear-shaped and reddish in color. The bark of the tree can be made into cloth and from this people make clothing. In building their houses, they make paper from the bark of the Fusang tree. They do not fight as they have no weapons." After further description of Fusang—prisons, marriage customs, the nature of the nobility and the king are all mentioned, though in the highly condensed, somewhat cryptic, style of the ancient Chinese—the account concludes: "Formerly, this country had no knowledge of the Buddhist religion, but during the Sung Dynasty, in the second year of the period called the 'Great Brightness' (A.D. 458) five priests of Pi-k-'iu from the country of Ki-pin (Kabul) journeyed to that country taking with them their Buddhist religious books and images and taught the people their Buddhist doctrine and to forsake rude customs and thus reform them."

Both Vining and Henrietta Mertz (whose *Pale Ink* is the most recent contribution to the Fusang literature) identify the Fusang tree as a plant native to Mexico, though they disagree on the nature of the plant. Vining argues that the description fits the prickly pear cactus. Mertz, however, who traveled extensively in the Americas to solve the mystery, believes it to be a particular type of Indian corn with red pear-shaped kernels.

Mertz (and to a lesser extent, Vining) cites recent archeological findings that point to the likelihood of trans-Pacific travel between Asia and the Americas well before the arrival of the first Europeans. The Meggers-Evans archeological study, for example, found remarkable similarities between the Valdivia phase pottery of the Ecuadorian coast and Japanese Jomon-ware dating from around 2500 B.C. Although such evidence flies in the face of the common assumption that Columbus "discovered" America, it is not at all improbable that Japanese fishermen found themselves stranded on the Ecuadorian coast thousands of years ago. Between 1800 and 1950, according to the California Academy of Science, ocean currents carried at least fifty Chinese and Japanese ships to the California coast.

Vining could not draw on twentieth-century archeology, but he did include numerous examples of Chinese and Mexican figures and designs that seem to have sprung from the same cultural mold. Vining's emphasis on this point gained credibility in 1953 when Gordon Ekholm published a paper identifying many "significant parallels" between Hindu-Buddhist and post-classical Mexican art. These include the motifs of a highly stylized lotus, serpent, bowl and sun. All these symbols have been used by Buddhists, and the fact that they suddenly appeared fully developed in Mexico in the fifth century A.D. makes it at least possible that they arrived with Hui Shan and his party of monks.

A perhaps more fanciful trail is the etymological one, which Vining follows with typical nineteenth-century exuberance. One of his more ingenious suggestions is that Guatemala may be derived from *Gautama* and *mala*, the Sanskrit word for rosary. In addition, Vining believes that Mayans may have taken their name from Queen Maya, Shakyamuni's mother. Mertz follows Vining with even greater ingenuity. If Hui Shan passed through a place, she reasons, its name may reflect this. She hypothesizes that the Chinese may have landed at Point *Hui*neme, California, then gone overland to *Saca*ton (from the prefix Saka, for Shakyamuni), and into Mexico where there are a number of cities with the prefix Hui: Wicam, pronounced Wee Sham), Huetama, Huichol, and Huizontla. Then there are also cities with the prefix Saka: Sacaton, Zacatlan, Zacatecas. Whatever one thinks of the value of this kind of etymology, the fact remains that Mertz has made a major contribution to the Fusang theory by providing a plausible route for the Chinese that matches many of the geographical details in the original account.

All this may well sound contrived and farfetched, but one takes pause on examining the *Hui*chol Indians. The Huicholes live near the Volcan de Colima, which matches a smoking mountain mentioned in Hui Shan's account. The Huicholes carry serpent-headed staffs and bowls called "Sakai-mona" which are decorated with a sun and serpent, and are considered religious healers by the people around them. The Huicholes so resemble the Chinese that the local Mexicans refer to them as "Chinois." Merz also points out that the performers in a yearly dance in the state of Sinoloa represent old white men with canes. The dance is said to go back at least a thousand years, and the local people, referring to the dancers as Chinelos, say it refers to the Chinese.

The dance of the Chinelos can be seen as a representation of a central American myth. According to the historian H.H. Bancroft, to whom Vining dedicated his book,

> although bearing various general names and appearing in different countries, the American culture-heroes all present the same characteristics. They are all described as white bearded men, generally clad in long robes; appearing suddenly and mysteriously upon the scene of their labors, they at once set about improving the people by instructing them in useful and ornamental arts, giving them laws, exhorting them to practice brotherly love and other Christian virtues, and introducing a milder and better form of religion; having accomplished their mission, they disappear as mysteriously and unexpectedly as they came; and finally they are apotheosized and held in great reverence by a grateful posterity.

Quetzalcoatl in Cholula, Votan in Chiapas, and Kukulcan in Yucatan are all examples of this figure, who may also include Pahana, the Lost White Brother of the Hopis.

De Guignes, Charles Leland, and Edward Vining had all been content to set Hui Shan in place of Columbus, but Mertz goes a step further. She suggests that it is not impossible that Quetzalcoatl and the other culture-heroes are legendary figures based on Hui Shan. Mertz argues that the description of Quetzalcoatl as a man who "was kindly, abhorred war, was adverse to cruelty, maintained the most exemplary manners, taught men to cultivate the soul, weave, reduce metals from their ores, and was all that could be considered supreme in a man," fits the description of a cultivated Chinese bhikshu such as Hui Shan. In addition, she adds, upperclass Chinese shaded themselves from the sun to keep their skin pale, and Quetzalcoatl is described as having light skin. Moreover, Hui Shan, like Quetzalcoatl, appeared suddenly and disappeared just as suddenly, after teaching the people to "forsake rude customs."

Tantalizing though this theory may be, it remains speculation. And yet, there are two recent discoveries which may convince even the most skeptical reader to postpone judgement. The first concerns a large rock carved with an elaborate swastika (a Buddhist symbol as well as an American Indian one) found on an old Indian trail in the Lakeside Mountains near California's San Jacinto Valley. When Mrs. Adelaide Wilson first came across the rock in 1914, it was covered by lichen and surrounded by a grove of sycamore trees near a small spring. Assuming that she had found an American Indian petroglyph, Mrs. Wilson and her husband brought two Cahuilla Indian friends to see it. "Very old," said Cornelio Luvo. "No one of our time has ever seen this one, but I have heard of it. My father's father said it was the people from the sea." Later the Wilsons showed the stone to the Indian leader Juan Costa, who also said, "This is one of those rocks that was made by the people from the sea." Mr. Wilson asked, "What people from the sea?" Juan smiled. "You know as much as I do," he said. "As much as any of us do. It is said they camped here long ago and that they came from the sea."

Still more recently yet another clue appeared—this time in the sea off the Palos Verdes Peninsula—when divers discovered thirty large circular rocks, weighing between 150 and 700 pounds apiece, with holes cut out of their centers. According to William Clewlow, head of the Institute of Archeology of the University of California at Los Angeles, the rocks may be anywhere from 500 to a thousand years old, and they may well have been used by the ancient Chinese as anchors.

All the evidence for Fusang is admittedly circumstantial—pieces of a jigsaw puzzle which has not yet been completed. But there are enough pieces, many of which do fit together, to remind us (paraphrasing William James), not to close our accounts with the past too quickly. Buddhism in North America may have had a far longer history and a far more profound effect than any but a few visionaries have dared to guess.

CHAPTER THREE

THE MINE OF SANSKRIT

I

Asia has played a part in America from the very beginning. Even if we dismiss trans-Pacific voyages as fanciful and ignore the migrations of Asian peoples across the Bering Straits as inconsequential prehistory, we still are left to begin with Christopher Columbus, whose passage to India ran aground on the New World. Though this fact is often considered simply a quaint historical coincidence, one which has left us nothing more significant than the linguistic irony that the people whom Columbus christened *Indios* still bear that name, it holds a deeper meaning, for behind that voyage, and the mercantile motives that financed it, lay an Asia that had been the jewel-like focus for millennia of European dreams.

It could be said that the existence of intricate and rich Asian civilizations—heathen though they may have been—demonstrated the possibility of alternatives to European society. Asia and America both shared the lure of being *not-Europe*, and many of the images Europeans cast on Asia, whether of riches, ancient, hidden knowledge, or dusky maidens, could be cast on America with equal ease. In the same way, the sudden appearance of literary utopias in the sixteenth and seventeenth centuries may be traced to the inspiration of very real voyages to both continents. "We sailed from Peru," began Bacon's *New Atlantis* in 1627, "where we had continued for the space of one whole year, for China and Japan, by the South Sea . . ."

There were, of course, important differences. Both Asia and America shared an immensity of scale, but Asia presented a tradition that had grown fixed and tyrannous with age, while America appeared as a new, limitless field within which men might create culture as they pleased. That America, as well as Asia, *already* possessed its own profusion of primeval cultures, was something scarcely any Europeans would allow themselves to notice. There may have been a few men of sympathetic mind among the first settlers, but they were powerless to stop the slaughter. In any case, there were few visible signs of "culture" such as written records, and where these did exist—as among the Mexicans—they were burnt as heretical.

Asian culture fared better. Asia had a sophistication, a long history of contact with Europe, and a skill in diplomacy that rendered her civilization more resistant to the worst excesses of the European barbarians. This was most true of China and Japan, both countries with a literate, historically aware culture that Europeans could feel ran parallel to their own. The rationalists of the eighteenth century saw China as an orderly, civilized, reasonable state.

The translations of Confucius, which were furnished by Jesuit missionaries, helped to create and confirm this view. To the *philosophes* and Deists of the eighteenth and seventeenth centuries Confucius was the Noble Sage, the philosopher who had discovered the laws of nature and morality and reason without recourse to belief in Divine Revelation or ecclesiastical authority. "We shall here see moral essays which are masterpieces," wrote the author of *La Morale de Confucius* in 1687. "Everything herein is solid; because that right reason, that inward verity which is implanted in the soul of men, and which our philosopher incessantly consulted without prejudice guided all his words." Here was proof of the Deist belief that reason resided in all men. "He seems rather like a doctor of revealed law," says the same author, "than like a man who had no light, but what the law of nature afforded him."

Some Europeans went so far as to consider China, because of its examination system, the model of a well-run egalitarian society—one that relied on merit rather than favor or birth to fill government posts.

When Eustace Budgell observed in 1731 that the Chinese practiced a "Maxim, which ought to be observed in every well-govern'd state; viz. that every Post of Honour or Profit in the Commonwealth, ought to be made the reward of Real Merit," he cited China to meet the often heard objection that such a system would prove impractical. "If any Modern Politician," he wrote, "should take it into his Head that this Maxim, however Excellent in itself, cannot possibly be observed in so large and populous a Kingdom as Great Britain; I beg leave to inform such a Politician, that at this very Time, this glorious Maxim is most strictly follow'd and observ'd in the *Largest*, and most *Populous*, and the best Govern'd Empire in all the *World*: I mean in *China*."

In France, Voltaire praised the Chinese for having perfected themselves in morals, political economy and agriculture, while King Louis XIV, looking towards Confucian theories of government to help him order an increasingly restive population, imitated a good Chinese emperor by guiding a plow during ceremonies opening spring planting. Other monarchs were less enthusiastic. When Christian Wolf addressed the University of Halle, and praised the Chinese Emperors Yao and Xun for "passing over their own Sons," and choosing as their successors "those they judged so equal to so great a Task," the king of Prussia gave him forty-eight hours, on pain of death, to quit the kingdom.

II

The king of Prussia, along with his cousin King George III, had reason to be disturbed, not with the revolutionary implications of Confucius, but with certain disturbances that signaled the beginnings of a new era. In 1773 the East India Company, then on the verge of bankruptcy due to the graft and corruption of its own officials, began shipping tea directly to America, avoiding the handling charges of European warehouses. The colonists, however, were not interested in the problems of the East India Company. Though the new method brought the price of tea down, it did not resolve the problem of English taxation on goods sold to the colonies, and on December 16, 1773 a small group of men masquerading as Indians boarded a ship carrying tea from Canton, and pitched it all into the waters of Boston Harbor. The English responded to the provocation with force, and before long they found themselves engaged in a full-scale colonial war.

In London, a small group of men, among them a brilliant young lawyer and linguist named William Jones, actively opposed the "military solution" to the American problem. Jones was known by his friends as "Oriental" Jones, "Persian" Jones and also, due to the breadth of his learning and the modesty and balance of his character, as "Harmonious" Jones. But from our vantage point the epithet of a leading contemporary Orientalist, A.J. Arberry, seems even more appropriate. Arberry calls him simply "The Founder." Men before him had given accounts, more or less accurate, of what they had seen in the Orient, but it was not until William Jones completed his work in India, that the scientific study of Oriental art and philosophy could be said to have even begun. Among Jones's lasting achievements are the founding of the Royal Asiatic Society, the discovery that Sanskrit and the European languages had a common origin in an earlier Indo-European language, and the first systematic essays in comparative religion and mythology. Equally important was his work as a translator and propagandist for Oriental literature, especially Persian and Sanskrit. Jones published the first translations of Hafiz and Rumi, and also introduced the great Sanskrit dramatist Kalidasa not only to Europe but to eighteenth-century India as well.

All of Jones's accomplishments culminated in his vision of the usefulness of Oriental studies for the West. At a time when nearly everyone considered the Orientals as titillating exotica, Jones saw, with a historical analogy that has proved prophetic, that the translation and study of Asiatic literature could come to play the same role in the modern world that the rediscovery of the Greek and Latin classics did in the renaissance of fifteenth- and sixteenth-century Europe. While many of Jones's pioneering efforts have been superseded, his vision of an "Oriental renaissance," (though he himself did not use that term) is still vital to an understanding of the intellectual and spiritual life of the West. We are just now becoming aware that the Orient is present in our world not simply as darkness, seductress, ancient wisdom, or any of the shadowy archetypes our psychologists have offered us, but as stimulus, leavening, or yeast—one might say sand, to the pearl of our own lives and culture. This vision of an Oriental renaissance appears in Emerson, Thoreau and Fenollosa, and when the historian Lynn G. White says that the introduction of D.T. Suzuki's work to the West may one day be counted as important as the rediscovery of Aristotle, or when Ezra Pound exclaims that China is our Greece, both men are embellishing and restating this key idea.

We should not assume from all this that Jones dwelt entirely in the universe of discourse. Jones also had an active political and legal career, one which brought him into an intimate relationship with the founders of America, and which, in turn, brought Americans into intimate contact with the Orientalist in Jones. Though the strand of Jones's orientalism has by now faded almost to invisibility, it is by no means a minor one in American intellectual history. In fact, were it not for the popularity of his work in eighteenth-century America, the Oriental weave which plays so prominent a part in the tapestry of Transcendentalism would have formed a very different design, or quite possibly, been absent altogether.

William Jones was born in 1736. His father, a member of the Royal Society, was a self-made man who had shipped out to the West Indies and written a standard book on navigation. He died while Jones was still a child, and William was raised by his mother. It is said that whenever the curious child asked a question his mother answered, "Read, and you shall find out." He was a small, somewhat delicate, high-strung boy who lost a year of school when he broke his thigh-bone in a childhood accident, but this only served to make him work harder, and his great gift for languages soon became apparent. At Harrow he augmented the required Latin and Greek with French and Spanish, and then learned Hebrew in order to read the Bible in the original.

At Oxford, Jones immersed himself in the Arabic manuscripts of the Bodleian library, and took the innovative step of engaging, out of his own limited funds, a Syrian to teach him the spoken language. Arabic led to Persian and Turkish, and his linguistic accomplishments became so well-known that when Christian VII of Denmark asked the English to provide him with a French translation of a Persian book, a history of Nadar Shah, the government called on Jones.

At first the young scholar refused. The eighteenth-century Persian was very different from the classical Persian he had studied, and furthermore Jones was repelled by what he took to be little more than a self-serving biography of a bloody tyrant. He relented, however, when the Danish king hinted that if no one in England could handle the job, he would be forced to turn to the French. After a year of tedious work, Jones sent the king a gold-stamped copy, and when Christian VII replied with a letter praising Jones to King George, he became famous overnight. The *Histoire de Nadar Shah* is important not so much for the quality of the rather literal translation, but for the ideas about the importance of Oriental studies that Jones introduced in the *Traite sur la Poesie Orientale*, which he wrote especially for the English edition. In this first version of the *apologia pro litteris orientalibus* to which he would devote his life Jones sketched out his argument. A mechanical imitation of classical imagery and themes, said Jones, had left European verse stale and lifeless. The introduction of fresh images and subjects drawn from Persian poetry would, he hoped, revive it. "The heroic poems of Ferdusi might be versified as easily as the Iliad," he wrote later in the *Dissertation sur la Litterature Orientale*, "and I see no reason why the *The Delivery of Persia* by Cyrus should not be a subject as interesting to us, as the anger of Achilles or the wandering of Ulysses." He urged those readers with "leasure and industry" to study Oriental languages so that they could join him in "Recommending to the learned world a species of literature which abounds with so many new expressions, new images, and new inventions." Perhaps the most eloquent plea appeared in his preface to the *Grammar of the Persian Language*:

> Some men never heard of the Asiatick writings and others will not be convinced there is anything valuable in them; some pretend to be busy, and others are really idle. We all love to excuse, or to conceal, our ignorance, and are seldom willing to allow any excellence beyond the limits of our own attainments: like the savages, who thought that the sun rose and set for them alone, and could not imagine that the waves, which surrounded their island, left coral and pearls upon any other shore.

Jones's translations of Firdausi, Attar, and Hafiz brought renown, but not a living. Sales were modest and there were not yet departments of Oriental language in the universities. After a year abroad as a tutor to Lord Althorp, during which time he read the Chinese *Shih Ching* (*Book of Odes*) in the Royal Library in Paris, Jones returned to England and resigned himself to studying law at the Middle Temple in London. What began as drudgery soon became a labor of love as the young Orientalist found the study of law unexpectedly congenial. He delighted in reading Blackstone, and developed a deep interest in English Common Law. At the same time he began to investigate comparative law, "the history," as he called it, "of the rules and ordinances by which nations, eminent for wisdom, and illustrious in arts, have regulated their civil polity." Both these studies—that of common and comparative law—would dovetail when Jones attempted to reform the British administration of law in India, but at this time he had, so he said, given up his Oriental studies as frivolous by comparison. Nevertheless, despite his best intentions (including storing his Oriental library in his Oxford room), he published five books of Oriental translations and essays during his years at the Middle Temple. Each time he decided that this would be his last.

By 1772, when Jones became a fellow of the Royal Society, it must have seemed that there was little that could stand in the way of a successful and prosperous career in law and government. His skill as a poet and linguist gained him admission to the select circle of Dr. Johnson's Club, where he joined men like Burke, the painter Joshua Reynolds, and the actor David Garrick for weekly luncheons at the Turk's Head in Soho. He was soon a familiar figure in the most advanced salons of the day, where his dancing, singing, and skill at the harp all combined with his promising career and his reputation as a translator of exotic Arabian poetry to make him one of the most eligible bachelors in London society.

Life was pleasant enough, but the political situation was turning ominous. At Bishop Shipley's country place in Asquith, where the conversation centered on the American problem, Jones met Benjamin Franklin and Joseph Priestley. Franklin in particular was a close friend of Bishop Shipley, a leading Whig who had spoken out against the government's American policy. Franklin and Jones were much taken with each other, and Franklin encouraged Jones's interest in the Bishop's daughter, Anna Maria, even though she was said to be already engaged, and Jones's financial situation was not yet secure enough for marriage.

As the American conflict dragged on, Jones's political activity increased. He ran unsuccessfully for a seat in the House of Commons on an antiwar platform, and crossed the Channel to confer with Franklin, who had become the American representative in France. His ostensible purpose was to gather material for an objective history of the American War, and at the same time to seek Franklin's help on behalf of John Paradise, a friend and client, whose Virginia estate was in danger of confiscation. His greater interest, though, lay in presenting Franklin with a compromise peace plan which would grant the colonies a separate form of government, but not independence, resulting in a "just commercial union." Jones wrote his ideas into a pamphlet called "A Fragment of Polybius," identifying himself as "a man unauthorized, unemployed, unconnected; independent in his circumstances, as much as in his principles," while Franklin was cast as "a philosopher named Eleutherian, eminent for the deepest knowledge of nature, the most solid judgement, most approved virtue, and most ardent zeal for the cause of general liberty." Franklin was pleased by the work, but told Jones that the plan had come too late. Nothing short of complete independence would satisfy the colonists.

Meanwhile, India threatened the Crown with as much difficulty as America. The French had agreed not to build any fortifications in India at the Treaty of Paris, but there was always the danger that with the support of the Indian rajahs, they could open a second front there. This, as well as the impending bankruptcy of the East India Company and growing civil disorder, prompted the English Parliament to pass a Regulatory Act which brought both the Company and its property under Government control. The Act also established a Supreme Court charged, among other duties, with protecting the interests of the natives. Four justices were appointed but by 1777, three years later, one had retired and two (like so many of the officials the Company had sent out) succumbed to the climate.

It took some months for the news to reach England, but as soon as Jones heard of the vacancies he let his availability be known. There could be no question of his qualifications. He knew Persian, had knowledge of Muslim customs and law, and was highly thought of in the legal world. The considerable salary of six thousand pounds a year, set high in the hope of rendering the justices immune to bribes, would enable Jones to attain the financial security necessary for marriage and a seat in the House of Commons after his retirement. At the same time, he would be able to pursue his Oriental studies in his leisure time. Finally, Jones hoped to demonstrate that a colony could be administered for the benefit of both natives and Europeans.

There was one problem. The king and his ministers were not anxious to have the brilliant young lawyer who opposed their American policy assume a position of power in distant India. To make matters worse, Jones's views had come to more nearly match Franklin's. During a second visit to Passy, Jones, Franklin and the French minister Verginnes debated whether common, that is, illiterate, men could comprehend the principles of representative government. Jones had written a pamphlet, *The Principles of Government, in a Dialogue between a Scholar and Peasant*, in which he argued the affirmative. It was published by the radical Society for Constitutional Information. The sheriff of Flintshire seized a second edition, published by Anna Maria's brother and William Shipley was indicted for publishing a work with the intent "to raise seditions and tumults within the kingdom." The trial, a landmark case in establishing the principle of freedom of the press, ended in acquittal, but this case, along with the popularity of Jones's pro-American poem "An Ode in

Imitation of Alcaeus," did not improve his chances for the judgeship. Nevertheless, the seat remained vacant, and his hopes were raised when he won praise for his translation of a book of Moslem law as Burke's assistant during the House of Commons hearings on India.

As the years passed, and no action was taken, his usually high spirits sank. There seemed no end to the tangle of shifting political alliances, feuds, promises and evasions he found himself caught in. He finally wrote Franklin, asking what prospects he might expect as a lawyer in Philadelphia. Franklin's response was undoubtedly cordial, since Jones next wrote Lord Althorp that if he were not soon put out of suspense, he would "accept a noble offer that has been made me by the noblest of men, among whom I may not only plead causes but make laws, and write them under the banks of my own river under my own oak."

On the morning of February 28, 1782, the House of Commons passed a resolution calling for an end to the American War. The king's answer, as Jones wrote Franklin, "was in substance, 'I do not want your advice, and will do as I please.' " This absolutist disregard for the will of the people seemed the last straw. "I have no wish to grow old in England," Jones wrote in the same letter, "for, believe me, I would rather be a peasant with freedom than a prince in an enslaved country." Franklin responded by furnishing Jones with a letter of introduction to Thomas Jefferson.

Jones planned to sail with John Paradise from France for Virginia, but at the last minute, when the ship was delayed, he learned that Anna Maria was not engaged to another man after all, and that a new minister had been named. Perhaps, he thought, he might yet reach India. The American War ended shortly after his return to London, but his enemies still blocked his appointment. Jones tried, as he had so many times, to reassure the Government. "As to my politics, which he has heard so much misrepresented," he wrote the king's minister, "his Lordship may be assured that I am no more a republican than a Mahomedan or a Gentoo, and that I have ever formed my opinion from what appeared to me, on the calmest inquiery, the true spirit of the Constitution." At last, after five years of waiting, the petitions of his highly placed friends convinced the king to overrule his nervous advisors, and on April 12, 1783, the newly-knighted Sir William Jones, with his bride Anna Maria, set sail from Portsmouth on the frigate, *Crocodile*, for the six month passage to India.

III

"I cannot conceive of a match more likely to be happy from the amiable qualities each of you possess so plentifully," Franklin wrote on the couple's departure, adding his hope that Jones would "return from that corrupting country, with a great deal of money honestly acquired, and with full as much virtue as you carry out with you."

Franklin's reference to "that corrupting country" was not merely hyperbole. Jones's character, as well as the generous salary of a judge, may have rendered him safe from bribery and graft, but there were still the dangers of the climate and disease and the constantly shifting political situation. Jones had vowed to remain aloof from domestic politics, and though his humanitarian ideals went far, he had no intention of extending them, in their most advanced form, to the Indians. He resolved the contradiction by observing that the Asiatics, while advanced in arts and letters, were far behind the Europeans in matters of government. "The religious manners and laws of the natives," as far as he was concerned, "precluded even the idea of political freedom." In fact, the Indians "were so wedded to inveterate prejudices and habits, if liberty could be forced upon them by Britain, it would make them as miserable as the cruelest despot."

Jones's feelings about the limitations of Indian political ideas did not, however, cloud his "boundless curiousity concerning the people of the East." He spent his time aboard the *Crocodile* reading Persian and law, and sketched an encyclopedic memoranda to himself, *Objects of Enquiry during My Residence in Asia*. The sixteen items included, "The laws of the Hindus and Mahomedans," "The Poetry, rhetoric, and morality of Asia," "Traditions concerning the deluge," "Music of the Eastern Nations," "The Best Mode of Governing Bengal," "Medicine, chemistry, surgery, and anatomy of the Indians," "The Shih-King or 300 Chinese Odes," and "The best accounts of Tibet and Kashmir." To this list he added, as if in afterthought, a few more prospects: an Arabic version of the Gospel of St. Luke, a Persian Psalms of David, and a History of the American War.

Shortly after Jones completed this list, the *Crocodile* made its first Asian port—the island of Hinzuan, just off the African coast. Jones lost little time in finding a native scholar to help him examine the Koran. A heated discussion took place, according to Lord Teignmouth, Jones's friend and biographer, in which Sir William "repelled the rude attack of Mussulman [Muslim] bigotry on the divinity of our Saviour."

Lord Teignmouth was, as Professor A.J. Arberry remarks, "pathetically anxious to prove Jones his own brand of evangelist," and his report of the incident reveals the anxiety which a man of Jones's sympathies evoked even in those contemporaries who most admired him. Lord Teignmouth went to great lengths in his *Memoirs* to still the rumors that must have circulated about Jones's faith in the "sublime doctrines of the Christian religion." "Had he been an infidel," states Teignmouth, "he would have smiled at the scoffs of Mussulman bigotry; and had he been indifferent to his faith, he would have been silent on an occasion, where he could expect neither candor nor concession from his antagonists."

Jones was neither infidel nor "indifferent to his faith," but neither was he the zealous missionary Teignmouth tries to make him. He himself did not waste much ink on the problem. It did not trouble him that mankind had many gods; they were all but names for the same One, and his sympathies for the Orientals ran deep. "I am no Hindu;" he wrote Earl Spencer in 1787, "but I hold the doctrines of the Hindus concerning a future state to be incomparably more rational, more pious, and more likely to deter men from vice than the horrid opinions inculcated on punishments without end." Nor was he a pure eighteenth-century rationalist. He did not view the universe as if it were a clockwork, and those who knew him considered him to be deeply religious. He was drawn to Asia not only as a scientist, but also as a poet.

IV

By the time the *Crocodile* reached India, Jones realized that the task he had set himself could not be accomplished by one man, no matter how prodigious his energy. The solution was to form a Society, like the Royal Society, that would be based on a scientific and systematic method. On January 15, 1784, only four months after his arrival, Sir William summoned thirty English administrators to the chambers of the Grand Jury Room of the Supreme Court of India. Jones introduced the scope of his vision to the assembled company by recounting his thoughts on the *Crocodile*. "At the mid-point" of his voyage, he said, while glancing at the ship's log one evening, when "India lay before us, and Persia on our left, while a breeze from Arabia blew nearly on our stern," he felt "an inexpressible pleasure in the midst of so noble an amphitheatre, almost encircled by the vast regions of Asia, which had ever been esteemed the nurse of sciences, the inventress of delightful and useful arts, the scenes of glorious actions, fertile in the forms of religion and government, in the laws, manners, customs, and languages, as well as features and complexions, of men."

The new Asiatick Society (Jones considered "Asiatick the classical and proper word, preferable to Oriental, which is in truth a word merely relative") would be "bounded only by the geographical limits of Asia." Within these it would study "MAN and NATURE: whatever is performed by the one, or produced by the other." Considering the range of the endeavor, the Society began modestly enough, steering, as Jones counseled, "a middle course between a languid remissness, and an over zealous activity." Papers were read at weekly meetings, and there was "but one rule, namely to have no rules at all." One question, however, the Founder passed over so quickly that we can well imagine its potential to cause what he diplomatically termed "differences of sentiment." "Whether you will enroll as members any number of learned natives," Jones left to be decided by ballot—sometime in the future.

The men enlisted by Jones were not professionals or specialists, but inspired amateurs. "A mere man of letters," he reminded readers in the first volume of *Asiatick Researches*, the journal published by the Society, "retired from the world and alloting his whole time to philosophical pursuits is a character unknown among European residents in India, where every individual is a man of business in the civil or military state, and constantly occupied either in the affairs of government, in the administration of justice, in some department of revenue or commerce, or in one of the liberal professions."

That Jones found enthusiastic support among these busy men was due in large measure to the influence of Warren Hastings, governor-general of India. Hastings had learned a fair amount of Persian, collected Indian art and manuscripts and liked to quote the *Geeta* in letters to his wife back in England. He had encouraged Charles Wilkins to translate the *Bhagavad-Geeta, or Dialoges of Kreeshna and Arjoon in eighteen lectures*—the first Sanskrit text translated directly into English. Others had followed Wilkins's lead. Francis Gladwin translated the *Institutes of the Emperor Akbar* from Persian, and when John Shore, later Lord Teignmouth, studied Persian translations of Sanskrit texts with the assistance of a Brahmin, he found that Hinduism "is pure Deism and has a wonderful resemblance to the doctrines of Plato."

But these men were the exceptions. Most Englishmen had little interest in Indian learning for its own sake. The more convincing motive was political. As Nathaniel Halhed wrote in the introduction to his *Gentoo Laws:*

> The importance of the commerce of India and the advantages of territorial establishment in Bengal have at length awakened the attention of the British legislature to every circumstance that may conciliate the affections of the natives or ensure stability to the acquisition. Nothing can so favourably conduce to these two points as a well-timed toleration in matters of religion and adaptation of such original institutes of the country, as do not immediately clash with the laws of the conquerors.

Hastings could use official funds to support translations of laws and codes, but little else. The actual situation, as Jones found it when he called the first meeting of the Asiatick Society, was expressed by John Shore in a letter to an Oxford friend. "Some books have lately been published," he wrote, "but the expense of printing them is so enormous and the reputation derived from the labours of translation so little that few attempts more will be made."

Still, it seemed inevitable, given the pervasive place of religion in Indian life, that the English would stumble on Indian spirituality. Jones himself was led to Sanskrit by the same reasoning that Halhed used to justify Indian studies to the British legislature. Jones's own research in common and comparative law led him to believe, like Halhed, that the Indians ought to be governed by "the original institutes of the country" (as long as these did not contradict English law) and he made this controversial idea the subject of his first charge to the Court. In order to bring this reform about, however, it would first be necessary to know what these laws were. Jones soon discovered that Halhed's *Gentoo Laws* was neither reliable nor complete. In addition, he could not find any oath that the Hindus would accept as proof against perjury, and he found himself at the mercy of pandits "who deal out Hindu law as they please." His one hope was that Wilkins would compile a complete digest of Hindu law directly from Sanskrit, but the translator of the *Geeta*, who had served in India since 1770, declined the honor in order to return to London. Jones was left to learn Sanskrit himself. Ironically, it was perhaps the only subject he had not included in his *Objects of enquiery*.

It was no easy matter, even for the most accomplished linguist in Europe. The only Sanskrit dictionary in existence, compiled by the Jesuit Father Haanxledon in the early eighteenth century, remained in manuscript, either unknown or unavailable to Jones, and he had only

Sanskrit-Sanskrit dictionaries and grammars to work with. The first Brahmins he approached at the Hindu University of Nadeya refused to even discuss the matter. (Apparently Wilkins's finding of a teacher in Benares had been nothing more than a fortunate accident.) Jones was refused a second time, even though he offered a considerable amount of money, and explained that he wanted only to help the Indians and had no intention of reading the sacred texts. (The Brahmins, it should be noted, were acting no differently from the English, who had prohibited the teaching of *their* language to Indians.)

Finally, Jones managed to persuade a medical practitioner of the Vaidya caste to instruct him, with the understanding that there were certain texts the teacher himself was not permitted to read. "Though not a Brahmin," Jones wrote of his teacher, "he has taught grammar and ethics to the most learned Brahmins, and has no priestly pride, with which his pupils in general abound." The work at first went slowly, but Jones's excitement grew as he completed his first exercise—a translation of the fables of the *Hitopadesha*. His studies were constantly interrupted by Court business, but there was no turning back. "I would rather be a valetudinarian all my life," he told a friend back in Calcutta, "than leave unexplored the Sanskrit mine which I have just opened."

V

By 1788, when the first volume of the *Asiatick Researches* appeared in Calcutta, the mine had already begun to produce ore of the highest grade. True, the first two samples—a translation of a land grant and literal translations of five monument inscriptions—were small, without much lustre, and of interest only to specialists, but the essay "On the Literature of the Hindus, from the Sanskrit," was another matter. "Whenever we direct our attention to Hindu literature," Jones wrote, there "the notion of infinity presents itself; and the longest life would not be sufficient for the perusal of near five hundred thousand stanzas in the Puranas, with a million more perhaps in the other works. . . ." The field was vast but Jones now had helpers; he had convinced the Brahmins of his good intentions and found "that the learned Hindus, encouraged by the mildness of our government and manners, are at least as eager to communicate their knowledge of all kinds, as we can be to receive it."

Jones may not have been, as he had to continually reassure his countrymen, anything like a *Gentoo*, but he was dedicated to learning everything he could from the Hindu pundits with whom he now conversed in Sanskrit. He could not bring himself, at least in print, to grant Hinduism equality with Christianity. But the resemblances he had seen between the gods of the Greeks and Indians led him to write in "On the Gods of the Greeks, Romans and Indians," (perhaps the first essay on comparative mythology) that there had been at one time "a general union or affinity between the most distinguished inhabitants of the primitive world. . . ." The Indian gods, he said, were not heathen idols, but forms "of those very deities who were worshipped under different names in Greece and Italy." Manu was Saturn; Indra, Jupiter. The discovery was a fortunate one. He could not have invented a better way of convincing skeptical, eighteenth-century Europeans of the value of Indian philosophy.

But it was not only the similarity between Greek and Indian gods that struck Jones. The lives of the Brahmin philosophers, whom Jones pictured as strolling through "groves and seminaries of learning" while "disputing in the forms of logick, or discoursing on the vanity of human enjoyments, on the immortality of the soul, her emanation from the eternal mind, her debasement, wanderings and final union with her source," also recalled the peripatetic sages of Greece. He found "all the metaphysicks of the old Academy, the Stoa, the Lyceum" in the six schools of the Hindus, and did not think it possible "to read the Vedanta . . . without believing that Pythagoras and Plato derived their sublime theology from the same fountain with the sages of India." It was here, rather than in any of the myriad forms of the gods, that Jones located the most sublime heights of Indian spirituality. "It must always be remembered," he told readers of the *Researches*, "that the learned Indians, as they are instructed by their own books, in truth acknowledge only one Supreme Being, whom they call Brahme, or the Great One in the neuter gender; they believe his Essence to be infinitely removed from the comprehension of any mind but his own. . . ."

Finally, it was the discovery of a correspondence, "too strong to have been accidental," between the gods and philosophies of Greece and India that led Jones to his fullest formulation of the Oriental renaissance. True, he had set forth numerous versions of the theme long before he left England. But it was only now, when he was face-to-face with Asia, that India could become Greece, and that what had before been a hopeful idea, closer to a plea than an actuality, could catch fire and become transformed into a universal vision.

"To what shall I compare my literary pursuits in India?" he wrote in 1787.

> Suppose Greek literature to be known in modern Greece only and there to be in the hands of priests and philosophers; and suppose them to be still worshippers of Jupiter and Apollo; suppose Greece to have been conquered successively by Goths, Huns, Vandals, Tartars and lastly by English; then suppose a court of juridicature to be established by the British parliament in Athens and an inquisitive Englishman to be one of the judges; suppose him to learn Greek there, which none of the countrymen knew and to read Homer, Pindar, Plato, which no other Europeans had ever heard of. Such am I in this country; substituting Sanskrit for Greek and the Brahmins for the priests of Jupiter and Vilimic, Vyasa and Kalidasa for Homer, Plato and Pindar.

VI

Jones had gone far in understanding Hinduism, but his ideas about Buddhism were necessarily clouded. Buddhism had long since disappeared from India by the time the English replaced the Moslems. If Jones had wanted to converse with Buddhist scholars, as he had with Brahmins, he would have had to go north to Tibet or south to Ceylon, Siam, or Burma. In fact, the scholarly study of Buddhism had not yet begun. The first Pali grammar, Eugene Burnouf's *Essai sur le Pali*, would not be published until 1826, and the discovery and translation of Northern Buddhist Sanskrit texts would have to wait for the civil servants who would follow the trail Jones had opened: first, Thomas Henry Colebrook, who was a judge of the Calcutta court of appeal and professor of Sanskrit at the East India Company's college in Fort William, and whose essay "On the Duties of a Faithful Hindu Widow" Jones would edit just before his death for the fourth *Asiatick Researches*; and then Brian Hodgson, who would send Sanskrit manuscripts to Calcutta, London and Paris from his lonely post in a hill-station in Nepal, one of these being the *Saddharma-pundarika* (or *Lotus of the True Teaching*) *Sutra*, which Eugene Burnouf in Paris would turn into a French version that would find its way to Ralph Waldo Emerson and Henry David Thoreau in Concord, Massachusetts. But all of this lay in the future. As the eighteenth century closed, the world's most learned Orientalist was not aware that India had once been the home of a great Buddhist civilization. That discovery would not take place until 1837, when James Prinsep, of the Calcutta Mint and *The Asiatick Society* would decipher the early Brahmi script of the Ashokan rock-edicts.

When Jones visited Bodh-Gaya in 1784, there were no Buddhist shrines, inscriptions, monasteries or pilgrims. Lord Teignmouth reported it was "famous as the birth place of Boudh, the author of a system of philosophy which labors under the imputation of atheism," but it was, as he also said, still "more famous for the annual resort of Hindu pilgrims from all parts of India, who repair to the holy city, for the purpose of making prescribed oblations to their deceased ancestors, and of obtaining absolution from all their sins."

It was for these reasons, more for lack of resources and information than of sympathy, that Jones's writings on Buddhism remain unsystematic, sketchy and incomplete. Not surprisingly, he seems to have adopted the Hindu view (which made of Buddha the ninth incarnation of Vishnu), though he was aware of Buddha's opposition to some of the excesses of Hinduism. He writes that the sacrifices offered in the name of Kali "gave such offense to Buddha." In his comprehensive essay "On the Literature of Hindus, from the Sanskrit," he had only this to say about Buddhism:

> We need say no more of the heterodox writings, than that those on the religion and philosophy of Buddha seem to be connected with some of the most curious parts of Asiatick History, and contain, perhaps, all that could be found in the Pali, or sacred language of the Eastern Indian Peninsula. It is asserted in Bengal that Amarsinha himself was a Baudda; but he seemed to have been a theist of tolerant principles, and like Abu'lfazl, desirous of reconciling the different religions of India.

Curiously, he thought that "Wod, or Oden, whose religion . . . was introduced to Scandinavia by a foreign race, was the same with Buddh, whose rites were probably imported into India nearly at the same time, although received much later by the Chinese, who soften his name into Fo." Jones does not say just who this "foreign race" may have been, but it seems from this passage that he either did not know or did not accept the Buddhist's version of the origin of their own religion.

Though Jones himself had no firsthand experience of Buddhism, the first of the *Asiatick Researches* did carry fairly reliable reports from Ceylon and Tibet. Tibet was the most difficult of all the Buddhist countries to reach. Oddly, it was also the country which yielded the most scholarly and accurate accounts of Buddhism. This was the result of the work of a few Jesuit (and later Capuchin) missionaries who had been drawn to Tibet in the early seventeenth century by rumors of Christians living there. Both Jones and his wife greatly enjoyed reading the collected papers of one of these men, the Italian Capuchin Francesco Orazio della Penna, who had lived in Lhasa from 1716 to 1732, and who had learned enough Tibetan to compile a dictionary that would be translated into

English in 1826. Father della Penna also translated Tsongkhapa's *Lam-rim chen-mo* (a basic stages-of-the-path text of the Gelugpa school, which he founded), as well as the *Pratimokshasutra*, but it is probable that these remained in manuscript, and that the "800 pages in quarto concerning the Mythology and History, both Civil and Natural, of Tibet" that Jones and Anna Maria read had come from selections included in the Capuchin missionary Antonio Giorgi's *Alphabetum Tibetanum Missionum Apostolicarum*, published in Rome in 1762.

Of more current interest to Jones and the Governor-General Warren Hastings was the account in the *Researches* of a government mission to Tibet by Col. Turnour. Hastings had dispatched an expedition to Tibet some years before, and the English had then been given a favorable audience by the Teesho Lama, who died in the intervening years. He had, however, recently reincarnated, according to Tibetan belief, and it was this Teesho Lama, now a young child not yet able to speak, with whom Mr. Turnour sought to establish (or reestablish) close diplomatic ties. For political reasons the Tibetans were not too anxious to allow the English party much access to the Tibetan court, but they did, finally, allow them a brief meeting with the young lama. Just before the audience, Tibetan officials told Turnour that the former Teesho Lama had been partial to the English, "and that the present one often tried to utter the name of the English." Like any good diplomat, Turnour did not trouble himself with the truth or falsehood of the doctrine of rebirth, but simply made use of it. "I encouraged the thought," he wrote, "hopeful that they would teach the prejudice to strengthen with his increasing age, and they assured me that should he, when he begins to speak, have forgot, they would early teach him to repeat the name of Hastings." At the request of the Teesho Lama's father, both Turnour and his companion, Mr. Saunders, wore proper English dress when they presented him with the customary "white pekong handkerchief," as well as a string of pearls and coral sent by Hastings.

The scene Turnour described could easily have taken on the sublime yet ridiculous tones of a comic opera. The Englishmen, after all, had journeyed thousands of miles to confront a child with whom they could not speak, and whose friendship in a previous incarnation they had to at least seem to acknowledge. But despite Turnour's initial remarks—which may have given the impression that he only humored the Tibetans out of political motives—it is clear from his description of the actual encounter that something else happened. The sophisticated Englishman had been surprisingly impressed and moved by the young lama:

> During the time we were in the room, I observed the Lama's eyes were scarce ever turned from us, and when our cups were empty of tea, he appeared uneasy, and throwing back his head and contracting the skin of his brow, he kept making a noise, for he could not speak, until they were filled again. He took out a golden cup, containing confects, some burnt sugar, and stretching out his arm made a motion to his attendants to give them to me . . . I found myself, though visiting an infant, under the necessity of saying something, for it was hinted to me, that notwithstanding he is unable to reply, it is not to be inferred that he cannot understand . . . I just briefly said, That the Governor-General on receiving the news of his decease in China, was overwhelmed with grief and sorrow, and continued to lament his absence from the world until the cloud that had overcast the happiness of this nation by his re-appearance was dispelled, and then if possible, a greater degree of joy had taken place than he had experienced of grief on receiving the first mournful news. . . . The little creature turned, looking steadfastly towards me with the appearance of much attention while I spoke, and nodded with repeated, but slow movements of the head, as though he understood and approved every word, but could not utter a reply . . . His whole regard was turned to us; he was silent and sedate, never once looking towards his parents, as if under their influence at the time; and with whatever pains his manners may have been formed to correct, yet I must own his behavior on this occasion appeared perfectly natural and spontaneous, and not directed by any action or sign of authority.

And yet, detailed and sympathetic as Turnour's account was, it did not include a single word about the Buddha or Buddhism. The Teesho Lama had made a powerful, somewhat inexplicable impression on the Englishman, but he did not try to discover what was behind that mood. The purpose of the visit had been political, not religious, and both the English and the Tibetans seemed to want it that way. The meeting suggested certain intriguing possibilities on both sides. When Turnour told Hastings about his impressions of the Teesho Lama, the governor-general at first allowed himself to wonder if the Teesho Lama were not indeed an incarnation of his predecessor, but he decided, upon further consideration, that it was actually "an extraordinary instance, of a kind never seen in the West, of the effect of education on the infant mind." The Tibetans, for their part were convinced that the visit had had a salutary effect on the Englishmen. As a contemporary Tibetan account had it: "Although [the visitors] were not knowers of the niceties of religion, by merely gazing [at the young Panchen Lama] an irresistible faith was born in them. And they said: 'In such a little frame there are activities of body, speech, and mind, so greatly marvelous and different from the other.' Thus they spoke with great reverence."

Still, the only author to write about Buddhism per se in *Asiatick Researches* was William Chambers, whose article "An Account of the Sculpture and Ruins of Mavilpuram" came from Ceylon, where Buddhism had survived first the Portuguese, then the Dutch and now the English. Chambers did not, like Jones, identify the Buddha with Wod or Oden, but with the Greek Mercury. He nonetheless made great advances on authors of the period by describing Sinhalese "priests" with a fair amount of accuracy. Reasoning from his observation that the Sinhalese priests are "of no particular tribe, but are chosen out of the body of the people," and "eat flesh, but will not kill the animal," Chambers drew the conclusion "that this is a system of religion different from the Veds," in many ways "totally inconsistent with the principles and practices of the Brahmins." In the same article Chambers suggested (probably the first scholar to do so) that Pali—or Balic, as he spelled it—was based on Sanskrit.

VII

The first number of the *Asiatick Researches* in which all these articles appeared was a great success. Jones's fame spread as seven hundred copies were sent to England while still others made their way to America. The volume fulfilled the expectations aroused by an earlier publication by Jones, the *Asiatick Miscellany* (edited by Francis Gladwin in 1785). The most popular pieces in this collection of "Original Productions, Translations, Fugitive Pieces, and Imitations, and Extracts from Curious Publications," were the hymns to Hindu gods like Kama, Narayana, Indra and Sarasvati, which Jones turned into English poems based on classical verse forms used by Pope, Gray and Milton. These "Hymns" were widely reprinted in American magazines, and the "Hymn to Narayana" made a deep impression on the young Ralph Waldo Emerson when he read it in 1820. Jones's other major effort in this vein was his translation of the *Gitagovinda*, which told of ". . . the loves of CRISHNA and RADHA, or the reciprical attraction between the divine goodness and the human soul. . . ." The translation was not quite complete, for Jones took it upon himself to omit "only those passages, which are too luxuriant and too bold for an *European* taste."

His major preoccupation was the work that had led him to Sanskrit in the first place—the translation of the *Manava-dharma-sastra*, the *Ordinances of Manu*. The book was to furnish the English with "a complete digest of Hindu and Mohammedan laws after the model of Justinian's inestimable *Pandects*, compiled by the most learned of the native lawyers, with an accurate verbal translation of it into English." It was very different from *Blackstone's*. "Manu" was the Hindu Adam, the first man, and the laws he had received, which governed the cosmos as well as society, formed the basis of the Hindu world view. The *Laws of Manu* contained twelve chapters divided into 2,684 articles; work proceeded slowly and laboriously, though by this time Jones had won the financial support of both the East India Company and the government. This enabled Jones to pay for the services of both the Moslem and Hindu pundits, who were now impressed with Jones's devotion to their literature and assisted him gladly.

It was from one of these friendly Brahmins that Jones heard of the *natakas*, a kind of Sanskrit literature that the Indian said resembled the plays performed by the English in Calcutta during the rainy season. The best of these was said to be *Shakuntala* by Kalidasa, and by the time Jones finished reading the play, he was convinced that he had uncovered one of the great masterpieces of world literature. Hastings may have felt the need to apologize for Wilkins's translation of the *Geeta*, by writing in the introduction, "I should exclude in estimating the merit of such a production all rules drawn from the ancient and modern literature of Europe," but Jones felt no compunction in calling Kalidasa "the Indian Shakespeare or Metastasio." When *Sacontala; or, the Fatal Ring: an Indian Drama* reached Europe in 1789 it created a sensation. Goethe read the German translation by G. Forster, and Shakuntala found a place in the prologue to Faust: "Wouldst thou the earth and heaven itself in one sole name combine?/ I name thee, O Shakuntala, and all at once is said." The play also had repercussions in India, where the discovery of the great playwright, whom most Indians had never heard of, sparked a national Indian renaissance. The Moghuls, the Indians realized, had superimposed a foreign culture on their own, as had the English. In taking Kalidasa from the narrow circle of Brahmins who guarded Sanskrit literature, and presenting him to the world as an equal of Shakespeare, Jones had given the Indians the key to unlock their own past.

As Jones's knowledge of Sanskrit increased, he began to see correspondences between it and many of the twenty-eight languages he had learned. By comparing the morphemes in European languages, Jones arrived at the formulation that is the foundation for comparative philology. "The Sanskrit language," he reported to the Asiatick Society in

1786, "whatever be its antiquity, is of a wonderful structure; more perfect than the Greek, more copious than the Latin, and more exquisitely refined than either, yet bearing to both of them a stronger affinity, both in the roots of verbs and in the forms of grammar, than could possibly have been produced by accident; so strong, indeed, that no philosopher could examine all three without believing them to have sprung from some common source, which, perhaps, no longer exists." This idea that there was an Indo-European family of languages, with an ancestor shared by both Europe and India, profoundly influenced Friedrich Schlegel. Schlegel, the first German Sanskritist, who learned the language from Sir Alexander Hamilton, one of the founding members of the Asiatick Society, when both men were interned by the French in 1803, went on to develop the field of comparative philology which became a cornerstone of the German Romanticism that would itself be so central to the American transcendentalists.

VIII

Jones planned to return to England in 1790, but he stayed on to finish the *Digest*. In 1793 Anna Maria's doctors pronounced her life in danger unless she returned to England immediately. She postponed her departure more than once, finally sailing at the end of the year. Jones planned to follow as soon as the work on the *Digest* was completed. He would retire on his comfortable income in England, and finally visit America. ("I shall not die in peace without visiting your United States for a few months before the end of the eighteenth century," he wrote Walter Pollard. "May I find wisdom and goodness in senates, arms and judicature which are power in your commons, and the blessings of wealth and peace equally distributed among all.")

But he had driven himself too hard. He died on April 24, 1794, with the *Institutes of Hindu Law; or the Ordinances of Manu, according to the Gloss of Culloca, comprising the Indian System of Duties, Religious and Civil*, ready for the press. Lord Teignmouth found him "lying on his bed in a posture of meditation . . . His bodily suffering, from the complacency of his features, and the ease of his attitude, could not have been severe; and his mind must have derived consolation from those sources where he had been in the habit of seeking it, and where alone, in our last moments, it can ever be found."

He was forty-eight years old. He had only been in India twelve years, but the mine of Sanskrit had been opened, and its riches made visible to the world. The voyage to America, which Jones never made, would be taken instead by his work.

CHAPTER FOUR

THE RESTLESS PIONEERS

I

It is often forgotten that many of the most distinguished New England fortunes were made in the early years of the nineteenth century by men in the East India trade. The Peabody, Sturgis and Russell families all did very well outfitting and sailing the new, fast clipper ships, and for a time there was no more fashionable Boston address than India Row, no more prestigious office than the one on India Wharf. But the main imports from India were cotton goods—Bengal Gingham, Madras Pattern, Gourypore Check—and the rise of the New England milltowns, along with the Protective Tariff in 1816, came close to destroying the trade.

That it did not was due mainly to the foresight and Yankee ingenuity of Frederic Tudor, who had hit upon the idea of selling ice to the tropics. In 1833, after testing the market in Martinique, Tudor dispatched his fastest clipper to India with one hundred and eighty pounds of New England ice in the hold. The natives were puzzled at first, and one, it was said, demanded his money back when he discovered that he had left his ice too long in the sun. However, Tudor soon convinced the Anglo-Indian community that ice was something they could not do without.

In the winter of 1846, as a young man named Henry David Thoreau watched, a hundred Irishmen up from Cambridge carved the blue ice of Walden pond into large blocks bound for India. He found himself contemplating a very different kind of East India trade, one that had summoned the Orientals themselves to his own backyard. He would write in *Walden*:

> Thus it appears that the sweltering inhabitants of Charlestone and New Orleans, of Madras and Bombay and Calcutta, drink at my well. In the morning I bathe my intellect in the stupendous and cosmogonal philosophy of the *Bhagvat Geeta*, since whose composition years of the gods have elapsed, and in comparison with which our modern world and its literature seem puny and trivial . . . I lay down the book and go to my well for water, and lo! there I meet the servant of the Brahmin, priest of Brahma and Vishnu and Indra, who still sits in his temple on the Ganges reading the Vedas, or dwells at the root of a tree with his crust and water jug. I meet his servant come to draw water for his master, and our buckets as it were grate together in the same well. The pure Walden water is mingled with the sacred water of the Ganges.

Though Thoreau always thought of the Orientals in the present, neither he nor Ralph Waldo Emerson had ever met a practicing Hindu or Buddhist. The Concordians stayed at home. They knew the Orientals from books, almost all of which were the results of the labors of the small band of Englishmen, Orientalists only in their spare time, who had gone out to India as civil servants and administrators. The *Bhagavad Geeta* that Thoreau read under the trees every morning at Walden had been translated by Charles Wilkins—the first work to be translated directly into English from Sanskrit. Even more important to the Concordians was Sir William Jones. It was from Jones's books, especially his translation of the *Laws of Manu*, and the essays in *Asiatick Researches*, that literate Americans, including Thomas Jefferson, drew their knowledge of Indian literature and comparative religion. In fact, the first American publication of a Sanskrit translation was of Jones's *Sacontala*, which appeared in 1805 in *The Monthly Anthology and Boston Review*. The *Review* was edited by a minister named William Emerson, who, like many of the liberal clergymen of the day, hoped that the new Indian scriptures would provide a kind of cross-culture proof for the historicity of Biblical events.

William Emerson's son, Ralph Waldo, was only seven when his father died. The library he left as his sole inheritance (and even that was eventually auctioned off) contained a fair collection of contemporary Orientalia: Lord Teignmouth's *Memoirs of Sir William Jones*, Robert Southey's *Curse of Kehama*, and Luiz Cameo's *Discovery of India*. All of these works were augmented with extensive notes and appendices taken from the *Asiatick Researches* that Jones had edited, and it is not unlikely that the young Emerson heard parts of them during family reading hours, or even read them himself.

In any case, when Ralph Waldo entered Harvard at the age of fourteen, he brought with him a well-developed, if conventional, interest in India. In one of his first college themes he argued with characteristic New England logic that it was the heat of India that was mainly responsible for her misery and superstition, and in 1820, as his first entry in his published *Journal*, he wrote, "The ostentatious ritual of India which worshipped God while still outraging nature, though softened as it proceeded West, was still too harsh a discipline for the Athenian manners to undergo."

There were those close to him, however, who had begun to entertain the notion that Asia might have something to offer the new culture. Emerson's Aunt Mary, a rather unusual and advanced Unitarian in her views, who had taken charge of his education after his father's death, would not go that far, but did write her nephew about the new Hindu philosophy she was reading. She was especially impressed with the reports about Ram Mohan Roy, the Indian religious reformer who had fashioned a universal theology from both Christianity and Vedanta, and who was quite popular in Unitarian circles.

Emerson answered his aunt with cautious interest. He was drawn, but not yet overcome. "I am curious to read your Hindoo mythologies," he wrote her in 1822, a year after his graduation.

> One is apt to lament over indolence and ignorance, when he reads some of these sanguine students of the Eastern antiquities, who seem to think that all the wisdom of Europe is twice-told lies hid in the treasures of the Brahmins and the volumes of Zoroaster. When I lie dreaming on the possible contents of pages as dark to me as the characters on the seal of Solomon, I console myself with calling it learning's El Dorado. Every man has a fairy land just beyond the compass of his horizon . . . and it is very natural that literature at large should look for some fanciful stores of mind which surpassed example and possibility.

In the following years, Asia nearly disappeared from Emerson's *Journals*. What, after all, could a young Unitarian minister make of a religion where, as he noted, "330 million Gods have in it each their heaven, or rather each their parlour, in this immense 'goddery'." Then there was the matter of the "teeming" Asian masses. The Social Reformer could not avoid pointing out that ". . . admiration paid by a few gazers to one's intellectual supremacy will hardly be counted in the eyes of the Philanthropists any atonement for the squalid and desperate ignorance of untold millions who breathe the breath of misery in Asia. . . ." Even at his most critical moments, though, he saw something else. His prose may have neatly dispatched those too "sanguine students" who expected the Brahmins to hold all the wisdom in the world, but he could still locate "learning's El Dorado" as a necessary function, if not a place, in the real world. "If the unknown was not magnified," he reasoned, "nobody would explore. Europe would lack the regenerating impulse, and America lie waste had it not been for El Dorado."

So "El Dorado," or India, or something India might stand for, if only in his mind, drew him on. He had become a minister as a matter of course, but that did not last long. The doctrinal reason for his departure was that he felt he could no longer administer the ordinance of the Lord's Supper, but that, it seemed clear to everyone, merely furnished the occasion. The unexpected death of his young wife, Ellen, from tuberculosis had affected him deeply, but it had also made it easier for him to leave, since he was now without family responsibilities. "The death of a dear friend, wife, brother, lover," he would write in *Compensation*, "somewhat later assumes the aspect of guide or genius; for it commonly operates revolutions in our way of life, terminates an epoch of infancy or youth which was waiting to be closed, breaks up a wonted occupation, or a household, or a style of living, and allows the formation of new ones more friendly to the growth of character." In any case, he did not hesitate to express his feelings. "How little love is at the bottom of these great religious shows," he wrote in his journal in 1831, "congregations and temples and sermons—how much sham!" In his own sermons he pointed more often to the divinity of man than to the divinity of Christ. "A trust in yourself is not the height of pride," he told his congregation, "but of piety, an unwillingness to learn of any but God himself." Therefore, he concluded, in language any Buddhist would have recognized, "the origin of self must be perceived."

His own thinking had come to be more and more influenced by the English and German Romantics—Goethe, Wordsworth, Coleridge, and

Carlyle, the last three of whom he met on a trip abroad. With her favorite nephew out of the country, Aunt Mary felt free to confide in his brother Charles: "It is far sadder than the translation of a soul by death of the body to lose Waldo as I have lost him. And now that he is far away I can complain. I do believe he has no fixed faith in a personal God!"

His aunt's fears were true, as far as they went, but she did not yet realize that he had replaced a personal God by a more universal one. "Prayer as a means to effect a private end is theft and meanness," he would write in *Self-Reliance*. "It supposes dualism and not unity in nature and consciousness." For Emerson, God, man and nature were all intimately connected. "We lie in the lap of immense intelligence," he wrote in the same essay, "which makes us organs of its activity and receivers of its truth."

When he returned to America from Europe, he found himself in great demand as a lecturer. If Aunt Mary thought him "confused & dark—a mixture of heathen greatness—pantheism—Swedenborgianism & German rationalism," his contemporaries saw him with greater clarity as the spokesman for that spirit of the age they called "the Newness." "We are all a little wild with numberless projects of social reform," he wrote Carlyle in 1840. "Not a reading man but has a draft of a new Community in his waistcoat pocket. I am gently mad, and am resolved to live cleanly. One man renounces the use of animal food; and another of coin; and another of domestic hired service; and another of the State; and on the whole we have a commendable share of reason and hope."

In Concord, where he settled with his wife Lidian, a circle gathered around him. "There was no club properly speaking;" F.W. Hedge later reminisced, "no presiding officer, no vote ever taken. How the name transcendental, given to these gatherings and the set of persons who took part in them, originated, I cannot say. It certainly never was assumed by the persons so called." The group had begun with four Unitarian clergymen discussing their dissatisfaction with Locke's philosophy, but soon included such nonclerical types as Bronson Alcott, whose experimental Temple School was run (while it lasted) on the Platonic assumption that children had minds and wisdom of their own, and Margaret Fuller, feminist and translator of Goethe's *Conversations with Eckermann*. There was much talk of Law, Truth, Individuality and Revelation, but the one concrete result of it all was the founding of a small magazine.

The first number of the *Dial* appeared in July 1840. Emerson's opening manifesto hailed it as "a Journal in a new spirit." The contributors were drawn, he said, "not so much [from] the pens of the practiced writers, as the discourse of the living, and the portfolios which friendship has opened to us." In addition to Emerson, these included Margaret Fuller, who served as editor, Ripley, Dwight, Parker and Alcott, who offered a selection of his rather didactic "Orphic Sayings." The *Dial* also carried an "Elegy," whose author was identified only by a terse, upright "T."

T. was, at twenty-three, the youngest in the group, the man about whom Emerson had written his brother Charles, "My Henry Thoreau will be a great poet for such a company; and one of these days for all companies." From their first meeting Emerson had taken a close interest in his Concord neighbor, and had hired him to do odd jobs around the house. It was Emerson's suggestion that prompted Thoreau to begin his voluminous, microscopically observed *Journals* ("Oct. 22, What are you doing now? he said—Do you keep a Journal? So today I make my first entry.") and it was in Emerson's library that Thoreau first came across the Orientals. He was completely taken; Sir William Jones's *Laws of Manu*, he wrote, "comes to me with such a volume of sound as if it had been swept unobstructed over the plains of Hindustan."

II

The *Dial* turned markedly towards the East when Emerson, with Thoreau as his assistant, reluctantly replaced Margaret Fuller as editor in 1842, and began to print a series of "Ethnical Scriptures." These were to be "selections from the oldest ethical and religious writing of men, exclusively of the Hebrew and Greek Scriptures. Each nation has its bible more or less pure." Emerson wrote, "None has been yet willing or able in a wise and devout spirit to collate its own with that of other nations, and sinking the civil-historical and their ritual portions to bring together the grand expressions of the moral sentiment in different ages and races, the rules for the guidance of life, the bursts of piety and of abandonment to the Invisible and Eternal;—a work inevitable sooner or later, and which we hope to be done by religion and not by literature."

Emerson's first offering to the elite circle of *Dial* readers (there were three hundred subscribers in 1842) consisted of selections from Charles Wilkins's translation of the *Heetopades of Veeshnoo Sarma*. Emerson had come in the years since college to appreciate the Hindus more and more. In 1843 the first copy of the *Bhagavad Gita* arrived in Concord. In a letter to Elizabeth Hoar, Emerson called it "the much renowned book of Buddhism, extracts from which I have often admired but never before held the book in my hands." That Emerson could mistake the *Bhagavad Gita* for a Buddhist work is symptomatic of the confusion that reigned about the differences between Hinduism and Buddhism. Yet when he did trouble to make the distinction, his sympathies lay with the Hindus.

His impressions of Buddhism were severe, to say the least. The root of his antipathy may be traced to an etymological misreading: the use of the term "annihilation" for "nirvana." Then, too, Buddhism never spoke of God as the Creator, nor did it help that the individual soul was said to be nonexistent. Emerson may have had no room for the idea of a personal God in the narrow or literal sense, but he could still speak of being "part and parcel of God." The idea of "annihilation," of "nothingness" froze him with its "icy light." "This remorseless Buddhism," he wrote in 1842, "lies all around, threatening with death and night. . . . Every thought, every enterprise, every sentiment, has its ruin in this horrid Infinite which circles us and awaits our dropping into it. If killing all the Buddhists would do the least good, we would have a slaughter of the Innocents directly." "*Buddhism*," he summarized in another entry: "Winter. Night. Sleep, are all invasions of eternal Buddh, and it gains a point every day. Let be, laissez-faire, so popular now in philosophy and in politics, that is bald Buddhism; and then very fine names it has got to cover up its chaos withal, namely trances, raptures, abandonement, ecstasy—all Buddh, naked Buddh." It was far too much, or rather far too little, far too absent, for a philosopher who could write that "Being is the vast affirmative, excluding negation, self-balanced, and swallowing up all relations. . . . The soul refuses all limits. It affirms in man always an Optimism, never a Pessimism."

Yet it is not all that neat. There were other times when the man who had called consistency the "hobgoblin of little minds" could speak of Buddhism with a friendlier voice. "The Buddhist is a Transcendentalist," he would say, because of "his conviction that every good deed can by no possibility escape its reward," and in the essay "Poetry and the Imagination," he set what he took to be Buddhist ideals against the coarse materialism of an industrial society: "Better men saw heavens and earths; saw noble instruments of noble souls. We see railroads, mills, and banks, and we pity the poverty of these dreaming Buddhists. There was as much creative force then as now, but it made globes and astronomic heavens, instead of broadcloth and wine-glasses."

It is in passages like this that Emerson seems to have forgotten his notions of Buddhist nihilism. The Concordians were at odds with their age, and they looked to the Orientals as an example of what their own best lives might be. The shadow of industrialism, "of railroads, mills, and banks," was already on them, and they sought models and inspiration from what they took to be men of a more bucolic and cultivated age. They found what they could not discover in the nearby mill-towns, in ancient Greece, China and India.

III

Emerson was a reluctant editor of the *Dial*, and before long he had ceded responsibility for the Ethnical Scriptures to Thoreau, who was enthusiastic about the project. "It is not singular," he wrote Emerson, "that, while the religious world is gradually picking to pieces its old testaments, here are some coming slowly after, on the seashore, picking up the durable relics of perhaps older books and putting them together again?" The first results of Thoreau's beachcombing were of high quality but predictable enough—passages from Jones's *Laws of Manu* and the sayings of Confucius. Far more of a find, though, was the Ethnical Scripture for the *Dial* of 1844, "The Preaching of the Buddha," taken, as Thoreau told his readers, "from one of the religious books of the Buddhists of Nepal, entitled the WHITE LOTUS OF THE GOOD LAW."

This was, in fact, the introduction of the *Saddharmapundarika*, or *Lotus Sutra*, to the English-speaking world. Thoreau had gone to a great deal of trouble to present this quintessential mahayana sutra to American readers. He had himself translated it from the French of Eugene Burnouf's *L'introduction a l'histoire du Buddhisme indien*, which had just appeared in Paris.

It is hard to imagine the impression that American readers unfamiliar with Buddhist doctrines may have received from the complex, exuberant imagery of the fragment of the *Lotus Sutra* Thoreau had translated. What, for example, could they have made of the statement: "What I have said is the supreme truth; may my auditors arrive at complete annihilation; may they follow the excellent way which conducts to the state of Buddha; may all the auditors, who hear me, become Buddhas."

IV

There is a sense in which Thoreau took the *Lotus Sutra* at its word: he followed "the excellent way which conducts to the state of Buddha," the way, that is, of contemplation and practice. He did not learn this from the Orientals, but it is fair to say that he received a good deal of encouragement from his reading acquaintance with them. His nature was always that of a contemplative, as Emerson's was that of a literary man. As early as 1841, while he was keeping Emerson's woodbox full, he confided to his journal, "I want to go soon and live away by the pond, where I shall hear only the wind whispering among the reeds. It will be a success if I shall have left myself behind."

He went, as men intent on meeting themselves have often gone, to the woods—though not too far. There was little keeping him by April of 1844. The last issue of the *Dial* had been published, Emerson having spent a final $300 in a vain attempt to keep it alive. Once again Emerson acted as benefactor. Thoreau built his ten-by-fifteen-foot cabin on one of the woodlots Emerson had bought just out of sight of Walden Pond.

Thoreau's Walden experiment had as many aspects as the man who lived it. Certainly one of them was to demonstrate how little one really needed to live well. But his primary purpose was to demonstrate something to himself, to "transact some *private business* with the fewest obstacles." This "private business" was in the nature of what we would call contemplation. Thoreau was constantly tracking his own nature, which to him was not necessarily other than nature itself. His method was quite simple:

> Sometimes, in a summer morning, having taken my accustomed bath, I sat in my sunny doorway from sunrise til noon, rapt in revery, amidst the pines and hickories and sumachs, in undisturbed solitude and stillness, while the birds sang around or flitted noiseless through the house, until by the sun falling in my west window, or the noise of some traveller's wagon on the distant highway, I was reminded of the lapse of time. I grew in those seasons like corn in the night, and they were far better than the work of the hands would have been. They were not time subtracted from my life, but so much over and above my usual allowance. I realized what the Orientals mean by contemplation and the forsaking of works.

One might say that Thoreau was pre-Buddhist in much the same way that the Chinese Taoists were. He forecast an American Buddhism by the nature of his contemplation, in the same way that a certain quality of transparent predawn forecasts a clear morning. He lost himself in nature as the Chinese painters did, by becoming one with nature. He was certainly not the only one of his generation to live a contemplative life, but he was, it seems, one of the few to live it in a Buddhist way. That is to say, he was perhaps the first American to explore the nontheistic mode of contemplation which is the distinguishing mark of Buddhism. Emerson had abstracted God into the Universe, the Over-soul, or infused Him through Nature with a capital "N." Thoreau was after the bare facts, the hard rock-bottom of existence. His journals were filled with details, precise observations and data. Emerson had an idea of what was real, Melville had ransacked the visible world for the symbols behind it, but Thoreau had no theories. He was content to wait and see what was there. There were many gods in Thoreau, as in all the pagans, but precious little God. Deity was not a problem one way or the other for Thoreau; it was more of a function than an absolute principle or existence. "I know that some will have hard thoughts of me, when they hear their Christ named beside my Buddha," he wrote in *A Week on the Concord and Merrimack Rivers*, "yet I am sure that I am willing they should love their Christ more than my Buddha, for the love is the main thing."

Thoreau was profoundly sympathetic, but he was not, in any sense of the word, a convert. He discovered in the Orientals something akin to his deepest spirit rather than another religion to replace the kind of Christianity in which, "The church is a sort of hospital for men's souls and as full of quackery as the hospital for their bodies." If he is with Buddha, he is also with Pan. "No god ever dies," he said in *A Week*. "Perhaps of all the gods of New England and of ancient Greece, I am most constant at his shrine." He is careful enough to warn us that "Every sacred book, successively, has been accepted in the faith that it was to be the final resting-place of the sojourning soul; but after all it was but a caravansary which supplied refreshment to the traveler, and directed him farther on his way to Ispahan or Baghdat." And to make certain we understand his meaning and do not merely trade a Western dogmatic for an Eastern one, he continues, "Thank God, no Hindoo tyranny prevailed at the framing of the world, but we are freemen of the universe, and not sentenced to any caste."

Yet this political consideration did not turn him from the East. After all, it was neither India nor ancient scriptures which drew Thoreau, but something much closer. ". . . .There is an orientalism in the most restless pioneer," he wrote, "and the farthest west is but the farthest east." He felt no need to struggle like Jones or Wilkins to master another language. "In every man's brain is the Sanskrit," was the way he put it. "The Vedas and their Agamas are not so ancient as serene contemplation. Why will we be imposed on by antiquity?. . . . And do we but live in the present?"

It was in the present that Thoreau met the Orientals. He did not seek them in another time or place, but he invited them to visit *his* town. "As for the tenets of the Brahmins," he wrote, "we are not so much concerned to know what doctrines they held, as that they were held by any. . . . It is the attitude of these men, more than any other communication which they make, that attracts us." The Orientals were ancient only in the sense that they were primeval, as fresh and luminous as "the hour before sunrise," and they were primeval only in the sense that Thoreau was. They lived as forest sages close to the heart of things. They were contemporaries.

Thoreau's most direct statement of identification with the Indian contemplative tradition came after he had left Walden. "Depend upon it that, rude and careless as I am, I would fain practice the yoga faithfully," he wrote H.G.O. Blake in 1849. "To some extent, and at rare intervals, even I am a yogi."

Not only Thoreau saw himself this way. His friend Moncure Conway also described his Walden life in a similar light: "Like the pious Yogi, so long motionless whilst gazing on the sun that knotty plants encircled his neck and the cast snake-skin his loins, and the birds built their nests on his shoulders, this poet and naturalist, by equal consecration, became a part of field and forest."

Thoreau's love for the Orientals was well-known to his contemporaries. Thomas Cholmondeley, a young Englishman who had come to Concord to meet Emerson in 1855, could think of no better gift to send Thoreau from England than a collection of Orientalia—"a nest of Indian books." Thoreau fashioned a case for the collection from river-board he had gathered during his canoe trips on the Musketaquid.

Thoreau died in 1862. When a friend asked him on his deathbed if he had made his peace with God, he responded, more like a Zen master than a Transcendentalist, that he was not aware they had quarreled. How deeply he had gone, and how closely his friends identified him with the Orientals, is apparent in the description John Weiss gave in 1865: "His countenance had not a line upon it expressive of ambition or discontent; the affectional emotions had not fretted at it. He went about like a priest of Buddha who expects to arrive soon at the summit of a life of contemplation."

V

On July 4th, 1855, Ralph Waldo Emerson received the paperbound first edition of a book of poems called *Leaves of Grass*. Six days later he wrote Sam Ward that the book was "so extraordinary for its oriental largeness of generalization, an American Buddh. . . ." He had never heard of its author, Walt Whitman, but he felt that the great American poet, free of Old World prejudice, had finally made his appearance. Whitman, however, had certainly heard of Emerson, and read him closely. As he reminisced to John Trowbridge in 1860, "I was simmering, simmering, simmering; Emerson brought me to a boil."

Emerson had once remarked to F.B. Sanborn that *Leaves of Grass* was "a mixture of the *Bhagavad-Gita* and the *New York Herald*"—the *Herald* being one of the more sensational tabloids of the day. And yet when Thoreau, meeting Whitman in New York City in 1857, complimented him that his work was "wonderfully like the Orientals," and asked if he had read them, Whitman's reply was a rather short: "No: Tell me about them."

It may be true, as scholars have it, that Whitman did not own a copy of the *Bhagavad-Gita* until the English cork-cutter, Thomas Cockburn Thomson, sent him one as a Christmas gift in 1857, but that hardly means he had not read it. There is Whitman's own statement in *A Backward Glance* that in preparation for his great work he had "absorbed . . . the ancient Hindu poems" along with Shakespeare, Ossian, Aeschylus, Homer, Sophocles and Dante. Like Thoreau, he had read them out-of-doors, "probably to better advantage for me than in any library or indoor room—it makes such a difference *where* you read," he said. As for his remark to Thoreau, we do well to remember that Whitman thought Thoreau a bookish man who wore a constant look of disdain, and that he also liked to give the impression that he was a raw original.

It was more probable that Whitman had read the Orientals, and swallowed them whole, along with everything else. While Emerson and Thoreau liked to use quotations from the Orientals as if they were precious jewels carefully set in the main stream of their work, Whitman embraced them all and plunged into a kind of ecstatic eclecticism that swept everything before it. "I do not despise you priests, all time, the world over," he wrote in *Song of Myself*:

> My faith is the greatest of faiths and the least of faiths,
> Enclosing worship ancient and modern and all between ancient and modern,
> Believing I shall come again upon the earth after five thousand years,
> Waiting repose from oracles, honoring the gods, saluting the sun,
> Making a fetich of the first rock or stump, powowing with sticks in the circle of obis,
> Helping the lama or brahmin as he trims the lamps of the idols,

Dancing through the streets in a phallic procession, rapt and austere
in the woods a gymnosophist,
Drinking mead from the skull-cup, to Shastas and Vedas admirant
minding the Koran . . .

In his late poem *Passage to India* Whitman turned from the New World he was always striking out for to celebrate "the infinite greatness of the past." ("For what is the present after all but a growth out of the past?") Whitman's India is, to begin with, real enough. There are "the streams of the Indus and the Ganges and their many affluents. . . . The flowing literatures, tremendous epics, religions, castes." And then there is his wonderful phrase that delicately expressed the relation between the old and new in Indian religion: "Old occult Brahma interminably far back, the tender and junior Buddha. . . ." The passage to India is not to "lands and seas alone" but to "primal thought. . . . Back, back to wisdom's birth, to innocent intuitions." It is an inward journey in which the soul has become India, "light of the light, shedding forth universes," and the passage to India has become a "passage to more than India!" It is in this last poem that the poet of the future New World comes face to face with the final reaches of that last journey:

Set forth—steer for the deep waters only,
Reckless O soul, exploring, I with thee, and thou with me,
For we are bound where mariner has not yet dared to go
And we will risk the ship, ourselves, and all.

The poem does not end there. It does not end; it goes on, even as the last line, "O farther, farther, farther sail!" goes on. And yet, Whitman always comes back to the world. In this he is perhaps more naively a Buddhist than any of the Concordians. This is how he concludes *Specimen Days*: "Perhaps indeed the efforts of the true poets, founders, religions, literatures, all ages, have been, and ever will be, our time and times to come, essentially the same—to bring people back from their persistent strayings and sickly abstractions, to the costless average, divine, original concrete."

VI

There were, of course, those who did not share either Whitman's or the Transcendentalists' high regard for the Orientals. Emerson's poem

Brahma may have tied a seamless knot of verse out of the Vedantic doctrine of identity in such lines as:

If the red slayer thinks he slays
Or if the slain thinks he is slain
They do not know the subtle ways
I keep, and pass, and pass again

But when the poem was published in the first issue of the *Atlantic Monthly* in 1857, no less a personage than Oliver Wendell Holmes attacked it as "the nearest approach to a Torricellian vacuum of intelligibility that language can pump out of itself," and the editor of Emerson's *Collected Poems* some years later tried to convince the author to suppress the poem entirely. Emerson refused, of course, but he remained somewhat aloof, above the battle. When he was asked to lend his name to a proposed American edition of *The Bhagavad Gita*, he refused, thinking "it not only some desecration to publish our daily prayers in 'The Daily Herald,' but also that those students who were ripe for it would rather take a little pains and search for it, than find it on the pavement." At any rate, he said, he thought it would be "as neglected a book, if Harpers published it, as it is now in the libraries."

William Henry Channing, however, had no such scruples when, in 1878, he sent a copy of his son-in-law's new book, *The Light of Asia, or The Great Renunciation, Being the Life and Teachings of Gautama, Prince of India and Founder of Buddhism*, to Bronson Alcott at the Concord Summer School of Philosophy. Channing's daughter, Fannie Marie Adelaide, had married the book's author, the English journalist and poet, Edwin Arnold, and Channing, an intimate of the Concord Circle, was straightforward in suggesting that Alcott have his friends review the work. "Poem and Poet should be widely known," Channing wrote Alcott, "and be heartily welcomed by the nation that providentially serves as mediator between Europe and Asia, to unite the East and West, the Ancient and Modern Ages, in unity."

Channing had selected the right man. Alcott was a tireless educator, popularizer and activist, with the reputation of being the most "idealistic" —that is, impractical—of the Concordians, chiefly, it seems, because he insisted on putting his theories of vegetarianism, progressive education and community living into practice. His interest in comparative religion was as strong as Emerson's or Thoreau's, but more grandiose. When *The Light of Asia* reached Alcott, the Summer School had just closed for the season, and it was too late to present it to the school, as Channing had suggested. But Alcott was so taken with the book that he moved quickly to have it printed in Boston from his own copy. "The book," prophesied Alcott, "will be read with great surprise by most, and raise curious questions in the minds of Christians generally."

Within six days after Alcott had received the book, F.B. Sanborn had published a review in the *Republican*: "Its poetic merits are considerable," he wrote, "but it has a higher value as an exposition in a sympathetic spirit of the true ideal that inspires the great philanthropic religions of Asia,—the harbinger, and, for half-civilized men, the compliment of Christianity."

Even Oliver Wendell Holmes was wildly enthusiastic, so much so that he waxed eloquent for twenty-six pages in *The International Review* about the poem which was "so lofty that there is nothing with which to compare it but the New Testament."

The immense popularity of *The Light of Asia* in America (it went through eighty editions and sold between a half million and a million copies) was due to the skill with which Arnold managed to retell the Buddha's story in a way that matched Victorian taste. His sources were scholars like Spencer Hardy, Samuel Beal and Max Muller, but he succeeded because he wrote a story, and not a tract or exposition. His Buddha is part romantic hero, part self-reliant man, and part Christ without being Christ. Arnold had been to India, and he made the most of its exotic setting. Indeed, his poem managed to combine sensuality and high seriousness with great skill. He titillated his readers with detailed descriptions of Siddhartha's palace life, where "Delicate dark-browed ministers of love . . . fanned the sleeping eyes of the happy Prince," and brought tears to their eyes with the scene in which Siddartha bids his wife and son farewell.

At the same time Arnold gave a fair outline of Buddhist thought as it was understood by the scholars of the day. He versified the doctrines of karma, the Four Noble Truths, and the Eightfold Path. By the time he wrote his poem Max Muller and other scholars had begun to question the prevailing view that nirvana was "annihilation," and Arnold concurred. As he said in his introduction, it was his "firm conviction that a third of mankind would never have been brought to believe in blank abstractions, or in Nothingness as the issue and crown of Being."

Perhaps Arnold went too far in making nirvana attractive to his reader. Indeed the lines

> . . . He is one with Life
> Yet lives not. He is blest, ceasing to be
> OM, MANI PADME, OM! the Dewdrop slips
> Into the shining sea!

may sound more Hindu or Christian than Buddhist. Nevertheless, it was from *Light of Asia* more than any other book that Americans first learned the story and the teachings of the Buddha.

However the successes and failures of Bronson Alcott are counted, and since he was the least published of the eminent Concordians he has too often been dismissed as simply foolish, it is certain that he succeeded in this one thing. The introduction of *The Light of Asia* to America through Concord marked the natural culmination of a process that had begun one hundred years earlier with another Englishman, Sir William Jones, and now Buddhism had become, for a while, what we might today call "a household word." It was time for the wheel to take another turn.

CHAPTER FIVE

GOLD MOUNTAIN AND RICE BOWL COUNTRY: THE FIRST CHINESE AND JAPANESE IN AMERICA

I

While the Transcendentalists were musing about Oriental wisdom in Concord, Asians themselves had begun to arrive three thousand miles to the west. In 1848, when gold was discovered at John Sutter's sawmill north of San Francisco there were only a handful of Chinese in America. But a year later three hundred Chinese met at the Canton Restaurant, and a group of Chinese merchants and traders, dressed in their finest silk robes and slippers, were received by the city fathers at Portsmouth Square. The merchants were presented with Christian pamphlets, printed in Chinese in Canton, which they glanced at politely, without much interest. "We have never seen a finer looking body of men collected together in San Francisco," reported the *California Courier*, "in fact, this portion of our population is a pattern for sobriety, order, and obedience to laws, not only to other foreign residents but to Americans themselves."

The merchants were the vanguard. By 1852, the gold rush had drawn twenty thousand Chinese. In 1860 one of every ten Californians was

Chinese, and by the end of the decade there were sixty-three thousand.

These first Asian emigres to America have often been pictured as a swarm of unskilled laborers, faceless and nameless coolies. But many of them brought essential skills to Gold Mountain, as they called it. Chinese carpenters brought their tools and built the first wood houses that could be moved from camp to camp. They brought their medicine, and a Chinese doctor, Ah Son, built a fifty-bed hospital at the mining camp of Yankee Creek. The Chinese also brought a tradition of working together, which enabled them to find gold in mines abandoned by the more individualistic Caucasians.

In 1867 teams of Chinese workers began laying track for the Central Pacific. They also wove the baskets that lowered them down the sheer cliff walls to dynamite and pick-axe the route through the Rockies and Sierra Nevadas. Chinese farmers grew vegetables, planted orchards and vineyards. Chinese fishermen harvested shrimp and other shellfish from the coastal waters, and Chinese workers built the levees and canals that drained the Sacramento River Delta. They worked as cooks, laundrymen, barbers and storekeepers. In all these occupations they proved themselves, as Mark Twain wrote, "quiet, peaceable, tractable, free from drunkenness, and . . . as industrious as the day was long."

And yet they were met, increasingly, by hatred and violence. Chinese miners and fishermen were subjected to a special foreigner's tax, and then often run off from their claims and fishing camps at gunpoint. In 1877 Chinese laundries were burned in San Francisco; in 1885 twenty-five Chinese were lynched in Rock Creek, Wyoming; and in 1884, the entire Chinese population of Tacoma, Washington was packed into boxcars and shipped out of town.

The law was not much help. In 1854 Judge Charles T. Murray of the California Supreme Court had refused to allow a Chinese witness to testify in a murder case involving two white men. Ever since the time of Columbus, reasoned the Judge, "the American Indian and the Mongolian or Asiatic were regarded as the same type of species"—a species inferior and without rights. Unprotected by their own government (which did not recognize the right of Chinese to emigrate until 1868) the Chinese in America were politically powerless. Though the U.S. Supreme Court at first overruled efforts to bar Chinese immigration, state and city lawmakers passed numerous anti-Chinese ordinances. Chinese laundrymen were not permitted to operate in wooden buildings; Chinese peddlers could not sell from baskets suspended by poles; shrimp fishermen were barred from using their fine-woven nets. During the 1870s the

Chinese question became an important issue in national politics, and in 1882 Congress passed the Chinese Exclusion Act—"the first departure," as Stuart Creighton Miller writes in *The Unwelcome Immigrant*, "from our official policy of open, laissez-faire immigration to be made on ethnocultural grounds."

In the eighteenth century Voltaire and Diderot had admired Chinese civilization for its refinement, rationality, order and wisdom—a view that in itself derived from Jesuit missionaries who had translated Confucius into Latin and moved in the highest circles of the Chinese court. But by the middle of the nineteenth century another image had come to the fore, "the basic image," as Stuart Creighton Miller wrote, "of a stagnating, perverse, semi-civilized breeding ground for swarming inhuman hordes." Part of this image came from the accounts American Protestant missionaries sent back to the hundreds of Christian newspapers that had mushroomed during the fundamentalist revival then sweeping through America. Seeking support and funds for their Chinese missions, the missionaries dwelt on the misery caused by Chinese heathenism: polygamy, footbinding, infanticide, gambling and numerous other depravities. As for religion: "the four marks of Paganism," said one missionary, "were Tauism, Boodism, ancestor worship, and opium addiction."

The opium addiction so often remarked upon by missionaries had actually been forced on the Chinese by the British in 1840. The Opium War opened China to commerce and Christianity at gunpoint; it also caused inflation and further weakened the reputation of the already unpopular Manchu emperor, especially along the Pearl River Delta in Kwangtung Province, where nearly all the emigres to Gold Mountain lived.

Kwangtung had always been the most open of China's provinces. It had also been the most independent and nationalistic. In 1850 it became once again the center of rebellion against the foreign Manchu dynasty. The leader of the Taiping Rebellion, the most nearly successful of these movements, Hung Hsiu-ch'uan, had read some Christian tracts, and received instruction from a Southern Baptist missionary. Hung Hsiu-ch'uan combined a belief in his own divinity as the brother of Christ with a millenarian cry for communalism and the end of the Manchu dynasty. He was also intensely anti-Buddhist. American missionaries, later disillusioned by Hung's belief in his own divinity, were at first enthusiastic. "So gratifying a scene of devastation I certainly never held before," wrote missionary Charles Taylor after visiting the rebels. "Here were gilded and painted fragments of images strewn about in every direction. The altars and tables, incense vases and candlesticks, Buddhist books and all the paraphernalia of idolatrous worship, were broken, torn, and scattered here and there in irrevocable ruin."

The farmers, fishermen and sailors of Kwangtung had a long history of going out to Malaysia, Borneo, Java and Vietnam. In the 1850s the chaos of civil war, rebellion, banditry, inflation, heavy taxes and shrinking lands made emigration to Gold Mountain especially attractive. Peasants taken prisoner during this period had been shipped out to Peru as coolies and were virtually slaves. But the men who shipped to America either paid their own passage or traveled with loans that would be paid back, with interest, from their work abroad.

In America they organized their life along familiar lines. In Kwangtung the most important social unit had been the family, and whole villages traced their descent from one ancestor. In Gold Mountain the Chinese formed organizations based on the districts from which they came. (Dialects from different districts were often incomprehensible.) These district organizations, the Five (later Six) Companies, formed the basis of Chinese social life. They acted as agents, provided new emigres with food and board, and served as a link with the home districts. The Chinese sent money back to their villages and often returned to marry and father children there. The tie continued even in death; Chinese who died in America were sent back to China by the Six Companies for burial.

The Six Companies were also centers for festivals and religious life. The first Chinese temple in San Francisco's Chinatown was built by the Sze Yap Company in the summer of 1853; a year later the Ning Yeong Company built the second temple, paying 16,000 dollars for decorations and furnishings alone. These company temples were housed on the top floors, where no one would be higher than the gods they enshrined.

By the end of 1875 there were eight temples in Chinatown; by the end of the nineteenth century there would be more than four hundred temples up and down the West Coast, wherever the Chinese worked and settled, from San Diego to Vancouver and inland to the Sierra Nevadas. Some, like the ones on the top floors of the Six Companies, were elaborate affairs, outfitted at great cost from China; others, dedicated to a single deity, such as the god of the fishermen, might be mere shacks, large enough only for a single person to kneel in. Some temples were situated in plain wooden buildings, others were decorated on the outside by the emigres themselves with the upturned eaves and brightly-colored trimming of pagodas. Nearly all were wood, and unlike the adobe missions of the Spanish in California, few have survived.

The temples played an essential part in the life of the Chinese. Most outside observers noted the offerings of food left before the deities and the bamboo divination sticks that were used in a way similar to the yarrow stalks of the *I Ching*. But a group of Chinese-American historians have recently suggested another, deeper dimension to the function of the temple:

> The temple symbolized a place where the Chinese laborer was a human being. It was a part of the culture which gave wholeness and meaning to existence. The temple symbolized harmony, balance, and justice. . . .

The deities residing there were

> sources of positive power who care and who generate within the heart of the worshipper the courage to go back out in an unbalanced world and work patiently while following the Tao.

Even such a seemingly ferocious figure as Kuan Yu, the god of war (and wealth) stood

> as the cosmic symbol that oppression of followers of the Tao will end, that balance will be restored, that good fortune and happiness will eventually come to those who do not use negative forces to attain life's end.

The Chinese temples reflected popular Chinese religion, which was a mixture of Taoism, Confucianism and Buddhism. For the most part the Chinese were remarkably tolerant in matters of religion and philosophy. They did not see the logic of worshipping one God above all others (as the Protestant missionaries had discovered). The Chinese could be Confucian rationalists (Confucius had said, "Respect gods and ghosts but keep them at a distance") or devotees of a particular local or family deity, or Ch'an (Zen) Buddhists striving for enlightenment in a monastery. But all subscribed to the Chinese proverb that cautioned: "One must not be blasphemous toward gods in whom one has no faith."

Buddhist deities were found together with Taoist gods in Chinese temples, but there were also a number of purely Buddhist temples. The Chinese were the first to bring the images of Shih Chia (Shakyamuni), A-mi-t'o (Amitabha), Yao Shih (Bhaishajyaguru), Mi Lo (Vairocana),

Wen Shu (Manjusri), and Mi Lo (Maitreya) to America. The most popular Buddhist deity was Kuan-yin, the bodhisattva of compassion, worshipped under various names in Japan, Korea, Tibet and Mongolia. One writer described her figure, found in a temple in Brooklyn Street, in 1892, "holding a Buddhist sutra in her hand, in an attitude of giving instruction to a child seated on her knee."

An equally important figure among the Chinese in America and China was A-mi-t'o, Amitabha, the buddha of the Western Paradise. A-mi-t'o had taken a vow that anyone who repeated his name with faith would be reborn in the Western Paradise, a buddha realm with perfect conditions for practicing the dharma and gaining enlightenment. Most Chinese lay Buddhists were followers of A-mi-t'o, and so belonged to the Pure Land school. According to instructions of the most accomplished Pure Land masters, the Pure Land of the Western Paradise was found in this world, within one's own mind. This interpretation led to a synthesis of Pure Land and Ch'an Buddhist practice in many Chinese monasteries, but most of the Chinese Buddhists in Gold Mountain were probably content with the faith that by occasional recitation of *Namu A-mi-t'o*, Amitabha's mantra, they would eventually be reborn in the Western Paradise.

The presence of Buddhist priests is mentioned in several accounts of Chinatown festivals and weddings. But if there were monks and priests in Gold Mountain, they seem to have concentrated on caring for temples and performing ceremonies. The Ch'an monks most likely did not travel to America from their isolated mountain monasteries; at least there is no mention of them.

The Chinese in general did not proselytize, and Chinese Buddhists in America followed the same pattern. But they did take to the courts when their right to practice Buddhism was challenged. In *Bitter Strength* Guenther Barth mentions the case of *John Eldridge vs. See Yup Company* in the spring of 1859, in which "The California Supreme Court preserved the public character of the Buddhist rite. . . . The Justices decided . . . that the court had no power to determine whether this or that form of religion or superstitious worship—unaccompanied by acts prohibited by law—is against public policy or morals." To their hostile neighbors the Chinese temples were "joss houses"—*joss* being a pidgin version of the Portuguese *deos*, god. Caucasians rarely visited the joss houses and then only as tourists at some of the more public temples in Chinatown. In an article published in the January 1878 issue of the *Warsaw Commercial Gazette* the Polish journalist (and later author of *Quo Vadis*), Henryk Sienkowicz, reported that "the entire Chinese population of San Francisco's Chinatown professes the principles of Buddhism." Sienkowicz took his readers on a guided tour of a Chinatown temple:

> . . . but we have not yet entered the most interesting places which are designated by multicolored paper lanterns. These are the Buddhist temples. . . . Let us go inside; everyone is allowed to enter here. Now we are really in China. A large room transformed into a temple is illuminated by colored lamps and multicolored window panes. In the corners stand silk umbrellas set on long handles, flags with suns, moons, and dragons, or long poles at the top of which are bronze emblems of indefinable forms. . . . In the center is erected the first altar in the form of a low, wide table on which stands a pair of silver dragons two feet high. . . . The main altar is the innermost part of the temple. There in the mysterious twilight . . . looms from behind the silk curtains the statue of a great Buddha in a sitting position . . . the expression on his golden-bronze colored face is a mixture of boredom and stupidity.

The contempt revealed in the last line reflects the Sinophobia of the day. To most Caucasians the joss houses conjured up dark mysterious sanctuaries where thick smoke from joss sticks (incense), obscured the air that was filled with heathen superstition and unspeakable rites. To the more barbarian outsiders, though, the joss houses were, as temples have always been, convenient targets for terror, and a number of anti-Chinese vigilante groups, such as the Order of Caucasians, thought nothing of burning the local Chinese temples to the ground.

An emblem of the attitude Americans took towards the religion of their Chinese neighbor exists today in two large vase-shaped pewter incense holders that stand before the statue of Kuan-yin, in a restored Nevada City Chinese Temple. The incense holders, brought from China at great expense by the Chinese miners who worked in the surrounding Sierra Nevada foothills, are still in good condition—except for a few jagged bullet holes punched through the soft metal, the result of a few random rounds fired into the local joss house by cowboys leaving the saloon on a Saturday night a century ago.

II

For hundreds of years the Tokugawa shoguns, having limited Europeans to a small Dutch outpost at Nagasaki, had pursued a policy of strictest isolation. Foreign ships in need of water and coal were routinely turned away, and shipwrecked sailors either returned to the West through the

Dutch port, or occasionally were executed as spies. In 1854, following the example of the British in China, the United States sent Commodore Perry and two fully-armed paddle-wheeled steamships to negotiate a treaty in which the Japanese would agree to "friendship, commerce, a supply of coal and provisions, and protection for our shipwrecked people."

In 1860 the first envoy to America, Shimmi Buzo-nokami, arrived in San Francisco. The official Japanese party, wearing hakama and carrying the two swords that all samurai were required to wear, proceeded on to Washington, where they presented a letter from the shogun to President Buchanan. On June 15th of that year they paraded down Broadway in New York City, observed by Walt Whitman:

> Over the Western seas hither from Niphon come,
> Courteous, the swarth-cheek'd two-sworded envoys,
> Leaning back in their open barouches, bare-headed, impassive,
> Ride today through Manhatten.

To Whitman the Japanese envoys prophesied the time when all of Asia—"the Originatress. . . . The nest of languages, the bequeather of poems, the race of eld"—would become renewed—"the sleep of ages having done its work"—by the American idea of "Libertad" represented by "My stars and stripes fluttering in the wind" over "the new empire grander than any before."

The Japanese were not so quick as Whitman to rejoice in the role Perry's gunships had forced upon them. It was not until eight years later, in 1868, the Year One of Meiji, that the government of the newly restored emperor, having defeated the shoguns, reluctantly granted permission for a few ordinary Japanese citizens to travel abroad.

The first hundred and forty-nine *gannen-mono* ("first year men") went out to work for three years on Hawaiian sugar plantations. Hawaiian planters had hoped that the Japanese would prove more dependable than the Chinese, who had demonstrated a tendency to leave the plantations in favor of city life and shopkeeping as soon as possible. But the Japanese, recruited from the streets of Yokahama, were not used to the harsh conditions of plantation work, and most of them fled to Honolulu. Of these only forty or so returned to Japan, while the rest remained and married Hawaiian women. This pleased King David Kalakaua, who considered the Japanese a Polynesian race, kin to Hawaiians, and he hoped they would revitalize a native population decimated by smallpox, measles and syphilis.

In 1881 King Kalakaua traveled to Japan accompanied by the sons of two missionaries. En route he surprised his two traveling companions by remarking that he considered himself an Asiatic, and by wondering aloud if it might not be a good idea to introduce Buddhism to Hawaii. In an interview with the emperor he suggested that Hawaii join Japan as part of a "Union and federation of the Asiatic nations and sovereigns" under the emperor's leadership. He also suggested that the two royal houses join together by a marriage between a Hawaiian princess, Kaiulani, then six, and the emperor's nephew. Accounts differ as to the response of the mikado, but he did later write King Kalakaua that he viewed the idea of a Japanese-Hawaiian union favorably.

King Kalakaua continued his world tour by visiting the United States in 1885. The American people were much taken by the "Merry Monarch" as he was called with reference to his jovial sociability, and Congress agreed to a treaty in which Hawaiian sugar and pineapple would be allowed to enter the United States duty free. The treaty spurred Hawaiian plantation owners to look once again towards Japan for workers.

The Japanese responded, but this time they insisted on a more favorable arrangement. The nine hundred and fifty-three workers who sailed from Tokyo in 1887 were mostly small farmers, and their working conditions were governed in some detail by a treaty which called for Japanese foremen, an interpreter, and hot water for daily baths. The Japanese *dekasegi-nin*, "go-out-and-earn-people," were under a three-year contract, and the Japanese assumed that they, and their money, would return. These first workers arrived in a celebratory mood, greeted by hula dancers, and King Kalakaua who gave a speech using the few Japanese words he had learned years before. The Japanese, in turn, impressed the Hawaiians with demonstrations of kendo and sumo wrestling.

The new workers were sent to outlying plantations where the work was long and hard, and overseers paid little or no attention to treaty agreements. Men fell in debt to company stores, and gambling, drinking and prostitution spread through the camps.

"Hawaii, Hawaii," went a song the Japanese made up as they worked in the hot sun, sweating under the heavy clothes they wore as protection against the thorny leaves of sugar cane.

> Like a dream so I came
> But my tears are flowing now
> In the canefields.

The Japanese government was disturbed enough to send Count Katsunoke Inouye to Honolulu to discuss the workers' conditions. The Hawaiian Foreign Office agreed to increase the number of interpreters, employ Japanese physicians, allow the workers to receive duty-free food from Japan, and also to sharply limit Chinese immigration to Hawaii. The emperor, Count Inouye told the Hawaiians frankly, did not want Chinese and Japanese to mingle abroad.

Meanwhile, in Japan, a young Jodo Shinshu priest who had also become concerned about the welfare of countrymen abroad sought an interview with Abbot Myonyo of the Hompa Hongwanji in Kyoto. There were already thousands of Japanese toiling in Hawaii without benefit of spiritual guidance, said priest Kagahi, and some of them had already died there with no one to conduct a proper Buddhist funeral. The abbot replied that so little was known about the conditions in Hawaii that a missionary effort would be premature, and besides, the missionaries of the Hongwanji were already preoccupied with Manchuria, Korea and South China. Nevertheless, he would not object if the young minister wanted to undertake an exploratory mission on his own.

Kagahi arrived in Honolulu on March 12, 1889. He began his investigation by discussing the situation with members of the Japanese community over cups of sake. He found Christian churches everywhere. There were also quite a few active Japanese-Christian missionaries, the most successful being the Reverend Mr. Miyama, who had made a name for himself by converting the Japanese consul and his family. There were a number of Chinese Buddhist temples dedicated to Kuan-yin and A-mi-t'o, but none for the Japanese. The situation was described by a group of Japanese Buddhists a few years later, in a petition to Hongwanji headquarters dated June 5, 1897: ". . . the religion here is dominated by Christianity. Towns bristle with Christian churches and sermons, the prayers of the missionaries shake through the cities with the church bells. To strong Buddhists like ourselves, these pressures mean nothing. However, we sometimes get reports of frivolous Japanese who surrender themselves to accept the heresy—as a hungry man does not have much choice but to eat what he is offered." To make matters worse, the Honolulu Buddhists reported that a number of "priests" masquerading as "special envoys from headquarters" had collected money from the faithful and then disappeared from the islands.

Though Kagahi had no permission to act as an envoy of the Hongwanji headquarters, he won the confidence of the Japanese community by his sincerity. He collected money door-to-door, and accepted a donation of a hundred and sixty dollars from two hundred workers returning to Japan. He went about his work quietly, but his activities, both social and religious, did not go unnoticed by the Christian missionaries, for the Hawaiian Evangelical Association warned against "a Buddhist organization among us, which encourages drinking."

Kagahi next took his campaign to the plantations, where he found his countrymen suffering "heavy burdens both in the physical and spiritual, distressed and wandering, as sheep not having a shepherd." By and large his mission was successful. Before he left Hawaii he had the satisfaction of seeing the completion of the first Japanese Buddhist temple in Hawaii—a small building on the corner of Pohahawai Avenue and Front Street in Hilo.

Kagahi returned to Japan in October 1889. Japanese Buddhist groups responded to his pleas with promises of financial help. But then Kagahi published a magazine article suggesting that Buddhist missionaries in foreign lands equate the Christian God with the Eternal Buddha, since both were but names for the same Absolute Reality.

In the near future more than a few Japanese Buddhists, looking for a way to make Buddhism "relevant" and "modern," would put forth the same argument, but at that time it was an unacceptable one. In order to strengthen the emperor's position, the new government had made Shinto the state religion, and had even attempted to destroy Buddhism with the cry of *Haibutsu Kishaku*—"Expell the Buddha; Destroy the Teachings." At the same time Western and Christian ideas had become fashionable among those who believed that Japan's only hope was to modernize quickly. The government had soon retreated to a position of religious neutrality, but the Buddhists were on the defensive and they did not take kindly to suggestions that they cover themselves with Christian top hats.

Kagahi was attacked for heresy; the funds that had been promised were withheld. Kagahi himself dropped out of sight, but the next year two more Jodo Shinshu priests appeared in Honolulu, and as the number of Japanese in Hawaii increased (there were about 25,000 in Hawaii by 1894), the officials of the Hompa Hongwanji could no longer ignore the need for an active missionary program. In 1896 the first official branch temple of the Jodo Shinshu was built within reach of five major sugar plantations in the town of Pauuhau on the island of Hawaii.

In 1892 Edwin Arnold, author of *Light of Asia*, had suggested to King Kalakaua's successor, Queen Liliuokalani that Hawaii form a union with Japan. The queen was interested but by then it was too late. A group of white Hawaiians, supported by U.S. Marines, staged a coup and founded the Republic of Hawaii. Japan sent a warship and protested to Washington, but the American government disclaimed responsibility. Six years later the islands were annexed by the United States. The planters had succeeded in protecting their economic interests. They had also given the United States a territory with a sizeable and growing Buddhist population—a territory that in the future would serve as an important stepping stone for Buddhist missionaries to the mainland.

The first party of Japanese immigrants to reach the mainland had arrived in 1869 as an advance party for Matsudaira Katamori, a feudal lord who had supported the Tokugawa shoguns against the emperor. The small group, led by a Dutchman, John Henry Schell, one of the lord's advisors, brought fifty thousand mulberry saplings, as well as bamboo shoots and tea seeds. They settled on six hundred acres near Sacramento, but few of the plants they had brought survived either the voyage or the dry soil, and the Wakamatsu Tea and Silk Farm Colony (named after the district Katamori had ruled) ended in failure after two years.

Only a few Japanese followed these early settlers; in 1870 the U.S. Census listed just seventy Japanese in America. Among these first visitors was Renshi Takuyu Unegami, a Buddhist priest who toured America in 1872, after studying Western religious organizations with four other ministers of the Hompa Hongwanji in Europe. By 1890 the number of Japanese immigrants had risen to 2,039; some had continued on to America after a stay in Hawaii, others had come directly from Japan. Nearly all were young, male and single—by all accounts an adventurous, hard-drinking group who found work in lumber camps, railroads, canneries and farms. Most Americans did not bother to distinguish them from the Chinese, but those who did began to say that the Chinese had been less troublesome. The Japanese seemed arrogant and overly sensitive. The Chinese had at least known their place, but the Japanese—backed by a strong military government—wanted to be treated as equals.

Unlike the Chinese, the Japanese did their best to adopt American customs. They dressed in Western clothes, and many studied English at the schools run by Methodist missionaries. On the whole they seemed content to leave Buddhism back in Japan—a state of affairs encouraged by Japanese officials who, like the consul in Seattle, Mr. Saito, believed that the introduction of a "foreign" religion to America would create "numerous problems" for the Japanese immigrants. In the future Japanese Buddhist churches would be central to Japanese-American life. But this was not the case in the 1890s. The official history of the Buddhist Churches of America stated bluntly: "Because of their youth and lack of responsibilities, the immigrants were not inclined to listen to religious instruction, and particularly not to the Buddhadharma."

Sir William Jones, from the original of Sir Joshua Reynolds

Ralph Waldo Emerson

Henry David Thoreau, 1856

Bronson Alcott at the School of Philosophy, Concord, Mass.

Sir Edwin Arnold, portrait, artist unknown, hanging in the Library of The Buddhist Society, London

Madame Blavatsky and Colonel Olcott in London, 1888

Anagarika Dharmapala in San Francisco

Soyen Shaku

Paul Carus

Edward Morse at the blackboard

Ernest Francisco Fenollosa

William Sturgis Bigelow

Kakuzo Okakura, photo in the Guest Book, 11th edition, October 1910

CHAPTER SIX

THE WHITE BUDDHISTS: COLONEL OLCOTT, MADAME BLAVATSKY AND THE THEOSOPHICAL SOCIETY

I

American spiritualism began modestly enough in 1848, when mysterious "rappings," startled the Fox family at their farm in Hydesville, New York. The two youngest Fox sisters, ages twelve and thirteen, devised a code which allowed questions to be answered, and eventually, having added table-turning, slate-writing and clairvoyance to their repertoire, joined P.T. Barnum. Before long a host of mediums had sprung up across the country, and by the 1870s the visitations from beyond, if that is what they were, had reached epidemic proportions, as if every disembodied spirit in the world had nothing better to do than make an appearance in the gas-lit parlors of nineteenth-century America.

Spiritualism occupied a central place in post Civil War America where it not only soothed the grief of bereaved relatives, but also gave assurance that there was, in fact, a world beyond death—a belief which science, with its insistence on tangible evidence, had called into serious question, and which religion, in its reliance on dogma and form, had failed to defend convincingly. It is true that the field was filled with a host of new Christian sects—revivalism, perfectionism, millennialism, and adventism, as well as the more secular heaven-on-earth communitarianism of Fourier, Robert Owen and John Humphrey Noyes. But these came and went with bewildering speed. Preachers and prophets had a way of moving on, replacing enthusiasm with discouragement and disillusion. Indeed, by 1870 so many flames of religious fervor had swept over the towns and villages of New York, that the state had become known as the "burned-over district."

To many people (eleven million in 1870), spiritualism held out the possibility of certainty. There were manifestations to be seen, there were rappings, bells and voices to be heard, and even "apports" (materialized objects) to be touched. This emphasis on phenomena invited scientific investigation, and in 1869 the London Dialectical Society sponsored an inquiry by a committee of distinguished scientists, the most celebrated being Sir Alfred Russell Wallace, who had developed the theory of natural selection along with Charles Darwin. To the consternation of the Society, the committee found the subject "worthy of more serious attention and investigation than it has hitherto received." In America similar research took place, and Horace Greeley, editor of the *New York Herald*, defended the Fox sisters against accusations of fraud. None of this convinced the scientific establishment, but the support of these few eminent men strengthened the spiritualist's hand, and though the press generally agreed with the *Saturday Review*'s characterization of spiritualism as "one of the most unequivocally degrading superstitions that have ever found currency amongst reasonable beings," public interest continued to grow.

II

One July day in 1874, when Colonel Henry Steel Olcott was sitting in his office working on a complicated case involving mechanical water meters and the Corporation of the City of New York, it suddenly occurred to him (for no reason he could ascertain) that he had not kept up with the spiritualist movement. The Colonel, as he was called, left his office and went around the corner to a newsstand, where he bought the current number of *The Banner of Light*, one of the more serious of the spiritualist journals. There he read an account of "certain incredible phenomena" taking place at the Eddy brothers' farm in Chittenden, Vermont. According to the *Light*, visitors to the farm "could see, even touch and converse with, deceased relatives who had found means to reconstruct their bodies and clothing so as to be temporarily solid, visible, and tangible." If this were true, thought the Colonel, it would constitute "the most important fact in modern science." He determined to go and see for himself.

Colonel Olcott spent only three or four days at the Eddy farm on his first visit, but he returned to New York convinced that the "animate statues" he had watched step forth from the upstairs closet (the dancing squaw Honto and the fierce Indian chief Santum being the most frequent) were indeed visitors from another world, and he said as much in an article published in the *New York Sun*. Colonel Olcott was not as well-known as Sir Alfred Wallace or Horace Greeley, but he was highly regarded as a man of utmost probity. During the Civil War he had distinguished himself by uncovering a ring of corrupt Army contractors, and had then gone on to serve as a special commissioner in the investigation that followed Lincoln's assassination. In any case, Olcott's report for the *Sun*, which attracted a good deal of attention, was "copied," as he said, "pretty much throughout the whole world."

Colonel Olcott returned to the Chittenden farm in the fall to write a more extensive series for the *New York Graphic*, accompanied by a staff artist. As the two men entered the Eddy dining room for lunch on October 14th, the Colonel stopped short at the sight of a large woman with a mop of short, crinkly blond hair. "Good gracious!" he whispered, "look at that specimen, will you." She was wearing a bright scarlet Garibaldian shirt which contrasted vividly with the dull browns and grays the other guests wore, and she was chatting in French with another woman. Olcott's articles had drawn many strange characters to the farm, but she was by far the oddest, and when the Colonel, who fancied himself something of an expert on physiognomy, immediately sat down opposite her so that he could study her features, he found himself looking into a pair of penetrating lapis lazuli eyes set deep in "a massive Calmuck face" that suggested "power, culture, and imperiousness."

After dinner, the Colonel followed her out to the porch, where she rolled a cigarette. "*Permettez-moi, Madame*," said the Colonel, striking a match. As he would remark later, their acquaintance "began in smoke, but it stirred up a great and permanent fire." The woman introduced herself as Madame Helena Petrova Blavatsky. She had come to the farm, she said, because of the articles by a Colonel Olcott, though she had worried that the Colonel might write about her—at which point the

Colonel introduced himself. Madame had nothing to fear, he told her; he would not write a word about her unless she consented.

Colonel Olcott and HPB, as she liked to be called, hit it off immediately. They became great chums and took long walks under the beeches, maples and elms, which were turning gold and crimson. "Her manner," Olcott later wrote, "was gracious and captivating, her criticisms upon men and things original and witty." They felt themselves part of the same social world, cosmopolitans and free-thinkers. HPB had been a great traveler; she had seen "many occult things and adepts in occult science." She had also fought with Garibaldi in Italy, in proof of which she had the Colonel feel the bullets still embedded in her shoulder and leg. Though she talked freely of her adventures, she did not yet allude to her own powers, or talk, as she later would, of Tibet and Himalayan Masters. She spoke rather as a "refined Spiritualist," one who criticized "the materialistic tendency of American Spiritualism" as "a sort of debauch of phenomena accompanied by comparative indifference to philosophy."

She took care to draw the Colonel out on his views of spiritualism and the occult. At times their discussions grew heated. Olcott had done his scientific best to prove that the Eddy phantoms were what they were said to be: visitations from the dead. He had searched William Eddy with the skill of a trained detective before the farmer entered the closet from which the apparitions appeared; he had sealed an upstairs window with wax stamped with his signet ring; he had engaged a mechanical engineer to examine the closet for trap doors and sliding panels; and he had measured and even weighed the phantoms.

HPB agreed with the Colonel that the phantoms were not, as the skeptics insisted, the results of trickery, fraud or hysterical hallucinations, but she disagreed with Olcott's interpretation. She argued that if the figures were genuine, they were nothing more than the "double" of the medium—William Eddy, in this case—escaping from his body, and "clothing itself with other appearances." Olcott held his ground, but he had to admit that he could not explain the strange fact that the nature of the phantoms had changed drastically since HPB's appearance. No longer were they American Indians, New Englanders and Europeans. Now the figures that took shape every night on the platform set up in the seance room were foreign, exotic, and all seemed known to Madame Blavatsky. There was a Georgian boy who had been a servant of the Blavatsky family in the Caucasus, and a fierce mustachioed Kurdish warrior brandishing a dagger and scimitar, whom Madame had known from her childhood, and last, in the Colonel's words, "a hideously ugly and devilish-looking Negro sorcerer from Africa, wearing a coronet composed of four horns of the oryx with bells at their tips," whom Madame, after some hesitation, finally remembered as the chief of a tribe of African jugglers she had encountered many years ago at a Ramadan feast in Upper Egypt.

It all made a very good story, and if Madame had ever been concerned that the Colonel would write about her, she must have changed her mind, for it did not seem to bother her in the least that in his next dispatch to the *Graphic* the Colonel was telling all of New York about the mysterious Russian woman whose sudden appearance on the scene had evoked such wonders.

III

Madame Blavatsky and Colonel Olcott saw a great deal of each other on their return to New York. Madame's first appearance in print, a letter to the editor of the *Graphic* defending the Eddy brothers, made her seem another ardent spiritualist, but it soon became clear that spiritualism, for her, was merely a convenient stepping stone. It (and the Theosophical Society which would come later) was meant to gradually "merge into and evolve hints of the teachings of the Secret Doctrine of the oldest school of Occult philosophy in the whole world, a school to reform which the Lord Gautama was made to appear." These teachings, said Madame, "could not be given abruptly." Spiritualism was a useful ally because it had "proved such a sore in the side of the materialists," and because it had broken the hold of science and orthodox, "theological" Christianity, but other than that it had produced (as Olcott wrote in an article inspired by HPB) "few things worthy of a thoughtful man's attention."

HPB did not deny the reality of phenomena—in fact, she had compromised herself more than once by defending mediums of dubious value—but she grew more and more critical of the "phenomenalism running riot," which, she said, had left "twenty millions of believers clutching at one drifting theory after another in the hope to gain truth." As it now stood, HPB considered spiritualism "unconscious sorcery," "for by allowing himself to become the helpless tool of a variety of spirits, of whom he knows nothing save what the latter permit him to know, he [the medium] opens, unknown to himself a door of communication between the two worlds, through which emerge the blind forces of Nature lurking in the astral light, as well as good and bad spirits."

Rather than place all hope in mischievous or confused "spirit guides," Madame suggested in an article in the *Spiritual Scientist* that all spiritualists would do better to investigate "the laws which lie back of the phenomena." These laws—HPB never spoke of "miracles"—could be found through the study of "the one positive science—Occultism," which Madame pictured as

> the mysterious lever of all intellectual forces, the Tree of Knowledge of good and evil of the allegorical paradise, from whose gigantic trunk sprang in every direction boughs, branches, and twigs, the former shooting forth straight enough at first, the latter deviating with every inch of growth, assuming more and more fantastical appearances, til at last one after the other lost its vital juice, got deformed, and, drying up, finally broke off, scattering the grounds afar with heaps of rubbish.

Although it was true that many of these Occult offshoots had existed throughout the world—Madame cited Homer, Moses, Hermes, Herodotus, Cicero, Plutarch, Pythagoras, Appolonius of Tyana, Simon the Magician, Paracelsus, Plato and the Count St. Germain, among others—the main root and trunk, "the whole truth," could be found "in one quarter, the Asiatic schools of philosophy." Therefore, explained HPB, she had come to America for only one reason: it was her mission to begin to "point the way eastward."

Other writers on esoteric and arcane lore had looked in more or less the same direction, but HPB differed because she spoke "from personal experience and practice" gained on her travels in the East. It was only there, she claimed, in "that cradle of Occultism," that one could still find schools of Adepts (sometimes called Masters, Sages or Mahatmas) who had been able to transmit the teachings of Occultism in unbroken purity for thousands of years. The exact locations of these schools or "lodges" were known only to Adepts, and, as Madame warned, "no one would be likely to find them out unless the Sages themselves found the neophyte worthy of initiation."

Despite HPB's hints that she had been one of the few—if not the only— Westerner in recent times to study with these Adepts, she did not put on spiritual airs. She smoked (tobacco continuously and hashish on occasion) and had a bawdy Rabelaisian wit. She was at once one of the boys (Olcott called her "Jack"), and an aristocrat who knew so little about cooking that she once tried to boil an egg by placing it on the bare coals. She was a complex, moody woman given to sudden alternations between flirtatious charm and violent outbursts. No one could be certain about her. Even Olcott, who had taken a room in her apartment ("the attraction of soul to soul, not that of sex to sex," he said) was at a loss. "She was such a bundle of contradictions, so utterly incapable of being classified like any of us common folk," he said, "that as a conscientious man I shrink from anything like dogmatic assertion."

Her door was open to all. "She neither meditated in seclusion," wrote the Colonel, "practiced austerities, denied herself the frivolous and worldly minded, nor selected her company." The decor of the "lamasery," as her apartment on Thirty-fourth Street came to be called, reflected HPB's style: intense, but with a self-sardonic twist. A gas lamp chandelier hung from the ceiling. Shelves and tables overflowed with exotic bric-a-brac: a mechanical bird, a wooden Buddha, Chinese fans, ivory cigarette holders. A mural of a jungle scene, complete with dried leaves and a mounted, snarling lion's head, covered one wall, while a bat spread its leathery wings over the doorway, and a stuffed monkey, wearing a dickey and grasping a page from Darwin's recently published *Descent of the Species* in one paw (this last being "a comment on materialistic scientists") stood in the center of the room.

It was here that Madame received, and, when the mood struck her, demonstrated a bit of magic for her guests. Astral bells and table rappings were standbys, but there were also more spectacular materializations and apports. Sometimes she seemed to brood, sunk sphinx-like in her big stuffed chair, while one of the constant stream of visitors demonstrated some aspect of mesmerism, mediumship, psychometry or magic. There was much talk of forming some sort of club or society, but nothing came of it until the evening of September 7, 1875, when one of the visitors, an engineer named Mr. Felt, delivered a lecture on "The Lost Canon of the Egyptians." Olcott was enthusiastic about Felt's claim that he had discovered a formula to summon minor spirits called "elementals" in his study of hieroglyphs, and he passed a note to Mr. Judge: "Would it not be a good idea to form a society to study this sort of thing," and Mr. Judge passed the note on to Madame, who nodded her assent.

After much discussion (the names Egyptological, Hermetic and Rosicrucian were rejected), the word "theosophy" was found in the dictionary, and on November 17, 1875, Colonel Olcott delivered the Inaugural Address of the Theosophical Society at Mott Memorial Hall. The original bylaws said only that "The objects of the society are to collect and diffuse knowledge of the laws which govern the universe," though both

HPB and William Q. Judge have testified that they at least had known from the beginning the threefold Objects adopted by the Society publicly in the 1880s:

> To form the nucleus of a Universal Brotherhood of Humanity, without distinction of race, creed, sex, caste, or color; To study the ancient and modern religions, philosophies and sciences, and the demonstrations of the importance of such study; and to investigate the unexplained laws of Nature and the psychical powers latent in man.

While Madame did not say so at the time, she later claimed that the "Society was founded at the direct suggestion of Indian and Tibetan Adepts." The Colonel himself believed that he had been in communication with the Masters ever since HPB had handed him a shiny, black, sealed envelope from the Master Tuitet Bey, of the Brotherhood of Luxor. Inside, in gold ink on green paper, Olcott read: "Brother Neophyte, we greet Thee. He who seeks us finds us. TRY. Rest thy mind—banish all foul doubt. We keep watch over our faithful soldiers. Sister Helen is a valiant, trustworthy servant. Open thy spirit to a conviction, have faith and she will lead thee to the Golden Gate of Truth." Other letters followed (the Colonel was eventually transferred to the Indian Section) but all of them paled beside the experience that Olcott had one evening while reading in his room in the lamasery.

"All at once," remembered the Colonel some years later, "as I read with my shoulder a little turned from the door, there came a gleam of something white in the right-hand corner of my right eye." The Colonel dropped his book in astonishment; he looked up to see

> an Oriental clad in white garments, and wearing a head-cloth or turban of amber-striped fabric, hand-embroidered in yellow floss-silk. Long raven hair hung from his turban to his shoulders; his black beard, parted vertically on the chin in the Rajput fashion, was twisted up at the ends and carried over the ears; his eyes were alive with soul-fire; eyes which were at once benignant and piercing in glance; the eyes of a mentor and a judge, but softened by the love of a father who gazes on a son needing counsel and guidance. He was so grand a man, so imbued with the majesty of moral strength, so luminously spiritual, so evidently above average humanity, that I felt abashed in his presence, and bowed my head and bent my knee as one does before a god or a god-like personage.

The Master seated himself in the chair across the table, and told the Colonel "that a great work was to be done for humanity, and that a mysterious tie, which could not be broken, however much strained it might be at times," had drawn him and HPB together. When the Master finally rose, Olcott suddenly thought, "What if this be but hallucination; what if HPB has cast a hypnotic glamour over me?" and wished that he might have "some tangible object to prove that he has really been here," but before the Colonel had given voice to his thoughts, the Master, shining with the soft gleam of an inner light had gone, leaving his turban, embroidered with a strange cryptograph, on the table.

The importance of this theophany for Olcott and the development of the Theosophical Society cannot be overestimated. Out of the experience came Olcott's "loyalty to the Masters behind our movement which the rudest shocks and the cruelest disillusionings have never shaken." Other than Blavatsky, Olcott was the only Theosophist to receive the honor of a personal visit from a Master, and it was largely because of his testimony and confidence that so many people were willing to at least believe in the possibility that the Masters, "the Elder Brothers of Humanity," were watching over "our dull pupil-race." "However others less fortunate may doubt," said the Colonel, "I KNOW."

Much to the Colonel's consternation, HPB stopped attending meetings as soon as the Theosophical Society seemed safely launched. The Masters, it seemed, had taken a decidedly literary turn. "I wrote this last night, 'by order,' " she told the Colonel one evening, handing him a few pages of manuscript, "but what it is to be I don't know." The pages remained in a drawer until she visited Professor Corson of Cornell and the project became clear to her. It was to be a book on "the history and philosophy of the Eastern Schools" and their relationship to modern science and philosophy. When she returned to New York, HPB plunged ahead as one possessed, sitting steadily at her desk until two in the morning. "She worked on no fixed plan," wrote Olcott, who served as her amanuensis after a day at his law, "but ideas came streaming through her mind like a perennial spring which is ever overflowing its brim." She had help, of course, from the visitors who came streaming through the lamasery—men like the rabbi who spent hours discussing the Kabbalah with her, and Dr. Alexander Wilder, self-taught authority on Plato, Hebrew and Greek—but the main portion of the work came to Madame through the Masters: sometimes, it seemed to Olcott, by way of possession (her handwriting would change drastically), and sometimes by presenting "astral doubles" of rare works not at hand. "Her pen would be flying over the page," observed the Colonel, "when she would suddenly stop, look out into space with the vacant eye of the clairvoyant seer, shorten her vision as though to look at something held invisibly in the air before her, and begin copying on paper what she saw."

The result was *Isis Unveiled, A Master-Key to the Mysteries of Ancient and Modern Science and Theology*. In it HPB had gathered all the underground strands of Western occultism, interpreted and ordered according to the master-key of Eastern philosophy. This philosophy was, by and large, based on the *Vedas*. But the philosophy of the *Vedas* itself was interpreted by another turn of the key, held this time by science.

The Adepts who personified the Vedic truth were not gods, or God, but men who, having taken a further step in spiritual evolution, had demonstrated "that by combining science with religion, the existence of God and immortality of man's spirit may be demonstrated like a problem of Euclid." There were no miracles in nature, and the Adepts, for all their occult powers, were not miracle-makers, but more like spiritual scientists who had mastered the objective cause-and-effect laws of the universe. The Masters thus became examples of the highest possibilities of spiritual evolution, just as *Homo sapiens*, in Darwin's vision, had become the highest product of natural selection. By making evolution the chief principle of her occultism, HPB had neatly transformed orthodox Christianity's arch-enemy into Theosophy's ally.

It took HPB two volumes and 2,600 pages to present her argument, with illustrations drawn from ancient religion, symbolism, mythology, science and newspaper clippings Olcott brought home with him. The Colonel held that "If any book could ever have been said to make an epoch, this one could," but the critics were not so kind. The *Sun* called it "discarded rubbish," the *Springfield Republican* thought it "a large dish of hash," and the *New York Times* refused to review it at all, having, as its editor admitted to HPB's publisher, Mr. Bouton, "a holy horror of Mme. Blavatsky and her letters."

None of it made any difference. The first edition of a thousand copies sold out within ten days.

Despite the success of *Isis*, the Theosophical Society seemed to have lost its way in America. Most of the spiritualists, disappointed by HPB's refusal to produce phenomena, drifted away. For a time, HPB considered making the Society a special lodge within the Masons, but then Olcott entered into a correspondence with Moljee Thackeray, an Indian he had met on a voyage to England in 1870, and a more interesting possibility appeared.

Thackeray belonged to the Arya Samaj, a society which at first seemed to have much in common with the Theosophical Society. The Arya Samaj (*Arya*, Noble; *Samaj*, Society) led by Swami Dayanand, a Hindu pundit and one of the first Indian nationalists, aimed to reform Indian society through a return to the teachings of the "original" *Vedas*. Olcott was led to believe that Swami Dayanand was "a Hindu Luther," and that he held the same views as the Theosophical Society regarding the impersonality of God—that God was "an Eternal and Omnipresent Principle which, under many different names, was the same in all religions." HPB hinted that the Swami was closely connected with the adepts of the Himalayan Brotherhood, and for a time the two societies were united, the Theosophical Society now going under the name The Theosophical Society of the Arya Samaj.

At the same time the Theosophists began a correspondence with two Sinhalese Buddhist monks, Sumangala, the High Priest of Adam's Peak, and a famous Pali scholar, and Meggittuwatte, a monk celebrated for his victory over a party of Christian missionaries who had made the mistake, as they later admitted, of challenging him to a three-day debate at Panadura. Meggittuwatte's victory had done a great deal to strengthen Buddhist resistance to repressive English laws and the attacks of the missionaries.

The Theosophical Society returned to autonomy when Olcott discovered that the Arya Samaj was not eclectic, like the Theosophical Society, but actually a new sect of Hinduism, based on the Swami's interpretation of the *Vedas* and shastras, and without, as the Colonel put it, "any benevolent interest expressed in the religious welfare of non-Vedic peoples." But it was still clear that powerful new forces were stirring in Asia, and that anticolonialism and nationalism were leading not only to a new political order, but to a revival of interest in the ancient religions as well. HPB now had no doubts about the direction the Theosophical Society ought to take, and neither she nor the Colonel seemed surprised when the Master Serapis informed them that they were to leave New York for India no later than December 17 of that year, 1878.

It was not easy for Colonel Olcott to leave behind the comfortable and congenial existence he had built up in New York. He was forty-six years old, and though he had been divorced from his wife for a number of years, he was not anxious to leave his two sons. In addition, the financial difficulties were formidable: he had to find a way to pay for the passage, and then to support himself and HPB in India. He came up with two or three speculative business ideas—among them an Indian trading company and a South American mining venture—but nothing came of them. He managed to procure a letter of recommendation from the president of the United States, and a special passport identifying him as a cultural and commercial ambassador, but the position was purely honorary, and did nothing to solve the financial problem. As December 17 drew closer, Olcott's doubts increased, but he had known ever since the night the Master had visited him that there was no turning back. As HPB had written him when he had asked to begin his studies under the Masters: "If you . . . agree to the word Neophyte you are cooked my boy and there is no return from it. . . . Patience, faith, no questioning, thorough obediance and Silence."

HPB herself prepared for the voyage by taking out American citizenship, an act calculated to reassure the British rulers of India that she was not, as rumored, a Russian spy. Finally, the lamasery furnishings were auctioned off, and Thomas Edison, who had discussed his psychic experiments with Olcott and become a member of the Society, sent an assistant to record the voices of HPB and other members of the Society on tinfoil discs. (Olcott planned to play these greetings in India on the phonograph he had recently bought.) At last the Colonel and HPB took a midnight carriage to the steamer *Canada*, having left General Abner Doubleday, the inventor of baseball, in charge of a Society that had, so it seemed, practically ceased to exist. The ship did not sail until the 18th, but they had, Olcott noted with relief, left American soil by the required date.

IV

"When we arrived in India, in February, 1879," HPB would write later:

> there was no unity between the races and sects of the Peninsula, no sense of a common public interest, no disposition to find the mutual relation between the several sects of ancient Hinduism, or that between them and the creeds of Islam, Jainism, Buddhism, and Zoroastrianism. As for any international reciprocity, in either social or religious affairs, between the Sinhalese and the Northern Buddhist nations, such a thing had never existed. Each was absolutely ignorant of the other's views, wants or aspirations. Finally, between the races of Asia and those of Europe and America, there was the most complete absence of sympathy as to religious and philosophical questions. The labors of the Orientalists from Sir William Jones and Burnouf down to Prof. Max Muller, had created among the learned

> a philosophical interest, but among the masses not even that. If to the above we add that all the Oriental religions, without exception, were being asphyxiated to death by the poisonous gas of Western official science, through the medium of the educational agencies of European administrations and missionary propagandists, and that the native graduates and undergraduates of India, Ceylon, and Japan had largely turned agnostics and revilers of the old religions, it will be seen how difficult a task it must have been to bring something like harmony out of this chaos, and make a tolerant if not a friendly spirit spring up and banish these hatreds, evil suspicions, ill feelings, and mutual ignorance.

The task was indeed difficult, as HPB said, but she did not make it any less so by the impression she gave the ruling British, who were nervous about Indian nationalism (the Sepoy Rebellion had been put down only twenty years earlier) and about Russia. The British in India were a caste apart, with their own language, social hierarchy, customs, and dwelling places, and when the CID (Criminal Investigation Division) discovered that HPB and the Colonel had taken a cottage in the native quarter of Bombay, where they fraternized with Indians connected with the Arya Samaj, the theosophists were put under surveillance. The Colonel's first public speech (HPB never spoke in public) to a densely packed crowd in Famaji Cawasji Hall seemed to confirm the government's suspicion. "The youth of India," thundered the Colonel, "will shake off their sloth, and be worthy of their sires. From every ruined temple, from every sculptured corridor cut in the heart of the mountains, from every secret vihara where the custodians of the Sacred Science keep alive the torch of primitive wisdom, comes the whispering voice, saying, 'Children, your Mother is not dead but sleepeth.' "

A.P. Sinnett, the editor of the influential *Allahabad Pioneer*, who had taken an interest in spiritualism while still in England, wrote HPB shortly after her arrival, and invited Madame and the Colonel to visit him at Simla, the summer capital of the British Raj. Sinnett was taken aback by HPB's uncouth ways, and he wondered why the Masters had chosen a channel so obviously unfit for bringing the message to the "right" people. He also found it hard to understand what HPB saw in the Indians, whom he considered, as he told her rather politely, "on a somewhat lower scale of cosmic evolution" than Europeans. Though HPB disagreed, (she would write Sinnett a few years later: "You want to write *esoteric* facts and you give instead English race prejudice. The Indians are immensely higher spiritually than Europeans, who may not reach their level for some milleniums yet. . . .") she and Sinnett still managed to forge an alliance. Sinnett was impressed by the rappings, astral bells and materializations that Madame seemed able to command at a snap of her fingers, and he introduced her to all the important people, including Allan O. Hume, former secretary of the government, and the wife of Major General Gordon, both of whom would figure in the Simla Eclectic Theosophist Society.

For her part, Madame not only satisfied Sinnett's appetite for phenomena, but also agreed to forward a letter he had written to the Masters. Within a few days Sinnett received a reply—not, as he had expected from Master Morya, but from another Adept, a Himalayan Brother, Khoot Hoomi Lal Singh, who came to be known as Master K.H. These letters (the originals are now in the British Museum) usually arrived by way of HPB, but they sometimes dropped, like falling leaves, from the ceiling above Sinnett's desk. The Mahatama letters, as they were called, were, on the whole, more metaphysical than the letters Olcott had so far received, and they formed the basis for two of Sinnett's books, the popular *Occult World*, published in 1881, and *Esoteric Buddhism*, published in 1883, about which more will be said later.

Having managed the difficult feat of establishing a beachhead for the Theosophical Society among both the British ruling class and their Indian subjects, HPB and the Colonel turned to Ceylon. Sinhalese Buddhism had been under attack by three successive waves of Portuguese, Dutch and British colonialism, and though the British seemed, on the face of it, milder than their predecessors, they had merely shifted from direct to indirect methods. Officially Queen Victoria had granted the Buddhists the freedom to practice their religion, but in practice only marriages which took place in Christian churches were recognized, which meant that children born of Buddhist parents were *ipso facto* illegitimate, a definite disadvantage when applying for any kind of official position. In addition, all schools had to be licensed by the government, which withheld state funds from any school that did not open the day with an hour of instruction from the authorized version of the Bible. The effect was that by the time the Colonel and HPB arrived in Ceylon there were four Buddhist schools in existence and 805 Christian ones.

Christian missionaries had always been an effective arm in the campaign to discredit Buddhism, and they had pursued a policy of challenging Buddhists to public debate for some time when they more than met their match with Meggittuwate Gunananda at Panadura in 1873. It was widely agreed that Gunananda, who was the most effective orator in Ceylon, had bested the Christians, particularly in the arguments about the creation of the world by a God and the existence of a personal, permanent soul, and it was as a result of reading a report of this debate that HPB and Colonel Olcott had opened a correspondence with Gunananda from New York. HPB had sent along the two volumes of *Isis Unveiled* as soon as they were published and Gunananda translated parts of the book, as well as some of HPB's letters, into Sinhalese. The material was read throughout the island with enthusiasm.

The Sinhalese Buddhists were, therefore, anxiously waiting to greet the Theosophists when they arrived at the coastal town of Galle on May 17, 1880. The harbor was lined with brightly painted fishing boats, a thousand flags flew in the sun, and a white cloth was spread out on the dock to lead them to their carriage. On May 25, HPB and the Colonel knelt before a Buddhist priest at a temple in Galle and performed the ceremony of "taking *pansil*"—the five lay precepts of undertaking to refrain from killing, lying, stealing, intoxicants, and sexual misconduct. They repeated the vows in Pali, as well as the refuge in Buddha, Dharma and Sangha, before a large crowd. "When we had finished the last of the Silas," Olcott wrote in his diary, "and offered flowers in the customary way, there came a mighty shout to make one's nerves tingle." It was the first time the Sinhalese had seen one of the ruling white race treat Buddhism with anything approaching respect, and it was (as far as we have been able to discover) the first time that Americans had become Buddhists in the formal sense—that is, in a manner recognized by other Buddhists.

Just what kind of Buddhists the Theosophists were is another question. As early as 1875, HPB had told W.Q. Judge in New York that she considered herself a Buddhist, and that the beliefs of the Masters "might be designated 'pre-Vedic Buddhists.' " Since, however, as HPB told Judge, "no one would now admit there was any Buddhism before the Vedas," it was best to think of the Masters as "Esoteric Buddhists."

Olcott's view, at least his view when they first reached Ceylon (now, more properly known as Sri Lanka), was similar. "Our Buddhism was that of the Master-Adept Gautama Buddha," he wrote in his diary then, "which was identically the Wisdom Religion of the Aryan Upanishads, and the soul of all the ancient world faiths. Our Buddhism was, in a word, not a creed but a philosophy."

The further implications of this approach were already being developed by the Master K.H.'s letters to A.P. Sinnett, which would result in the publication of Sinnett's *Esoteric Buddhism* in 1883. "In proportion as Buddhism retreats into the inner penetralia of its faith," Sinnett would write, "these are to be found to merge into the inner penetralia of other faiths. The cosmic conceptions, and the knowledge of Nature on which Buddhism not only rests, but which constitute esoteric Buddhism, equally constitute esoteric Brahminism." In the Theosophic version of Buddhism, then, Gautama Buddha was one of a long line of Adepts, who were masters of that occult science which lay at the root of all true knowledge.

Still, according to the information Master K.H. sent Sinnett from his Himalayan retreat, Buddhism most closely served the Theosophical purpose, since even in its exoteric form "Buddhism has remained in closer union with the esoteric doctrines than any other popular religion." There were, however, important distinctions to be made within Buddhism itself. "The fact is," Sinnett wrote, "that Ceylon is saturated with exoteric, and Tibet with esoteric, Buddhism. Ceylon concerns itself merely with the morals, Tibet, or rather the adepts of Tibet, with the science, of Buddhism."

It was not a view the most learned Sinhalese bhikkhus would accept, but neither they nor the Theosophists cared to argue the issue. If the Theosophists balked at accepting Buddhism (or any religion, for that matter), as "a creed," they nevertheless accepted it as "philosophy," albeit with a certain eccentricity, and the Sinhalese were satisfied to accept them as allies. In any case, the Colonel was in his element. He and HPB proceeded overland to Colombo in triumph, the Colonel lecturing to thousands in temples, halls and impromptu outdoor meetings. Though government agents and missionaries did their best to obstruct them, the two-month tour was a huge success, resulting in the formation of seven branches of the Buddhist Theosophical Society of Ceylon.

V

David Hewivitarne met Colonel Olcott and Madame Blavatsky at the close of their first public meeting in Colombo. At fourteen he was already something of a firebrand. He had been introduced to the Founders by his uncle and father, both ardent Buddhists and active members of the young Buddhist Theosophical Society. David's maternal grandfather had donated the land which supported the first Buddhist monastic college in Ceylon, and, before his birth, his mother had offered flowers and incense to the Buddha and the devas in the wish that her child might be a son who would restore Buddhism to its rightful place in Ceylon.

David Hewivitarne, who would become known throughout the Buddhist world as Anagarika Dharmapala, was born on September 17, 1864, in the Pettah district of Colombo. His early childhood was spent in a household steeped in traditional Sinhalese Buddhist piety. Every morning and evening he recited the three refuges and five precepts with his family before a wooden replica of the great stone Buddha at Polonnaruwa, and at the age of nine he took the brahmacharya vows from his father who counseled him to sleep little and be content with whatever came his way. Later, he frequented Kotahena Temple, where Meggittuwate Gunananda delivered fiery denunciations of Christianity on Saturday evenings, and where he first heard about the two Westerners who had formed the Theosophical Society, and who had befriended the Sinhalese Buddhists.

His formal schooling plunged him into a very different world. His parents were ardent Buddhists and nationalists, but they were also middle class and had no choice but to send David to the aggressively missionary Christian schools. At Saint Benedict's Institute, which he entered at the age of ten, short prayers to the Virgin Mary were recited every half hour, and Buddhist children were required to attend a special class once a week. He next attended the Anglican Christian Boarding School, where church services were held every morning and the students recited Bible verses from memory every day. Young Hewivitarne was critical of the Bible, especially the Old Testament, but he was a diligent and gifted student and by the time he met the Theosophists he knew Exodus, Deuteronomy, Numbers, Joshua, The Four Gospels and the Acts of the Apostles by heart.

His teachers naturally considered him promising material for conversion, but David delighted in using his knowledge of Scripture to point out inconsistencies in Christian doctrine. He developed a sharp eye for hypocrisy, being particularly repulsed by the behavior of the boarding master of the Anglican school, who enjoyed shooting small birds after he had taken a few drinks.

The headmaster of St. Thomas's Collegiate School, which he next attended, was a strict disciplinarian who caned Hewivitarne for taking a day off to celebrate Wesak, the full moon day of the Buddha's birth, enlightenment and parinirvana. Then in March 1883, a Sinhalese Catholic mob, white crosses painted on their foreheads, attacked a Buddhist procession as it passed St. Lucia's Church on the way to Kotahena Temple. David Hewivitarne did not return to St. Thomas's.

He continued his education in the Pettah Library. He read in ethics, psychology, philosophy, history and biography. He felt a special kinship with Keats and Shelley. Of the latter's *Queen Mab*, he said, "I have never ceased to love its lyric indignation against the tyrannies and injustices that man heaps on himself and its passion for individual freedom." He wondered if the English poets, rebels like himself against the orthodoxies of Christianity, had been reborn on earth or in the deva worlds, and he thought of finding their reincarnations so that he could introduce them to the dharma they had never had the chance to hear. He did his best to track down bhikkhus and yogis who might have attained arhatship, or who had gained *abhijna*, psychic powers that sometimes resulted from yogic training, but never found anything more than rumors and stories. Apparently Sinhalese bhikkhus had abandoned the practice of meditation long ago, and the orthodox position was that liberation through meditation was no longer possible. One could only study the Scriptures and follow the Precepts with the hope of achieving a more felicitous rebirth.

It was not enough. Hewivitarne longed for something more, for a teacher who had direct experience of spiritual practice. In 1883 he felt he had found what he had been looking for in A.P. Sinnett's *Occult World*, the book which first introduced the Theosophical Masters to the reading public. He was further encouraged by an article on "Chelas and Lay Chelas" (*chela* is the Sanskrit term for disciple) which he read in *The Theosophist*. The article announced the establishment of an esoteric section, The Himalayan School of Adepts, within the Theosophical Society, and Hewivitarne wrote to Theosophical Headquarters, now in Adyar, India, to request admission. Here, it seemed, were accomplished Masters who could instruct him in the techniques and practices which had been lost or neglected by the Sinhalese Buddhists.

Colonel Olcott and Madame Blavatsky returned to Ceylon in January 1884 to organize legal action against the organizers of the Catholic mob, and Hewivitarne, though underage, was initiated into the Society with his grandfather as sponsor. Madame Blavatsky devoted hours to the young man, who was completely taken with her and her tales of the Masters M. and K.H. who directed the Society from their Himalayan caves. Whatever doubts he may have had were completely dispelled when HPB quoted the message A.P. Sinnett had received from Master K.H.: "THE ONLY TRUE REFUGE FOR HIM WHO ASPIRES TO TRUE PERFECTION IS THE BUDDHA ALONE."

HPB soon informed her new protege that Master K.H. had sent her a special message about his future. Hewivitarne was to return to Adyar and prepare himself for advanced occult studies under the personal tutelage of HPB herself. David's father at first gave his permission, but he changed his mind after having an inauspicious dream on the eve of his son's departure. Both the High Priest Sumangala and Olcott sided with the father, but HPB turned everything around by announcing that not only would she be personally responsible for David's safety, but that he would die if he were not permitted to accompany her.

HPB and David had been in Adyar only a few weeks when HPB took another of her sudden turns. The two had an intimate little chat during which she discouraged his interest in psychic powers and the occult. There was no need for him to study Occultism, after all, she said, since all that was necessary could be found through the study of the Pali Scriptures. She gave him her blessing and instructed him to devote his life to the good of humanity. Somehow it did not seem to surprise the aspiring chela that the Masters had sent him back to Ceylon rather than on to Tibet. In his mind, as in the minds of most Sinhalese, the cause of the Theosophical Society was identical to the cause of the Buddhist revival. "In those days," he wrote years later, "the Theosophic atmosphere was saturated with the aroma of the devotion of the Himalayan Masters to the Lord Buddha. . . ."

VI

Colonel Olcott had returned to Ceylon in the spring of 1882. The lack of Buddhist schools seemed to him the most serious obstacle the Sinhalese faced and, to raise money for a Buddhist Educational Fund, he set out on a tour of the countryside. The enthusiasm inspired by his first visit had waned, and that fact, in addition to the poverty of most of the Sinhalese, made it difficult to raise a substantial sum. Then too, the Colonel had come to the realization that most of the Sinhalese knew almost as little about their religion as did most Europeans, and they were therefore susceptible to the slanders and exaggerations of the missionaries. The Colonel decided to correct the situation by writing a Buddhist catechism—a small, easily understood book which would spell out the basic tenets of the Buddhist faith. In preparation, Olcott read some ten thousand pages on Buddhism in French and English translation. Olcott went over the Sinhalese manuscript word by word with Sumangala, high priest of Sripida and Galle, and Principal of the Vidyodaya College, who gave it his *imprimatur* only after days of discussion. Olcott made no references to Adepts or other peculiarities of Theosophical belief, nor did he try to interpret Buddhism according to the *Vedas*, Occultism or Western ideas of religion.

In the introduction to the catechism, he suggested that the word "Buddhism" itself was only a Western term; "Buddha Dharma," he said, was the best name for it. Nor should it be thought of as a religion. "The Sinhalese Buddhists," he wrote, "have never yet had any conception of what Europeans imply in the etymological construction of the Latin root of this term. In their creed there is no such thing as a 'binding' in the Christian sense, a submission to or merging of self in a Divine Being." Unlike Blavatsky, who looked to India and the Masters for inspiration, it seems clear that Olcott had begun to view the world through Buddhist eyes.

Olcott returned for the third time in 1883. He was concerned to find the Catholics attracting converts by performing healings; he knew the power of Lourdes. He suggested to the Buddhists that they ought to practice healing in the name of Lord Buddha, but the bhikkhus told him that they knew nothing about such things. Then one day, while Olcott was collecting money for the fund, a cripple named Cornelius Appu brought a small donation. Something made the Colonel try a few surreptitious passes over the man's arm. It was not the first time the Colonel practiced the magnetic passes made popular by Professor Mesmer. As a young man he had successfully anesthetized a woman who had her tooth pulled. Later in the day the man returned to tell the Colonel that he could move his arm a little. Olcott began regular treatments and within a few weeks, Appu's arm had improved so much that he was able to sign a statement attesting to his cure. Word spread quickly, and everywhere he went Olcott was met by crowds hoping that the "White Buddhist," as he had become known, could help them. The Colonel kept it up for a number of years, until finally the strain grew too great and the Masters suggested that he retire.

The culmination of Olcott's efforts for the Sinhalese occurred in 1884 when the Colonel traveled to London in order to present a petition to the secretary for the Colonies on behalf of the Sinhalese. The credentials he carried from Washington doubtless helped, though they conferred no real power, but the success of this mission was due more to the force of his personality and the authority of his arguments. When he left London, the secretary had revoked the laws that had made it necessary for the Sinhalese to don top hat and frock coats to be married in Christian churches, and Wesak (the holiday young Hewivitarne had been caned for observing) was proclaimed an official holiday. To the Sinhalese, it seemed that the American Theosophist had single-handedly restored their religion and culture to them.

Meanwhile, with Olcott and HPB still in London, the Theosophical Society in India had run into trouble. The society had greatly extended its influence in the five years since the Founders had arrived from New York. The alliance with Swami Dayanand and the Arya Samaj, always an uneasy one, had finally ended when the swami accused the Theosophists of embracing Buddhism at the expense of his Vedic fundamentalism, but the Theosophical Society had by then established itself as a strong, if nonpolitical, influence on the growing Indian nationalist movement. It attracted both progressive Englishmen, like A.O. Hume, who saw home rule as ultimately desirable, as well as educated Indians. In the spiritual field, Swami Dayanand had been replaced by the more scholarly and philosophical approach of a Brahmin scholar named T. Subba Row, who wrote a number of articles on Indian religious themes for the Society's magazine, *The Theosophist*. Then, too, HPB had managed to surround herself with a number of Hindu disciples, the closest being a Brahmin named Damodar, who created something of a stir by announcing in *The Theosophist* that he had renounced his caste in favor of the principles of equality and brotherhood as taught in Theosophy.

All this made the government and the missionaries especially watchful. But the real danger came from within. In 1879 a certain Mrs. Coulomb, who had sheltered a shipwrecked HPB in Cairo many years before, arrived destitute, along with her husband, in India. HPB, never one to forget an old friend, took in the Coulombs—the woman as housekeeper and the husband as gardener and carpenter. The Coulombs did not get on well with the rest of the Adyar residents, and with the Founders away in London the situation turned ugly. The Coulombs left, with a great deal of bitterness on both sides. Nothing was heard from Mrs. Coulomb until the Christian College Magazine published an article she had written, "The Collapse of Khoot Hoomi," in which the housekeeper published certain letters, allegedly from HPB, which made it appear that HPB had forged the Master's letters. The Coulombs also wrote that they had acted as confederates for many of HPB's demonstrations of psychic phenomena, and Mr. Coulomb claimed that he had built a sliding panel in back of the shrine where the Masters deposited their letters.

That was only the first round. In London, the newly-formed Society for Psychical Research (SPR) announced plans to investigate the Theosophical case. HPB and the Colonel were interviewed willingly enough in England, along with other witnesses. Then Richard Hodgson, a young university graduate, went out to India for three months. The atmosphere was not one to encourage an impartial investigation. The Coulomb charges had brought everyone's doubts and fears to the surface, and Hodgson found the Theosophical community in disorderly retreat. A.O. Hume, second in command of the Simla Eclectic Theosophical Society (the branch to which the most well-placed English belonged) stated that while some of the phenomena attributed to HPB were genuine, some were fraudulent, as the Coulombs had claimed. Hodgson's report in volume III of the *Proceedings of the SPR* supported the Coulombs, stating that "all the marvelous narratives put forward as evidence of the existence and occult powers of the Mahatmas are to be explained as due either (a) to deliberate deception . . . or (b) to spontaneous illusion, or hallucination, or unconscious misrepresentation or invention on the part of the witness."

As for HPB, "For our part," wrote the distinguished scientists on the committee, "we regard her neither as the mouthpiece of hidden seers, nor as a mere vulgar adventuress; we think she has achieved a title to permanent remembrance as one of the most accomplished, ingenious, and interesting imposters in history."

Madame Blavatsky arrived in Adyar in December, ready for battle. The letters, she said, were pure fabrications. Mr. Coulomb had built the sliding panels into the shrine while HPB had been in England. Furthermore, the Coulombs were in the pay of the missionaries who had published their attack. She intended to sue for libel immediately.

Olcott and the other members hesitated. They argued that HPB's only defense would be to produce the Masters or other phenomena in court, something she had always refused to do. To begin with, it ran against occult principles, and besides, Olcott argued, the courts of the British Raj had been waiting for an opportunity to destroy the Society, and HPB could not expect a fair trial. Finally, the Theosophical Society (as HPB herself had repeatedly emphasized) did not depend upon her ability to create miracles on demand. HPB held fast; her honor and the honor of the Masters was at stake. But without the support of her friends there was little she could do. She was forced to accept the recommendations of a special convention: the Theosophical Society would not take the case to court, and Madame Blavatsky submitted her resignation as corresponding secretary. As far as she was concerned the Society had failed its first crucial test.

The affair wounded her deeply. She sailed for Europe on March 30, 1885, so ill that she had to be carried on board. The ship stopped over at Ceylon, and David Hewivitarne, who had been working tirelessly at the headquarters of the Colombo Buddhist Theosophical Society, visited her for the last time. He remained loyal to the end, believing that HPB and the Masters were Buddhists who had been betrayed on all sides, and he, at least, would never abandon them.

VII

European scholars of the time considered Ceylon to be the home of the purest Buddhism in Asia—by which was meant the Buddhism that most closely resembled the original doctrine of the Buddha and the early Sangha. The man most responsible for this view was Thomas Rhys-Davids, an English civil servant who had been led, like Sir William Jones, to master the classical language of Ceylon in order to interpret native law. Rhys-Davids had been asked to settle a dispute arising from the death of a bhikkhu. The question seemed to be whether his assistant or another monk should take his place; the answer, Rhys-Davids was told, lay in a body of law called the Vinaya, which could only be read in Pali. The bhikkhu who taught Pali to Rhys-Davids, Unnanse Yatramulle, made a deep impression on the young magistrate. ". . . He was sinking into the grave from the effects of a painful and incurable malady," Rhys-Davids wrote in tribute some years later.

> I had heard of his learning as a Pali scholar . . . and was grateful to him for leaving his home under such circumstances to teach a stranger. There was a strange light in his sunken eyes, and he was constantly turning away from questions of Pali to questions of Buddhism. I found him versed in all the poetry and ethics of the Suttas and was glad to hear him talk. There was an indescribable attraction about him, a simplicity that filled me with reverence.

Inspired by his teacher, Rhys-Davids collected a complete version of the Tripitaka as it existed in palm-leaf manuscripts. He directed his attention especially to the suttas, then lying, in his words, "buried and unpublished." He returned to England, and in 1881 announced the formation of the Pali Text Society, which he modeled on the Early

English Text Society. The Pali Text Society scoured the libraries of Europe and Ceylon for palm-leaf manuscripts, and then transliterated the Pali into Roman letters. "No other course was reasonable," wrote Davids's wife, Carolyn Rhys-Davids, "since Buddhism was not of one country, hence of one script, only." Both the Pali Text Society and the Sacred Books of the East series, edited by Max Muller, published the fruits of Rhys-Davids's work.

For Rhys-Davids and the Pali Text Society, the Pali scriptures as found in Ceylon, Burma and Siam represented the most authentic record of what the Buddha's "original" teaching had been in India. The Northern, so-called mahayana schools were, in this view, degenerations corrupted by superstition and priestcraft. Some of this had also crept into Southern Buddhism, but on the whole the Pali Canon presented the pristine teaching of the Buddha. Rhys-Davids saw Southern Buddhism as "Protestant Buddhism"—scientific, rational and reasonable, while Northern Buddhism was more like Roman Catholic Buddhism—that is, filled with ritual, recourse to saints (bodhisattvas) and run by priest-craft. Therefore, the sensible way for a Westerner to approach the problem of Buddhism was to find a way back to the original teaching of Gautama, to discover the earliest texts in existence. These were, nearly all scholars of the day believed, in Pali.

Colonel Olcott took a broader view. He hoped to bring all the world's Buddhists together under a common banner. He would find those principles on which they could agree, rather than spend his time ferreting out differences. It was obvious to him that a united Buddhist movement would have more power in the world than the fragmentary one that now existed. His concern, then, was more political than scholarly.

Emblematic of the Colonel's vision was the Buddhist flag he designed with Sumangala in 1889. "It was a splendid idea," the Colonel wrote in his diary, "and I saw in a moment its far-reaching potentialities as an agent in that scheme of Buddhistic unity which I have clung to from the beginning of my connection with Buddhism."

The Colonel's *Buddhist Catechism* had already been a step in that direction: it had been translated in Japan and India, and into nearly every European language. The flag, "which could be adopted by all Buddhist nations as the universal symbol of their faith, thus serving the same purpose as the cross does for all Christians," would come, thought the Colonel, as a "powerful reinforcement." The Sinhalese, Olcott wrote in his diary, "had hit upon the quite original and unique idea of blending in the flag the six colors alleged to have been exhibited in the aura of the Buddha, namely, sapphire-blue, golden-yellow, crimson, white, scarlet, and a hue composed of the others blended (*prabhasvara*)." On Wesak of that year it flew from almost every temple and Buddhist household in the island. Olcott considered the flag "one of the prettiest in the world," and he was pleased to find, on visiting the Tibetan ambassador to the viceroy in Darjeeling, that the colors were the same as the flag of the Dalai Lama.

VIII

In 1888 a committee of young Japanese Buddhists dispatched the poet Noguchi to invite the Colonel to Japan. "We are praying Colonel Olcott to come and help us," Noguchi told the annual convention of the Theosophical Society in Adyar, "to come and revive the hope of our old men, to put courage in the hearts of our young men, to prove to the graduates of our colleges and universities, and to those who had been sent to America and Europe for education, that Western science is not infallible, and not a substitute, but the natural sister of religion. . . ."

Olcott, Noguchi and Dharmapala (whom the Japanese had also invited) left from Colombo. The Sinhalese Buddhists held a festive farewell meeting at the Theosophical Hall in Colombo. Sumangala Nayaka Maha Thera invoked the Triple Gem and the devas to bless the mission, and presented the Colonel with a Sanskrit letter for the heads of the Japanese Buddhist Committee. As far as anyone knew, this letter was the first official communication to pass between the Northern and Southern branches of Buddhism in many centuries. The letter expressed fraternal greetings and the hope that the Buddhists of Asia would unite for the good of the whole Eastern world.

The party was met at Kobe by representatives of the seven leading schools. It was an auspicious beginning, but Olcott soon discovered that the Shin Shu (Pure Land) school intended to finance his visit without consulting the other schools. He countered with the demand that his tour be sponsored by a joint committee composed of representatives of all the schools. The Japanese were not immediately responsive, and finally the Colonel "gave notice that unless they did form such a joint committee, I would take the next steamer back to my place of departure. I am not sure," he wrote, "but that those venerable pontiffs, spiritual teachers of 39,000,000 Japanese, and incumbents of about 70,000 temples, must have thought me as dictatorial a fellow as my countryman Commodore Perry."

The Colonel had his way, and at a joint meeting at the Choo-in Tendai temple in Kyoto, he read Sumangala's Sanskrit letter (a Japanese translation had been provided each dignitary). It was December, and Dharmapala had never before experienced such cold. He had fallen ill as soon as he reached Japan, and an attack of rheumatic fever made it necessary for him to watch the proceedings from a wheelchair. Much of his visit was spent in a Japanese hospital, where he met with Japanese Buddhists and officials, and was cared for by students of the Bungakurio Military Academy.

Olcott went on to give seventy-five lectures in the next three months. According to his estimate, he spoke to 187,000 people. He told the Japanese that the tide of world opinion had turned toward Buddhism, due, in large part, to the publication of books by Western authors. He cited Edwin Arnold's *Light of Asia* as especially important, and somehow came up with the estimate that there were at least fifty thousand Buddhists in America. The Japanese newspapers covered his tour extensively, and in one town a kite bomb exploded streamers calligraphing "Olcott san has come" across the sky. At one point he was requested to repeat the five precepts in Pali before a statue of the Buddha. "I could not help smiling to myself," he noted in his diary, "when thinking of the horror that would have been felt by any of my puritan ancestors of the seventeenth century, could they have looked forward to this calamitous day." He was sure that, had he "been born among them at Boston or Hartford, I should have been hanged for heresy on the tallest tree."

Toward the end of his tour, the Colonel made an attempt to found a Japanese Buddhist Section of the Theosophical Society. He felt that this way all the sects could be brought under the umbrella of the organization whose motto, "There is no religion higher than Truth," symbolized a god-like neutrality towards sectarian rivalry. The Japanese were interested, but insisted that sectarian rivalry was so strong in Japan that only an outsider who was also a Buddhist (i.e., only Colonel Olcott) could bring this about.

Olcott liked the idea enough to propose to HPB, now working in Europe on her magnum opus, *The Secret Doctrine*, that he resign the presidency of the Society to "build up an International Buddhist League that might send the Dharma like a tidal wave round the world." HPB cabled back immediately: if he resigned his office, she would abandon the Society. Even this would not have stopped him, he wrote later, "if a far higher personage than she had not come and told me that the Buddhist scheme must be postponed, and that I must not leave the post confided to me." The Masters, it seemed, still watched over the Theosophical Society, and the Buddhist League would have to remain "a great and splendid work that lies in the hand of the future."

Despite his sickness, Dharmapala had managed to see something of Japan. He was especially impressed with the great buddha in Kamakura. For Dharmapala, as for many of the Asians struggling against cultural and political imperialism, Japan provided almost the only example of an Asian country that had maintained its integrity—"a sovereign star," as Dharmapala called it in one of his speeches, "in a continent of servitude."

Still, he had his doubts. Attending a parade in his honor at the Bungarikio Military Academy, he worried about the mixture of Buddhism and militarism that allowed the highly disciplined cadets to march under the Buddhist flag the Colonel had designed. He also found it strange that Japanese priests, who were permitted to marry, led such worldly lives. Nevertheless, these were only details, and when he left, he carried with him a warm reply to the Sinhalese from the Japanese Buddhists, expressing the hope that in the future the two divisions of the Buddhist world might come to know each other more intimately. Olcott himself returned to Colombo a few months later, accompanied by three Japanese priests who intended to study Pali and Southern Buddhism.

IX

The three priests were not the first Japanese to study Buddhism in Ceylon. Two years earlier, on March 8, 1887, a twenty-eight-year-old Zen monk named Soyen Shaku had boarded a German steamer at Yokohama and reached Colombo three weeks later.

Soyen Shaku had been ordained a Zen monk in 1871, at the age of twelve. Every evening he gave his old teacher, Ekkei Zenji, a massage. "My teacher loved silence and spoke very little to other people," he wrote later in an autobiographical fragment, "especially to a mere boy, so he seemed like an antique statue, inaccessible, with no means for my approach. The only opportunity I had to see him smile was when he took a cup of sake, while watching the gold fish in the pond, but even then he spoke neither to me nor the gold fish."

In 1875 one of Soyen's teachers died. The monks stayed within the temple grounds for forty-nine days. The Rohatsu sesshin (held to commemorate the Buddha's enlightenment) followed. "All of us tried as best we could to forget everything else," said Soyen, "and just devote ourselves to meditation." For two nights Soyen sat under the Bodhi tree growing behind the window of the Founder's room. The snow covered him completely. "It was in that seclusion," Soyen later remembered, "that I attained real faith as a Zen monk which Buddha or devil could never deprive me of."

Soyen was devoted to Zen, but he was not narrow. He studied at Miidera, a Tendai temple, for six months. Then he studied with Gisan, the patriarch of a whole line of modern Zen masters. Gisan was then seventy-six. "Most of the time he was in bed with a little reading table by his side, his eyebrows bushy and snow white. His voice was as clear as a young person's. In his everyday life he was like a grandfather to us, though in his sanzen [Zen interview] he was very severe."

Soyen received dharma transmission in 1884, at the age of twenty-five. When he passed a particularly thorny koan overnight, Kosen, his teacher, is said to have remarked, "He is a born Bodhisattva." It was the kind of praise hardly ever heard in the Zen world.

Kosen had studied Confucianism before becoming a Zen monk, and it is likely that this training allowed him to be more interested in "worldly" learning than most Zen masters of his time. At the beginning of the Meiji era he was appointed the superior overseer of religious teaching in the Educational Bureau. At the same time he became patriarch of Engaku temple at Kamakura, which he opened to lay students of Zen. Many of these lay students were also students at the new Western-style universities which had just been founded, and as the group grew, Kosen formed them into a lay society called *Ryomakyo-kai: kai*, meaning "society," and *ryomakyo* meaning "abandonment of the concepts of both objectivity and subjectivity." Though Kosen did not intend it, this society would eventually play a crucial role in the development of Zen in America.

With Kosen's encouragement, Soyen studied at Keio University from 1884 to 1886. It was the logical time for him to settle down to a career in the temple; instead he took the unheard-of step of going west to Ceylon.

At first everything seemed strange: the birds and animals were unlike any he had seen before and even the grass was different. Instead of the pine trees he was used to, there were palms everywhere, and while Soyen wrote to his teacher that he was himself "somewhat black," he noted that comparing him to the Sinhalese was like comparing a heron to a crow. In addition both men and women wore their hair piled on top of their heads with circular combs, and the men wore red and white striped skirts. It was all very new. "The only familiar sound," he wrote his teacher somewhat plaintively, "is the sound of the dogs barking, just as they do in Japan."

Even his fellow monks made him feel different. They wore three pieces of clothing, and carried a wind fan in their right hands and an umbrella in their left. They walked over burning sands with their bare feet, carried iron begging bowls instead of money. He could not even join them in their begging rounds because he was not used to the heat, and so he had to buy his food.

He began to learn the Pali alphabet, which he found "very difficult." He felt himself "just born in this country," with his senses not yet working very well. "I feel like I am surrounded by fences," he wrote, "or like I am scratching an aching foot on the outside of my shoe." When some Sinhalese bhikkhus came to visit him, they could not converse, and he felt "like a queer person in a circus."

Nevertheless, he had come to learn something, and he threw himself into the situation completely, as he had done with his Tendai studies. Years later he would confide to his student Nyogen Senzaki that he had gone to Ceylon to learn how the hinayana Buddhists practiced the Precepts, but when he tried to explain it to his teacher he put it less simply. "My purpose in coming," he wrote Kosen, "is to hide myself from the world of name and fame, wrapped in the light of attainment, whatever it may be. According to the history of Zen, many teachers mingled with beggars, the working class, and farmers for many years, for the same reason, to hide themselves, so I am trying to follow them in this peculiar way of the nineteenth century." His only regret, he hastened to add, was that he could not see his teacher in his advanced age. "When I think of it, tears come from my eyes, remembering the 3,000 miles of ocean extending between us."

Before too long he was able to follow the bhikkhu's way of life—"a real beggar's life, as Buddha prescribed." At night the grass was his bed, the stones his pillow. When it rained, "I shrank myself up like a turtle, smiling at my own appearance." He followed the rule against taking anything except hot water or tea after the noon meal. He ate thin porridge in the morning, and at midday "rice without even one piece of teacake." Even so, he did not feel hungry at all.

At first he thought it strange that the bhikkhus, who followed the Vinaya so strictly, ate meat offered on their begging rounds. When the monks told him, "If you do not hear the killed victim's suffering voice or do not know that the killing was made especially for you, then the meat is clean," he worried that this justification would reach the Japanese sangha, and he asked Kosen not to tell the monks in Japan about the Sinhalese custom.

For the most part, he was greatly impressed by the Sinhalese. He knew that some Japanese, "intoxicated with European ways, with study, politics, learning, and building," might call the Sinhalese "barbarians," but he knew that the Sinhalese "treasure the real Dharma, even though it may be Hinayana in form. All the monks," he wrote, "keep the Precepts strictly and act as examples of the ethical life for the rest of the people, who respect and pay homage to them. When I think of the Japanese Buddhists," he confessed, "both priests and adherents, I must say I feel ashamed."

By 1888 he was under some pressure to return to Japan. "Please consider my situation," he wrote Kosen, "and permit me to stay here for a while longer. I am not thinking even a bit about myself, but I want to gather material to spread the teaching for others. . . .After attaining Bodhidharma's teaching and now to spend time studying Hinayana teaching is a very queer action which no Zen monk would approve," he admitted, "and now you my teacher scold me for this, and it is all true. I am like one casting off the gorgeous robes of a king and replacing them with the torn rags of a beggar."

He did not, even for a moment, forget his Zen. When he saw the relic of Buddha's tooth at Kandy he felt it was "nothing but dried real teeth, very human and with no real feature." But when he showed the bhikkhus a Buddha relic he carried with him from Japan (it was, he said, "a lovely blue color") they laughed, and told him it was merely artificial jewelry. He blushed, and politely said nothing, but he recited Bukko's poem in the depth of his heart:

> My sarira wraps up heaven and earth,
> Do not try to poke over cold ashes searching for it!

"If I expressed my Zen with such words as Bukko's," he wrote Kosen, "the 60,000 monks of Ceylon might be in danger of losing their minds."

Finally, he assured Kosen that he did not seek to make himself an example to others. "I only put myself in the position of the wanderer in the *Saddharmapundarika Sutra*, and am experiencing difficulties which no one would realize or practice in Japan and China. There are some reasons which are the motive for this action," he concluded, "but I will not talk about them until I fulfill my part well."

After three years Soyen Shaku returned to Japan and began teaching in the Nagata Zendo. The next year his teacher Kosen died, and Soyen took his place as Zen master of Engakuji. In 1892 he received an invitation to the World Parliament of Religions, which was to be held in Chicago as part of the Columbian Exposition of 1893. He decided to go even though his disciples, monks and laymen alike, opposed the journey, thinking it improper for a Zen priest to set foot in such an uncivilized country. His letter of acceptance was put into English by a young university student who had recently begun to study at Engakuji—a certain D.T. Suzuki.

X

Colonel Olcott had visited Burma for the first time in 1885. The Burmese had not suffered from colonialism as much as the Sinhalese had, and consequently did not seem to have the same need for the Colonel's services. The Burmese put the Colonel through a public examination on Buddhist doctrine before his first public talk—nothing to wonder at, according to Olcott, "considering what a marvel, almost an impossibility, it must have seemed to them that a *pucca* white man (that is, a pure-blooded not a mixed one) should come and, at that sacred shrine, in open day and in the presence of thousands of Burmans, avow himself a Buddhist from conviction, without ulterior motive." The Colonel passed his test satisfactorily, and before leaving Rangoon he established three separate sections of the Theosophical Society—one for Buddhists, one for Hindus, and one for Europeans interested primarily in psychic phenomena.

In 1890 a Burmese Buddhist group asked the Colonel's advice about their plan to send a party of bhikkhus to Europe. Olcott found the idea "admirable," but premature. He took the position, which the Burmese accepted, that Asian Buddhists ought to agree on a common platform before sending missionaries to the West.

The Buddhist League had come to nothing, but the Burmese inspired the Colonel to try once more. This time he called for a meeting of Asian Buddhists to take place at Adyar, directly following the annual Theosophical Convention of December 1890. Delegates from Ceylon, Burma and Japan met for two weeks, after which the Colonel presented a draft of Fourteen Buddhist Beliefs "upon which all Buddhist sects could agree if disposed to promote brotherly feeling and a mutual sympathy between themselves." Though the document was signed by all the delegates present, they had no real authority, and so the Colonel set out, once again, to unite the Buddhist world. Ceylon, where the Colonel was authorized to admit people into the Buddhist faith, was no problem. Burma proved more difficult. The Colonel had to kneel for hours on the hard wood floor of the great Council Hall at Mandalay while he discussed the Fourteen Beliefs, before the royal high priest would sign the document. Japan required all the Colonel's diplomatic skill. Shaku Genyu, head of the joint committee that had been formed during the Colonel's first visit, as well as of the Shingon school, listened patiently, and then told the Colonel that the Fourteen Beliefs might be acceptable as far as they went, but that the mahayana contained infinitely more.

"If I should bring you a basketful of earth from Mount Fuji, would that be a part of your sacred mountain?" asked the Colonel. Shaku Genyu said that it would. "Well, then," said the Colonel, "that is all you accept, that these propositions be accepted as included within the body of Northern Buddhism, as a basketful of its mountain, so to speak." The Colonel then went on to win the imprimatur of priests of the Zen, Nichiren, Jodo and Tendai schools.

XI

Dharmapala remained in India. Despite HPB's advice that "what he needed could be found in Pali," he had been frustrated in his attempts to find someone with actual meditation experience. He had, however, studied the *Visuddhimagga* and the *Satipatthana Sutta* closely, and meditated every morning on his own. At the Adyar Convention he joined the Esoteric Section of the Theosophical Society, making him, at least in theory, a student of the Mahatmas under the direct guidance of HPB. But Madame Blavatsky remained in Europe, where she formed her own Blavatsky Lodge in London, and Dharmapala, instead of taking instruction from the Masters, finally received guidance from "an old Burmese gentleman" with the Burmese delegation.

After the convention Dharmapala and Kozen Gunaratna (one of the Japanese priests who had accompanied Olcott back to Ceylon) traveled together in India. Both men had read an article by Sir Edwin Arnold, author of *The Light of Asia*, and were inspired to make a pilgrimage to Buddhist sites. Arnold himself had recently toured India and was shocked by the state of the Buddhist holy places. The Deer Park at Sarnath was desolate, but the Buddhist temple at Bodh-Gaya was in near ruins. Bodh-Gaya, where the Buddha had achieved enlightenment, had been owned by Shaivite Hindus for three hundred years, and priests still performed Hindu pujas under the bodhi tree. In an article written for the *London Daily Telegraph*, the poet described what he had found in

> the spot dear, and divine, and precious beyond every other place on earth, to all the four hundred million Buddhists in China, Japan, Mongolia, Assam, Cambodia, Burma, Arakan, Naupal, Thibet and Ceylon. . . . If you walked in that spot which all these scores of millions of our race love so well you would observe with shame and grief . . . ancient statues plastered to the walls of an irrigating well. . . . Stones carved with Buddha's images . . . used as weights in the levers for drawing water. . . . I have seen three feet high statues in an excellent state of preservation, buried under rubbish . . . and the Asokan pillars, the most ancient relics of the site—indeed, "the most antique memorials of all India,"—which graced the temple pavement, are now used as posts of the Mahant's kitchen.

In a two-hour interview with Colonel Olcott's mentor Sumangala, Arnold described the deplorable neglect of Bodh-Gaya. They devised a plan for an international committee of Buddhists to petition the queen's government in India to buy the temple and site from the Mahant and restore it to Buddhist hands.

"I think there never was an idea which took root and spread so far and fast as that thrown out thus in the sunny temple-court at Panadura amid the waving taliputs," wrote Arnold. "Like those tropical plants which can almost be seen to grow, the suggestion quickly became an universal aspiration, first in Ceylon and next in other Buddhist countries."

The Light of Asia had done more than any other book to popularize the story of the Buddha's life in the West. Now, instead of introducing Buddhism to the west, Arnold introduced the world's Buddhists to each other. Without meaning to, Arnold had found the key Olcott had been searching for. The struggle for Bodh-Gaya would unite the Buddhist world more than any number of committees, flags or common principles could ever do. Since there were scarcely any Buddhists left in India, Bodh-Gaya became the responsibility of Buddhists everywhere.

Anagarika Dharmapala and Kozen Gunaratna spent a few days sightseeing in Bombay and Calcutta. They visited a well-known yogini, Maji, in her cave on the banks of the Ganges, and then went on to Sarnath, where Dharmapala thought it a great pity that there were no Buddhists to preserve the stupas and stone carvings from vandals. Dharmapala had been moved by Arnold's descriptions of Bodh-Gaya, but nothing that he had read prepared him for the effect the ruined temple would have on him.

"After driving six miles, we arrived at the holy spot," he wrote in his diary.

> Within a mile you could see lying scattered here and there broken statues of our blessed Lord. At the entrance to the Mahant's temple on both sides of the portico there are statues of our Lord in the attitude of meditation and expounding the Law. How elevating! The sacred Vihara, the Lord sitting on his throne and the great solemnity which pervades all round makes the heart of the pious devotee weep. How delightful! As soon as I touched with my forehead the Vajrasana a sudden impulse came to my mind. It prompted me to stop here and take care of this sacred spot, so sacred that nothing in the world is equal to this place where Prince Sakya Sinha gained enlightenment under the Bodhi Tree. When the sudden impulse came to me, I asked Kozen priest whether he would join me, and he joyously assented, and more than this, he had been thinking the same thing. We both solemnly promised that we would stop here until Buddhist priests came to take charge of the place.

Given the keys to a Burmese rest house (the only sign of Buddhist interest in Bodh-Gaya), Dharmapala went into action. He fired off dozens of letters and articles for Buddhist publications. His own funds were nearly exhausted, but he vowed not to leave, even if he were to die of starvation. Much of his time was spent in practicing meditation, and the atmosphere of Bodh-Gaya, as well as his state of deep devotion had a powerful effect on him. On February 17, he wrote in his diary, "This night at 12 for the first time in my life, I experienced that peace which passeth understanding." For the next forty years, until his death in 1933, the battle for Bodh-Gaya would be at the center of Dharmapala's life.

Dharmapala stayed at Bodh-Gaya for six weeks, long enough to realize that in order to gather support he would have to travel. The Mahant, it turned out, was not very eager to sell the temple and its revenues. The government would have to be convinced to bring pressure to bear; money would have to be collected; international Buddhist opinion raised. Dharmapala set out for Burma and Ceylon. En route he learned that Madame Blavatsky had died in London. He felt the loss irreparable, and wondered who would be able to take her place. Without Blavatsky there would be no communication with the Masters, and the Theosophical Society would be no more than a hollow shell.

On May 31, 1891, Dharmapala founded another society, The Bodh-Gaya Maha Bodhi Society, in Colombo. Sumangala was president, Olcott director, and Dharmapala (considered too young to hold such august posts) was secretary. The Society had one paramount aim: to return Bodh-Gaya to the world's Buddhists, most of whom, after an initial burst of enthusiasm, seemed content to forget the whole affair. Nevertheless, Dharmapala persisted, and seven months later, on July 15, the day before the full moon, when the Buddha had preached his first sermon, he reached Bodh-Gaya with four Burmese bhikkhus, who raised the Buddhist flag and took up residence in the Burmese rest house. Dharmapala tried to buy a small plot of land from the Mahant, but negotiations grew so complicated that every step seemed only to increase the confusion. Finally, Dharmapala organized an International Buddhist Conference at Bodh-Gaya. Delegates came from Chittagong, Ceylon, China and Japan. The Japanese delegates reported that Japanese Buddhists were willing to raise the money necessary to buy the temple from the Mahant, and the delegates drafted plans to collect money for a Buddhist university and the translation of Buddhist texts into Indian vernaculars. The conference had been planned to coincide with the visit of the lieutenant governor of Bengal, but Dharmapala made the tactical error of flying the Japanese flag next to the Buddhist one, and consequently the lieutenant governor, sensitive to Japanese ambitions in Asia, stayed away. He further told Dharmapala that, as far as the government was concerned, the temple belonged to the Mahant.

The first issue of the *Maha Bodhi Journal* appeared in May of 1892, edited by Dharmapala. Colonel Olcott contributed "The Sweet Spirit of Buddhism," and Dharmapala wrote "A United Buddhist World," and "The Mahayana School of Buddhism," in which he argued that the Theravadin school was not, as Sir Monier Williams believed, of the hinayana, but actually "belongs to the oldest school of the Mahayana." Only the eighteen schools could be said to belong to the hinayana, said Dharmapala, because "they taught the incomplete doctrines"—a view which foreshadowed that of recent scholars. The quotations on the masthead announced the missionary fervor of the modern international Buddhist movement in the words of the Buddha as recorded in the *Mahavagga* of the Vinaya: "Go ye, O bhikkhus, and wander forth for the gain of the many, the welfare of the many, in compassion for the world, for the good, for the gain, for the welfare of gods and men. Proclaim, O

Bhikkhus, the doctrine glorious. Preach ye a life of holiness, perfect and pure."

In Chicago the Reverend Dr. J.H. Barrows, chairman of the World Parliament of Religions, read the Journal, and invited its editor to represent the Buddhists of Ceylon.

Dharmapala at first felt himself unqualified, but his friends argued that conviction about the Buddha Dharma was more important than scholarly knowledge, and urged Dharmapala to attend. Colonel Olcott, on the other hand, thought the Parliament a grand waste of time. His attention was absorbed by Asia and, since HPB's death, with the schisms that threatened the Theosophical Society. Finally Dharmapala decided to go. Sumangala Maha Thera gave his blessing and authorized him to represent the Buddhists of Ceylon. With this, Olcott reluctantly assented, and wrote to Annie Besant (HPB's successor in London), and the Theosophical representative to the Parliament, to keep an eye on his protege. His parents supplied him with a new suit and money, and Dharmapala at last boarded the *Brittania*, carrying a Buddha relic, a small image of the Buddha, and twenty thousand copies of the Five Precepts that HPB and the Colonel had recited in Colombo just thirteen years before.

CHAPTER SEVEN

HISTORY IS REPEATING ITSELF: THE WORLD PARLIAMENT OF RELIGIONS

To the men who organized it, the World Parliament of Religions represented the culmination of a great vision. No one, said Dr. John Henry Barrows, liberal Protestant minister and chairman of the Parliament, could claim the idea as his own, for its roots went back to the days of Paul and Jesus. It was the modern missionary movement, whose origins Dr. Barrows traced to the founding of the British Empire in India that provided the spark for this Parliament. Their work had "opened a new field for evangelization, and a new field for scholarship." As Barrows pointed out, it was only about a hundred years, since the time of Sir William Jones, "that the mother tongue of all the languages of modern Europe—the Sanskrit—had been added to the list of 'the learned languages' cultivated by scholars." Yet in that time most of the scriptures of the world's great religions had become available, and the growth of what Barrows called comparative theology had brought about nothing less than "a larger conception of human history, a new and more religious idea of divine providence through all ages and all lands."

The Christians still argued that the highest development of the religious impulse could be found only in Christianity, but it was from their own missionaries that the most effective work in comparative religion had come. The missionaries had learned the languages and compiled the dictionaries and grammars that led to a deeper knowledge and appreciation of the very people they had come to save.

The majority of the delegates and audience at the Parliament were Christians. But the non-Christian Asian religions were also very present. Japan and India—whose representatives included Hindus, Parsis, Sikhs and Jains—had sent the largest delegations, but China, Siam and Ceylon were also represented. No less momentous, for the Western delegates, was the fact that nearly all the warring sects of Christendom had also appeared together on the same platform, reviving, once more, the almost forgotten dream of a united Church. Nothing like it had ever been seen before, and few thought that Anagarika Dharmapala had overstated the case when he called the Parliament (in a letter from Calcutta) "the noblest and proudest achievement in history, and the crowning work of the nineteenth century."

The Parliament had been planned as the spiritual expression of the Columbian Exposition of 1893—"the most comprehensive and brilliant display," as Barrows put it, "of man's material progress which the ages have known." To house the Exposition an entire city had been built along the shores of Lake Michigan. The gleaming palaces of the "White City" recalled the great empires of the past—Greece, Rome, Egypt, renaissance Italy. They had all, so it seemed, culminated in this moment, in the heartland of this new republic. "And since," said Barrows, "it is as clear as the light that the Religion of Christ has led to many of the chief of and noblest developments of our modern civilization, it did not appear that Religion, any more than Education, Art or Electricity should be excluded from the Columbian Exposition."

Of course there were those who thought otherwise. Some objected "that Religion is such in its nature that it cannot be exhibited." Others said that "there could be no Congress of Religions without engendering the animosities which have embittered much of man's past history." The archbishop of Canterbury declined his support because "the Christian religion is the one religion" and he did not see "how that religion can be regarded as a member of a Parliament of Religions without assuming the equality of the other intended members and the parity of their position and claims." At least one missionary considered the idea blasphemous. "Let me warn you not to deny the sovereignty of your Lord by any furtherance of your agitation in favor of a Parliament not sanctioned by His Word," the Reverend E.J. Eitel thundered from his post in Hong Kong.

But for the most part the response to the more than ten thousand letters the organizers had sent throughout the world overwhelmed even the most optimistic of them. It was felt everywhere, Barrows wrote, "that the tendencies of modern civilization were toward unity." Advocates of the new science of comparative religion were naturally enthusiastic, and Professor Max Muller, editor of the Sacred Books of the East, sent greetings and a paper from Oxford. Christian support came from various quarters. Some churchmen felt the Parliament would once and for all demonstrate the superiority of the Christian revelation for which Buddha, Confucius and Zoroaster had merely prepared the world. Others believed that the liberal ideas of the Parliament would further Christian missionary efforts since, as Rev. T.F. Hawks wrote from Shanghai, "no greater obstacle exists to the success of foreign missions than the unchristian and antagonistic attitude of missionaries to other faiths and philosophies."

There were many reasons given for participating in the Parliament, but there was one that had the breadth needed to unify all the others. "Religion," said the chairman, "like the white light of Heaven, has been broken into many colored fragments by the prisms of men. One of the objects of the Parliament of Religions has been to change this many colored radiance back into the white light of heavenly truth."

A noble sentiment, no doubt, and one that had been gaining ground for some time. Yet it was not the white light but the radiance of the "many colored fragments" that caught the eyes of the four thousand men and women who witnessed the pageantry of the opening ceremonies in the Great Hall of Lake Michigan on a bright September morning. The delegates entered under the flags of their respective nations while the crowd cheered. Cardinal Gibbon, the representative of the Roman Catholic Church, sat in the center of the platform, in bright scarlet robes. Next to him sat Swami Vivekananda, the university-educated disciple of the illiterate Bengali mystic, Sri Ramakrishna. Vivekananda was "clad in gorgeous red apparel, his bronzed face surmounted with a huge turban of yellow." On the other side of the Cardinal sat B.B. Nagarkar of the Brahma-Samaj, in orange and white, and next to him Anagarika Dharmapala, "swathed in pure white, while his black hair fell in curves upon his shoulder." The Chinese and Japanese delegates were "arrayed in costly silk vestments of all the colors of the rainbow." Meanwhile the

Protestant ministers and their invited guests, looking on from the rear of the stage, formed "a sombre background in their dark raiment."

As Clarence Eddy struck the organ, first a few voices, and then the whole assembly, broke into the words of the Psalm 100:

> Before Jehovah's awful throne
> Ye nations bow with sacred joy:
> Know that the Lord is God alone;
> He can create and he destroy.

Then the opening speeches began: Charles Bonney, president of the Parliament, Archbishop Feehan, P.C. Mozomoodor and the Chinese commissioner to Washington, Pang Kwang Yu. The honor of delivering the concluding speech for the opening ceremonies fell to Anagarika Dharmapala. A reporter for the *St. Louis Observer* described the moment in detail:

> With his black, curly locks thrown back from his broad brow, his keen clear eye fixed upon the audience, his long brown fingers emphasizing the utterances of his vibrant voice, he looked the very image of a propagandist, and one trembled to know that such a figure stood at the head of the movement to consolidate all the disciples of Buddha to spread "the Light of Asia" throughout the civilized world.

For Dharmapala the "universal" message which the Christians claimed they alone possessed had been proclaimed first by the Buddha (as he would point out later) long before Christ. But in his opening speech he contented himself with placing the Parliament in the context of Buddhist history. Dharmapala declared that the Parliament "was simply the re-echo of a great consummation which the Indian Buddhists accomplished twenty four centuries ago." This was the Council of Ashoka—the proceedings of which had been "epitomized and carved on rock and scattered all over the Indian Peninsula and the then known world." As a result of that parliament, Dharmapala announced, Ashoka had sent "mild disciples of Buddha, in the garb that you see on this platform, to instruct the world." The Buddhists sent into the world by Ashoka, said Dharmapala, had taught Asia the "noblest lessons of tolerance and gentleness," and they had now begun to bring the same message to the West. "I hope," he concluded, "in this great city, the youngest of all cities, this program will be carried out, and that the name of Dr. Barrows will shine forth as the American Asoka." It was clear, as the reporter had noticed, that in Dharmapala the Buddhists had found a spokesman who was in every way a match for the most skillful Christian missionary.

The first speaker to touch on Buddhism, aside from Dharmapala's opening remarks, was the Honorable Pung Kwang Yu, who was attached to the Chinese legation in Washington. Pung Kwang Yu—the "Yu" being an honorific for "scholar"—spoke as an orthodox Confucian for whom religion was noticeable chiefly for the mischief it invariably caused. "Every attempt to propagate religious doctrines in China," he told the assembled representatives of the Parliament, "has always given rise to the spreading of falsehoods and errors, and finally resulted in resistance to legitimate authority and in bringing dire calamities upon the country." As for Buddhism in particular, Pung Kwang Yu said that the great number of Buddhist works translated into Chinese (a load that would "cause an ox to sweat") "only treat of the methods of obtaining release from this world, and have not a word to say concerning the arts by which this world is ruled." Since Confucianism concerned itself above all with the question of social relations and conduct, it was "impossible that there should be any conflict between the teachings of Buddha and the affairs of state."

Nevertheless, the Confucian viewed Buddhism with a lofty disdain, though he did admit that the esoteric books were profound and abstruse. After all, Confucius himself had said, "We cannot as yet perform our duties to men; how can we perform our duties to spirits." What good was it then, to spend time on metaphysical abstractions? Taoist and Buddhist priests, said the imperial commissioner, were "given to speculations on the invisible world of spirits, and neglectful of the requirements and duties of life. For this reason," said Pung Kwang Yu, "they are employed by public functionaries to officiate on occasions of public worship, and at the same time they are despised by the Confucianists as the dregs of the people."

He turned on the Christians next. They paid no attention to Chinese customs; they proselytized among the lower classes; encouraged converts to shamefully neglect their aged parents; and worst of all, they ignored the proper order of things by holding church services where men and women worshipped together.

With diplomatic restraint, Pung Kwang Yu closed by reminding his audience of the plight Chinese immigrants still endured in America. "I have a favor to ask of all the religious people of America," he said on the last day of the Parliament, "and that is that they will treat, hereafter, all my countrymen just as they have treated me. . . . The majority of my countrymen in this country are honest and law-abiding. Christ teaches us that it is not enough to love one's brethren only. I am sure that all religious people will not think this request is too extravagant." The audience cheered, and Dr. Barrows announced that he would impart the message to the government, adding that he hoped the result would be an end to "the obnoxious Geary law," this being the current version of the Chinese Exclusion Act.

On the third day of the Parliament the Japanese Buddhist layman and translator Zenshiro Noguchi introduced most of the Japanese Buddhist delegation, including the Rinzai Zen master Soyen Shaku, and representatives of the Jodo Shinshu, Nichirin, Tendai and Esoteric schools. "Shall I offer you Japanese teapots and teacups, or silk fabrics, pictures, fans?" he asked. "But all these are only materials which fire and water can destroy. Rather, I would offer something which the elements cannot destroy, the best of all my possessions. Buddhism."

He had brought with him "many thousand copies in English of Buddhist works"—*Outlines of the Mahayana As Taught by Buddha*, *A Brief Account of Shin shu*, *A Shin shu Catechism*, the *Sutra of Forty-Two Sections* and two other short sutras. The party had also presented the chairman with "four hundred copies of the complete Buddha's Shaka Sutras in Chinese translations made from the original Sanskrit." He hoped that the sutras would be translated into English, and he regretted that at present "there is no Mahayana doctrine, which is the highest order of Buddhist teaching, translated into English." In order to understand the mahayana, he said, it would be necessary to learn Chinese or Japanese. Or, he added diplomatically, the Japanese would have to learn English.

The next speaker, Kinzai R.M. Hirai, spoke excellent English, but, as Barrows said, he "seemed at the outset to have some misgivings as to the reception which his message of rebuke of the un-Christian dealing of Christians toward his people would meet with in a Christian audience." Hirai spoke on a subject which was a very sensitive one for the Japanese—namely, their treatment in America. Japanese citizens were barred from entry to universities and public schools by the San Francisco School Board. What were the Japanese to think of Christian morality, he asked, "when there are men who go in procession hoisting lanterns marked 'Japs must go'? If such be Christian ethics, we are perfectly satisfied to be heathen." "Loud applause followed many of his declarations," reported the *Chicago Herald*, "which grew as the delegates were exposed to a thousand cries of 'Shame!' as he pointed out the wrongs which his countrymen had suffered through the practices of false Christianity. When he had finished Dr. Barrows grasped his hand, and the Rev. Lloyd Jones threw his arms around his neck, while the audience cheered vociferously and waved hats and handkerchiefs in an excess of enthusiasm."

By the fourth day, when Kinzai Hirai read Horin Toki's paper on *The History of Buddhism and Its Sects in Japan*, the crowd had grown so large that it was necessary to hold overflow meetings in the adjacent Hall of Washington. Toki took great pains to differentiate the three Buddhist yanas, or vehicles (preliminary, hinayana and mahayana), insisting all the while that the "truth of the three yanas is the same, the difference being in the minds of those who receive it."

On the evening of the fifth day His Royal Highness Prince Chandradat Chudhadharn, the brother of the king of Siam, explained that "Dharma is a Sanskrit word meaning 'the essence of nature.' What is to be hoped for," the prince said, "is the absolute repose of Nirvana, the extinction of our being, nothingness." The prince made use of the familiar Buddhist analogy of the man who is frightened by a piece of rope lying on a dark path, until he realizes it is not a snake, but only rope.

"It is precisely the same with ourselves, our lives, our deaths, our alarms, our cries, our lamentations, our disappointments, and all other sufferings," said the prince. "They are created by our ignorance of eternity, of the knowledge of Dharma to do away with and annihilate all of them."

On the afternoon of the sixth day Z. Noguchi read a paper on "Buddhism" by Banryu Yatsubuchi, who worried that "there are no proper technical words in English to convey my thoughts." Trying to interpret a religious discourse, said Yatsubuchi, "is like scraping a sore through shoes." Reverend Yatsubuchi had cause for concern. His discourse was based on the Tendai school, and while most of the earlier speakers had emphasized the human qualities of Shakyamuni, he chose to tell the audience that "space has no limit, the worlds are innumerable, the Buddhas are numberless."

It was Yatsubuchi who first introduced the teachings of Esoteric Buddhism to America. In gradual teaching, he said, "one can reach the truth by accumulating good works and taking off evil deeds, but in sudden teaching one is requested to understand the reason of passion is Buddhahood, birth and death is Nirvana, and our present body is Buddha." This last teaching, he explained, "is the Secret one which was preached by Buddha Dainichi, and explained by the great Japanese Sage, Kobo."

In comparison, the speech by Soyen Shaku, the first Zen master in America, was matter of fact, and down to earth. (Soyen Shaku's paper was read by Barrows from an English translation prepared in Japan by his student, D.T. Suzuki.) Its subject was "The Law of Cause and Effect, as Taught by Buddha." Not once did he mention satori or koans. "Cold and warmth come alternatively, shine and rain change from time to time without ever reaching an end," he said. "Again, let us close our eyes and calmly reflect upon ourselves. From morning to evening we are agitated by the feelings of pleasure and pain, love and hate. . . . Thus the action of mind is like an endless spring of water. And if we ask for an explanation of these marvelous phenomena? Why is the mind subjected to constant flux? Why does everything change?"

"For these," said Soyen, "Buddhism offers only one explanation, namely the law of cause and effect. Buddhism considers the universe as having no beginning and no end." Finally, he reminded his audience that "our sacred Buddha is not the creator of this law of nature, but is the first discoverer of the law."

Judging from accounts in the official *History of the Parliament*, Soyen Shaku was not one of the more charismatic figures present. For one thing, he did not speak English at the Parliament, but even if he had, his talks were not the kind designed to excite crowds. Dharmapala, on the other hand, spoke English charmingly, with an accent that to American ears sounded as musical as an Irish brogue. His appearance fit Western conceptions of how a spiritual person should look, and the ladies especially were taken with him. It was repeated more than once that with his long hair and cropped beard he resembled no less a personage than Christ. His garb, which he had designed himself, further enhanced his appeal. He wore trousers of yellow India silk, covered with a toga-like garment of the same material. As the leader of International Buddhism, he spoke with a passion and devotion that stirred his audience. Of all the Easterners present only Vivekananda drew as much attention.

In a talk after the opening ceremonies, Dharmapala launched into a favorite theme of nineteenth-century Buddhist reformers: that it was Buddhism, not Christianity, that could heal the breach between science and religion. The argument began with the one fact about Buddhism that puzzled and annoyed Christians more than any other. There was no God, no Creator in Buddhism, and thus no need for miracles that contradicted "scientific" facts. "Speaking of Deity in the sense of creator," Dharmapala told his audience, "Buddha says there is no such thing."

In a second talk, entitled "The World's Debt to Buddha," Dharmapala, standing now with an ancient statue of the Buddha on a table beside him, spoke with the same fervor he had used to defend his ancestral faith against the Christian missionaries in the jungles of Ceylon. "Ancient India, twenty-five centuries ago, was the scene of a religious revolution, the greatest the world has ever seen," he said, in an implicit attack on Christian claims.

> And now, history is repeating itself. Twenty-five centuries ago India witnessed an intellectual and religious revolution which culminated in the overthrow of monotheism, priestly selfishness, and the establishment of a synthetic religion, a system of life and thought which was appropriately called Dharma, philosophical religion. All that was good was collected from every source and embodied therein and all that was bad was discarded. The tendency of enlightened thought of the day all the world over is not toward theology, but philosophy and psychology. The barque of theological dualism is drifting into danger.

There were more Buddhist lectures: Dharmapala read a paper sent from Ceylon by High Priest Sumangala, praising Colonel Olcott's work; Soyen Shaku delivered an impassioned plea for "Arbitration Instead of War;" Zitsuzen Ashitsu of the Tendai school pointed out that "Many Europeans and Americans who studied Buddhism with interest unfortunately have never heard of Mahayana. . . . They are entirely ignorant of the boundless sea of Buddha's doctrine welling just beneath their feet;" and Yoshigirai Kawai of the Nichirin sect explained that even ignorant men and women, who cannot read and write can surely attain to the state of Buddhas, if they sincerely repeat "*Namu-myo-ho ren-ge-kyo.*"

After listening respectfully to the Buddhists, the Christian missionaries took their turn. The Reverend S.G. McFarland, posted in Bangkok, said that since the Buddhist "acknowledges no *Creator*, no *Great First Cause* . . . he has no Guide and no *Almighty Helper*" and so "the certain and dreaded future is a dark and mysterious and unknown and unknowable state." Reverend M.L. Gordon of the Christian Doshisha University of Kyoto argued that Buddhism could not be considered a "Final Religion" because it did not include the idea of a soul, and hence there was no place for a "personal, individual existence in a future life." Furthermore, since the Buddhists had no conception of a "Creator and Preserver" they also had no "sense of personal sin against a personal God, who is both a loving father and righteous judge." "It is one of the commonest testimonies of Buddhists who have afterward become Christians," said Reverend Gordon, "that sin as a personal burden was unknown to them."

The speeches and discussions went on for sixteen days—morning, noon and night—but the delegates did manage some moments away from the lecture halls. There were receptions in grand Chicago homes, the foreign delegates arriving at one of them in the electric launches that were one of the most popular features of the Exposition. But for the most part the Buddhists concentrated on their work, and when not on the lecture platform in the main hall, both Dharmapala and Mr. Hirai spent many hours in special "inquiry rooms" surrounded by curious and eager members of the audience.

Of all the acquaintances Soyen Shaku and Dharmapala made at the Parliament, none was to prove more important to the development of Buddhism in America than the German emigre Dr. Paul Carus, editor of *The Monist* and Open Court Press, and author of books on religion and science. Like Dharmapala and Soyen Shaku, Carus believed that Buddhism was more fitted than Christianity to heal the breach that had opened between science and religion, since it did not depend on miracles or faith. Soyen Shaku's talk on cause and effect supported his views on the matter, and after having spent some time in discussion with the Zen master, Dr. Carus invited him to his home in LaSalle, Illinois, a small town some ninety miles southwest of Chicago. There Carus proposed that Soyen help him translate and edit Open Court's new series of Oriental works, but Soyen refused the offer (he was, after all, the abbot of an important Zen monastery), suggesting in his stead, that Carus invite Daisetz Teitaro Suzuki, the young student who had translated his Parliament lectures in Japan.

Carus also became friends with Dharmapala, though he had reservations about Anagarika's fiery temperament. (During one meeting Dharmapala had asked how many of his listeners had read the life of Buddha, and when only five people raised their hands, he thundered, "Five only! Four hundred and seventy-five millions of people accept our religion of love and hope. You call yourselves a nation—a great nation—and yet you do not know the history of this great teacher. How dare you judge us!") Carus also had doubts about Dharmapala's obsession with Bodh-Gaya; he did not think the cause would win sympathy from the American public. But despite his reservations, Carus had to admit that Dharmapala made a most effective propagandist, and Carus became a founder of the American branch of the Maha Bodhi Society.

The Parliament ended in a blaze of glory with the Lord's Prayer and the five hundred members of the Apollo Club singing "America." The Christians were pleased. "The Parliament has shown," Barrows announced, "that Christianity is still the great quickener of humanity . . . that there is no teacher to be compared with Christ, and no Saviour excepting Christ. . . . I doubt," he said, "if any Orientals who were present misinterpreted the courtesy with which they were received into a readiness on the part of the American people to accept Oriental faiths in place of their own."

But the last word had yet to be said. A few days after the Parliament ended, September 26th to be exact, Anagarika Dharmapala lectured in the Athenaeum Building, under the auspices of the Theosophical Society of Chicago, on the subject of Buddhism and theosophy. As usual, the hall was packed. "As the audience was about to go," reported the *Journal of the Mahabodhi Society*,

> the announcement came from the platform that an unusual event was about to take place. C.T. Strauss was about to be admitted to the faith of Buddha. The ceremony was simple, yet impressive. Mr. Strauss took his place upon the platform before the priest, Dharmapala pronounced in Sanscrit the formula oath of Buddha. Mr. Strauss repeated it after him. That was all. It was ended in a moment, and Mr. Strauss was an accepted and approved Buddhist of the Maha-Bodhi Samaj.

So it was that Charles T. Strauss of 466 Broadway, a New York City businessman, born of Jewish parents, not yet thirty years old, long a student of comparative religion and philosophy, found himself—in the words of Dharmapala's biographer—"the first person to be admitted to the Buddhist fold on American soil."

CHAPTER EIGHT

IN THE WAKE OF THE PARLIAMENT

I

Some time in 1887, in the hills above Santa Cruz, California, a certain "Philangi Dasa" took a vow to publish *The Buddhist Ray* for a period of seven years. To Dasa, editor of this first Buddhist periodical in America, the Parliament of Religions proved a rousing success—not for Christians like the cardinal of Boston, who, Dasa reported, had "tried to stampede the Parliament in favor of Christianism by waving a Bible over his head and yelling," but for the Buddhist brethren, especially Brother Dharmapala, who "ungrudgingly shook hands with the many hundred Christian women who thronged about him for that purpose, and wrote his name in their autograph albums, and on their fans: very wise actions," as Dasa commented, "that will tend to decrease the contributions to the missionary funds the coming Christmas, and will also make the Christian maiden less shy of a Buddhist lover."

The tone was one that had not been heard before from an American writing on Buddhism—ironic, light, saucy, self-assured. Philangi Dasa was a one-hundred-percent American Buddhist. He had spent some time as a Theosophist, but he was now inclined to agree with Dharmapala, who had told him that the Society had begun to "christofy Blavatsky and belittle Buddha." Not that it bothered him all that much. "The truth is," he wrote in the *Ray*, "that the Society in this country needs a god, and I believe Blavatsky will make as good a god as any being or shadow. Rather than worship Jehovah I would worship Blavatsky. She taught 'theosophy' and practiced the Noble Law of the Buddha and when a soul does that, worship is not too great a reward."

Very little is known about the editor of the *Ray*, except that his real name was Vetterling. He was a printer by trade and he published the *Ray* from his cabin in the mountains above Santa Cruz, California. "We believe ours to be the first Buddhist baby born in Christendom," he wrote from his retreat, which he had named Buddharay, "an historic place, being the first in the West, in a Christian land, from which the Buddha's Noble Doctrine had been heralded." When the *Santa Cruz Surf* wrote that the editor of the *Ray* was thought to be "a gentleman, who for a number of years has lived in a delightful nook in the Santa Cruz mountains and has devoted himself closely to study," Dasa reprinted the notice with the emendation that his "study" generally consisted of "woodchopping, digging, hoeing, planting, printing, etc."

In addition to editing the *Ray*, Dasa had also written a book called *Swedenborg the Buddhist*, which was published in Los Angeles and then translated into Japanese by Kakichi Ohari. "As the Christian Swedenborgians have pronounced the author of this work 'a fool, imbecile, rough, drunk, woman hater, atheist and devil,' " wrote Dasa of his own book, "it stands to reason that there must be some truth of an unusual order in it. The edition is selling rapidly, and a second edition of 15,000 copies is ready."

The Buddhist Ray was clearly a labor of love. It was finely printed in two columns, its pearl-grey cover displaying a rising sun, from within which shone a Sanskrit OM, along with the subtitle, "A Monthly Magazine Devoted to the Lord Buddha's Doctrine of Enlightenment." Every issue of the *Ray* reprinted articles of interest to Buddhists, both pro and con, culled by the editor from contemporary newspapers and journals.

Some were presented without comment; for example, from the *New York Journal:*

> It is no uncommon thing to hear a New Yorker say he is a Buddhist nowadays. A few years ago such a statement would have caused wonder, but today it evokes no surprise. There are several hundred

Buddhists here, and every one of them is a man remarkable for his intelligence.

Other times, the editor was not above speaking his mind directly:

> A subscriber has asked us to publish the Buddhist creed. We are extremely happy to say that Buddhism has no creed. His majesty the Devil would long ago have swallowed Buddhism, had it had a creed. He has thus far swallowed all organizations with Creeds, Boards of Control, and Directors, anointed and unanointed; and because of their presence in his belly, he is now noisomely flatulent in the world;—as heard and seen in the pulpit and in the religious press! Dear subscriber;—Buddhism has come West, not to tickle surfeited palates with 'old-church' or 'new-church' hash, but to teach men to think righteously and to act righteously, that they may become spiritual freemen!

After the Parliament, Dharmapala visited Dasa at Buddharay in Santa Cruz, and suggested that Dasa speak in public and in general make himself a more visible propagandist. "We cannot follow brother Dharmapala's advice," he wrote in the *Ray*, "for the reasons we gave him while he was at Buddharay: first, because our skin is too light, and the Americans would take us for an Irish or American high caste Brahmin of the Theosophical Society, and second, because we have no mahatmic credentials from the Himalayas, a serious obstacle indeed."

On the final page of the last issue, December, 1894, Philangi Dasa withdrew from view. "As the seven years have now elapsed," he wrote, "and my vow has been fulfilled, I now extinguish *The Buddhist Ray*." Nothing quite like it has come our way since.

II

Anagarika Dharmapala sailed for India via Japan and China from San Francisco on October 10, 1893. In Hawaii a small party of Theosophists, carrying fruit and flowers, came aboard his ship: Dr. Auguste Baptise Marques, secretary of the Australian Theosophical Society (and later French consul), and two middle-aged ladies. One of these, Mrs. Mary E. Foster, a wealthy and prominent woman, descended on her mother's side from Hawaiian royalty, confided that she suffered greatly from an uncontrollable temper, and though the meeting lasted only a few minutes, whatever advice or instruction Dharmapala gave Mrs. Foster apparently made a deep impression, for in time Mary Foster became the chief source of financial support for Dharmapala's activities. Before her death in 1926, she would contribute more than a million rupees to the cause.

When Dharmapala reached Japan at the end of October, he was met at the Tokyo railway station by a hundred Japanese priests, including Z. Noguchi, who had been one of the Japanese delegates to the Parliament. Though he campaigned in Japan six weeks, Dharmapala finally had to leave without the monetary support he had hoped for. He went on to Shanghai, where he addressed a gathering of Chinese monks, and to Siam, but met with no more success than in Japan. "The true spirit of Buddhism has fled," he wrote in his diary, "and only a lifeless corpse is to be seen in Buddhist countries of the Southern school." The Sinhalese, however, welcomed him with elephants, drums and a procession of monks. Later, back in Bengal, he found Olcott occupied with the case of W.Q. Judge (accused by Annie Besant's party of forging letters from the Masters), and the Bengalis full of questions about Vivekananda. "I told them," he wrote in his diary, "of his heroic work and the sensation he is creating in America."

Dharmapala had returned to Bodh-Gaya with a gift from the Japanese—a seven-hundred-year-old statue of the Buddha—which he planned to enshrine in the temple. The Hindus refused permission on the grounds that the Buddha was the ninth incarnation of Vishnu, and the temple line therefore Hindu. After a few days of meditation Dharmapala decided to place the image in the temple anyway. He was met by a party of the Mahant's men armed with clubs, the statue was thrown from the temple to the courtyard below, and a series of court cases followed once again. The statue, in the meantime, was housed in the Burmese Rest House, until the British demanded that it be moved out of Bodh-Gaya and placed in a museum. It was the ultimate insult. "O ye gods," Dharmapala wrote Carus in despair, "Justice has fled from British India!"

Dharmapala returned to America in 1896 at the invitation of Paul Carus, though he had misgivings. He was afraid, he wrote Carus, that he would "not get a serious hearing from the people. They have been taught in their mother's lap the self doctrine of theological Christianity; and the teachings of Buddha are in direct conflict with the dogmatic thesis of the Bible." He admitted that Buddhism and Christianity seemed to have much in common in terms of ethics and teachings of "divine love." But these were minor points. "In broad principles," he insisted flatly, "we disagree." Christ as a personal Saviour had to be given up.

"Still," he felt, "there is nothing like making an effort to liberate the mind from its theologic slavery."

Dharmapala's first post-Parliament lecture tour took him across the nation: he spoke to audiences in New York, Chicago, San Francisco, Grand Rapids, Cincinnati, Duluth, Minneapolis, Iowa City, Des Moines, Dayton and Columbus. The weather was severe, and the audiences not as large as he had hoped, but the newspaper reports were good, and everybody, it seemed, wanted to hear him talk on the same subject: "The Reconciliation of Buddhism and Christianity." He complied, but in his diary noted that ". . . these so-called Christians live in killing each other, hating each other, swindling each other, introducing liquor and vice where they hadn't existed." Women still composed a majority of his audience. His biographer writes, "Several American women attempted to seduce the handsome young ascetic, but all their efforts to soil the radiant purity of his character failed, and instead of the words of endearment which they had hoped they heard from his unsullied lips only the Word of the Buddha."

He agreed with Carus that a proposed visit to America by Colonel Olcott and the Siamese Prince Bhikkhu Jinavarawansa could result in "a triumphant unfurlment of the Buddhist flag in America." At the same time he insisted on remaining aloof from the dispute between Judge and Besant, though each side tried to gain his support. When he returned to Ceylon he suggested to Olcott that it was time for the Ceylonese Buddhist Theosophical Society to drop the "Theosophical." Olcott had already resigned from the Maha Bodhi Society, and though Dharmapala continued to revere Blavatsky, his break with the Theosophical Society was now complete.

In San Francisco, in May of 1897, Dharmapala officiated at the first Wesak celebration held in America. While thirty-seven candles symbolizing the thirty-seven principles of wisdom burned before an image of the Buddha, four hundred people listened to Dharmapala chant the *Mangala Sutta* from a palm leaf manuscript.

For the most part Dharmapala concerned himself more with broad social issues than with the problem of training individual students. On his third visit to America, during the years 1902-1904, he visited technical schools. (Tuskegee and Carlisle especially drew his attention.) He was convinced that the East needed the technology of the West, just as the West needed the dharma of the East. Mrs. Foster supplied the funds for an industrial school at Sarnath.

It was during this visit that he attended a lecture by William James at

Harvard. "Take my chair," Professor James said when he recognized Dharmapala, dressed in his yellow tunic, seated in the hall. "You are better equipped to lecture on psychology than I." After Dharmapala's talk outlining the major Buddhist doctrines, Professor James turned to his class and announced, "This is the psychology everybody will be studying twenty-five years from now."

In 1925 Dharmapala went to London, and purchased a house to serve as a British vihara. He continued on to San Francisco, where he spoke at a meeting held by a Japanese Zen monk named Nyogen Senzaki, and met with Mrs. Foster, who promised to support the London center with a monthly stipend. On his last evening in San Francisco, Mrs. Foster (she was then eighty-one) asked him to chant, and he, remembering Mrs. Foster's temper, which had been the cause of their meeting, recited an English version of Buddhaghosa's verses on anger from the Visuddhimagga:

> . . . Why frettest thou where no occasion is?
> Because at every moment states break up,
> Those aggregates which caused thee harm have ceased.
> With which of these art thou in anger now?

Seven years later, on January 16, 1933, Anagarika Dharmapala, weakened by heart disease, received the full ordination of a bhikkhu from a party of Sinhalese monks. Dharmapala vowed, just before his death, that he would be reborn in a Brahmin's family in Benares to continue the battle for Bodh-Gaya. "Let me die; let me be born again; I can no longer prolong my agony," he said in the months he was dying. "I would like to be reborn twenty-five times to spread Lord Buddha's Dharma." In 1949—sixty years after Dharmapala had first seen Bodh-Gaya—the new government of an independent India returned the site of Shakyamuni's enlightenment to Buddhist hands.

III

After the close of the Parliament, Soyen Shaku and another Japanese priest spent a week with Paul Carus and his family at their home in LaSalle, Illinois. The two men discussed religion and philosophy. "This 19th century of ours is the preparatory stage for a religious reformation," Soyen wrote Carus after he had returned to Japan. "It is incumbent on we who believe in the reformation to eradicate the folly of sticking to delusions, and to enhance the glory of the truth. . . . Before the truth there should never be such discriminations as Christianity, Islam, or Buddhism, much less the differences of races, customs, or languages. . . ." Like Carus, Soyen had a knack for presenting Buddhism as a rational and scientific religion. With his own students, he was very much the traditional Rinzai Zen master, who used koans extensively, but it is unlikely that he ever discussed the subject with Paul Carus or other Westerners. That would be left to his student, D.T. Suzuki.

Soyen Shaku and Carus kept up their friendship through correspondence, and when Carus had the page proofs of his book *The Gospel of Buddha*, he sent them on to Soyen. Carus did not read Pali, Sanskrit, Japanese or Chinese, but his library included every available book on Buddhism in English, French and German, and Soyen, who had spent a year in Ceylon, approved of the way Carus had referred to both hinayana and mahayana sources in the *Gospel*. Though the *Gospel* was the subject of some criticism—most notably from the scholar Oldenberg—it became Carus's most widely read work, and was translated into a number of languages. Like Colonel Olcott's *Catechism*, it was even used by Asian Buddhists. As D.T. Suzuki wrote, "before the publication of *The Gospel of Buddha*, Buddhism had been treated in too scholarly a manner or too popularly. Dr. Carus combined the spirit of science and philosophy, and his sympathy went beyond mere interest. Then he was able to check himself from becoming a fanatical sympathizer, and presented Buddhism impartially and justly."

Suzuki translated the book for a Japanese edition to which Soyen Shaku supplied the introduction. He credited the new Western interest in Buddhism with "The advanced state of modern science, the indefatigable researches of Western Sanskritists, and a powerful interest in comparative religion." But he also added a word of caution for the Japanese reader. All the Western books then being read in Japan (and he named Max Muller's *Nirvana*, Swedenborg's *Buddhism*, Olcott's *Catechism* and Arnold's *Light of Asia*) had "the peculiar excellence" of the author's genius, said Soyen, but "as for the final and ultimate truth of Buddhism," he was "not sure whether they had understood it or not."

D.T. Suzuki, the man who served as Soyen Shaku's translator, was born in the town of Kanazawa, two hundred miles north of Tokyo, in 1870. Suzuki's father was a physician with a fondness for the Chinese classics. As a member of the samurai class, his privileges had been abolished by the Meiji restoration and Suzuki grew up in a kind of genteel poverty. His father's death in 1876, when Suzuki was only six, made the family's situation even more difficult. One of the brothers found a job teaching and the mother took in boarders, and at the age of eighteen, having finished elementary and high school, Teitaro Suzuki found a job teaching arithmetic, reading, writing and English in a small fishing village. (Suzuki had taught himself English from books, and when he reached America some years later he was surprised to find that while his vocabulary was adequate, his grammar was almost entirely Japanese.)

After his mother died, he made his way to Tokyo and the Imperial University, where he took courses without enrolling in a degree program. He had begun to wonder about his karma—why his father had died while he was still young, and why he had started life with so many seeming disadvantages. His family belonged to the Rinzai school of Zen, as did most samurai, and thus it was natural that he turn to Zen for an answer to his questions.

He began his Zen training with Setsumon-roshi, but his first important teacher was Kosen, the father of modern Zen, who was then eighty-one. Kosen gave Suzuki the koan of "one hand," and when Kosen died in 1892, Suzuki continued his training with Soyen Shaku, Kosen's dharma heir, who had just returned from Ceylon. Suzuki did not become a monk, but just the same, for the next four years, as a lay-disciple, he lived the strict life of a novice monk at Engakuji.

Soyen gave the young scholar the koan *Mu*. "I was busy during these four years," Suzuki remembered nearly seventy years later,

> with various writings, including translating Dr. Carus's *Gospel of Buddha* into Japanese, but all the time the koan was worrying at the back of my mind. It was, without any doubt, my chief preoccupation and I remember sitting in a field leaning against a stack of rice and thinking that if I could not understand *Mu* life had no meaning for me. Nishida Kitaro wrote somewhere in his diary that I often talked about committing suicide at this period, though I have no recollection of doing so myself. After finding that I had nothing more to say about *Mu* I stopped going to sanzen with Shaku Soen [Soyen], except for the sosan or compulsory sanzen during a sesshin. And then all that usually happened was that the Roshi hit me.

"Ordinarily," continued Suzuki, "there are so many choices one can make, or excuses one can make to oneself. To solve a koan one must be standing at an extremity, with no possibility or choice confronting one. There is just one thing which one must do."

Suzuki's crisis came about when it was finally settled that he would go to LaSalle and work on the *Tao Te Ching* with Dr. Carus. "I realized," he said, "that the *rohatsu-sesshin* that winter might be my last chance to go to sesshin and that if I did not solve my koan then I might never be able to do so."

He put all his spiritual strength into the sesshin, and finally, towards the end of the fifth day, when "there was no longer the separateness implied by being conscious of *Mu*," a bell sounded, he was awakened from his samadhi, and he answered all of Soyen Shaku's questions except one. The next morning he answered that one too. He remembered that night, walking back to his quarters in the temple, "seeing the trees in the moonlight. They looked transparent and I was transparent too."

Soyen acknowledged Suzuki's realization by giving him the lay Buddhist name "Daisetz," which means "Great Simplicity" (in his later years Suzuki liked to tell people that it meant "Great Stupidity"), and soon arrangements were being made for Suzuki to go to America and work with Carus at The Open Court Publishing Company in LaSalle. "My Dear Friend and Brother," Shaku Soyen wrote Carus from Kamakura on February 2, 1897, "T. Suzuki will leave Yokohama by the steamer 'China' . . . and be expected to visit you at LaSalle within the last two days of the month if everything goes well about his journey. . . . He is a honest and diligent Buddhist, though he is not thoroughly versed with Buddhistic literature, yet I hope he will be able to assist you. . . ."

Suzuki himself arrived in San Francisco at the end of February, 1897. He was apparently detained for some time by the immigration authorities who found some signs of tuberculosis. Both Carus and Dharmapala, who was then in California, expressed their concern to officials, and after a period of observation Suzuki was allowed to proceed on to LaSalle, Illinois.

The Open Court Publishing Company, and the journal *The Monist*, had been started in 1887 and continued to be financed by Mr. Edward Hegeler, a zinc manufacturer, who had originally come to America from Bremen. Hegeler had started the Open Court to promote a forum based on a scientific philosophy called Monism, and he was particularly interested in reconciling science with religion. In 1888 Dr. Paul Carus married Mr. Hegeler's daughter, Mary, and became editor of Open Court, whose authors included John Dewey, Charles Pierce, W.T. Harris, Bertrand Russell, Pierre Janet, Ernst Haeckel and Max Muller. The Open Court was one of the first publishers to bring out inexpensive, paperback editions of the classics—Aristotle, Spinoza, Kant and Leibniz among them.

D.T. Suzuki took up residence in the Carus's large house where he found, somewhat to his surprise, that his duties included helping out around the house: "drawing water from the well, chopping fire wood, carting in earth, going on errands to the grocery, and even cooking, if need be." In good weather he enjoyed cycling out into the countryside where he could read in pleasant surroundings. (He was studying, among other things, Whitney's *Sanskrit Grammar*.)

His first assignment was to help Carus with the *Tao Te Ching*. Carus knew no Chinese, but he wanted this translation to be a scholarly one and he had Suzuki supply a character by character gloss, as best he could, but Suzuki found himself unable to check Carus's use of Teutonic abstractions. "The Chinese are masters in reproducing the most subtle changes in their innermost feelings," Suzuki wrote of this first collaboration with Carus. "Thus in order to translate passages from Lao-Tzu, I had to explain to Dr. Carus the feeling behind each Chinese term. But being himself a German writing in English, he translated these Chinese ideas into abstract conceptual terms. If only I had been more intellectually equipped then," he thought later, "I might have been better able to help him understand the original meaning."

In order to supply a corresponding Chinese text, Suzuki cut out the Chinese characters from Chinese and Japanese books, and pasted them in the proper places on the manuscript pages, which were then reproduced photographically.

Suzuki received three dollars a week and room and board for his work, which, in addition to his domestic duties, soon included practically every job that needed doing in a small family publishing house. He learned to type and read proofs—a job, he wrote Soyen, only slightly less slavish in America than in Japan—and he edited and took photographs. His main duties remained in the field of translation; as soon as the *Tao Te Ching* was finished, he spent his mornings translating Ashva-ghosha's *The Awakening of Faith in the Mahayana*.

It was in LaSalle that he began work on *Outlines of Mahayana Buddhism*, his first book in English. Both Soyen Shaku and Paul Carus had tried to present Buddhism to the West as a single ethical and scientific system, but Suzuki directed attention to the organic, evolutionary nature of Buddhism. "Let us ask," he wrote in the *Outlines*, "whether there is any religion which has shown some sign of vitality and yet retained its primitive form intact and unmodified in every respect. Is not changeableness, that is susceptibility to irritation, the most essential sign of vitality?" But it was not these ever-changing forms that constituted the kernel of the matter for Suzuki. "Mahayanism," he wrote, "is not an object of historical curiosity. Its vitality and activity concern us in our daily life. It is a great spiritual organism; its moral and religious forces are still exercising an enormous power over millions of souls; and its further development is sure to be a very valuable contribution to the world-progress of religious consciousness."

Western scholars had been distracted, fascinated, and misled by the multitude of doctrines, deities and practices in the mahayana. Such exuberant tropical profusion and multiplicity, it was thought, represented nothing more valuable than a good example of how degenerate the once-pristine teachings of the Buddha had become. But Suzuki was able to weave the web of mahayana doctrines into comprehensible patterns because he had himself directly experienced the continuity of every thread: as he expressed it, "that element in religion which remains unchanged throughout its successive stages of development and transformation."

The awakening he had experienced during his last rohatsu sesshin in Engakuji continued to work within him in America. There had been still another step, another turn. "This greater depth of realization," he wrote, "came later while I was in America, when suddenly the Zen phrase *hiji soto ni magarazu*, 'the elbow does not bend outwards' became clear to me. 'The elbow does not bend outward' might seem to express a kind of necessity, but suddenly I saw that this restriction was really freedom, the true freedom, and I felt that the whole question of free will had been solved for me."

It was here in LaSalle that he came to see the direction that he would travel. "Innen [karma]," he wrote to Soyen at the beginning of more than sixty years of writing, "are indeed beyond our thought."

> An idea that has no immediate effect, after being received by somebody may later be of help to him in entering the Way of Enlightenment . . . all of a sudden flashing across his mind. The old Buddhist saying, "The merit of hearing the Buddha's teaching even once, is infinite, even if one falls short of believing it," refers to this truth. I am not particularly fond of argument, but as I am firmly convinced of this truth, I occasionally express myself. It is my secret wish that if my thoughts are beneficial to the progress of humanity, good fruits will, without fail grow from them in the future. . . .

IV

Carus, meanwhile, was doing his best to present Buddhism in a way that would be palatable to Westerners. Like Olcott, he believed that the majority of Asian Buddhists had lost the true spirit of the Buddha's teaching. His response to this problem was not to ally himself with the Theravadins, as the English Pali scholars had done, but to adopt a comparative stance. *The Open Court* magazine, was not, like the *Ray*, exclusively Buddhist, but it did serve as a kind of round table of Buddhist thought and as a vehicle of communication for American and Asian Buddhists. Carus invited articles from Japanese mahayanists, Sinhalese Theravadins, American sympathizers and Western scholars. Max Muller appeared often in the pages of *The Open Court*, and Carus and Professor Oldenberg kept up a running argument, Oldenberg accusing Carus of cavalierly ignoring the realities of Asian Buddhist practice, and Carus holding that Oldenberg's strictly philological approach, while valuable, often missed the point.

In addition to books such as the *The Gospel of the Buddha* and *Buddhism and Its Christian Critics*, Carus wrote a number of tales with Buddhist themes. One of these, *Karma, A Story of Buddhist Ethics*, was translated into Russian by Count Leo Tolstoy, and when *Karma* was retranslated into other European languages, Tolstoy was credited as author.

"I deeply regret not only that such a falsehood was allowed to pass unchallenged," Tolstoy wrote Carus,

> but also the fact that it really was a falsehood, for I should be very happy were I the author of this tale. It is one of the best products of national wisdom and ought to be bequeathed to all mankind, like the *Odyssey*, the *History of Joseph*, and Shakyamuni. This Buddhistic tale seems to shed light on a new side of the two fundamental truths revealed by Christianity, that life exists only in the renunciation of one's personality, and that the good of men is only in their union with God and through God with one another.

Carus was a prolific writer; he published more than sixty books in his lifetime, in addition to editing two journals. But he did not limit his advocacy of Buddhism to the printed page. He provided Dharmapala with contacts, advice and a certain amount of financial aid for his American tours, in addition to serving as a founding member and then as president for the American Maha Bodhi Society. At the same time he did not think it wise to introduce Americans to Buddhism by way of a zealous battle for a shrine in India, and he was uncomfortable with the depth of Dharmapala's bitterness towards the authorities of British India. After all, had not the Buddha renounced violence, in thought and deed?

One of Carus's closest Buddhist friends was the Countess de Canaverro, also known as Sister Sanghamitta who had been converted by Dharmapala and opened a girls' school and orphanage called Sanghamitta Convent in Ceylon. Later, when differences of opinion with Dharmapala forced her to leave the convent, Sister Sanghamitta married, but that did not last either, and she retired to a farm in New Jersey. Through it all, she and Carus kept up a close correspondence.

Carus had given a great deal of thought to the problem of westernizing Buddhism, and he came to the conclusion that the introduction of music would be most helpful. Carus adapted a number of verses from the *Dhammapada* and other sources to Western music—Beethoven, Chopin and German folk songs. It was, Carus admitted, a "bold innovation," and one which provoked strong opposition from another of his Buddhist correspondents, the Scottish monk, Ananda Metteya. Metteya, head of an order called Buddhasasana Samagama (International Buddhist Society), was editor of *Buddhism*, a magazine with a circulation of three thousand. "Here I think you forget," he wrote Carus from his Rangoon headquarters, "that to the Buddhist music is one of the gross abstractions of the senses, which his Religion teaches him to abstain from as one of the fertile causes of the rise of emotional feeling."

Carus took up Metteya's objections seriously. He pointed out that the Buddha had taught a middle path between the extremes of sensuality and ascetism, and that music, like poetry could be used to express "high and noble as well as low and vulgar thoughts." He also referred Metteya to a passage from Suzuki's translation of *The Awakening of Faith*, in which Ashvaghosha was said to have converted the people of Pataliputra by composing a tune whose "melody was classical, mournful, and melodious, inducing the audience to ponder on the misery, emptiness, and non-atman-ness of life." Then, too, said Carus, the paintings in the Ajanta caves pictured monks with guitars and other musical instruments, and "the classical music of Europe is pervaded by the deep religious spirit which may very well be regarded as Buddhistic. Chopin's Nocturne, Opus 37, could not be better described than as a longing for Nirvana."

Ananda Metteya remained unconvinced, but Carus found a number of allies in California. His most enthusiastic supporter was one Rt. Reverend Mazzinanda, swami lord abbot of the Buddhist Church in Sacramento.

Mazzinanda was eighty-five years old when Carus wrote to him in 1911. His father had been a Parsi, his mother Bengali. Mazzinanda claimed to have studied with the Dalai Lama until 1853, to have become a monk in 1847 at the age of twenty, then to have traveled to India in the company of three other monks (two Russians and a Tibetan), and from there to have gone on to his European education at Oxford, Heidelberg, Paris and London. In 1893, he said, he had attended the Parliament of Religions in Chicago, reaching California in 1903.

Dressed in a orange burnoose and turban, with a flowing scarlet robe over it, and over that a yellow robe, Mazzinanda celebrated Buddhist High Mass, as he called it, Lhasa-style, twice every Sunday in the frame house at 418 O Street in Sacramento. He had converted more than three hundred people to Buddhism in "many years of terrible struggle," helped, he told Carus, by the inspiring music and words he had composed especially for Americans (for example, *Nearer My Buddha to Thee*). "Some probably have the idea that it savors too much of the Christian form of worship," he said, "but I do not see it in that light. Buddha taught when in Rome, do as the Romans do."

V

The first Japanese Buddhist missionaries to reach the continental United States arrived in San Francisco on July 6, 1898, five years after the Parliament had closed. Within a week the two missionaries—Reverends Eryu Honda and Ejun Myamoto—had met with thirty young Japanese men at the home of Dr. Katsugoro Haido, and on July 30 of the same year a ceremony in the Pythian Castle Auditorium at 909 Market Street celebrated the founding of the Bukkyo Seinenkai, or Young Men's Buddhist Association.

It was an auspicious beginning, but when the two ministers reached Seattle, they found the Japanese Consul, Mr. Saito, less than enthusiastic. "When I discussed the proposed Buddhist missionary work in the United States," Reverend Honda remembered some thirty years later, "Consul Saito, with an expression of annoyance on his face and while thumbing through a number of documents, asked whether the United States government would allow the entrance of a foreign religion. He also expressed his feelings about the numerous problems which might arise from the entrance of a foreign religion when the Japanese and Americans are presently coexisting peacefully."

When the two missionaries returned to Japan they found the Hompa Hongwanji leaders divided. Consul Saito's reluctance was not to be overlooked, and then there was the question of the great distance of America from headquarters. There was also concern that if the Hompa Hongwanji announced the beginnings of missionary efforts, and then had to withdraw, the organization itself would lose face.

It was at this point that a formal petition, signed by eighty-three members of the Young Men's Buddhist Association reached the Hongwanji Headquarters. The petition, addressed to the lord abbot, asked that the Hompa Hongwanji send a missionary to San Francisco to establish a branch temple in America.

> For those of us living in the United States there is no possibility of basking in the Compassionate Life of the Buddha. Not only are we unable to hear about the Buddhadharma in general, we are cut off from enlightenment through the teaching of Jodo Shinshu. Thus we are unable to understand and appreciate the heart and mind of Shinran Shonin. How we lament at such a state of affairs. Who would not lament? In the eight directions are non-Buddhist forces surrounding the Japanese Buddhists, and we cannot be at ease. It is as if we are sitting on the point of a pin; no matter how we move, we will be pricked. Our burning desire to hear the Teachings is about to explode from every pore in our body. . . .

Such a passionate plea could not be ignored. A compromise of sorts was reached by announcing only that a missionary would be sent to the Buddhists in San Francisco (rather than that Buddhist missionary activity in America had begun) and on September 1, 1899 Doctor Shuei Sonada, head of the Academy of Literature of the Hompa Hongwanji of Kyoto, and his disciple Reverend Kakuryo Nishijima, arrived at the Occidental Hotel in San Francisco. The two priests were photographed by the *San Francisco Chronicle* in the hallway of the hotel wearing their robes. The *Chronicle* reported that the priests had come "to convert the Japanese and later Americans to the ancient Buddhist faith. They will teach that God is not the creator, but the created, not a real existence but a figment of the human imagination, and that pure Buddhism is a better moral guide than Christianity."

The first Hongwanji Branch Office opened at 807 Polk Street on September 23. Soon there were study classes on Saturday, lectures on Sunday and a full program of social services—welfare, employment offices, a medical clinic and a dormitory for new immigrants. As Japanese farmers moved into central California, branches were established in Sacramento, Fresno and Vacaville.

At first glance, there did not appear to be much contact between the Japanese Buddhists of California and their Caucasian counterparts. But in San Francisco, the Hompa Hongwanji Branch Temple conducted a special lecture and service in English on Monday evenings almost from the beginning, and a certain Doctor Norman, a particular friend of Reverend Sonada, was especially helpful in the early days. "In spite of the unfavorable comments made about the Buddhist group," says the official history of the Buddhist Churches of America, "he did much to gain the favor of the American public." On the 16th of April 1900, Doctor Norman and Reverend Sonada joined with five San Franciscans—remembered now only as McIntyre, Hayes, C.F. Jones, E.R. Stoddard and Agnes White—to form a group known as The Dharma Sangha of Buddha. The Sangha grew to twenty-five Americans and twenty Japanese, and began publishing an English language bimonthly *The Light of Dharma*. Dharmapala, Suzuki and Carus all contributed to *The Light*, and The Dharma Sangha of Buddha used Carus's musical settings in their services.

During the same turn-of-the-century year Mary E. Foster attended the opening ceremonies of the new Jodo Shinshu Temple of the Original Vow in Honolulu, and Paul Carus, in LaSalle, brought out D.T. Suzuki's first book, a translation of *Ashvagosha's Discourse on the Awakening of Faith in the Mahayana*. It was also the year that Sigmund Freud published *The Interpretation of Dreams*.

CHAPTER NINE

THE BOSTON BUDDHISTS: AN INTERLUDE

I

On March 16, 1877, Harvard Zoologist Professor Edward Morse, having ridden across America on the transcontinental railroad, boarded the steam-and-sail ship *City of Tokio* for Yokohama. Morse was in search of brachiopods, which he wanted to study along Darwinian lines. He had only been in Japan a few days when a casual glance out of a train window led him to discover the neolithic Omori shell mounds—an event that marked the beginning of Japanese archeology. The authorities at The Imperial University of Tokyo were impressed, and they asked Morse to organize a department of zoology and museum of natural history. By the time Morse got to the brachiopods that summer, he had become the first of a number of Bostonians to fall under the spell of Japan. "Never will these first impressions of wandering through a Japanese town be effaced," he wrote in his diary. "The odd architecture; the quaint open shops, many like the cleanest cabinets; the courtesy of the attendants; the novelty of every minutest object; the curious sounds of the people; the delicious odor of cedar and tea filling the air. About the only familiar features were the ground under our feet and the warm, bright sunshine."

Morse returned to Boston and Salem for a brief visit in November. The lectures he gave at the Lowell Institute turned a whole generation of select Bostonians—Percival Lowell, Henry Adams, Dr. C.G. Weld and Isabella Gardner, among others—towards the island kingdom so unlike Boston. Morse returned to Japan in April 1878, along with his family. He was followed shortly by two American teachers he had recruited for the Imperial University—the physicist T.W. Mendenhall, and Ernest Francisco Fenollosa, who was to teach political economy and philosophy.

Fenollosa, then twenty-five years old, had been born in Salem in 1853, a year before Perry's ships had forced the Japanese to end three hundred years of isolation. His father had arrived in America with a touring Spanish military band; his mother, who had died when he was eleven, came from an old Salem family which had been engaged in the East India trade. At Harvard Fenollosa did very well. He graduated first in philosophy, read Hegel and formed a Herbert Spencer club. After a two year graduate fellowship and a short stay at the Divinity School, he took up drawing and painting at the Boston Museum of Fine Arts, at the same time attending the first of Professor Charles Eliot Norton's lectures in the new field of art history.

The American professors arrived in Japan at the crest of Japanese enthusiasm for things western. They were domiciled with their families (Fenollosa had married Lizzie Millet of Salem) in spacious houses on the grounds of a former feudal estate. The Imperial University had an international faculty. The director, Dr. Murray of Rutgers, was an American. German professors staffed the Medical School, while English, French, German and Chinese instructors taught languages. The students had been carefully selected; some had already studied abroad, others had been given special preparatory classes in English. Fenollosa's students were eager to have him expound Hegel and Spencer, while Morse found it "delightful to explain the Darwinian theory without running against theological prejudice as I often did at home." In fact, the new doctrine of evolution was grasped quickly by the Japanese, and one of Fenollosa's students, Inouye Enryo, a Buddhist scholar and Pure Land priest, would soon make use of it to argue that Buddhism was more suited to the modern world than Christianity. "To Inouye," writes George Sansom in *The Western World and Japan*, "the Hegelian dialectic was analogous to the analytic logic of the Tendai sect, and the doctrine of Karma (which had attracted Huxley's attention) was an anticipation of the development hypothesis then finding favor in Occidental countries. With regard to Christianity his line of argument is that any form of theism must be unacceptable to Western philosophy and science. Therefore Christianity is false, but Buddhism is true."

This was just the sort of thing that the Christian missionaries in Yokohama had been afraid would result from Morse's Darwinism and Fenollosa's evolutionary philosophy. They did their best to counter the professors, some of them going so far as to pray for Morse's soul. But the students were unaffected. They were not interested in Christian polemics, but in Western science and philosophy. The very survival of their nation, it seemed, depended upon their ability to digest the new knowledge of the West as quickly as possible.

Meanwhile the Americans had become equally enthusiastic about Japanese culture. Morse, whose tastes in Western art leaned to marching bands, surprised everyone by becoming an avid and expert collector of Japanese pottery. He also became the first Westerner to study tea, and even managed to learn to sing Noh—disciplines he undertook, so he said, to learn "things from the Japanese viewpoint."

Fenollosa turned to art. Japanese woodblock prints had already led avant-garde painters like Manet, Lautrec and Van Gogh to brighten palettes and flatten perspectives. But the Japanese themselves had been puzzled by Western interest in work they considered merely commercial. The government, meanwhile, had imported Italians to teach in the art department of the Imperial Engineering College, and brushes, the chief medium of Japanese culture for thousands of years, were replaced by pencils in the primary schools. As for the traditional paintings and sculptures by masters like Sesshu, these were, for the most part considered something from a feudal past the Japanese seemed in a hurry to forget.

But it was just this art, which he found in Tokyo curio shops, that impressed Fenollosa most. He was not disturbed, as were the few Westerners who had seen such works, by lack of realism or apparent distortions. As a student of Hegelian aesthetics he recognized that the idea expressed by a painting was the important thing—not its success in making a mechanical imitation of nature. He recognized that the Chinese and Japanese painters were masters of space and line; that which is left out being equally, if not more important, than that which is included.

Fenollosa's real education began when a Japanese student, just returned from Harvard, introduced him to Marquis Kuroda and his collection. The Marquis had said, "An American cannot judge. This art is beyond him," but he had nevertheless allowed Fenollosa to spend hours looking at works by Sesshu and Motonobu. Then Fenollosa met members of the Kano and Tosa families, formerly court painters to the Tokugawa shoguns. He studied their collections and traditions. With the help of two of his students, Nagao Agari and Kakuzo Okakura, who would later write *The Book of Tea*, he read biographies of great masters and began to apply the principles of Professor Norton's art history to Sino-Japanese art. It quickly became apparent that he was dealing with a tradition as great as that of Western art, and that the old notion "so generally and so lightly taken, that China has remained at a dead level for hundreds of years" was entirely false.

By 1882, Fenollosa had learned enough to lecture the aristocrats of the Ryuchkai club on the superiority of traditional Japanese art to "modern cheap Western art." "Despite such superiority," said Fenollosa, "the Japanese despise their classical paintings, and with adoration for Western civilization admire its artistically worthless modern paintings and imitate them for nothing. What a sad sight it is! The Japanese should return to their nature and its old racial traditions, and then take, if there are any, the good points of Western painting."

The lecture had a profound effect—helped, no doubt, by the fact that there were more than a few Japanese with ideas similar to Fenollosa's, who were quick to put the foreigner's prestige to good use. In any case, the pendulum suddenly swung the other way. Within a few years Fenollosa had organized a number of clubs for traditional painters and connoisseurs. The government ordered the art department of the Engineering College closed, and Western style works were banned from an official exhibition held in Uyeno Park. In 1884 the committee for art education, of which he was a prominent member, recommended that schools return to teaching by traditional methods. Finally, he was named, along with Okakura, an imperial commissioner of fine arts. But the most important proof of his acceptance, for him, was being adopted into the Kano family. His name, written in Chinese characters, was Kano Yeitan—Endless Seeking.

Fenollosa's research led him inevitably to the Buddhist temples around Kyoto and Nara. He studied Chinese scrolls and discussed Zen with the abbot of Daitokuji. At another temple he discovered one of the earliest relics of Tendai sculpture, a large ceramic Buddha's head, in an ash barrel. By 1884 he was able to write to Morse back in Salem that he had compiled what he believed to be "the first accurate list of art treasures kept in the central temples of Japan."

His greatest moment came when he and Okakura convinced the priests of Horiuji temple to open the gates of the Yumedono Pavilion. No one had seen the contents for two hundred years, though in 1868 some Shinto priests, taking advantage of the anti-Buddhist climate attempted entrance, only to be frightened off by a clap of thunder. The priests were certain that nothing less than an earthquake would occur now, but Fenollosa, armed with government letters and orders, insisted, and the priests reluctantly yielded. "I shall never forget our feelings as the long disused key rattled in the dusty lock," he wrote.

> Within the shrine appeared a tall mass closely wrapped about in swathing bands of cotton cloth upon which the dust of ages had gathered . . . our eyes and nostrils were in danger of being choked with the pungent dust. But at last the final folds of the covering fell away, and this marvelous statue, unique in the world, came forth to human sight for the first time in centuries. . . . We saw at once that it was the supreme masterpiece of Korean creation.

It is no wonder, then that Fenollosa came to consider his work, as he wrote Morse, "just as important at bottom as much of that which the world's archeologists are doing in Greece and Turkey." Of course, he admitted, in words similar to the ones used by Sir William Jones a century earlier,

> people don't see the practical importance of Eastern civilization for the world with the same vividness as they do that of Greek culture. . . . But from the point of view of human history as a whole, it is absolutely indispensible. I expect the time will come when it will be considered necessary for a liberally educated man to know the names and deeds of man's great benefactors in the East, and the steps of advance in their culture, as it is now to know Greek and Latin dates and the flavour of their production.

His own collection, he hoped, would be "safely housed forever in the Boston Art Museum," though that desire placed him in something of a moral quandary. "Already people here are saying that my collection must be kept for the Japanese," he wrote Morse. "I have bought a number of the very greatest treasures secretly. . . . And yet, if the Emperor or the Mombusho [Department of Education] should want to buy my collection, wouldn't it be my duty to humanity, all things considered, to let them have it? What do you think?"

Actually, Morse had already expressed his thoughts on the subject. One evening he and Fenollosa and Doctor William Sturgis Bigelow (a Harvard Medical School doctor who had accompanied Morse to Japan instead of practicing medicine in Boston) had been showing each other the results of the day's collecting in a small country inn, when Morse fell unaccountably silent. "Many fine things of Japanese art are now on the market like those we are buying," he said finally. "It is like the lifeblood of Japan seeping from a hidden wound. They do not know how sad it is to let their beautiful treasures leave their country."

Okakura, their translator, was sitting off to one side, listening. He had studied English at the Research Center for Foreign Books, which had been founded by the shogunate in 1856. He had also studied painting with Seiko Okuhara, a woman of advanced views who sometimes wore men's clothing and lived in Ueno district, Tokyo's bohemian quarter. As a member of the Shi-shu-sa (Poetry-Wine Group), who modeled themselves on the ancient Chinese poets, Okakura had developed a fondness for sake and good company. His romantic temperament was equal to Fenollosa's, and it is said that the moment he heard Morse's words he vowed to convince the authorities back in Tokyo to reverse the situation. The result was the passage of the National Treasures Law of 1884. By that time, however, Fenollosa's collection had already been sold to Dr. C.G. Weld, who deposited it as the Weld-Fenollosa Collection in the safety of the Boston Museum. Apparently neither the Moshumbo nor the emperor had offered to buy the work, at least not quickly enough. Morse's pottery, more than 40,000 pieces, of every period and style, followed some years later, as did Bigelow's sword-guards and lacquer. It had taken less than ten years for the three men to give Boston what was probably the greatest collection of Far Eastern art in the world.

II

It is most likely that Fenollosa first met Sakurai Keitoku Ajari ("Bishop") during one of his temple expeditions. The Ajari, whom Fenollosa called his "most inspired and devoutly liberal teacher in matters religious, the lofty living exemplar of the spiritual knighthood," was the head of Hoyugoin Temple at Miidera on Lake Biwa. Sakurai belonged to a branch of the Tendai school that had been founded in 864 by Chiso Daisho. Chiso had been a great painter, and the particular branch of Tendai he founded, which specialized in the teachings of Shingon (Esoteric) Buddhism, had imported many of the Chinese T'ang portraits, as well as other works of Tendai art that Fenollosa greatly admired.

Fenollosa was an active, energetic man, and it was the image of the bodhisattva—one who takes "a vow as early as baptism to lead the strenuous path of battling for the right, to consecrate one's career throughout any number of necessary incarnations to loving service"—that most inspired him.

Bigelow, on the other hand, shared neither Fenollosa's passion for action in the world or his sense of the dramatic. He had done some collecting, he had quietly financed many of Fenollosa's most important acquisitions, but he lacked, as Fenollosa said, ambition. He was wealthy enough not to have to carve out a career for himself, but he was also too restless and sensitive to settle for the constricted life of a good Boston club-man. Like Dr. Peter Alden, the character in Santayana's novel *The Last Puritan* (said to be based on Bigelow), he had given up medicine to heed the admonition, "Physician, heal thyself." It was a cure he hoped to bring about by performing some of the more esoteric rites and disciplines of the Shingon school

The Ajari believed, as Fenollosa wrote, "that the Western spirit was nearly ripe to receive the lofty doctrine which Eastern guardians have preserved for its precious legacy," and on September 21, 1885 both Fenollosa and Bigelow received the precepts—the san-ki-kai—of Tendai Buddhism.

The Ajari began by outlining the approaches taken by the three vehicles or yanas. "In the small vehicle," Fenollosa wrote hastily in pencil while Okakura translated, "there is the desire to subdue desires and become free of them, whereas in the Daijo, the mahayana, the desire is to become a true Buddha. So distinction is from the beginning." "In Shingon," he continued, "they practice the three secrets of the mind, body, and mouth; but not in Daijo, where they only meditate."

"One of the most difficult things in Shingon practice," Fenollosa had written in his notebook,

> is not to think of the reality of the image. They are apt to think that the image of Fudo for instance is really Fudo. But their thought must not dwell on the image; they must think only of the truth which they have developed from their mind. They must not think that there is or is not a Fudo. This is necessary since, as a necessary result of the three secrets, a Fudo will come out before them. But to think of this Fudo so coming is injurious. The image should be thought of as a trick. In the spring, flaming mist is seen across large fields. Not a reality. . . .
>
> This is what is said to beginners but some ways of meditating are secret and can't be told. . . . In secret religion, the descent from teacher to teacher is very important.

III

On June 3, 1886, Henry Adams and his traveling companion, the painter John LaFarge, set out for Japan in the comfort of a private car, courtesy of Adams's brother Charles, president of the Union Pacific. LaFarge sketched the West, while Adams read up on Buddhism. In Omaha, a young reporter interviewed the two distinguished gentlemen. "He got the better of us," Adams wrote his friend John Hay, "for when in reply to his inquiry as to our purpose in visiting Japan, LaFarge beamed through his spectacles the answer that we were in search of Nirvana, the youth looked up like a meteor, and rejoined: 'It's out of season!' "

The exchange set the tone for the trip. That he would feel himself out of season, either too early or too late, was somehow inevitable. Only six months earlier, Adams's wife Clover had committed suicide over the death of her father. It was an event so devastating that he refused to ever mention it; it did not even appear in his autobiographical masterpiece, *The Education of Henry Adams*. In one of his less guarded moods, he once admitted that, all questions of Nirvana aside, he "hungered for annihilation."

There is no mention in Adams's letters that he met Fenollosa's or Bigelow's teachers. Apparently Fenollosa's high-handed manner managed to sour Buddhism, as well as Japan, for him. "He has joined a Buddhist sect," Adams reported. "I myself was a Buddhist when I left America, but he has converted me to Calvinism with leanings towards the Methodists."

Still, there were moments when he saw things with less jaundiced eyes. He agreed with LaFarge that the Dai Butsu was "the most successful colossal figure in the world," and he borrowed a Japanese priest's camera to photograph it. The tombs at Nikko he thought well worth a journey of over twenty miles of muddy roads, in ninety degree heat, still weak from a bout of cholera. "One feels no impulse to exert oneself," he wrote after that particular trip, "and the Buddhist contemplation of the infinite seems the only natural mode of life."

But it was the bodhisattva Kuan-yin that touched both men most deeply. It would not be too much to suggest that this was Adams's first glimpse of the goddess—"by essence illogical, unreasonable, and feminine" —he would so movingly celebrate in *Mont-Saint-Michel and Chartres*. "Of all the images that I see so often," he wrote, "the one that touches me most—partly, perhaps, because of the Eternal Feminine—is that of the incarnation that is called Kwan-on, when shown absorbed in the meditations of Nirvana."

It was this figure that Adams thought of when he returned to America and devoted himself to the problem of his wife's memorial. He and LaFarge conferred with Okakura (who was now in Boston) about the symbolism of the bodhisattva Kuan-yin and Adams retained the famous sculptor, St. Gaudens. Stanford White agreed to design the foundation and headstone. The "Buddha grave" was to somehow fuse the art of East and West, and to embody "the acceptance, intellectually, of the inevitable." Still painfully sensitive about his wife's death, Adams did not make St. Gaudens's work any easier. He absented himself entirely from the artist's studio after providing St. Gaudens with photographs of Chinese buddhas, and relied upon LaFarge to convey, more or less, what he wanted by reading stories to St. Gaudens about the bodhisattva. When the sculptor asked Adams to review his preliminary work, Adams sent LaFarge in his place. St. Gaudens, attempting to put it all together, scribbled in his notebook: "Adams. Buddha. Mental repose. Calm reflection in contrast with violence of nature." Five years after the initial commission he succeeded. The seated, robed figure was considered St. Gauden's finest work.

"His first step on returning to Washington took him to the cemetery known as Rock Creek," Adams wrote in the *Education*,

> to see the figure which Saint-Gaudens had made for him in his absence . . . so that, as spring approached, he was apt to stop there often to see what the figure had to tell him that was new; but, in all that it had to say, he had never once thought of questioning what it meant. He supposed its meaning to be the one commonplace about it—the oldest idea—known to human thought. He knew that if he asked an Asiatic its meaning, not a man, woman or child from Cairo to Kamchatka would have needed more than one glance to reply. From the Egyptian Sphinx to the Kamakura Daibuts; from Prometheus to Christ; from Michael Angelo to Shelley, art had wrought on this eternal figure almost as though it had nothing else to say. The interest of the figure was not its meaning, but in the response of the observer.

IV

When Fenollosa returned to America in 1890 to become the first curator of the collection he had sold to Dr. Weld, the Emperor Meiji presented him with the Order of the Sacred Mirror. "You have taught my people to know their own art," the mikado said. "In going back to your country, I charge you to teach them also."

That was exactly what Fenollosa had in mind—that, and a great deal more. The magnitude of his vision took expression in the long symphonic poem *East and West*, first read before the Phi Beta Kappa society at Harvard in June 1892, and then rushed into publication in time for the 1893 Columbia Exposition, which Fenollosa attended as a member of the fine arts jury. *East and West* begins with Alexander the Great's near conquest of India, then traces the separated histories of both hemispheres—the West, masculine, softened by Christianity, and the East, feminine, steeled by the samurai spirit of spiritual knighthood. Fenollosa considered the Japanese the heirs of the best in Chinese culture, which he identified as the Buddhist illuminations of the T'ang and Sung dynasties.

The conclusion of the poem, "The Future Union of East and West," prophesied that "Within the coming century the blended strength of Scientific Analysis and Spiritual Wisdom should wed for eternity the blended grace of Aesthetic Synthesis and Spiritual Love." "This stupendous double antithesis," Fenollosa considered, "the most significant fact in all history."

Fenollosa gave a good deal of thought to his place in this grand scheme. "I must take a *broad view* of my position in America," he began an 1891 memorandum. To begin with, he reminded himself, "that however much I may sympathise with the past civilizations of the East, I am in this incarnation a man of Western race, and bound to do my part toward the development of Western civilization."

In practical terms, his strategy was to work through art, or, more exactly, art education, which was still a new concept in American educational circles. As curator of the Boston Museum's Department of Far Eastern Art, Fenollosa mounted a series of exhibitions: a critical retrospective of Hokusai's prints, sixteenth-century screens with gold backgrounds, selections from Samuel Bing's Paris collection, and a hundred Chinese Buddhist paintings from the eleventh and twelfth century lent by Daitokuji, the great Zen temple in Kyoto.

But he was not content to move only in the rarefied air of Boston art museum patrons. He must be careful, he warned himself, not to "ignore the economical questions of the day, nor the terrific problem of the world's suffering, sin and disease." Like Morse, he had been impressed by the high level of taste which even the poorest Japanese peasant enjoyed, and he hoped to find a way to bring a similar aesthetic sensitivity to the American masses. The answer seemed to lie in universal art education, incorporating crafts. "The function of art," he wrote, "must be used so as to brighten and gladden the lot of the poor, social rearrangement giving them leisure to cultivate taste, like the Japanese peasant." In this way, Fenollosa believed, the poor themselves would eventually transform their cities and homes.

It is likely that Fenollosa's ideas about art education would have remained solely in the realm of theory if Arthur Wesley Dow, a young landscape painter and teacher from Ipswich, Massachusetts, had not come across a book of Hokusai's sketches in the Boston Public Library, and been led to seek out Fenollosa at the museum. Dow became Fenollosa's assistant and the two men began a long collaboration—Fenollosa providing the philosophical and theoretical material, and Dow turning it all into a practical method of art education that would make sense to children, teachers and local school boards.

In many ways, the Dow-Fenollosa system paralleled the new theories John Dewey was beginning to develop in Chicago. There were two basic approaches to art education, as Dow saw it: the Analytic, in which "the pupil learns to draw, but defers expression until he has attained proficiency in representation," and the Structural, in which "Self expression begins at once, involving all forms of drawing and leads to appreciation." In practical terms, Dow drew a sharp distinction between *studying* objects to make an accurate representation, and *composition*, the "*expression of an idea* . . . with all the parts . . . so related as to form a harmonious whole." The former, while a necessary discipline, was imitative, while the latter called forth "the need of a new faculty which is but imperfectly developed, in short, the ability to *compose*, the *creative* faculty. . . ." "We have educated our children," as Fenollosa put the matter, "too much to think, to little to see and feel wholes."

In 1895 Dow began teaching composition at Pratt Institute in New York; four years later he published *Composition, A Series of Exercises Selected From a New System of Art Education*, illustrated with work from Whistler, Sesshu, Hiroshige and the Kanos. Dow was named director of Columbia University Teachers College Fine Arts Department in 1903. It was a position of immense power, directly in the mainstream, and the teachers and administrators who studied at Columbia carried Fenollosa's ideas into classrooms across the nation.

In 1914, a young woman named Georgia O'Keefe studied with Dow at Columbia. She read Fenollosa's *Epochs of Chinese and Japanese Art*, and came into contact with Fenollosa's ideas about universal art education. O'Keefe eventually became an important figure in the circle of modernists that gathered around Alfred Stieglitz, whom she married. The art historian Barbara Rose (in the *New York Review of Books*) notes that Fenollosa "was instrumental in reviving the interest in Oriental concepts that the Transcendentalists had begun to explore during the mid-nineteenth century, drawing on European Romanticism and Eastern Religion," and believes it is "likely that Fenollosa is a missing link between the artists of the Stieglitz circle and the Transcendental writers."

Fenollosa's ideas about art, education and poetry would have a far-reaching effect on American culture. But during the early years of the nineties, when he was still formulating his attack, it was Buddhism that he took as a measure of the best man could achieve. The drawing rooms of once-Puritan Boston were just then awash with mysticism, occult fancies and Eastern Religion. At Harvard, Professor William James, seized with the idea that "there is a continuum of cosmic consciousness, against which our individuality builds but accidental fences, and into which our several minds plunge as into a mother sea or reservoir," was beginning the research that would become, in 1902, *The Varieties of Religious Experience*. Mary Baker Eddy's Christian Science, which owed more than a little to Indian metaphysics, was spreading quickly. It was, as Lilian Whiting, Boston correspondent for the *New Orleans Times-Democrat*, put it, enough to make one think "we are the heirs of all ages, and it is in America that the next round of humanity will take place."

On November 16, 1894, Professor Rhys-Davids, president of the Royal Asiatic Society and founder of the Pali Text Society, began a six-week series of lectures on Buddhism at the Lowell Institute. Rhys-Davids held the view that the ancient Pali texts and the Theravada Buddhism of Southeast Asia represented the purest original forms of *buddhism*, while mahayana Buddhism, with its profusion of images, beliefs, practices and priests, represented a later, more corrupt form.

It was a view which, as Lilian Whiting explained to her readers, "represented the exact opposite of that held by Professor Fenollosa, who is also an expert on the subject." Fennollosa presented his own view to Miss Whiting (at her request) one evening, namely, that Buddhism was "a progressive religion," one that continued to grow and develop in time. "Professor Davids," said Fenollosa, "contemplated it as it existed in ancient times."

But it was not Rhys-Davids, whose scholarship Fenollosa acknowledged with the greatest respect, that provoked Fenollosa's scorn. The Englishman's views were at worst limited. The real danger, he felt, came from those who confounded Buddhism with Theosophy and occultism, and the chief offender, at the moment, was the popular novelist and man-about-town Marion Crawford. Fenollosa thought Crawford's novel *Casa Braccio* a cheap attempt to "work the occult 'boom' for all it may be worth." What Crawford called "Buddhism," Fenollosa wrote Isabella Gardner, was nothing more than "theosophy mixed with a little diluted Hegel . . . neither Buddhist nor Eastern, but a mixture of German Transcendentalism and English 'Psychical Research.' No Buddhist," Fenollosa pointed out, "talks about Universals, Absolutes, Macrocosms, Essence, Pure Being; at least as the foundation for his practice."

Fenollosa and Sturgis Bigelow were probably the first Americans to have studied (and practiced to some extent) mahayana Buddhism with a qualified teacher, and Fenollosa did his best to dispel the common assumption that Buddhism selfishly taught a way to save one's self.

> 'Ultimate continuous survival' [quoting Crawford] seems a singular paraphrase for 'salvation.' Such a selfish basis for religion is quite foreign to true occult Buddhism. 'The first object of all religious practice' is not 'to liberate one's own soul,' but to sacrifice one's self for the love of others.
>
> A true man or woman, whose life radiates sunshine and sweetness, who is sound at the core through love, and devout through reverence for all ideals, may never have had an occult ecstasy, a metaphysical illumination, or a mystic sign, and yet may be nearer Christ, Buddha, Life Eternal, than many an advanced mystic. My Buddhist teacher expressly declared this. So mysticism is not the only 'way,' not necessarily even the best way and certainly not the normal 'way.' Pride in a little occult knowledge is about the only cause which delays liberation well-nigh eternally.

In 1895 Fenollosa's Boston career came to an abrupt end when he divorced his wife to marry Mary McNeil Scott, a young Southern lady, who worked as Fenollosa's assistant at the museum and had lived for a time in Japan. The scandal was too much for Boston, even a Boston "enchanted by mysticism." Fenollosa resigned his position at the museum and moved to New York, where he married Mary Scott.

After a year in New York, the Fenollosas set out for Japan. Fenollosa still had friends there, but things were not the same. Japanese nationalism had risen; Westerners, even one decorated by the emperor, were no longer so eagerly sought after. Okakura, who had lived with a married woman, found himself embroiled in a scandal not unlike Fenollosa's. His enemies made good use of the affair, and he was forced to resign his post at the Tokyo Fine Arts Academy. By 1897 Fenollosa considered himself fortunate to have signed a year's contract as an English teacher at the Tokyo Higher Normal School.

Despite his financial difficulties and the shifting political situation, Fenollosa thrived in Japan. He and Mary lived in Kyoto beside the Kamo River. "Life was carried on in a purely Japanese way," wrote Mary Fenollosa. "There were no other foreigners except Mrs. Fenollosa (myself), and the menage consisted of two Japanese servants, a student-interpreter, and one of the Professors of Chinese Poetry from the University of Tokio. Japanese artists, priests, and poets began to frequent the place. There were many visits, on our part, to the homes of these, and also to temples. . . ." Fenollosa, accompanied now by Mary, continued his Buddhist studies at Miidera with Chiman Ajari and Keiyan Ajari, successors to Sakurai Ajari.

It was during this period that Fenollosa turned his attention to Chinese poetry, Japanese Noh drama and the I Ching. He and Mary went to as many Noh plays as possible, and Fenollosa began collecting their texts. "This is the first time I have lived," said Fenollosa. "There seems no end to the material that is offering itself here. Of all the foreigners, only one remained to visit on rare occasions—Lafcadio Hearn, a shy, solitary man, blind in one eye, certainly no Bostonian.

Hearn's early life had been as homeless as any wandering monk's. He had been born in Greece, raised in Ireland by a great aunt, schooled briefly by Jesuits in France. At the age of nineteen he had arrived penniless in New York, made his way to Cincinnati, taken up printing and newspapering, and then settled in New Orleans, where he wrote exotic tales under the influence of Flaubert, Baudelaire and Pierre Loti.

In 1890, after a sojourn in Martinique, he went to Japan on assignment for *Harper*'s. He already had an interest in Buddhism, which he believed to "accord with scientific opinion better than does any other religious hypothesis," but it was, as Kenneth Rexroth has noted, Buddhism as "a way of life," and "the effects of its doctrines upon the daily actions and common beliefs of ordinary people" that most interested him. He studied and wrote lucidly of what he called the "higher Buddhism," but he took an equal interest in Shinto and folk-religion. He did not find it strange that the Japanese thought each rock, tree and mountain to have its own residing spirit. He delighted in Japanese ghost tales and stories of the supernatural—without, however, falling prey to Theosophy or occultism. He visited the Fenollosas fairly often, but he lived apart from the Western colony for the most part. Finally, in 1895, he took the unheard of step of becoming a Japanese citizen, taking the name Yakumo Koizumi.

The Fenollosas returned to America for the last time in 1900. They moved to a mansion near Mobile, which they called Kobinata, after their Japanese home. The rooms were divided with screens from Fenollosa's collection, and the walls were hung with prints and kakemonos. Fenollosa spent a good part of the year traveling and lecturing, on the Chautauqua circuit, to thousands of people in small towns throughout the country. Mary Fenollosa published a number of novels under the pen-name "Sidney McCall," one of the most successful being *The Dragon Painter*—a book based on the life of Kano, Fenollosa's friend and favorite artist.

In 1906, the Fenollosas established a permanent base in an apartment on Twenty-third Street in New York City. It was here that Fenollosa sat down at his desk, cancelled his lectures and worked feverishly for three months to complete a rough pencil draft of his life-work, the *Epochs of Chinese and Japanese Art*. The final revision, Fenollosa told Mary, would have to wait for another visit to Japan. In 1908, during a tour of European museums with a group of students, Fenollosa died suddenly of a heart attack. His ashes were taken to Japan, and placed under a grove of cryptomeria trees on the grounds of the temple at Miidera.

V

Bigelow had returned to Boston along with Fenollosa in 1890. He had remained in Japan for seven years, returning only after the death of Sakurai Ajari. To all appearances it seemed that little had changed. Bigelow resumed a refined life bounded by clubs and close friendships that moved within a select circle. He was, befitting a practitioner of the esoteric Shingon school and a good Bostonian, quite reticent about his spiritual life. (When Theodore Roosevelt first met Bigelow in Paris in 1887, he wrote to Lodge, "He was most charming; but Cabot *why* did you not tell me he was an esoteric Buddhist? I would have been spared some frantic floundering when the subject of religion happened to be broached.")

His closest tie was with the young poet George Cabot "Bey" Lodge, the son of his old friend, Senator Lodge. Bey was of that generation of nineties Harvard poets whose sensitive natures seemed too finely tuned for life in the real, hearty world. Henry Adams gives a picture of this period in the biography he wrote—somewhat as a duty and a favor to the young poet's family.

> Early in his college course, the young man had acquired a taste for Schopenhauer . . . but another of his literary attractions was the strong bent of his thought towards oriental and especially Buddhistic ideas and methods. At about the same time it happened that Sturgis Bigelow returned to Boston . . . and brought with him an atmosphere of Buddhistic training and esoteric culture quite new to the realities of Boston and Cambridge. The mystical side of religion had vanished from the Boston mind, if it ever existed there, which could have been at best, only in a most attenuated form; and Boston was as fresh wax to new impressions. The oriental ideas were full of charm, and the oriental training was full of promise. Young Lodge, tormented by the old problems of philosophy and religion, felt the influence of Sturgis Bigelow deeply. Bigelow was an intimate of the family, and during the summer his island of Tuckernuck, near Nantucket, was the favorite refuge and resource for the Lodges.

The young poet seems to have been nearly the only person in Boston (except for Okakura, who started working in the Boston Museum in 1905) to whom Bigelow confided the extent of his involvement in Buddhist practice. Bigelow did his best to share what he had learned from his teacher with Bey, instructing him in meditation, yet he worried about his lack of qualifications. In terms of practice and commitment, Bigelow had gone deeper than any of the Bostonians, but he found it difficult to continue his practice with no one to advise him. He often felt, as he put it, "like a five-year-old child with a Masune sword."

Bigelow left Tuckernuck for his last trip to Japan on July 20, 1902. He attended the formal ceremony in which Nayaboshi became the chief abbot of Homyoin, marked the thirteenth anniversary of Sakurai Ajari's death and received a certificate making him one of the lineal transmitters of the Bodhisattva-shila discipline. He would have gone on to become a priest, writes a biographer in *The Saturday Club*, "had not the condition of his health prevented his taking the final vows." In 1908, Bigelow was appointed lecturer on Buddhism at Harvard. His Ingersoll lectures of that year marked the beginnings of his modest career as a spokeman for Buddhism.

When Theodore Roosevelt (whose career Bigelow had encouraged) became president, Bigelow used his influence to promote understanding between Japan and America. He argued against anti-Japanese legislation and encouraged Roosevelt to read about *bushido* (the code of the samurai), and also to look into judo. As it turned out, Bigelow's efforts had very real effects. In 1905 Roosevelt managed, through Bigelow's urging, to have a number of anti-Japanese laws repealed.

In August of 1909, Bey Lodge died at Tuckernuck while Bigelow was in Europe. He had left two books of poetry, the last of which, *The Song of the Wave*, contained two versions of a sonnet called "Nirvana"—the poems were "the result," as Bey had written Bigelow some years earlier, "of an hour's practice last night." Bey had died at the age of thirty-five, and the shock of his death further weakened Bigelow's already precarious health.

In 1913 Okakura Kakuzo died at the age of fifty-two. Okakura had been an advisor to the Chinese and Japanese collection in the Boston Museum since 1905 and an intimate of Isabella Gardner at Fenway Court, where Mrs. Gardner had built a small meditation room and study for his personal use. He and Bigelow had often gone to galleries and concerts together, and with Okakura's death (and Fenollosa's continuing estrangement from Boston) Bigelow found himself even more isolated.

In a reflective, autumnal mood he donated his more than 26,000 pieces of Japanese and Chinese art to the Boston Museum. With Bey Lodge and Okakura gone, Bigelow's feeling of spiritual loneliness grew more acute. He had a deep connection to his teachers, but they were too far away to be much help. He had an understanding of what "practice" meant in the Buddhist context, but no one to share it with, no one to guide him and no one to give him a sense of balance and humor. Looking back on his life it strikes one that it was this isolation from his teachers, and most poignantly, from the third jewel, the Sangha, which must have made his own practice so difficult. He knew too much to be content with the easy sort of sentimental Theosophical Buddhism that satisfied some of his contemporaries, and we can take his dissatisfaction with himself as a measure of his own deep commitment.

William Sturgis Bigelow died on October 5, 1926. He remained divided between two countries even in death. He was laid out in the dining room of his house at 56 Beacon Street in his Buddhist robes. But during the proper Episcopal funeral at Trinity Church the coffin remained closed. Half his ashes rested in Mt. Auburn Cemetery, and half, as he had willed, were sent, along with the ritual objects he had used for his Shingon practice, to Homyoin temple. There, returned at last, William Sturgis Bigelow Gesshin received a proper Buddhist funeral.

VI

Mary Fenollosa had been left with the unfinished work of her husband. In 1910 she returned to Japan, and with the help of Agari Nagao and Kano Tomonobu, she managed to complete the *Epochs of Chinese and Japanese Art*—that "single personal life impression," which presented Chinese and Japanese civilization as "one great working of the human mind under wide variations. . . ."

When Mary Fenollosa brought the finished manuscript to England for publication in 1912, she met a young expatriated American poet by the name of Ezra Pound, and when she returned to America she sent him the manuscripts and notes of the literary work that had engaged Fenollosa during his last years in Japan.

The rough word-for-word versions of Chinese poems (with prose paraphrase) reached Pound at a crucial point. Most people at the time, as Fenollosa had written, considered Chinese poetry "hardly more than amusement, trivial, childish, and not to be reckoned in the world's serious literary performance." But for Pound the Chinese texts opened up a new direction. The Chinese poets did not moralize, or explain, nor were they didactic—instead they treated the object directly, as the Chinese painters did. The early Chinese poets, said Pound, were "a treasury to which the next centuries may look for as great a stimulus as the Renaissance had from the Greeks. . . . The first step of a renaissance, or awakening, is the importation of models for painting, sculpture, and writing. . . . The last century discovered the Middle Ages. It is possible that this century may find a new Greece in China."

Pound found the manifesto for his version of the oriental renaissance in Fenollosa's notes—a short, highly condensed essay called *The Chinese Written Character As A Medium For Poetry*. The central argument of

Fenollosa's essay (which Pound had published) was that the pictographic nature of the Chinese ideogram was ideal for poetry, since it was not abstract, but based on a concrete image, or series of images superimposed on each other. The character for "East," to give one example, was, according to Fenollosa, composed of two images—one representing a pine, the other the sun. Thus instead of the abstraction "East" which brings no concrete image before the mind's eye, the Chinese portrayed the (rising) sun (caught) in the branches of a tree. Professional sinologues have had a field day demonstrating the fallacy of this argument (only a small fraction of ideograms work this way), but that does not change the fact that the essay provided a lucid and necessary *ars poetica* for the great modernist breakthrough of early twentieth century Anglo-American poetry. "We have here not a bare philological discussion," wrote Pound, "but a study of the fundamentals of all aesthetics. In his search through unknown art Fenollosa, coming upon unknown motives and principles unrecognised in the West, was already led into the many modes of thought since fruitful in 'new' Western painting and poetry. He was a forerunner without knowing it and without being known as such."

If *The Chinese Written Character* provided Pound and the imagists with a theoretical basis for their poetry, then Pound's versions of Fenollosa's glosses, published in 1915 as *Cathay*, demonstrated what could be done in practice. The nineteen poems in *Cathay* changed the face of Anglo-American poetry forever; and though scholars have found it relatively simple to demonstrate that the Fenollosa-Pound versions were filled with linguistic blunders, no one has cared to refute T.S. Eliot's statement that "Pound invented Chinese poetry for our time."

From the viewpoint of American Buddhist history, the period of the *fin-de-siecle* Boston Buddhists remains an interlude—"a most interesting transitional period," in the phrase Fenollosa himself used to describe the Japan of the late eighties and early nineties. Though both Fenollosa and Bigelow lectured and wrote on Buddhism, neither of them had the inclination—or the training—to introduce Buddhist practice on a more practical level. (Bigelow's one attempt to transmit his Buddhist faith was crushed when Bey Lodge died at thirty-five.) And unlike other Buddhists of the same period (the Theosophist Henry Steel Olcott, the Asian missionaries such as Anagarika Dharmapala and Soyen Shaku), neither Fenollosa nor Bigelow nor Okakura founded any organizations or left any Buddhist disciples. Homyoin temple, and the intricacies of Tendai and Shingon, remained in Japan.

Fenollosa was the most active and missionary of all the Bostonians. If it is true, as Lawrence Chisolm writes in *Fenollosa and the Far East*, that at the time he took the precepts with Sakurai Ajari, Buddhism "involved aesthetic and philosophical exploration rather than personal conversion," it is also true that by the time he returned to Japan for the last time his Buddhism had deepened and matured.

In any case, it was Buddhism that Fenollosa identified as the true genius of Eastern civilization. In the *Epochs* he saw China's history, "her fate and her curse," as the record of "a growing antagonism" between the Confucian scholars, (who he thought of as Puritans and pedants) and the Buddhists and Taoists "who entered with joy and hopefulness upon a new life, new religious sanctions, and a new art. . . ." The exemplar of this progressive, non-Confucian strain in Chinese culture was, for Fenollosa, Li Po (Fenollosa used his Japanese name, "Rihaku"), whose poems made up the major portion of *Cathay*. "The poetical wealth of the man and of his day," Fenollosa wrote again in the *Epochs*, "is proved by the fact that nature, man, ethics, Taoist fancies and Buddhist devotion, all enter his verses as natural friends, and all pulsing with sympathy toward the social betterment and freedom of man."

Interestingly enough, it was on just this point that Pound most radically diverged from Fenollosa. By the time of the *Cantos*, Pound had turned Fenollosa's version of Chinese history completely around. It was now Confucius who represented the highest of Chinese civilization, while the Buddhists—now called "Buddhs" in that slurring ethnic shorthand of the *Cantos*—came to stand for the enemy. Since most critics have approached Fenollosa in reverse through Pound, it is not surprising that the importance of Buddhism in his own work and life has been either overlooked or minimized.

Still, it remains true that ultimately it is in the field of cultural transmission that Fenollosa and his circle (to borrow Van Wyck Brooks's phrase) have had the greatest effect. It was through the play of the intellect, *logopoeia* as Pound called it, that these late blooms of the New England Puritan-Transcendental tradition—urbane, civilized, cultivated men—happened to bring to fruition the vision of an oriental renaissance Sir William Jones had planted more than a century before. "Translation," as T.S. Eliot wrote of the Fenollosa-Pound version of Noh plays, "is valuable by a double power of fertilizing a literature: by importing new elements which may be assimilated, and by restoring the essentials which have been forgotten in traditional literary method. There occurs, in the process, a happy fusion between the spirit of the original and the mind of the translator: the result is not exoticism but rejuvenation."

And such a translation is a necessary prerequisite for the wordless act of transmission that is so central to the continuity of mahayana Buddhism. Without the finger of language, it would be impossible to even point at the moon.

BOOK II

CHAPTER TEN

HOLDING THE LOTUS TO THE ROCK: 1905-1945

I

Enroute to America

Like this boat on the spring ocean
A monk comes or goes by the karma-relation
The horizon seems to be extending endlessly
The current, however, takes us to the New World
Yesterday, the whales swam around us.
Today the clouds shut off the sight of old Japan.
Following in the course of Bodhi-Dharma
From the West to the East I go.
Then, turning to the South, I may visit
India and Ceylon again, making a pilgrimage like Sudhana
Before long, our boat will enter the Golden Gate
And the sea-gulls, perhaps, may guide me to the destination.

Thus wrote Soyen Shaku aboard the steamer Cleveland, which carried him, along with eighty Japanese immigrants, to America.

It was June 1905, twelve years since he had attended the World Parliament of Religions in Chicago. Now he was returning to America as the personal guest of Mr. and Mrs. Alexander Russell of San Francisco.

Soyen Shaku was the only Zen master in Japan with any interest in teaching foreigners, and by the time the Russells had visited him at Engakuji during a round-the-world cruise, he had already permitted three Americans to join the monks in the training hall. From these Americans, who ate barley gruel with the monks and sat a full sesshin, Soyen had learned something about how to guide foreigners in Zen. He was happy to accept the Russells' invitation, which, he felt, would provide him with another opportunity to teach Zen to foreigners. Mr. Russell was a wealthy, civic-minded businessman with interests in mining, rubber and real estate. Mrs. Russell had traveled widely in the Orient, where (she once told a reporter) she had "studied all religions, taking what I think is best from each."

The Russells lived out on the Great Coast Highway, some miles from San Francisco, with seven adopted children. The House of Silent Light, as Mrs. Russell called her establishment, stood on a high bluff overlooking the Pacific. It was surrounded by a wooden fence that sheltered the traditional Japanese garden from the wind. Entrance was gained through a Japanese-style peaked gate. Over the gate the Russells hung a wood plaque, carved with Soyen Shaku's calligraphy of the Chinese characters for "silent light." Soyen Shaku's room was specially furnished in Japanese style.

The isolation of the Russells' residence, along with Mrs. Russell's interest in the Orient, gave rise to rumors that the Russells harbored some strange cult—rumors Mrs. Russell did her best to dispel. She told a newspaper reporter:

> There is nothing new or original in what we're trying to do. It is our desire to reach a high spiritual plane by means of meditation so incumbent on absolute tranquillity. Though we live quietly we're still vitally interested in the joys and sorrows of the world and our home is always open to neighbors and friends. . . . But I've never forsaken Christianity, and there is a small chapel in the house. I teach no "isms," preach no propaganda, and there is no colony here—just a family of nine.

Mrs. Russell had asked Soyen Shaku to teach her family Zen, and during the nine months he was their guest Soyen Shaku did just that. "The daily life of the family is thoroughly religious," he wrote friends in Japan. "Three times a day they practice Zen meditation, sing hymns ringing a hand bell, and have simple meals with the accompaniment of Western music. The whole family, even servants, abstain from meat, wine, and smoking." Mrs. Russell became the first American to begin koan study. Most of the Japanese Zen establishment had thought it impossible for Americans, let alone an American woman, to comprehend something as Japanese as Zen, but Soyen Shaku met their objections with a poem addressed to Mrs. Russell that alluded to the famous Sixth Patriarch of Chinese Zen:

> The Fifth Patriarch told a new monk,
> Southern monkeys have no Buddha nature,
> That monk proved he had Buddha nature
> By becoming the Sixth Patriarch;
> In any part of the globe
> Where there is air, a fire can burn.
> Someday my teaching will surely go to the West,
> Led by you.

II

Soyen Shaku was joined at the Russells' by a young student of his, a monk named Nyogen Senzaki. Senzaki's mother had been Japanese, his father either Chinese or Russian. He had been born and orphaned in Siberia, where a passing Japanese monk had found him lying next to his mother's frozen body. He was adopted by a shipwright named Senzaki, and then came under the care of a Soto Zen priest and Kegon scholar who began teaching him the Chinese classics, along with Buddhism, at the age of five. By the time he was eighteen Senzaki had read the entire Chinese Tripitaka. He studied both Soto Zen and Shingon, and then studied with Ushima Shaku who had revived the study of the Vinaya school in Japan. He had known impermanence from the beginning, and he cultivated it throughout his life. He was fond of likening himself to the mushroom—"without a very deep root, no branches, no flowers, and probably no seeds."

While still in Tokyo, Senzaki had begun a friendly correspondence with Soyen Shaku. Then, in 1896, he presented himself at the gates of Engakuji. On seeing Senzaki, Soyen told an attendant, "That strange monk does not look so healthy. Take good care of him."

Senzaki was indeed ill. He had tuberculosis, and had to spend a year isolated in a little hut. Soyen Shaku visited him there occasionally, and once Senzaki asked him, "What if I should die?" "If you die, just die," Soyen answered, and after that Senzaki's health began to improve.

Senzaki's first impression of Soyen Shaku had been of "severe penetrating eyes and a stern mouth . . . all very different from the kindliness he had displayed in his letters." Soyen was dressed in a yellow robe, and he sat with his palms folded as Senzaki bowed three times. They drank tea together, and Soyen told Senzaki that "all rules and regulations should be signed in blood. . . . But," he continued, "we do not have to do that these days. I have read and answered your letter and we understand each other, so from now on you come for personal guidance at the proper time, or at any time, even if I am in bed, you may shake me awake and do sanzen if you wish."

Senzaki stayed five years. For a time, he shared his room with a young lay-student, D.T. Suzuki. He fought hard "on the battlefield of koans, most of the time defeating myself," but he never took advantage of Soyen's invitation to wake him up at any time for sanzen. That, Senzaki said later, would have been "like visiting a lion's den."

Instead of becoming a priest at a village temple or staying on as a monastery monk, Senzaki left Engakuji to found a kind of nursery school. He called this school the "Mentorgarten," a name which reflected the inspiration he had received from reading the German Froebel's books on the new idea of the "kindergarten." Though he was still a monk, he did not indulge in giving the children religious instructions or ceremonies. Rather, he "guided and watched over them, helping them learn about nature while they were playing." At times, he allowed himself to call their attention to a "sunrise or sunset, or the different shapes of the beautiful moon, or the stars scattered in the heavens."

It was hardly the usual course for a Zen monk to take, but Soyen Shaku stood behind him. "Monk Nyogen tries to live the Bhikshu's life according to the teaching of Buddha," wrote Soyen in a 1901 introduction to Senzaki's book *A Grass in the Field*,

> to be non-sectarian with no connections with cathedral or headquarters; therefore, he keeps no property as his own, refuses to hold a position in the priesthood, and hides himself from noisy fame and glory. He has, however, the four vows—greater than worldly ambition, Dharma treasures higher than any position, and loving kindness wealthier than church properties. He walked out of my monastery and now wanders around the world meeting young people, gradually associating with their families and so tries in making religion, education, ethics and charity as the steps to climb to the highest. He is still far from being a 'Bodhisattva Never-Despise,' but I consider him as a soldier of the crusade to restore the peaceful Buddha-land for the whole of mankind and all sentient beings. . . .

Senzaki seems to have come to America with the idea of raising funds for the Mentorgarten. But he was also unhappy both with the institutional form Buddhism had taken in Japan, as well as with the militant nationalism that gripped Japan during the Russo-Japanese War of 1905. In any case, he arrived in America soon after Soyen Shaku and went to work at the Russells' as a houseboy. For reasons that are not entirely clear, both he and Soyen seem never to have discussed their student-teacher relationship with others. Senzaki washed dishes, did laundry, cleaned the house. He worked hard, but he was, as he remembered, "a real greenhorn," and though he knew enough English to read Carlyle's *Sartor Resartus* in his spare time, he had trouble understanding the spoken language. Finally, the housekeeper decided that she had had enough, and she sent Senzaki on his way with a five-dollar gold piece.

That same evening Soyen Shaku accompanied Senzaki on his way to a Japanese hotel in San Francisco. They were walking through Golden Gate Park when Soyen stopped, set down Senzaki's suitcase, which he had been carrying, and said, "This may be better for you instead of being hampered as my attendant monk. Just face the great city and see whether it conquers you or you conquer it." Then he turned quickly away, said goodbye and disappeared into the evening fog. It was the last time Senzaki ever saw him.

Mrs. Russell asked Soyen to give occasional talks for her friends. Daisetz T. Suzuki, who had just arrived from LaSalle, translated. Soyen's talks were based on the *Sutra of Forty-Two Chapters*, a short compendium of Buddha's sayings which Indian Buddhists had used to introduce Buddhism to China in A.D. 67. In addition to the informal talks at the Russells', Soyen also spoke before audiences of Japanese immigrants—at the Buddhist Mission and Japanese Consulate in San Francisco, and in Fresno, Sacramento, San Jose and Oakland. In September 1905, he and D.T. Suzuki visited Los Angeles, where nine hundred Japanese and one hundred Americans attended a lecture at Turner Hall.

In March of 1906, Soyen Shaku and Daisetz Suzuki set out across America. They traveled by train, and Soyen Shaku described his impressions in a series of poems as the unfamiliar landscape flew by:

No dust clings to the peaks of the Rocky Mountains
Heaven and earth are all white
I watch additional snow falling

From my seat in the train
I feel like I am facing the Sublime Itself.

As they continued, he wrote:

My mind runs smoothly
Like the Mississippi river where I am now
Morning sun reflects a pink color upon the snow
Probably the snow is fragrant like flowers.

In Illinois, he enjoyed a reunion with Carus ("the American Vimalakirti [who] does not cling to silence," but "writes and lectures constantly on the Gospel of Buddha") and Hegeler, his old friends from the days of the Parliament. "When two harp players meet," he wrote to Carus, "There are no strings needed/In their instruments." He saw the great torrent of Niagara Falls as "washing away human delusions." But it was not only nature that struck him. In New York City he saw the

High buildings stand like a mirage
A heavenly bridge passes over the dragon-waters
It is greater than a rainbow.
The spring breeze has no concern with noises of human beings
I stand alone with the Statue of Liberty.

Soyen Shaku saw America as a natural place for the dharma to grow and evolve. The talks he gave to American audiences as he toured the country presented the public with its first comprehensive view of the mahayana. First, he had to correct the still prevalent notion that Buddhism was negative and life-denying. Even so knowledgeable and sympathetic a man as Dr. Barrows had recently published a lecture claiming that "the goal which made Buddha's teachings a dubious gospel is Nirvana, which involves the extinction of love and life, as the going out of a flame that has nothing else to feed upon."

The problem, as Soyen saw it, was that Barrows (along with most other Western scholars), took the hinayana as the whole of Buddhism. They saw the "negative side of Nirvana" well enough, but they had no notion that "the positive side of Nirvana consists in the recognition of Truth."

Like his friend Carus, Soyen emphasised the rational and intellectual nature of a Buddhism "always willing to stand before the bar of science." But Soyen was a roshi, a Zen master, able to speak with authority on the role that meditation played in Buddhism. The practice of *dhyana* (the

Sanskrit term Soyen used) was not "trance or self-hypnotism," nor was it "a sort of intense meditation on some highly abstracted thoughts." "What it proposes to accomplish," said Soyen, "is to make our consciousness realize the inner reason of the universe which abides in our minds. Dhyana strives to make us acquainted with the most concrete and withal the most universal fact of life." Just how this was to be done Soyen did not say. He did not provide any instruction on the technique of dhyana, and though he had allowed Mrs. Russell to work on koans, he never discussed the subject in his public talks.

After nine months in America, Soyen returned to Japan via Europe, India and Ceylon, where he had lived as a bhikkhu twenty years before. Daisetz Suzuki went back to his work with Carus in LaSalle. Two years later Suzuki himself returned to Japan by way of London, where he translated Swedenborg into Japanese, and Paris, where he spent his days at the Biblioteque nationale, copying out portions of the ancient manuscripts Sir Aurel Stein had uncovered in the Tun-huang caves in Central Asia.

Nyogen Senzaki, meanwhile, remained behind in San Francisco. He worked for a time as a "George," that is, a Japanese house-boy. He read all the books in English on Buddhism he could find in the San Francisco Public Library, and he meditated by himself in Golden Gate Park. (Soyen Shaku had told him to work for Americans, and not to utter even the "B" of Buddhism for seventeen years.) After a while, he supplemented his domestic work by teaching English and Japanese in Oakland. In the earthquake of 1905, he lost all the letters—more than thirty—that Soyen had written him, and in 1908, after a wave of anti-Japanese hysteria swept the city, he, along with most other Japanese "boys," lost his job. He found work with the others, on a farm outside the city. His comment on that year: "Sun all day on head, very hard on us."

But he was a mushroom, as he had said. He could wait, When the time was right, when conditions were proper, he would appear as if from nowhere, and he would do whatever had to be done.

III

In September of 1906 a second party of Zen Buddhists arrived in San Francisco. This group was led by Sokatsu Shaku. Like Daisetz Suzuki, Sokatsu had been a student of Kosen, the great Meiji Zen master, and then of Kosen's successor, Soyen Shaku. Sokatsu had practiced hard at Engakuji for ten years. When he finished his Zen training at the age of twenty-nine, he told Soyen that he wanted to become a monk, but did not care to live in a temple. "Normally monks live in temples so they can obtain food and drink," Soyen told him. "If there is no food," Sokatsu answered, "I shall eat nothing. I believe that where there is Buddhism there is food and where there is no food there is no Buddhism."

Sokatsu covered his head and most of his face with the big mushroom-shaped straw hat of the traveling Zen monk, put on straw sandals, packed all his belongings into a little box strapped on his back, and embarked on a pilgrimage of great Zen temples. Then he continued on to Burma and Ceylon, as Soyen had done, and lived with barefoot sadhus in India for two years. When he finally returned to Japan, Soyen called him to his room and told him, "You have acquired the great wisdom of Buddhism. Now you must complete the Four Great Vows which you made and turn the wheel of supplication for the benefit of others."

Years ago Kosen had founded the Ryomokyo-kai, a lay-Zen group in Tokyo. Nothing like it had ever existed in Japan. The group had long since dispersed, and Soyen now charged Sokatsu: "You must go to Tokyo for the purpose of reviving it, blowing once more the bellows and rekindling the flame to forge those laymen who wish to attain enlightenment."

Sokatsu spent the next three years studying the character of the people of Tokyo. Then with the help of four friends from Engakuki, he built a small temple in a converted farmhouse on the outskirts of Tokyo. Soon he had ten or fifteen lay-disciples—most of them students, artists and intellectuals. There were also, and this was almost unheard of, a number of women.

The members of the Ryomokyo-kai sat in the zendo every morning at six. They attended *sanzen*—a one-to-one encounter between master and student—before leaving for their jobs or classes at nine. Sesshins were held once a month, and Sokatsu gave *teisho*—a formal commentary by a Zen master—every Sunday. In July, when there was a month-long sesshin, the laymen lived as monks.

One of Sokatsu's students during this period was a young artist by the name of Shigetsu Sasaki—later known as Sokei-an. When Sokei-an began study at the Romoyoko-kai, Sokatsu asked him how long he had been studying art. "Six years," said Sokai-an.

"Carve me a Buddha," Sokatsu said.

After fifteen days, Sokei-an returned with a statue of a Buddha. Sokatsu looked it over. "What is this?" he said, and he threw it out the window into a pond. It seemed unkind, Sokei-an remembered years later, "But it was not. He meant me to carve the Buddha in myself."

Sokei-an had been trained as a dragon-carver. At the age of fifteen he had gone on a tour of mountain temples, paying his way by repairing the temple dragons. After that, he had attended the Imperial Academy of Art to study painting and sculpture. When he was twenty-four years old, Sokei-an was drafted during the Russo-Japanese War, and spent eight months on the battlefields of Manchuria.

Shortly after he returned to Tokyo, Sokatsu summoned him to his room. "I am going to America," he said. "Will you come with me?"

Before they left, Sokatsu arranged for Sokei-an to marry one of the women members of the group, Tomoko Sasaki, a student at the Tokyo Women's College, then the only college for women in Japan. Sokei-an and Tomoko were married in a Buddhist ceremony, which was quite unusual, most marriages in those days being Shinto affairs. The group also included a philosophy graduate named Zuigan Goto, Sokatsu's eldest disciple.

"And so in September of that year, 1906," as Sokei-an recounted some years later,

> Sokatsu Shaku sailed for the United States with six disciples, including myself. As several of his former disciples had become students in the University of California we first settled in Berkeley. We laughed heartily at our Roshi when, at the University Hotel in Berkeley, he used a knife and fork for the first time. We watched his face as a plate piled with corned-beef and cabbage was placed before him. His expression was more serious than ever as he struggled to eat this food, which was certainly not the customary food for a monk! This was our first lesson in "When in Rome do as the Romans do. . . ."
>
> One day he [Sokatsu Shaku] announced that he had bought ten acres of land in Hayward, California, about two hours by trolley from Oakland. When our group reached there we found a farmhouse, a barn, an emaciated cow and ten acres of worn out land. Sokatsu's eldest disciple, Zuigan Goto, now President of Rinzai University in Kyoto, Japan, had seen in a newspaper an advertisement for the sale of the farm and had been sent by our teacher to purchase the property from the farmer, who certainly must have had no regrets in parting with it! We had confidence in Zuigan because he was a graduate of the Department of Philosophy of the Imperial University of Tokyo. But the land which he had purchased was absolutely exhausted land. The cow, also, was exhausted!
>
> Under such conditions we began our lives as farmers. On clear days we worked hard in the fields cultivating strawberries. On rainy

> days we meditated. Our neighbors made fun of us. There was not a real farmer among us; all were monks, artists, or philosophers.
>
> The day finally arrived when Zuigan drove to market the wagon piled with crates of the strawberries we had grown. A market man picked out one of the smallest of our strawberries and cried in a derisive voice, "What do you call this, school-boys?" "It is a strawberry," we replied. Showing us a strawberry almost the size of his fist, he said: "This is what is called a strawberry! You had better send your produce to the piggery!"

A stormy meeting with Sokatsu followed that night. Sokei-an argued that a thorough study of the Zen records had not fitted the group for such work. The argument grew more intense and Sokei-an left the group to return to San Francisco, where he studied oil painting at the California Institute of Art.

In the spring the rest of the group also abandoned the farm and returned to San Francisco. Sokei-an apologized to Sokatsu, and rejoined the group. The first American branch of the Ryomokyo-kai was located on Sutter Street, and later moved to Geary. There were about fifty Japanese students who attended meetings, as well as a few Americans. Zuigan Goto translated for them.

Two years later, Sokatsu was called back to Japan for six months by Soyen Shaku. He returned to San Francisco for another year and a half, then left for good. All his disciples, except Sokei-an and Tomoko, went with him.

For a time Sokei-an worked repairing Buddhist statues in a store which imported Chinese sculpture. Then a friend of his with a farm in the Rogue River Valley of Oregon invited him to visit, and in February of 1911, Sokei-an walked across the Shasta Mountains through the snow into Oregon. During the day he and his friend dynamited tree stumps and transplanted trees. Every night, from the first of May to the end of September he took his dogs and walked along the riverbed to a rock that had been chiseled flat from the current over thousands of years. Then he practiced meditation until the first train whistle woke him at five in the morning.

He next made his way to Seattle. He and Tomoko (they had apparently separated and then reunited) took a shack on an island off the coast and lived among the Indians. They had two children, and in 1914 Tomoko, pregnant again, decided to return to Japan. Sokei-an remained in the United States.

"For several years," said Sokei-an, "I led a wandering life, finally reaching the city of New York in 1916, when I was 34." Sokei-an spent his first night in New York at the Great Northern Hotel on West Fifty-seventh Street. The next day he went by the Yamanaka Company to find work; they sent him to Mr. Mori's shop on East Twenty-third Street, and he worked there at night carving ivory and wood, painting boxes and repairing art.

Sokei-an began to frequent Greenwich Village; he let his hair grow long, and met people like the English magician, Aleister Crowley, and Maxwell Bodenheim, with whom he translated the poems of Li Po. These were printed in *The Little Review*, the magazine which Jane Heap and Margaret Anderson published, and which Ezra Pound helped to edit from England. (It was the same *Little Review* that first ran Fenollosa's *Chinese Written Character*.)

Sokei-an had also begun writing sketches for *Chuokoron*, one of the leading Japanese newspapers. Kotsubo Utsubo, who knew him at that time, wrote a memoir in 1958 in which he characterized Sokei-an's writings as "frank conversations on the way of life of the common people in America, his writing crisp, clear, and unusual." A collection of his sketches, *American Yawa* (American Night-Talks) and *Kyoshu*, a book of poems, were published in Japan, and as a result, Sokei-an became something of a literary figure in Tokyo.

And then one day he suddenly realized that he had to see his teacher. Ruth Fuller Sasaki, who would later become Sokei-an's wife and disciple, described the event:

> While his interest in Zen kept on during this period, he was learning a lot about life. And then in 1919, in the summer, on an awfully, awfully hot day in July, he was walking down the street and suddenly in the street he saw the carcass of a dead horse, and something happened to him psychologically and he went straight home to his rooms and packed up his things and got a ticket for Japan and went back to Sokatsu.

He resumed his studies with Sokatsu and rejoined Tomeko and their three children in Japan. But he was not happy, and he returned to America. For the next few years, he went back and forth between America and Japan. He worked as an art restorer and woodcarver in Seattle and New York. And then on one crossing he threw his chisel into the middle of the Pacific, and resolved to complete his Zen training.

He rented a small house near the Ryomokyo-kai and intensified his practice with Sokatsu. He completed his Zen training at the age of forty-eight. In 1928 Sokatsu authorized him to teach.

Sokatsu told Sokei-an that from now on his life would be devoted to teaching Zen. "Your message is for America," he told him. "Return there!"

IV

In 1910 Senzaki began in the hotel business. He started as a porter, worked his way up to clerk, then manager. He seemed to have gained experience without losing his innocence. For example, he never could understand why some customers would rent a room, stay in it only a few hours, and then leave. Why was it, he wondered, that they never stayed to sleep?

In 1916 he managed to buy a hotel with the help of a business partner. Senzaki tried, but he was not a good businessman. When the hotel lost money, he gave it up and became a cook. At the same time he continued teaching Japanese, and also wrote about Zen for Japanese newspapers.

One night, November 1919, Senzaki woke from his sleep shivering with cold. He lit a stick of incense and meditated until dawn. Two days later a newspaper arrived from Japan. Soyen Shaku had died at the age of sixty-one. From that time he marked Soyen Shaku's death every year.

In 1922, seventeen years after he had first arrived in America, he dared to "utter the 'B' of Buddhism." He hired a hall with twenty dollars he had saved from working as a houseboy and gave his first lecture. He had translated a talk by Soyen Shaku, "First Steps in Meditation," for the occasion. But his English was so heavily accented that he had to write the words down on a blackboard. At the end of the lecture he asked people to leave their names and addresses.

From then on he would hire a hall whenever he had the money. Sometimes he would simply speak on Buddhism in a friend's parlor. He called the various meeting places "the floating zendo." The only image was a six-hundred-year-old painting of Manjusri, the bodhisattva of wisdom whose figure sits on the altar of all Zen meditation halls. He had it on loan from a Japanese art dealer.

In 1927 a brother monk by the name of Mamiya visited San Francisco for three days. When he returned to Japan he raised three hundred dollars for the "floating zendo." Within a month Senzaki had spent the money on hiring a hall and buying chairs for people to sit on. Senzaki had established a zendo—one he would carry "as a silkworm hides himself in his cocoon," for thirty more years.

V

Sokei-an had been authorized to teach Zen, but he was not a Zen priest, which was exactly the way his teacher, Sokatsu, wanted it. Sokatsu had spent his life building the lay Zen lineage of the Ryomokyo-kai that Kosen had begun, and he wanted his successors to be laymen. Sokei-an, however, felt that Americans would not take a layman seriously as a Zen teacher, and he wanted to return to New York as a priest. He also felt, as did most other Zen Buddhists, that the teaching could not be transmitted by laymen. Practiced, yes, but not passed on from one generation to the next.

Sokei-an insisted. Sokatsu retorted that in any case Sokei-an had not mastered Go, flower arrangments, tea ceremony or calligraphy—all necessary accomplishments for a Zen priest and roshi. But Sokei-an would not back down. He shaved his head, put on robes, and had himself ordained by Aweno Futetsu, a priest of the Ryosen line of Daitokuji. At that, Sokatsu grew furious, and the two never spoke to each other again.

Sokei-an returned to New York with no money, and no place to live. For a time he supported himself by writing a series of articles for a Japanese paper on the different ethnic groups in the city. He stayed away from his friends in Greenwich Village, and lived with an Italian family in Little Italy, a Portugese family somewhere else and a Negro family in Harlem.

His first attempt to propagate Buddhism ended in disaster. He built a shrine in a room he shared with a friend, and then went around to his neighbors in the apartment house to talk about Buddhism. "Not only would no one listen to him," according to Kotsubo Utsubo's memoir, "but they were all annoyed. The situation became so bad that they could no longer remain in the apartment, but they had to move elsewhere."

Finally, he went to Mr. Mia, a Japanese businessman with the Yamanaka Company. Mr. Mia had studied Zen himself, and he gave Sokei-an five hundred dollars and found him a place to live. At the same time, five Japanese men living in New York formally petitioned the Japanese headquarters of the Ryomokyo-kai to allow Sokei-an to begin a New York branch.

"I had a house and one chair," said Sokei-an years later, "And I had an altar and a pebble stone. I just came in here and took off my hat and sat down in the chair and began to speak Buddhism. That is all."

On May 11, 1931, Sokei-an and three others signed the incorporation papers for the Buddhist Society of America. Meetings were held at Sokei-an's apartment on 63 West Seventy-third Street. In the beginning, Sokei-an spoke to eight students. Four years later, in 1935, the group had grown to fifteen. Sokei-an had shown a few students the cross-legged posture for zazen, which they practiced at home, but at the meetings they all sat in chairs. The meetings began when a Mrs. Helen Scott announced that Sokei-an Sasaki, abbot of Jofuku-in, would speak. Sokei-an then entered the room and the members meditated together for half an hour. After meditation those students who had been given koans would meet with Sokei-an in a small ante-room separated from the larger room by a folding door, upon which he had pasted some pages from a sutra.

By 1938, the group had doubled. There were now thirty. Sokei-an was determined, but he was not in a hurry. It had taken around three hundred years for Zen to take root in China, and he felt it would take at least that long in America. He likened the difficulty of the enterprise and the patience required for it to holding a lotus to a rock, waiting for it to take root.

VI

In 1931 Senzaki moved his "floating zendo" to Los Angeles. The money for the move to Turner Street, where he held his meetings, came from the Japanese community, and Senzaki kept up the practice he had started in San Francisco of instructing Japanese on one night and Americans on another. Senzaki had followed Soyen Shaku's advice during his years in San Francisco. He had met the challenge of the great city head-on. He had immersed himself in the world, even while he studied and practiced and prepared himself to teach Buddhism. Now in Los Angeles, it was Senzaki the monk that appeared once more. "A Buddhist monk is celibate and leads the simplest life possible," he wrote a friend sometime later. "He never charges for any kind of work he does, being only too grateful to do something for his fellow men. He accepts used clothes or old shoes and wears them. Any excess of food or money he gives away. He sleeps quietly without worries, having none in his possession."

It was not easy to help Senzaki, since he would usually give away anything he did not need immediately. A favorite ploy among his students was to leave a five-dollar bill inside the meditation bell. But when Senzaki found it, he would immediately invite the person who had left it to join him for dinner at a nearby cafe. Senzaki did not need much, but he knew how to enjoy himself.

The zendo in Los Angeles had two names—the Mentorgarten Meditation Hall, in English, and the Tosen-zenkutsu ("Meditation Hall for the Eastern Dharma") in Japanese. Like Sokei-an, Senzaki did not try to teach his students the traditional cross-legged posture. They sat in chairs for an hour's meditation, heard a short lecture from Senzaki, and then chanted the Four Vows. There was no "socializing." Everyone left in silence except those who stayed behind to speak with Senzaki privately. There was no statue of Buddha, just a painting of Manjusri before which Senzaki recited sutras three times a day. "But I do not mean to pray to this Bodhisattva," he reassured his students. "A true Mahayanist never worships anything but his own true inner self. The recitation is an expression of our prajna, perfect understanding, and nothing else."

The Mentorgarten had no connection with the world of official Japanese Zen, for Senzaki did not have much respect for the Japanese Zen establishment. Most Japanese priests, he wrote in an article for a Japanese newspaper, smoked, chased after money and did not practice celibacy. "I do not know what Japanese Buddhists now believe," he wrote, "but I do know that those who understand Buddhism, whether in Burma, Ceylon, China, or America, do not consider anyone as a monk who does not live the life of a monk, no matter whether he may rank as a Bishop, Archbishop, or Cardinal. True Buddhists consider such titles as mere business labels."

If most priests were businessmen, then most temples were little more than "the main offices of their respective sects, something like those of chain stores." An abbot of a monastery had visited Senzaki in Los Angeles and told him that he should not ordain Americans without having a license from the Japanese government. (Buddhist temples in Japan were licensed and registered with the government.) But Senzaki pointed out that the first monks and nuns in Japan had taken self-ordination. "Why not deal with Buddha directly," he said, "without the necessity of a middle man, high priest, or cathedral? The ordination of a Buddhist," he continued, "is not under the control of any sect. Anyone who has been ordained a Buddhist for ten years, no matter what sect, has authority to ordain others."

Senzaki's attitude offended a number of priests in Japan, but it seemed quite natural in California. He taught Zen because he felt it approached the true meaning of Buddhism most directly. But at the same time he remained removed from the sectarian squabbles that had become endemic among Japanese Buddhists. Once a year he led his students and friends on a Buddhist pilgrimage of Los Angeles, which by now had temples of most of the Japanese sects. By 1938 there were two Zen temples, two Shin temples, a Jodo temple, a Nichirin temple and a Shingon temple serving the Japanese community of Los Angeles. When Senzaki led his pilgrimages he visited each one, offered incense and recited a short poem. Sometimes the resident priest would also deliver a talk.

Senzaki also made the Mentorgarten into a place for the study of Japanese art and culture. He introduced his students to haiku writing (they did it in English, around the kitchen table), tea ceremony and flower arranging. His circle at this time included Samuel Lewis (later to become well-known as a teacher of Sufism), Paul Reps, who collaborated with Senzaki on a translation of *The Gateless Gate* and a number of other books, and G. Manly Hall, the esoteric philosopher who would later found the Philosophical Research Society and Library in Los Angeles.

Senzaki's main supporter in Los Angeles was Mrs. Kin Tanahashi, the proprietor of a Japanese confectionery. (The two had become friends when Senzaki took care of Mrs. Tanahashi's handicapped son.) In the fall of 1934, Mrs. Tanahashi was reading *Fujin Koron*, a Japanese magazine, when she came across some poems and diary entries by Nakagawa Soen, a young Japanese Zen monk. Mrs. Tanahashi showed Soen's work to Senzaki, and the two men began a correspondence. Like Senzaki, Soen had become disillusioned with the Japanese Zen establishment, and he was then living by himself on a mountain, Dai Bosatsu Mountain, practicing zazen, eating wild plants and making his prostrations to the sun as it rose every morning. Senzaki had gone his own way in "this strange land" (as he often referred to America) for thirty years when he began his correspondence with Nakagawa Soen. Now at last he had found someone who understood his rather unorthodox approach. Perhaps this Soen might be the one who would someday continue his work.

VII

Sokei-an and Senzaki knew each other quite well, but they watched each other like two tomcats across the continent. Senzaki told one of his students once that there was not one koan Sokei-an couldn't answer, but also told him, "I remember once when Sokei-an looked at me and said 'Senzaki-san, I think you are an egotistical ass.' "

Samuel Lewis said, "In this pair, Sokei-an and Senzaki, I saw something that was too much for me. It was a cosmic thing and I often wondered whether it was love or hate."

One of Senzaki's students, a motion-picture actor by the name of Mr. Money, had the impression that "Sokei-an was the only man in the world that could 'get through' to Senzaki. . . . Sokei-an had what it took to tell Senzaki off, and he was fearless in speaking his mind."

Senzaki, however, could more than hold his own. He had once told Sokei-an off, and threatened to slap his face. "I acted as I did because I was the only one carrying the needed weight or influence necessary to get through to him or reveal a strong human trait he had yet to overcome," Senzaki told Mr. Money, "And it was the same with Sokei-an. He carried the needed weight or influence and when he had something to say to me, on my human nature or ego, I listened."

VIII

In 1934 an American named Dwight Goddard, citing limitations inherent in both Senzaki and Sokei-an's approach, founded an organization called the Followers of Buddha, an American Brotherhood. Goddard had been a missionary with the American Board stationed at Foochow, China, when he first visited a Buddhist monastery at Kushan. He began reading about Buddhism, took a first, tentative trip to Japan, and then returned to China in 1925 to spend some time at Karl Ludwig Reichelt's Christian-Buddhist monastery in Nanking. In 1928 he returned to Japan to learn more about the "experiential" side of Buddhism. For the next eight months he lived in Kyoto at Shokoku-ji, where Taiko Yamazaki-roshi allowed him to join the monks during evening zazen, and bestowed upon him, "although somewhat out of the regular order, the insignia of a 'monk-novice.' "

Goddard's monastic experience in both Japan and China convinced him that both Sokei-an and Senzaki were on the wrong track with their lay approach.

> Their method was to have regular lectures and meditation services, [wrote Goddard of Sokei-an and Senzaki] but the poor support they received limited their efforts. They had many learners, but few became devoted converts. The weakness of this method seems to be

> that coming under the influence of Buddhism for only two or three hours a week and then returning to the cares and distractions of the worldly life, they fall back into the conventional life of the world.

The Followers of the Buddha, Goddard's answer to the problem, was an attempt to found an American monastic order. The organization had two homes—Goddard's farmhouse in Thetford, Vermont, and a West Coast retreat—an old homestead of forty acres, planted with fruit trees and vines, surrounded by the Santa Barbara National Forest. The backbone of the Brotherhood would be the Homeless Brothers—celibate renunciants, who "must have resolved, definitely, to give up everything that hinders the attainment of enlightenment by means of the practice of Dhyana." The presence of ladies at the refuge was not encouraged, since they were considered hindrances to the Brothers' attempts to live "a tranquil life." Lay members would be responsible for the support of the Brothers. "The need of the different classes of members for each other is mutual," wrote Goddard. "The Brothers need the material gifts of the Lay members, the Lay members need the spiritual help of the Brothers."

The American Brotherhood was not very successful. For one thing, Goddard's strictly monastic style ran against the American grain. Then, too, Goddard's plan to bring over a Ch'an master from China never materialized, and he himself did not have the training and mastery of either Senzaki or Sokei-an. The Followers of the Buddha seems to have ended before it ever really got underway. In 1934, the first and only resident in Santa Barbara was Lay Brother Joseph Cresson.

Goddard's publishing efforts had much greater effect. *ZEN, A Magazine of Self-Realization* (later subtitled simply *A Buddhist Magazine*) had commenced publication from Thetford, Vermont in 1930. In 1932 Goddard published the first version of his most enduring and influential work. *The Buddhist Bible* was an anthology of Buddhist scriptures. Some Theravadin material was included but selections from what Goddard called the Dhyana Sects—Ch'an, Zen and Kagyu—predominated. Goddard, with his collaborator, the Chinese bhikshu Wai-tao, translated and edited the *Heart*, *Shurangama*, *Diamond* and *Lankavatara Sutras*, among other seminal mahayana texts.

"*The Buddhist Bible*," wrote Goddard, "is not intended to be a source book for cultural history and historical study." Rather it is "designed to show the unreality of all conceptions of the personal ego." Its purpose is "to awaken faith in Buddhahood as being one's true self and nature; to kindle aspiration to realize one's true Buddha nature; to energize effort to follow the Noble Path, to become Buddha."

That *The Buddhist Bible* at least partly succeeded in all this was a measure of Goddard's devotion and commitment. Originally self-published from Thetford, Vermont, *The Buddhist Bible* went through numerous editions. According to Huston Smith, "No other collection has quite taken its place . . . for the reader who is looking for scholarship and meaning, coverage and control—all four—I know no alternative that is its equal."

IX

Daisetz Teitaro Suzuki and Beatrice Erskine Lane, a Radcliffe graduate and Theosophist, were married in Japan in 1911. The couple lived in a small house in the compound of Engakuji until Soyen Shaku's death in 1919. They then moved to Kyoto where Suzuki taught Philosophy of Religion at Otani University. There the Suzukis founded the "non-sectarian mahayana" English-language journal, *The Eastern Buddhist*, and in 1927 the English publisher, Rider, brought out Suzuki's *Essays in Zen Buddhism* (First Series), many of which had first appeared in *The Eastern Buddhist*. (Beatrice Lane Suzuki's *Mahayana Buddhism* was published in England in 1938.)

The publication of the *Essays* (a Second and Third Series followed shortly) secured Suzuki's reputation in England, and in 1936, when he was nearly seventy, he left Japan to lecture in England at The World Congress of Faiths.

D.T. Suzuki impressed many people in England with his disarming combination of playfulness and scholarship, but perhaps none more than a young man by the name of Alan Watts, who found Suzuki to be (as he wrote in his autobiography) "about the most gentle and sophisticated person I have ever known, for he combined the most complex learning with utter simplicity."

Alan Watts, who was then editor of *Buddhism in England*, had been born in 1915, in the village of Chislehurst, Kent. And yet, almost from the beginning, "the East" had been a presence in his life. Alan's mother was a teacher in a school that catered to the daughters of missionaries, and Alan had grown up surrounded by images and curios which the girls' parents had presented to his mother. His childhood reading drew him further afield. Kipling's *Kim* made him feel that there was more to Buddhism than to Christianity, and when he came across a small replica of the great Kamakura Daibutsu in a curio shop, he bought it at once, finding the expression "neither judgmental or frantic, but stately and serene."

By the time young Watts met Francis Croshaw, "a vague and wealthy man of uncertain behavior," he had already come to the conclusion that conventional English life, epitomized by bowler hats and nine-to-five jobs in London, was not for him. Mr. Croshaw had an extensive library and he lent Watts Edwards Holmes's *The Creed of the Buddha*, as well as Lafcadio Hearn's *Gleanings In Buddha Fields*—which gave Watts "such a convincingly different view of the universe from the one I had inherited that I turned my back on all I had been taught to believe as authority." He had also found, tucked into the pages of Holmes's book, a small yellow pamphlet on Buddhism by Christmas Humphreys, a London barrister who was the leading light of the Buddhist Lodge in London.

Watts wrote to Humphreys. A lively correspondence ensued, and at the age of fifteen, Watts decided that he "had to get out from under the monstrously oppressive God the Father," and declared himself a Buddhist. It was some time before Watts was able to meet Mr. Humphreys, and when he finally did get to London, accompanied by his father (who followed his son's intellectural development closely), the members of the Lodge were astonished to find their correspondent a boy of sixteen.

Watts never bothered to attend a university. Instead, he moved down to London, where he continued to read voluminously—D.T. Suzuki, Blavatsky, Nietzsche, Havelock Ellis, Bernard Shaw, Lafcadio Hearn, Dwight Goddard, Carl Jung. He published a small booklet on Zen, a distillation of Suzuki's scattered writings, and took on the editorship of the Lodge's journal, *Buddhism in England* (later, *The Middle Way*).

He met all sorts of people at the Lodge. Tai-hsu, the Chinese Buddhist reformer, who was struggling to modernize the Chinese sangha, Nicholas Roerich, the Russian painter, mystic and Tibetologist, Krishnamurti, who had inherited the torch of Theosophy from Annie Besant and then renounced it, and Frederic Spiegelberg, the German Orientalist. All of them, it seemed, were passing through London on their way to America.

It was at this time, when Watts was in his twenty-first year, that D.T. Suzuki appeared at the World Congress of Faiths, and it was also at this time that Watts met "a vivacious and talented young woman" by the name of Eleanor Everett. Eleanor had come to London to study piano, fresh from Japan, with her mother, an impressive and rather grand lady named Ruth Fuller Everett.

Ruth Fuller Everett was married to the prominent Chicago attorney, Charles Everett. She had spent some time at the Nyack, New York ashram of one Pierre Bonnard, a "phenomenal rascal-master" (according to Watts) who taught his students, including a number of New York socialites, hatha yoga and "tantra." It was possibly at this ashram that Ruth first heard talk about Zen, and in 1930, when she and her husband stopped in Japan during a world cruise, they were introduced to D.T. Suzuki, who gave her a copy of his *Essays* (Second Series), and demonstrated the basic rules of sitting.

She returned to Japan two years later, and this time Dr. Suzuki introduced her to Nanshinken-roshi, the Rinzai master of Nanzenji. Allowed to join the monks for their morning sittings, she stayed for three and a half months. Her purpose, as she thought of it later, "was simply to see, by practicing according to the exact method that I was taught, as it was practiced in the Sodo, whether this method would produce any results for a foreigner or not."

Her question must have been answered in the affirmative, for when she settled in New York in 1938 she became one of the principal supporters of Sokei-an's group, the Buddhist Society of America, as well as the editor of the society's journal, *Cat's Yawn*. That same year Alan Watts and Eleanor Everett were married at the Parish Church in Earl's Court, even though both Eleanor and Ruth, and Alan and his father (who had become treasurer of the London Lodge) were all Buddhists. A Buddhist wedding did not seem to be socially acceptable.

Watts and Eleanor arrived in New York shortly after their marriage. They lived in an apartment adjacent to Ruth's place on the upper West Side, close to Sokei-an's small apartment-temple on West Seventy-fourth. Since Sokei-an was the only Zen master available, Watts put aside his "lone-wolf" inclinations for the moment and asked to be accepted as Sokei-an's student.

The two worked together for several weeks, but Watts felt uncomfortable with Sokei-an's teaching style and stopped attending sanzen. For one thing, Sokei-an was using the koan system of Hakuin, the eighteenth-century Rinzai master who had systematized koan study. As Watts understood it, this method required that every koan had to "be answered in a specific way—which seemed to be hunting for a needle in a haystack." He much preferred, he decided, the more spontaneous Zen of Bankei and the Chinese masters like Hui-neng and Ma-tsu.

Watts also found it strange that Sokei-an did not teach his students the formal style of doing zazen, nor did he hold zazen sesshins at his temple. Sokei-an's teaching seemed confined to sanzen, the interview between disciple and teacher. What instruction there was in formal zazen—for

Watts and others—came from Ruth Fuller Everett. Sokei-an had been content to have people sit in chairs before the meetings, but when Ruth Everett became active in the group she "began to upbraid him, literally, about this matter of not sitting." ("Well, at least I have to have the roof over my head," he told her. "If I put them down on cushions and made them do zazen, I would have no roof over my head.") But he was actually happy to have people sit cross-legged, if they were ready and willing, and under Ruth Everett's urging the younger, more enthusiastic members began showing up for zazen at eight in the morning.

It was, however, in sanzen and teisho that Sokei-an seems to have made the greatest impression. "Sokei-an was a most remarkable teacher in sanzen," Ruth Everett wrote. "He was utterly transported out of himself when he sat in the roshi's chair. And you had the feeling before him that this was not a man, this was an absolute principle that you were up against."

> When I was, in recent years, asked if we were given "instruction" in Zen [said Mary Farkas] my considered answer had to be "no." To those of us who received Sokei-an's teaching, the word "instruction" must be a misnomer, for his way of transmitting the Dharma was on a completely different level. . . . It was, of course, his SILENCE that brought us into IT with him. It was as if, by creating a vacuum, he drew all into the One after him.

Sokei-an spoke extremely slowly; his pauses sometimes seemed to last forever. His accent was pronounced—a hindrance to some, an added attraction to others, as Mary Farkas noticed, but his teisho was always dramatic. As she explained:

> Sokei-an played not only the human roles, but also the animal, mineral, and vegetable as well. Sometimes he would be a huge golden mountain, sometimes a lonely coyote on the plains. At other times a willowly Chinese princess or Japanese geisha would appear before our eyes. . . . There was something of Kabuki's Joruri, something of Noh's otherworldliness, something of a fairy story for children, something of archaic Japan. Yet all was as universal as the baby's first waaah.

Watts meanwhile had decided to "study with Sokei-an without his knowing it." He had, after all, the most unusual opportunity of observing a Zen master "in his personal life," since Sokei-an often visited the hotel where both the Wattses and Mrs. Everett had their apartments. Watts noticed, among other things, that Sokei-an "never fidgeted nor showed the nervous politeness of ordinary Japanese, but moved slowly and easily, with relaxed but complete attention to whatever was going on." Sokei-an and Ruth Everett had begun to spend a great deal of time together. (Charles Everett, her husband, had died in 1940.) Ruth was working hard with Sokei-an translating the *Sutra of Perfect Awakening*, but there were also many social occasions. A photograph of the period shows the two couples, Alan and Eleanor, Sokei-an and Ruth, out for the evening on the boardwalk at Atlantic City—mother and daughter looking like sisters in their long evening gowns, Watts resembling a young, handsome David Niven in his tuxedo, and Sokei-an, also in evening clothes, but wearing glasses, and a large false nose and moustache, looking very much like a Japanese Groucho Marx. Alan had gotten his wish—he had managed to study a Zen master "in his personal everyday life"—in fact, so it seemed, a Zen master in the first bloom of romance. Alan and Eleanor found themselves the "fascinated witnesses" of Sokei-an's and Ruth Everett's "mutually fructifying relationship—she drawing out his bottomless knowledge of Buddhism and he breaking down her rigidities with ribald tales that made her blush and giggle."

Watts had begun to give seminars in New York. A mailing to members of the Jungian Analytical Psychology Club of New York brought five students to a seminar on "The Psychology of Acceptance." Word soon spread, and before long there were more students, an editor from *Harper's* stopped by to listen, and his first American book appeared, *The Meaning of Happiness*, (subtitled: "The Quest for Freedom of the Spirit in Modern Psychology and in the Wisdom of the East"). It was well-reviewed in the *Times* and other papers, but it did not fit the current mood. The German army had just crossed over into France.

Watts was now twenty-six and faced with the dilemma of making a living in his adopted country. Ruth not unreasonably thought that her bright young son-in-law might do well to obtain a Ph.D., and go into teaching. Watts discussed this step with Marguerite Block, editor of the *Columbia Review of Religion*, but she suggested, instead, that Watts write a long and learned article for the *Review*.

"The Problem of Faith and Works in Buddhism" appeared in the May 1941 issue. The article was a discussion of the old argument about the relative merits of act and faith, but cast in Buddhist terms—the self-power (*jiriki*) of the Zen school as opposed to the other-power (*tariki*) of the Shin. Watts argued that the two positions were, in fact, complementary, since koans could not be solved until one had given up all effort, and since the Amitabha of the Shin "need not be considered as 'other' in the theistic sense, but simply as that true or real Self, which, like the heart or the brain, is other than the ego and will." For Watts all this had "momentous consequences" since he realized "that if you substituted 'Christ' for 'Amitabha,' Zen, Jodo Shinshu, and Christianity were all approaching the same point by different routes."

Eleanor had fallen into an ever-deepening depression, and one day, having stopped to rest at St. Patrick's Cathedral, she found herself staring at "a completely vivid vision of Christ." Eleanor's vision coincided with Watts's "growing realization that Christianity might be understood as a form of that mystical and perennial philosophy which has appeared in almost all times and places," and he began to think that he might best fit into Western society as a Christian minister. He chose the Episcopalian Church—he was, after all an Englishman—as the most satisfying of the churches, both for its ritual and its liberality. There were difficulties, such as Watts's lack of an undergraduate degree, but he had read and published widely, and he finally enrolled as a "special student" at Northwestern's Seabury-Western Theological Seminary. He did not think that he was abandoning Buddhism for Christianity; it was just that the Anglican communion "seemed to be the most appropriate context" for him to do his work in Western society. At the time, there did not seem any other place for him to go.

X

In November of 1941 Sokei-an and the First Zen Institute moved into new quarters, provided by Ruth Everett, on East Sixty-fifth. This was the beginning, said Sokei-an, of "his second period of work in New York." On December 7 Pearl Harbor was attacked. A few days later the FBI began to round up Japanese "security-risks." Buddhist priests were given special attention and the American Buddhist Society, unknown to Sokei-an and his students, was put under round-the-clock surveillance. Both Sokei-an and Mrs. Everett were questioned extensively by the FBI, but meetings were allowed to continue. Then, on July 15, 1942, Sokei-an was taken to an internment camp.

Sokei-an was not in the best of health and the conditions in the camp did not help matters. He kept busy by carving a walking stick with a dragon emblem, which he presented to the colonel in charge. It was by fighting, he would tell his students later, that people came to know each other.

Ruth hired a well-placed lawyer and one of Sokei-an's former students,

George Fowler, then a commander in the Navy, testified in his favor. He was released, and Sokei-an and Ruth Everett were married in 1944. But Sokei-an's health had been seriously weakened by the camp experience. He had once said, "It is an unhappy death for a Zen Master when he does not leave an heir," and now he said that he wished he had five more years to complete the work he had begun in America forty years before. He did, however, charge Ruth Fuller Sasaki (Sasaki being Sokei-an's family name) with two tasks: he wanted her to find a Rinzai Zen master from Japan to take his place at the Society and he wanted her to complete his translation of the *Rinzai-roku*—something that would only be possible for someone who had completed formal Zen study. Having looked to the future as best he could, Sokei-an died on May 17, 1945. "I have always taken Nature's orders," he said, "and I take them now."

XI

In the days following Pearl Harbor, everything "Japanese" became suspect. At first, only the leaders of the Japanese community on the Pacific Coast were arrested and detained. Buddhist ministers in particular were singled out. (The FBI did not distinguish between Shintoists and Buddhists: both were considered to owe allegiance to the emperor of Japan.) Teachers at Japanese language schools, newspaper editors and anyone associated with martial arts clubs or other Japanese cultural organizations were also rounded up.

As American losses in the Pacific increased, the outcry to remove all "Japs" from the West Coast increased. Occasional sightings of Japanese submarines off Santa Barbara and the Northwest coast added to the hysteria. Stories of a Japanese Fifth Column engaged in espionage and sabotage raced through the Pacific Coast. In fact, there was not one instance of espionage or sabotage by the Japanese in America. But even this was used to strengthen the cry against the Japanese-Americans, and Earl Warren, then Attorney General of California, argued that the Japanese were simply waiting until they could strike "with maximum effect." Even those who believed the Japanese-American community to be loyal Americans argued that, given the climate, it would be safer for the Japanese if they were removed from the coast. The fact that many of the Japanese were American citizens did not seem important.

On February 19, 1942, President Franklin Delano Roosevelt, acting on the recommendation of General John Dewitt of the Western Defense

Command, signed Executive Order 9066. Suddenly the entire West Coast Japanese community found itself ordered to report to assembly centers for "relocation." Stores were boarded up, houses abandoned, farmland and orchards rented out and furniture sold—all at a great financial loss. The shock and shame of the sudden dislocation—that is, the "psychological damage"—was incalculable. By 1943, 110,000 Japanese-Americans, both citizens and noncitizens, infants and grandparents, had been removed to internment camps where they lived surrounded by barbed wire, watchtowers and armed guards.

Nyogen Senzaki was sent to Heart Mountain, a camp in the desert of Wyoming, along with ten thousand others. Perhaps, he thought, the relocation could be seen as another example of the eastward movement of the teachings. "A government must practice its policy without sentiment," he wrote in a poem:

> All Japanese faces will leave California to
>   support their government
> This morning the winding train, like a big
>   black snake,
> Takes us away as far as Wyoming.
> The current of Buddhist thought always runs
>   eastward.
> This policy may support the tendency of the
>   teaching.
> Who knows?

It was, indeed, a time of great uncertainty. Before leaving Los Angeles Senzaki had entrusted his robes to an American student, since he could not tell when, if ever, he might return. But he carried his floating zendo along with him, and he established a sitting place in the small cabin (twenty by twenty) that he shared with a man, his wife and their small child. Perhaps ten or twelve people joined him for his meetings and meditation. "They are the happiest and most contented evacuees in this center," he wrote to one of the twenty or thirty American students with whom he continued to correspond. (He also managed to send out a lecture every month to his Mentorgarten students.)

Nakagawa Soen had planned to visit Senzaki in Los Angeles in 1941. That was now impossible, but the two men, who had never met in person, agreed to face each other across the ocean at a certain time on the twenty-fifth of every month (Dai Bosatsu day), and bow to each other in greeting. It would take more than a war to keep them apart.

On July 2, 1945, the Supreme Court ruled against any further restriction of Japanese-Americans. More than 40,000 had already relocated to places like Colorado, Illinois and Utah. Those who returned to the West Coast found the neighborhoods they had lived in filled with new immigrants from the South and Mexico. To anyone who cared to see, it was clear that the *nisei* and *issei*, second and first generations, had demonstrated their loyalty under the most trying circumstances. The battle record of the all-Nisei 442nd Combat Regiment—one of the most bloodied and decorated units in the European theater—had demonstrated that. But there were still many who did not care to see. Farms that had been leased had been abandoned and orchards that had taken years to grow had died. The Nichirin temple in Los Angeles, where more than six-hundred families had stored their belongings, had been looted.

Senzaki returned to Los Angeles and took up temporary residence at the homes of various students. He was, once again, homeless, as he had been when Soyen Shaku had walked through Golden Gate Park with him in 1905, and now, on October 29, 1945, he marked the anniversary of his teacher's death, as he had done each year, with a poem:

> For forty years I have not seen
> My teacher, So-yen Shaku, in person.
> I have carried his Zen in my empty fist,
> Wandering ever since in this strange land.
> Being a mere returnee from the evacuation
> I could establish no Zendo
> Where his followers should commemorate
> The twenty-sixth anniversary of his death.
> The cold rain purifies everything on the earth
> In the great city of Los Angeles, today.
> I open my fist and spread the fingers
> At the street corner in the evening rush hour.

Sokei-an in his apartment, New York City, late 1930s

Nyogen Senzaki and Nakagawa So-yen [Soen]

Ruth Fuller Everett [later Sasaki] and Georgia Foreman, Japan, 1933–1934

Dwight Goddard

Christmas Humphreys, Alan Watts and D.T. Suzuki in the Rembrandt Hotel, London, 1958

Gary Snyder, Berkeley, Summer 1955

Jack Kerouac, 1957

Philip Whalen and Allen Ginsberg, San Francisco, August 1971

Shunryu Suzuki-roshi

Hakuun Yasutani-roshi

Philip Kapleau-roshi

Joshu Sasaki-roshi

Eido Shimano-roshi

Gyoun Aitken-roshi

Zentatsu Baker-roshi

Jakusho Kwong-sensei

Kobun Chino-sensei

Katagiri-roshi

Taizan Maezumi-roshi and his two senior disciples, Bernard Tetsugen Glassman-sensei (on roshi's left) and Dennis Genpo Merzel-sensei

CHAPTER ELEVEN

THE FIFTIES: BEAT AND SQUARE

I

In March of 1947 two young Americans working with the International Military Tribunal in Tokyo followed a Japanese friend up a steep flight of stone steps to a small house on the grounds of Engakuji temple. The man they had come to meet, D.T. Suzuki, was not expecting visitors, and before he rose to greet them, Philip Kapleau and Richard DeMartino had a chance to watch him through the glass-panelled sliding *shoji* of his study. Richard DeMartino remembers the scene: Suzuki "sitting on his knees, Japanese fashion, in front of a Western typewriter, on which he was pecking away with the index finger of either hand, a little clean-shaven old man in a black kimono wearing down over his eyes, a Western style green bookkeeper's eyeshade."

D.T. Suzuki had spent the war years in scholarly seclusion, his wife and co-worker Beatrice Lane having died in 1939. Now he felt it was time to return to America for an extended visit, and in 1949, with DeMartino as aide-de-camp, he flew to Honolulu to take part in the Second East-West Philosopher's Conference. He taught at the University of Hawaii for a year, and then in 1950 Richard Gard, a graduate student, arranged a temporary appointment at the Claremont Graduate School in Pasadena—a post Suzuki needed to enter the country. But at the last minute, Claremont was unable to come up with Suzuki's living expenses, and in desperation Gard turned to Bishop Takahashi of the Los Angeles Shingon temple. The Bishop called a meeting of several Buddhist leaders in Los Angeles and the needed funds were raised from the Japanese-American community.

After teaching for a year at Claremont, Suzuki arrived in New York. He lectured at the Church Peace Union and in private homes, but he had no regular academic appointment until Cornelius Crane, of Crane Bathroom Fixtures, subsidized a series of seminars at Columbia. Crane, who had sat at Daitokuji, stipulated that auditors be allowed to attend Suzuki's seminars, and because of this Suzuki's students included psychoanalysts and therapists—Erich Fromm and Karen Horney, among them—as well as artists, composers and writers. And there were also people such as Mary Farkas and Philip Kapleau, then a businessman, who were simply interested in what Suzuki had to say about Buddhism.

At these seminars the seeds of the so-called Zen "boom" of the late fifties were sown. Of the artists and intellectuals present perhaps the one most profoundly influenced by Suzuki's Zen was composer and writer John Cage. Cage was then thirty-eight. His avant-garde music had been widely praised, but he himself was full of doubts, "confused," as he said in a recent interview, "both in my personal life and in my understanding of what the function of art in society could be." Cage's friends had recommended psychoanalysis, but Cage found that Suzuki's seminars (which he attended for two years) and the study of Buddhism served as well.

Although Suzuki told Cage that he had nothing to say about music or art, Cage still felt Suzuki had led him to see music "not as a communication from the artist to an audience, but rather as an activity of sounds in which the artist found a way to let the sounds be themselves." This in turn, thought Cage, could "open the minds of the people who made them or listened to them to other possibilities than they had previously considered. . . . To widen their experience; particularly to undermine the making of value judgements."

To accomplish this aim, Cage decided to compose music "with a means that was as strict as sitting cross-legged, namely the use of chance operations," thus shifting his responsibility "from that of making choices to that of asking questions." Audiences found the results of Cage's chance compositions (as well as other pieces, such as *4'33"*, in which the performer sat silently at the piano for that length of time) irritating and outrageous, but ultimately thought-provoking.

Suzuki took the Hua-yen or Kegon doctrines of the *Avatamsaka Sutra* as the starting point of his Columbia seminars. Kegon taught the interdependence of all things, and Dr. Suzuki, along with other Buddhist scholars, considered it the high point of Buddhist thought. "Kegon is believed to have been the expression of the Buddha in his enlightenment," Suzuki told his class. "All other teachings were given by the Buddha to his disciples after he had come out of the enlightenment. In Kegon he made no accommodations to his hearers."

Neither did D.T. Suzuki make such accommodations. Teaching for Suzuki, in addition to being a way of earning a living, was a way of thinking out loud about whatever books or translations he happened to be working on, and it was not uncommon for him to lose students as he crisscrossed the blackboard with a bewildering maze of diagrams and notes in Japanese, Sanskrit, Chinese and Tibetan. Mary Farkas, who audited the class occasionally, remembers counting as many as a dozen people sleeping in their chairs one afternoon. Not that it bothered Suzuki. Once, John Cage tells, a low-flying plane drowned out Suzuki's voice in mid-sentence, but Suzuki simply continued speaking, without bothering to raise the level of his voice.

II

It had been nearly thirty years since Mrs. Sasaki, then Ruth Fuller Everett, had been introduced to her first Zen teacher, Nanshinken-roshi, by Doctor Suzuki in Kyoto. Now, in 1949, she returned to Kyoto to complete her husband's unfinished work: first, to find a teacher to take his place at the First Zen Institute in New York, and second, to finish the translations of the *Rinzai-roku* and other key Zen texts. She would need luck and persistence to find a qualified roshi willing to come to New York, but to translate Zen texts Mrs. Sasaki would have to master the language of the original koan texts—a colloquial form of T'ang and Sung dynasty Chinese, prickly with slang and forgotten idioms. In addition, she would have to complete her own Zen training. Mrs. Sasaki began by taking up residence in a small house on the grounds of Daitokuji, starting intensive language study and attending sanzen with

Zuigan Goto-roshi, who had first accompanied Sokei-an to America in 1906.

Back in New York, the members of the First Zen Institute did their best to continue without a teacher. They held readings of Sokei-an's lectures, and meetings were led by senior members. When Mrs. Sasaki returned to New York for a brief visit in 1952 she told the remaining members of the Institute that though she would continue to search for a suitable teacher, the prospects were not very promising. As far as she could see, the members of the First Zen Institute of America were on their own. The Institute moved downtown to Waverly Place, the library was put in storage and the zendo opened only on certain days.

In the winter of 1954 Asahina Sogen, the abbot of Engakuji, Soyen Shaku's monastery, visited America. It had been ten years since any one at the Institute had spoken with a Zen master, and during his brief visit the abbot did what he could. He wrote their names in calligraphy, then showed them the proper way to do walking meditation, gave instructions in breathing, and demonstrated the proper use of the *kyo-saku* (literally "waking stick"). Finally he shed his formal robes and corrected sitting postures with "lightning precision." He cautioned against "dead sitting," using the *nyo-i* (a wand whose graceful curve suggests proper posture) given him by Soyen Shaku. "A symbol of freedom," he said, holding it out. "Suppleness is very important. We say, if it is supple, it is alive. If it is rigid, it is dead." Toward the end of the evening, while eating ice cream and drinking tea, the abbot demonstrated the shout of Rinzai's *Ho*! "To give a 'Ho!' is agreeable in the quiet night air of New York," he said, and then departed, leaving the members of the Institute once more on their own.

In February of the following year, on the twenty-fifth anniversary of the founding of the Institute, Mrs. Sasaki arrived in New York with Isshu Miura-roshi, who she hoped might succeed Sokei-an Sasaki. With Mrs. Sasaki as translator, Miura-roshi delivered a series of eight lectures on the koan system of Hakuin Zenji, the eighteenth-century master who had developed the koan system most commonly used in Rinzai Zen. There had been a great deal of nonsense written about koans by experts who had never studied koans themselves, Mrs. Sasaki said, and Miura-roshi's lectures (published in 1965 as *The Zen Koan*) were aimed at clearing up some of the most commonly held misconceptions.

For the first time since Sokei-an's death in 1945, students were able to work on koans with a roshi. Sanzen, Mary Farkas remembers, "was no longer something written about in a book or happening to mysterious persons on a remote mountain. It was a blow in the solar plexus, human beings encountering in a wilderness, the opening of unknown eyes."

Mary Farkas followed Miura-roshi back to Japan to see what could be done about arranging a more permanent stay. She was enthusiastic, but over the years she had seen the extent to which Americans could twist Zen to match their own ideas, and she sometimes had doubts about the wisdom of doing anything at all, and she expressed her misgivings to Mrs. Sasaki. "Well that's true," answered Mrs. Sasaki, after a moment's thought, "but then what else would people spend their time doing?" When Mary Farkas asked Zuigan Goto-roshi, "Don't you think we have made some progress in this last half century?" he replied encouragingly, "Yes, you could say you have taken a step."

III

After his return from the Heart Mountain Camp in 1945 Nyogen Senzaki had settled into a small corner apartment on the top floor of the Miyako Hotel. The Miyako was located in the heart of Little Tokyo, on the corner of San Pedro and First Street, and Albert Saijo, a young nisei who had been fifteen when he first met Senzaki in Heart Mountain, remembers it being "filled with whores, pimps, and numbers runners." Senzaki's apartment consisted of a tiny kitchen and a larger bed-sitting room whose walls were covered with books and philodendron twining in and out of the bookcases.

It was here, with the sounds of traffic floating up from the streets below, that Senzaki set up second-hand chairs, acquired from a funeral parlor, for the meetings of the postwar Mentorgarten. On Sundays a fairly substantial Japanese congregation chanted sutras. During the week the English-speaking meetings continued much as they had for the last twenty-five years. People meditated on the wooden chairs (Senzaki marking off the periods with wooden clappers every fifteen minutes), recited the Four Vows and then listened as Senzaki gave a short talk or reading from one of the translations he was working on. Then tea, along with a Japanese confection, and the meeting would be over. As before, socializing was discouraged, and if Senzaki found people lingering too long after a meeting, he would suggest that it was time to go home.

The most important event of the postwar years, as far as Senzaki was concerned, was the arrival of Nakagawa Soen in 1949. The two men, who had corresponded for fifteen years and had bowed across the ocean to each other every Dai Bosatsu Day during the War, first met face to face on San Francisco's Pier 42. "There is a saying of Zen," Senzaki told the group that had gathered to greet Nakagawa Soen at the Theosophical Society Library, "that it is better to face a person than to hear his name. But there is another saying: It is better to hear the name than to see the face. I don't know which one applies to our case, but at any rate we are both contented and happy."

Soen began his talk at the Theosophical Library by referring to the original Three Objects of the Theosophical Society: to form the nucleus of a Universal Brotherhood of Humanity, to encourage the study of comparative religion and philosophy, and to investigate the unexplained laws of nature and the powers latent in man. Then he quoted Soyen Shaku's 1906 lecture, in which the pioneer Zen master had said that after studying Buddhism for more than forty years, he had begun to understand that "what I had understood is that, after all, I do not understand anything." Since it was the two-hundredth anniversary of Goethe's death, Soen added a passage from Faust which ended:

> Already these ten years, I lead,
> Up and down, across and to and fro,
> My pupils by the nose, and learn
> That we in truth can nothing know!

"This," announced Soen, "is exactly the point of Zen," and then he suddenly brought his hand down on the table with a sharp crack and asked his startled audience, "Who is hearing this sound?" Obviously, he said, no one Japanese or American. "The master of hearing," then, was "without distinction of race, creed, sex, caste, or color," and the "nucleus of the Universal Brotherhood of Humanity" was "probably nothing but just hearing this sound." But to truly understand what this means one must "ask and ask until you reach the bottom," then "all of a sudden, when the bottom is broken through, you will realize what 'the unexplained laws of nature' really are, and you will be able to acquire an understanding of 'the powers latent in man!' " It was a clear explanation of the way koan practice works, but one wonders what the founders of the Theosophical Society, Colonel Olcott and Madame Blavatsky, would have made of it all.

In the early fifties one of Senzaki's most devoted students was a young man named Robert Aitken. Like Senzaki, Aitken had spent the war years in internment. As a young civilian construction worker on the island of Guam he had been captured by the Japanese at the beginning of the war and taken to a detention camp outside of Kobe, Japan. Aitken was interested in haiku, and one of the guards in the Kobe camp, aware of this, loaned him a book, *Zen and English Literature*, by R.H. Blyth, which had just been published in Japan by the Hokuseido Press.

Reginald Horace Blyth was a friend and disciple of D.T. Suzuki. He had followed Suzuki's lead by looking for the core of Zen in sources that were hardly traditional—Shakespeare, Wordsworth, Don Quixote, Blake and Whitman, for example. The result of this exploration, *Zen in English Literature*, was a tour de force, a grand cultural leap that succeeded in illuminating both Western literature and Zen by examining each in the light of the other.

The book was a revelation to Aitken. He read it over and over in the camp at Kobe feeling as if he were reading Shakespeare, Basho, Blake and Whitman "for the first time." "The world seemed transparent," Aitken remembered years later, "and I was absurdly happy despite our miserable circumstances." Aitken read through the book at least ten times. When the guard finally took it back, Aitken felt as though he had lost his best friend. Then in May of 1944 all the camps around Kobe were combined and Aitken suddenly found himself face to face with the author of *Zen and English Literature*.

Blyth was an Englishman who had originally gone out to India. Finding himself repelled by the colonial mentality of his countrymen, he had moved on to Korea, which was occupied at that time by the Japanese. In Seoul, Blyth taught English at a Japanese-run college, and studied Zen with Kayama-roshi, the abbot of a branch temple of Myoshinji, a Rinzai temple. He moved to Japan in 1940 with his Japanese wife and had been interned along with other nationals of enemy countries at the beginning of the war. *Zen and English Literature*, his first book, had been written in the early days of his internment, and he had now begun work on a series of books on haiku.

During the fourteen months that they were confined together Blyth and Aitken spent many hours in conversation about haiku, Japanese culture and Zen. Blyth had a rather cavalier attitude about the necessity for zazen, and the two men did not practice. Nevertheless, Aitken was inspired to find a teacher and practice zazen after the war.

Upon his release Aitken returned to Hawaii, finished his B.A. in English literature at the age of thirty, married and then spent a semester studying Japanese language and literature at Berkeley. During the

Christmas vacation of 1947, Aitken and a friend took a trip south to Ojai, where they hoped to find J. Krishnamurti, who, Aitken thought, would be "about as close as I could get to Zen in this country." But Krishnamurti was away in India, and Aitken and his friend continued south. At P.D. and Ione Perkins Bookstore in Pasadena they found Richard Gard working as chief clerk while studying for his doctorate in Buddhist Studies at Claremont. Gard and Aitken had known each other at the University of Hawaii before the war, and Gard told Aitken about Nyogen Senzaki.

Aitken went right over to the Miyako Hotel in Little Tokyo and knocked on Senzaki's door. He found Senzaki alone in his room. Senzaki showed Aitken a photograph of Nakagawa Soen, and Aitken asked Senzaki if the purpose of zazen were self-realization. Senzaki said it was. By the time the visit was over Aitken had decided that this was what he wanted to do, and he returned to northern California for his wife.

There was not a great deal of instruction beyond Senzaki's talks. "Mostly," remembers Aitken, "we learned from his wonderful manner, his kindness, and his modesty." He gave Aitken a Buddhist name, "Chotan," meaning "Great Abyss," and quoted Meister Eckhart to him: "The eye with which I see God is the very same eye with which God sees me."

"Show me that eye!" Senzaki said. Aitken worked very hard on this koan, and one day he walked into his room with an answer: he simply closed his eyes.

"Oh, ho!" Senzaki cried. "Well then, where does it go when you sleep?" Aitken couldn't answer, and years later, even when he was working on a different koan with another teacher, the question would pop up into his mind.

The Aitkens returned to Hawaii, where Aitken began work on a master's degree in Japanese literature and, in 1950, with the recommendation of D.T. Suzuki, he obtained a fellowship for a year's study in Japan.

In Japan Aitken lived with the Blyths for a time while he audited classes at Tokyo University. Then he attended two sesshins at Engakuji with Asahina-roshi. It was his first experience with true zazen (he had sat in a chair with Senzaki) and his knees became so swollen that he could only walk a few steps. Asahina-roshi did not speak English, and his monks had no experience in dealing with foreigners, so Aitken got in touch with Nakagawa Soen. Soen was a highly accomplished haiku poet, and he and Aitken got along very well. Aitken moved into his monastery as a lay monk.

Soen was then still the attendant of his teacher Yamamoto Gempo-roshi. Asahina-roshi had translated Senzaki's Meister Eckhart verse into the more traditional koan "Show me your original face and eye," but Gempo-roshi felt that was too complicated and gave Aitken *Mu*—a koan which would occupy him for many years to come. Gempo-roshi was then quite old. Like Senzaki and a number of other Zen teachers and monks, he had been an orphan. His foster parents had been poor farmers, and because he had contracted a disease that left him blind at an early age, he had grown up illiterate. In his early twenties, Gempo had made a pilgrimage of the thirty-three temples which Kobo Daishi, the founder of Shingon in Japan, had set up on the island of Shikoku. The pilgrimage was strenuous, and Gempo collapsed with hunger and fatigue at the gate of the one Zen temple on the pilgrimage. The priest of the temple, who nursed him back to health, so impressed him that he became a monk, and during the course of his training he regained his sight and finally learned how to read and write. He was considered a very good teacher, but somewhat unorthodox and idiosyncratic. His country accent was so pronounced that the monks themselves could only understand about a third of what he said in teisho, and Nakagawa Soen used to say of his teisho on the *Mumonkan*, "This is not *Mumonkan* Teisho, but Gempo Goroku"—*goroku* meaning personal or random writings.

Yamamoto Gempo-roshi retired soon after Aitken arrived, and when Nakagawa Soen-roshi was installed as his successor and abbot of Ryutakuji, Aitken was there, reciting *dharanis* (Sanskrit chants) along with everybody else. Soen had put on the abbot's double kimono of white Babutai silk. He wore a purple robe and a *kesa* (outermost Buddhist robe) that had originally belonged to Hakuin. Under all this finery, in his underclothes, he had hidden a letter from Senzaki, with a congratulatory poem. The fact that he had known beforehand "that all the Sangha in America were meditating for me," he wrote Senzaki, "strengthened me tremendously," and he felt, as he chanted during the ceremony, that his voice could be heard in Los Angeles.

IV

Dr. Suzuki began to settle into his New York life around 1953 when Miss Mihoko Okamura, a nisei student in his class at Columbia, persuaded him to leave his spartan quarters in Butler Hall for the comfort of her parents' apartment on West Ninety-fourth Street. Miss Okamura's father, Frank Okamura, worked as a gardener at the Brooklyn Botanical Garden, and Mrs. Okamura was happy to prepare the *mochi* and *yudofu* that were Dr. Suzuki's favorite dishes. Miss Okamura became Dr. Suzuki's constant and lifelong companion, assisting him as secretary, typist and editor, and generally devoting herself to his welfare. It was she who prepared the thick green powdered tea he had imported from Japan, and though Suzuki worked surrounded by great piles of books and papers, Miss Okamura could find whatever Dr. Suzuki needed at a moment's notice. She took his calls and arranged his schedule—a crucial function, since Dr. Suzuki seemed constitutionally incapable of refusing any of the requests for aid, advice or encouragement that increasingly came his way.

Without any effort or care on his part, Dr. Suzuki had become a figure. He was interviewed on television, profiled in the *New Yorker*, even featured in *Vogue*. His age, wit and air of gentle, bemused, scholarly abstraction caught the public imagination, but it was Dr. Suzuki's character above all else that impressed those who met him. Thomas Merton spoke for many people when he said of D.T. Suzuki: "In meeting him one seemed to meet that 'True Man of No Title' that Chuang Tzu and the Zen Masters speak of. And of course this is the man one really wants to meet. Who else is there? In meeting Dr. Suzuki and drinking a cup of tea with him I felt I had met this one man. It was like finally arriving at one's own home."

Suzuki was also well known for his books which were now increasingly available in paperback. He had written a number of books for specialists, but most were essays addressed to the intelligent cosmopolitan in a style at once rambling, humorous and direct. It was as if one overheard him thinking to himself in his booklined study late at night, digressing now and then to pursue a fascinatingly abstruse detail, or chuckling to himself as he translated an old Chinese Zen story. It was a unique voice. No one else could speak of spiritual life with such a lively mixture of authority and informality.

Suzuki knew better than anyone how misleading it could be to conceptualize Zen Buddhism, but he was willing to take the chance and point the finger of words and concepts at the inexpressible moon. In this he followed William James, an early and important influence. James had classified the various elements of the mystical experience; in the same way, Suzuki categorized *satori*: irrationality, intuitive insight, authoritativeness, affirmation, exhilaration and momentariness.

Suzuki had been careful to emphasize that Zen was Zen *Buddhism*. But at the same time he refused to limit Zen to any time, place or doctrine. "As I conceive it," he wrote, "Zen is the ultimate fact of all philosophy. That final psychic fact that takes place when religious consciousness is heightened to extremity. Whether it comes to pass in Buddhists, in Christians, or in philosophers, it is in the last analysis incidental to Zen." It was this universalization of Zen that made it possible for all kinds of people to see Zen in all kinds of places.

Indeed, by the latter half of the fifties, the idea of Zen had become so popularized that it achieved the status of a fad. "Zen has always been credited with influencing Far Eastern Art," Mrs. Sasaki observed somewhat ironically from Kyoto in 1959. "But now the discovery has been made that it was existing all along in English literature. Ultra-modern painting, music, dance, and poetry are acclaimed as expressions of Zen. Zen is invoked to substantiate the validity of the latest theories in psychology, psychotherapy, philosophy, semantics, mysticism, free-thinking, and what-have-you. It is the magic password at smart cocktail parties and bohemian get-togethers alike."

One of the more serious attempts to confront Zen was the 1957 Conference of Zen Buddhism and Psychoanalysis, in which D.T. Suzuki was the featured speaker. More than fifty analysts converged on Cuernavaca for the week-long workshop. As early as 1934 Carl Jung had recognized that Zen and psychotherapy had a common concern, namely spiritual "healing" or "making whole," and that the Zen master and psychoanalyst fulfilled a similar role in the individual's search for wholeness. Like psychology, Zen Buddhism spoke of mind and consciousness. D.T. Suzuki himself had attempted to use Western psychological terms to explain Zen Buddhism, but he was critical of the limitations inherent in the analytic method of psychology: "Finally, as a matter of fact, there is no beyond, no underneath, no upon in our consciousness," he wrote in *An Introduction to Zen Buddhism*. "The mind is one indivisible whole and cannot be torn into pieces. When the koan breaks down all hindrances to the ultimate truth, we all realize that there are no such things as hidden recesses of mind, or even the truth of Zen appearing all the time so mysterious."

Unlike psychology, Zen was a spiritual discipline. Referring to a term shared by both Zen and psychology, he told the assembled analysts at Cuernavaca,

> Psychologists talk a great deal about spontaneity, but what they are talking about is a child-like spontaneity, which is by no means the spontaneity and freedom of an adult human being. As long as he is unable to give up his childish freedom, he will need the help of a psychologist, but he can never expect to be free and spontaneous if he does not go through years, perhaps many decades of self-discipline, at the end of which he will have reached the stature of a fully matured manhood.

While the lectures at Cuernavaca did much to legitimize the on-going dialogue between Zen and psychoanalysis, as usual it was Suzuki's presence, even more than his words, that mattered most. Erich Fromm remembers after the first two days of the conference, "a change of mood began to be apparent. Everyone became more concentrated and quiet. At the end of the meeting a visible change had occurred in many of the participants. They had gone through a unique experience; they felt that an important event had happened in their lives, that they had waked up a little and that they would not lose what they had gained."

Fromm himself was left with a particularly poignant memory. One afternoon, noticing that Suzuki had taken a longer than usual break from the hard chairs and speeches, Mrs. Fromm and Miss Okamura went out to look for him. "They could not find him anwhere," Fromm writes, "and just as they began to become a little worried, they saw him sitting under a tree, meditating. He was so relaxed that he had become one with the tree, and it was difficult to see 'him'. . . ."

V

In September of 1957 Dr. Suzuki, having retired from Columbia in June, joined the philosopher and Zen scholar, Shinichi Hisamatsu for an extended stay in Cambridge, Massachusetts. Dr. Hisamatsu, a disciple of the Japanese philosopher Kitaro Nishida, was giving a series of lectures on Zen at the Harvard Divinity School. Dr. Hisamatsu was steeped in German metaphysics and even graduate students familiar with the subject, found his lectures difficult to follow.

Among those attending Dr. Hisamatsu's lectures were Elsie and John Mitchell. The Mitchells had just returned from Japan where they had recorded the chanting and services at Eiheiji for Folkways Records. The Mitchells were somewhat frustrated by the theoretical nature of Dr. Hisamatsu's lectures, and one evening, after a talk at the Newton Andover School of Theology, they asked him about the practice, as opposed to the theory, of Zen. Dr. Hisamatsu offered to provide instruction, and under his guidance a small group began practicing at the Mitchells' new house on Craigie Street in Cambridge. They fixed up one room as a zendo, and began collecting books for a Buddhist library. (This library would eventually comprise more than twenty thousand volumes.) The first participants were mostly Japanese graduate and postgraduate students from Harvard-Yenching Institute, where Elsie Mitchell tutored English. There was one student who belonged to the Soto school (*shu*), two who belonged to different branches of the Shingon-shu and a Jodo-shu minister from Hawaii, whose by no means wealthy congregation had managed over the years to save enough to send him to do graduate work at the Harvard Divinity School. The few American members of the group were, Elsie Mitchell remembers, "rather fiercely non-organizational." They all had one thing in common: an interest in zazen.

Dr. Hisamatsu returned to Japan after six months ("just," Elsie Mitchell remembers, "as he was beginning to understand the Western mind") and various members took turns leading zazen, among them Reverend Hirioka, a Shingon priest. The group incorporated as the Cambridge Buddhist Association in 1959. Dr. Suzuki, who lectured occasionally to the group, agreed to serve as president with the provision that he not be required to attend meetings or take on any duties.

The members of the Cambridge Buddhist Society adopted the Soto style of "just sitting." For one thing, there was no roshi, and a roshi was necessary for koan practice. Then, too, the group consisted largely of people who were already Buddhists and the Soto style of "just sitting" or concentration on breathing, was one that could be practiced by all the members.

Elsie Mitchell returned to Japan a number of times and began to study with Rindo Fujimoto-roshi, the abbot of Sho-so-an, a small Soto temple with a dirt floor zendo. Fujimoto-roshi had studied koans with Sogaku Harada-roshi, but he had come to the conclusion that, valuable as such practices might be, the Soto approach of just sitting was "the most natural way."

In 1960 Elsie Mitchell supervised the translation of a lecture Fujimoto-roshi had given to a group of laymen in Japan. The draft of this translation was sent back to Japan, retranslated and checked by the roshi. But when Mrs. Mitchell showed the manuscript to friends, she found that even though the language had been simplified and the more technical points dropped entirely, most of them could not make anything out of sentences such as "Both original enlightenment and practice are different names for the same thing, and so belief in original enlightenment is realized in the form of zazen practice or discipline." So she added an introduction explaining that the basic Buddhist approach to zazen was "neither a technique to achieve something or get somewhere, a do-it-yourself psychotherapy, a tranquilizer, or a way to stimulate the 'creative unconscious.' " Using zazen as a means to an end, wrote Mrs. Mitchell, was not the Buddhist approach. Rather, Buddhist zazen was a way of life.

A thousand copies of *The Way of Zazen* were printed and handbound in Japan. When the Mitchells went down to pick them up at the Boston Customs House, they were sure that most of them would stay in the boxes they had been shipped in. But within a year, to everyone's surprise, they found that the first edition had completely sold out. Apparently there were now at least that many people who were interested in learning how to "just sit."

VI

In 1956 Daitokuji granted Mrs. Sasaki permission to build a library and a small sixteen-mat zendo next to the house she had occupied since 1949, and the First Zen Institute of America opened a branch in Kyoto. Mrs. Sasaki now had a place to put into practice her firm conviction that serious students of "traditional transmitted Rinzai Zen" had no other choice than to train in Japan.

The difficulties in undertaking this training were immense, and only a very few foreigners were able to even attempt it. For one thing, the first year would have to be devoted to language study and to learning how to sit "with the proper posture and breathing" that roshis normally expected of sanzen students. Then there was the difficulty of finding a roshi willing to work with foreigners, and, finally, there was the problem of making a living. "Zen study demands full time and a free mind," Mrs. Sasaki warned. "Worries about livelihood and other matters are a serious hindrance."

Despite these formidable obstacles, there were a few who found a way to pursue Zen study. Robert Aitken and Philip Kapleau made their way to Nakagawa Soen's monastery, and Walter Nowick became a close student, and eventually a successor of Zuigan Goto-roshi. Nowick had studied music at Julliard and was able to support himself during long years of intensive study by playing concerts and teaching piano, both to private students and at Kyoto Women's University.

Mrs. Sasaki hoped that the Western students who trained in Japan would be able to bring true Rinzai Zen back to the West, "equipped with Western-trained intellects and a wide-open Zen eye." They would also (again hopefully) be in a position to "clearly distinguish Zen's eternal essence, valid for men of all times and all places, from the cultural patterns in which it was now embedded."

For this, as well as for the study of Zen itself, it would be necessary to translate the major Rinzai Zen texts from both Chinese and Japanese masters. A cross-cultural team of dedicated scholar-practitioners was called for: Westerners with long experience in Zen training as well as a knowledge of Chinese and Japanese, working alongside Asians also trained in Zen, and with a knowledge of European languages. This approach had in fact been successfully used by Indian, Chinese and Tibetans in the great Buddhist translation projects of the past, but nothing like it had ever been attempted in the modern era.

To begin the work Mrs. Sasaki first recruited Professor Yoshitaka Iriya, Head of the Department of Chinese Literature at Nagoya University, and the leading scholar in the field of colloquial T'ang and Sung Chinese. Though Professor Iriya was said to be totally uninterested in Buddhism, Mrs. Sasaki convinced him to take on the post of director of research. In the years to come the translation team included Philip Yampolsky, a Buddhist scholar from Columbia, Seizan Yanagida of Hanazono University and Burton Watson, also of Columbia. For a time the secretary and assistant was Gary Snyder, a young poet and graduate student in Oriental languages from Berkeley.

In addition to English translations of basic Zen texts, koan and classical Chinese poetry collections used in Zen study, the staff worked on a grammar of T'ang-Sung colloquial Chinese, indexes and a Zen dictionary. With so many hands involved and with such a scrupulous regard for scholarly accuracy, the work went slowly. But Mrs. Sasaki was determined. It was necessary, as she said, "To know the Zen of the past for the sake of the Zen of the future."

VII

One afternoon in 1953, a young poet named Allen Ginsberg visited the First Zen Institute which was then still housed in Mrs. Sasaki's elegant uptown apartment. Mrs. Sasaki was in Japan at the time, and Ginsberg occupied himself by perusing the Zen paintings, records and books in the library. But he did not stay very long: the whole atmosphere of the place made him uncomfortable; it was, as he remembered years later, "intimidating—like a university club." Ginsberg had only recently discovered Buddhism and Chinese philosophy in the New York Public Library. "I had only the faintest idea that there was so much of a kulcheral heritage, so easy to get at thru book upon book of reproduction," he wrote Neal Cassady in California.

He had also begun to read, he wrote Cassady, "a little about their mystique and philosophy which I never did from a realistic viewpoint before. . . . I am working eastward from Japan and have begun to familiarize myself with Zen *Buddhism* thru a book (Philosophical Library Pub.) by one D.T. Suzuki (outstanding 89 yr. old authority now at Columbia who I will I suppose go see for interesting talk)."

What impressed Ginsberg most in his reading of Suzuki was the description of satori. Five years earlier Ginsberg had heard a voice he took to be William Blake's reciting "Ah! Sunflower" in his Harlem apartment, while outside the blue sky and ancient crumbling buildings seemed alive with "the presence of a vast, immortal, intelligent hand." The vision had left him at once inspired and shaken. Satori, he now thought, "seemed to be the right fitting word for what I had actually experienced so that I got interested in Buddhism."

Jack Kerouac also came to Buddhism in a library. He had just finished writing *The Subterraneans*, a novel about an unhappy, drastic love affair, in three benzedrine-powered days and nights. "I didn't know what to do," he told Al Aronowitz for his *New York Post* series on the beat generation in 1959. "I went home and just sat in my room, hurting. I was suffering, you know, from the grief of losing a love, even though I really wanted to lose it.

"Well, I went to the library to read Thoreau. I said, 'I'm going to cut out from civilization, and go back and live in the woods like Thoreau,' and I started to read Thoreau and he talked about Hindu philosophy. So

I put Thoreau down and I took out, accidentally, *The Life of Buddha* by Ashvagosa [sic]."

That was the beginning. In the years to come, as Kerouac drifted back and forth across America, the pages of his unpublished novels heavy in his pack, his interest in Buddhism would continue to grow. The first of the Buddha's Four Noble Truths especially (all existence is suffering) gave him a philosophical basis for understanding his life and the lives he observed all around him. While visiting the Cassadys in California he found and devoured Dwight Goddard's *Buddhist Bible* in the San Jose library. He also read all the sutras he could lay his hands on, as well as Patanjali, the *Vedas*, Lao-Tzu and Confucius. He took extensive notes while reading the *Buddhist Bible*, and when he typed it all up he found that he had more than a hundred pages. He called it *Some of the Dharma*, and thought of it as kind of an ongoing study for both himself and Ginsberg, who was now in Yucatan.

Back East he moved into his mother's house in Richmond, New York and read the *Diamond Sutra* every day. He began memorizing and reciting sutras, and he carried Goddard's *Buddhist Bible* with him everywhere, even on the subway. He began to discipline himself in meditation, first brewing a cup of green tea, then locking the door to his bedroom (his mother disapproved) and finally sitting down on a cushion, painfully crossing his legs for twenty minutes or so—and then forcing himself to remain seated another minute. He now considered the football he had played in high school and Columbia as preparation for his new life.

> Practicing meditation and realizing that existence is a dream [he wrote Ginsberg] is an athletic, physical accomplishment. Now I know why I was an athlete, to learn perfect physical relaxation, smooth strength of strong muscles hanging ready for Nirvana, the great power that runs from the brow to the slope of shoulders down the arms to the delicately joined hands in Dhyana, the hidden power of gentle breathing in the silence.

In the spring of 1955 he went south to North Carolina where his sister's family lived. During the day he cut wood and cleared land. At night he sat up late at the kitchen table after everyone else had gone to bed and worked on the three Buddhist books he now had going: *Some of the Dharma* (which had become an elaborate scrapbook of musings, *pensees*, sutra extracts, aphorisms, haikus), *Wake Up*, a biography of the Buddha, and *Buddha Tells Us*, a collection of translations "of works done by great Rimbauvian Frenchmen in the Abbeys of Tibet." None of it was publishable of course, though The Philosophical Library did offer to bring out the translations collected in *Buddha Tells Us*, if Kerouac could guarantee sales of six hundred copies at $3.50 each.

Then in July of 1955 his fortunes began to turn. Malcolm Cowley finally convinced Viking to bring out *On The Road*.

VIII

Allen Ginsberg first read *Howl* at the Six Gallery in San Francisco in March of 1955. Kerouac sat on the side of the tiny platform, drinking wine, and "giving out little wows and yesses of approval and even whole sentences of comment with nobody's invitation but in the general gaiety nobody's disapproval either."

The Six Gallery reading became, in retrospect, the beginning of what journalists would soon call the San Francisco Renaissance. To the poets who read along with Ginsberg—Michael McClure, Philip Lamantia, Philip Whalen, Gary Snyder, with Kenneth Rexroth as master of ceremonies—the response to the reading marked the recognition that they were part of a new and growing community of like-minded people.

Kenneth Rexroth, the elder statesman of the San Francisco literary scene and a self-taught translator of Chinese and Japanese poetry, had brought the poets together by suggesting that Allen Ginsberg look up Gary Snyder in Berkeley. Ginsberg and Snyder hit it off right away, discovering a common interest in the works of William Carlos Williams and Pound. As Ginsberg told Kerouac, he thought that Snyder was the only person he had met on the West Coast "with any truly illuminated intelligence."

To the Easterners Kerouac and Ginsberg, Snyder embodied the mythical genius of the Far West. He had spent most of his childhood on a small farm outside Seattle. By the age of thirteen he had started hiking around the high country of the Cascades. Around that same time, he wandered into a room filled with Chinese landscapes at the Seattle Art Museum. "They blew my mind," he remembers. "My shock of recognition was very simple: 'It looks like the Cascades.' The waterfalls, the pines, the clouds, the mist looked a lot like the northwest United States."

On scholarship at Reed, Snyder studied anthropology, linguistics and literature, with special attention to American Indian studies. He had become aware of Buddhism—along with Hinduism, Taoism and Confucianism—around 1949, and first heard about Zen from a Reed student who had briefly been a student of Senzaki's. In the fall of 1951, on his way to graduate school at Indiana University, he came across a copy of D.T. Suzuki's *Essays in Zen Buddhism* in a San Francisco bookstore. He bought a copy, put it in his rucksack and continued hitching on.

Suzuki's *Essays* gave Snyder a sense of how Taoism, Buddhism and Hinduism were interrelated. "The convergence that I really found exciting," he remembers, "was the Mahayana Buddhist wisdom-oriented line as it developed in China and assimilated the older Taoist tradition. It was that very precise cultural meeting that also coincides with the highest period of Chinese poetry—the early and middle T'ang Dynasty Zen masters and the poets who are their contemporaries and in many cases friends—that was fascinating."

Snyder taught himself to sit by reading and looking at statues of buddhas and bodhisattvas. He corrected his posture as he went along, since he discovered that sitting became painful, and his breathing didn't feel right, if he wasn't sitting correctly. From the very beginning, he felt that sitting was "a completely natural act." After all, he reasoned, both primitive people and animals were "capable of simply just being for long hours of time. . . . I wasn't expecting instantaneous satori to hit me just because I got my legs right," he says. "I found it a good way to be."

After a semester at Indiana, Snyder left to work as a fire lookout in Washington. The job suited him perfectly. "For those seeking jobs which leave time for study and zazen," Snyder wrote to the First Zen Institute's *Zen Notes* in 1955, "I can recommend a lookout as an excellent place for anybody with yamabushi tendencies and some physical and mental toughness. There are lakes, meadows, flowers, cliffs, glaciers, many bear and deer, and clouds both below and above you. I found an excellent period for zazen between sunrise, 4:30 A.M. and the radio check in at 8:00 A.M."

In 1952 Snyder left Indiana and enrolled in the Oriental Languages department at the University of California at Berkeley. Having discovered that the T'ang Dynasty tradition of Zen he had read about in Suzuki was "still alive and well in Japan," he had decided to work on the two languages—Japanese and T'ang Chinese vernacular—that would enable him to experience it first hand.

When Ginsberg and Kerouac met Snyder he was living in Berkeley in a small shack about a mile from the backyard cottage Ginsberg (briefly a graduate student in English) shared with Kerouac. In *Dharma Bums*, Kerouac described visiting Snyder (as "Japhy Ryder") a few days after the Six Gallery reading. Of Snyder's cottage, Kerouac wrote,

> nothing in it but typical Japhy appurtenances that showed his belief in the simple monastic life—no chairs at all, not even one sentimental rocking chair, but just straw mats. In the corner was his famous rucksack with cleaned-up pots and pans all fitting into one another in a compact unit and all tied and put away inside a knotted-up blue bandana. . . . He had a slew of orange crates all filled with beautiful scholarly books, some of them in Oriental languages, all the great sutras, comments on sutras, the complete works of D.T. Suzuki and a fine quadruple-volume edition of Japanese haikus. . . . A few orange crates made his table, on which, one late sunny afternoon as I arrived, was steaming a peaceful cup of tea at his side as he bent his serious head to the Chinese signs of the poet Han Shan.

(Snyder's translations of the Chinese Zen mountain-recluse Han Shan's poems were later published as *Cold Mountain Poems*.)

Kerouac, Ginsberg, Snyder and Philip Whalen, a poet who had been with Snyder at Reed, spent a lot of time back and forth between the two houses—"having dinner together, or just sort of hanging around together there in the yard and writing and talking and drinking wine and having a good time," Whalen remembers. Everybody was reading R. H. Blyth's four-volume collection of haikus, and trading back and forth modern American versions of their own. In Ginsberg's phrase "We had 'dharma confrontation' with koan and spontaneous tongue."

Except for Snyder, who sat regularly on his rolled-up sleeping bag for half an hour or so every morning, and Whalen who sat occasionally, the Buddhism was mostly literary. Kerouac's sitting remained idiosyncratic. "He was incapable of sitting for more than a few minutes at a time," remembers Whalen. "His knees were ruined by playing football. . . . They wouldn't bend without great pain, I guess. He never learned to sit in that proper sort of meditation position. Even had he been able to, his head wouldn't have stopped long enough for him to endure it. He was too nervous. But he thought it was a good idea."

Ginsberg was still looking backward to the kind of visionary experience that had overwhelmed him in Harlem years before. "Nobody knew much about zazen," he said later. "It was a great tragedy. If somebody had just taught us how to sit, straighten the spine, follow the breath, it would've been a great discovery."

On Friday nights Snyder and Whalen had begun attending a study group at the Jodo Shinshu Berkeley Buddhist Church. The discussion concentrated on basic Buddhist philosophy. The study group was made up of the Reverend Imamura and his wife Jane, Bob and Beverly Jackson, a high school teacher and his wife who had both studied with

Senzaki in L.A., Alex Wayman, a graduate student in Tibetan at Berkeley, and Will Peterson, the printmaker and editor of the group's magazine, the *Berkeley Bussei*, and, as Gary Snyder remembers, "a number of really sharp Japanese-American Nisei and Sansei." Kerouac and Ginsberg dropped by a number of times to read their poems, some of which were printed in the *Bussei*.

It was at the study group that Snyder first met Alan Watts, who had come over from San Francisco to give a talk one Friday night. Watts had made the West Coast his home, having left the Episcopal church and his wife behind. He had begun to teach at the American Academy of Asian Studies—which was, as Watts described it in his autobiography, "one of the principal roots of what later came to be known, in the early sixties, as the San Francisco Renaissance." Frederic Spiegelburg had been its director until 1952, when the Academy had run out of funds, and Watts took over as chief administrator. The faculty consisted of Tokwan Tonda, a Japanese trained in Tibet, who brought a Tibetan woodblock Tripitaka to the small library, Haridas Chaudhuri, a professor of philosophy from the University of Calcutta, and Judith Tyberg, Sanskritist, and (like Spiegelburg and Chaudhuri) a follower of Sri Aurobindo. Visiting lecturers included Buddhists such as D.T. Suzuki, G.P. Malalasekera, Bhikkhu Pannananda from Thailand, the Zen master Asahina Sogen, the Thera Dharmawara from Cambodia and Ruth Fuller Sasaki "who entranced the whole student body with her formal and definitive lecture on the use of koan in Zen meditation." Watts introduced Snyder to Mrs. Sasaki, with the result that she arranged a scholarship-grant for him to study Rinzai Zen in Japan and work as a secretary with the translation team at the First Zen Institute of America in Japan.

Kerouac remained something of a loner amid the constant talk and partying. Few if any of his closest friends felt the way he did about Buddhism. Ginsberg was put off by Kerouac's gloomy harping on the First Noble Truth. "I resented and resisted the nothingness," he remembers. Snyder thought Kerouac was an important writer and was impressed that he had studied so much Buddhism on his own. Still, there were important differences in the way the two men saw things. They were, as Jack wrote, "two strange dissimilar monks on the same path." Kerouac insisted on the primacy of the First Noble Truth, and he thought Snyder's Mahayana Zen tricky and intellectual.

In 1956 Kerouac and Snyder shared a little cabin on the slopes of Mount Tamalpais. It was here, while he was waiting to go up to Washington as a fire lookout, that Kerouac wrote *The Scripture of Golden Eternity*, the clearest and most direct expression of his Catholic Buddhism. Years later he remembered the circumstances of composition: "Gary Snyder said, 'All right, Kerouac, it's about time for you to write a scripture.' " He wrote it in pencil, for once violating his own rule against revision, "because it was a scripture. I had no right to be spontaneous."

The Scripture is Kerouac at his best, and one of the most successful attempts yet to catch emptiness, nonattainment and egolessness in the net of American poetic language. *The Scripture of the Golden Eternity* is tinged, rather than colored, by occasional Catholic images of saints, heaven and roses, but for the most part its sixty-four verses, paragraphs teetering breathtakingly between prose and poetry, might have been written by a lyrical American Nagarjuna, the double and quadruple negations laying bare an empty, shining golden eternity, in which "nothing will be acquired, at last."

Kerouac wrote in (22):

> Stare deep into the world before you as if it were/the void: innumerable holy ghosts, bhuddies/and savior gods there hide, smiling. All the/atoms emitting light inside wavehood, there is/no personal separation of any of it. A Hummingbird/can come into a house and a hawk will not: so rest/and be assured. While looking for the light, you/may suddenly be devoured by the darkness/and find the true light.

IX

Gary Snyder sailed for Japan on May 15, 1956. Mrs. Sasaki introduced him to Isshu Miura-roshi, and he spent his first year in Japan at Shokokuji, serving as the roshi's personal attendant, cooking, studying Japanese and teaching the roshi English. When Miura-roshi accompanied Mrs. Sasaki to visit the First Zen Institute in New York he instructed Snyder to continue his studies with Sesso Oda-roshi, Zuigan Goto-roshi's successor at Daitokuji.

Mrs. Sasaki had been very busy in Japan, but she had not had an easy time of it. Goto-roshi wanted her to return to America and Europe as a Zen missionary, but Mrs. Sasaki had stuck by her conviction that her proper role consisted in completing the immense tasks of translation she had begun, as well as in providing a place for Westerners to prepare themselves for traditional Rinzai practice. She was, in any case, a rather aloof person and public proselytizing was not her forte. Goto-roshi, however, did not expect a sanzen student to disobey his instructions, and he expressed his displeasure. For five years Mrs. Sasaki did not attend sanzen, though she did continue to sit zazen and to send the roshi the appropriate gifts on the appropriate occasions. There was much gossip about all this on both sides of the Pacific, none of it making her work any easier. Then, unexpectedly, Goto-roshi sent Mrs. Sasaki a note thanking her for one of the gifts and inviting her for tea. His anger had vanished, and within a year Mrs. Sasaki was once more attending sanzen.

Mrs. Sasaki was ordained a priest at Daitokuji in 1958. She was sponsored by Oda-roshi, since Goto-roshi had retired. Everything was carried out in the most traditional manner, except for the fact that Mrs. Sasaki did not, as was customary, have her head shaved.

X

In 1955 Nyogen Senzaki returned to Japan for the first and last time. Senzaki visited Soyen Shaku's grave at Kamakura, but he stayed mostly at Ryutakuji, avoiding the Rinzai Zen establishment, as stubborn and independent in Japan as he had been all the years in America. It had been nearly half a century since Senzaki had left Japan for San Francisco with Soyen Shaku, and though he had grown used to American ways, he never lost his emotional tie to his homeland.

The monks at Ryutakuji were all curious about their roshi's friend from America, and one of them, a young man named Tai Shimano (now Eido Tai Shimano-roshi, Zen master of the Zen Studies Society in New York), remembers that he was very moved by "this elderly man, with his exotic looking silver hair, his vital voice, and the strangely accented Japanese" with which he delivered a talk to the assembled monks.

Through Senzaki's close connection with Soen-roshi, a number of Americans, such as Robert Aitken and Philip Kapleau, had appeared at the gates of Ryutakuji. Because Tai Shimano knew some English, it became his job to explain the details of monastery life to visiting foreigners. Tai Shimano himself was a product of Rinzai monastery training. Born into a samurai family, he had learned the *Heart Sutra* by the age of nine, and the ways of the *sodo*—the monk's training hall— were second nature to him. He was, he remembers, "constantly astonished" by the requests of the foreign students, and by the great difference between "East and West, monastic and lay life."

After the closing ceremony of the summer sesshin of 1957, Soen-roshi summoned Tai Shimano to his room. Senzaki was growing old, said Soen, and he needed an attendant. Soen asked Tai Shimano if he would like to go to America for about a year. "It would be a wonderful experience," Soen assured him, and Tai Shimano thought it over for two days. Soen had occasionally talked about American Zen, how he considered it fresher and more enthusiastic than Japanese Zen. Finally, Tai Shimano decided to go and he spent a full day writing Senzaki. Senzaki wrote back that Mrs. Tanahashi, one of his students from Los Angeles was visiting Japan, and suggested that Tai Shimano and she meet. "When she arrived," Tai Shimano remembers, "the three of us sat together in the roshi's room. Soen-roshi made ceremonial tea. We shared one bowl. Then we took each others hands. It was our silent wish that we might be able to meet this way some day in America."

On May 7, 1958 a telephone call came during morning zazen. Soen-roshi left his seat to answer it and did not return. After morning sanzen, Soen told Tai Shimano that Senzaki had died that morning. They knelt and chanted the Four Vows together.

Senzaki's last rites, like his life, were conducted in his own way. His body was laid out in a mortuary filled with flowers, and twelve Japanese priests chanted and placed a memorial tablet on a shrine that had been set up for the occasion. That much was conventional. Then someone announced that a talk by Senzaki would be played. A record table had been set up on top of a piano, and from it the mourners were startled to hear Senzaki's voice, loud and clear, first in Japanese, quite cheerful, talking and laughing. Then a woman named Seiko-an read Senzaki's "My Last Words," a statement that he had first written in 1936 and since revised many times. During the reading, Senzaki could be heard correcting Seiko-an's pronunciation. Clearly he knew exactly how he wanted it done.

> I imagined that I was going away from this world, leaving all you behind and I wrote my last words in English. Friends in the Dharma, be satisfied with your own heads. Do not put on any false heads above your own. Then, minute after minute, watch your step closely. These are my last words to you.
>
> [He went on, since, as he said, he felt that he owed some explanation.] Each head of yours is the noblest thing in the whole universe. No God, no Buddha, no Sage, no Master can reign over it. Rinzai said, "If you master your own situation, wherever you stand is the land of Truth. How many of our fellow beings can prove the truthfulness of these words by actions."
>
> Keep your head cool but your feet warm. Do not let sentiments sweep your feet. Well trained Zen students should breathe with

> their feet, not with their lungs. This means that you should forget your lungs and only be conscious with your feet while breathing. The head is the sacred part of your body. Let it do its own work but do not make any "monkey business" with it.
>
> Remember me as a monk, nothing else. I do not belong to any sect or any cathedral. None of them should send me a promoted priest's rank or anything of the sort. I like to be free from such trash and die happily.

Then people lined up to offer incense. "The halls, the side rooms, every stitch of space . . . was filled with people," wrote Katherine-Edson Mershon. "People of all kinds and descriptions, races and creeds. That to me was really the tribute."

Senzaki's ashes were placed in the Japanese cemetery in east Los Angeles. Within sight of his stone stood the memorial and the graves of the soldiers of the 442nd Nisei Combat Battalion. Soen's calligraphy of Senzaki's name had been carved on the face of the stone, and on the back, in English, Senzaki's admonition to "Keep your head cool but your feet warm. . . ." He had said he would bury his bones in America, and he had done just that.

Soen had been present at Senzaki's funeral, and afterwards he led two memorial sesshins. Robert Aitken who served as *jishi* (attendent) for the first sesshin (Soen-roshi doubled as *jikijitsu*—monk in charge of the meditation hall) believes this to have been the first full seven-day sesshin in America conducted in a regular manner, though it was still somewhat irregular. "Everybody found it very difficult," he remembers, "everybody was unaccustomed to the regimen; it was hard to learn not to talk and to keep their minds centered."

Soen-roshi returned to Japan a few months after Senzaki's funeral. Aitken had divorced his first wife and had married Anne Hopkins, whom he had met at the Happy Valley School in Ojai where he had been an English teacher, and she an administrator. The couple now returned to Hawaii. They started a second-hand bookshop in Honolulu's Chinatown, specializing in Hawaiiana and Asian religion. Aitken kept a list of all the people who had bought books on Buddhism, which meant that they had a ready-made mailing list when Soen gave them the go-ahead to start a Zen sitting group. Four people attended the first meeting in the Aitken's living room in October of 1959.

Gary Snyder returned briefly to America in 1958. He had spent the last few years training with Oda-roshi at Daitokuji, and when he moved back into the shack above Locke McCorkle's house in Mill Valley, a small informal *zazenkai*, a zazen group, took shape. Gary sat regularly in the evenings and he was joined by a few friends—Claude Dahlenberg, who had been the janitor at the Academy of Asian Studies, the poet Lew Welch, a roommate of Snyder's and Whalen's at Reed, and Albert Saijo, who had come up from Los Angelos where he had studied with Senzaki. The cabin came to be known as "Marin-an," a Chinese-Japanese-American pun. "Ma" in Chinese is horse; "rin" is a grove; "an" is Japanese for hermitage. Since there were horses pastured around it and it was located in Marin County, they called it "Horse Grove Hermitage."

When Snyder went to Japan, Albert Saijo and Lew Welch maintained the little temple zendo. "I agree with you about the importance of the zendo," Welch wrote Snyder, "[I] will conduct the sesshins with absolute punctuality and strict form and dignity even if no one shows but me. All the rest of American Zen is talk." Marin-an lasted only a short time, and then Albert Saijo, Lew Welch, Bill McNeill and Phil Whalen—and later Joanne Kyger and Claude Dahlenberg—moved into East-West House, a large turn-of-the-century wooden building on the corner of Post and Buchanan in San Francisco, right around the corner from the Soto Zen Mission (where Tom Fields and Dahlenberg would later meet and study with its new priest, Shunryu Suzuki). Around Thanksgiving, 1959, Jack Kerouac showed up after appearing on the Steve Allen Show, and Lew and Albert drove him back East in Lew's new Willys Jeepster. They traded haiku all across the country, collected years later in *Trip Trap*.

When they reached New York, they found Ginsberg and Orlovsky in their apartment on East Second Street, hit the Cedar Bar and the Five Spot packed for Ornette Coleman. They even went to The First Zen Institute for an evening service. "The Buddha on the altar was offered marble cake and an orange," remembers Saijo. "We were served marble cake and tea."

A special "Zen" edition of the *Chicago Review* had appeared in the summer of 1958. The issue included Snyder's essay "Spring *Sesshin* at Sokoku-ji," Alan Watts's "Beat Zen, Square Zen, and Zen," "Meditation in the Woods" by Jack Kerouac, D.T. Suzuki's translation from the Chinese *Sayings of Rinzai*, Ruth Fuller Sasaki's translation (also from the Chinese) "Chia-Shan Receives the Transmission from Boatman Priest Te-Ch'eng," a "Mentorgarten Dialogue" by Nyogen Senzaki, and articles by Dr. Shinichi Hisamatsu, Akihiso Kondo (a Tokyo psychoanalyst), "Zen and the Work of Wittengenstein," by Paul Wienpahl, a poem of Philip Whalen's, and one of Franz Kline's black-and-white abstractions—all the emerging lines of the new American Zen gathered together.

Snyder's essay gave a bird's-eye view of what went on during a week of intensive zazen: "One's legs may hurt during long sitting. . . . The mind must simply be placed elsewhere." "Zen aims at freedom," wrote Snyder in describing how the jikijitsu might knock anyone not seated properly right off his cushion, "but its practice is discipline."

It was just this paradox which provided Alan Watts with the basis for his essay. "Beat Zen, Square Zen, and Zen" could only have been written by Watts. After all, as he would write in his autobiography, "it had often been said, perhaps with truth," that his "easy and free-floating attitude to Zen was largely responsible for the notorious 'Zen Boom' which flourished among artists and pseudointellectuals in the late 1950's, and led on to the frivolous 'beat Zen' of Kerouac's *Dharma Bums*, of Franz Kline's black and white abstractions, and John Cage's silent concerts."

Watts himself was in many ways more Taoist than Buddhist, and his essay located the roots of Zen in T'ang Dynasty China and "the old Chinese masters steeped in Taoism." He quoted Lin-chi: "Just be ordinary and nothing special. Eat your food, move your bowels, pass water, and when you're tired go and lie down. The ignorant will laugh at me but the wise will understand."

Having established that Zen was the creation of China and not of Japan, Watts could take aim at both the extremes—beat and square. The spirit of Lin-chi's words, he commented, is far from the strict boarding-school style of Japanese monasteries. As for the Western followers of official Japanese Zen—who were now studying in Japan and would soon return with "certificates to hang on the wall"—they could be considered "square" because they were seeking "the *right* spiritual experience, a *satori* which will receive the stamp (*inka*) of approved and established authority."

Watts admitted Beat Zen to be "a complex phenomenon"—ranging from a use of Zen for justifying sheer caprice in art, literature and life to a very forceful social criticism and "digging of the universe" found "in the poetry of Ginsberg and Snyder, and rather unevenly in Kerouac." (As an astute editor footnoted: "Mr. Snyder seems to have gone square. Witness his essay, page 41.") "But," as Watts said, "Beat Zen is always a shade too self-conscious, too subjective, and too strident to have the flavor of Zen."

Not that Watts was overly concerned about either of the extremes, for he took "the experience of awakening which truly constitutes Zen" to be "too timeless and universal to be injured." Hopefully, in any case, both square and beat Zen would "so complement and rub against each other that an amazingly pure and lively Zen will arise from the hassle."

But in the end it finally came to one thing: "If you really want to spend some years in a Japanese monastery, there is no earthly reason why you shouldn't. Or if you wish to spend some time hopping freight cars and digging Charlie Parker, it's a free country." To that characteristically American conclusion, Watts could not resist adding another, equally characteristic Chinese one:

> In the landscape of spring there is neither better
>   nor worse;
> The flowering branches grow naturally, some long,
>   some short.

Gary Snyder returned again to Japan in the spring of 1958. For the next seven years he would attend sesshins and live periodically in the monastery with Oda-roshi, whom he later described as "an especially gentle and quiet man—an extremely subtle man, by far the subtlest mind I've ever been in contact with." Oda-roshi's teishos were delivered "in so soft a voice nobody could hear him." ("Several years after Oda roshi had died," Snyder later told an interviewer, "one of the head monks, with whom I had become very close, said to me, 'You know those lectures that Oda-roshi gave that we couldn't hear? I'm beginning to hear them now.' ")

While Snyder was working right in the heart of what Watts would have called square Zen, Kerouac was back in New York, finally having achieved the success and recognition he had dreamed of so many years before. *On the Road* had at last—ten years after it was written—been published to critical acclaim. Kerouac was celebrated, ridiculed, parodied and sought after. By all accounts the sudden fame did not serve him well. He drank increasingly and even with a best-seller to his credit, was not able to find a publisher for *Mexico City Blues*, *The Subterraneans*, *Dr. Sax* or *Visions of Neal*. What his publisher wanted was another *On the Road*, and the editors at Viking suggested that Kerouac write something especially for his generation, in simple prose sentences, telling "what it was all about." Kerouac complied by writing *The Dharma Bums* in ten days and nights at his mother's house in Florida, in a straightforward, fairly conventional style. Just as *On the Road* had been built around Neal Cassady, so *The Dharma Bums* was constructed around Gary Snyder.

The novel protrayed Snyder and Kerouac's friendship, and the poetry-and-buddhist milieu of the time. But it also contained a prophetic vision that Snyder had passed on to Kerouac, a vision of the next generation, waiting, like Maitreya, for the coming sixties:

> I see a vision of a great rucksack revolution [Japhy says], thoussands or even millions of young Americans wandering around with rucksacks, going up to mountains to pray, making children laugh, and old men glad, making young girls happy, and old girls happier, all of 'em Zen lunatics who go about writing poems that happen to appear in their heads for no reason, and also by being kind, and also by strange unexpected acts keep giving visions of eternal freedom to everybody and to all living creatures. We'll have a floating zendo, a series of monasteries for people to go and monastate and meditate in . . . wild gangs of pure holy men getting together to drink and talk and pray, think of the waves of salvation can flow out of nights like that, and finally have women too, wives, small huts with religious families, like the old days of the Puritans. . . .

The day *The Dharma Bums* was published, Kerouac, Ginsberg and Peter Orlovsky were on their way to an elegant penthouse party in honor of Kerouac's new novel, when Kerouac stepped into a phone booth and called up D.T. Suzuki. Kerouac said he would like to stop by for a visit, and Suzuki asked when he wanted to come by. "RIGHT NOW!" Kerouac yelled into the receiver, and Suzuki said, "O.K." Kerouac, Ginsberg and Orlovsky all trooped over to the brownstone on West Ninety-fourth that Suzuki shared with the Okamuras.

"I rang Mr. Suzuki's door and he did not answer," Kerouac wrote in a reminiscence published in the *Berkeley Bussei*, the magazine of the Berkeley Young Buddhist Association, in 1960,

> —suddenly I decided to ring it three times, firmly and slowly, and then he came—he was a small man coming slowly through an old house with panelled wood walls and many books—he had long eyelashes, as everyone knows, which put me in the mind of the saying in the Sutras that the Dharma, like a bush, is slow to take root but once it has taken root it grows huge and firm and can't be hauled up from the ground except by a golden giant whose name is not Tathagata—anyway, Doctor Suzuki made us some green tea, very thick and soupy—he had precisely what idea of what place I should sit, and where my two other friends should sit, the chairs already arranged—he himself sat behind a table and looked at us silently, nodding—I said in a loud voice (because he had told us he was a little deaf) "Why did Bodhidharma come from the West?"—He made no reply—He said, "You three young men sit here quietly & write haikus while I go make some green tea"—He brought us the green tea in cracked old soupbowls of some sort—He told us not to

forget about the tea—when we left, he pushed us out the door but once we were out on the sidewalk he began giggling at us and pointing his finger and saying "Don't forget the tea!"—I said "I would like to spend the rest of my life with you"—He held up his finger and said

"Sometime."

CHAPTER TWELVE

AND ROUND: THE SIXTIES

I

"Where there is practice there is enlightenment." This above all was the message Shunryu Suzuki-roshi brought to America. To be sure, it was not as simple as it sounded—as even the most casual glance at Dogen's *Shobogenzo* would show. But it was direct. It cut everything away that might prevent getting on with the work at hand—the past and the future, the fear of failure and the hope of success. To daydream about the wonderful person one will become when enlightened is not true practice, to bemoan the past that had led to one's wretched present is not true practice. True practice might be big enough to encompass past and future, but it could happen only in the present moment, this breath, going out, coming in, "like a swinging door," as the roshi put it.

So they sat. The roshi walked around silently behind them correcting posture, tilting a chin in, moving a shoulder a little to the left or right, adjusting the fingers that formed the mudra, left over right, thumbs barely touching, so that only the thinnest tissue of paper could pass through, just so, not too loose, not too tense. The Zen masters of the previous generation, Senzaki and Sokei-an, had not given the physical posture so much attention. Their students had sat in chairs, they were older people, their bones were stiff, their muscles tense; somehow it had never seemed possible that they could *sit*, imperturbable. But these youths of the sixties had dropped the old rigidities: they had practiced yoga, they ate brown rice, they wandered through the woods. They had done all that and suspected—at least the ones who made their way to the Soto Zen Mission in San Francisco—that all those trips were not enough, or, actually (as they would start to say after a little Zen) *too* much. It was all extra. Just to sit. Just to eat. Just to sleep. Just to work. Just to carry water and cut wood, as the old Chinese master said—that's the miracle.

II

Shunryu Suzuki flew from Tokyo to San Francisco on May 23, 1959. A photograph taken at the departure shows him waving happily in the bustling airport, a bouquet of flowers in one hand, a package in the other, wearing his black robe and sandals over white *tabis*. His face was lit by a smile curved like a waxing moon. He looked completely at home in the international bare modern spareness of the departure area, and very happy.

Shunryu Suzuki was met at the San Francisco airport by the congregation of Sokoji—for the most part elderly middle class Japanese-Americans in neat dark suits and matronly dresses. Sokoji itself ("Soko" meaning San Francisco, "ji" temple) had been founded in 1934 by Hosen Isobe, a Soto Zen missionary who had previously established temples in Korea, Hawaii and Los Angeles. Shunryu Suzuki was the sixth priest to arrive from Soto headquarters in Japan.

The temple—which was also designated as a Soto Zen Mission—was located in an ornate wooden building at 1881 Bush Street, in that part of San Francisco known as Japantown. The building, Sephardic-Moorish in design, with a big soaring tower and arabesque-like carvings on the facade, had been originally built as a synagogue during the 1890s. Next door, in a smoky, windowless room, was the neighborhood go club—a kind of unofficial community center for the men who played there every evening until their children came to tell them it was time to come home. Sokoji had nearly been lost during the war when all its members had been interned, but they had somehow managed to continue the mortgage payments from the camps, and when the war was over, the building was still theirs.

For most of its existence Sokoji, like most of the Asian-American Buddhist temples, had remained, in Alan Watts's words, "a circumscribed service center for the Japanese community" which "gave no substantial alternative to what was already being offered in the Presbyterian and Methodist churches." Things had begun to change with Shunryu Suzuki's predecessors, Hodo Tobase and his assistant Kazumitsu Kato. Tobase taught some Americans calligraphy, and Kato and Watts (teaching then at the American Academy of Asian Studies) shared their love of good cooking and spent hours reading the *Rinzai Roku* and Bankei together.

Even before Shunryu Suzuki's arrival a few Americans had begun attending services at Sokoji. One of these, a member of the First Zen Institute of America in New York, had read lectures by Sokei-an, the Institute's founder, to a small group on Friday nights, a practice which was discontinued when Shunryu Suzuki arrived. "We have a new priest," he wrote his friends back East, "who speaks English fairly well, and he is a grand person. Everyone at our temple is more than happy to have him as a teacher." They sat facing the wall, "all lights out except the candle on the altar. Sensei walks around with a big stick—quite a few get good whacks." There were between twelve and thirty people sitting together on Wednesday nights when the letter was written in 1961, several of them "boys that look like beatniks with beards, sweat shirts, and some with sandals, but I must say they seem sincere."

Shunryu Suzuki himself was quoted by a journalist as saying, "My first young person was a girl who turned up and said, 'My husband wants to go to Japan to study Zen.' I replied, 'Instead, he should stay here and see. Why don't you study too.?' "

In any case, within a few years the number of Americans who had come to Sokoji had increased dramatically. To all of them he said the same thing: "I sit at five-thirty every morning. You are welcome to join me."

Like most Japanese Zen priests, Shunryu Suzuki was following his father's profession. The position was, in effect, almost hereditary. But unlike most priests in his position, Shunryu Suzuki had not become his father's disciple. Instead he "left home" at the age of thirteen to study with Gyakuju So-on-roshi, a disciple of his father, and a strict disciplinarian. Out of five disciples during this period, Shunryu Suzuki was the only one not to leave. At the age of nineteen he completed high school at a school connected to Komazawa Buddhist University, and then went on to the university itself. In his junior year he boarded with an Englishwoman, a Mrs. Ransome, who had tutored the crown prince. Mrs. Ransome did not think much of Buddhism, and she liked to tease her boarder about his religion, but by the time he graduated and continued his Buddhist training at Eiheiji, Mrs. Ransome had become his first student. It was at this time that Suzuki's desire to go to America and teach first manifested. He felt, as Richard Baker, one of his closest disciples said, "that Buddhism needed some fresh opportunity, some place where people's minds weren't made up about Buddhism." But Shunryu Suzuki's teacher did not like the idea, and so he asked, as a kind of second choice, if he could go to Hokkaido, which was a frontier region only recently settled. When he was refused again, Suzuki settled down in Japan, became the priest of a temple called Zounji, and then, after his teacher died, of Rinso-in, his teacher's temple.

During the Second World War Shunryu Suzuki was conspicuous by his refusal to help the government inspire the populace with the proper samurai spirit. (Japanese soldiers were often sent to temples for a quick course in zazen before being sent off to the front.) Instead, Suzuki formed a local discussion group that discussed the implications of militarism. He never spoke much about what had happened during the war, but he apparently continued to speak out and even publish some of his talks. When the war was over and the occupation army revoked the teaching licenses of all Zen priests who had actively supported the war, copies of his lectures were accepted as evidence in his favor, and he was able to keep his license to teach high school English.

After the war, Shunryu Suzuki worked hard to rebuild his country. He fulfilled his teacher's wishes by completing the restoration of Rinso-in—a task which took longer than usual since he insisted that everything be done by using the traditional methods of carpentry. He also reestablished two kindergartens. His first wife had died before the war, and he married the principal of one of the kindergartens, Mitsu Matsuno. When he accepted the three-year temporary appointment as priest of Sokoji everyone was surprised and after two and a half years in America, his wife and youngest son were sent to bring him back. But they also stayed, and when it finally became clear that he would not return, his eldest son, Hoichi, replaced him as head of Rinso-in.

Zazen was the heart of what Shunryu Suzuki taught. Legs crossed, back straight, chin in, eyes half-open, looking down, hands folded. Body erect and relaxed at once. Attention on breathing, counting one to ten, and back again. Just sitting like a frog on a lilypad on the round black *zafus* (cushions) that Shunryu Suzuki had brought from Japan—at first on the benches downstairs, then in the small zendo he had built upstairs, and then, as that became crowded, along the balconies.

This sitting was in itself the expression of Buddha nature. "According to the law of Buddha," Shunryu Suzuki quoted Dogen Zenji, the patriarch of Soto Zen, "body and mind are originally one; essence and form are not two." In other words, the posture of zazen itself was not different from the attitude of mind it proclaimed. "These forms are not the means of obtaining the right state of mind," Shunryu Suzuki told the students who joined him in the early morning. "To take this posture is itself to have the right state of mind."

Just sit. There was nothing to be achieved. No grand vision, no wonderful breakthrough to be pointed out or sought. In one lecture he talked about a woman who had come to him because she lost her temper with her child; she wanted to know if doing zazen would change that. "Roshi laughed a lot about that," a student remembered, "the idea that Zazen would change anyone. He said he was a very lazy boy and now he was a very lazy man." "So long as your practice is based on a gaining idea," he said, "you will have no time actually to gain your ideal. Moreover, you will be sacrificing the meat of your practice."

D. T. Suzuki, decades earlier, had made satori and Zen synonymous; Shunryu Suzuki now did something similar with "practice," an English word that he gave a Buddhist spin.

And yet few people, it must be admitted, felt like Buddha the moment they sat down, or, at least, like they *thought* Buddha might feel. Not to do anything proved difficult enough. There may have been levels of relaxation in counting the breath, but there were also levels of boredom, irritation, pain, anxiety. Like most worthwhile activities, zazen proved easier to begin than to continue. It did not provide much in the way of entertainment. But then, that was the point.

"When a fish swims in the water there is no end," Shunryu Suzuki quoted Dogen. And then went on:

> It is very interesting that there is no end. Because there is no end to our practice it is good. Don't you think so? Usually you expect our practice to be effective enough to put an end to our hard practice. If I say just practice hard for two years, then you will be interested in our practice. If I say you have to practice your whole lifetime then you will be disappointed. You will say, "Oh Zen is not for me." But if you understand that the reasons you are interested in this practice is because our practice is endless, that is true understanding. That is why I am interested in Buddhism. There is no end.

III

Right from the start it was clear that Shunryu Suzuki was at home in America. It did not bother him that his students scarcely knew anything about Buddhism or Zen culture. That was in a certain way an advantage. As beginners they had already glimpsed one of the essential points—what the Japanese called *shoshin*, "beginner's mind." Spiritual practice in the West had long been associated with great accomplishments and mysterious powers. But as Suzuki-roshi explained, "In the beginner's mind there is no thought, 'I have attained something.' When we have no thought of achievement, no thought of self, we are true beginners."

It was an inspired move of cross-cultural jujitsu. By identifying beginner's mind with Zen practice, Shunryu Suzuki reversed in one stroke the inferiority Americans so often felt towards the overwhelmingly "mysterious" and complex traditions of the Orient. What might have seemed a problem became instead possibility. "In the beginner's mind," as he said, "there are many possibilities; in the expert's mind there are few."

But being open to the creative possibilities of American Buddhism did not mean making things easier. Suzuki-roshi lectured in English on traditional, difficult texts, *The Blue Cliff Record* (a classic collection of koans) and the *Lotus Sutra*. There were sesshins first on weekends, and then, in 1962, a full seven-day sesshin. Slowly, he began to add elements of what he called "the rigid formal way of practicing Zen." Long-established rules governed every move in the zendo, and the observation of these rules cut right across the grain of American individualism—the notion that freedom meant, as Suzuki-roshi said, "physical freedom, the freedom of activity." But it was just this notion, according to the logic of Zen training, that caused suffering. "It is not a matter of good or bad, convenient or inconvenient," as roshi explained. "You just do it without question. That way your mind is free."

He even went so far as to suggest—much to everyone's amazement—that American Zen ought to have more rules than Japanese Zen. "You think two-hundred and fifty precepts for men and five hundred for women is awful and that it should be made simpler," he said. "But I think you will have more difficulty in practicing zazen in America than we do in Japan. This kind of difficulty should be continued forever or we will not have peace in the world."

He declined to say what additional precepts he might have had in mind ("I don't want to disturb your zazen," he told the student who asked) but he did increase the number of bows after zazen from three to nine. When it was suggested that this might discourage some people, he answered, "It is true, very true. I know people will be discouraged. I know we are causing a lot of discouragement for American people when we bow nine times, when they bow only three times in Japan. I know that very well. So I bow nine times here in America."

Shunryu Suzuki's thesis at Komazawa Buddhist University had been on bowing, and his own teacher, Gyakuju So-on had a big callous on his forehead from bowing. "He knew he was an obstinate, stubborn fellow," explained Suzuki-roshi, "and so he bowed and bowed and bowed." Bowing was particularly important for Americans, he thought, because American culture lacked forms to show respect to a Buddha—"a human being who was not a god and who nevertheless attained perfection." But, of course, buddha was everywhere. "Sometimes we bow to dogs and cats; sometimes the teacher bows to the student." He said, "You should be prepared to bow, even in your last moment. Even though it is impossible to get rid of our self-centered desires we have to do it. Our true nature wants us to."

So there were rules—etiquette, decorum. These did not change for anyone. If you wanted to sit in the morning, you were there, on your zafu, by five-thirty. There was freedom, but within form. As Suzuki-roshi explained it, in an astute analysis of that generational conflict that obsessed the decade, older people might understand what the *Heart Sutra* meant when it said, "emptiness is form," and younger people might understand what it meant when it said, "form is emptiness," but both were necessary.

There was no traffic to speak of at five twenty-five in the morning when the students crossed Bush Street to sit at Sokoji, but they waited at the corner before the deserted street until the light clicked into green, and then, and only then, did they walk across within the white crosswalks. It was something their contemporaries only a few blocks away in the Haight-Ashbury would never have thought of doing.

IV

Hakuun Yasutani-roshi reached America three years after Shunryu Suzuki-roshi. He was by then seventy-seven years old, a tall skinny hawklike man with large ears that stuck out, as one observer said, like teacups. In some ways it could be said that Yasutani-roshi's Zen was complementary to Suzuki-roshi's—the other side of the mirror, so to speak. While Suzuki-roshi went quietly about his work at Sokoji waiting for people to come and sit with him, Yasutani-roshi crisscrossed America seven times between 1962 and 1969. For the most part, he stopped only long enough to hold sesshin.

Yasutani-roshi had at one time been in charge of his own *sodo*, but he had come to feel, as Robert Aitken has written, "that the Dharma could best be maintained among people of the workaday world." He soon had students all over Tokyo where he "could often be seen," as Philip Kapleau remembers, "trudging about in a tattered robe and a pair of sneakers on his way to a zazen meeting, his lecture books slung over his back, or standing in the crowded inter-urban trains."

Because of Yasutani-roshi's interest in teaching lay people outside the monastic setting, it was natural for foreigners to seek him out. Both Robert Aitken and Philip Kapleau, who trained with Yasutani-roshi for eight years, had been sent to him by Soen-roshi, and it was these two men, along with Soen, who laid the plans for Yasutani-roshi's first trip to America. Yasutani-roshi's interpreter and assistant was the young monk, Tai Shimano-sensei, a disciple of Soen-roshi's, who had been the resident monk at the Koko-an Zendo in Hawaii since 1960.

While Suzuki-roshi had stressed the dailiness of zazen and community, and scarcely mentioned satori or *kensho* (literally "seeing into one's nature"), Yasutani-roshi was most in his element conducting sesshins, which were for him as for his teacher, Harada-roshi, preeminently opportunities for people to experience kensho. Yasutani's sesshins have been described (and sometimes criticized) as having created a pressure-cooker atmosphere. Certainly they were intense—hard-driving attacks on reality which spared nothing to push the student through the first barrier of *Mu*. For Yasutani kensho was the beginning of real Zen practice, and he expected one or two people to have at least a glimpse of it nearly every sesshin.

Yasutani-roshi's first sesshin in America did not disappoint him. It took place in Honolulu in 1962 with twenty sitters. Tai Shimano-sensei, the resident monk at Diamond Sangha who had been studying English at the University of Hawaii for the previous two years, translated and served as jikijitsu. "To experience kensho is crucial," Yasutani-roshi said at the beginning of the sesshin, "but we are so lazy. Therefore, during sesshin we have to set up a special atmosphere so that all participants can go straight ahead toward the goal. First, absolute silence should be observed. Second, you must not look around. Third, forget about the usual courtesies and etiquette." He then added it would probably be necessary to use the kyosaku rather frequently. "That five-day sesshin," Eido-roshi has written, "was as hysterical as it was historical." By the time it was over, no less than five people had experienced kensho.

Hakuun Yasutani-roshi was born in 1885, clutching—as he told the story—a tiny rosary bead a Buddhist nun had given his mother to swallow as a talisman for her unborn child. At the age of five, head shaved, Yasutani-roshi entered a temple where he learned the alphabet, arithmetic, and the *Heart Sutra*. He attended public school until he became a novice in a Soto temple at the age of thirteen, attending at the same time, first a Soto-run seminary and then a teacher-training school. Married at the age of thirty, he began a long career as an elementary school teacher and principal—a period which Robert Aitken saw as "a foundation for, rather than just postponement of his future career of Zen teaching. The understanding he always showed for the problems of laymen as Zen students, and his capacity to communicate readily with women probably grew out of his own domestic and social periods during those early years."

While teaching school, Yasutani-roshi continued his own Zen study with different Soto teachers, but he was troubled by their apparent indifference to kensho. "It is clear from public records," he wrote later, "that all patriarchs who succeeded Shakyamuni, without a single exception, experienced kensho. Why is it that beginning with Nishiari Bokusan and continuing through his distinguished and talented successors, no one can speak to the central point of whether or not there is such a thing as kensho. Why is it that they do not show us the way to kensho? Why don't they guide us? I could not understand."

To Yasutani-roshi, Dogen's dictum that enlightenment and practice were one had been used by many Soto priests without proper attention to the "enlightenment" side of the equation. "The fact that they [Soto teachers] dealt with satori in vague generalities," wrote Philip Kapleau, "made its actual realization seem remote, chimerical." Nevertheless, Yasutani-roshi perservered in his practice and eventually returned full-time to the Soto clergy with an appointment as specially dispatched priest for propagation of the Soto sect. The assignment required him to lecture extensively around Tokyo, and the increased responsibility seems to have pushed Yasutani's doubts to a breaking-point. "I was altogether a blind fellow," he wrote later, "and my mind was not yet at rest. I was at a peak of mental anguish. When I felt I could not endure deceiving myself and others by untrue teaching and irresponsible sermons any longer, my karma opened up, and I was able to meet the master Daiun Shitsu, Sogaku Harada-roshi. The light of a lantern was brought to the dark night, to my profound joy." It was 1924, and Yasutani-roshi was thirty-nine years old.

Harada-roshi was one of the foremost exponents of a movement (with roots in the Meiji) of Soto teachers who had studied koan with Rinzai masters. The Zen that Harada-roshi developed was in some ways eclectic, but it also developed its own style. There was a great emphasis on the first kensho—so much so that students who passed through the first barrier, usually *Mu*, were recognized in a ceremony at the end of sesshin, something that was never done in the Rinzai school. Harada-roshi also did much to modernize and demystify Zen. In traditional Zen, introductory instructions were rarely given, the student being left to find his own way, no matter how long it took, but Harada-roshi began his sesshins with introductory lectures that spelled out as much as possible the proper approach to Zen practice.

Harada-roshi's monastery, Hosshinji, was located on the northern coast of Japan. (When he was offered the abbotship of a temple in a warmer climate, Harada-roshi refused, saying that the cold at Hosshinji drove men into the pits of their stomachs, where reality could be found.) Anyone who thought of Zen as quiet or tranquil would have been shocked by the atmosphere in Harada-roshi's zendo. During sesshins the jikijitsu exhorted sitters to do their utmost, and the kyosaku was used unsparingly, like a whip, to goad practitioners on. It was exactly what Yasutani-roshi had been waiting for. He attended his first sesshin with Harada-roshi in 1925. Two years later his doubts about kensho were dissolved, and by 1938 he had completed koan study. He received inka in 1943.

Like his master Harada-roshi, Yasutani-roshi had little use for the sectarian arguments between the two major Zen schools. "Rinzai and Soto Zen have their respective strong and weak points," he wrote, "but since strong points are liable to change into weak points and evils, by correctly learning each kind of Zen the strong points of both are taken in, and one is saved from the easily engendered short-comings and ill effects of both. . . . Then, each may devise his characteristic methods of guidance without imitating anyone, in accord with the times and adapting to the country."

Yasutani-roshi had gotten a late start, but once he received inka from Harada-roshi he worked ceaselessly. Having spent the years until he was forty raising a family of five children and teaching school, he now devoted himself to teaching lay people. By 1954, when his organization, the Sanbo Kyodan (Fellowship of the Three Treasures) became independent of the Soto school, there were more than twenty-five zazenkai around Tokyo and its environs.

Nakagawa Soen-roshi had first met Yasutani-roshi at Hosshinji. (Though a roshi and abbot of Ryutakuji, Soen used to put on his old monk's robe and go to Hosshinji to do sesshin with Harada.) The two had become close friends, and when Soen-roshi's mother had fallen ill in 1962, preventing his planned tour of America, he asked Yasutani-roshi to take his place.

Yasutani-roshi's first sesshin on the mainland was held in Los Angeles, with the assistance of Tai Shimano-sensei and Maezumi-sensei (now Hakuyu Taizan Maezumi-roshi of the Zen Center of Los Angeles), a young monk who had come to the Los Angeles Soto Zenshuji temple in 1956. (Zenshuji, headquarters of the Soto school in America had been founded by Hosen Isobe, the same missionary who founded Sokoji in San Francisco in 1934.) Maezumi-sensei's father, Hakujun Kuroda-roshi, was the head of a Soto temple, and Maezumi had been ordained there at the age of eleven. He had studied Oriental philosophy and Japanese literature at Komazawa University, and trained at Sojiji, one of the two major Soto monasteries. At the same time, he had begun, at the age of sixteen, to study koans with Koryu Osaka-roshi, a lay Rinzai master with a dojo in Tokyo. In 1955, he received dharma transmission (*shiho*) in the Soto school from Kuroda-roshi.

Maezumi-sensei had spent his first two years in America boarding with a family in Pasadena while studying English at the city college. He continued his studies for a short time in San Francisco, and then returned to take up his duties as a priest at Zenshuji. He was kept very busy there attending to the needs of the Japanese congregation. He continued zazen practice on his own, and studied the *Shobogenzo* with Reirin Yamada-roshi, then Soto bishop of America. He had also become friendly with Nyogen Senzaki. Senzaki had only two years to live then (it was 1956) but in that time, he made a deep "autumnal" impression on the young priest.

By the time Yasutani-roshi arrived in Los Angeles in 1962, Maezumi-sensei had begun to hold weekly zazen meetings at Zenshuji. It was also at this time that Maezumi-sensei began to study koans with Yasutani-roshi, who urged him to return to Japan periodically to complete his training. Maezumi-sensei's resumption of intensive training was so important to him that later, when he looked back on the nearly ten years he had spent in America previous to his meeting with Yasutani-roshi, he would shake his head over those "wasted years".

After visiting Nyogen Senzaki's grave in the Japanese cemetery in east Los Angeles, Yasutani-roshi and Tai Shimano-sensei flew to Pendle Hill, a Quaker retreat center in Pennsylvania, for the next sesshin. Few of the participants had ever practiced zazen, and everybody brought their own cushion, each one a different color and size. "It was colorful; indeed, it was chaos!" remembers Shimano-sensei, and one graduate student in philosophy from nearby Temple University left after the first day, leaving a note on his pillow: "If I were to stay for the five days, my philosophy would be totally crushed." The party held another sesshin in New York City, and then continued on to Boston, where the Cambridge Buddhist Society organized a sesshin in a Cape Cod house.

Yasutani-roshi's sesshins were powerful and difficult. Shimano-sensei, in charge of the zendo, ran a very tight ship, Rinzai-style, with lots of yelling and shouting. He was generous with the kyosaku, and when the *dokusan* (soto term for sanzen) bell was rung there was a race, people falling, running, to see the roshi. Nothing was held back; the chanting at the services was from the gut, as loud as possible. "You had to be very strong to sit through them, just to sit through them," recalls Charlotte Beck, now Joko, a priest with Maezumi-roshi; "they were murder."

Yasutani-roshi did not pay very much attention to what went on in the zendo during sesshin; he left that to the jikijitsu and the people organizing the details. He communicated with people individually as they came into the dokusan room. He did not speak much English—though he delighted in using the few words he did have—and he had to use an interpreter (often Maezumi-sensei) for both dokusan and teisho. But he did not rely on words only: "He mimed," Robert Aitken has written, "as clearly and as humorously as Marceau or Chaplin." In fact, his dokusan were of two types: one with words (beginners naturally chose that) and one without.

After Yasutani-roshi's second trip to America in 1963, he and Shimano-sensei embarked on a round-the-world tour. At Bodh-Gaya, Yasutani-roshi realized a longtime dream by sitting in zazen under the Bodhi tree; at Sarnath a Sinhalese monk gave the two Japanese priests the traditional yellow robes worn by Theravadin monks. "We removed our Japanese-style monk's robes and wore the ones he gave us in the traditional way covering only our left shoulders," wrote Tai Shimano. "Suddenly two thousand five hundred years vanished, leaving a skinny old Buddhist monk, after years of practice, standing on the very ground of Buddha's first sermon, as though he were listening to the Four Noble Truths."

By 1964, the situation had progressed to the point where Yasutani-roshi was considering retiring in Hawaii. A group of people who had attended his sesshins on the East Coast had begun to sit together at the American Buddhist Academy, the California Bosatsukai (formed by students of Senzaki and Soen-roshi) had become more active and Koko-an was growing. A house was purchased by the Koko-an group in a rural area of Oahu and every weekend was spent on renovations. But Yasutani-roshi's Japanese students prevailed upon him to postpone his retirement, and at the same time U.S. immigration officials, testing for tuberculosis, discovered a spot on Yasutani's X-ray, so a permanent visa was not possible. The plan was dropped and Yasutani continued his yearly trips.

Tai Shimano-sensei, meanwhile, had been pondering a nineteenth-century Japanese-Hawaiian popular song that went:

> Should I go to America
> Or should I go back to Japan
> Here in Hawaii I wonder and it is hard to decide.

For the most part, he reflected, the Japanese in Hawaii had stayed right where they were. But he thought Hawaii more of a place for retirement or vacations than for Zen. Soen-roshi left it up to him, and finally he decided to go on to New York. He arrived at Kennedy Airport on New Year's Eve, 1964, carrying a small Buddha statue, a kyosaku and one suitcase. No one met him, but he stayed at a friend's apartment, and soon found his own apartment on the Upper West Side. There was nothing in the apartment except for the Buddha image he placed on the empty mantle.

Shimano-sensei began meeting with the small group that had begun zazen practice in a room at the American Buddhist Academy. In front of the Academy building on Riverside Drive stood a large statue of the founder of Shin Buddhism, Honen, wearing a large straw hat, walking with a staff—a gift from a group of Buddhists in Hiroshima. The founder of the American Buddhist Academy, the Reverend Hozen Seki was a small, gentle but determined man who had come to New York with the hope of making the Shin teachings available to people outside the Japanese community. In this he had been only moderately successful, but he was very open-minded and did what he could to help other Buddhist groups. He had known Sokei-an in the forties, and had been close friends with D. T. Suzuki during Suzuki's Columbia years. D.T. Suzuki, in fact, had a lifelong interest in Shin Buddhism, and he regarded the way of *tariki* (other power) as complementary to the way of Zen *jiriki* (self-power). He had been a frequent visitor at the American Buddhist Academy, and had delivered a series of lectures there, later published as *Shin Buddhism*.

As the Reverend Seki told Shimano-sensei, when he had first come to New York there had been no Buddhist temples there at all. The only Buddhist group in existence, except for Sokei-an's small band, had been the Buddhist Fellowship of New York, a study group that met in Carnegie Hall for discussion under the leadership of Boris Erwitt, a Russian emigre. Seki was only challenged. He spent his first year in New York rowing in Central Park, listening to lectures at Columbia, observing New York and New Yorkers. "Well, Reverend Shimano," he now said, "be patient for ten years. No rush at the beginning."

Tai Shimano was patient—he was, after all, a Zen monk—but he was also of samurai stock, a young man with a strong body and great determination. His karma had been linked to America from the early days in Ryutakuji—first with Soen-roshi, and through him Nyogen Senzaki, whose attendant he almost became, and then the Koko-an Zendo and Yasutani-roshi. They had all dug the foundation. It was time to build.

The group moved from their borrowed room at the Buddhist Academy to Tai-Shimano's apartment. People had to bring cushions and blankets, until Shimano-sensei showed some of them how to cut and sew black cloth for zafus. To raise the money for the rent Shimano-sensei went out to look for a job, the first time in his life he had had to do such a thing. A sympathetic manager at the Bank of Tokyo offered him a position as a chauffeur for visiting businessmen, which he turned down, and then came up with a job compiling all the Japanese names from the Manhattan phone book for a mailing list. Tai Shimano could work on it in his own time. The first month's rent was paid.

The Sangha grew. Shimano-sensei lectured on Zen at the New School for Social Research, then moved into a larger ground-floor apartment on West End Avenue that had once been a doctor's office. Once a month they sat all weekend, and the necessary accouterments for a zendo began to appear as if by magic. In San Francisco to meet Yasutani-roshi on one of his trips, Shimano found a huge gong. When he struck it, the sound was deep and profound. The inscription matched. The gong had been cast in 1555 for Daitokuji. The antique dealer wanted a thousand dollars for it. Shimano had two hundred fifty dollars in his account. The dealer took that and gave him three months to pay. Some time later he passed a bronze Buddha image in the window of a New York antique store. It was the perfect size for the new zendo. When he saw it gathering dust in the shop, he could think only of taking it back to the zendo and offering incense. The cost was much too high, but a member of the group offered to buy it. When Shimano-sensei had bathed it, he found an inscription stating that it had been made for a branch temple in Empukuji in Chichibu, the temple where he had first been ordained.

As the group grew, Shimano-sensei felt the need for some kind of more substantial organization. Friends told him that it was essential the group become a legal, tax-exempt organization. But the cost of the legal work involved seemed substantial. Tai Shimano happened to remember the existence of the Zen Studies Society, the organization that Cornelius Crane had set up to encourage the work of D. T. Suzuki in 1956. The purpose of the Society was to "introduce the cultural, educational, and spiritual aspects of Zen Buddhism to the West." One of Shimano-sensei's friends, Dr. Bernard Phillips, was a member of the Society's board of directors and chairman of the department of religion at Temple University. Though the Society had become virtually nonexistent with the death of Mr. Crane in 1962 and the return of D. T. Suzuki to Japan, it still had a legal existence. Dr. Phillips introduced Shimano-sensei to the Society's lawyer, Mr. George Yamaoka. Papers were signed. Shimano-sensei became a board member. The Zen Studies Society had no assets or property. "There was," as Tai Shimano remembers, "nothing for him to turn over to me and there was nothing to take over." He thought it an auspicious beginning for a Buddhist organization.

V

By 1965 Philip Kapleau was ready to come back home. He had spent thirteen years in Japan—first with Soen-roshi, then as a lay monk at Hosshinji under Harada-roshi, and finally with Yasutani-roshi. It had not been easy. He had begun the first philosophical phase of Zen study in 1948 when he met D. T. Suzuki while working as a court reporter for the International War Crimes Tribunal, and had then become one of the inner circle following Suzuki's lectures at Columbia. But philosophy, even Zen philosophy, had not helped the feeling of futility he experienced on returning to his work in Connecticut as a court reporter after living through the war crimes trials at both Nuremberg and Tokyo.

Following the advice of a Japanese friend who had told him, "Zen's not philosophy, it's a healthy way to live. If you really want to learn Buddhism in Japan and not just talk about it, your whole life will be transformed," he returned to Tokyo at the age of forty-four. The first two Zen masters he sought out refused him because he could not speak Japanese. His fervent protest that he had thought Zen "a teaching without reliance on words and letters" did no good. Finally Soen-roshi took him in. He permitted Kapleau to stay at Ryutakuji and allowed him to "sit, kneel Japanese style, or use a chair." Kapleau then entered Hosshinji, where he learned to sit cross-legged despite excruciating pains in his legs, back and neck, and where he sat through his first sesshin. He stayed at Hosshinji for three years as a lay-monk until he was forced to leave "because of failing health exacerbated by the austere and tense atmosphere and the poor diet."

He continued his training, on Soen-roshi's advice, with Yasutani-roshi. Since Yasutani-roshi had no monastery, Kapleau, like the other lay students, lived in his own quarters, and his health improved. Yasutani-roshi had told Kapleau, "It is your destiny to carry Zen to the West. Don't quail or quit in spite of the pain and hardship." In the summer of 1958, during his twentieth sesshin with Yasutani-roshi, Kapleau "threw [himself] into Mu with such utter absorption that *I* completely vanished." His kensho experience left him, as he noted in his diary, feeling "free as a fish in an ocean of cool, clear water after being stuck in a tank of glue . . . and so grateful." He remained in Japan, training further with Yasutani-roshi—who ordained him as a Zen priest—and acted as Yasutani-roshi's translator during dokusan for the growing number of Westerners who had come to Japan.

Dokusan had always been the most private of encounters, but Yasutani-roshi now gave permission for Kapleau to make detailed notes of the exchanges between roshi and student—something that Kapleau, with his training as a court reporter, his now fluent Japanese and his long Zen training was uniquely suited to do. Working with Koun Yamada-roshi, a cigar-smoking hospital administrator who was Yasutani-roshi's closest disciple, Kapleau compiled a book, *The Three Pillars of Zen* that included transcripts of dokusan, Yasutani-roshi's *sozan* (introductory talks before sesshin, an innovation of Yasutani-roshi's teacher, Harada-roshi) and translations of other Zen writings. The book also included descriptions of kensho experiences by Yasutani-roshi's Japanese and American students. It was the first book written by a Westerner from within the Zen tradition, and the fact that Kapleau had convinced Yasutani-roshi to give him permission to use the dokusan interviews along with the kensho experiences, made the book unique in any language. *The Three Pillars of Zen* made it clear that zazen was at the heart of zen, and gave instructions on how to begin sitting. It made it possible for people who had never met a Zen teacher to begin practicing on their own.

The Three Pillars of Zen was first published in Japan in 1965, just as Kapleau was preparing to return to America. The book was read by Chester Carlson, the patent attorney and founder of the Xerox Corporation, and his wife, Doris, who belonged to a Vedanta study group in Rochester. The Carlsons were impressed. They bought five thousand copies of the *Three Pillars* and distributed them free to public libraries; they also invited Kapleau to visit them in Rochester. Kapleau had been away from the States so long that he felt a little lost when he first returned. He traveled to promote *The Three Pillars of Zen* (which had now been published in America), but he made Rochester his base. Mrs. Carlson had asked him to lecture to her study group, which was made up of twenty women and two men, most of them in their middle forties. "They were very eclectic," remembers Kapleau, "into about anything that came along." He taught them to sit zazen—they had been meditating in chairs—and was pleasantly surprised, remembering his own difficulties, that they were able to sit cross-legged without too much trouble. But the group was not easily converted. When no one came to Sunday morning zazen, Kapleau discovered that most of the women were at church.

Soon, through his book and the lectures Kapleau was giving around the country, another kind of student began to show up at a house Kapleau and a few students had rented on a tree-lined street in a residential area of Rochester. They quickly supplanted the older members of the study group as the main force of the Zen Meditation Center of Rochester, which Kapleau founded in 1966. The new, younger students "just took to it like ducks to water," Kapleau remembers now, "going barefoot, the whole thing of being close to the earth, the natural thing—particularly at that time."

Kapleau had realized as soon as he had returned to America that Zen could not take hold if it were seen as something foreign and exotic. Americans might be willing to go along with a Japanese teacher using

Japanese words and customs, but it was not a natural thing to do when the teacher was American. During a pilgrimage to Southeast Asia he had seen how Buddhism had taken a different form in different cultures. Surely the same transformation would have to take place in America.

Yasutani-roshi conducted occasional sesshins in Rochester during his trips to America, but in-between Kapleau was on his own. He began to experiment—with English versions of sutras for chanting in the zendo, a more Western style of dress, designed for sitting comfort, Western Buddhist names for people who took precepts, and "ceremonies, forms, and rituals that are in accord with Western traditions." When he suggested to Yasutani-roshi that the Rochester Center translate the *Heart Sutra* into English, Yasutani-roshi was not pleased. "Oh what a battle I had with my teacher on that," Kapleau remembered many years later. "He was very much against it."

Yasutani-roshi countered that the Sino-Japanese of the *Heart Sutra*, chanted daily in every Zen monastery, "had evolved from centuries of chanting; it was fluent and could be easily learned; the meaning of the words was secondary. In short, there was no need for an English version." He took "an equally dim view" of Kapleau's other proposals.

The *Heart Sutra* of the Prajnaparamita (Perfection of Wisdom) had originally been written in Sanskrit. Koreans, Chinese and Tibetans all translated and chanted it in their own languages. Kapleau, who had the tenacity to stay for thirteen years in Japan, would not yield. He argued that Soto Zen had not really spread in Japan until Keizan, the second patriarch of the Soto School, changed the Chinese forms Dogen had brought with him into Japanese ones. Of course, one had to know what to keep as essential and what to discard as mere cultural accretion, but Kapleau was certain that his long training and residence in Japan would "preserve me from throwing out the baby with the bath water."

In any case, the question of the *Heart Sutra* and other details of cultural transformation cut like a blade between the two men who had worked together for so long in Japan. The break, when it came in 1967, was painful and final. The two men never spoke to each other again. It was a traumatic event. After thirteen years in Japan, Philip Kapleau was on his own. He was determined to find a way for the Zen of his teacher to grow to maturity in America.

VI

As Eido Tai Shimano-roshi and others have observed, 1960 marked the point when American Zen turned from the intellectual to the practical. By the mid-sixties more than a score of Zen groups had appeared in the soil watered by Soyen Shaku, Sokei-an, Senzaki, D. T. Suzuki and all the others, like mushrooms after a spring rain.

To survey the terrain:

In Maine, Walter Nowick, former Juilliard student and member of the First Zen Institute of New York, had become dharma successor of Zuigan Goto-roshi after years of study in Japan. Goto-roshi had instructed him to wait ten years before teaching, a period he spent working his potato farm in Maine, teaching music at a nearby university and to private students (many of them Japanese, who had followed him to America) and being very quiet. Only the inner circle of Zen people knew anything about the first American to receive full transmission in an orthodox line of Rinzai Zen.

In Boston, the Cambridge Buddhist Society continued. Nakagawa Soen-roshi, Yasutani-roshi and Shunryu Suzuki-roshi all visited.

In New York, the First Zen Institute of America, which moved into a brownstone on East Thirtieth Street, continued to be guided by Sokei-an's teachings under the leadership of Mary Farkas, whose *Zen Notes* kept track of the emerging scene. Isshu Miura-roshi, having accepted ten of the Institute's students as his disciples, taught quietly in a New York apartment. As he told Tai Shimano, who had found him at the age of sixty with "a few enthusiastic students," "If I can sow even one real seed, if not a half seed, in America, that's enough." Tai Shimano-sensei's Zen Studies Society continued to expand, with connections to both Soen-roshi and Yasutani-roshi. A few years later, in 1967, the Reverend Nakajima, a young Soto priest, who had studied in Ceylon, would begin to hold zazen in the same Upper West Side apartment that Tai Shimano had occupied.

In Philadelphia, Dr. Albert Stunkard organized a Zen group with ties to Yasutani-roshi, Soen-roshi, and Tai Shimano. Also in Philadelphia, Dr. Kyung-Bo Seo, working on a doctorate at Temple, began to teach Korean Buddhism to a small group.

In Washington, D.C., another Zen group was associated with the Zen

Studies Society. There was also the Washington Buddhist Vihara, a Theravadan group that had a small party of monks in 1966.

In Rochester, Philip Kapleau's Zen Meditation Center of Rochester continued to grow.

In Chicago, the Reverend Gyomay Kubose, a Shinshu minister established a zazen group. Like Reverend Seki in New York, Kubose looked forward to a time when Americans would practice *nembutsu* (the recitation of Buddha's name), along with Zen, as Buddhists had in China. So far, as he wrote, Shinshu had not made much of an impact because it had been largely confined to Japanese communities, and because of its "Christian-like presentation." But in fact—as D. T. Suzuki had pointed out in his talks at the American Buddhist Academy—Shin was very different from Christianity, and tariki, other power, was the true self. In fact, the Buddhist Churches of America, the name of the Jodo Shinshu congregations, had attracted a few Americans, and some had even become ministers; but for the most part their influence was confined to the communities where they lived.

In San Francisco, in addition to the increasing numbers studying with Suzuki-roshi, a smaller group had begun to work with the Chinese Ch'an master, Hsuan Hua, about whom more will be said later.

In Hawaii, the Diamond Sangha continued to grow under the guidance of Robert Aitken, with connections to both Yasutani-roshi and Soen-roshi. In 1965 Mr. Katsuki Sekida, a lay Buddhist leader from Ryutakuji, Soen's monastery, arrived to serve as translator and a teacher of zazen.

In Los Angeles, by 1967 Maezumi-sensei's group had moved out of Zenshuji and rented a house on Serrano Street in the Wilshire district. For a time there was talk of their joining with Suzuki-roshi's group, but in the end they remained independent, and in 1968 they incorporated as the Los Angeles Zendo (now Zen Center of Los Angeles). Yasutani-roshi also began to hold sesshins at the Los Angeles Zendo, the first being held in 1967. Shortly after a visit from Maezumi-sensei's brother, Kuroda-sensei, the Los Angeles Zendo was registered as a Soto temple and sodo with the name Busshinji—"Buddha Truth." During 1970 Maezumi-sensei made two extended trips to Japan in order to continue his training with Yasutani-roshi. Maezumi-sensei received inka from Yasutani-roshi at the end of the second extended visit.

Meanwhile, another Zen master, Joshu Sasaki-roshi, had arrived in Los Angeles. All these men—with the exception of the peripatetic

Nakagawa Soen-roshi and Hakuun Yasutani-roshi—had one thing in common: they had all come to stay.

When Joshu Sasaki-roshi had left Japan, in fact, he had undergone the traditional ceremonies of permanent departure—like Senzaki he said that he was going to bury his bones in America. He had been a monk of a Rinzai Zen temple of the Yoshenji line, and then the resident monk of a small mountain temple, Shoju-an in Nagano prefecture. He arrived in Los Angeles in June of 1962, apparently because two people, a Dr. Harmon and Gladys Weisberg, had asked for a Zen teacher.

Joshu Sasaki-roshi was then—and still is—a short, round man with a pugnacious nature and a full belly-deep laugh. He arrived in Los Angeles with a Bible in one sleeve of his robe and an English dictionary in the other. He must have looked at the Bible because he has been especially active in teaching zazen at Catholic monasteries, but he soon decided that he was too old—or busy—to do much about learning English, and he still, eighteen years later, delivers his teisho in Japanese—a Japanese that is, according to his present translator, Shinzen Young, immensely difficult to translate. As Sasaki-roshi said, "If you want to explain enlightenment, you have to make up a new language." Writes Young,

> A perfect knowledge of Japanese and a thorough familiarity with the Sanskrit and Sino-Japanese Buddhist technical vocabulary are necessary but not sufficient requisites for translating Sasaki-roshi, for he has created his own 'idiolect,' a unique personal language. . . . One must always be aware that he employs both everyday words and Buddhist technical terms entirely idiosyncratically. For him words become synonyms with bewildering ease. . . . To appreciate this mode of expression one must be able to break former associations to words and listen many times without struggling to make it make sense.

Sasaki-roshi first lived in a tiny one bedroom frame house in the Los Angeles suburb of Gardenia. The garage served as zendo and the bedroom as sanzen room. The roshi himself slept on a mattress in the living room. With no experienced students to help, he had to run the whole show himself. He was jikijitsu during zazen, roshi during sanzen, and, often, *tenzo* (cook) in-between. As more people came out to Gardenia, he ran into a peculiarly American problem: the neighbors complained that the streets were blocked by cars and they had no place to park. For a while, meetings rotated between various students' homes, until 1966 when the roshi established Cimarron Zen Center in the mission-style compound of a Los Angeles former estate.

Sasaki-roshi used traditional koans in an untraditional way—or to be more precise, he transformed traditional koans into the American idiom, "How do you realize Buddha nature while driving a car?" for example. He used an interpreter in teisho, but not in sanzen, where his limited but direct English served its purpose. His Zen was active. He translated shunyata, emptiness, as zero, but he did not stop there. As he said when he first arrived in Los Angeles, "It was the historical Buddha, Shakyamuni, who discovered that Zero exists through the *activity of Zero*. This Zero-activity is also called the activity of emptiness."

When he first came to America he saw the country as "ripe for spiritual revolution, since the young were not prisoners of tradition." But he also worried that many of the students who came to him were "social failures," and that though they were bigger than the Japanese "their navels are much more diminished." Certainly none of them laughed as he did, and he recommended standing up and laughing out loud, from the belly, first thing in the morning, and once, when he was asked why he came to America he replied, "I let other people do the teaching. I came to have a good time. I want Americans to learn how to truly laugh."

To a certain extent, the Zen Buddhists of the sixties presented a united front. But just beneath the smooth surface, none of it ever becoming public, there were stirrings of scandal, disagreements, rivalries, hints of incompetence. This man, fresh from the monastery and used to the conventional morality of Japan, had been swept off his feet by the freedom of American women, and had slept with one or more of his students. Someone else was not really qualified to teach. This one knew nothing of koans, that one nothing of shikantaza. Lurking in the background were centuries-old traditions of sectarian rivalry between the Soto and Rinzai schools in Japan, a rivalry that most of the men who came to America had very little patience for, but which seemed, nonetheless, to have a strong influence on how they thought. A major controversy was the running skirmish between those who emphasized going straight for kensho and those who stressed that "practice and enlightenment were one."

Most of this was rather unsettling for American students to discover.

Of course, Buddhism had always been rather argumentative within itself. "Dharma combat" was a tradition in Zen especially; one which, it was fair to say, kept the teaching alive and everybody on their toes. Still, not everything said was on the level of the battles recounted in the old koan collections, and it was sometimes shocking for wide-eyed Americans to discover that the man with whom their friend was training was thought by their teacher to be, say, "a Zen teacher passing around a bar of iron claiming it is gold." American students had been universally praised for being open, fresh, without preconceptions. That much was agreed. But what was not said in public, but must often have been said in private, was that these same wonderful innocents were also perhaps rather too naive about the whole business. Buddhism has no central licensing agency, no pope, no board of elders. Each school had its own system, but even so, "permission to teach" could mean many things, and one man's enlightened master was another man's fool, or worse yet, charlatan.

And yet, shocking or disillusioning as it may have been, it made for a certain liveliness. Once, when Joshu Sasaki-roshi, a pure Rinzai man, gave a public talk at the University of California in Berkeley, he was asked in the question period if there were anywhere in the Bay area where one could study Zen. The roshi said no, not as far as he knew, and invited the questioner to visit him at the Cimmaron Zen Center down in Los Angeles. There was a surprised, audible reaction from the audience, many of whom were students and friends of Suzuki-roshi's San Francisco Zen Center, which by then had more than one branch in the Bay area, and Sasaki's translator, a Japanese-American doctor, hastened to add, "The roshi means that there is nowhere else where one can study his particular line of Zen," which was true enough. But it certainly appeared—to some at least—that the roshi had rather enjoyed the stir his blunt answer had caused.

VII

Things had changed quite a bit since the fifties when the circle Kerouac sketched in *The Dharma Bums* had been small enough to be included in the backyard of a Mill Valley party. During the "Zen boom" of that time it was said that Zen talk could be heard at every cocktail party. If people talked loosely of Zen now, their tongues were likely to have been loosened by something other than a dry martini: grass, acid or at least strobe lights. Sokoji itself—and its American offshoot, which went by the name of the San Francisco Zen Center—was only a stone's throw from Haight-Ashbury, the crossroads of the cultural transformation that had swept across America.

The spiritual atmosphere of the new generation was eclectic, visionary, polytheistic, ecstatic and defiantly devotional. The paper of the new vision, *The San Francisco Oracle*, exploded in a vast rainbow that included everything in one great Whitmanesque blaze of light and camaraderie. American Indians, Shiva, Kali, Buddha, Tarot, Astrology, Saint Francis, Zen and Tantra all combined to sell fifty thousand copies on streets that were suddenly teeming with people. When the *Oracle* printed the *Heart Sutra*, they did a double spread of the Zen Center version (complete with Chinese characters), but in the borders were two very naked goddesses, drawn in the best Avalon Ballroom psychedelic. The beats had dressed in existential black-and-blue; this new generation wore plumage and beads and feathers worthy of the most flaming tropical birds. If the previous generation had been gloomy atheists attracted to Zen by iconoclastic directives—"If you meet the Buddha, kill him!"—these new kids were, as Gary Snyder told Dom Aelred Graham in an interview in Kyoto, "unabashedly religious. They love to talk about God or Christ or Vishnu or Shiva."

Snyder himself had gotten a firsthand look at the counterculture when he'd returned from Japan for a short visit in 1966. He was just in time for the first Be-In at Golden Gate Park, where he was joined by a number of friends from the early days. Allen Ginsberg was there, (dressed in white, bearded), as were Lawrence Ferlinghetti and Michael McClure. Kerouac was conspicuous by his brooding absence. He wanted nothing to do with it all. Hippies horrified him. When a bunch of kids showed up at his mother's house in Northampton, Long Island with jackets that said *Dharma Bums* across the back he slammed the door in their faces. His last visit to San Francisco had been written down in *Big Sur*, one of his most powerful novels. It was the story of a nervous collapse, of a man looking into the abyss of his success and seeing his friends poisoning the water in the stream he was drinking from. The culmination of the novel came when Kerouac, shuddering with the D. T.'s outside Ferlinghetti's cabin (where he'd gone for a rest) had a vision of the Cross. As far as he was concerned, there was the ring of truth in the remark Japhy Ryder had made to old Ray Smith, which he'd edited out of *The Dharma Bums* at the last minute: "You old son of a bitch, you're going to end up asking for the Catholic rites on your death bed."

But now, at the Be-In, with the sun shining through a deep blue sky and thousands of people at ease in all their finery on the meadow,

Snyder read his poems, and Ginsberg chanted the *Prajnaparamita*, which he'd learned from Gary during his recent trip to Japan and India, to clear the meadows of lurking demons. Even Shunryu Suzuki-roshi appeared briefly, holding a single flower.

Also present on the stage that afternoon were two former Harvard psychology professors, Timothy Leary and Richard Alpert, enthusiasts of the new psychedelics. Whatever else LSD became in time, at that moment it was the messenger that led a fair number of people into the dazzling land of their own mind. What had begun as the private discovery of a few intellectuals and experimenters had spread in a flash, and for a split second of history it was as if the veil had been rent and all the archetypes of the unconscious sprang forth. More often than not—for reasons no one could explain—these came in the guise of the gods and goddesses of the Hindu pantheon. Somehow they fit: the posters for the new bands and ballrooms, with their lush color and wavy flowing lines, were right at home next to popular religious Hindu posters of blue-hued baby Krishna standing on a glowing white lotus.

There were those who claimed psychedelics had changed the rules of the game, and that the mystic visions once enjoyed only by saints could now be had by anyone. In any case, it was obvious to the university researchers at Harvard, who had searched the scientific literature in vain, that the scriptures of Buddhism and Hinduism contained descriptions that matched what they had seen and felt. So Timothy Leary had recast the verses of the *Tao Te Ching* in a book called *Psychedelic Prayers*, and had taken the *Bardo Thodol*, the *Tibetan Book of the Dead*, as a guidebook for the archetypal psychedelic drama of ego-death, journey and rebirth.

"Those who do not have the time or money to go to India or Japan," Gary Snyder wrote in an essay "Passage to More than India," "but who think a great deal about the wisdom traditions, have remarkable results when they take LSD. The *Bhagavad-Gita*, the *Hindu Mythologies*, the *Serpent Power*, the *Lankavatara Sutra*, the *Upanishads*, the *Hevajra Tantra*, the *Mahanirvana Tantra*—to name a few texts—become, they say, finally clear to them. They often feel that they must radically reorganize their lives to harmonize with such insights." At times, as Snyder noted, the psychedelic experience led straight to meditation. "In several American cities," he wrote, "traditional meditation halls of both Rinzai and Soto are flourishing. Many of the newcomers turned to traditional meditation after initial acid experience. The two types of experience seem to inform each other."

And yet, there were crucial distinctions to be made. Long before acid,

Zen masters had dealt summarily with visions that arose during meditation. It made no difference whether these *makyo*—as they were called—were visions of bodhisattvas. They were to be ignored. Some Zen masters were even said to have plunged students with particularly stubborn *makyo* into tubs of icy water.

Still, it was impossible for any roshi to ignore the question of LSD and its relationship to Buddhism. Koun Yamada-roshi, Yasutani-roshi's chief disciple in Japan, was said to have tried it only to report, "This isn't form is the same as emptiness; this is emptiness is the same as form." Suzuki-roshi may have said, as Gary Snyder told Dom Aelred Graham, that "people who have started to come to the zendo from LSD experiences have shown an ability to get into good zazen very rapidly," but he also said in New York, as Harold Talbott, Graham's secretary, told Snyder, "that the LSD experience was entirely distinct from Zen." In any case, it seemed that in practice Suzuki-roshi mostly ignored it. When Mary Farkas of the First Zen Institute asked him what he thought of the "Zen-drug tie-up we kept hearing so much of," she gathered from his reply "that students who had been on drugs gradually gave them up and that highly structured and supervised activities left little opportunity and lessened inclination."

But not everyone was so tolerant. In New York a student walked into the zendo on acid, sat on his zafu until he felt enlightened enough to get up off his cushion in the middle of zazen, then knelt in front of the teacher, rang the bell, and walked off nonchalantly into the small rock garden in back of the zendo. The teacher followed, and the two stood locked eye-ball to eye-ball, until the teacher asked, "Yes, but is it real?" and the student, who seemed to have held his own till then, fled. After that, there was a rule that no one could sit zazen who used LSD in or out of the zendo.

Others in the Zen world were as concerned. In Japan, D. T. Suzuki wrote an essay as part of a symposium on "Buddhism and Drugs" for *The Eastern Buddhist* in which he warned that the popularity of LSD "has reached a point where university professors organize groups of mystical drugtakers with the intention of forming an international society of those who seek 'internal freedom'. . . . All this sounds dreamy indeed," wrote D. T. Suzuki, "yet they are so serious in their intention, that Zen people cannot simply ignore their movements."

If Dr. Suzuki sounded the alarm, the Americans were more moderate in their reactions. Ray Jordan, a former student of Senzaki's and then an assistant professor of psychology, had written in *Psychologia*, that "LSD might be a useful aid both to the realization of prajna and to the development of meditational practice," but a sesshin with Yasutani-roshi had since convinced him that he had been mistaken. The sesshin had "included a moment which the Roshi identified as kensho," and Jordan was now able to testify that "even the deepest and most powerful realizations associated with LSD were weak and dim compared to the reality and clarity of sesshin events. . . ." Jordan admitted that "in a small number of cases psychedelic experiences may have revealed to persons the everyday presentness of the Pure Buddha Land [but] from that point on the psychedelics are of no value whatsoever insofar as the Way is concerned. Without relying on anything one must walk step by step, moment by moment in the daily reality of the Pure Land."

Alan Watts was more sympathetic. He pointed out, to begin with, that everybody must speak for himself since so much depended on the "mental state of the person taking the chemical and circumstances under which the experiment is conducted." In Watts's case, these had been benign, and LSD had given him "an experience both like and unlike what I understood as the flavor of Zen." His mind had slowed, there were subtle changes in sense perception, and most importantly, "the thinker" had become confounded so that it realized "that all so-called opposites go together in somewhat the same way as the two sides of a single coin." This in turn had led to an experience of what the Japanese Buddhists called *ji-ji-mu-ge*, the principle of universal interpenetration.

But if one were not trained in yoga or Zen, warned Watts, this insight might lead one to believe either that "you are the helpless victim of everything that happens to you," or that, like God, you are "personally responsible for everything that happened." To go beyond this impasse, one needed either "an attitude of profound faith or letting-go to you-know-not-what." In that case, "the rest of the experience is total delight . . . what, in Buddhist terms, would be called an experience of world as dharmadhatu, of all things and events, however splendid or deplorable from relative points of view, as aspects of symphonic harmony, which, in its totality, is gorgeous beyond belief."

And yet, the most interesting part of the experience for Watts was not this ecstatic and sublime state, but the moment of return to the ordinary state of mind. There "in the twinkling of an eye" lay the realization "that so-called everyday or ordinary consciousness is the supreme form of awakening, of Buddha's anuttara-samyak-sambodhi." But this realization, remembered clearly enough, soon faded. "It is thus," concluded Watts, "that many of us who have experimented with psychedelic chemicals have left them behind, like the raft which you used to cross a river, and have found growing interest and even pleasure in the simplest practice of zazen, which we perform like idiots, without any special purpose."

It was left to Robert Aitken to describe the new psychedelic-influenced generation in detail. The early members of Koko-an Zendo, Aitken remembers, had been former Theosophists. The turning point had come in 1963 or 64 "when utter strangers would come into the dojo, bow at the entrance, seat themselves and sit like stones through the first period, and then at kinhin time they would get up and fall down."

Aitken couldn't figure it out. They sat as if they'd been doing it for years, but when the time came for them to do kinhin, it was obvious that their legs had fallen asleep, a common occurrence among novices. It turned out, as he later discovered, that word had gone around that the Koko-an Zendo was a good place for tripping.

In 1967 the Aitkens bought a house on the island of Maui in anticipation of Aitken's retirement from the East-West Center at the University of Hawaii. The long-haired young had begun to flock to Maui by then, and many of them had rented rooms in a house the Aitkens had bought. Since the Aitkens continued to rent out rooms, they became intimately acquainted with the new generation, and Aitken was able to sketch out their characteristics for *The Eastern Buddhist* symposium with some appreciation. Those from "the yogic end of the counter-culture," he wrote, "had a consuming interest in illuminative religion, a sense of wholeness and essence, a love of nature, a devotion to poverty and asceticism, a sensitivity to one another, and a desire to 'get it on,' that is, to practice rather than simply to talk."

Many of these were interested in zazen, and the Aitkens decided to establish a branch of Koko-an on Maui. In its first stages, Maui Zendo served "as a kind of mission to the psychedelic Bohemia." "Virtually all the young people who knock on our front door have tried LSD, mescaline, or psilocybin," he wrote—a situation which he thought true for the San Francisco Zen Center as well as other groups across the country.

The Maui Zendo soon became known as "a place where you could get your head together," and a regular zazen schedule was begun. But the turnover was enormous. "The thing that created this marvelous spirit also destroyed it," Aitken says now, "and that was the dope." The regular use of marijuana, Aitken had observed, "destroyed the sense of proportion," while LSD, as he had written in his essay, seemed to "shatter much of the personality structure, and the impulse of the moment assumed paramount importance."

It was, finally, the "human problem of distraction" that Aitken found most crucial. "The new gypsies," he found, "blow like leaves in the wind, now in Mendocino, now at San Francisco, then all the way to Maui, then back to the mainland, always with a convincing reason that may be no more than a faint interior or exterior impulse." Zazen was a natural corrective to this, and the Maui Zendo began to develop more and more in the direction of a training center.

VIII

But why so many drifting, and at this time? Only Aitken, of all the symposium contributors, saw fit to mention the fact that the "Summer of Love," and all that implied, had occurred during a long and unpopular war. "Suppose the American government had begun 15 years ago to develop viable alternatives to a war economy?" he asked. "Would the drop-out movement be so significant today? And would those who did drop out with drugs have the same conviction that society is a bummer? We must raise such questions and accept the likelihood that severe social stress may prompt experimentation to begin with, and may color the drug experiences and subsequent attitudes."

Aitken himself worked as a draft counselor during the Vietnam War, despite the fact that when a student at Koko-an asked Yasutani-roshi, "If my country calls me to serve in the war in Vietnam, should I go or not?" the roshi had replied, without hesitation, "If your country calls you, you should go."

"I could not agree with my Roshi," Aitken would write some years later. Nevertheless, my "faith in him did not waver a jot. I knew he and I grew up in altogether different circumstances—he in the jingoistic fervor of the Chinese and Russian wars,—I in the Humanist world of doubt. Our responsibility to each other lay in reaching a contact at a place deeper than culture or history." As it turned out, Yasutani-roshi and the anti-draft party reached a kind of truce; neither pursued the matter.

Wars, as Sokei-an Sasaki had remarked at the beginning of the Second World War some twenty years earlier, have a way of bringing countries closer together. Vietnam was for the most part a Buddhist country, though the Catholicism brought by the French had firmly established itself. There were mahayanists who had entered from China, both Pure

Land and Zen sects, as well as a Theravadin influence from Southeast Asia. Vietnamese Buddhists had taken an active and visible part in their country's struggle. They seemed to constitute an alternative to both the Catholic American-backed government of Prime Minister Diem and to the National Liberation Front. Buddhists were a real force, and the United States government found it politic to take notice of them.

The State Department even went so far as to establish an Office of Buddhist Affairs. The man picked to organize the new section was Richard Gard, the Buddhist scholar from Claremont who had been instrumental in arranging D. T. Suzuki's postwar visit to America, and an old acquaintance of Aitken's. Gard had been working for some years as an Asian specialist with the United States Information Service when he was informed one afternoon that he had been chosen to brief Secretary of State Henry Cabot Lodge on Buddhism. He would have, he was informed, exactly ten minutes of the secretary's time. Gard thought it over and figured that to fit even the barest outline of Buddhism into ten minutes he would have to speak about sixty words a second.

As it turned out, the secretary of state already knew something about Buddhism. He told Gard that he'd had a cousin, William Sturgis Bigelow, who had been a Buddhist. "In that part of our family, we've heard about Buddhism," he said. "There's nothing at all wrong with it." The secretary then sat down at his desk and pulled out a legal-sized yellow pad. An aide reminded him that he had only ten minutes. Lodge waved him away. "If it's important, let's hear about it," he told Gard. Gard suggested, among other things, that if the secretary wanted to find out about Buddhism, he might consider meeting with Buddhist leaders in Asia, something no one in the State Department had ever done before. Lodge agreed, and in 1963 he met with Japanese and Vietnamese Buddhists—much to their surprise.

It was the first time since the days when Lodge's cousin, William Sturgis Bigelow, had given his close friend, Theodore Roosevelt, a copy of *The Religion of the Samurai*, along with advice on Japanese affairs, that someone sympathetic to Buddhism had access to Washington. When the Sinhalese Embassy made a formal protest about an advertisement which pictured a pair of sandals, soles up, next to a Buddha image, and when other Buddhists protested the marketing of a perfume in a Buddha-shaped bottle (the perfume issuing forth when the figure's head was squeezed), the matter was brought to Gard. While he was without any real power, he was able to communicate the State Department's recommendations. In the same way, he informed MGM that the department did not think it appropriate for them to go ahead with plans for an extravaganza, of Biblical proportions, on the life of the Buddha.

But these were minor matters. In Vietnam, Buddhists were engaged in a life-and-death struggle against the repressive measures of President Ngo Dinh Diem's government. This struggle was most dramatically brought to the attention of the Vietnamese—and the world media—by the self-immolation of Thich Quang Duc in Saigon on May 11, 1963. The practice, originally introduced to Vietnam from China and based on passages in three Indian mahayana sutras, was traditional but rarely practiced in Vietnamese Buddhism. According to one authority, "it was practiced in the northern parts of Vietnam as late as 1950, by monks who had attained the highest degree of meditative perfection."

But it now became an image of the ultimate anguish of that war: a monk, sitting in meditation, hands clasped in the mudra of meditation, body ablaze, brought into American homes by newspapers, magazines and television. According to Dr. Thich Thien-an, a Buddhist monk and scholar (later the founder of the International Buddhist Meditation Center in Los Angeles), he and twenty thousand other Buddhist monks, nuns and intellectuals had been arrested in the middle of the night by the Diem government. Nobody knew they had been arrested and they all expected to die at any moment. Dr. Thien-an himself was led out blindfolded a number of times. "That was an emergency case," he said of the monks who burned themselves. "I was released from jail by those monks who died, because when those monks burned themselves, then newspapers, magazines, and television reported it. Then the United Nations sent an investigation delegation to Vietnam." Dr. Thien-an—with many others—was released the night before the delegation arrived. "In Vietnam," he said, "we consider the first monk to do that a bodhisattva. At that time, if no one had done that, then all of us would have died in jail and nobody would have known." He was aware that many people were put off by what they considered a bizarre act of sacrifice. "In Buddhism, the first important precept is not killing," he said, "not killing oneself and not killing others. But in such an emergency there was no other way. They were using their bodies like a lamp for help."

A few American Buddhists responded with sympathy. The San Francisco Zen Center held a memorial service for Bhikshu Quang Duc and sent a letter to Washington urging action to prevent further persecution of Buddhists in South Vietnam. The Rochester Zen Center held a sesshin dedicated to those who had suffered in the war, and collected donations for relief work. In New York City, the Reverend Boris Erwitt, an ordained Shinshu minister, led a demonstration outside the United Nations, which made the six o'clock news, and towards the end of the decade, Gary Snyder, Richard Baker and a few members of the San Francisco Zen Center protested by sitting zazen in front of the chain-link fence of the Oakland Navy Yard. And in Hawaii, Robert Aitken actively worked with the antiwar movement.

At the same time, the nonviolent wing of the peace movement found an ally in the Vietnamese Buddhist Zen monk Thich Nhat Hanh, who toured America with Jim Forrestal of the Resistance. Thich Nhat Hanh, in turn, wrote a meditation manual for activists. The method recommended mindfulness of breathing.

Other examples of the effect of the war on American Buddhists could be given, but for the most part opposition was an individual matter. Buddhists as Buddhists did not follow the path of social action as so many Christians did. In the midst of all the turmoil, it seemed that sitting still might be the most effective and practical thing anyone could do.

IX

By the fall of 1966 close to a hundred and fifty people were sitting zazen and attending lectures at the San Francisco Zen Center; fifty or sixty sat at least once a day, and eighty people, twice as many as the previous year, had attended the seven-day sesshin. Dainin Katagiri-sensei had joined Shunryu Suzuki-roshi as the assistant priest at both Zen Center and Sokoji (after five months at Zenshuji, the Soto temple in Los Angeles), and in 1967 Kobun Chino-sensei would also arrive to help. As Zen Center itself grew, it naturally spawned a number of satellite centers run by senior students of Suzuki-roshi's: Mel Weitsman in Berkeley, Bill Kwong in Mill Valley and Marion Derby in Los Altos.

The Los Altos group had started out in Marion Derby's living room. In 1966 they decided to convert Marion's garage into a zendo. Suzuki-roshi was very active in the reconstruction, designing the zendo with carpenter William Stocker, picking out the boards for the zendo floor at the local lumberyard and thoroughly enjoying himself cutting and sawing the boards. The *tatami* platforms were constructed at the height of a chair, with one removable section, so that one of the members, unable to use a zafu because of a back problem, could sit in a chair facing the wall at the same height as everyone else—an arrangement that Suzuki-roshi hoped would also encourage older people to attend the sittings.

Every Thursday morning at the Haiku Zendo in Los Altos—so named because it had space for seventeen zafus, the number of syllables in haiku—Suzuki-roshi talked informally. These talks, usually no longer than fifteen minutes, were addressed to a group of lay people who seemed to have little in common except the ability to rise early enough to come to morning zazen.

"Usually Roshi started off in a general, rambling way," one participant recalls, "with no particular subject in mind. After two or three minutes he would discover his subject and continue on into his talk." Mostly he talked about practice and zazen: how to do it, even while living in the suburbs. He showed them how to include their difficulties, as a skillful gardener (to use a favorite metaphor) welcomed and made use of weeds. "We pull the weed and bury the weed near the plant to give nourishment to the plant," he said one morning. "So even though you have difficulty in your practice, even though you have some waves while you are sitting, the weed itself will help you. You should not be bothered by the weeds you have in your mind. You should rather be grateful, because eventually they will enrich your practice."

No one in the West had before spoken so directly and intimately about sitting. Marion Derby recorded, transcribed, and rough-edited the talks. People thought they might make an interesting book (the working title was "Morning Talks at Los Altos"), and Richard Baker took on the project, but because of his duties as president of Zen Center he turned over most of the work to Trudy Dixon. Trudy Dixon, along with her husband, the painter Mike Dixon, had been one of the earliest of Suzuki-roshi's students, and when she began work on Suzuki-roshi's manuscript she was already ill with the cancer that would take her at the age of thirty.

Suzuki-roshi had taught high school English in Japan, and had attended adult education courses in English shortly after his arrival in San Francisco, but his English remained idiosyncratic—he had, after all, only been speaking the language for seven years. Trudy Dixon was a gifted poet, but more than that, she grasped the essentials of her teacher's mind; the process of her dying had intensified her understanding and practice. The book she fashioned, *Zen Mind, Beginner's Mind*, had a fresh, early morning quality to it. Suzuki-roshi spoke with a spare voice, unpretentious and humorous. It was, in fact, an American Buddhist voice, unlike any heard before, and yet utterly familiar. When Suzuki-roshi spoke, it was as if American Buddhists could hear themselves, perhaps for the first time.

Trudy Dixon died before *Zen Mind, Beginner's Mind* was published ("Because of your complete practice your mind has transcended far beyond your physical sickness," Suzuki-roshi would say at her funeral, "and it has taken full care of your sickness like a nurse."), but she had done her part to bring the words of her teacher to thousands of people. From now on, whenever anyone wondered what to read to learn about the practice of Zen, they would most likely be referred to this book of "informal Zen talks."

X

"Suzuki-roshi," remembers Richard Baker, "at first tried to make practice available and possible in people's ordinary way of life. But after a few years he found that almost no one was getting it, so he hoped to establish a traditional monastery in an isolated place in the mountains or country-side." In 1966 Richard Baker located a parcel of land that seemed perfect for what roshi had in mind: a hundred and sixty acres of wilderness in the middle of Los Padres National Forest on the eastern slope of the Coast Range that runs from Carmel to Santa Barbara. Plans to purchase the undeveloped land had barely begun when an adjoining property, Tassajara Hot Springs, became available. It lay nestled in a deep mountain canyon, at the dead end of twenty miles of a twisting, turning, switchbacking dirt road that climbed to 5,000 feet before dropping to Tassajara Canyon. It was as remote as any Chinese or Japanese mountain temple, but it included complete, if aging, facilities: a hot springs, guest cabins, a stone lodge and kitchen.

People had been visiting Tassajara for centuries. The walls of a cave in the sheer cliffs above Tassajara Creek had been decorated with white hand prints by Indians. Indians had also used the hot springs for purification and healing. Spanish hunters followed—"Tassajara" is Spanish for "a place for drying meat." In the 1870s William Hart built a shale dining room, bath house and a few cabins; the next owner, Charles Quilty, Jr., brought in Chinese laborers to cut the road, and by the 1890s a four-horse stage was making the trip from Salinas three times a week.

Like everyone who had ever lived in Tassajara, Bob and Ann Beck, who owned it in 1963, had a special feeling for the place. Tassajara had always served as a retreat, and the Becks liked the idea that the hot springs would be run by people familiar with the traditions of Japanese bathing. The Becks appreciated that Zen Center kept Tassajara open for guests (many of whom had been coming for years) during the summer years. Zen Center, for its part, felt that the presence of guests would "help Zen develop more realistically in relation to American life." Given all this, the Becks did their best to make it possible for Zen Center to buy Tassajara by offering the most favorable terms.

Still, the sum needed was considerable, especially for a group made up of young members without great financial resources. But the time was right. As Robert Aitken wrote from Hawaii, "The development of the Tassajara Zen Mountain Center in a deep American forest marks the transition of expatriate Buddhism to a native religious discipline—the fulfillment of eighty years of Western Buddhist history."

Encouragement and support came from many quarters. Nancy Wilson Ross: "I can think of no project of greater cultural significance in our country's present culture." Paul Lee, Professor of Philosophy, UCSC: "The establishment of a Zen monastery in the wilderness area near Carmel Valley is an important event in the history of religion in America." Huston Smith: "Our preoccupation with the way things ought to be calls for places where, resonating, we can rejoice in the way they *are*. Therefore, the Zen Mountain Center." Gary Snyder: "Looking and walking over the ridges and meadows, swimming the cold river holes and hot spring pools of Tassajara—I know this is the place it has to be. The Indians had it before. The Coast Range Mountains are rugged like Chinese Mountains—the dry rockiness, warmth, and shady groves are like India. There are numbers of fine people ready to make use of the right place. We can't let this slip by." And, finally, Alan Watts: "It is time for us in America to realize that the goal of action is contemplation. Otherwise we are caught up in mock progress, which is just going on toward going on, what Buddhists call samsara—the squirrel cage of birth and death. That people are getting together to acquire this property for meditation is one of the most hopeful signs of our time."

Contributions came from more than a thousand people and many artists and performers gave benefits. Gary Snyder, back from Kyoto now, read at the Fillmore from the on-going *Mountains and Rivers Without End*, sitting half-lotus in front of the microphone, accompanied by a light show put together by the Mahalila Mandalagraphers. Alan Watts lectured to five hundred people in the Avalon Ballroom; Charlotte Selver and Charles Brooks gave a weekend workshop with Suzuki-roshi on sensory awareness; Ali Akbar Khan played. There was even an "Zenefit" as the poster proclaimed, at the Avalon Ballroom, by hometown bands—Big Brother and the Holding Company, the Grateful Dead, and Quicksilver Messenger Service. Not everybody was ready to get up before five in the morning to sit in a Zen monastery, but a lot of people seemed to want a place where they could do it if they ever wanted to.

Zen Buddhists have always had a deep feeling for nature, for "mountains and rivers without end." "The color of mountains is Buddha's pure body/The sound of running water is his great speech," Su Dongpo had written in the thirteenth century, and Suzuki-roshi said, "Nature is a true teacher of Zen." At Tassajara it almost seemed that one had stepped into a Chinese painting. There was only one phone line, Tassajara One, and that was often down. The place roared with silence. Tassajara was beautiful, awe-inspiring, grand, elemental, a perfect place for Zen study.

But it was also—and this too was necessary for Zen practice—a difficult place, a place of extremes. (". . . .But not all who enter the mountains see them as they really are," Suzuki-roshi had continued. "Only a man who knows himself can see the true nature of mountains.") The mountains that towered around the narrow canyon were indeed majestic; they were also enclosing, confining. One did not stroll up them. The canyon itself had the feeling of a great stone zendo that threw one back on oneself, continually. The air was clear, the sky at night luminous with stars. But temperatures were extreme. In the summers the dry California heat could reach above a hundred, but in the winters, when the sun took its time clearing the high mountain walls, the early mornings chilled the bone. Summers it rarely rained and a spark of lightning could set off raging forest fires in a moment; in spring the melting snow and rain could flood Tassajara Creek or turn the road into an impassable river of mud, which was just what happened the first April a crew from Zen Center worked at Tassajara. They were cut off from the outside for three weeks, and not even a four-wheel drive Toyota truck, hastily purchased in San Francisco, could get through.

It was on the coldest days that the students appreciated the famous Tassajara hot springs most. These were reached by way of a Chinese-curved bridge that spanned the creek. The two large concrete baths were lit by kerosene lamps in late afternoon, when the winter sun had already dropped behind the mountain walls. There was no heat to speak of at Tassajara, and the steaming baths served admirably to warm bodies stiff with cold and work, just as the hot Japanese baths had always done in

Zen temples. For Dogen Zenji every detail of daily life was sacred, an opportunity to practice, and so verses were tacked up in the bathhouse, which the students would recite after bowing before a small shrine.

Tassajara Zen Mountain Center opened in July of 1966 when Suzuki-roshi, Katagiri-sensei, Chino-sensei, Maezumi-sensei and Bishop Togen Sumi-roshi, head of the Soto School in America, held a ceremony to install the Buddha on an altar in the zendo. The *shuso* (head monk) for the first practice period was Richard Baker, who had had his head shaved, becoming a monk and a priest in a ceremony the night before. (A shaved head, Suzuki-roshi told a reporter, was "the ultimate hair-style.")

Suzuki-roshi called Tassajara a "baby monastery," but it was not really a monastery in the Western sense of the word. It was a place for intensive Zen training, not a lifetime retreat from the world. In this respect, it was identical to Japanese Zen monasteries or training temples—with one important difference. There were men and women at Tassajara. This was a fundamental departure from the traditions of Asian Buddhism. Married couples had their own quarters, while single men and women lived in dormitories. The arrangement seemed to work very well, and the Tassajarans wondered why it had never been tried before.

The three-month practice period that began in July was a custom that went back to the time of the Buddha. In those days the monks had wandered most of the year until the rainy season, at which point they settled down together to practice meditation in retreat. The custom had continued in most Buddhist countries, and formed the basis for the three-month intensive-training periods in Chinese and Japanese monasteries. It was, as Suzuki-roshi said, "one of the foundations of Zen Buddhism . . . and indispensable for the existence of Zenshinji" (Zen Mind/Heart Temple, the Japanese name given Tassajara.)

It was traditional in Japan for new students to do *tangaryo*, to sit seven days by themselves, with breaks only for meals. This seemed somewhat harsh, since few students had extensive sitting experience, and it was decided to begin with a *tangaryo* of three days, and then five days at a later date. Even so, most students found it one of the most difficult things they had ever done. Suzuki-roshi said only, "Be prepared to sit" by way of instruction. From four o'clock in the morning to ten o'clock at night, with nothing but the sound of Tassajara Creek outside of the stone walls they faced, the students were left to themselves. It was required only that they stay on the cushion—just how was left to the individual. Of the seventy who said they would start, fifty-five finished.

Tassajara followed the traditional way, but Suzuki-roshi also liked to give his students space. ("The way to control a cow," he had said, "is to give it a big meadow.") There was a lot of discussion in the beginning about whether to wear robes, what language to chant in, how strict the schedule ought to be, and what kinds of practices to include.

In the end, they found themselves following a modified version of the rules Pai-chang had formulated for Zen monasteries in China nearly a thousand years before. The Indian sangha had at first been composed of monks who begged for a living, as rishis and sadhus had always done in India; later Indian Buddhism had been supported by wealthy lay people and royalty. But in China, Buddhism was a foreign religion, at times in competition with both Confucianism and Taoism. Deprived of secure government patronage, Chinese Buddhist monks supported themselves: thus Pai-chang's famous rule, "A day of no work is a day of no eating." Chinese Ch'an (that is, Zen) monks grew rice, cut their own wood and cooked their own food, and many of the encounters between master and student that later became recorded as *koans* took place in the field or kitchen.

Manual labor—*samu*—was an essential part of Zen training. Suzuki-roshi himself was a skilled mason with a fondness for working with stone. At Tassajara he worked on the stone wall that supported the bridge, and began a rock garden. Though small, he was able to outlast students twice his size. Someone observed that he was always at rest, except when directly pushing or guiding a stone to its proper place. He himself said only that he was probably too attached to hard work.

If it was true that Tassajara gave people who had only seen the roshi occasionally in San Francisco an opportunity to spend more time around him—("The teacher," as Suzuki-roshi said at the beginning of the first practice period, "works and practices under the same conditions as the students. But there is some difference. The student perceiving this difference is shown the way to the Buddha in himself and the Buddha in his teacher.")—it was also true that the schedule was the teacher. It, and the rules that governed group practice, made the student realize that, as roshi had said, again at the start of the practice period, "To live in this world means to exist under some condition moment after moment." It was only by learning to exist in these conditions with "flexibility of mind" that the student could discover "the imperturbable mind which is beyond concepts of personal or impersonal, formal or informal."

The high-pitched wake-up bell rang at four in the morning. Then came the clack of a wooden mallet against the *han*, a rectangular rough wooden plank, a sound that continued in a tattoo of ever-increasing intensity for three rounds, giving students fifteen minutes to stumble along the kerosene-lantern-lit path to the zendo. Two periods of zazen followed, the morning chants (in Japanese and English) and then breakfast, a three-hour work period, another period of zazen, lunch, rest, study, more work, the baths, a service, supper, lecture by the roshi, and finally, another two periods of zazen. Each period of the day was signaled by one of the percussion instruments traditional to Zen monasteries—a bronze bell (*densho*), handbell, the han and the thunderous roll of the buddha drum. All these, so important to the atmosphere of Tassajara, had been sent as a gift from Soto Zen Headquarters in Japan.

Japanese monastery food was vegetarian and rather meagre by American standards—white polished rice and pickles predominated. The so-called Zen macrobiotic diet was in vogue during the mid-sixties. (Philip Kapleau told his students in Rochester that the only time he had ever seen Japanese monks rebel was when they were served brown rice at the suggestion of a visiting American.) After some experimentation, the chief cooks, Bill Kwong and Ed Brown, came up with a reasonable diet. The food was vegetarian, brown rice being served fairly often, along with cheese and eggs. Miso soup, with its high protein content, was daily fare, and the morning gruel, concocted of rice cooked along with the previous days leftovers, proved surprisingly tasty. Bread was whole grain, freshly baked, and thick.

The Tassajara cuisine was eventually collected by Ed Brown into two cookbooks, *The Tassajara Bread Book* and *Tassajara Cooking*. More than just collections of recipes, the cookbooks managed to give the feel of "kitchen practice." The Tassajara cookbooks sold—and continue to sell—a large number of copies. It was these books, more than anything else, that introduced people across America to Tassajara and the spirit behind it—a circumstance that would probably have greatly pleased Dogen, who put the most advanced monks in charge of the kitchen, and who wrote *Tenzo Kyokun*, a work devoted to the subject.

On workdays lunches were taken outdoors at wooden tables under the watchful eyes of big blue Steller's Jays, who tested mindfulness by swooping down on any morsel of food left unguarded for a moment. On more formal occasions such as sesshin, meals were eaten in the zendo using *oryoki*—a set of three bowls (the largest representing the Buddha's begging bowl) that lie nestled one inside the other, with a linen napkin, dishcloth, spoon, chopsticks and *setsu* (bowl cleaner) in their own cloth case, the whole covered by a final cloth, which unfolded forms the base on which the three bowls are set.

An oryoki meal begins with three rolls of the Buddha drum announcing an offering of food first to the Buddha on the shrine. Food is served down the line to the accompaniment of chants and *gasshos* (palms together), eaten with mindfulness, silence and speed. When the wooden clappers are struck, the closing chants begin, and the servers enter with hot water or weak tea, which is used to clean the empty bowls. (It is understood that everything taken must be eaten.) The bowl-cleaning water is passed from one bowl to the other, cleansing each in turn, and part is drunk and part poured into a bucket which will in turn be emptied into the garden. A few morsels of food are put into a bowl and taken out to be offered to the hungry ghosts who will claim their due later in the evening in the form of raccoons and other small animals, and then the bowls are replaced inside each other, the various cloths refolded and laid on top, and the outer cloth retied.

The entire process is fast, efficient and wonderfully self-contained; it is also a moving and dramatic ceremony—a ceremony in which the most ordinary act of eating, stripped down to its essentials, becomes meditation. It is also a gauge of mindfulness since a moment's inattention will throw a person out of rhythm with everyone else in the zendo. Of course at first not everyone saw oryoki in such favorable light. More than a few thought they were being "programmed" but by the end of the practice period, *The Windbell*, Zen Center's magazine, reported that "many students left Tassajara feeling that the most important thing they'd learned there was how to eat in a satisfying and simple manner."

The practice period ended with a seven-day sesshin, which itself ended with formal dharma dialogue with Suzuki-roshi. A few days later the *Shuso* ceremony was held. In Japan it had often degenerated into a merely formal occasion. But this was not the case at Tassajara. Kobun Chino-sensei instructed the students to ask "questions which demonstrated their own understanding of Zen and which probed the understanding of the Shuso." Reported the *Windbell*, "Something was obviously expected from the Shuso and the zendo was charged with skeptical excitement—how can a student answer questions usually asked a roshi."

After the Shuso had chanted, offered incense, received the bamboo-root vajra staff from Suzuki-roshi, and announced, "I am ready for your questions," Bill Kwong rose, "leaped to his feet, stamped and shouted *KWATZ*: Then he turned slowly and formally and walked toward the door. There was a tense pause and the Shuso asked, 'Do you have anything else to say?' The student turned, stamped, and walked back, bowed to the Shuso, and sat down." Another student: "What do you make of my transparency?" Answered by: "What transparency? You seem to be there to me, I can't see the wall through you." After more questions, the first practice period at Tassajara and in America ended. From that day on there has never been a year without one. As Kobun Chino-sensei said, "In a vale of these deep mountains a disciple of Buddha comes to teach. Let us hear congratulations."

The importance of Tassajara as the first true mountain-home of the American Buddhist practice was underlined by the visit of Yasutani-roshi, Nakagawa Soen-roshi, Tai Shimano-sensei and Maezumi-sensei in the summer of 1968. The two roshis had just finished a sesshin in Ojai, and Soen-roshi, Yasutani-roshi and Tai Shimano-sensei were on their way to New York to open the New York Zendo Shoboji (Temple of the True Dharma) in a renovated carriage house on East Sixty-seventh Street. Soen-roshi sent a large buddha, "The Endless Dimension Universal Buddha" that had been discovered at Ryutakuji; he also carried with him a smaller Healing Buddha and Maitreya Buddha also from Ryutakuji, and a portion of Nyogen Senzaki's ashes.

The party first shared a hot bath with Suzuki-roshi. Suzuki-roshi and Kobun Chino-sensei then conducted an informal funeral service for Nyogen Senzaki, and Soen-roshi gave a short talk about Senzaki and offered a portion of Senzaki's ashes to Tassajara. They then drove to the top of the mountain and walked out on a freshly cut trail to the peak where Soen-roshi conducted an impromptu full-moon ceremony. As they formed a circle, clapping their hands, chanting the *Heart Sutra* and dancing, the full moon came up over the peak, and Soen-roshi scattered Senzaki's ashes on top of a peak indicated by Suzuki-roshi. A few years later, part of Suzuki-roshi's own ashes would be scattered on the next peak.

Another portion of Nyogen Senzaki's ashes was carried to New York, where it was enshrined in the new zendo; other portions rested in Los Angeles and Honolulu. The dust of his body was now scattered across America, in all the places people practiced the dharma he had taught so long and quietly.

A year earlier the last of his fellow pioneers had joined him. Ruth Fuller Sasaki died in 1967. A year before that, in 1966, Senzaki's fellow student at Engakuji, D. T. Suzuki, had died in Kamakura, working at his desk to the very end, at the age of 96. His last words reflected the growing influence of Shin Buddhism on his thought: "Don't worry! Thank you! Thank you!" An era had ended.

XI

Students returning to San Francisco after the first practice period at Tassajara found themselves at loose ends. This was to be expected after such a prolonged period of intense meditation, but the question still arose of how to continue in the city the practice they began in the mountain fastness of Tassajara. Group practice (which the Japanese likened to a bagful of potatoes: each one cleaning the other by rubbing against it) had been an important part of the training at Tassajara, and it seemed a natural step for people to begin to live together in the row of frame houses across the street from Sokoji. (San Francisco, in any case, had a history of communal living, and the city at that time was peppered with more than a hundred urban communes.)

The Zen households helped, but something more was needed. Zen Center now seemed like a child that had outgrown its parents' home. The congregation of Sokoji had been a most gracious host in the best Japanese tradition, but sharing Sokoji with the Japanese congregation also meant sharing it with a Women's Auxiliary, a three-man band that practiced Monday nights, a women's judo class on Thursdays and Japanese movies on weekends. Both parent and child agreed it was time to leave home.

In 1969 Zen Center found and bought a large red-brick building, the Jewish Women's Club residence, on the corner of Page and Laguna Streets. Page Street, as it was called, came complete with a large hotel-style kitchen and dining room, rooms for seventy people in its two upper stories and a courtyard that Suzuki-roshi planned to turn into a rock garden. The move scarcely interrupted the schedule. The trucks were loaded after the morning sitting at Sokoji and unloaded that afternoon at Page Street in time for the evening sitting in the new basement zendo. The next day they began to hold services in the new Buddha Hall, situated on the first floor of the building, looking out on Page Street. Now anybody walking past in the early morning or late afternoons could hear the steady heartbeat of the *mokugyo*, the deep and high of the bells, and the steady monotones of the chanting, "Form is emptiness, emptiness is form. . . ."

The neighborhood itself presented more than a few problems. This was not Japantown, where the people knew that a shaved head meant a Buddhist priest. The area had one of the highest crime rates in San

Francisco, and the people, for the most part poor and black, didn't know what to make of the group that had just bought the building. At first the Zen Center members, good college-educated liberals for the most part, kept the door open. But when the neighborhood kids took to hanging out in the building, followed by their older brothers and sisters, the situation grew edgy. There were thefts and random outbreaks of violence. There is one story about some heavy-looking dudes showing up in the hallway one afternoon just as Suzuki-roshi was leaving the zendo. "Hey, man," one of them demanded, pointing to the roshi's kyosaku. "What you do with that stick?" Roshi looked up—his questioner was at least twice his size—and glaring fiercely said, "I hit people with it." Everybody froze, and then roshi brought the stick down to the tough's shoulder, as slow and gentle as a falling feather.

But not everyone could play with the situation so skillfully. A year before there had been a problem with people midnight-raiding the refrigerator at Tassajara. Tatsugami-roshi, a great, craggy-faced, ex-sumo wrestler and former head of training at Eiheiji, had been in residence at Tassajara then, and he proposed that the students simply "put locks on the doors and take them off your minds." Some had seen it as defeat, but they had gone ahead and done it, and now—after much discussion—they reluctantly did the same thing at Page Street.

Of course all the problems were actually another form of the *genjo koan*—the root koan, that arises out of everyday life—and as such were to be welcomed. "To have a strong practice in comfortable surroundings is difficult," said Suzuki-roshi. "But when you practice with various difficulties that practice has a lot of strength in it. . . . When we practice in the midst of the difficulties of our neighbors and our own difficulties, then we will have good practice."

It had been eleven years since Suzuki-roshi had come to America, and it was time now for older students to help out. There were the problems with the surrounding community, and there were also all the new people, some merely curious, some desperate, some burned-out, who were now appearing at the door to Page Street in ever-increasing numbers.

Suzuki-roshi had already ordained six people as first-order priests; now he decided to hold a lay ordination. It was not, as he said at the ceremony, "to give some special idea of lay Buddhist because all of us are Buddhists, actually . . . but the time has come for us to strive more sincerely to help others." He admitted that he wasn't sure just what a "lay ordination" was—the term itself being rather contradictory—just as he wondered when he first came to America about the proper form of an

American Buddhism that was "not exactly priest's practice and not exactly laymen's practice," but he was willing to see how things would develop. The thirty-six people who took the lay ordination sewed their own *rakusus*—the small rectangular bib-like vestment that symbolized the Buddha's patchwork robe—out of nineteen jigsaw-shaped pieces of black cloth, reciting *namu ki e butsu* ("I take refuge in the Buddha") with every stitch. "I think this is a good example of the Buddhist way," said Suzuki-roshi. "Even though we are busy there is some time to practice the most formal practice. Even though all human beings in the city are busy, there is no reason why they cannot practice our way. If all join our practice of being a Bodhisattva, the result will be great."

"In the East," as Suzuki-roshi said, "the main effort we make to solve problems is to work inside ourselves. But here in the West we try to solve problems actively, by action outside of ourselves. The real way to help others should be a combination of the so-called Eastern and Western ways."

The idea was not new, but as the Zen Center settled into their inner-city home, they would become particularly skillful and effective in blending the two approaches. Organic vegetables from Green Gulch—a Zen Center farming community and monastery just over the Golden Gate Bridge in Marin county—would be sold (at prices the neighborhood people could afford) in the Green Gulch Green Grocery, across the street from the center, along with bread from a Zen Center-run bakery. After some debate, Green Gulch Green Grocery would sell soft drinks as a concession to a neighborhood taste; the line would be drawn at alcohol and cigarettes. The Zen Center also became active in the local neighborhood organizations, finally founding the independent Neighborhood Foundation. Their sophistication and experience in organizing skills would enable them to help the community secure a neighborhood park, and also to develop a program to help maintain low rentals in the area.

Within a short time Page Street—along with Tassajara and, later, Green Gulch—had become kind of a showcase or pilot project of the emerging American Buddhism. At Page Street the regular day-to-day regimen of traditional Soto practice was combined with American community life. A few people spent all their time working there while others spent their days at outside jobs. Businesses began to develop, first being Alaya Stitchery, first an in-house supplier of zafus and zabutons, (cushions used for sitting practice), and then a shop with its own line of clothing and designer-colored zafus.

Zen Center became an almost obligatory stop for every visiting Buddhist, many of whom spoke or gave workshops there. Lama Govinda and his wife Li Gotami showed their painting and photographs at Page Street, and Buddhist scholar Edward Conze, the foremost translator of the Prajnaparamita literature, gave seminars. The first Tibetans to arrive in America also found a welcome at Zen Center—Tarthang Tulku and Lama Kunga, who started their own centers in Berkeley, and Sonam Kazi, a Sikkimese layman and meditation master. Chogyam Trungpa, Rinpoche, who met Suzuki-roshi at Tassajara in 1970, found Suzuki-roshi

> my accidental father, presented as a surprise from America, the land of confusion. All his gestures and communications were naked and to the point as though you were dealing with the burning tip of an incense stick. At the same time, this was by no means irritating, for whatever happened around the situation was quite accommodating. He was very earthy, so much so that it aroused nostalgia for the past when I was in Tibet working with my teacher. . . . It was amazing that such a compassionate person existed in the midst of so much aggression and passion.

Suzuki-roshi spent the winter-spring practice period of 1969 convalescing at Page Street from a bout with influenza. In January he returned to Japan for six months. Richard Baker, along with his wife and child, had been studying Buddhism and Japanese culture and language in Kyoto, and he now accompanied Suzuki-roshi to Rinso-in, where Suzuki-roshi formally acknowledged him as his dharma heir.

When Suzuki-roshi returned to America, he had his gall bladder removed. In the summer of 1971, he went up to Tassajara, seemingly in better health. In fact, he had cancer of the liver and the doctors were not very hopeful, but he and his wife decided not to say anything to his students for awhile. While he was at Tassajara, he went on as if nothing were the matter. Even though the temperature was in the hundreds, he followed the regular schedule, worked in the rock garden, held dokusan, lectured far into the night and began preparing for the lay ordination of fifty-five students—a task that entailed selecting Buddhist names and writing out calligraphy on the backs of rakusus and lineage papers.

His wife tried to slow him down, but she had a hard time doing it. He seemed to enjoy the game like a mischievous child, and when he was working in his rock garden he sometimes stationed his jisha as lookout, instructing him to whistle when he spotted Mrs. Suzuki. One afternoon he got the whole kitchen staff, as well as a number of other people, to help make *udon* (noodles) for a dinner party he was planning for a few older students. Suzuki-roshi kept adding to the dough they were rolling out on the freshly-scrubbed kitchen floor, until the whole kitchen was filled with *udon*. When Mrs. Suzuki appeared, and tried to get him to leave for an afternoon nap, Suzuki-roshi refused and they had what sounded like an argument in Japanese. Mrs. Suzuki stomped out and Suzuki-roshi happily continued to add more dough. An hour or two later she returned, this time with a look of steely determination in her eyes, grabbed her husband by the arm and pulled him out the door. Suzuki-roshi laughed and waved goodby, and all of Tassajara ate noodles for a week.

But he was very sick. "People say that Buddhism is dying in Japan," he had said at a lecture in San Francisco some weeks earlier. "*But when something is dying it is the greatest teacher*." So he went on and on. Driving back from Tassajara to San Francisco, he stopped at the St. Francis Retreat House where Yasutani-roshi, Soen-roshi and Tai Shimano-sensei were holding sesshin. He took part in the closing ceremony, and Soen-roshi made tea for him in a bowl he had brought from Jerusalem.

He returned to Page Street and his bed in a quiet, sunny room overlooking the courtyard. He left it only once, for the Mountain Seat Ceremony in which he installed Richard Baker as his successor and chief priest of Zen Center.

Richard Baker had been one of Suzuki-roshi's earliest students. He had gone to Harvard, worked at Grove Press in New York and then pursued a master's in Oriental History at Berkeley, where he had organized a number of important conferences for the University Extension—among them the celebrated Berkeley Poetry Conference and the first LSD conference.

Sometime after he met Suzuki-roshi, Baker was having a beer in a North Beach Mexican restaurant with a friend who suddenly turned to him with great conviction and had said, "You know, Dick, if we were really serious, we'd drop everything and just study Buddhism." Baker had looked across the table and realized that his friend didn't mean it—it was just something he'd said—but the words went right through him, and he realized his friend was right, whether he meant it or not. He had felt, as he once said, "like I had just dropped a thousand suitcases." The next morning he went to Zen Center and began sitting regularly.

Now, nearly ten years later, he found himself outside Katagiri-sensei's home, leading a procession down Page Street, to the accompaniment of bells and drum. He was wearing a blue and gold phoenix-emblazoned robe given him by Suzuki-roshi and holding a horse-hair fly whisk, as he stopped to offer incense and *gathas* (verses) at various stations: the door to Page Street, the shrine in the Buddha Hall and zendo, Suzuki-roshi's room.

The Mountain Seat Altar was a large platform assembled at one end of the Buddha Hall. The sangha was in front, kneeling on the tatami; the invited guests—Lama Kunga, Abbot Hsuan Hua from Gold Mountain Temple, Sasaki-roshi from Los Angeles, to name just a few—were seated in chairs around the room. Suzuki-roshi appeared then at the head of the procession, half-carried by his son. He was shockingly thin and frail, banging on the tatami with his staff. The drum stopped. Baker-roshi (as his master had acknowledged him) stood, offered incense, and recited his gatha:

> This piece of incense
> Which I have had for a long long time
> I offer with no-hand
> To my Master, to my friend, Suzuki Shunryu-daiosho
> The founder of these temples.
> There is no measure of what you have done.
>
> Walking with you in Buddha's gentle rain
> Our robes are soaked through,
> But on the lotus leaves
> Not a drop remains.

Katagiri-sensei gave the authentication verse for Suzuki-roshi. Zentatsu Myoyu Baker's sermon was to the point: "There is nothing to be said." Wrote one observer:

> Suzuki-roshi was helped to his feet and moved to the front of the altar to make his bow. But when he turned to face the people there was on his face an expression at once fierce and sad. His breath puffed mightily in his nostrils, and he looked as if he strove vigorously to speak, to say something, perhaps to exhort his diciples to be strong in their practice, or to follow Richard Baker with faith; no one can say. He faced the congregation directly as if to speak and instead rolled his staff between his hands sounding the rings twice, once looking to the left and once to the right side of the hall. It was as though some physical shock had passed through the hall; there was a collective intake of breath, and suddenly, everywhere people were weeping openly. All those who had been close to the Roshi now realized fully what it would mean to lose him, and were overcome with a thoroughly human sorrow. As their Master falteringly walked from the Hall, still marking each step with his staff,

> everyone put his hands palm to palm before his face in the gesture of gassho, and bowed deeply. And that was all. Very simple and direct, the ceremony had lasted little more than an hour.

Shunryu Suzuki-roshi died two weeks later, early in the morning of December 4, 1971, just after the opening bell of the Rohatsu sesshin that celebrates Buddha's enlightenment. His wife, son, and successor, Baker-roshi, were with him at the time. He had been in America for nearly twelve years—a complete cycle according to the Chinese calendar—and in that short time he had discovered the authentic voice of American Buddhism and cleared the ground for the first American Buddhist community. His life was complete.

Yasutani-roshi died two years later, on March 28, 1973, at the age of eighty-eight, three days after conducting a *jukai* (lay ordination) ceremony for about thirty people in Kamakura. He left the Sanbo Kyodan in the hands of Koun Yamada-roshi, his principal dharma successor, a lay roshi who commuted everyday from Kamakura to his job as a hospital administrator in Tokyo. His work in America was continued by Taizan Maezumi-roshi at the Zen Center of Los Angeles who had received *inka* from him in 1970, as well as by Philip Kapleau in Rochester, Eido-roshi in New York and Robert Aitken in Hawaii.

Sokei-an, the Zen pioneer who had first come to America in 1906, had once said that bringing Zen to America was like holding the root of a lotus to rock. By the end of the sixties, thanks to the work of Shunryu Suzuki-roshi and Hakuun Yasutani-roshi, no one could doubt that the lotus had taken hold.

CHAPTER THIRTEEN

WHEN THE IRON BIRD FLIES

I

At dusk on March 17, 1959, Tendzin Gyatso, the Fourteenth Dalai Lama, disguised as a Tibetan peasant, slipped out a backdoor of the Norbu Lingka Summer Palace, and passed through the lines of the Chinese troops surrounding Lhasa. He was met on the banks of the Kyichu river by a party of Khampa (East Tibetan) horsemen, and two weeks later crossed the Himalayas into India. By the time the Chinese sealed the border close to a hundred thousand Tibetans had followed him into exile.

India was not an easy country to be a refugee in, but it was the birthplace of the Buddha and the home of the religion the Tibetans valued above all else. Tibetan Buddhism was, for the most part, Indian Buddhism. Indian Buddhists had founded the first Tibetan monastery, Samye, in the seventh century; all four major schools of Tibetan Buddhism traced their origins back to Indian masters; and the Tibetan Tripitaka had been translated directly from the Sanskrit by teams of Tibetans and Indians. Of course there had not been any Buddhism in

India for more than seven hundred years—not since the great Buddhist university of Nalanda had been razed to the ground by the Moslem armies invading from the north. But by that time a large part of the Indian Buddhist tradition, both written and oral, had safely been transferred to Tibet. Now that refuge, too, had been destroyed. If Tibetan Buddhism was to survive and grow, it would have to do so, once more, from the land of its birth.

Tendzin Gyatso, the Fourteenth Dalai Lama, had been two when the search party from Lhasa reached his parents' modest farmhouse in a small village in the province of Amdo, near the Chinese border. They had been led to the house in the customary way—by a vision the previous Dalai Lama's regent had seen reflected in the sacred waters of lake Palden Lamoi Latso. The regent had seen a small boy standing in a courtyard before a house exactly like this one—there had been the same black-and-white dog, the same tiled roof, the same oddly shaped drain spouts and though the leader of the search party, the abbot of Sera monastery, had come disguised as a servant, the child seemed to recognize him at once. Furthermore, Tendzin Gyatso could speak the refined Lhasa dialect of the court, and when he was shown a number of ritual objects that had belonged to his predecessor, the Thirteenth Dalai Lama, and asked to choose between them and exact replicas, he unerringly picked the authentic ones.

The state oracle of Nechung confirmed the choice, and there were other tests, all no doubt important, but what most impressed observers, such as Sir Charles Bell, the British representative in Lhasa (and a close friend of the Thirteenth Dalai Lama) was the way the young boy from a peasant family in Amdo took everything quite casually and easily, as if he had expected it all. Tendzin Gyatso obviously felt, as he himself said later, very much at home in the role of the Dalai Lama.

Tendzin Gyatso's immediate predecessor, the Thirteenth Dalai Lama, had done his best to bring Tibet safely into the modern world. He had managed to maintain Tibetan independence in the face of foreign intrusion by the British, who dispatched an expeditionary force to Lhasa under Sir Francis Younghusband in 1904, and by the Chinese, in 1910. The Thirteenth Dalai Lama had instituted reforms in land distribution and taxation, and he had curbed the power of the largest monasteries. He had sent Tibetans to study abroad, and had opened an English school in Lhasa in the 1920s. He had also introduced electricity to Lhasa and brought the first motor car (carried piece by piece over the Himalayas), to Tibet. But he had died in 1933 leaving an ominous prophecy. A high incarnation in a monastery in Outer Mongolia had been killed by the Communists and the monks were forbidden to practice their religion: the same thing, the Thirteenth Dalai Lama said, could be expected to happen in Tibet, and on a much wider scale.

Tendzin Gyatso was sixteen when the Chinese Army entered Tibet on October 7, 1950. Despite his youth, he assumed his role as Dalai Lama. For nine years he tried to reach some understanding with the Chinese, but the situation continued to deteriorate. A revolt broke out in the Eastern province of Kham, and then spread to Lhasa. When the Chinese invited the Dalai Lama to their camp for a theatrical performance, asking him to come without his usual entourage or his personal body-guard, the Tibetans feared the worst, and surrounded his palace, the Potala. Fighting broke out, and it was at the height of this crisis that the Dalai Lama left Lhasa.

When the Dalai Lama reached India he was a tall, rather thin man, bespectacled, with the stooped scholarly shoulders of one who has spent many hours bent over his books. He wore the closely cropped hair and maroon robes of a Tibetan monk, and had especially long and graceful arms, one of the signs, it was said, of an incarnation of the Dalai Lama. He was a serious and earnest man, but wore his authority lightly, with a detached, almost bemused air.

To Tibetans, the Dalai Lama was not only the political ruler of their country, he was also the incarnation of Avalokiteshvara, the bodhisattva of compassion. The basis of this rebirth was considered to be the bodhisattva vow of mahayana Buddhism—a deep motivation, strengthened through lifetimes of spiritual practice, to delay one's own entry into nirvana in order to liberate all sentient beings. Such a person was considered to have already realized his own nature as without self or ego, and yet still took rebirth for the sake of others. The Indian Buddhist Shantideva had expressed this vow in his classic *Bodhicaryavatara*: "As long as there are migrators in cyclic existence, may I remain—removing their suffering."

Tibetan Buddhists are taught to consider everything that happens in life, good or bad, as part of their path, and the Dalai Lama found the experience of being a refugee to be quite useful, in a spiritual sense. He had done his best to be realistic in Tibet, but his position had made it difficult. As he said in a recent interview,

> Being a refugee is a really desperate, dangerous situation. At that time, everyone deals with reality. It is not the time to pretend things are beautiful. That's something. You feel involved with reality. In peace time, everything goes smoothly. Even if there is a problem, people pretend that things are good. They can practice that during a peaceful or smooth time. During a dangerous period, when there's a dramatic change, then there's no scope to pretend that everything is fine. You must accept that bad is bad.

The situation was tragic; the Chinese had swifly and brutally suppressed the revolt of 1959, a half million people lost their lives, and Tibetan culture had been nearly eradicated. Monasteries had been transformed into barracks, and many of the ancient texts of Tibetan and Indian Buddhism burned, or used as fodder for mules. To the Chinese, Buddhism and feudalism were one and the same, and both had to be destroyed.

There was not much the Tibetans in India could do. Some Khampas, the fiercely independent Eastern Tibetans, harassed the Chinese with guerilla actions in the border regions, but they were hopelessly outclassed militarily, being no match for Chinese airplanes and machine guns. Prime Minister Nehru had offered sanctuary, but he could not recognize the Tibetan government-in-exile. To do so would have further endangered India's relationship with China, already threatened by a long-standing border dispute. The rest of the world looked away. No one wanted to risk a war with China over an obscure country like Tibet.

II

For the most part the Tibetan exiles, following the lead of the Dalai Lama, faced their situation philosophically. They were nationalists; they would do everything they could to regain their country, but first they were Buddhists. "From a deep point of view," the Dalai Lama said, "while we don't have our independence and are living in someone else's country, we have a certain type of suffering, but when we return to Tibet and gain our independence, then there will be other types of suffering. So, this is just the way it is." This was not pessimism, he explained, though it might look that way, but realism—"Buddhist realism." Facing the facts in this way did not mean giving up in despair. On the contrary: "These sorts of thoughts," he said, "make me stronger; more active."

In any case, there was a great deal to do. To begin with there was the very real question of survival. Food and medicine were both in short supply; the camps were dangerously overcrowded. The Tibetans were accustomed to living at very high altitudes; in the heat and humidity of the low Indian plains many of them came down with tuberculosis and emphysema. Then there was the problem of livelihood: the Tibetans had to find ways to make a living in India. At the same time there was the larger, more complex question of how Tibetan culture itself could survive and grow in the completely new conditions of modern India.

To the Dalai Lama, as to other Tibetans, the future of Tibetan culture (which was indistinguishable from Tibetan Buddhism) depended on the future of the young *tulkus*. The tulkus were, like the Dalai Lama, enlightened teachers who had consciously taken rebirth for the benefit of others still caught in the wheel of samsara. The Dalai Lama was the best known of the tulkus, but they existed in all the schools of Tibetan Buddhism. (They are referred to as *rinpoche*, "precious jewel.") In Tibet the tulkus had received a rigorous and thorough training in all aspects of Buddhism. Often they would study closely with a guru they had themselves instructed in a previous lifetime, so that the teaching of a particular lineage passed back and forth, each tulku taking a generational turn as teacher and student, sage and child. In this way the continuity of the teaching had been assured, but in the present situation nothing was being done.

The welfare and training of the young tulkus was naturally of special concern to the Dalai Lama, and he directed his concern to Mrs. Freda Bedi, then working with the Central Social Welfare Board of the Indian government. Mrs. Bedi was most sympathetic. She had recently completed a vipassana meditation course with Mahasi Sayadaw in Burma. When she had heard about the Tibetan refugees streaming into India on her return to Delhi, she had gone out immediately to take a firsthand look at the conditions in the camps. Something about the Tibetans touched her deeply, and she had vowed, then and there, to devote the rest of her life to their welfare.

Freda Bedi was a formidable woman who took her vows seriously. She had been one of the first women to graduate from Oxford, where she had met her husband, Baba Bedi, a direct descendant of Guru Nanak, founder of the Sikhs, and also an ardent Indian nationalist. It was traditional for descendants of Guru Nanak to marry outside the Sikh community, and usually they married Brahmins. Instead, Baba Bedi married Freda and brought her back to the Punjab. There they began a family and took an active part in the struggle for Indian independence against the British. Baba Bedi spent about fifteen years in prison. Freda herself was detained for a shorter time along with her children. When independence finally came in 1949 Freda became a leader in the fight for women's rights in the Punjab. Eventually she became a high-ranking official in the Social Welfare Board under Nehru.

Freda Bedi was just the person to do something about the education of the young tulkus. Despite nearly thirty years in India—many of them spent in active opposition to her native land—Freda Bedi had managed to retain the best qualities of the traditional English schoolmistress. Furthermore, she had already taken one young tulku, Chogyam Trungpa, Rinpoche, under her wing and into her home in Kalimpong.

Chogyam Trungpa was then about twenty. He was the Eleventh Trungpa, and as such the abbot of the Surmang group of monasteries, which were a part of the Karma Kagyu school. He had led a large party of three hundred refugees out of East Tibet in a dramatic escape; toward the end they had had to eat boiled leather and to travel by night to elude Chinese patrols. In Kalimpong he had begun to learn English, exhibiting at the same time a remarkable ability to encounter and absorb the culture of the West. His English tutor was a young, Oxford-educated Englishman by the name of John Driver who had come out to India in 1956. Driver had written his dissertation on the Nyingmapas and was now studying with Dingo Khyentse, Rinpoche. It was Driver who first inspired Trungpa Rinpoche to think of teaching in the West.

When the Young Lama's Home School was established in New Delhi, the Dalai Lama appointed Freda Bedi as principal and Trungpa Rinpoche as spiritual advisor. Each of the four major schools sent about ten tulkus along with a lama to act as instructor. Early mornings were devoted to chanting and services, and because the tulkus of each school performed their own devotions in adjoining rooms, the usual cacaphony of drums, handbells, horns and chanting was multiplied fourfold. Then came the basics of a good traditional Tibetan education—Buddhist doctrine, Tibetan history, language, spelling, poetry, astrology, and calligraphy.

Afternoons were reserved for English classes. Since this was the only Western education offered at the school, the tulkus used their English lessons to find out as much as they could about the Western world. Jane Warner, a young American who had come to India to study Buddhism, and taught English at the school, found the tulkus especially bright and mature—whether or not you happened to believe in the idea of tulkus. "There were endless questions," she remembers. " 'What, the world's not flat, it's round?' They would gather things from the *National Geographics*. They were constantly working, using their heads. When you talked to them it was almost effortless for them to learn. They would come in sometimes with an almost five or six syllable word from *National Geographic*. I would explain what the word was, and then when they were leaving the class they would make up a sentence using the word and throw it back to me. It was already a part of their vocabulary."

When the Young Lama's Home School dissolved a few years later, more than half its students eventually made their way West, though not all taught dharma. Some simply took up ordinary jobs in cities like New York or Toronto, where they became businessmen, factory workers or cab drivers.

The Tibetan exiles in India, meanwhile, had begun to form their own communities. The Tibetans were devoted to their religion—indeed their whole society had been organized around it. But at the same time they were a very earthy, practical, good-humored people. Now, despite the hardship of their exile, they set about rebuilding their lives with great energy. They began farming and formed cooperatives to resume their traditional crafts, such as weaving rugs and sweaters. They had always been skillful traders, located as they were on the caravan route between India and China, and they continued to engage in trading in India.

Communities in Tibet had often been grouped around a particular lama or monastery, and to a certain extent this pattern continued in India. The Dalai Lama and many from the Gelug (Yellow hat) sect settled in Dharamsala, where the Tibetan government-in-exile made its headquarters.

The Nyingmapas were the oldest school of Tibetan Buddhism, tracing their lineage back to Padmasambhava, who had introduced Tantric Buddhism to Tibet from India in the eighth century. While there were Nyingma monasteries and monks (Mindroling, for example, was known throughout Tibet for the purity of its practice and discipline) the Nyingmas had a strong tradition of family-centered lay practice. They were in some ways the least organized of the great orders, and many Nyingma lamas were married men who lived and taught in small temples located near villages. There were also many Nyingma yogis, who practiced in the mountains far from the monasteries.

The head of the Nyingma sect was His Holiness Dudjom Rinpoche, an incarnation of Shariputra, a disciple of the Buddha, as well as of Dudjom Lingpa, a great yogi and *terton* (a discoverer of texts hidden by Padmasambhava for discovery at a future time), and Khyeu Chung

Lotsawa, one of the original twenty-five disciples of Padmasambhava. Dudjom Rinpoche wore his hair long, in the manner of the yogis, was married, with a family, and dressed in a simple grey cotton chuba, albeit of the finest weave. He was a great scholar as well as meditation master, and while in exile he completed a *History of the Nyingmas*, in Tibetan. He made his home, with his family, in Darjeeling.

The youngest of the heads of the Tibetan orders was His Holiness Sakya Tridzin of the Sakya order. Like the head of the Nyingmapas, Dudjom Rinpoche, the Sakya Tridzin was a layman who wore his hair long. He had escaped to Sikkim from the province of Sakya at the age of fourteen. There he had learned his first English words, and then had gone to Darjeeling where he had continued his studies in Madhyamika philosophy, logic, Prajnaparamita and Abhidharma. He spent a year in Mussoorie recovering from tuberculosis, and then in 1964 he founded the Sakya Centre in Mussoorie as his main monastery. In 1967, at the age of twenty-two, he gave the *lamdre* (stages of the path) teaching for the first time to four hundred monks and about a hundred lay people. The next year he founded the Sakya Rehabilitation Settlement in a region which, except for its heat, reminded the refugees of their home district of Sakya. By this time his English had become fluent with the help of a number of Westerners who had arrived to help with the rehabilitation work and to study Buddhism.

Rangjung Rigpe Dorje, the Sixteenth Karmapa, had accompanied the Dalai Lama and other Tibetan dignitaries to Peking for talks with the Chinese in 1957, and what he had seen there had apparently convinced him that the end was near, for he had left Tibet earlier than the others. Because of this he had been able to bring out many of the religious treasures—thangkas, ritual objects, images and texts—that had been gathered by the Karmapas at Tsurphu monastery for the last seven hundred years. The Kagyus, of whom His Holiness Karmapa was the head, had been active in the Himalayan kingdoms of Bhutan and Sikkim for hundreds of years, and the Karmapa built his new main monastery, Rumtek, in Sikkim, at the invitation of the royal family. The Karmapas had been the first lineage of tulkus, that is, the first Karmapa had been the first enlightened teacher to predict the time and place of his rebirth—in his case, by a letter written before his death. This practice had been continued by all the succeeding Karmapas. The Karmapas were renowned for their ability to discover and identify tulkus, whose education traditionally came under their care. Rumtek thus became the place where all the young Kagyu tulkus went for the training, as well as being the seat of the Gyalwa ("victorious;" a title often used) Karmapa.

It was also the place where Freda Bedi went when the Young Lama's Home School disbanded. She and her husband had not lived together for some time; her daughter had married and her son had graduated from college. And so, with her family's blessing, Freda Bedi became a nun—Sister Gelongma Khechog Palmo—under the Gyalwa Karmapa.

Her protege, Chogyam Trungpa, Rinpoche, set sail aboard the P & O Line for England, where he had received a Spaulding Scholarship to attend Oxford. He arrived in England in 1963, along with Akong Tulku, a lama his own age who had been part of his escape party. After Tibet and India, he found England "very strange—unlike anything I had ever seen before." He had thought it would be kind of a "stark modern realm." Indeed, he was impressed by its cleanliness and sense of order, but what struck him most was that it "turned out to have its own dignified culture." The Westerners not only had their own traditional culture, but a very rich one indeed.

Ensconced in a suite of rooms at Oxford, the young Eleventh Trungpa studied, among other subjects, comparative religion and philosophy. Some of the lectures were difficult to follow, but with the tutorial help of John Driver, he delved into Plato and other Western philosophers.

The monastery of Surmang had contained a rich collection of Tibetan art, and while in Tibet, Trungpa Rinpoche had greatly enjoyed Tibetan painting, as well as calligraphy. At Oxford he pursued his aesthetic interests by taking classes in oil painting, sketching and art history. He found the medieval art of the West similar to Tibetan art—both involved "a very precise discipline, that when you paint you know how to do it exactly," but he was also fascinated by the way modern art "cut through all hesitations to freely express whatever strange things came out of one's head." He began going down to London every week to look at the oil paintings and sculpture in the museums. But it was not only the art of the West that caught his eye. He was also drawn to the art of China and Japan, especially Japan, and he began taking lessons in the Sogetsu school of flower arranging from an Englishwoman named Stella Coe.

Trungpa's training in meditation had given him, as he said recently, "a general sense of inquisitiveness and also an open mind." Whatever he saw and did—from lectures on art to reading Plato to attending parties in London—was "taken in, as a learning process, always, so that everything was recorded as if in a notebook." The young Eleventh Trungpa, Tibetan man-about-town, did not miss much.

But it was not enough. Trungpa Rinpoche had been found and enthroned by the Gyalwa Karmapa eighteen months after his birth in February 1939. He had taken the shramanera (novice) precepts at the age of eight, the same age he had gone into retreat, accompanied only by his cook-attendant and tutor, to meditate on Manjushri for one month. A year later he met his principal guru, Jamgon Kongtrul of Sechen, "a big jolly man, friendly to all without distinction of rank, very generous and with a great sense of humour combined with deep understanding." Jamgon Kongtrul had told the young Trungpa how happy he was to return the teaching he had received from his predecessor, the Tenth Trungpa ("to return the owner's possessions," as the Tibetan expression went). At the age of eleven Trungpa had begun the ngondro, preliminary practices for the vajrayana teachings. At the age of fourteen he had conducted his first full empowerment (*wangkur*) which he had previously received from Jamgon Kongtrul, the sixty-three-volume *Rinchin Terdzod* (*The Mine of Precious Teachings*); it lasted for three months.

He was, thus, steeped in Buddhism, or, as he would put it years later, "pickled in Buddhism." Now, having felt out the situation in India and England, he began to look for a situation in which to present the teachings. Visits to Prinknash Monastery and Stanbrook Abbey had convinced him that the contemplative life could still be practiced in the West, and when Ananda Bodhi, the senior bhikkhu of the English Sangha Vihara, suggested that he and Akong Tulku take over Johnstone House, a retreat house in Dumfriesshire, Scotland, the Tibetans went out to investigate. Trungpa found the air and the rolling hills of the remote area fresh and invigorating, and after a few more visits the center was turned over to the two young Tibetans. They renamed it Samye-Ling Meditation Centre, after the first Tibetan monastery founded by Padmasambhava in the eighth century. It was, Trungpa remembers, "a forward step. Nevertheless, it was not entirely satisfying, for the scale of activity was small, and the people who did come to participate seemed to be slightly missing the point."

III

It was not really very surprising that the students who found their way to Dumfriesshire to study with the Eleventh Trungpa should have missed the point, either slightly or by a wider mark. To many, Tibet had come to represent the quintessential land of mystery and miracles—a point of view given wide currency, first by Madame Blavatsky and the Theosophists in the nineteenth century, and then further popularized by mystical romances such as James Hilton's *Lost Horizon*, which had become a best-seller and a movie in the thirties.

It was a corollary of this view that Tibet was an isolated and secret land. Certainly it is true that, given Tibet's geography, vastness, altitude and climate, it was forbidding enough to outsiders. But it was hardly an isolated country—rather, the Tibetans lived at a crossroads of the Buddhist world. They took their Buddhism mainly from India; they had also received teachings from China, Khotan, Afghanistan and probably Persia. Tibetan teachers themselves had crossed the Himalayas to establish monasteries in Bhutan, Sikkim, Ladakh, and Nepal.

Tibetan lamas had converted the fierce Mongol warriors to Buddhism, and when the Manchu dynasty took power in China, Tibetans served as spiritual advisors to the emperors of China. Marco Polo had met Tibetan lamas at the court of the great khan in the thirteenth century, as had William of Rubruck, when he sought unsuccessfully to enlist the Mongols' aid against the Moslems. By the seventeenth century a number of Christian missionaries, both Jesuit and Capuchin, had reached Lhasa. One of these, the Jesuit father Ippolito Desideri took up residence at Sera monastery in 1716, where he learned Tibetan and produced a translation of Tsongkhapa's *Lam rim chen mo*. But Desideri was recalled to Rome, and his work disappeared into the Vatican library.

There were other visitors to Tibet during the early days of the British raj, but it was not until the middle of the nineteenth century that a true picture of Tibetan Buddhism began to emerge—due mainly to the extraordinary, singleminded devotion of one man, the Hungarian Csoma de Koros.

Csoma de Koros came from a poor family of the old Magyar nobility and had to support his own education. He accomplished this by tutoring and learning to live with extreme simplicity. Even so, he did not complete his university education at the University of Gottingen until he was thirty-four. Then, turning his back on the comfortable professorship that awaited him at home, he set out to fulfill a student vow to discover "the origin and language of the Hungarians," whom he took to be related to the Hungars of Mongolia.

Csoma set out on foot for Asia in November of 1819—he carried only a small bundle, a walking stick and one hundred florins in his pocket. He worked on his Arabic in Alexandria, continued overland to Mesopotamia disguised as an Arab, floated on a raft to Baghdad, and finally reached

Teheran in 1820. Taking the name of "Sikander Beg," ("Gentleman Alexander") he reached Kabul in 1822, and then crossed the mountains to the capital of Ladakh. Unable to find a pass through the Himalayas he turned back to the Kashmiri border, where he was befriended by the English explorer William Moorcroft. Moorcroft listened to his plans, and presented him with a copy of Father Georgi's *Alphabetum Tibetanum*. This was a rather garbled primer of Tibetan printed at Rome in 1762 from material gathered by the Capuchin missioneries in Lhasa.

Csoma now determined to learn Tibetan. He studied the *Alphabetum* closely, and found a Tibetan-speaking resident of Kashmir with whom he could converse in Persian. Then he set off once more, this time to the mountains to the northeast. There he won the trust of a lama at the monastery of Yangla, and from June 1823 to October of the next year, he sat in a cell, nine feet square, with nothing but a sheepskin cloak to protect him from the freezing cold, reading through volumes of Tibetan Tripitaka—"the basis," as he later reported, "of all Tibetan religion and learning."

He arrived at the hill station of Sabathu in late November of 1824 (with an abstract of the Tripitaka and the beginnings of a Tibetan-English dictionary), clad in a blanket, looking like no European the English officers had ever seen. He was politely detained at the hill station while the authorities wondered what to do with this strange looking man. Csoma said that he merely wished to continue his studies; in return all results—a dictionary, grammar and outline of Tibetan literature—would belong to the British government. The British viceroy in Bengal, Lord Amherst, agreed, and de Koros was granted a stipend of fifty rupees a month.

It was not very much, even in India. Csoma returned to the Tibetan frontier regions and continued his labors, working, as his biographer says, "in penury and solitude," complaining only that the Royal Asiatic Society had not sent the books he had requested. Years later, when the Society finally did make him a grant for that purpose, he returned the money. He had far surpassed the information the books contained.

Putting aside his dream of reaching Mongolia, he eventually completed his dictionary and grammar, published by the government in 1834. He had come to a sympathetic understanding of Buddhism, reflected in a number of articles he wrote for the *Asiatic Researches*. He also urged other scholars to study Tibetan, which he considered to be "the orthodox language of Buddhism, just as Latin is that of the Church of

Rome." "The principal seat of Buddhism," he wrote, at a time when most scholars paid heed only to the Pali texts, "is in Tibet."

Csoma had spent six years in the Tibetan frontier, and another eleven working in India. In 1842, having completed his obligations to his English benefactors, he set out again for Lhasa, and then, hopefully, Central Asia—the origin, he still believed, of his race. He got as far as Darjeeling, where he died of fever. Nearly a century later, in 1933, Japanese Buddhists pronounced him the first Western bodhisattva for the selfless work that had "opened the heart of the Western world to an understanding of Buddhism."

De Koros was followed by a number of writers on Tibetan Buddhism. In 1895 the missionary L.A. Waddell published a detailed and influential study of *The Buddhism of Tibet or Lamaism*. A good English Protestant, he judged Tibetan Buddhism to be mostly "contemptible mummery and posturing," and most Western scholars followed the lead. Tibetan Buddhism, in all its baroque exuberance, with its priestcraft, rituals, mantras, magic, monasteries, mystics and hermits—to say nothing of the scandalously shocking portrayals of deities in ritual intercourse—was a pitiful degeneration from the pristine purity of the Theravadins and the Pali texts. Even so sympathetic a writer and observer as the American professor J.B. Pratt could justify leaving Tibetan Buddhism out of his otherwise complete *Pilgrimage of Buddhism* by explaining, in 1924, that, "I have said nothing whatever of the Buddhism of Tibet, Nepal, and Mongolia. This has not been due to lack of space but to deliberate intention. The form of religion which prevails in these lands is so mixed with non-Buddhist elements that I hesitate to call it Buddhism at all."

The tide began to turn, however, in 1927, the year that saw the publication of *The Tibetan Book of the Dead* (*Bardo Thotrol*) by Oxford University Press. (That same year, coincidentally, the first series of D.T. Suzuki's *Essays in Zen Buddhism* was also published in England.) *The Tibetan Book of the Dead* was edited and compiled by W.Y. Evans-Wentz, an American scholar who had taken his degree in the field of folklore at Oxford after work at Stanford and the University of Rennes. During his research for his first book, *Fairy-Faith in Celtic Countries* (published by Oxford in 1911), Evans-Wentz had found evidence of belief in rebirth among the Druids. Thereafter the subject of rebirth held special interest for him, and he developed an interest in Gnostic Christianity and Indian religion. Evans-Wentz was a trained anthropologist, but he did not hold himself aloof from his sources. He had gone to the East in the twenties, "wandering," as he wrote "from the palm-wreathed shores of Ceylon, and thence through the wonder-land of the Hindus, to the glacier-clad heights of the Himalayan Ranges, seeking out the Wise Men of the East. Sometimes I lived with city dwellers, sometimes in jungle and mountain solitude among *yogis*, sometimes in monasteries with monks; sometimes I went on pilgrimages as one of the salvation-seeking multitude."

Evans-Wentz met the actual translator of the *Tibetan Book of the Dead*, Kazi Dawa-Samdup in Gangtok, Sikkim, in 1919. (The introduction had been made by the chief of police of Darjeeling.) Kazi Dawa-Samdup, then headmaster of the Gangtok School, was at work on an English-Tibetan dictionary. He had served as interpreter to both the British Government in Sikkim and the Tibetan Plenipotentiary in India, and had been a member of the political staff of the Thirteenth Dalai Lama during his stay in India in 1910. Kazi Dawa-Samdup had once hoped to lead the life of a monk or hermit, but since he was the eldest son, family duties had taken precedence, and he had become instead a lay disciple of the Bhutanese hermit Guru Norbu. (Like many Bhutanese, Norbu was a member of the Drukpa Kagyu school.)

Evans-Wentz became, by his testimony, a disciple of Kazi Dawa-Samdup, and though Evans-Wentz knew little, if any, Tibetan, the two men worked closely together to prepare the English edition of the *Tibetan Book of the Dead*. Despite Evans-Wentz's best efforts to "act simply as the mouthpiece of a Tibetan sage," he was unable to refrain completely from seeing Tibetan Buddhism through the lens of the comparative religion and folklore in which he had trained at Oxford. Tibetan Buddhism offered him a living example of an underlying worldwide "wisdom-religion," traces of which he found in Gnosticism, Egyptian religion, Greek mysteries, Hinduism and yoga. As a result, his version contained certain inaccuracies: the diction, for example, with all its "ye's" and "thou's," suffered from Biblical rhetoric, and Evans-Wentz had failed to adequately distinguish between Hindu and Buddhist terminology.

Still, the *Book of the Dead* was the first tantric Buddhist text presented to the general public without apology. It was actually a *terma*—a text hidden by Padmasambhava until the proper time for its discovery. When it was published in 1927 it created, as Carl Jung wrote in his "Psychological Commentary" to a later edition, "a considerable stir in English-speaking countries." He himself spoke of it with the highest praise. "For years," he wrote, "ever since it was first published, the *Bardo Thodal* has been my constant companion, and to it I owe not only many stimulating ideas and discoveries, but also many fundamental insights." What most impressed Jung was the clarity of the book's psychology, the way it instructed the dead, as well as the living, to recognize all appearances and visions, whether beautiful or terrifying, as the reflections of consciousness. It was this consciousness itself which the authors of the *Tibetan Book of the Dead*, whoever they may have been, saw as the clear light of buddha nature within each person. Evans-Wentz saw this as the luminous truth central to the vajrayana or "esoteric" Buddhism of Tibet. It was Evans-Wentz's greatest achievement to be one of the first to thus identify Tibetan Buddhism as the culmination of the Buddhist path. Tibetan Buddhism, he argued, was not "in disagreement with canonical, or exoteric, Buddhism, but related to it as higher mathematics to lower mathematics, or as the apex of the pyramid of the whole of Buddhism."

By the late fifties there were a number of scholars who were inclined to agree with him. Kazi Dawa-Samdup had died in Calcutta in 1922, but Evans-Wentz had gone on to edit other of his translations and collaborate with other translators to publish texts by Padmasambhava, on the Nyingma method of meditation, and Kagyu texts on the six yogas of Naropa and the life of Milarepa. The Russian, G. Roerich, had translated the *Blue Annals*, a Tibetan history of Buddhism, and Giuseppe Tucci of Rome had produced his monumental *Indo-Tibetica* and *Tibetan Painted Scrolls*. In 1959 two important translations appeared with a timeliness that made it almost seem as if they had been planned to welcome the first of the refugees: the Englishman David L. Snellgrove published a scholarly edition of the *Hevajra Tantra*, the first complete tantra to appear, and Herbert V. Guenther, a Vienna-trained Buddhist scholar with formidable linguistic gifts published an edition of Gampopa's *Jewel Ornament of Liberation*. The *Jewel Ornament* was a step-by-step manual of the Buddhist path written by the founder of the Kagyu school in the twelfth century, and was the clearest and most accessible Tibetan manual yet to appear. The *Hevajra Tantra*, however, was something else again. It was, Edward Conze noted, rather puzzling and disappointing. The text by itself, said Conze, "must remain relatively barren, since a knowledge of the Sanskrit and Tibetan alone cannot prove the clue to the Tantric systems which are essentially psychological in their purpose and intention." It was a groundbreaking work in terms of scholarship, but only made it clearer than ever that the understanding of the tantras depended on the oral instructions, and training, of a qualified teacher.

It was precisely at this point, of course, that Western scholars had access to their Tibetan counterparts. Scholarship in Tibet—which meant primarily Buddhist scholarship—had a long and active tradition. Tibetan scholars, working with Indian pundits, had translated the whole corpus of Indian Buddhist literature—and had done so very accurately. Exact equivalents to the Sanskrit terms had been worked out and then codified, a situation that did not yet exist in the West, where there were still, for example, any number of terms in use for a particular word. So successful had been the teams of Tibetan *lotsawas* (translators) and their Indian counterparts that scholars were able to reconstruct portions of lost or destroyed Sanskrit texts from their Tibetan translations almost word-for-word. This was, in fact, what had most interested Indian Sanskritists about the Tibetan refugee scholars, and in 1962 the Indian Government had asked the Tibetan authorities to appoint one scholar from each of the major schools to teach at Sanskrit University in Benares. One of the most active and energetic of these teachers was the representative of the Nyingmapas. Tarthang Tulku was a tall, rangy man from the East Tibetan province of Kham, home of the Khampa horsemen and nomads, and it was easy to picture him riding over the broad Tibetan plains. His father had been a Nyingma lama, doctor and astrologer, and Tarthang had been recognized as an important incarnation from Tarthang monastery. For thirteen years he had traveled widely through the wildest sort of country, studying with twenty-five different gurus of all four schools, but concentrating on the Nyingma teachings. He had escaped in 1959 to Bhutan and India, and then gone on to Sikkim to study further with his root guru Dzongsar Khyentse, Rinpoche.

Khyentse Rinpoche told him, at their last meeting, to continue his own self-development and to share what he had learned with the world. His first step in this direction—in addition to his teaching at the Sanskrit University—had been to found a press in India. Tibetan books had been printed by means of woodblocks (xylographs) that had to be carved with a great deal of skill and devotion. Tibetans had gone to India for an alphabet for the express purpose of printing the Buddha's word, and books were, therefore, highly sacred objects. The oblong Tibetan pages were unbound, and secured between two wooden boards and then wrapped in silk. The pages and coverings were often illuminated and ornamented with jewels, as they had once been in medieval Europe. Tarthang Tulku had brought many rare books with him from Tibet, and he began reprinting these in India. Eventually he published more than twenty-five texts, which were used in India by the Tibetans for their religious practice and study and were also sent to various libraries throughout the world. Tarthang Tulku hoped they would serve as a seed for an eventual flowering of the dharma.

It was not long before a few American scholars appeared on the scene.

One of the first of these was Dr. Turrell Wylie of the University of Washington Inner Asian Program (endowed in part by the Rockefeller Fund and Department of Defense, which had suddenly realized the potential usefulness of languages such as Vietnamese, Chinese and Tibetan). Dr. Wylie was looking for a Tibetan scholar who could collaborate with his group at the university, and a Bengali acquaintenance of his suggested that the university would do well to invite a Sakya lama, since the Sakyapas were reputed to be the most scholarly of all the schools. As it turned out, the Bengali knew of a renowned Sakya scholar, the Venerable Deshung Rinpoche, abbot of the Sakya Tharlam Monastery, and he arranged an introduction.

The Sakya library had been the largest and most complete in Tibet. Because it had been located fairly close to the Indian frontier, many leading Indian scholars had sought refuge there when Nalanda had been destroyed. The Indians had brought their libraries with them, and some of them had become proficient enough in Tibetan to translate their own works into that language. Deshung Rinpoche had visited the Sakya library as a young man. He had been amazed to find hundreds of thousands of books stacked thirteen stories high, and at first he had been so overwhelmed that he just made his prostrations and left. But soon he returned, and spent about three years reading in the great library. (Years later, when Deshung Rinpoche first visited New York and saw the skyscrapers, the first thing that came to his mind were the great stacks of books in the Sakya library.)

At the University of Washington, Deshung Rinpoche and a few other Sakya lamas worked with scholars such as Dr. Wylie, Leon Hurvitz, Agehananda Bharati (then writing his book on *The Tantric Tradition*), E. Gene Smith and Edward Conze. Deshung Rinpoche (whom Dr. Conze found to be "a nugget of pure gold") taught Tibetan and Buddhist philosophy and worked, with the other Sakya scholars, on an English-Tibetan dictionary. His closest student was Gene Smith, who in time became one of the few experts able to unravel the history of the various Tibetan lineages and schools.

But for the most part, Deshung Rinpoche did not teach dharma—at least not in the traditional sense. He was in his fifties and he had not learned English, nor, at his age, did it seem likely he would, and the only Westerners around who spoke Tibetan were anthropologists with little interest in Buddhism. When a few graduate students and others came to ask him about teachings and initiations and so on, he advised them to go to India where the great lamas now lived—to the Dalai Lama at Dharamsala, the Sakya Tridzin, or Dingo Khyentse, Rinpoche, a holder of both Sakya and Nyingma teachings. For the time being, Deshung Rinpoche quietly continued his own meditation, remaining, as he put it, "alone with his Buddhism."

Deshung Rinpoche and other Sakyas at Seattle had actually been preceded by a Tibetan Buddhist teacher, who was not, strictly speaking, Tibetan. This was Geshe Wangyal, a Kalmuk Mongolian, who arrived in the town of Freehold Acres, New Jersey, in 1955. Freehold Acres had been settled by a community of displaced Kalmuks who had been brought there after World War II by the Tolstoy Foundation. The Mongolians were almost all adherents of the Gelug school, and when Geshe Wangyal made his appearance there were already four or five Buddhist temples serving the surrounding community. Geshe Wangyal stayed in one of these at first, but the local temples functioned more or less as churches and community centers and Geshe Wangyal seemed to have something else in mind. Before long he had moved out and obtained a charter from the Dalai Lama for the Lamaist Buddhist Monastery of America—the first Tibetan monastery open to Americans in this country.

Geshe Wangyal had studied at the great monastery of Drepung in Lhasa. Drepung was one of the major centers of the Gelugpas, the most recently formed of the Tibetan schools, having been founded in the fourteenth century by Tsongkhapa. Tsongkhapa had stressed the necessity for a thorough and long study—ten or fifteen years was not unusual—of the sutras and Madhyamika dialectic and logic. Public debates were an important part of Gelug training. The debates were lively affairs, one monk sitting cross-legged in the courtyard, while his opponent, rosary swinging from his arm, would stride back and forth presenting a challenge, and then leaping forward with a clap of his hands to signal the time for response. The culmination of the scholastic phase of Gelugpa study was the degree of geshe, roughly equivalent to a doctorate in theology. It was only after many years of such study that a Gelugpa could, if he wished, go on to the practice of the tantras.

Geshe Wangyal's root guru had been Lama Dorjieff, an influential and politically powerful Buriat Mongol. Dorjieff had been a tutor of the Thirteenth Dalai Lama, and he had, it was said, done his best to convince the Dalai Lama that Russia was the location of Shambhala—the mythical kingdom Tibetans believed to be the home of an enlightened society.

During the twenties Dorjieff had hoped that things would be better for the Mongolian Buddhists under Communism than under the Orthodox Christian regime of prerevolutionary Russia. At first the Communists allowed him to move freely among the Mongolians. But in the thirties the government reversed its policy; Buddhism, though it may have done away with God, was still considered a reactionary religion. The government even suppressed the celebrated school of St. Petersburg Buddhologists—Stcherbastky who had done groundbreaking work on the Buddhist theory of "dharmas," and Obermiller, another Buddhist scholar. Lama Dorjieff himself was kept under house arrest in the monastery he had built in St. Petersburg, until his death there in 1941.

Geshe Wangyal had firsthand experience with communism. At the age of nineteen he had worked with Lama Dorjieff in St. Petersburg, he had been in Peking in the thirties and had seen with his own eyes what happened in Outer Mongolia. So when the Chinese first entered Kham in 1951, he had left immediately, even though most Tibetans were not alarmed. He had always looked towards America as the best place to teach Buddhism, and he had in fact begun to study English, first in Lhasa and then in Peking. It took him four years to secure a visa, and during that time he traveled widely, visiting Paris, Hanoi and Hong Kong, among other places.

His Kalmuk friends helped to build a ranch style house in Freehold Acres (the first of many) and Geshe Wangyal eventually brought over four lamas from India: Geshe Sopa, Lama Kunga (a Sakya), and two young tulkus. He supported them by teaching in the Altaic Languages Department at Columbia, to which he commuted by bus once a week.

At that point three Harvard students—Christopher George, Jeffrey Hopkins and Robert Thurman—discovered Geshe Wangyal and began coming down from Cambridge. Geshe Wangyal welcomed them, but he did not make any extravagant promises. Nor did he have much patience with talk about higher teachings or a higher consciousness. "I don't know about all that," he said. "But I've been a scholar, I've read a few interesting books, and if you want to learn to read these books, OK." In return, he said, his students could teach the four lamas English. The Kalmuks in the community were amused and somewhat puzzled by this arrangement. They were not used to the idea of their lamas teaching Americans; and the older members did not very much like the idea. One of the early American students remembers, "They seemed to believe that because the Buddhists hadn't invented the automobile there was something wrong with Buddhism."

Thurman himself had just returned from Asia. He hadn't even paid any attention to Buddhists while he had been looking, not very seriously, "for something like a Sufi master, someone out of Gurdjieff's *Meetings With Remarkable Men*." "I had the cushiest time in Asia," he recalls. "I was the first hippie as far as the Asians went. There were no Americans they had seen who weren't in the Army or something. So for them to see Americans who were absolutely broke, early acid movement by-products staggering around—they thought we were faquirs or something and they were very nice to us; they would give us food, and say, 'Oh yes, you're religious now.' "

But if the Indians were taken in, Geshe Wangyal was not. "He was very critical of me. He was very much into the mundane, saying 'What are you wearing these ridiculous Afgani pants for, and why don't you have some shoes on?' " "You can't travel the path of the Dharma," he told Thurman, "that's difficult. You can't even travel on a bus without everybody freaking out."

The first thing that Thurman and the others had to do, said Geshe Wangyal, was to learn Tibetan—a language whose grammar has still eluded comprehensive explanation by generations of linguists. While learning Tibetan, they began reading texts with Geshe-la (as he was affectionately called)—first simple ones, and then, as their facility grew, progressively more advanced ones. The traditional preliminary to Tibetan (vajrayana) practice consisted of one hundred thousand prostrations—but here, as one student quipped, "Instead of prostration, there was translation."

Not that it was all intellectual. For one thing, Geshe-la worked with each student individually, and he had a way of creating a situation which would bring out all sorts of negative emotions: jealousy, anger, self-pity. Then, as one student recalls, "When you had understood what was happening, resolved this ego problem, he knew it immediately and he would say OK, bring your book, and he would read and read the very passage dealing with that particular thing."

Next to translation and chess (which he loved to play) Geshe-la's greatest love seemed to be building. He looked the scholar, a small man with a wispy Chinese-style chin beard and a face like beaten gold, but he was also a very practical, hands-on man, and he always had one building project or another going—nothing exotic, no traditional Tibetan architecture, just the kinds of things that were built in suburban New Jersey. Geshe-la himself wielded hammer and saw with gusto, seemingly oblivious to the obstacles and problems that sprang up everywhere. There was never enough money, the cement truck would arrive at the wrong time, and because Geshe-la insisted on making up the plans as he went along, nobody ever knew what would happen next. (More than one student, discovering that the last line of shingles on a roof did not fit because Geshe-la had insisted the whole job be done by eye, thought ruefully of Milarepa's stone towers.) So it went.

In Tibet the Gelugpas had emphasized the importance of a strict monastic training; indeed the Gelug school had been a reform movement that sought a return to the monastic purity of the Kadam school brought into Tibet in the eighth century by the Indian master Atisha. Geshe Wangyal ran his place as a monastery. Women studied and took their meals there, but they slept and lived in a small nearby house. And while he did everything he could to encourage the Tibetan and Mongolian monks to live a more-or-less traditional monastery life, he did not encourage his American students to follow them. In fact, when Robert Thurman announced that he wanted to be ordained, Geshe Wangyal refused, and when Thurman pressed him, he said that he would not do it, but if Thurman really wanted ordination, he could go to India and ask the Dalai Lama. So Thurman went, but before he left Geshe Wangyal insisted that he leave his full set of "civilian" clothes—suit, shirt and tie-safely in Geshe Wangyal's closet.

In Dharamsala the Dalai Lama ordained Thurman as the first American Tibetan Buddhist monk. He stayed for some time, studied Nagarjuna and became unusually fluent in Tibetan. But finally, having wearied of the endless ecclesiastical politics around the Dalai Lama, and having decided that this was not, after all, what he was meant to do for the rest of his life, he returned to New Jersey. And there was his suit, neatly pressed, waiting for him just as he had left it.

Geshe Wangyal had always encouraged his students to attend graduate school, and now Thurman returned to Harvard. Within a few years he earned his doctorate with a translation from the Tibetan of a thorny Madhyamika text by Nagarjuna. Jeffrey Hopkins also obtained his doctorate, and when Lama Kensur Lekden, the abbot of the Tantric College of Lower Lhasa, came to America in 1968 to teach at the University of Wisconsin, Jeffrey Hopkins served him as translator. The University of Wisconsin Program in Indian Studies, which was headed by Richard Robinson, an enthusiastic Sanskritist and Chinese scholar, was then the liveliest place in America for Buddhist studies and, with the possible exception of Seattle, perhaps the only place for a young Buddhist scholar who did not think it unseemly to practice the subject he taught. Geshe

Sopa also taught there. Lama Kunga founded the Ewam Choden Sakya Center in Kensington, California.

Thurman and Hopkins have since become two of the more active Buddhist scholars in America. Recently they and other students of Geshe Wangyal founded the American Institute of Buddhist Studies, an attempt "to bridge academia and Buddhist philosophical teaching."

Despite the presence of lamas in Seattle, New Jersey and Wisconsin, American Buddhists saw the sixties primarily as the decade of Zen. But the mostly long-haired young who made the overland journey to Nepal and India were intrigued by the Hindus, the Tibetans and a new generation of Theravadins. The reckless Western pilgrims prepared the ground for the lamas, yogis, and no-nonsense Theravadins who would be welcomed to the chastened America of the seventies.

They had hunted holy men in gompas, ashrams, riverbanks, monasteries, jungles and caves. They had found the Tibetans and traded them Timexes for chubas and skullcups, taught them English, helped with relief work and took every initiation possible. They sat by ghats in Benares watching corpses split open on funeral pyres; they bathed in the muddy Ganges at dawn; they fasted—eating only fruit or rice or nothing. They smoked ganga in chillums with naked Shaivite sadhus. A fair number burned out, ending up talking to the gods they sought. They finally stumbled back to America, culture-shocked and time-warped, bringing with them, whether they knew it or not, a hint of the dharma that would follow.

IV

Allen Ginsberg and Gary Snyder, as usual, had been there early on. They met in India in 1962 along with Peter Orlovsky and Joanne Kyger, the California poet whom Snyder had married in Japan. There they made their pilgrimage to all the Buddhist holy places—Bodh-Gaya, where they saw the Tibetans circumambulating the temple and whirling prayer wheels; the Deer Park at Sarnath, where the Buddha gave his first discourse. Everybody kept a journal and Gary Snyder recorded their meeting with the Dalai Lama thus:

> Allen & Peter asked him at some length about drugs & drug experiences, and their relationship to the spiritual states of meditation. The Dalai Lama gave the same answer everyone else did: drug states are real psychic states, but they aren't ultimately useful to you

> because you didn't get them on your own will and effort. For a few glimpses into the unconscious mind & other realms, they may be of use in loosening you up. After that, you can too easily come to rely on them, rather than undertaking such a discipline as will actually alter the structure of the personality in line with these insights. It isn't much help to just glimpse them with no ultimate basic alteration in the ego that is the source of lots of the psychic-spiritual ignorance that troubles one. . . . Then the Dalai Lama & I talked about Zen sect meditation, him asking "how do you sit? how do you put your hands? how do you put your tongue? where do you look?"—as I told or showed him. Then he said, yes, that's just how we do it. Joanne asked him if there couldn't be another posture of meditation for westerners, rather than cross-legged.

"He said, 'It's not a matter of national custom' "—which Snyder thought, "about as good an answer as you could get."

LSD was still news in countercultural circles. Tibetan art fit right in. Zen was all black and white but Tibetan Buddhism with its brilliant, multi-hued thangkas was as vivid as any psychedelic vision. To young Westerners the deities in Tibetan art were representations of certain structures in the mind, archetypes, eternal beings, gods and goddesses—a view held by C.G. Jung, that great preface-writer to both D.T. Suzuki and Evans-Wentz.

In any event, it was assumed that the Tibetans, having profound experience in the mysterious workings of the mind, would have something illuminating to say about this new drug. Ginsberg had experimented with LSD in the days when Timothy Leary was still at Harvard. Allen had at first been enthusiastic, but lately his visions had become frightening, and he wondered if he ought to discontinue his experiments. Ginsberg visited Dudjom Rinpoche in Kalimpong, and said to him, "I have these terrible visions, what should I do?" Dudjom Rinpoche sucked air through his mouth in a traditional Tibetan sign of sympathy, and said, "If you see anything horrible, don't cling to it; if you see anything beautiful, don't cling to it." And that was that. As far as Ginsberg was concerned, his advice made sense and jolted him out of the trap he had caught himself in.

Of all the Westerners to make their way to India during the sixties, perhaps the one most prepared to meet the Tibetans on their own ground was the monk and poet Thomas Merton. Father Merton had been a sophisticated young man at the beginning of a promising literary career when, in his last year at Columbia, he had converted to Catholicism. In 1941 he had entered the Trappist monastery of Gethsemani near Bardstown, Kentucky where he lived for the next twenty-seven years.

The Trappists lived a life of silence, communicating when necessary by an elaborate sign language. They arose at two in the morning; meditated and chanted the Psalms in choir, celebrated Mass at four, more prayer and liturgy followed, then a reading period. At seven, bread and coffee for breakfast. Lunch consisted of cheese, vegetables, bread and milk. Most of the daylight hours were taken up by manual labor; the silence of the abbey was punctuated by the buzz of chain saws, tractors and the clump of work boots down the stone halls.

Merton had gone into Gethsemani intending to abandon everything, including literature, for a life of silent contemplation and prayer. But monastic life brought out the poet in him, and when he confessed to his superior that he had begun writing, the Order, to his surprise, encouraged him to continue. So he led a dual life as cloistered monk and literary man. Inside Gethsemani he was Father Louis; to the outside world he was Thomas Merton, author of the best-selling autobiography, *Seven Story Mountain*.

Thomas Merton would publish sixty books—poetry, translations, essays, journals, biographies, polemics. Though he rarely left the grounds of Gethsemani, Merton was better informed and more active in areas of social and political injustice than most people living in Manhattan. He wrote in the tradition of Gandhi about race relations, peace and the dangers of nuclear war. He supported the Vietnamese Buddhist monk Thich Nhat Hanh and Catholic activists like the Berrigan brothers in their opposition to the Vietnam War.

In the late fifties Merton had begun to explore the similarities between the Western and Asian contemplative traditions. He had corresponded with a number of orientalists, but the greatest influence had been D.T. Suzuki, whom he met in 1964 and who had remarked that Merton understood Zen better than any other Western student.

Merton believed that however much the contemplative traditions of both East and West might differ, they both took as their primary aim the transformation of man's consciousness through the practice of spiritual disciplines—something that was desperately needed in a world drifting towards war and destruction. He sought therefore to open communication between contemplatives who had so far remained divided along religious and monastic lines.

"If the West continues to underestimate and to neglect the spiritual heritage of the East," he wrote in *Mystics and Zen Masters*, "it may hasten the tragedy that threatens man and his civilizations. . . . The horizons of the world are no longer confined to Europe and America. We have to gain new perspectives, and on this our spiritual quest and even our physical survival may depend."

The communication between East and West could only take place, he felt, under what he called Asian conditions of non-hurrying and of patient waiting—in contrast to "the Western passion for immediate visible results." It demanded therefore that Western contemplatives "live and share those traditions, as far as we can, by living them in their traditional milieu."

Though Merton had ostensibly been given permission to leave Gethsemani to attend a meeting of Catholic monastic orders in Bangkok, the journey to Asia was in reality a pilgrimage which he had dreamed about for a long time. He went, he said, "as a pilgrim who is anxious to obtain not just information, not just 'facts' about other monastic traditions, but to drink from ancient sources of monastic vision and experience. I seek not only to learn more about religion and monastic life, but to become a better and more enlightened monk myself."

Merton arrived in India at a crucial point in his life. After serving ten years as spiritual director of novices he had finally been granted permission to live in a hermitage on the grounds of Gethsemani. Still he felt the need for an even more eremitical life, and on his way to Asia he had visited Alaska and the California coast searching for a spot that would be as far removed as possible from the business of the monastery and the increasing demands of fame.

He arrived in Calcutta on October 19, 1968. The next day, "quite by chance," he met his first Tibetan—Chogyam Trungpa, Rinpoche, recently returned to India with his young English secretary who had taken the Tibetan name Kunga Dawa. "The important thing," Merton noted in his journal, "is that we are people who have been waiting to meet for a long time."

He continued on to Dharamsala where he found "the Tibetans all over the mountains in huts, houses, tents, anything. Prayer flags flutter among the trees," he wrote in his journal. "Rock mandalas are all along the pathways. 'OM MANI PADME HUM' is carved on every boulder."

On November 4 he had his first audience with the Dalai Lama. The two met as monks—they talked about religion and philosophy and different forms of meditation and the Dalai Lama advised Merton to get a good grounding in Madhyamika. During Merton's second audience they discussed the nature of shunyata "and the empirical existence of things grounded in shunyata." "A lot of it, at first, was rather scholastic," Merton noted, but when Merton said that he thought it "important for monks in the world to be living examples of the freedom and transformation of consciousness which meditation can give," the Dalai Lama demonstrated the correct Buddhist meditation posture, and they began to talk about objects of concentration and how the mind itself could be the object of concentration. "It was a very lively discussion," wrote Merton afterwards, "and I think we all enjoyed it. He certainly seemed to." In fact, the Dalai Lama suggested that Merton return on Friday to talk about Western monasticism.

At the third audience the Dalai Lama "asked a lot of questions about Western monastic life," and whether "the monks continue to progress along a spiritual way, toward an eventual illumination, and what were the degrees of that progress? . . ." Merton "sort of hemmed and hawed a bit, and said 'Well, no, that's not quite what the vows are all about.' " But he found it interesting, as he later told the abbots assembled in Bangkok, "that this is what he *thought* the vows should be about." Actually, Merton thought that St. Benedict's concept of *conversio morum*—"conversion of manners" could be interpreted "as a commitment to total inner transformation of one sort or another—a commitment to become a completely new man."

Finally Merton asked the Dalai Lama for his ideas on Marxism and monasticism, which was to be the subject of his talk in Bangkok. "The Dalai Lama is in no way a fanatical anti-Communist," Merton later reported. The abbots of the larger Tibetan monasteries had refused to do anything, for example, to give land to people who needed it, and this, the Dalai Lama had said, "precipitated the disaster and it had to happen."

At the end of it all Merton felt that they had become very good friends and also recognized "a real spiritual bond between us." For his part, the Dalai Lama remarked that Father Merton was a "Catholic geshe"—the highest possible praise from a Gelugpa.

Sonam Kazi was the translator during Merton's audience with the Dalai Lama. Sonam was a Sikkimese layman who had gone to an English Catholic secondary school, and then continued his studies in psychology in Delhi. As a young man he had suffered from unaccountable bouts of depression and had figured out his own method of introspection, of looking into the mind that got depressed. This had led to an interest in meditation, and when he was posted to Lhasa as part of the Sikkimese diplomatic legation he spent his time off visiting many different gurus. He had been most impressed by one teacher, Jetsun Lochen Rinpoche, a hundred-year-old woman who lived in a hermitage about a day's ride from Lhasa. She had sent him to Dudjom Rinpoche, head of the Nyingmas, and he had become a disciple.

Sonam Kazi was a devoted follower of Dzogchen ("Great Perfection"), the esoteric tradition that the Nyingmas considered to be the ultimate teaching which could lead to the attainment of buddhahood in one lifetime. The first human teacher of Dzogchen was the Indian Garab Dorje (born in A.D. 55); the teachings were brought to Tibet in the eighth century by Padmasambhava and Vimalamitra, and it was this approach rather than the more gradual and scholastic one of the Gelugpas that Sonam Kazi urged Merton to investigate. "At least he asked me if I were willing to risk it, and I said 'Why not?' . . . the question is finding the right man," Merton wrote. "I would certainly like to learn something by experience and it does seem that the Tibetan Buddhists are the only ones who, at present, have a really large number of people who have attained to extraordinary heights in meditation and contemplation."

Sonam Kazi was not the only one urging Merton to investigate the direct path of Dzogchen found in the Nyingma school—Lobsang Lhalungpa, a Tibetan scholar fluent in English, was very interested in the Nyingma form of meditation, as was E. Gene Smith, the American Tibetologist who had studied with Deshung Rinpoche in Seattle and was now in India publishing Tibetan texts for the Library of Congress.

Merton met a number of lamas in addition to the Dalai Lama, but none impressed him as much as the Nyingma lama Chatral Rinpoche. "They were both monks of zero pretence," Harold Talbott remembers, "and they saw eye to eye." Chatral Rinpoche was a master of Dzogchen, and he lived in a little gompa high in the hills above Ghoom. He dressed like a Bhutanese peasant, with a red wool hat tied around his chin.

The two monks talked for two hours about all sorts of things—"but all leading back to dzogchen, the ultimate emptiness, the unity of shunyata and karuna, going 'beyond the dharmakaya' and 'beyond God' to the ultimate perfect emptiness. He said he had meditated in solitude for thirty years or more and had not attained to perfect emptiness," wrote Merton, "and I said I hadn't either."

On December 3 his pilgrimage reached a kind of culmination at Polonnaruwa, Ceylon, where there are three figures carved out of a cliff—the Buddha, reclining at his parinirvana; and next to him, Ananda, the Buddha's closest disciple, standing with arms crossed; and lastly, a buddha seated in meditation.

> Looking at these figures, I was suddenly, almost forcibly jerked clean out of the habitual, half-tied vision of things, and an inner clearness, clarity, as if exploding from the rocks themselves, became evident and obvious. . . . The rock, all matter, all life, is charged with dharmakaya . . . everything is emptiness and everything is compassion. I don't now when in my life I have ever had such a sense of beauty and spiritual validity running together in one aesthetic illumination. Surely, with Mahabalipuram and Polonnaruwa my Asian pilgrimage has come clear and purified itself. I mean I know and have seen what I was looking for. I don't know what else remains but I have seen and have pierced through the surface and have got beyond the shadow and the disguise. This is Asia in its purity, not covered over with garbage, Asian or European or American, and it is clear, pure, complete. It says everything; it needs nothing. And because it needs nothing it can afford to be silent, unnoticed, undiscovered. It does not need to be discovered. It is we, Asians included, who need to discover it.

On December 10, 1968, Thomas Merton delivered his talk on "Marxism and Monasticism" to the assembled Catholic abbots at the conference in Bangkok. He recounted how a French revolutionary student leader he had met once told him, "We are monks also." Merton went on to say that the monk, like the revolutionary, is "essentially someone who takes up a critical attitude toward the contemporary world and its structures," with the fundamental difference that the Marxist sought to change economic substructures, while "the monk is seeking to change man's consciousness."

> What is essential in the monastic life is not embedded in buildings, is not embedded in clothing, is not necessarily embedded even in a rule. It is concerned with this business of total inner transformation. All other things serve that end. . . .
>
> And I believe that by openness to Buddhism, [he concluded] to Hinduism and to these great Asian traditions, we stand a wonderful chance of learning more about the potentiality of our own traditions, because they have gone, from the natural point of view, so much deeper into this than we have. The combination of the natural techniques and the graces we have and other things that have been manifested in Asia and the Christian liberty of the gospel should bring us all at last to that full and transcendent liberty which is beyond mere cultural differences and mere externals—and mere this and that.

These were to be Thomas Merton's last words. When he had finished his talk he went back to his hotel room, and sometime within the next two hours, while standing on the stone floor, possibly after taking a shower, he touched a large electric fan—either to turn it on or to move it closer—and the full force of two-hundred and twenty volts shot through him.

"In death Father Louis' face was set in great and deep peace," the Trappist delegates wrote to their brothers at Gethsemani, "and it was obvious that he had found Him Whom he had searched for so diligently." The monks wore white vestments at the Requiem Mass, "to testify to our belief that this was an occasion of great happiness as we rejoiced in the knowledge that our brother had truly gone to God."

Thomas Merton's body was returned to Gethsemani, where it was buried in a spot marked only by a simple white wooden cross. The pilgrimage was complete.

Chogyam Trungpa, Rinpoche had been on his way to Bhutan from his meditation center in Scotland when he met Thomas Merton at the Central Hotel in Calcutta. The two men had spent only a few days together, but they grew very close and talked about collaborating on a book that would bring the vajrayana and Catholic traditions together. "Father Merton himself was an open, unguarded, and deep person," Trungpa wrote later, and when he heard about Merton's death he had felt it as "a tremendous loss, to me personally and to the world of genuine spirituality."

Trungpa Rinpoche had been invited to visit Bhutan by the queen, whose son he had been tutoring in Buddhism while the boy was a student at Ascot. In Bhutan he undertook a retreat at Tagtsang, in a cave where Padmasambhava had meditated more than a thousand years before.

The cave was large and seemed filled with the presence of Padmasambhava, whom the Tibetans of all schools revere as "Guru Rinpoche"—Precious Guru—and whom the Nyingmas in particular consider a second Buddha. He is said to have been born fully enlightened from a lotus, as his name Padma (lotus) Sambhava (born) suggests. His biography is filled with accounts of his often outrageous and miraculous exploits.

At the beginning of his ten-day retreat Trungpa Rinpoche reflected on his life and thought particularly about the problem of propagating the dharma in the West. He invoked Guru Rinpoche and the Kagyu forefathers, asking them to provide a vision of the future. "For a few days nothing happened," he wrote later. "Then there came a jolting experience of the need to develop more openness and greater energy. At the same time there arose a feeling of deep devotion to Karma Pakshi, the second Karmapa, and to Guru Rinpoche. I realized that in fact these two were one in the unified tradition of Mahamudra and Ati."

He was "filled with the vivid recognition of their oneness," and in two days he composed a new *sadhana* in twenty-four pages—a meditation text that is recited and practiced by tantric Buddhists either in groups or alone—called the *Sadhana of Mahamudra*. "Its purpose was to bring together the two great traditions of the vajrayana as well as to exorcise the materialism which seemed to pervade spiritual disciplines in the modern world. . . . otherwise true spirituality could not develop. I began to realize that I would have to take daring steps in my life."

Returning to England via India, he met with the Karmapa and the Dalai Lama, and also made the acquaintance of Mr. James George, the Canadian high commissioner to India. Mr. George had been involved in the Gurdjieff work and he was a close and sympathetic student of Buddhism. Mr. George had been interested in the Tibetan myth of Shambhala for a long time, and he asked Trungpa Rinpoche what he knew about it.

"I shall never forget an evening in our house in New Delhi, in 1968," he wrote years later,

> when we had the now well-known Tibetan teacher, Trungpa Rinpoche, staying with us. We had been asking him about the Tibetan tradition of Shambhala. To our astonishment he replied very quietly that, although he had never been there, he believed in its existence and could see it in his mirror whenever he went into deep meditation. That evening in our study he produced a small circular metal mirror of the Chinese type and after looking into it intently for some time, began to describe what he saw. Within a circular range of high snowpeaked mountains there was a green valley with a beautiful city where extraordinary people lived, cut off from the outside world by their own volition. In the middle of the city there was a little palace or temple on top of a hill composed of terraces. Around this hill there was a square-walled enclosure, and around this again other enclosures where people lived and where there were temples and gardens, chotens and other sacred monuments. It sounded "out of this world," but there was Trungpa in our study describing what he saw as if he were looking out of the window.

Trungpa Rinpoche's interest in the legend of Shambhala would manifest itself years later in America, but for the time being he returned to England and Samye-Ling, where he found his application for British citizenship had been approved. He himself was now a Westerner—the first Tibetan ever to become a British subject.

Although ready to commit himself fully to teaching in the West, he was unsure of how to proceed. "I went through several months of ambivalence," he wrote later, "of feeling pushed forward and pulled back simultaneously, unable to respond clearly in spite of a series of small warnings." Then one day while he was driving through Northumberland he blacked out at the wheel of his car and smashed through the window of a joke shop. He was taken to the hospital, seemingly unconscious. "In spite of the pain, my mind was very clear; there was a strong sense of communication—finally the real message had got through—and I felt a sense of relief and even humour." When he came to, twenty-four hours later, he discovered that the left side of his body was paralyzed.

"When plunging completely and genuinely into the teachings," he wrote, "one is not allowed to bring along one's deceptions. I realized that I could no longer attempt to preserve any privacy for myself, any special identity or legitimacy. I should not hide behind the robes of a monk, creating an impression of inscrutability, which, for me, turned out to be only an obstacle. With a sense of further involving myself with the sangha, I determined to give up my monastic vows. More than ever," he wrote, "I felt myself given over to serving the cause of Buddhism."

CHAPTER FOURTEEN

IN THE LAND OF THE RED MAN

I

One day in 1967 a young Berkeley graduate received a letter from Tarthang Tulku in Benares. "Dear Joel," he read, "I don't know if you remember me. I don't remember you. But if we met, I probably liked you very much. My wife and I are trying to come to America now. Can you help us?"

Joel did remember. He had met this Tibetan, Tarthang Tulku, while wandering around Benares Hindu University. They had met only once and spent about four hours together, just talking. Nothing very special had happened; Joel couldn't remember anything he had learned from the conversation. But Tarthang Tulku's directness and simplicity touched him and he wrote back and sent a little money. The correspondence continued, and then one day a letter from Tarthang arrived from Paris, and then another from London and then one from New York: "Hi Joel! I'm here in New York! I'm coming to California soon!"

Tarthang Tulku and his French-Egyptian wife Nazli arrived in Berkeley in February of 1969. Berkeley was full of swamis, sufis and yogis, and Esalen and the Human Potential therapies that had crystallized around it were at their height. It was the tail end of the sixties and Berkeley was not exactly virgin territory, but the comet of new consciousness was still visible in the sky.

The most active Buddhist presence were the Zen Buddhists. Shunryu Suzuki-roshi's Zen Center, just across the Bay Bridge in San Francisco, had established a Berkeley branch. But there were few Tibetans—and none in Berkeley, nor in America with the youth (Tarthang was in his early thirties) of Tarthang Tulku.

Tarthang had heard in India and Europe that America was a very new country, very materialistic and that "Americans are only interested in dope and sex." But he found "that Americans, particularly young people, have a true heart. There is sincerity and much interest in truth and spiritual life." Within a short time a small group had formed around him and begun the Tibetan Nyingma Meditation Center, "the first Vajrayana congregation in America."

The Tibetans considered the vajrayana (tantric path) to be the shortest, most direct route to enlightenment. It attempts to reach the top of the mountain, to use a Tibetan metaphor, by a direct ascent of the cliff; but although the way is direct and quick, it is also perilous and demands full commitment, a great deal of discipline and willingness to face the most unpleasant truths about one's life. The need for a knowledgeable and trustworthy guide who has made the ascent himself is thus particularly stressed. (The guru is in fact considered a fourth refuge, in addition to the Buddha, dharma and sangha.) The vajrayana places great emphasis on *upaya*, skillful means, and the vajrayana path is described as one with a multitude of techniques available.

The skillful tantric practitioner was said to achieve liberation through the very things that obscured the vision of the ordinary man, and because the tantric path rejects nothing it can make use of anything. Tantric practices engage the body, speech and mind, and can include chanting, visualization, elaborate rituals, meditation with and without form, physical exercises, intensive philosophical study and much more. To the Tibetans the vajrayana represented the culmination of the Buddhist path. It stood in relation to the earlier *yanas* (vehicles) of hinayana and mahayana as the fruit of a tree stood to its trunk and branches. The Tibetan word for tantra is *gyu*, continuity. The word tantra itself comes from a Sanskrit cognate that means to weave, and the tantric view of life is one in which all aspects of life are woven and knit together. Compared to the stark elegance of Zen, the vajrayana presented a flowery exuberance.

It was a rich feast, no doubt, and more than a little overwhelming. The students who first gathered around Tarthang Tulku began exactly where a group of beginning vajrayanists in Tibet would have begun, with the first of the tantric preliminary practices, a hundred thousand prostrations. These prostrations were not in the style of Chinese or Japanese bows—where only the head and knees touched the ground—but full out, so that the practitioner's whole body lay on the ground. These were done while reciting the fourfold refuge and while visualizing the refuge tree, which consisted of Padmasambhava in the center, the successive gurus of the Nyingma lineage, as well as hosts of arhats, buddhas, bodhisattvas, dakinis and dharmapalas.

It was not by any means an easy practice. Suzuki-roshi had run into problems when he increased the number of bows after zazen from six to nine. Now here was this affable Tibetan suggesting that people who were truly serious about practicing the vajrayana do a hundred thousand prostrations. Aside from the sheer difficulty of the physical act, which was considerable, the prostrations brought up a great deal of resistance. They demanded openness and surrender. The openness seemed easy enough for people to relate to, at least the idea of it, but surrender was something else again. To whom or what was one surrendering, sweating and aching, time after time, seemingly forever. Wrote one student, "Westerners may liken these prostrations to the Israelites worshipping the Golden Calf, or the heathen worshipping primitive animistic gods."

And yet there were a fair number of spiritual adventurers desperate or willing enough to try it. Perhaps some of them were drawn into it by mere curiosity or a love of the exotic. But the repetitive, sheer physical labor, the barbaric reality of it, soon took care of any mystical daydreams about great yogic powers. Prostrations brought one down to earth, quite literally. They were hard work.

In Tibet these preliminary practices had often been done in retreat. But in America they were more often sandwiched in between jobs, university classes, taking care of the kids. They could be finished in a few months or they could take years. It all depended on the person doing them. In any case, they were only the first of the preliminary practices. When they were finished they were followed by the rest of the *bum nga* ("five one hundred thousands" preliminary practices), all of which involved their own visualizations: a hundred thousand repetitions of the Bodhisattva Vow, a hundred thousand repetitions of the Vajrasattva mantra, a hundred thousand offerings of a mandala representing the entire universe, and guru yoga, involving a hundred thousand repetitions of Guru Padmasambhava's mantra.

The vajrayana had many practices at its disposal, but as Tarthang Tulku made clear, "Meditation is the essence of the Buddha Dharma. . . .It involves the development of our own human consciousness. Meditation should have an important place in our daily life. Discussing it and thinking about it won't help. We must practice. In the beginning meditation seems separate from us but eventually it becomes our own nature."

The students who first came to the four-hour-long classes Tarthang Tulku conducted in a small house, at eight-thirty Saturday mornings, began by accustoming themselves to the seated meditation posture. In addition to meditation, the classes included chanting and prostrations, which gave them a distinctly tantric flavor. The principle mantra *Om Ah Hum Vajra Guru Padma Siddhi Hum*, invoking the blessing of Padmasambhava, was chanted slowly, with great longing and devotion. To Tibetans in general, but especially to the Nyingmas, Padmasambhava was particularly suited to help people during the dark age he had prophesied. The Tibetans considered the practice of his *sadhana*, as Tarthang Tulku explained, "especially important and effective in times plagued by excessive materialism and strong desires. Quite obviously, then, these practices have great practical relevance to our present age."

The typical Nyingma situation was a community of family groups centered around a lama who was often married himself. The Nyingmas had thus developed forms of practice suitable to lay people. "Like the characteristically open-minded American," said Tarthang, "the Nyingmapas have always been adaptable to different social conditions, or free from rigid, dogmatic stances, and can interact harmoniously with other philosophical and meditative approaches. . . ."

The basis for the Nyingma's flexibility had been established by Padmasambhava. Prophesying that "when the iron bird flies, and horses run on wheels,/The Tibetan people will be scattered like ants across the World,/And the Dharma will come to the land of the Red Man," Guru Rinpoche (as the Tibetans called him) had hidden certain teachings called terma (treasures) throughout Tibet. Some were buried in caves, others at the summits of high mountains. They were meant to be recovered, it was said, when they were needed for a specific situation. (The best known terma, at least in the Western world, was *The Tibetan Book of the Dead*.) The tradition of terma meant that the Nyingma were not bound by a fixed and immutable set of texts; the teaching was alive and thus could always develop and adapt to meet a new situation.

And yet this did not mean that the teaching would be popularized, watered down, or made palatable to Western tastes. "In establishing the Vajrayana in America," wrote the editors of *Crystal Mirror*, the Nyingma Meditation Center's journal, "no adaptation of the practices done in Tibet has been made. We believe that success and longevity of the Teachings depend on their being presented in the purity of their original form."

Within a few years Tarthang's group had grown large enough to buy and renovate a run-down fraternity house near the campus of the University of California. For two solid months they worked with Tarthang Tulku to transform the building into the Nyingma Meditation Center's home, Padma Ling, place of the Lotus. A more settled pattern began to emerge now: an hour of prostration and sitting every morning; walking meditation, chanting and prostrations in the evening. Rituals were held—pujas, sutra readings and other liturgical practices were conducted regularly. Rituals were observed on the same days they had been in Tibet, according to the Tibetan lunar calendar. All the chanting was in Tibetan—a practice that made it necessary for students to take at least introductory classes in the language. Some students began translating prayers and texts with Tarthang Tulku.

At the end of only three years Tarthang Tulku could say, "Before I came here no one knew the Vajra Guru Mantra, or had heard of Padmasambhava. But since I came to America there are, I may say, hundreds of people praying the Vajra Guru Mantra. Also they understand what Vajrayana means, very basically." And it was true. Padmasambhava had come to America just as he had come to Tibet a thousand years before; it was not as wild as Tibet; but who could doubt it needed taming. Padmasambhava, the Lotus-Born Guru, real and transparent as a rainbow, who had brought the vajrayana to Tibet, had now brought it to America.

II

Chogyam Trungpa, Rinpoche arrived in North America in January of 1970. He and his wife, Diana, flew first to Toronto where they lived in a small apartment while waiting for their American visa. Then they crossed the border to a farm in Barnet, Vermont that had been purchased by a few American students who had studied with him at Samye-Ling. There, at Tail of the Tiger (they had consulted the *I Ching* for the name), Trungpa found "an undisciplined atmosphere, combining the flavors of New York City and hippies." Everybody wanted to jump into advanced tantric practices right away. He told them, "Please sit; sit a lot."

In May he set out for New York and California on a lecture tour. He found a country in the midst of what seemed to many like a spiritual renaissance. But to him it was a spiritual supermarket. The shelves were bursting with gurus and swamis and roshis. Trungpa cut through it all. America suffered, he said, from spiritual materialism: "deceiving ourselves into thinking we are developing spiritually when instead we are strengthening our ego-centricity through spiritual techniques." Getting high—whether through grass, spiritual practices such as fasting, chanting, yoga or whatever—was simply not the point. His appearance was disquieting and puzzling to many, for he presented an entirely different picture from other teachers. He ignored health food and ate whatever he wanted, from Japanese haute-cuisine (in New York he managed to find an all-night sushi bar off Forty-second Street) to good old English roast beef. He also drank and smoked without apology, and sampled all the good things that Western civilization had come up with, from the halls of Oxford to the then-fashionable psychedelics—which he laughingly characterized as a kind of "double illusion" or "super samsara."

In July, Trungpa settled down in Boulder where he had been invited to teach at the University of Colorado. As word spread—through his lectures, seminars and books (*Meditation in Action*, a collection of talks, was published in America in 1970, and *Cutting Through Spiritual Materialism* in 1973) people began sitting and studying together at urban meditation centers called Dharmadhatus, which sprang up in New York, Boston, Berkeley and Los Angeles. In Boulder students rented a house which Rinpoche named Anitya Bhavan, "House of Impermanence," and then organized a city center called Karma Dzong—*dzong* meaning fortress and *karma*, buddha-activity. A number of the students in Boulder were drawn from a hard-living, dope-smoking, back-to-the-land commune called the Pygmies, and they formed the nucleus of the group who first settled a sparse, pine-and-rock-studded valley in northern Colorado that gradually, under Rinpoche's tutelage, grew into the Rocky Mountain Dharma Center.

Rinpoche was always at least one or two hours late for his lectures, and because of this his early scene involved a great deal of hanging out, socializing and gossipy boredom. But it all had a purpose. "By the time he finally arrived," one student remembers, "his audience was very ready to hear what he had to say, they had so exhausted the resources of their own self-entertainment." This boredom was the subject of many of his early discourses. There was nothing, he liked to point out, more boring than meditation. "In order to follow the spiritual path," he wrote in *Meditation in Action*, "one must first overcome the initial excitement."

The discipline increased slowly but deliberately. People began group sittings, and went for month-long retreats in cabins built at Tail of the Tiger and the Rocky Mountain Dharma Center. Trungpa adapted certain parts of the Zen tradition such as the use of zafus, the round sitting cushions used in zazen (though his were red and yellow) and he combined "just sitting" with walking meditation, though even here he introduced a characteristic note of uncertainty, since the periods of sitting-and-then-walking were not regular. Students never knew if the sitting were to last three hours or fifteen minutes before an equally uncertain period of walking meditation—usually no longer than twenty minutes—would "rescue" them from stiffness or boredom or obsession of mind. Still, the rules in a typical Dharmadhatu were rather relaxed compared to the rules of a Zen meditation hall. There were no monitors—sitters took turns ringing the bell that signaled the end of a sitting period—and one was allowed to move. It was not uncommon to see someone sitting on a zafu, feet flat on the mat, and head in hands, in a position more reminiscent of Rodin's Penseur than Shakyamuni Buddha.

A few early students, having previously sat zazen, complained about the loose, relaxed style, and then discovered that without the help of the external rules that Zen gave them their concentration was not as tight as they had thought. Boisterous parties often followed long meditation sessions, and students with purist attitudes found themselves swept like so many autumn leaves into the chaos. But the parties and social life were mixed with a growing sitting practice and close intellectual study of basic Buddhist principles. No matter how outrageously some nights might end, the next morning everyone woke to the sound of the conch, and it was back to the meditation hall, back to "square one," as Trungpa put it, "the place where you actually were the morning after, and not where you thought or imagined you ought to be."

There was indeed something uncompromising about Trungpa's approach. When asked why he smoked cigarettes, he said that it might be important for people to see. No one could escape spiritual practice by thinking that they had to become "pure" before they could begin. When Allen Ginsberg (who had met him as they both hailed the same taxi in New York) asked him if the Hindu-style heart chakra mantra meditation he had learned from Swami Muktananda was suitable for him, Trungpa answered laconically, "Probably not." Whatever Trungpa did or said became part of the path, and for many of his students the same kind of inescapable quality began to emerge. "Meeting him was like meeting yourself," said one student, "which was not always pleasant; few of us, looking into the mirror of our own breath, found ourselves to be quite as fair as we had imagined." Yet something stuck and people continued sitting, studying, finding time and money for retreats and later for *dathuns*, month-long meditation intensives, and then for the seminary, a three-month period of study, meditation and living at close quarters.

As more people began to practice, a certain degree of organization became necessary. Karma Dzong, Tail of the Tiger, the Rocky Mountain Dharma Center, and all the urban Dharmadhatu centers had developed along their own lines. In early 1973 Trungpa Rinpoche established Vajradhatu, a nationwide organization consolidating all the centers and activities. Soon Dharmadhatu memberships required that students sit two full days a month. Study groups had been a part of the scene from the first but now study became more systematic. A Vajradhatu Education Office was set up, and many of the drop-out academics and graduate students found themselves developing rather large study programs, complete with syllabi, teaching materials and examination questions.

In October of that year the first Vajradhatu Seminary took place at a hotel in Jackson Hole, Wyoming. The seminary was a three-month practice and study session. "Some scholars would say that in order to attain enlightenment you have to be a great scholar," Rinpoche said in one of the talks he gave every evening. "And others would say that in order to attain enlightenment you don't have to know anything at all, anything whatsoever, intellectually. One has to just practice meditation, keep going in that direction. These two approaches seem to be rather incomplete. We cannot rely on one or the other method."

The seminary study was based on the three yana approach—the first lectures outlined the hinayana, then went on to the mahayana, and finally the vajrayana. The seminary was the first time Trungpa Rinpoche spoke openly of the vajrayana—a subject he felt could only be understood after students had a thorough intellectual grounding and a certain amount of experience in hinayana and mahayana practice, discipline and study. He had, so he said, "been waiting to discuss this topic for a long time, in fact practically since I've been in this country."

Trungpa Rinpoche's exposition of the vajrayana was based on the teachings of Jamgon Kongtrul Lodro Thaye, the brilliant nineteenth-century teacher, who had collected and revitalized the teachings of all the many sects. Jamgon Kongtrul had synthesized a vital and eclectic movement called Rime ("unbiased"). Trungpa Rinpoche's root guru, Sechen Kongtrul, was an incarnation of Jamgon Kongtrul.

Trungpa Rinpoche began by discussing the samaya vow—the vajrayana commitment to the guru, and then spoke about the various tantras from the kriya yoga to the final ati yoga, or dzogchen. Trungpa Rinpoche felt that presenting the vajrayana in America was not to be taken lightly. "In order to launch Vajrayana in America," he said,

> we must give repeated warnings about the dangers of tantric practice. Giving many warnings is much more compassionate than presenting the vajrayana outright.
>
> I hope you'll be able to relate what you have studied and learned to others, but there's an exception. I would like to keep the tantric things that we discussed private. As you know there are no terribly embarrassing things contained in it. It's just the same old Buddhist stuff in many ways. But somehow the whole basic thing creates a lot of power, and it contains an enormous amount of magic and energy. We should be very careful.

He had prepared his students for four years before he called the small group of people to his house at Four Mile Canyon some months after the first seminary had ended, and gave them the transmission and permission to begin the first of the preliminary practices.

III

During his first few years in Berkeley, Tarthang Tulku concentrated on working with a small group of students at Padma Ling, the home of the Tibetan Nyingma Meditation Center. Padma Ling was an open airy building, surrounded by extensive gardens planted with fruit trees and flowers and filled with Tibetan prayer-flags. Peacocks and golden pheasants added a sense of repose and regal spaciousness. The students who lived there with Tarthang Tulku and his family were all serious and committed to the traditional training, and they worked, for the most part, very hard—both at their practices and at running the center and keeping up with various activities, such as the Tibetan Aid Project and Dharma Publishing (which Tarthang Tulku founded in 1969). It was assumed that the future teachers of the Nyingma in America would come from their ranks, though this would depend on their willingness and ability to complete a three year retreat traditionally required of Nyingma lamas.

At the same time more and more people had begun to attend the monthly weekend seminars Tarthang Tulku gave at Padma Ling. Many of these people were mental health professionals, particularly those influenced by Abraham Maslow's "Third Force" of humanistic psychology. Alan Watts, who was one of the first visitors to Padma Ling, had written some years earlier that Eastern religion actually had more in common with psychotherapy than with Western forms of religion and philosophy, and many of the therapists who attended Tarthang Tulku's lectures agreed with him. Maslow had inaugurated a new direction in psychology by focusing on health instead of disease. Maslow's studies of healthy, "self-actualizing" individuals, had led him to a serious consideration of what he called "peak experiences." In his last book, Maslow had characterized individuals who had such experiences as having achieved a high level of growth and maturity. He found that they led lives which reflected wholeness, simplicity, order, effortless energy, completion and dichotomy-transcendence. This description had much in common with the definition of a Buddha as one who had reached the highest development of his human potential—to use a term in vogue at the time. It was thus possible for some psychologists to see enlightenment as the ultimate state of mental health.

Because of the increasing interest among psychologists and others in the mental health field, Tarthang Tulku established a secular educational school called the Nyingma Institute. The purpose of the Institute was "the transmission of the psychological, philosophical, and experiential insights of the Nyingma lineage" to professionals, academics and the general public. The most rigorous academic standards would be combined with the practice of meditation, which was an essential part of Tibetan educational philosophy.

The Nyingma Institute opened in June of 1973 with a six-week Human Development Training Program, aimed specifically at Western therapists and psychologists. The Institute building itself, a former fraternity house that clung Tibetan-style to the Berkeley hillside, had been purchased only a month before the seminar began and so when the fifty-two participants arrived to find the students from Padma Ling still hard at work cleaning and making last-minute repairs, they were handed mops and brooms. "This was not the smoothly staffed American institution they were used to," wrote Gay Gaer Luce. "Our very arrival was an immediate lesson in the Buddhist secret of survival, a philosophy which urges the acceptance of life as it is, rather than an effort to meet expectations."

The program began with two solid days of meditation, chanting (which Tarthang felt Americans particularly receptive to), visualizations and a series of yoga-like exercises called *kum-nye*. Then Tarthang Tulku, seated cross-legged before the class, began to ask a few simple questions. "What is thought? What is the difference between calmness and stillness? What is sound?" "We gave the articulated answers one might expect from a group of educated professionals," reported Dr. Luce. "But as we listened to ourselves we began to get the message: what we accept for answers is simply the reduction of one concept or construct for another. We knew little about the experience of sound—although we were sitting in a relatively noisy room over a street with some traffic."

Rinpoche presented a barrage of exercises drawn from the vajrayana. He asked them to "sit in a chair for three hours and ask, 'What is the self-image.' You will get an answer," he said, "and then ask again, 'What is the self-image?' " He had people look into a mirror at the reflection of their own eyes for three hours at a time; he instructed them not to say 'yes' for a week; to keep silent for a weekend; he had them gaze at a white Tibetan letter on a black background until they could visualize it clearly; he told them to count every thought they had for an hour. (Dr. Luce came up with more than a thousand.)

Nothing was taken for granted. Rinpoche challenged some of the most basic assumptions of Western therapy, particularly the fixation of analysis on past events at the expense of attention to the present. He was particularly puzzled by the way children and adults blamed their parents for their own unhappiness. Buddhists, he pointed out, considered a certain amount of suffering and dissatisfaction as a natural, inevitable part of life. It was, after all, the First Noble Truth, the beginning of the spiritual path, and the basis for insight and work on oneself.

Then, too, he found it hard to understand the alienation and lack of caring that seemed to be so much a part of life in the Western nuclear family. The basis of Buddhist compassion was an understanding that all beings, at one time or another, had been each to the other parent and child. So he assigned another exercise: go as far back as possible and remember the way your parents gave birth to you, fed, clothed, diapered and supported you as an infant. Then he instructed them to visualize "their sufferings, their impoverished or neglected lives, and especially feel the loneliness of old people, so fragile and overlooked."

The exercises were indeed powerful, but the most important thing was that they did not stand alone as isolated techniques. "These Tibetan exercises," wrote Dr. Luce, "are integrated into a whole philosophy of life, one that had little sentimentality about death, pain, dirt, or human nastiness. These are not to be avoided, but seen and accepted. Enlightenment is said to be the ability to live with reality as it is, which means that one must peel away the culture's veneer over the nature of survival or life's brevity."

The themes of awareness and compassion ran through it all. The therapist must study himself as well as the patient in order to do any good at all. "The master, teacher, or therapist," said Tarthang Tulku, "is a person who can understand each level of human consciousness, through his own experience, as well as having received oral instructions. . . . there are no gaps between him and another person. He can put himself totally in the place of the patient. In other words, he is not treating somebody else; in a way, he is treating himself."

The first Human Development Training Program gave the Institute a rather spectacular start. That fall saw the beginning of a more traditional program of classes and seminars in Buddhist philosophy, psychology, and Sanskrit and Tibetan language study. The key scholar connected with the Institute was Dr. H.V. Guenther, Head of the Department of Far Eastern Studies at the University of Saskatchewan, who taught Buddhist philosophy and worked closely with Tarthang Tulku on translations of Nyingma texts by such masters as Longchenpa (*Kindly Bent to Ease Us*) and Jigme Lingpa.

Dr. Guenther was, in a sense, the Sir William Jones of our times—he had learned Chinese at the age of nine in Vienna and had then begun Sanskrit. He had originally learned Tibetan to read Sanskrit texts that were available only in their Tibetan translations, and went on to become an acknowledged Western expert in the language. In 1951 he had gone to India where he first taught Russian at Lucknow and then Indology, Buddhism and Tibetology at the Government Sanskrit College in Varanasi. There he became one of the few scholars in the world to be interested in indigenous Tibetan Buddhist literature and philosophy—particularly the ancient forms preserved by the Nyingmas, which he speculated had entered Tibet not from India, but from somewhere in inner Asia, possibly Khotan.

This theory caused controversy in scholarly circles, but was nothing compared to the controversy around Dr. Guenther's translations. For his translations Guenther used the technical language and concepts of modern philosophy and depth psychology; for example, "Mahakala is the black lord of transcending awareness; compassion is achieved in goal attainment which is the communion of the cognitive, communicative and manifestation patterns realized in Buddhahood." Agehananda Bharati, author of *The Tantric Tradition*, criticized this translation saying, "Psychology is bad enough in psychological writing, but intolerable in any other genre: mixing jargon metaphors from various disciplines in this manner is aggravating . . . interpretation of any text must be of one piece, with one metaphor-type from any specific discipline for the interpretation." Nevertheless, Dr. Guenther was recognized, as Hugh Richardson says, "as a true fortress of Tibetan Buddhism—so large it seems unassailable." Once when he was challenged to prove that his translation of a certain term was justified, he invited his opponent to his office where he had, as he said, "shoeboxes filled with index cards cross-referencing Tibetan usages of technical terms." Dr. Guenther may have been maddening to read at times—his renditions could be alternately illuminating and obscure—but no one seriously concerned with Tibetan Buddhism could ignore him, and his presence at the Nyingma Institute assured it a place on the map as an important center for Buddhist studies.

IV

Naropa Institute began when Trungpa Rinpoche met with some of his students in his little trailer at Rocky Mountain Dharma Center to talk about starting a school. Rinpoche thought of Naropa as "a hundred year project," modeled on the ancient Indian Buddhist University of Nalanda, which drew students—Buddhist and non-Buddhist alike—from all over Asia. Though Nalanda had been Buddhist inspired and run, its curriculum had included secular subjects such as logic, poetry, arts and sciences. (Naropa, a great pandit and head of Nalanda, had left the university in search of a guru; he subsequently became one of the forefathers of the Kagyu school.)

The premise of Naropa Institute was that clear, hard thinking is central to a sane spiritual journey; what was needed was a crossroads where the intellectual-critical mind of the West and the way of experience and meditation of the East could meet head-on—"a place where intellect and intuition could come together," according to the brochures and catalogues which were mailed out for the first summer session in

1974, announcing courses on meditation, T'ai-chi, tea ceremony, thangka painting, Tibetan and Sanskrit, madhyamika philosophy, anthropology, physics and cybernetics. A number of luminaries were enticed to teach: there was Trungpa Rinpoche, of course, and Ram Dass, author of the best-selling *Be Here Now*, the story of the journey of Harvard psychology professor Richard Alpert from LSD researcher to Hindu holy man.

Then there was Professor Herbert Guenther who taught "The History of the Kagyus," and Agehananda Bharati who flew in to give a lecture on "The Future (if any) of Tantra," and concluded that, "Lastly, where can tantra happen? It can happen only in America and Western Europe . . . and maybe it has started right here in Boulder, Colorado 80302." Gregory Bateson, originator of the double-bind theory of schizophrenia and author of *Balinese Character* and *Steps to an Ecology of Mind*, taught a course on "The Evolutionary Idea;" Allen Ginsberg, now a student of Trungpa Rinpoche, who had given him the Buddhist refuge name "Lion of Dharma," taught a course on "Spiritual Poetics" and performed a spontaneous, linked verse poem with Trungpa Rinpoche. The night Nixon resigned, John Cage gave the first performance of *Empty Words - Part IV*, consisting of a mix of vowels, consonants and silences culled by chance operations from the *Journal of Henry David Thoreau*. (Slide projections of drawings from the *Journal* slowly appeared and disappeared throughout the performance.) There were lectures, classes, concerts, readings, performances, debates and colloquiums, and although Naropa Institute had started as a fairly modest project, it seemed that every day another course, reading or workshop was added—the Institute seemed to have its own momentum.

At first about one or two hundred students were expected. Then, as responses to the catalogues began pouring in, the estimate was revised to five hundred. As it turned out, two thousand people came to Boulder for the first summer session in 1974. Trungpa Rinpoche and Ram Dass were the biggest draws. They taught in a big, carpeted former bus garage on the hot summer nights (Rinpoche on Monday and Wednesday, Ram Dass on Tuesday and Thursday) in a kind of *mano a mano*—Rinpoche in his shirtsleeves, cautioning, demanding, inspiring cynicism, cutting through spiritual materialism, handling his vajra (a ritual scepter) like a reverse lightning rod; and then Ram Dass, bearded and bhakti, starting every lecture on the *Bhagavad Gita* by leading eight hundred people in chanting and singing kirtans (devotional chants)—the course culminating in an all-night Shiva chant on the outskirts of Boulder.

Probably half of the two thousand students had been drawn by Ram

Dass and there were certain ideological differences between the Hindus and the Buddhists, which were reflected in their styles. The Boulder Buddhists thought the Hindus too full of love and light; the Hindus thought the Buddhists cynical and rowdy. The Hindus were vegetarians and clean living; the Buddhists smoked, drank, ate meat and hung out at Tom's Tavern across the street from Karma Dzong. But everybody got along, more or less, and went to parties and talked all night in the motel-like townhouses that Naropa had rented for the summer, and swam and sunned in the townhouse pools and went back and forth between Ram Dass and Rinpoche's lectures, like so many ping pong balls, words and concepts about no-words and no-concepts floating around in their minds. Some students even found time for all-day sittings.

Of course there was too much going on for most people to pay attention to any one thing. But that was the point. "There is a particular philosophy of Naropa," said Rinpoche to Ram Dass in a panel discussion at the end of the summer,

> which is not so much trying to bring it together, like a spoon of sugar in your lemonade so that it becomes more drinkable, but the point is more like a firework—not so much that each will fight with each other in the destructive sense, but that there is an enormous individualism in terms of the doctrines and teachings that are presented. All of them are valid but at the same time there is a meeting point which takes place in a spark.

V

Jack Kornfield and Joseph Goldstein began their collaboration when they met at Naropa. Their paths had been strikingly parallel: both had gone to Southeast Asia in the Peace Corps, both had studied there intensively in the Theravadin tradition of Buddhism, both had returned to America at about the same time and both had begun teaching. Joseph had studied in Bodh-Gaya with an Indian named Munindra-ji, Jack as a bhikkhu in Thailand with the forest monk Achaan Chaa. Joseph had been famous in India for sitting patiently with Munindra in Bodh-Gaya, sticking with it—watching, watching, watching, as was the way in vipassana (insight) meditation; watching his mind, watching his breath, watching his feelings, watching his pain, his pleasure, his hope, his bliss, his hunger—watching whatever rose into the field of his consciousness—

while everybody else passed through, sat for a day, a week, a month maybe, and then went on, perhaps to Neem Karoli Baba, Ram Dass's guru, an old man wrapped in a blanket, and then to Nepal and Kathmandu and maybe back to Benares and then on to take a vipassana course somewhere with Goenka.

Joseph's teacher in Bodh-Gaya, Anagarika Munindra, was a tiny Bengali about half as tall as Joseph. Munindra had been active in the Maha Bodhi Society and in 1949, when India gained independence, the new government asked him to take charge of the Buddhist temple in Bodh-Gaya. He accepted it, thinking that he would now be able to complete the work that Anagarika Dharmapala had left unfinished. In 1957 he took a six month leave of absence to practice meditation with Mahasi Sayadaw in Burma. He remained in Burma for seven years, reading the entire Tripitaka in Pali and training as a teacher and monk with Mahasi Sayadaw. Then he returned to India and became an anagarika—a homeless one—and established an international meditation center at Bodh-Gaya where a few Westerners, among them a tall, ex-Peace Corps man named Joseph Goldstein began to practice.

While Joseph was sitting at Bodh-Gaya, Jack Kornfield was practicing vipassana deep in the jungles of Thailand. His teacher, Achaan Chaa, was a very strict and traditional bhikkhu, a forest monk, who had walked for a number of years as an ascetic, begging his food and sleeping under the trees. Though he taught a fair number of Westerners who found their way to his forest hermitage in northeast Thailand, he had not made any allowances for them. They followed the Vinaya, all of the two-hundred-and-fifty rules that Buddha had listed for his monks in the beginning, and they lived a very simple life—eating once a day, sweeping the forest paths and meditating.

Jack returned to America in the robes of a Theravadin monk a year or so before Naropa began, but he found it impossible to keep his vows as a forest monk and decided to return to lay life. Usually this was done in a ceremony with other bhikkhus, but since there were no other bhikkhus in Boston, Jack conducted the ceremony himself in a Thai Wat that had been reconstructed and placed in a museum.

He drove a taxicab for a while and eventually decided to return to graduate school in psychology. Then one day Jack met Trungpa Rinpoche at a cocktail party in Cambridge and Rinpoche invited him to come to Naropa for the summer to teach a course on Theravadin meditation.

Meanwhile Joseph, back from teaching with Munindra in Bodh-Gaya, wrote to Naropa about teaching vipassana there, but they replied that they had already asked someone else. At the same time Ram Dass was making preparations for his course on the *Bhagavad Gita* and wanted Joseph, who he had met at Bodh-Gaya, to teach vipassana as part of the course. He had heard that Joseph was back in America but didn't know how to find him. Then a few days before the summer session began, Ram Dass and Joseph ran into each other in a Berkeley restaurant and Ram Dass told Joseph that he wanted him to teach in Boulder. They left the next day.

When Jack and Joseph met in Boulder they discovered that they were teaching along the same lines. Even though no one had heard of them their meditation classes were very popular; indeed, one student described them as the "dark horses of the summer." A number of students were drawn to the straightforwardness and simplicity of vipassana, and wanted to study more intensively. So in the fall of 1974 Joseph and Jack (as people started to call their teaching team) put together a course for one month at a rented campground. People took the five precepts of not killing, not stealing (traditionally not taking what is not given), no sexual misconduct (interpreted during a retreat as celibacy), not lying (interpreted as keeping noble silence) and abstinence from intoxicants. Participants ate before noon and practiced mindfulness not only during meditation, but during every activity.

For the next few years Joseph and Jack lived a peripatetic existence, traveling around the country and holding courses, some of them as long as three months. Then in 1976 a group of Theravadins bought a mansion-like red brick building that had served formerly as a Catholic seminary just outside the town of Barre, Massachusetts.

The Insight Meditation Center, as they called it, was run by a staff of volunteers. Students cooked the vegetarian food, answered the phones, did the office work and kept up the grounds. They worked for a year at a time before someone else would take their place, and they followed the five precepts. Students who attended retreats at Barre paid seven dollars a day for food and lodging and were asked to give *dana* (donations) to help defray costs and support the teachers. The system worked very well and within a short time the Insight Meditation Center was one of the few Buddhist retreats in the country to operate in the black.

Unlike most meditation centers in America, the Insight Center was not built around the charisma of a single teacher. It was run by the sangha along with a kind of cooperative of teachers trained in the vipassana tradition. This was possible because even though there are many varieties of vipassana, they are all based on what are traditionally called the four foundations of mindfulness: of the body, of feelings, of mind and of the objects of mind. The differences, says Joseph, "really have to do with the objects you choose to develop awareness on. Some of the techniques use all four foundations as an object, some of the techniques use one or some combination of them."

Munindra favored starting with mindfulness of all four objects in a kind of choiceless awareness—at least if it seemed the student could handle it. If not, the practice concentrated first on mindfulness of breathing and picked up the other objects as the practice ripened. This was the approach that Joseph encouraged new students to take. "As the practice matures," he says, "the labels drop away, and with them the need for any specific fixed object. Then it happens that whatever rises in consciousness—there's awareness."

The actual practice of this kind of "bare attention" sounded quite simple, perhaps even simplistic. But it is hard to concentrate on just one thing—attention, without clinging, to the passing show of what everyone takes to be a permanent, abiding self. "In the beginning," says Joseph "it's as if someone is watching all these objects. The progression of insight is that when the mind becomes still, mindfulness begins to observe the watcher, to see that actually there is no watcher. There's just watching. That's also a process of arising and passing away—*anicca*, impermanence. And as it develops further, the observer and the observed come together, and there's not that sense of separation and duality."

But it took time and work, even if the work was the nonwork of letting go. Vipassana retreats tended to be long—two weeks was considered the minimum. "Two weeks gives you a good amount of exposure to the range of changes," Joseph says,

> from the confusion to being high to more confusion to working through that—so that people get a chance to experience that no one state is "it," and that the real teaching is the balance of mind behind the changes. This is the most important teaching. A few days sitting usually involves just experiencing pain, which could be simply discouraging. One week gives the breakthrough to getting a little high and coming to the false conclusion that this is what meditation is all about. But two weeks, we've found, gives enough exposure to enough ups and downs so that you can see the balance between particular states—which is the whole message.

Within a few years the elders of the Theravadins began to arrive at the Insight Meditation Center: Anagarika Munindra, the Venerable Mahasi

Sayadaw, the forest monk Achaan Chaa and others. The Theravadins in Southeast Asia were the most monastically oriented of all Buddhists and stuck close to the letter of the Vinaya rules. But the Americans who had trained with them had either not returned as bhikkhus or had returned to lay life shortly after arriving back in America. Joseph thought they might be starting a lineage that would be "preserved outside the monastic continuum—a whole new experience of the dharma unfolding." On their last trip to Burma, Joseph and Jack had asked the abbot of one of the strictest Theravadin orders whether they should adhere to the traditional rules in their monastery at Barre. He told them that they didn't have to take all the rules over because they might not all be appropriate. "He told us to use whatever form was appropriate to remember that any form can become a trap, and that even in Burma some of the bhikkhus were too attached to the rules."

On Mahasi Sayadaw's visit to Insight Meditation Center he prepared to give students short interviews as was the custom at the courses in Burma. Jack asked him how many students he thought he and his instructors could "check"—which is the term they use—and they replied that they could handle thirty an hour, that is, one every two minutes, which was how many Jack assigned. The students whose names were posted on a list outside the meditation hall got in line and waited, practicing mindfulness of standing and waiting. At the end of the hour the Bhikkhu U Jannaka had seen eight students and U Pittaka had seen about twelve. Jack Kornfield commented to them, "Pretty different teaching Westerners than Burmese," and the bhikkhus had to agree. They felt that the real difference was one of concentration, and that this was because the Burmese had more faith in the practice to begin with and so didn't worry so much about whether what they were doing would be effective. Thus the Burmese were able to develop concentration in the initial stages much more quickly; from the interviews, the monks saw that most Westerners had not gone very far beyond the hurting knee state.

Along with concentration the vipassana teachers saw motivation as a problem in developing practice. As Joseph said, "There is not the same belief in rebirth in different realms in America as in Burma, so people do not seem to have the same motivation to practice." The Sayadaw listened thoughtfully, but he did not have any easy answers. "It is very difficult to explain to people what the Buddha taught," he said. "Bad karma, miserable rebirth, good karma, good life . . . means they have a chance to practice. All you can do is teach what the Buddha said. It is not only in America. Few practice. Even in Burma there are more people who do not practice meditation than people who do."

VI

Tarthang was the first and most visible Nyingma teacher in America, but he was not the only one. Sonam Kazi, the Sikkimese lay meditation master who had served as the Dalai Lama's translator for many Westerners, including Ginsberg, Snyder and Thomas Merton in India, arrived with his wife and daughter in San Francisco in 1970. He was sponsored by the Alan Watts Society for the Study of Comparative Philosophy. The Kazis visited the Nyingma Institute, Zen Center, Tassajara and Esalen, where Sonam moderated as Alan Watts and Tarthang Tulku engaged in a genial debate about the necessity for effort in Buddhism. (The debate ended before it began when Alan Watts's opening question, "What must you do to attain enlightenment?" was answered by Tarthang's "Nothing," and Watts was at once delighted and stopped in his tracks.)

While in India, Sonam had met a number of people who were interested in Gurdjieff. These people were deeply involved in the Work, as they called it, but felt that after Mr. Gurdjieff's death the life had gone out of the organization and they were looking for a new direction. So they invited Sonam Kazi to New York where they held a series of exploratory meetings. They were upper middle class, older and more settled than, say, the students who had first gathered around Tarthang in Berkeley, and though most of them eventually drifted away, they formed the nucleus of what became the Longchen Nyingthig Society.

Sonam Kazi was very much a layman, proof that one could live the life of a tantric yogi while existing in the world. In fact, the beauty and uniqueness of the vajrayana, as he saw it, lay partly in the fact that one did not have to renounce the world and spend years in a monastery in order to realize the true nature of mind. "A tantric yogi," he would tell the New Yorkers gathered before an elaborate Tibetan-style shrine in a living room somewhere on the Upper West Side, "knows how to meditate in either a palace or a cave."

Sonam preferred, as did many Nyingmas, to work quietly, without publicity or fanfare, with a small group of people. New members would come by word of mouth—that is, by karma. He was highly accomplished in dzogchen and eloquent about its virtues, but he left the details of ceremony and ritual to his wife Tsede-la, who had been a close disciple of the great woman tantric teacher, Jetsun Lochen Rinpoche in Tibet. Not that he ignored these aspects. He felt strongly that the teachings should be presented to Americans in a complete way, just as they had been presented to him in Tibet, and when someone would object—as someone often did—that they were interested in the nonconceptual aspects of dzogchen and not the preliminary practices and ceremonies and rituals that went along with it, he would answer that the vajrayana was like a finely woven carpet, and one could not pick and choose one thread or color over all the others without running the danger of unravelling the whole design.

He had a great appreciation for other traditions—especially Zen and Krishnamurti—both of which had something in common with the dzogchen approach, but like most Tibetans, he had absolutely no interest in mixing traditions, and he viewed the American predilection for eclecticism with some disdain. "You only end up," he said, "with a concoction like chop suey."

Sonam Kazi had also studied with Lochen Rinpoche in Tibet, but his root guru was Dudjom Rinpoche, and in 1972 Sonam invited him to visit the United States, making him the first of the heads of the four Tibetan orders to visit America. His Holiness Dudjom Rinpoche visited the Nyingma Institute and the Longchen Nyingthig Buddhist Society in New York; he conducted refuge and bodhisattva ceremonies and gave a few public talks in New York and Berkeley. But it was not until he returned for a longer visit in 1976 (this time at the invitation of New York poet John Giorno, who had become his disciple in India) that he established his own center, Orgyen Cho Dzong, and began to teach in the west on a regular basis.

Dudjom Rinpoche himself gave an impression of vast space and quiet, yet at the same time he acted with simplicity and directness and a kind of domestic warmth. He wore his long hair knotted in the back, in the traditional style of Nyingma yogis, and he dressed with unassuming elegance in a plain, light grey, cotton chuba. But when he performed pujas and empowerments (initiations), he sat regally on a brocade-covered throne, constructed Tibetan-style by his New York students, and he wore whatever ceremonial crown and robe was appropriate for the occasion.

When His Holiness Dudjom Rinpoche traveled around the country on his second visit in 1976, he spoke about the nature and place of the vajrayana, particularly the dzogchen teachings, in relation to the hinayana and mahayana. "We could illustrate the different paths of the teaching of the Buddha with an example," he said.

> A group of men, finding a poisonous tree in a field, immediately rush to it and cut down the tree because they know that consuming it would be fatal. Not only do they cut it down, but their fear of it is so great that they cast the poisonous tree far away and also uproot it from the very depths so that the poisonous tree will not grow back. This represents the approach of the hinayana. The poison is an allusion to the poisonous passions, or rather the ignorance which is the basis of them. And the people gathered in the field who uproot the poisonous tree and cast it away are the followers of the hinayana.
>
> While the first group of people is engaged in uprooting the tree, there arrives on the scene a braver group of people, or a more clever group of people, rather, who see how painfully the earlier group of people is engaged in cutting down the poisonous tree . . . and the second group of people say, "You needn't go to such trouble to uproot that tree. We understand the poisonous tree is fatal if consumed, and so we believe in cutting down the tree. But instead of bothering to uproot the tree, you should simply apply the antidote. That is, if you pour very hot water over it, the root will be burnt, and after that, if you apply hot ash, the root will never grow into a tree again.
>
> This second group of people are students of the mahayana, or the bodhisattva path. They do not go to the lengthy and meticulous extent of removing every aspect of our poisonous defilements, but instead apply the antidote for every poisonous act. For instance, anger is counteracted by compassion and love.
>
> At that point there arrives a doctor who is, in fact. in search of a poisonous tree. He says; "This is the very tree I have been looking for. I am trying to make a medicine for which I require this very poison tree."
>
> This is an example of the secret mantrayana, or tantra, where the effort is not to remove or abandon or dissolve the poisonous defilements but instead to see that in these poisonous qualities there is wisdom. These impurities can be transmuted and transformed into wisdom.
>
> And then a beautiful peacock descends into the field and upon seeing the poisonous tree, immediately consumes it with delight, and immediately transforms its poisonous quality into beauty. Such is the approach of dzogchen—or ati yoga—seeing the defilement, recognizing instantly its wisdom quality, consuming it and transforming it into the grace of realization. Although ati yoga or dzogchen is the highest approach yet if not followed properly it can be dangerous. It can be dangerous to eat poison when we are not peacocks. In order to be like this peacock one should first gain depth in view, and also be able to maintain the continuity of awareness in meditation, and in addition, one's actions themselves should be impeccable.

So for Dudjom Rimpoche, as indeed for all the Tibetans, the final teaching of vajrayana was "secret," not because it was a mysterious or hidden truth reserved for a spiritual elite, but because it was dangerous without the preparation and personal guidance of a guru.

Americans had a hard time with the Tibetan emphasis on the importance of the teacher, for there was nothing comparable in their culture. The apprenticeship system was perhaps the closest analogy, but even then apprenticeships were limited to learning a specific craft or skill, and did not entail the same kind of personal faith and devotion to the instructor. People might believe in God, or an ideal or a scientific theory, but in America one did not place complete trust in another human being. Still, the Tibetans who had come here felt that the sudden appearance of the vajrayana in America—which seemed to have happened almost overnight—showed "the karmic link that America had with the secret mantrayana teachings of Guru Padmasambhava."

As Sogyal Rinpoche, a young, Oxford-educated lama, said, "This particular era is very turbulent and everything is kind of gross, but it is exactly in this kind of field that Guru Padmasambhava's compassion and power works best. And another point is that in this turbulent period, whatever one does is speeded up. Karma keeps pace with the twentieth century and Padmasambhava keeps pace with it also. He is the Buddha of our time and cuts through our neuroses and skillfully relates the dharma to the frustrations of our age." And Dudjom Rinpoche had added, "The uniqueness of Guru Rinpoche's line is that we do not totally have to change our lifestyle or take on the stricter precepts as found in Hinayana. Working skillfully on ourselves and not totally giving up our worldly goods leads quickly to attainment."

According to the Tibetans the vajrayana had first been taught by the Buddha to a certain King Indrabhuti—as a response to the king's plea that he would never be able to give up his kingdom and all the pleasures that came with his station. It was not hard, then, to see twentieth century America as the land of King Indrabhuti, where distractions were actually opportunities to practice and awaken, and Dudjom Rinpoche for one found it no problem at all to make his home on the top floor of a brownstone in the richest, busiest, most distracting city in the world. His students might talk about "getting away" to meditate, but he was fine where he was; in fact, he rather liked it.

VII

When the word reached Boulder that Rangjung Rigpe Dorje, His Holiness the Sixteenth Karmapa, the head of the Karma Kagyu order, was coming to America, the students of Trungpa Rinpoche saw their teacher change almost overnight. This man who had divested himself not only of his robes, but seemingly of anything that was even remotely Tibetan, who smoked, drank, spoke their language and hung out with them was now carefully inspecting swatches of the finest brocade; instructing them how to starch white curtains with rice water; assembling dinner services from the best crystal, china and silver; sending them in search of gold-leaf chopstick rests; designing an elaborately carved, Tibetan-style throne; preparing a menu that included the finest Chinese cuisine as well as salted and buttered Tibetan tea, *tsampa* and *mo-mos*.

As the day of the Karmapa's arrival approached, Trungpa Rinpoche had driven himself into a high exhaustion; he had gone without sleep for days on end, personally overseeing the smallest details, at times taking vacuum cleaner, needle and thread, and iron in hand. Nothing was spared, including himself.

His Holiness the Sixteenth Karmapa arrived in New York on September 18, 1974, the year of the Wood Tiger. He was met by Chogyam Trungpa, Rinpoche who held the traditional sticks of burning incense, and was presented with garlands of flowers by Trungpa Rinpoche's students. It had been six years since His Holiness and Chogyam Trungpa Rinpoche had last seen each other, and the Karmapa had doubtless heard lots of stories, some true, some exaggerated, about how this former monk had immersed himself in the Western world. But now as they met His Holiness smiled broadly, and it was clear that everything was all right.

The Karmapas and the Trungpas went back a long way. The founder of the Trungpa lineage, the great siddha Trungmase Togden, had been a close disciple of Teshin Shekpa, the fifth Karmapa in the fourteenth century, and had received many oral teachings from him. The fourth and the tenth Trungpas had been especially close disciples of the Karmapas of their time, and the Karmapas and the Trungpas had always maintained a close relationship. The Karmapas had traditionally been charged with recognizing the important tulkus of the Kagyu lineage, and in 1939, at the age of sixteen His Holiness had had the vision which resulted in the discovery of Chogyam Trungpa, Rinpoche.

His Holiness was a plump, round-faced man in his early fifties. He wore the sleeveless maroon-colored robes of a Tibetan monk and his hair was cropped very short. He did not speak any English, nor did he do much teaching, in the sense that Trungpa Rinpoche or Tarthang Tulku taught. He just was, and that seemed more than enough. When he smiled everything around him seemed bathed in sunlight. "It's really wonderful to have His Holiness in one's presence," said Sister Palmo (the former Freda Bedi) who had accompanied His Holiness to America. "He is full of laughter and he couldn't be less serious. He streams great love to everyone and all who see him go back feeling better simply for having seen him." The Karmapa told an interviewer that he had no message for "Americans in general," but to those who came to him, the Karmapa "would impress on them a consciousness of their state of impermanence and that they should try to develop their understanding of Buddhist teachings and their practice of sitting meditation." When a reporter asked him the classic, "why had he come to America," he replied, speaking through his interpreter, "The Lord Buddha preceded me. If there was a lake, the swans would go there." It was not by the truth or subtlety or profundity of his words that he won people. There was something else. He was, as Trungpa Rinpoche said, a dharma king, and wherever he was seemed to reflect an inner splendor and ease. The police who escorted him in New York ended up by asking for his blessing and wearing little red protection cords he gave them, and more than one press conference ended the same way.

The power and the spiritual presence of the Karmapa was most apparent in the ceremonies and pujas he performed—especially in the Black Crown Ceremony. The origins of the Black Crown Ceremony went back to the first Karmapa, Tusum Khyenpa, the founder of the Karma Kagyu Order. He had been a student of Gampopa, who himself had been a student of the great poet and yogi Milarepa. Tusum Khyenpa spent many years in solitary retreat, and when he finally attained enlightenment it is said that a host of dakinis presented him with the knowledge of the past, present and future, and celebrated the event by offering him a black crown woven from their hair. According to the teaching, the crown has been present, though invisible, above the heads of every Karmapa from that time on.

The second Karmapa, Karma Pakshi, was an adept in tantric practice and renowned as a siddha. He was the teacher of Kublai Khan at the imperial court of China—a position held by all the succeeding Karmapas until the tenth. The Emperor Yung-lo, a spiritually gifted disciple of the Fifth Karmapa, had had a vision of the black crown. Desiring to share the vision with ordinary people, he ordered a replica made and presented it to the Karmapa.

All the Karmapas since that time had worn the black vajra crown during the Black Crown Ceremony, just as the sixteenth Karmapa did when he performed the ceremony for the first time in North America on the afternoon of September 21.

The ceremony began with the nine monks who had accompanied the Karmapa playing Tibetan horns and chanting in low, gutteral tones. Then His Holiness seated himself cross-legged on a thick cushion on the brocade-covered throne that Trungpa Rinpoche's students had prepared for him, and put on the ceremonial meditation hat of Gampopa. The monks performed three prostrations before His Holiness, and then, requesting that he assume his transcendental form of Avalokiteshvara, the bodhisattva of compassion, they offered a metal disc with rice, a mandala symbolizing the entire universe. They then chanted the sevenfold service, which consists of prostrations, offerings and prayers, and which ends with a dedication of the merits of the ceremony to all sentient beings.

Responding to the monk's supplication, His Holiness removed the hat he was wearing, and began to enter into a deep meditation. One of the monks handed him a box, from which His Holiness removed the crown, which was wrapped in a silk cloth. He carefully unwrapped the cloth, and with the horns resounding, removed the crown. Then, taking a deep breath that seemed to move him into another dimension, he placed the gleaming blue-black crown slowly on his head. He held it there lightly, with one hand. Then he took a crystal rosary in his other hand, and recited "om mani padme hum," the mantra of Avalokiteshvara, the bodhisattva of compassion, one hundred and eight times.

He was the same man who had walked into the room and seated himself on the throne, but he was also someone or something else—an unmistakable and regal being of power and serenity and compassion. It was a moment of extraordinary simplicity, directness and powerful clarity. Then he seemed to sigh, the horns stopped, he removed the crown, wrapped it once again in its silk covering, replaced it in its box and the ceremony was over.

The people who had been watching got up from their chairs and formed a line. One by one they stepped forward and the Karmapa blessed each person with a touch on the head as they filed past, sometimes with a small reliquary, sometimes with a stick with ribbons, sometimes with his hand; and the monks handed everyone a small, red protection cord, which was to be worn around the neck as a reminder of the occasion. The ceremony was always the same; it had not changed since the days of the Fifth Karmapa, and would be repeated for thousands of Americans across the country.

The Karmapas were famous in Tibet for their ceaseless activity in propagating the dharma. Many Karmapas traveled in huge tent camps of several thousand people, both inside Tibet and outside it—in China, among the Mongols, and in the frontier lands of Bhutan, Sikkim and Nepal. Now as the Sixteenth Karmapa traveled across America, not on horseback, but in a fleet of limousines chauffeured by students of Trungpa Rinpoche, the lodgings prepared for them along the way, with brocade-covered walls, fine Tibetan and Chinese rugs, wall hangings and thangkas, were reminiscent of the interior of the tent of a nomadic dharma king.

They went first to Vermont, to Tail of the Tiger (now a contemplative community), where His Holiness blessed the land, performed a long Mahakala puja, and where, at the request of Trungpa Rinpoche he gave Tail of the Tiger a new name—Karme-Cho kyi ling (Karme-Choling for short) which meant "the Dharma Place of the Karma Kagyu." Then on to Ann Arbor, where he met with Swami Muktananda and took part in a discussion about Hindu and Buddhist tantra. In Boulder he performed the Black Crown Ceremony for the Karma Dzong community, as well as a series of lineage abhishekas (empowerments), and he recognized his first tulku born in the West—Trungpa Rinpoche's son, Surmang Tenga Rinpoche, as the incarnation of one of the Karmapa's teachers.

The Karmapa also wrote and delivered the following:

> Proclamation to All Those Who Dwell Under the Sun Upholding the Tradition of the Spiritual and Temporal Orders
>
> The ancient lineage of supreme Trungpa incarnations, beginning with the great siddha Trungmase Chökyi Lodrö, has given rise in every generation to a great being who performed nothing but sacred action. Awakened by the vision of these predecessors in the lineage, this present disciple of mine, Chökyi Gyatso Trungpa Rinpoche, has carried out the vajra holder's discipline in the land of America, establishing his students in liberation and ripening them in the dharma. This wonderful truth is clearly manifest.
>
> Accordingly, I empower Chökyi Gyatso as *Vajra Holder* and *Possessor of the Ultimate Lineage Victory Banner of the Practice Lineage Teachings of the Karma Kagyü*. Let this be recognized by all people of both elevated and ordinary station.

For Chogyam Trungpa, Rinpoche the visit of His Holiness had come at just the right time. Trungpa Rinpoche had worked very hard to prepare his students for the vajrayana—he had nursed and scolded them through the hinayana discipline of sitting, and he had befriended and encouraged them into mahayana warmth and generosity. Now, after four years, just as the first "tantra group" was beginning the first of the preliminary practices, he had been able to introduce them to the head of the lineage, a true dharma king, someone who was, as Trungpa Rinpoche put it, "one of the most revealing, enlightened tantric feast creators of all."

Before His Holiness's visit Trungpa Rinpoche's students in Boulder (and around the country) had taken pride in being "American Buddhists," without all the ritual trappings and Tibetan paraphernalia. But now they had met His Holiness and had seen the manner in which Rinpoche prepared and took care of his teacher. They had been introduced to the next step, especially important among the Kagyus, of devotion—the relationship, as Trungpa Rinpoche said, "which makes the student persist in this long, difficult, and often extremely painful voyage of discovery."

Certainly everything in the Boulder community had become more formal, more elegant, more vivid and more celebratory during his visit. Nor did that change after he left. The shrine room had been redone in brilliant reds and golds and banners hung from the walls. Ritual became more evident, especially in the advanced practices, and the suits and ties and shining shoes that people had worn for their audiences with His Holiness were now worn to dinner parties and seminars. Rinpoche's annual birthday party, which had been a rather wild affair in the old days now included formal toasts and ballroom dancing. Some people were shocked by the turn of affairs and left, but for most it was just another part of their training.

"The teaching was definitely upgraded by Rinpoche," said Ken Green, a Vajradhatu director.

> We were introduced to mahamudra, which is dealing with the phenomenal world. The mahamudra teaching is not to shy away, but to participate and celebrate, to step out further, willing to be psychologically rich and dignified. From the practitioner's point of view we are talking about dealing with form very directly, which means how a person eats, the way he dresses, how you furnish your home. All that becomes part of the path; it is no longer superficial. There's an element of ritual that begins to enter one's life.

But if His Holiness had made an impression on the students, they had also made one on him. "His recent visit to America was a very special acknowledgement that American students can receive the teachings of the vajrayana in the fullest sense," Rinpoche said after His Holiness had left the country. "He is very excited about the ground work that has been prepared already. So I think it is a real historical event when a Buddhist leader begins to acknowledge the potential of Western students. He felt that he could bless them and sow further seeds on the ground we have prepared."

VIII

Kalu Rinpoche was a yogi. Like Milarepa, he had lived for years in a cave in Tibet, and he had only come out when his root guru had insisted it was time for him to teach. He avoided the large monasteries with all their administrative headaches, and instead became master of the three-year retreats at a small meditation center.

With the Communist takeover of Tibet he fled to India, where he settled down contentedly in a tiny cell in a small monastery near Darjeeling, and eventually accepted a small, run-down monastery near Sonada. It had originally been a Gelugpa monastery, and even though Kalu Rinpoche was a Kagyu he never bothered to remove from his room the images of Tsongkhapa (the founder of the Gelugpas) and his two chief disciples.

The first thing he did in Sonada was to build a hut for a three-year retreat. It wasn't much—the roof was made from biscuit tins, the walls were papered with pages from Western magazines, and the temple room was underground; but it was occupied immediately by a succession of Tibetan, Bhutanese and Sikkimese monks, and by the time Thomas Merton visited Kalu Rinpoche in 1968 there were sixteen people, fifteen men and one woman, doing the three-year retreat at Sonada.

Kalu Rinpoche first visited France and America in 1971 at the request of the Dalai Lama, the Karmapa and the many Westerners who had met him in India. He formed a number of centers for the practice of a Chenrezig (Tibetan for Avalokiteshvara) sadhana. He gave that particular meditation, he said, because it developed compassion, and because while it contained all the elements in the higher vajrayana sadhanas, it didn't entail the same high-voltage risks. Even when students of Kalu

Rinpoche went on to other practices they continued to practice the Chenrezig meditation.

His principal center in North America was established in Vancouver, Canada and when he returned home to Sonada his students traveled down to Seattle and asked Deshung Rinpoche to teach in Kalu's absence. Deshung Rinpoche had not taught dharma since his arrival at the University of Washington in 1961, and at first he refused. But one of Kalu Rinpoche's students asked him if he didn't think it a good idea that Kalu Rinpoche had established dharma centers in North America, and Deshung Rinpoche said yes, he thought it was very good. So he was trapped, and he began to make periodic trips up to Vancouver. There he taught not only dharma, but also Tibetan, which the students studied diligently, in order to talk to him without a translator and also because Kalu Rinpoche thought it would help them to practice and understand the dharma more effectively.

When Kalu Rinpoche saw that some of his Western students were strongly committed—some of them had completed the preliminary practices three or four times, and had managed to learn Tibetan as well—he began thinking about the possibility of setting up a three-year retreat for Westerners. In 1974 he discussed the idea with a few close disciples, and then, of course, word leaked out and others came to him and said that they wanted to do it too. Rinpoche replied that he would consider it if they completed the preliminary practices, learned Tibetan and got together enough money to support themselves for the three years. A small group of people began then to make preparations, although they had no idea how or where the retreat might take place.

As it turned out, the first three-year retreat for Westerners began in 1976, in France, where Kalu Rinpoche had been given some land. The first group of sixteen—eight men and eight women—started out by building the retreat facilities themselves. None of them had ever built anything before and most of the work had to be done by hand, but they got it built in about four months: two separate compounds, one for the men and one for the women, each with eight cells around a central courtyard, with a main temple, a kitchen, a bathroom and a special room for the yoga exercises that would come later. The buildings were constructed from cinder blocks and the individual cells were unheated—"that," as one retreatant said, "was a last minute surprise from Rinpoche."

The retreatants slept sitting up in a big box, wrapped in blankets. Still it was cold in France during the winter, and the cells hadn't been that well-constructed. The cinder blocks held the damp and the doors were not flush, and during the cold French months the retreatants woke more than once to find snow drifts in their cells.

The retreat began with a sadhana to one of the protectors which lasted for two weeks. Then they spent four months on the entire ngondro—the preliminary practices. Since everyone had done the Kagyu ngondro at least once, they did the ngondro of the Shangpa school (which traced its origins back to Niguma, the siddha-consort of Naropa) and which was the particular school that Kalu Rinpoche headed. They practiced shamatha for two months—one month longer than usual—and then they began to practice various sadhanas, usually for a few months at a time. They covered a lot of territory because the retreat was actually something like a survey course of the different practices.

Their day began at four each morning, with shortened versions of the preliminaries, and then a session of sadhana practice until six, at which time there was an offering, and then at six-thirty they all came together—the men in their temple, the women in theirs—to do a group Tara puja until nine when they had breakfast. Then another meditation until lunch, one after lunch, another group puja and then dinner and the final night session. That was it. Of course they had some time off—once a year, on the Tibetan New Year, they shortened their practice by two sessions. And there were a few highlights when the routine was broken, such as visits by Kalu Rinpoche, His Holiness Karmapa or His Holiness Dudjom Rinpoche. The only people they saw were their fellow retreatants, in their separate compounds, the cook, a student of Lama Kalu's, and their instructor, Lama Tenpa, who spoke only Tibetan and who lived in a little hut halfway between the men's and women's retreats.

"At the beginning," remembers Sarah Harding, a young woman from Malibu who was part of the first group,

> the whole thing seemed like hardship, especially with the cold and the prostrations coming at first. I was the only one from a warm climate, and suffered a lot more, but still it was tremendously cold—you'd put down a cup of tea in your room and in a few hours it would be ice. And at first things weren't working, like hot water and electricity. It all gave you a feeling of deprivation, waking up at four in the morning and not being able to lie down to sleep. But you get used to anything, and by the end I was just feeling guilty for being so peaceful and comfortable. It seemed like a vacation, all those poor people out there working, and I have nothing to do but this—really, in the beginning it felt like a hardship and in the end it was not. And you get used to the cold. And you get used to waking up. The hard part for me was that even at the end of three years you don't feel like the mind is behaving itself.

> I think it gave me a much more practical understanding. I had thought, oh there would be all these high kinds of meditative states I would achieve, and that doesn't happen; you know, it's hard to meditate. And I stopped thinking of meditation and practice as a kind of deep absorption or magical something—it just becomes a real nitty gritty sort of thing. We can see that in any great teacher—we say, "he's so down to earth"—but it doesn't really make sense until you start to practice and see that it's really a part of life—practical and sane and not full of far out trips; more than anything else the retreat brought that home to me. And being with other people, that works through a lot of bad habits—stubbornness and a lot of anger and things like that, just as processes in my head—throwing yourself against a brick wall again and again, you kind of get broken in. You want to be able to be angry and have pride and you can't maintain it on a retreat. It's just broken down and that really carries over.

At the end of the retreat, Kalu Rinpoche returned and told the sixteen men and women that they were now lamas and that he wanted them to teach—something that most of them had not expected and did not feel prepared to do. But first they had a few free days to spend in the countryside—"it was just like this wonderful dream that couldn't go wrong," Sarah recalls. "Colors were vivid and anything that anyone said sounded fantastically interesting."

A few of the retreatants elected to return for another three years. Rinpoche sent Lama Sarah Harding back to her hometown of Los Angeles to assist a lama at his center in Pasadena. The lama spoke hardly any English, so she was kept busy translating and taking care of endless administrative details. The center, which was supposed to support her, was barely able to support itself, so she went to work, for the time being, as a receptionist. It wasn't easy but she managed. As she says, "Suddenly Rinpoche trusted us, and you kind of had to live up to it."

When they first came out of retreat only a few Westerners expressed interest in doing the retreat themselves. "There were a lot of empty rooms there;" remembers Sarah, "they were all waiting to see what happened to us. Then suddenly, within a couple of weeks, it was just swamped. People were waiting and a whole other retreat had to be built in Sweden. So many people were asking Kalu Rinpoche's permission to do the three-year retreat that plans were made to build one in Vancouver, and another in New York, and still another in Oregon, all of them with waiting lists." Apparently the retreatants passed the test.

IX

The moment Trungpa Rinpoche saw Narayana there was a flash of recognition and he knew. Narayana was Thomas Rich, a close disciple of Swami Satchidananda and an ebullient Italian-American from Passaic, New Jersey—"a colorful personality with lots of smiles, possessing the charm of Hindu-American diplomacy," as Trungpa Rinpoche saw him then. It was 1971 and he was in Boulder to invite Trungpa Rinpoche to a World Enlightenment Festival.

Narayana went back to Los Angeles where, along with a close friend named Krishna (Ken Green), he was in charge of Swami Satchidananda's Integral Yoga Institute. He wrote a long letter to Trungpa Rinpoche. "During our visit last week I remarked that you were not what I expected," he began.

> This is my third attempt to write to you, the other two being inadequate expressions of what I had experienced through our contact. After our talk I found myself in a state of quiescence. In itself that is not so new for me, but this calm was deeper, more weighty. The people around me remarked that I seemed different. All I could reply was that our contact was such that all my petty concerns about life became unreal. I have been talking about you ever since. . . . Someone had asked me to ask you why you smoked or drank but the question was absurd in light of your consciousness of the truth. And like any real contact with another, I became again conscious of my infinite self. . . . Forgive this clumsiness.
>
> All I am trying to say is that I am open to you and I have been deeply touched by your divinity, so much so that all I have to do is think of you and my mind clears and thought subsides. This creates in me a willingness to experience you more fully. I am aware that an opening like this is rare in my life.

Narayana Rich and his friend Krishna Green met Rinpoche again. Rinpoche told them they were welcome to study with him, but to first get the blessings of Swami Satchidananada, and in 1971 they drove from California to New York for an interview with their guru. "You'll always be my children," he said, and sent them on their way.

In 1971 Narayana, and his wife Lila, and Krishna and his wife Helen, moved to a house near Tail of the Tiger in Vermont, where they started Trikaya Bakery. "The special feature of our bread," remembers Krishna, "was that you couldn't cut it. It would crumble at the touch of a knife."

In the winter of 1971 Rinpoche gave his copy of Gampopa's *Jewel Ornament of Liberation* to Narayana and told him in confidence that he would one day be his vajra regent. Krishna, Helen and Lila were also told but none of them really knew what it meant. "There was a quality of mystery," says Ken Green. "What does 'Vajra Regent' mean? Rinpoche hardly talked about it—it was brought up two or three times during the whole period before the Regent was acknowledged. That is very much how the Vajracarya [Trungpa Rinpoche] works. Unsaid, allow people to use their intelligence, to use the space."

In 1974 Trungpa Rinpoche brought Tail of the Tiger, Karma Dzong and the urban meditation centers—Dharmadhatus—together under the umbrella of Vajradhatu. Ken Green and Thomas Rich were among the board of directors, and Thomas Rich's training now took a new form. He became an administrator in an organization that grew very quickly. There were three contemplative and retreat centers—Tail of the Tiger (later Karme-Choling), Rocky Mountain Dharma Center and Dorje Khyung Dzong, the most remote of all, in southern Colorado. There was Nalanda Foundation, a nonsectarian educational foundation comprising Maitri, an experimental therapeutic community in Connecticut and Naropa Institute. There was insurance, rent, phone bills, financing, and always, fundraising. There was Ashoka Credit Union, the Alaya Preschool and the Mudra Theater Group. Rinpoche worked closely with Narayana. "He is arrogant and humble, resourceful and impatient," Rinpoche said, "and always willing to regard his position as a further training process. Working with him takes no struggle, and he is quick to apply what he has learned." There was no time off for Thomas Rich. It was, as he once said, "like living in a fishbowl." One of the things people noticed about him was that unlike some of the other administrators he did not hold on to personal or administrative territory; he seemed rather to delight in finding people to take over jobs that had been his. He worked very hard, and then let go.

On August 22, 1976 six hundred people watched as Thomas F. Rich, Karma Chokyi Dawa Legpai Lodro Osel Tendzin Chogle Namgyel, Karma Moon of Dharma Excellent Intellect Radiant Holder of the Teachings Victorious in All Directions, was empowered by Trungpa Rinpoche as his vajra regent (*dorje gyaltsap*), "to act on my behalf in propagating Buddhadharma and the vision of the three yanas throughout the world." The onlookers were startled to hear the traditional ceremony end with the "V for victory" (and vajrayana) theme from Beethoven's Fifth.

This was not the end of Osel Tendzin's training, but an intensification.

He began to teach, and Rinpoche would continue to watch him very carefully over a period of years. "My training of him has been primarily through close and critical observation," Rinpoche says. "My empowerment of the Vajra Regent was the starting point of planting the seed in his mind that he was and could become a good product of vajrayana or of the sanity of the Buddhist practice altogether."

There were varying reactions among the Sangha. Some people couldn't see it at all. Osel Tendzin had been too much one of them, another American, round-eyed and mustached, with a fondness for golf. But mostly, as Trungpa Rinpoche said, "People were deeply moved that a future holder of the lineage could be from America."

A few years after the empowerment, a reporter asked Osel Tendzin why he had been chosen as the vajra regent. "It was basically my lack of ambition," he said. "I never wanted to be anything. All I liked to do was daydream in a passionate way. He [Trungpa Rinpoche] felt I wouldn't build a nest for myself, as a self-styled guru, that I wouldn't corrupt the teaching. . . ."

His Holiness Karmapa agreed. On his second visit to America he confirmed Trungpa Rinpoche's choice: "the supreme vidyadhara Trungpa Tulku Chokyi Gyatso has appointed his chief disciple, Osel Tendzin, as his Gyaltsap. This I fully acknowledge and rejoice in. Accordingly, let everyone offer to him due respect."

Trungpa Rinpoche wrote in a poem,

> I hand you my power.
> If I grow you grow.
> Your childishness is the ground where you can take
>   part in the power.
> Your inquisitiveness is magnificent.
> There is need for a further growing tie with heaven
>   and earth.
> I have given you the space:
> The very blue sky,
> The clouds and the suns and the moons are yours.
> But you are confused—
> Could you use your responsibility as a golden joke or
>   a vajra scepter?
> It is very heavy.
> But I think you can hold it.
> You, my son,
> Take your Swiss Army knife—
> Make a samurai sword out of it.

His Holiness the Dalai Lama

The Translator and the Editor: Lama Kazi Dawa-Samdup and W.Y. Evans-Wentz taken in Gangtok, Sikkim, 1919

Geshe Wangyal

Thomas Merton, early 1960s,
at Abbey of Gethsemani

Tarthang Tulku

His Holiness Dudjom Rinpoche

Joseph Goldstein and Jack Kornfield,
Barre, Mass., July 1981

Anagarika Munindra, Barre, Mass., July 1981

His Holiness the Gyalwa Karmapa

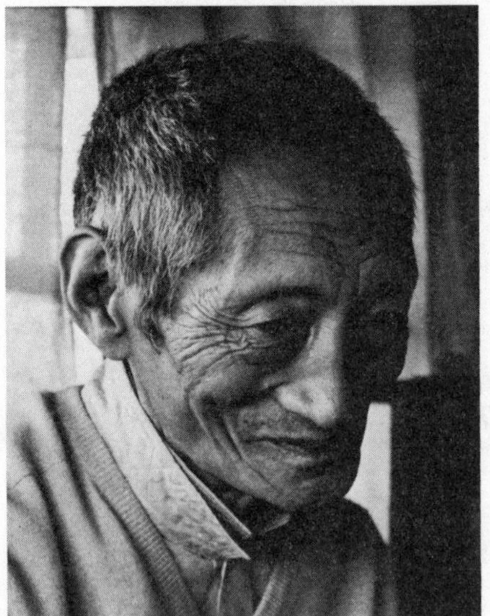

Kalu Rinpoche

His Holiness Dilgo Khyentse Rinpoche and Chögyam Trungpa, Rinpoche

Tripitaka Master Hsuan Hua

Ku San Sunim, Los Angeles, 1981

Soen-sa-nim [Seung Sahn]

D.T. Suzuki

Alan Watts

The Venerable Thich Thien-an

CHAPTER FIFTEEN

THE OTHER ZEN AND THE PURE LAND: THE CHINESE, KOREANS AND VIETNAMESE

I
The Chinese

The Chinese were actually the first Buddhists to reach America, whether the date is marked by the legendary party of monks who accompanied Hui Shan in the fourth century or from the immigrants of the 1860s. But it was not until Tripitaka Master Hsuan Hua began teaching the five schools of Ch'an, T'ien-t'ai, Vinaya, Esoteric and Pure Land in San Francisco's Chinatown in 1962 that the full range of Chinese Buddhism came into view in America.

Hsuan Hua was born in northeast China in 1908. At the age of eleven, while walking across a field near his village, he found a child's corpse wrapped in straw. He had never seen death before and he asked his mother, who was a devout Buddhist, what it meant. She said that all human beings eventually die. Hsuan Hua wanted to know if there was any way to escape death, and a stranger, who happened to be visiting, told him, "The only way to escape is to practice the Tao (Way) so as to enlighten one's mind and understand one's inner self." Hsuan Hua resolved then to become a monk. His mother was pleased, but she asked him to wait and care for her and his father.

He was a model of filial piety until his parents died. Then he took the vows of a novice, and sat in meditation in a little hut beside his mother's grave for three years. He ate only one meal a day and never laid down to sleep. One night the villagers saw a bright light coming from Hsuan Hua's hut. They rushed to the cemetery with buckets of water, but when they arrived there was no fire. There was nothing but Hsuan Hua sitting quietly, deep in meditation.

In 1947, at the end of World War II, Hsuan Hua made a pilgrimage three thousand miles across China to pay homage to the great master, Venerable Abbot Hsu Yun (Empty Cloud), who was then one hundred and nine years old. Hsu Yun recognized Hsuan Hua's enlightment, and transmitted the mind-seal of the Wang Yei lineage to him, an event that Master Hua commemorated with a verse:

The noble Yun saw me and said, "Thus it is."
I saw the noble Yun and verified, "Thus it is."
The noble Yun and I both thus,
Universally vow that all beings also be thus.

In the summer of 1949 he fled the Communist revolution and emigrated to Hong Kong. He arrived penniless and immediately went into retreat in a mountainside cave where he spent two weeks sitting on a flat rock in full lotus position. Within a short time a stream of Buddhist refugees fleeing from the new Communist regime began to pour into Hong Kong. They had left suddenly, the landholdings of the larger monasteries had been confiscated, the smaller temples turned into government offices and some senior monks had been executed as "landlords." They left behind sutras, images and all the other dharma treasures that had been accumulated over hundreds of years.

Hong Kong was mainly Christian. Most of the monks were elderly, and desperately in need of food, shelter and clothing. Master Hua left his cave and raised funds to provide for them. He also built temples and lecture halls, reprinted sutras and taught the dharma.

In 1959 word came that the Venerable Master Hsu Yun had died in China at the age of one hundred and twenty, and Master Hua left Hong Kong, first for Australia, where he taught Chinese at a university, and then for America, where some of his Chinese disciples had founded the San Francisco Buddhist Lecture Hall in 1958.

He began his life in America in Chinatown, waiting patiently until those who had "conditions" (that is, karmic links) with him appeared. He was first known only in the Chinese community, but gradually word spread that an enlightened Ch'an master was living in Chinatown, and Americans, many of them graduate students in Chinese, began to come around. The master was then living and teaching in the tiny fourth floor room of the Buddhist Lecture Hall that once been a Taoist temple on Waverly Place, and it was there, in the summer of 1968 that he held his first ninety-six day long Dharma Assembly on the *Shurangama Sutra*.

Everyone lived together in that one room, listening to the master's lectures, eating one meal a day, studying Chinese, meditating, chanting and working; at night some of the people slept sitting up in the meditation posture on the roof. At the end of the session the master said, "This year the Dharma flower will bloom in America—a five-petalled flower." In 1969 five students who had attended the Assembly accompanied the Master to Keelung, Taiwan, where they received the shramanera (novice), bhikshu and bodhisattva ordinations. When they returned to America their shaved heads were marked with the five incense burns customary for ordination and they wore the flapping brown T'ang Dynasty robes of the orthodox Chinese monks.

In the winter of 1970, Master Hua and the Sino-American Buddhist Association (which replaced the original Buddhist Lecture Hall) renovated a large, red-brick, former mattress factory in the Mission District of San Francisco, and called it Gold Mountain Monastery—Gold Mountain being the name of a monastery in China and also the name that the first Chinese immigrants had given America. Gold Mountain was very much a traditional Chinese monastery. It was there, on June 7, 1972, that master Hua and the five American bhikshus conducted the first ordination ceremony in America—lasting one-hundred and eight days in this case. According to the *Mahavamsa* (the "Great Chronicles" of Ceylon), King Mahanama had said that Buddhism could not truly be said to have taken root in a country until a native-born son could be ordained in his native land by his countrymen. Now that condition had been met.

In 1976 the Sino-American Buddhist Association purchased the 237-acre Mendocino State Hospital for the Criminally Insane, just outside of Ukiah, California, which they called the City of Ten Thousand Buddhas. They installed an eighteen foot statue of Avalokiteshvara in the meditation hall and tranformed the two hundred eighty cells of Mendocino's state maximum security prison into cells for monks at Tathagata Monastery. A building on the other side of the property became Joyous Giving House Convent. They also established Dharma Realm University, a nonsectarian institution which provides a Buddhist atmosphere where someone might study engineering as well as the Chinese classics.

At Gold Mountain all five schools of Chinese Buddhism are taught and practiced: the vinaya (discipline) schools emphasize the two hundred fifty rules of conduct for bhikshus and bhikshunis, and the five precepts for lay disciples; the T'ien-t'ai school stresses sutra study and recitation; the Esoteric school involves the use of mantras and dharanis; the Pure Land school, based on faith that anyone who recites the name of Amitabha will be reborn in the Pure Land (a Buddha-field from which it would be comparatively easy to attain enlightenment), practices through chanting; while the Ch'an (Zen) school uses sitting meditation and *kung-an* (koan) work.

Westerners are often surprised at the union of Ch'an and Pure Land. These two methods seem logically inconsistent, Pure Land being based on faith and "other power" and Ch'an on the great doubt and "self power." Furthermore, the Pure Land doctrine seems more Christian than Buddhist—"like a fairy tale," as one student said to Master Hua, "where by simply relying on Amitabha our problems will be effortlessly solved."

But for the Chinese Ch'an masters, the Pure Land practice of chanting Amitabha's name with single-mindedness was a valuable, expedient means, one through which the cultivator could realize that the Pure Land was his own true nature. Ch'an and Pure Land were complementary rather than contradictory. "The most important point of recitation is to melt the drift of false thoughts so that one becomes pure and spotless like the driven snow," Master Hua told his American students, and the practice at Gold Mountain frequently includes sessions where Amitabha's name, *namo-om-i-t'o-fa*, is chanted—or sung—melodiously in Chinese manner.

These recitation sessions, which sometimes last as long as a month, often precede a week or more of the strictest Ch'an sessions. At that time there is silence throughout the meditation hall, while cultivators sit with the kung-an, "Who (or what) is reciting the Buddha's name?" from 2:30 in the morning until midnight. Periods of sitting alternate with occasional lectures by the master and with brisk walking—which sometimes breaks out into running.

Life at Gold Mountain Monastery and at the City of Ten Thousand Buddhas follows the most severe practice of all American Buddhist communities. Bhikshus and bhikshunis live apart and adhere closely to the Vinaya. They rise at 3:40 in the morning for a program that includes bowing, chanting, services, meditation, language study (Mandarin Chinese, Sanskrit and European languages) and work. They eat one vegetarian meal a day, and many of them sleep in the meditation posture at night. ("Difficult for your legs for the first year or two," says Bhikshu Heng Lai, "but it's really beautiful. Your head is clear all night long.") These "bitter practices," as they are called, are an important part of the training under Master Hua, who succinctly sums up their value in the saying, "Bitter practice, sweet mind," and though at first they seem impossible, many who undertake them find that with time they become quite natural.

Master Hua emphasizes sutra studies and delivers a lecture on a sutra at the City of Ten Thousand Buddhas every day of the year. These lectures, sometimes also given by senior students, are simultaneously translated into Chinese or English. The monks and nuns of Gold Mountain have also been active in translation, and the Buddhist Text Translation Society, which was founded by Master Hua in 1970, has published a number of exemplary translations. The scholarship and accuracy of these translations are of the highest order since translations are checked and rechecked by no less than four different committees. The goal of the Translation Society is to publish the entire Tripitika in English, as well as in other major European languages.

Chinese Buddhists often spent several years wandering through China on pilgrimages that entailed ascetic practices and self-imposed hardship. Heng Ju, a bhikshu from Gold Mountain, revived this ancient practice when he undertook a bowing pilgrimage from San Fransicso to Seattle in the fall of 1973. An adventurous, ex-Navy submarine mechanic, Heng Ju had been inspired by the bowing pilgrimage that the Venerable Master Hsu Yun had taken across China in the 1880s. Master Yun had bowed, knees, elbows, forehead and hands to the ground once every three steps, six thousand miles across China. The pilgrimage had taken six years, and during it Master Yun had attained a single-minded radiance and clarity of mind that far surpassed anything he had ever known.

The first time Heng Ju tried the practice he left Gold Mountain late at night without a word to anyone. He had bowed for five miles, from Market Street to the foot of the Golden Gate Bridge. He had stopped traffic, been shadowed by the police and finally returned to the monastery, his body exhausted, wondering if he had not, at last, gone completely mad. Yet, as he said, "there was something about the experience that was impossible to describe, but which felt like it was reaching to the core." He decided to try again, this time with the master's advice and blessing. He would bow for his own cultivation and would dedicate his efforts to the cause of world peace.

Accompanied by Bhikshu Heng Yo, who carried a pack with food and camping gear, Heng Ju left San Francisco on October 16, 1973. He bowed through rain, sleet and sun, through all the small towns along Highway 1, past laundromats, taverns, schools, shopping centers and gas stations. He suffered poison oak, blisters, sunburn and swollen knees. The first hundred miles were the worst. "We were plagued with terrible weather and lack of equipment, and I began to think that what we had set out to do was just too big, that it was totally impossible to bow a thousand miles in America for world peace." Their outlandish appearance—shaved heads, robes and bowing—seemed at first to outrage people. "Bowing a thousand miles from San Francisco to Seattle was a relatively easy task," Heng Ju said when they had completed the trip. "What is hard is trying to explain it to people." At first they handed out a three-by-five card:

> Because people are constantly suffering due to the enmity and fighting among themselves, and because they fail to realize the quiescent wisdom of their own nature, Dharma Master Heng Ju, a Buddhist bhiksu (monk) is making a pilgrimage for world peace and harmony . . . in the hope that he may evince a response from the Buddhas, Bodhisattvas, and devas (gods) so they will prevent violence and fighting and protect and maintain peace in the world.

But they soon found it was better to talk to everyone individually. So they spoke with reporters, truck drivers, school kids, loggers, tourists, highway patrol men (who tried to run them in), born-again Christians (who tried to convert them) and a few local Buddhists. As their trip progressed—three steps, one bow; five or six miles a day—they found that the increasing coverage of newspaper and television did a great deal to explain to people who they were and what they were doing. Earlier in the trip someone had thrown a can of beer at them from a speeding car and once a drunken driver tried to run them down. But by the time they got to Gold Beach, Oregon they were greeted by a sign on the marquee of a sporting goods store saying "Welcome Heng Ju & Heng Yo. Have a good trip."

On Saturday, July 20, 1974, nine months after they had begun, Heng Ju and Heng Yo completed their thousand-mile pilgrimage. They were met in Seattle by Master Hsuan Hsu, and the assembly from Gold

Mountain as well as many others who had come together to celebrate a gathering for world peace.

When Heng Ju spoke he recited a verse that the master had given to him on the day of his departure.

> Practicing what is difficult to practice
> is the conduct of the sage:
> Enduring what is hard to endure is the
> genuine patience.
> All Buddhas throughout the ten directions
> have walked down this road.
> The eighty thousand Bodhisavttvas have
> followed right along.
> Blow the magnificent Dharma conch and
> raise up the cry;
> Shake your precious tin staff, transform
> stingy greed.
> Your work complete, and result full, a
> return midst song of triumph
> Then I'll give my disciple a meal of
> berry pie!

The story, which everyone knew, was that six days after taking the vow to eat only one meal a day, several years prior to his bowing journey, Heng Ju had slipped out of the monastery and eaten a whole batch of pastries. One berry pie was left, and he wrapped it up, put it in his pocket and returned to the monastery. By evening he had begun to think about the pie, and he thought about it all through the abbot's lecture that night. About ten o'clock, when everyone was asleep, he climbed out the bathroom window, on to the fire-escape and up to the roof, where he began to eat.

> But just at that moment [he said] I looked over at the fire escape to see someone else climbing up onto the roof! I stood there terror-struck, with a mouthful of pie. There was no place I could run. It was the Master! I stood there unmoving for a moment. . . . Then I began walking around in a circle on the rooftop as if in deep contemplation. The Master, too, began to circle the roof as if in deep contemplation but he was going in the opposite direction. We passed each other twice without looking at each other, but on the third lap I looked up and saw him grinning like a Cheshire cat. He said four words, "How does it feel?" That was the famous berry pie incident. The Abbot has been kidding me about it for years now.

When Heng Ju and Heng Yo got back to the monastery after their pilgrimage—they had bowed an extra hundred fifty miles up to the site of a projected monastery, just for good measure—they were welcomed by a dharma assembly: ceremonies, festivities, dharma talks and a vegetarian feast. Heng Ju ate only one thing, a whole berry pie, presented by the abbot. As he said at the end of his talk that day. "Today you have all had a chance to see a bhiksu who bowed a thousand miles for a piece of pie."

II
The Koreans

Korean Buddhism began in the fourth century when the Kyo (sutra teaching school) was brought from China. During the next two centuries Korean monks who had trained and realized enlightenment at the Ch'an monasteries of T'ang Dynasty China returned and established practice centers on nine mountains. These gave rise to the Nine Schools of Korean Zen which is pronounced *Son*. Korean Zen was practiced with great vigor, and many Korean Zen masters and monks went to China and Japan where Korean Buddhist art and architecture also achieved great heights. Many of the early temples in Japan were designed and built by Korean craftsmen, and Korean painting, which had a vivid, primitive and direct quality, became highly prized in China and Japan.

During the Yi Dynasty (1392-1910), however, Confucianism was the state religion, and Buddhism was severely restricted. In 1910 the Japanese occupied Korea and they too interfered with the Korean Buddhists. They reserved approval of abbots for all major monasteries and tried to force Korean Buddhists to follow the Japanese forms of Buddhism, mainly by putting pressure on monks to marry. Though the majority of monks did marry, the Korean Buddhists fought the Japanese and worked to revive the original Korean Buddhist spirit.

During this period of nationalism and struggle against the Japanese, a young boy named Lee Duk An joined the underground movement. He was sixteen years old and a student in a technical school. Lee Duk An's first underground assignment was to build a shortwave radio to contact the Free Korea Army in Manchuria. When the radio was discovered, he was jailed for six months, and only the fact that his school principal came from the same town as his Japanese judge saved Lee Duk An from the death sentence. Today Lee Duk An is the Zen master Seung Sahn (Soen-sa-nim), the most active and influential Korean Buddhist teacher in America.

After the defeat of the Japanese in World War II, Korea was divided between the Russians and Americans, and Soen-sa-nim, disillusioned with politics, went up into the mountains to read Socrates, Spencer and Rousseau. A friend suggested Oriental philosophy, so he read Confucius, and then somebody gave him a copy of the *Diamond Sutra*. "Ah! Buddhism's number one," he said, and went on to become a monk.

He went up into the mountains again, this time with only the *Shin Myo Chung Ku Tai Tarani*, the mantra of original mind energy. He ate powdered pine needles, bathed in the icy mountain streams and chanted for twenty hours a day. Demons, ghosts, tigers and snakes came to attack him, and visions of buddhas and bodhisattvas beguiled him. On the last day of his hundred-day retreat his body disappeared and he understood that everything he saw—trees, rocks, clouds, sky and crows—was his true self.

After this he encountered Zen Master Ko Bong, one of the fiercest and wildest Zen masters in Korea. Master Ko Bong would only teach when he was given something to drink, and then only laymen and nuns, because, he said, monks were too lazy. People weren't sure whether Master Ko Bong was crazy or enlightened, but no one could defeat him in dharma combat.

Soen-sa-nim asked Master Ko Bong how to practice Zen. Master Ko Bong said, "A monk once asked Jo-ju Su-nim, 'Why did Bodhidharma come to China?' Jo-ju said, 'The pine tree in the front garden.' What does this mean?" Soen-sa-nim understood, but he was not trained in dharma combat so he could only reply. "I don't know." "Keep this don't-know mind," said Ko Bong. "That is Zen practice."

Soen-sa-nim then went to Su Dok Sa monastery where he took part in the hundred-day training session. Towards the end of the session he noticed that the monks' practice had grown lax, so he decided to stir things up. Somebody had been stealing firewood and rice from the monastery, and Soen-sa-nim was put on watch. One night he removed all the pots and pans from the kitchen and laid them out in a circle in the courtyard; another night he turned a small Buddha-image to the wall; then he hung a national treasure incense burner from a persimmon tree. Next time he was discovered—in the act of arranging seventy pairs of nun's shoes neatly in front of the abbot's room.

That morning he stood before an assembly of monks and nuns. The nuns voted for expulsion. The monks voted to give him another chance, since he was a new monk and so young, as long as he made a formal apology. First he bowed to Master Duk Sahn, who whispered, "Keep up the good work." The abbess told him he had caused more than enough commotion in the monastery. He said, "The whole world is full of commotion. What can you do?" Then he bowed to Master Chun Song and said, "I killed all the Buddhas of past, present, and future. What can you do?" "Aha!" said Master Song, and shot a question at him. Soen-sa-nim replied, and at the end of the dharma combat Chun Song jumped up and down, laughing, "You are enlightened! You are enlightened!" Everyone was astounded. Soen-sa-nim, then twenty-one years old, had been practicing little more than a year.

He immediately set out for Seoul and Master Ko Bong. On the way two other Zen masters acknowledged his enlightenment. When he entered Ko Bong's room he bowed and said, "All the Buddhas in the three worlds have turned out to be a bunch of corpses. Let's have a funeral ceremony." "Prove it!" said Ko Bong. "Here are the leftovers from the wake," said Soen-sa-nim, putting out a bottle of wine and some dried fish. "Let's have a drink," said Ko Bong. "Give me your glass," said Soen-sa-nim. Ko Bong held out his hand. "That's not a glass, that's your hand." Ko Bong laughed. "Almost done," he said. "But I'm going to check."

Soen-sa-nim responded to every koan like lightning. "The last one," said Ko Bong: "The cat eats cat food, but the cat bowl is broken. What does it mean." Again Soen-sa-nim answered without hesitation. Ko Bong just shook his head. Soen-sa-nim was outraged; four Zen masters had acknowledged his enlightenment. He tried again. "Nothing doing," said Ko Bong. Finally the two men locked eyes, glaring at each other. Soen-sa-nim growled like a tiger. They stared at each other in silence for fifteen minutes. Suddenly the answer shot forth from the depths of Soen-sa-nim's mind. Tears of joy filled Ko Bong's eyes. "You are the flower; I am the bee," he cried. On January 25, 1949, Soen-sa-nim received the transmission from Ko Bong—the only one Ko Bong ever gave. "Someday Korean Buddhism will spread through the world through you," he said. "We will meet in five hundred years."

Soen-sa-nim went back to Su Dok Sa. When war broke out he was drafted into the South Korean Army for five years. After the war ended, he cut his hair and became abbot of a temple in New Seoul, mostly so he could have a place to care for Ko Bong, who was getting old.

He eventually spent nine years in Japan and Hong Kong, founding temples and teaching. In 1972, with no money and no English, he took a plane to America, to Los Angeles, where there was a large Korean community. One of his fellow passengers was a Korean who taught at a university and also owned a laundry in Providence, Rhode Island. He offered Soen-sa-nim a job repairing washing machines. The Zen master accepted on the spot.

In Providence Soen-sa-nim worked twelve hours a day at the laundry and began to learn English. He met Professor Leo Pruden of Brown University's Buddhist Studies Department, and gave a few talks there, with Professor Pruden translating from Soen-sa-nim's Japanese. After a while two of Professor Pruden's students moved into Soen-sa-nim's apartment. Soon a small group had gathered, and one day they told Soen-sa-nim that they wanted him to quit his job in the laundry and teach full time. "OK, you like, I like," he said, and the Providence Zen Center began to take shape.

The Koreans are an earthy mountain people, less formal than the Japanese, and Soen-sa-nim was a relaxed, seemingly happy-go-lucky sort of fellow; he was broad and round and resembled a Ho Tai, the Chinese god of fortune and children who loves to dispense gifts. This in itself was an attraction to some who had been put off by what they saw as the rigid adherence to form in Japanese Zen. "I think that's why some Americans seek out Korean teachers," an early student of Soen-sa-nim's said:

> To smash through that whole cultural thing. Korean and Chinese masters teach in very funky situations. They're not into lovely Zen gardens, they just let them grow with a lot of dirt around and they just get into hard training.
>
> About a month after Soen-sa-nim came to Providence, we were in a small, funky apartment in the black section of Providence, and Soen-sa-nim hung a cheap pin-up calendar he got in the mail from Korea. We could see this stupid calendar hanging on the wall every time we did walking meditation. But when we asked him to take it down he said, "Those ladies are great bodhisattvas, every time you get annoyed they are hitting you."

By 1974 Soen-sa-nim had enough English to confront his students in dharma combat and to recount Zen stories. Soen-sa-nim thought that Americans had certain advantages over Orientals when it came to Zen. "Zen means believing in yourself one-hundred percent," he said, "and for believing in yourself the American way is better than the Oriental system. The child is soon independent of the parents, whereas in the Orient you remain dependent on society—always dependent on something." Yet this very quality created another problem. "The American mind is tough and self-reliant," he said, "but stuffed full of opinions. The Zen mind is not dependent on Buddha, on dharma, on God—not dependent on anything. Depend on yourself! The American way is excellent—if you can only let go of your opinions."

So he prescribed "medicine"—chanting and bowing. "Every morning we bow 108 times. Every morning and evening we chant for half an hour. It is very easy to keep a clear mind during the bowing and chanting because they are nonthinking actions. When we bow, we just bow; when we chant, we just chant. By bowing and chanting together, we put our likes and dislikes aside and become one mind." Chanting, said Soen-sa-nim, was very good for "a people filled with thinking and addicted to meaning." Oriental medicine made use of the problem to effect the cure, and this was a case in point.

For the Koreans who attended the temples founded by Soen-sa-nim—particularly Tah Mah Sahl in Los Angeles and the International Zen Center in New York—chanting was the normal practice. Soen-sa-nim set great store by what he called "together action" and one of his dreams is to bring Korean and American Buddhists together. Some of his students went to Korea to practice, and in America his temples were used by both Americans and Koreans alike. The Koreans, for the most part, were devout ladies who came on Sundays to chant the name of Kwan Sae Um Bosal (Kuan-yin, Avalokiteshvara), to make offerings and to occasionally put plastic flowers on the altar. They also cooked elaborate, vegetarian, Korean food for the monks.

Korean chanting, like Chinese chanting, is musical and very lively. When there is a Zen *kido* (a chanting retreat which lasts anywhere from a day to a week) everybody brings along their favorite instrument. In addition to the wooden *mogok* used to keep time in the meditation hall, there are tambourines, maracas, wooden sticks and bells—anything that will serve to keep the beat going, and the Koreans do not feel constrained to stand or sit still.

The Americans join in at the *kidos*, but they are somewhat out of their element. For them Soen-sa-nim is a Zen teacher, and it is the sitting that commands their greatest attention. Practice is intensified by one-hundred day retreats in the mountains and by the week or week-end long sessions called "Yong Maeng Jong Jin"—which means "when sitting to leap like a tiger." At that time, students meet privately once a day with Soen-sa-nim in interviews that may last anywhere from five to twenty minutes. It is then that the sword of dharma combat is unsheathed—a sword that for all its sharpness is a blade of compassion. One evening, after a dharma talk at the Cambridge Zen Center, a student asked Soen-sa-nim, "What is love?"

Soen-sa said, "I ask you: what is love?"
The student was silent.
Soen-sa said, "This is love."
The student was still silent.
Soen-sa, "You ask me: I ask you. This is love."

Though Soen-sa-nim has ordained a number of monks, the major thrust of his far-flung centers in Cambridge, New Haven, New York, Los Angeles, Berkeley and other places, remains lay practice—as is true for nearly every Buddhist group in America though there are exceptions, Gold Mountain being the main one. From the viewpoint of the orthodox bhikshu sangha (which the Koreans reformed after the Japanese occupation ended) neither lay people nor married monks can safeguard or transmit the lineages of Korean Son (Zen) that have been kept fresh and alive ever since Korean monks returned from T'ang China to the Nine Mountains in Korea. This is the responsibility of the orthodox monastic sangha, who have preserved the hard training, absolute dedication and rigorous life of the original Ch'an communities through all the vicissitudes of the Korean sangha.

Korean Buddhism was restricted, to a greater or lesser extent, for more than five hundred years, and then nearly turned inside out by a foreign power. Yet in all the Buddhist countries of the world, it is only in the still remote mountains of Korea (or more precisely, South Korea) that the life of the original Ch'an community continues to this day.

Until recently, this aspect of Buddhism remained right there, in the mountain temples. During the fifties and sixties Americans interested in practicing in a Zen monastery went to Japan, not Korea. Starting in the sixties, however, the remote temples began to play an important role in the lay Buddhist revival in Korea, serving as retreat and teaching centers. One of the masters most active in this bhikshu-lay interchange is the Venerable Ku San Sunim of Song Kwang Sa Monastery (Vast Pines Monastery).

Ku San Sunim was born in 1910. He worked as a barber until the age of twenty-eight when he became a monk under Master Hyo Bong, one of the most celebrated Zen masters of his era. The majority of Korean Zen practitioners work with one kung-an, often *Mu*, or "What is this," until they attain full realization, and Ku San held his kung-an before him constantly. After seven years of hard practice, both in meditation halls and hermitages, Hyo Bong certified his first major awakening. Four years later Hyo Bong transmitted the dharma to Ku San.

Ku San Sunim served at National Sangha Headquarters in Seoul, but then, realizing that he was not quite finished, returned to his hermitage. He practiced harder than ever now, never lying down, standing in one position for days on end, and meditating with a knife tied on a stick under his chin to prevent him from dozing off. At last, after three years, at the age of fifty, he achieved the great awakening.

In general, Korean Zen masters never left their monasteries. Ku San Sunim, however, had been active in the movement to revitalize Korean Buddhism, and he often traveled to speak before lay Buddhist groups around Korea.

In 1972 Ku San Sunim came to America for the dedication of the Korean Buddhist Sambosa (Temple of the Three Treasures), which had been built in the Carmel Valley of California by Reverend Han Sang Lee, a Korean layman. At his first Formal Dharma Discourse in America (given, as is traditional, in Chinese), the master ascended the High Seat, struck his staff three times, and said, "Throughout the length and breadth of the world, people in all societies say 'I,I.' But actually what is this 'I'? Clearly, all men need to realize this 'True-I.' When you can truthfully say, 'With one stroke I can knock down the Empire State Building; in one gulp I can swallow the entire Pacific Ocean,' then and only then will you have realized it."

One American followed Ku San Sunim back to Song Kwang Sa, and became a monk; others followed and soon Vast Pines Monastery became the first traditional temple to make a place for a Western sangha. The first Western bhikshus and bhikshunis had to learn both Korean and classical Chinese. They sat in the meditation hall (on cushions on a stone floor, heated by a wood fire below) for fourteen hours a day, raised the Great Doubt with the kung-an (koan)—"What is this"—that Ku San had given them, ate kim chee (pickled cabbage, a staple of Korea) and rice, and worked along with the other monks in the rice or grain fields. During the practice times all work stopped and they sat for twenty hours a day, and one week they sat straight through, not sleeping at all. With the exception of the one telephone (installed after much discussion) life was the same as it had been a thousand years before.

Ku San Sunim returned to America in April of 1980, this time with two bhikshunis (one French and one from Scotland) as translators. A few Americans, former bhikshus, were also on hand to help out. Ku San Sunim led a week-long meditation session to mark the tenth anniversary of the Korean Buddhist Sambosa Temple in Carmel. He also dedicated Korea Sa in Los Angeles as a branch temple of Song Kwang Sa.

There are about eighty thousand Koreans in Los Angeles, making it the largest Korean city in the world next to Seoul. When Ku San Sunim held a seven-day series of lectures and practice for people wishing to take the bodhisattva precepts, the hall of the new temple was packed every night. Most of those attending were Koreans from the surrounding community, but the abbot of the new temple, Hyun Ho Sunim speaks English, and he, along with Ku San Sunim and Americans who have trained at Song Kwang Sa in Korea, are determined to make Korea Sa a place where Americans can study Korean Zen.

Koreans may be the most recent arrivals on the scene, but because of the continuing vigor and strength of their monastic sangha, as well as the devotion and support of the lay community, they promise to play an important part in the unfolding pattern of American Buddhism.

III
The Vietnamese

The Venerable Dr. Thich Thien-an, Vietnamese Buddhist monk and scholar, first came to the United States in 1966 as a visiting professor of language and Oriental philosophy at UCLA. Dr. Thien-an had planned to return to Vietnam in 1967, but a group of American students came to him, immigration forms in hand, and pleaded with him to stay. "In Vietnam there are many capable teachers of Buddhism," they said, "but here in America there are very few. If you return to Vietnam, who will teach us?"

He began to teach in a rented house in Hollywood. A scholar with formidable credentials (he had received his doctorate in Oriental literature from Japan's prestigious Wasada University) and a Zen master trained in the Lin-chi (Rinzai) tradition, he was gentle and completely approachable—"a Zen master without a bark," as one student said. He would do whatever needed to be done with a big smile and without a second thought, whether it was washing dishes during a meditation retreat, stamping garbage in the dumpster or teaching a course on sutras.

As more students gathered around him he formed the International Buddhist Meditation Center in an old wooden house just south of Vermont Avenue, in a neighborhood that had once been black, was now mostly Mexican, and was fast becoming Korean and Thai. Shortly thereafter he founded the College (later University) of Oriental Studies. Vietnamese Buddhism was based mainly on Chinese Buddhism—it had the same union of Zen and Pure Land and sutra study—but it also had a

Theravadin tradition among the Khmer (Cambodian) minority in the Mekong Delta, and also as a result of increased contact with Southern Buddhist countries. During the war, the Vietnamese Buddhists—both Theravadin and Mahayana—had joined to oppose the Catholic Diem government repression, first in an Intersectarian Committee for the Protection of Buddhism and then in the United Buddhist Church of Vietnam. Vietnam thus became the only Asian country where Theravadins and Mahayanists worked in active collaboration.

This broad ecumenical approach was reflected in all of Dr. Thien-an's work. He ordained monks and nuns, who were celibate, shaved their heads, wore robes and worked at the center; but he also ordained married people, who did not shave their heads and who wore robes only at the center. This last group he likened to Protestant ministers, and he felt that their work was particularly important for the spread of Buddhism in the West.

The University of Oriental Studies, which Dr. Thien-an founded in October of 1973, also followed an ecumenical path. Dr. Leo Pruden and Shinzen Young, who both had studied Shingon in Japan, taught at the college, as did a number of Theravadin monks. Geshe Gyaltsen, a Gelugpa, taught Tibetan and Tibetan Buddhism, and Song Ryong Hearn, a distant relative of Lafcadio Hearn, who had trained in Korea, taught Zen meditation. Visiting Buddhist scholars gave workshops at the college, and a large number of Buddhist dignitaries and leaders who visited Los Angeles—such as the Dalai Lama and the Gyalwa Karmapa—were often received there. On these occasions Dr. Thich Thien-an exhibited still another side. He had a fondness for pageantry and ceremony, which provided an excuse for people to come together, and he led processions in brightly colored robes, wearing a tall lotus-shaped hat, with red and blue ribbons, and carrying an ornately wrought staff.

In 1975 Saigon fell, and Dr. Thien-an (who had been jailed with other Buddhists in 1963 by the Diem government) found himself suddenly swept back into the shifting current of Vietnamese politics. "I remember going into his room and sitting with him during the eleven o'clock news," one of his students recounts. "He would just sit quietly in absolute silence, watching. He never talked about it, but I could tell the suffering he was going through about his country." After that the phone never stopped ringing. In the beginning he accepted collect calls from anyone anywhere in the world, until the phone bill soared beyond the center's capacity. In those days he was the only Vietnamese monk of any prominence living in the country—and he had become an American citizen—so the United States government asked him to help with the massive resettlement program for Vietnamese refugees. "He had never intended to get involved with the Vietnamese community in America," says one student.

> He never thought there would really be one—his real passion was work with the American people because he saw the United States as being the repository of the dharma, and hoped that it would be possible to bring Buddhism from the West to the East, when Asia was again ready for the teachings. But when Saigon fell and the refugees needed help, he didn't hesitate, even though it meant the International Buddhist Meditation Center and the university would suffer from the divided energy. He just was the embodiment of compassion, and so he did whatever his duty was, whatever had to be done.

When the first Vietnamese refugees arrived, Dr. Thien-an immediately sent his American monks and nuns to Camp Pendleton. Sister Karuna Dharma recounted:

> When those refugees came in they expected to come to a country where there was no Buddhism, and so all that some of these people brought with them were sutras and maybe a change of clothes. We held Buddhist ceremonies right across from the processing center in Camp Pendleton, and as soon as they could break away they would come running over because they had seen an American in a Buddhist robe, and those people would just grab hold of you and hold onto you and weep openly and unashamedly, because, they'd say to you, "I never expected to find Buddhists in this country, I never expected to be able to raise my children in a Buddhist culture."

Dr. Thien-an—and the Vietnamese monks and nuns who worked along with him—were the only hope for the refugees, particularly the Buddhists, who were suffering both physically and emotionally from the transplant to America. Vietnam had been at war continuously for forty years; people had been born, had raised families, had had grandchildren and had never seen peace. There were age-old political divisions and distrust among the refugees. Dr. Thien-an transcended it all. He raised funds to buy apartment buildings to house the refugees, and he took one building with a central courtyard, painted it yellow, and built a Vietnamese-style temple on one floor. Buddhist temples in Vietnam were centers of social life, and this temple served the same function for the Vietnamese in Los Angeles. On holidays, especially New Year's, the courtyard was hung with bright yellow and red streamers, everybody offered incense before the gleaming white statue of Quam Am (Kuan-yin) and the kids threw firecrackers while the monks' chanting blared over loudspeakers from the temple upstairs. They were a long way from Vietnam, but the refugees had found a home.

Dr. Thien-an never rested. Everyone and everything demanded attention: students, monks, nuns and lay people; the university and meditation center; the Vietnamese—especially the old people who would never learn English and needed help with everything. Somehow Dr. Thien-an made it all work.

On November 4, 1978, the International Meditation Center held a vigil of fasting, chanting and meditation for Thich Thien Minh, a Vietnamese Buddhist leader who had died eighteen days earlier in prison in Vietnam. In January of 1979 Dr. Thien-an and a group of Vietnamese and American monks, nuns and lay people set out from San Pedro for international waters in a sixty-five foot motorized sailboat. Once there they held a service for the next wave of refugees, the so-called "boat people." The service was for the boat people who had died at sea, as well as for the suffering of the remaining refugees. "The significance of conducting the ceremony out at sea was felt by all of those participating," said an American monk. "There was a sense of oneness with the dispossessed who lost sight of land and were at the mercy of the boundless ocean." Several buckets of ocean water were brought back to the Vietnamese temple, and chanting, prayers and offerings continued there for a week.

In September of 1980 Dr. Thien-an complained that he did not feel quite right. Doctors found a brain tumor and operated, then discovered that it had metastasized from a cancer of the liver. Dr. Thien-an went back to work. On the evening of November 21, 1980, he called Sister Karuna to his house, saying, "It is urgent." He had been vomiting blood. He insisted on putting on clean robes. In the car his robes were soon covered with more blood. She sped through the streets of Los Angeles. He put his hand on her arm. "It's OK," he said. "Slow down. Don't go so fast." He died on the morning of November 23, 1980. The hundred thousand Vietnamese Buddhists in America had lost the first American Vietnamese patriarch. His American students lost their teacher. "He was our strength, the foundation of our practice, and while he taught us that all things are impermanent, that we must never cling to anything, he remained the strong, sure guide in our lives. We never dreamed we could lose him so soon after finding him." The motorcade to the cemetery was five hundred cars long. Sister Karuna Dharma, who had been his disciple for twelve years, became the abbess of the International Buddhist Meditation Center. The Venerable Dr. Thich Man-Giac took his place as supreme abbot of the Vietnamese Buddhist Churches in America.

"It's hard to discuss now," said Sister Karuna after Dr. Thien-an's death, "but it seems to me that in the future, when we look back at the development that American Buddhism took, we're going to find that Vietnamese Buddhism—which related so well to political concerns such as human rights—was a great influence in the development of American Buddhism. Hundreds of years from now I think historians are going to say, 'Look at this, this tiny little country brought forward at that time a man who profoundly affected American Buddhism in a way we never thought was possible.' "

☆ ☆ ☆

Ten years later, things had come full circle, as another Vietnamese monk, Thich Nhat Hanh, spoke softly to a group of twenty Vietnam veterans during a "retreat for reconciliation and healing."

Thich Nhat Hanh talked about the School of Youth for Social Service he had founded in Vietnam in 1964, which trained social workers to rebuild bombed villages. Because he and other Buddhists had pursued a middle way, calling for reconciliation and an end to the war, they were attacked by both sides. "Many workers in the school were killed," Thich Nhat Hanh said. "I myself escaped death in a very narrow way. The fact that I'm alive and sit here is a miracle. Now I realize that those of us who have touched the war, who have experienced the war directly, have a duty to bring the truth of the war to people who don't have direct experience. We are the best people to do it."

For the first few days the veterans practiced mindfulness of breathing, eating, and walking in silence. "We reflect our society, and in order to see what potential we have for peace, joy, and happiness, we have to look into ourselves," said Thich Nhat Hanh. "We have to see also the potential of war, of violence in ourselves, in the body of our collective consciousness. So practicing looking deeply, we will be able to see, and that kind of insight will have a liberating power. We will know what to do and what not to do in order to bring about change in our society and our consciousness."

In the evenings, and toward the end of the retreat, they met in small rap groups to talk about their experiences. During one of these discussions, a Vet confessed that he had killed five Vietnamese children in an ambush. Ever since then he could not bear to be alone in a room with children.

Thich Nhat Hanh replied that "at this very moment there many children who are dying in the world. There are children who die just because they lack a single pill of medicine. If you are mindful, you can bring that pill to that child, and you can save his life. If you practice like that for five times, then you will save five children. Because what is to be done is to be done in the present moment. Forty thousand children die every day because of the lack of food. Why do you have to cling to the past to think of the five who are already dead? There are those who are dying now. You have the power to change things by touching the present moment."

At the end of the retreat a middle-aged man who had set fire to a Vietnamese village twenty years before spoke to a refugee Vietnamese monk who now lived in Los Angeles. "I want to apologize for being a part of destroying your country," he said, "and to all the people you probably helped after I made them homeless."

The monk bowed, palms joined, knees and head to the ground. "I have been a monk for many years and I thought I could control my emotions but today I cannot," he said. "During the war, I used to give funeral services for the families of the dead, but my heart was hard, like ice, because the suffering was too great. Then I got a telegram saying my own brother had been killed, and I knew true suffering. Today the voice of Jesus Christ speaks through you and the Buddha flower opens in you."

No one can say what will happen in a hundred years. But at this moment—and life can only be found in the present moment, as Thich Nhat Hanh says—it does indeed seem that Vietnamese Buddhism, as personified by this gentle and fearless monk, will have a great impact on American Buddhism.

CHAPTER SIXTEEN

THE CHANGING OF THE GUARD

I

The procession carrying the body of Chogyam Trungpa, Rinpoche, was heralded by the wails of a lone bagpiper playing "Farewell to Nova Scotia," and the slow, steady heartbeat of a deep bass drum, followed by the hoarse, guttural cries of Tibetan horns. As a crowd of more than three thousand students and guests watched in silence, the procession emerged from the fog-bound forest and passed beneath the red Tori Gate, which marked the entrance to the upper meadow and the cremation site at the Karme-Choling retreat center in northeastern Vermont.

The body was carried in a palanquin—a canopied, silk-curtained upright box—on the shoulders of eight of Trungpa Rinpoche's closest students, and covered with a round white parasol. The palanquin was then lifted into the ornately painted cremation stupa for a high lama—a *purkhang* (literally "corpse house")—which stood twenty-five feet high and was surmounted with a gold spire.

The fire offering was performed by monks led by three of the four regents of the Kagyu school—Shamar Rinpoche, Jamgon Kongtrul Rinpoche, and Gyaltsap Rinpoche, as well as Dilgo Khyentse Rinpoche, one of Trungpa Rinpoche's teachers and the head of the Nyingma school. This much was traditional. There were, however, a number of innovations, befitting the cremation of a teacher who had done so much to bring Buddhism, particularly the Tibetan vajrayana, into a new country and time. To begin with, the fire offering was also performed by a contingent of American Buddhists, who had reached that level of practice in their study with Trungpa Rinpoche. These practitioners performed the same liturgy as the monks and lamas, making the same fluid mudras with bell and vajra, albeit a bit less gracefully, and attempted the same visualizations and formless meditations. However, the Americans chanted the liturgy in an English version that had been painstakingly translated by Trungpa Rinpoche and a dedicated group of scholarly students. The American *tantrikas* were also nearly all lay people who had found time to complete the difficult and time-consuming preliminary practices of Tibetan Buddhism while holding jobs and raising families, and they were also evenly divided between men and women. Thus, though everything had been done properly, according to ancient tradition, there were certain changes—changes that were more or less assumed to be natural and necessary to both Tibetan mentors and their American students.

Trungpa Rinpoche had died on April 4, 1987, at the age of forty-seven, in Halifax, Nova Scotia, where he had moved the international headquarters of the Vajradhatu Buddhist Church. Officially, it was said that he had died from cardiac arrest and respiratory failure. That was technically correct, but many people, including some of his closest and most devoted students, thought that his death was related to, if not caused by, his legendary drinking. From the traditional Tibetan point of view, however, Trungpa Rinpoche was not an ordinary man but a bodhisattva, an enlightened master who had vowed to take rebirth in order to liberate all sentient beings. Because of this, all his actions, no matter how problematic they may have looked from a conventional point of view, were to be taken as teachings.

Trungpa himself, however, seemed to have little doubt about either the timing or meaning of his death. "Birth and death are expressions of life," he wrote in a message read after his death. "I have fulfilled my work and conducted my duties as much as the situation allowed, and now I have passed away quite happily. . . . On the whole, discipline and practice are essential, whether I am there or not. Whether you are young or old, you should learn the lesson of impermanence from my death."

The death of Chogyam Trungpa, Rinpoche, did indeed underscore the truth of impermanence. It was now painfully clear that another era in the history of American Buddhism had come to an end with the passing of many of the first-generation teachers who had been trained in Asia. Trungpa Rinpoche had been preceded by Shunryu Suzuki-roshi, the founder of the San Francisco Zen Center, in December 1971; Hakuun Yasutani-roshi, Philip Kapleau's teacher, died in 1973; His Holiness the Gyalwa Karmapa, head of the Kagyu school, passed away in Zion, Illinois, in 1981; in 1984 Nakagawa Soen-roshi, Nyogen Senzaki's dharma brother and the teacher of Eido-roshi and Maurine Stuart-roshi, died at Ryutakuji. That same year Lama Thubten Yeshe left his center in Kopan, Nepal, to die among his many Western disciples at Vajrapani Center in Boulder Creek, California, where he was cremated according to tradition. Two years later, a Spanish child, Osel Hita Torres, was recognized as his reincarnation by his disciple Lama Zopa and the Dalai Lama.

In 1987—the year of Trungpa Rinpoche's death—His Holiness Dudjom Rinpoche, head of the Nyingma school and a *terton*, or revealer of hidden teachings, died at the age of eighty-two at his center in Dordogne, France; his body was later enshrined in his temple in Bodhanath, Nepal. That same year Deshung Rinpoche, the Sakya lama who had come to Seattle twenty years before, died in Bodhanath. Two years later, Kalu Rinpoche, the modern Milarepa, died at his monastery in Sonada, India, at the age of eighty-four. During his four tours of North America, he taught the dharma, as he said, "in a traditional way, without combining it with any other viewpoints," and trained many Western lamas in the full three-year retreat. On March 1, 1990, Dainin Katagiri-roshi died at the Minnesota Zen Temple in Minneapolis. He had come to assist at the Soto Zen Headquarters in Los Angeles in 1963 and had then worked closely with Suzuki-roshi in San Francisco. Three months before his death, he had completed the ceremonies marking the completion of training for twelve Zen priests, one Japanese and eleven Americans. And finally, Dilgo Khyentse Rinpoche, one of Trungpa Rinpoche's principal teachers and advisors, died in September, 1991, at the age of eighty-one, in Bhutan.

Because so many of these great pioneers had left American teachers, it was easy to think that American Buddhism had finally come of age.

But it soon began to seem that it had entered a period of adolescence—an awkward, aggressive adolescence marked by acute growing pains. A number of teachers, both American dharma heirs and their Asian teachers, fell into a very American trap, namely abuse of power—particularly in sexual and financial areas—and thus found the details of their personal lives subject to an equally American scrutiny and outrage. To many American Buddhists, both students and teachers, it seemed that the meeting of East and West heralded by the heady sixties and early seventies had turned into nothing less than a head-on collision.

II

The signs of trouble had first appeared publicly in 1983 at the San Francisco Zen Center, long thought of as the very model of a modern Zen center. Under the guidance of Suzuki-roshi's Dharma heir, Zentatsu Baker Roshi, Zen Center had grown enormously, both in size and influence. Zen Center consisted of three major centers: Page Street, a residential center in San Francisco; Green Gulch, an idyllic farm and lay center nestled in a valley next to Muir Beach, on the slopes of Mount Tamalpais; and Tassajara, the mountain retreat center. The community businesses, which included the Green Gulch Grocery, the Tassajara bakery, Alaya stitchery, and Green's, a highly successful gourmet vegetarian restaurant overlooking San Francisco Bay, were all staffed by Zen students, many of whom also lived in either Page Street or Green Gulch.

The initial spark that set off what would soon become a raging conflagration was the revelation that Baker-roshi had been having an affair with a married woman student. This turned out to be the proverbial straw. In the meetings which followed, a number of people came forth to reveal other "secret" affairs. There were also charges of financial improprieties, or at least inappropriateness, relating to the Roshi's three residences in San Francisco, Tassajara, and Green Gulch; his mode of transportation, a white Audi; his extensive library (triplicated at each residence); his art collection; and so on. It was also said that he was using his office to further his own ambitions—that he spent so much time with friends like Governor Jerry Brown, Esalen director Michael Murphy, and *Whole Earth Review* publisher Stuart Brand that he had neglected both his own practice and teaching responsibilities. In short, he lived far too fast and well, while longtime students languished in low-paying jobs that were supposed to be "good for their practice."

A series of anguished meetings and confrontations followed, but clear communication seemed to elude both the Zen master and students who had spent fifteen or twenty years practicing to gain clarity of mind. In the end, Baker-roshi left for Santa Fe and then moved to Crestone, Colorado, where he began teaching a few old and some new students under the auspices of the Dharma Sangha.

Much discussion centered on the faults and sins of Baker-roshi, as well as on the "conspiracy of silence" which allowed many senior students, who had known that much was amiss, to say nothing. But it also became clear that at least part of the problem had been caused by the characteristically American form, the Zen Center. Shunryu Suzuki-roshi had once remarked that Americans were neither monks nor lay people but something in between. Zen Center had tried to find a way to combine the intensity of monastic practice with an American community open to both men and woman. Though many of the most serious practitioners were ordained as priests, shaving their heads and wearing robes, they were not celibate and thus as Zen Center had grown and matured, so had their families.

In Japan, Zen priests typically married and took on the job of running a temple after a three- or four-year course of training in a monastery. In America, however, training seemed to go on forever, and after ten or fifteen years it was hardly surprising that many priests and residents came to think of the Zen Center as their home and community. There were, in any case, few if any affiliated temples for priests to minister. What, then, did a Zen priest who had lived in a Zen center for ten or fifteen years of training and studying *do* when he or she realized that enlightenment wasn't going to strike like lightning and solve everything? For some Zen students, it now began to seem that they had paid a rather high price for their youthful idealism. They had learned how to sit zazen, they had the security of community, but they had neglected careers and professions. They had not learned how to make their way in the world. They had not grown up.

The Zen center turned, for the moment, to professional "facilitators." Communications experts and psychologists were invited to give workshops. Some students found disturbing but illuminating parallels between Buddhist centers and alcoholic and dysfunctional families, in which—as one Zen Center member put it—"we've learned all too well how to keep silent and how to keep secrets."

In response, students sought ways to make Zen Center more open and democratic. New Board members were elected instead of being appointed. The biggest departure from tradition had to do with the new abbott. Reb Anderson, a dharma heir of Baker-roshi, was hired for a four-year term.

Nearly ten years later, Norman Fischer, a Zen priest who taught and lived at Green Gulch, reflected on the turmoil. "Teacher-student relationships come out of the fabric of the society that produced them," he wrote in the *Buddhist Peace Fellowship Newsletter*. "The Roshi comes out of the Sino-Japanese-Confucian worship-your-ancestors tradition. Put that beautiful Roshi in the middle of our Freudian Oedipal will-to-power tradition and it is little wonder that people are going to be confused for a hundred years or so."

III

Before long, the problems at the San Francisco Zen Center began to seem less of an isolated incident than part of a pervasive pattern. In the next few years a rather large number of Zen teachers found themselves in a similar compromised position. Maezumi-roshi admitted to an affair with a senior student and, as a result of concern about his drinking, entered an alcohol treatment center. (He later said that he had learned much from that whole experience, not only about himself but about American culture as well.) The supposedly celibate Korean Zen master Seung Sahn (Soen-sa-nim) revealed long-term relationships with two students. A supposedly celibate elderly teacher visiting the Insight Meditation Center was confronted after he made advances to a female student. As the "conspiracy of silence" was broken, more and more women came forward to reveal problems with a number of other teachers, some of whom denied the accusations or simply remained silent. In 1985 Jack Kornfield published in *Yoga Journal* the results of a survey he had made on the "Sex Lives of the Gurus." Kornfield, a highly respected teacher of vipassana and the holder of a Ph.D. in clinical psychology, revealed that out of fifty-four Buddhist, Hindu, and Jain teachers he had interviewed, thirty-four had had sexual relationships of one kind or another with students. Half of the students, whom Jack also spoke with, said that they felt that the relationship had "undermined their practice, their relationship with their teacher, and their feelings of self-worth."

The most shocking revelation came in early December of 1988, when members of the Vajradhatu Board of Directors instructed teachers in local centers to inform the sangha that Osel Tendzin, the Regent appointed by Trungpa Rinpoche, had AIDS and had apparently not informed his sexual partners, and to recommend that anyone who thought he or she might be at risk be tested. "Since none of us believes the Vidyadhara taught magical 'protection' against natural cause and effect," as one Board member later put it, "this seemed like a necessary minimal step to take to protect people's health." As it turned out, one of the Regent's partners, a young man in his twenties, did contract the virus, apparently from him, and then inadvertently passed it on to a girlfriend; it was also said that some members of the Regent's inner circle had said nothing about his condition, even though they had been aware of the Regent's ongoing sexual activity for some time.

Many people, not surprisingly, reacted with anger and a sense of outraged betrayal. Some reflected as well on the part that they had played in the tragedy. "The Vidyadhara made it clear to his closest students that the Regent is not a fully realized person and that it is our responsibility to be clearly critical of him," one senior student wrote in a letter that was widely read in the sangha. "The recent events have made it clear to us that over the years we have not fulfilled this responsibility. This, our own ignorance and laziness, has allowed things to be brought to a painful point."

When the news first became known in the Vajradhatu sangha, I had the opportunity to meet with the Regent face to face. He was in San Francisco, just having left a long retreat, and was preparing to speak to the sangha at the local center in Berkeley. Sitting across from him in a living room, with four or five other close and concerned students present, I asked, "So what happened?" His answer was direct and spontaneous: "I was fooling myself," he told me. The next day, in a closed meeting of the Vajradhatu sangha, he expressed "tremendous remorse at any pain I have caused," though he was careful not to use the "A" word, as he put it.

"Thinking I had some extraordinary means of protection, I went ahead with my business as if something would take care of it for me," he said. As for explaining how such a thing could have happened, he was inscrutable. "It happened," he said. "I don't expect anybody to try to conceive it." In a subsequent letter to the sangha, he wrote, "As Lord Buddha said, there is no fault so grievous that it cannot be purified."

Many students, including the Board of Directors, asked the Regent to withdraw from teaching and the leadership of Vajradhatu. He refused. To do so he said, "would violate the oath I took with my guru, and it would also violate my heart."

The sangha itself was deeply divided. There were those who wanted the Regent to resign or be removed by the Board. Others thought that the Regent had expressed sufficient remorse and that it did no good to blame or "demonize" him. Still others suggested that the Regent's plight was not unconnected to the risks inherent in Trungpa Rinpoche's "crazy wisdom" tradition, which included outrageous and unconventional behavior as part of its repertoire. When the Board of Directors was unable to reach a consensus on how to proceed, they consulted Tibetan elders in Nepal and India. Letters and long-distance phone calls were translated from English into Tibetan, from Tibetan into English. With rumors and accusations flying back and forth between Asia and America, the Tibetan teachers emphasized that the most important thing of all was for students to continue their practice and preserve the harmony of the sangha. To this end, they suggested a traditional Tibetan solution: they advised the Regent to go into retreat.

For more than a year, there was continual turmoil. The Board, still unable to reach a consensus, was effectively paralyzed. The Regent took up residence in Ojai, California, along with his family and a band of loyal students. Though he engaged in intensive practice, he continued to act as both spiritual and administrative head of Vajradhatu. Consequently, two Vajradhatus now existed, one in Halifax, where the Board resided, and one in Ojai. There were endless community meetings and countless long-distance phone calls. Those who stayed—and there were many—did their best to make sense of the situation. When the Regent and the Board of Directors blocked the community's newspaper, *The Vajradhatu Sun*, from making any mention of "the current situation," which had by then been reported in the *New York Times* as well as many other papers, students published an "independent" journal called *Sangha*.

In the end, the Regent did finish his days in retreat. On August 26, 1991, the morning after Osel Tendzin died in a hospital in San Francisco, Jamgon Kongtrul Rinpoche was at Karme-Choling in Vermont, completing the Vajrayogini initiation for over two hundred students who had completed their preliminary practices. The next day he announced the appointment of Osel Mukpo, Trungpa Rinpoche's eldest son, as the spiritual leader of Vajradhatu. The Sawang, as he was called, who was twenty-seven, had spent the last five or six years in India and Nepal, learning Tibetan and studying with one of his father's teachers, His Holiness Khyentse Rinpoche, as well as others. A year later, in the winter of 1992, Tai Situ Rinpoche announced that he had recognized the twelfth incarnation of Trungpa Rinpoche, an eighteen-month-old child in eastern Tibet.

IV

The unraveling of institutional Buddhism, as painful as it has been, has resulted in a valuable reexamination of the place of Buddhist practice in American society. At the very least, such problems have cut through romantic projections and thrown American Buddhists back on their own meditation cushions.

There is no doubt that many people have been hurt and disillusioned, but this disillusionment has also done much to dispel illusion—which is, perhaps, another way of talking about enlightenment. The Western apprehension of Eastern religion in general and Buddhism in particular has actually been a series of misapprehensions. "Buddhism" was one thing to Emerson and Thoreau, another to the Theosophist Colonel Olcott, still another to the beat Zen enthusiasts of the fifties, the wide and wild-eyed psychedelic youth of the sixties, and the serious Zen students and disciplined yogis who sat at the feet of roshis and Tibetan lamas during the seventies and eighties.

Surveying the wreckage of so many reputations and lives, one wonders if this is something new or merely something very old and deeply hidden, unspoken of, that has only now begun to come to light. During the eighties it began to seem that anyone in a position of power—clergymen, therapists, doctors, lawyers, teachers, and politicians—might also be tempted to abuse that power. As Peter Rutter, M.D., writes in *Sex in the Forbidden Zone*, "Sexual violation of trust is an epidemic, mainstream problem that reenacts in the professional relationship a wider cultural power-imbalance between men and women."

Viewed within this larger context, the "fall" of a teacher turned out to be a rich source of political, psychological, and spiritual lessons. Politically, as Dr. Rutter says, it mirrored the power imbalances inherent in a patriarchal society. Psychologically, it underscored the responsibility that the phenomena of "transference" placed on therapist or teacher. And spiritually, it stripped away the veil of dependency on teacher and group, bringing practitioners back to the critical self-awareness and self-reliance crucial to the teachings of the Buddha, who said, "Do not believe in anything simply because you have heard it. Do not believe in traditions because they have been handed down for many generations. Do not believe in anything simply because it is found written in your religious books. Do not believe in anything merely on the authority of your teachers and elders, but after observation and analysis, when you find that anything agrees with reason and is conducive to the good and benefit of all, then accept it and live up to it." (Yvonne Rand of the San Francisco Zen Center says that this quotation should be "tatooed on our eyelids.")

The general disillusionment also made practitioners reflect on the difficulties of the path itself, for, as Trungpa Rinpoche liked to remind his students, there were no guarantees. Every level of spiritual insight seemed to cast a corresponding shadow. The closer one got to the heart of the matter, the more furiously the forces of ignorance and habitual pattern fought back. The Buddha was tempted by both the demons and daughters of Mara just before he broke through to final, complete enlightenment; Satan offered Christ the whole world as he wandered in the desert.

The contemporary Western world provided its own characteristic temptations, of course. Jet-set spirituality speeded up and magnified all the possibilities. In addition, some Western Buddhist teachers fell into one of the subtlest of the Zen sicknesses: attachment to emptiness. A little bit of enlightenment, Western Buddhists were finding out, could be a dangerous thing, especially if it led to a feeling of transcendental invulnerability. No wonder Bodhidharma had warned about "one who thinks only that everything is void but is ignorant of the law of causation. . . ."

The response of the Buddhist community to all this was as varied as the community itself. There were calls for an explicit code of ethics and institutional safeguards, for statements by the sangha affirming that sexual abuses would not be tolerated. There were cautions against self-righteousness ("the shadow of the shadow"). There were pleas for reconciliation and understanding. There were suggestions that erring teachers avail themselves of the ancient monastic tradition of confession before the sangha.

Through all the confusion, hurt, and rhetoric, one important difference between Judeo-Christian morality and Buddhist morality could, perhaps, be glimpsed. The "cause" of evil in Buddhism was not sin, original or otherwise, but ignorance—and all sentient beings, inasmuch as they had not yet realized their true nature, were subject to it. Indeed, the path existed only because ignorance existed.

The responsibility for both teachers and students, then, was not to judge and condemn but to work on themselves and help each other dispel the clouds of ignorance in order to uncover the sun of their common buddha-nature. Easier said then done, of course. But the tradition went all the way back to Shakyamuni. Thich Nhat Hanh, one of the most consistent voices for reconciliation, told the story of a pirate, Angulimala, who believed he would gain all he desired by stringing a necklace with the knuckles of a hundred hands. When he encountered the Buddha, he was filled with remorse, but he felt it was too late for him to change his ways. "It is never too late," the Buddha replied. "The ocean of suffering is immense, but as soon as you turn around, immediately you can see the other shore."

V

As the twentieth century comes to a close, it is clear that North America (despite all the problems of individuals, organizations, cultural collision, and an underlying racism) has become something of a preserve for threatened and endangered Buddhist lineages, as well as providing new possibilities for still-secure lineages from Japan, Thailand, or Sri Lanka. So it is that Asian Buddhists who have not communicated for hundreds or even thousands of years now find themselves sitting next to each other in a new home: Theravadins from Southeast Asia; Zen and Pure Land Buddhists from China, Japan, Korea, and Vietnam; and Vajrayana or Tantric Buddhists from Tibet and Mongolia have all put down roots in North America. A century after the World Parliament of Religions in Chicago there are at least a million people in America who call themselves Buddhists.

The simultaneous coexistence of all these forms of Buddhism is of major consequence for North American Buddhism. First of all, many American Buddhists have explored more than one tradition and are therefore in a position to take a critical look at sectarian claims of superiority. In addition, American Buddhists have already witnessed a fair amount of cross-lineage and cross-cultural borrowing. At the same time, this cross-lineage borrowing has underscored the essential unity of the buddhadharma. American Buddhists, as beginners, have found a basic

Buddhism that lays a common ground for nearly all Buddhist schools. There also appears to be a basic Buddhist practice. Nearly every lineage recommends beginning with some form of the breath awareness meditation, which is called *shamatha*, "peacefulness" in Sanskrit.

It does not seem likely, however, that North America will end up as a melting pot of American Buddhism—which would be a case, perhaps, of the whole amounting to less than the sum of its parts. Rather, it seems, North American Buddhism will continue to be a pluralistic Buddhism, a Buddhism in which there is much dialogue and exchange, but also a great diversity and plurality of skillful means. Buddhism in North America—or North American Buddhism—includes the most traditional unassimilated devotional forms of emigrant communities from Southeast Asia; the "assimilated" Buddhism of the Japanese-American Pure Land Buddhist Churches of America; Vietnamese, Korean, Chinese, Japanese Zen centers; Theravadin vipassana centers; and Tibetan Buddhist centers of all four Tibetan lineages. And all of *these* range from the very traditional (or even fundamentalist) to the extremely innovative. (Toni Packer, Kapleau-roshi's dharma heir, no longer calls her center Zen or Buddhist, though students continue to sit.) There are also numerous grass-roots or floating sanghas ranging from weekly sitting groups that move from one urban apartment to another, to the rural Ring of Bone Zendo, whose members, as Gary Snyder says, view themselves "not as a 'Zen center,' but as a sort of mountain peasant Buddhist temple, with a community approach."

Then, too, there are all the other ways in which Buddhism continues to be taught and to exert an influence on the culture. A recent anthology includes more than forty contemporary American poets associated with Buddhism. The Buddhist-Christian dialogue continues with an ongoing theological encounter organized by Masao Abe and John Cobb, as well as various academic conferences held in Berkeley, Hawaii, and Boston. Buddhist scholarship itself also shows continuing vitality. Many young scholars have managed to combine university training with Buddhist practice, something that was nearly unheard of and even suspect in the previous generation. The Kuroda Institute, which is connected with the Los Angeles Zen Center, has organized conferences and published translations and studies in the area of Zen and Japanese Buddhism. Tibetan studies have also profited from the new crop of scholar-practitioners. Jeffrey Hopkins and Robert Thurman, two former students of Geshe Wangyal, headed important programs, Hopkins at the University of Virginia and Thurman as Je Tsongkapa Professor of Tibetan and Indic

Studies at a newly endowed chair at Columbia University. Matthew Kapstein, also of Columbia, assisted Gyurme Dorje in translating Dudjom Rinpoche's magnum opus, *The History and Fundamentals of the Nyingma School*. And The Naropa Institute, founded by Chogyam Trungpa in 1974, became the first "Buddhist-inspired" college to receive accreditation, in 1986.

VI

Generalization of any kind seems to dissolve in the face of such cultural and religious diversity. And yet it does seem safe to suggest that lay practice is the real heart and koan of American Buddhism, for it is this aspect more than any other which defines the revolutionary direction of the emerging American Buddhism. It is true, of course, that lay practice has had a long and honorable place in Buddhism ever since the time of the Buddha; but it is also true that with certain exceptions, such as the Pure Land school, Buddhism has depended on the monastic sangha for its continuity.

Most Western Buddhists, however, have little interest in supporting monks and nuns. Indeed, the idea of "the transference of merit," whereby the support that lay people give monks and nuns is transformed into merit leading to future benefit seems to run counter to the spirit of most North American Buddhists, who tend to see Buddhism as a do-it-yourself religion. Americans want to practice themselves.

One of the most revolutionary aspects of this new American lay practice, of course, is that it includes women. In recent years, specifically feminist critiques of male-oriented forms of Buddhism have proliferated through conferences, journals, and books. A number of American women teachers have also emerged—Ruth Denison, Sharon Salzberg, and Jacqueline Mandell in the vipassana community; the late Maurine Stuart-roshi, Toni Packer, Jan Chozen Bays, Joko Beck, and Yvonne Rand in the Zen tradition; and Tsultrim Allione and Pema Chodron in the Tibetan tradition.

Some of these teachers have been content to work within the traditional male-dominated structures. Here, too, generalizations that follow gender are hard to make. Some teachers, such as vipassana teacher Sharon Salzberg, are staunch traditionalists. Others, however, have experimented with specifically "feminist" or feminine forms and approaches—a less macho, more receptive, less hierarchical form of Buddhism. Maurine Stuart-roshi was quite comfortable with the so-called macho or samurai style of Rinzai Zen, but she also was known to put down the stick and massage the shoulders of a slumping meditator during sesshin. Ruth Denison, a vipassana teacher and head of the Dhamma Dena Center (named for a female disciple of the Buddha) has added sensory awareness movements to her retreats. This may sound like a small thing, but it is unprecedented for vipassana students.

Denison and others also hold retreats solely for women. "We are not women gathering as a group against men," says Denison. "But to find our own strength and new responsibilities, we need this time to be by ourselves."

Some, like Sandy Boucher, argue that women's spirituality is different from men's. "Women need more attention to skillfull means," Boucher writes in *Turning the Wheel: Women Creating the New Buddhism*.

Not all women agree, of course. Karuna Dharma, disciple of Thich Thien-an, told Lenore Friedman, the author of *Meetings with Remarkable Women: Buddhist Teachers in America*, "I've had women try to convince me that experiences in meditation are different in women than they are in men. I think that's malarky. Each individual experience is different, and certainly gender is involved for a part of it, but only part of it. And I'm not sure it's the most important part."

Whether or not women are "creating the new Buddhism," as the subtitle of Sandy Boucher's book claims, they are certainly playing an important role in that transformation. Conferences at The Naropa Institute, at the Providence Zen Center, and in San Francisco have experimented with nonhierarchical formats for communication first explored by the women's movement, and explored issues such as the abuse of power, the role of women in Buddhist communities, the integration of Buddhist practice with raising a family, and allowing more room for the expression of feeling and emotions in practice.

At the end of her book, Boucher imagines a woman at a Western Buddhist center in the year 2015 looking back. It is kind of a feminist version of the "rucksack revolution" vision which Jack Kerouac put in *The Dharma Bums* in 1957, and well worth quoting at length:

> At first we communicated the efforts that had already been made: the altering of the language of chants and sutras to eliminate male bias, the insistence that women equal in number to men be allowed to give lectures and perform religious offices, the creation of support structures to give mothers the opportunity to do their spiritual practice, the incorporation of body movement into practice situa-

> tions, the allowing of psychological content as a useful point of focus in practice, the integration of group therapy into the schedule of activities of a center, the very *acknowledgement* of therapy individual or otherwise as useful; the recognition of autonomous women teachers and establishment of women-led centers and retreats. Those who particularly understood the synthesis of Buddhism with Native American beliefs communicated their awareness, for it was realized that the native religions connect us to our land. . . .
>
> All this information and speculation came together, forming an immensely rich stew. Everyone—women and those men who care—ate to satiety. And from this nourishment syntheses were made, plans and visions issued. People began to see how the Dharma could be lived out and transmitted in ways more beneficial than before. . . .

VII

Jack Kornfield would certainly qualify as one of those "men who care." In a 1988 essay, "Is Buddhism Changing in North America?," he identified three key themes: Democratization, Feminization, and Integration ("The most frequently asked question of my fifteen years of teaching has been: How can we *live* the practice in our American lives?"). "It will take a great deal of courage on the part of North American Buddhists to face the areas where Buddhism, in its structures and practices, is not working," Kornfield wrote. "To make a place for the Dharma that is open and true, we will need to look honestly at such difficult issues as abuse of power and authority, alcohol, sexuality, money, and our political responsibilities. . . . Similarly, we have to examine ourselves. So many of us come to practice wounded, lonely, or in fear, wanting a loving family as much as enlightenment. . . ."

The study at Spirit Rock, a Marin County vipassana retreat center affiliated with the Barre center in Massachusetts, will reflect these new concerns. In addition to the bare-bones sitting of vipassana, Spirit Rock will include "teachings on right livelihood and service, on right speech and communication, as well as more emphasis on the development and expression of compassion in all aspects of life—through Buddhist peace work, through family life, through ecology."

Like Boucher (and many others), Kornfield makes a strong plea for the integration of psychotherapy and Buddhism. "There were major areas and difficulties in my life, such as loneliness, intimate relationships, work, childhood wounds, and patterns of fear that even deep meditation didn't touch," he wrote in *Inquiring Mind*, the journal of the vipassana community. "It's important we put out the message that for most people sitting practice doesn't do it all. At best, it's one important piece of a whole deep path of opening."

Many American Buddhists have also found the twelve-step programs that have grown out of Alcoholics Anonymous to be another valuable "piece" of their path. (Thich Nhat Hanh has said that the twelve-step programs sound like American dharma.) The twelve-step approach has also offered American Buddhists an interesting model of an indigenous grass-roots, nonhierarchial, leaderless, spiritually based self-help structure which encourages open, nonjudgemental communication ("No cross-talk!"). Indeed, some American Buddhists have found startling similarities between the way alcoholic families denied that father or mother had a drinking problem and the way entire communities denied that their teachers were in trouble. In both systems, so it seemed, family and community members "enabled" their parents and teachers to continue drinking, thus making it harder for them to confront the depth of their problems and seek help.

VIII

Since lay people live in society, the question of social action has also become one of the most important marks of the new American Buddhists, who argue that the traditional stance of political noninvolvement (or complicity in the status quo) adopted by most Asian groups is not appropriate for American Buddhists living in a democratic society. Like feminists, "engaged" Buddhists are drawn from many different sanghas. Many have gathered around the Buddhist Peace Fellowship, a group dedicated to bringing the Buddhist point of view into the peace movement, as well as making Buddhists more aware of social and ecological issues

"Many people have taken action, but if their state of being is not peaceful or happy, the actions they undertake only sow more troubles and anger and make the situation worse," says Thich Nhat Hanh. "So instead of saying, 'Don't just sit there; do something," we should say the opposite, 'Don't just do something; sit there.' We sit there and we get more lucid, more peaceful, and more compassionate. With that state of being our actions can become meaningful to the world." Thich Nhat Hanh and other engaged Buddhists, therefore, have emphasized the development of mindfulness, insight, and calm—of inner peace—as primary. Thich Nhat Hanh also suggests that engaged Buddhists cultivate the half-smile of the Buddha. "A tiny bud of a smile on your lips nourishes awareness and calms you miraculously," he says. "Smiling means we are ourselves. To meditate well means we have to smile a lot. Your smile means you are being gentle with yourself. This is the most basic kind of peace work."

At the same time, however, Thich Nhat Hanh and others point out that Buddhists who do practice meditation can make a real difference in the struggle against social injustice. "People might be used to distinguishing between contemplation and action," Thich Nhat Hanh explains. "But I think in Buddhism, these two cannot be separated. To meditate is to be aware of what is going on—in yourself and the world. If you know what is going on, how can you avoid acting to change the situation?"

So far, "engaged Buddhists" constitute a small but powerfully creative force in the emerging American Buddhism. The Buddhist Peace Fellowship has held a number of national conferences and training sessions, sponsored a fact-finding trip to Nicaragua, taken part in demonstrations, and publishes a lively national journal. During a national march for peace in New York City, members of the Minnesota chapter of the Fellowship organized an all-day sitting in a small park across from the United Nations.

Other "hands-on" projects have been initiated by various centers throughout the country. John Daido Loori-sensei, abbot of the Zen Mountain Center, has been active in making Zen available in prisons, even holding a sesshin "inside." Bernard Tetsugen Glassman-sensei of Zen Center of New York, in Yonkers, believes that just as Zen in Japan incorporated flower arranging and the martial arts, Zen in America "will pick up Western tendencies toward social engagement." ZCNY runs a training program for homeless people in the gourmet bakery that supports the community, and has begun an innovative model project, Greyston Family Inn, which trains minority workers to remodel abandoned apartment buildings, which they will then live in. Joanna Macy, a Buddhist scholar who has written extensively on Sarvodaya, a Buddhist grass-roots village community organization in Sri Lanka, gives workshops on despair and empowerment, especially in the areas of nuclear waste and ecology issues. In San Francisco, Issan Dorsey, who had come to Zen after a career as a female impersonator, street hustler, and hippie commune leader, opened the Maitri Hospice for AIDS patients next door to the Hartford Street Zendo. When he was installed as abbot of Hartford Street Zen Center—and dharma heir of Baker-roshi—in 1989, he declared, "The doors of Hartford Street Zendo remain wide open. While I remain within this place, the door shall never be closed to any living thing." Then he went back to work, leading zazen, teaching Buddhism, fund raising, cutting through bureaucratic red tape, and nursing patients, until he, too, succumbed to AIDS a year later, at the age of fifty-seven.

IX

It is perhaps not entirely unrelated to the vicissitudes of American Buddhism during the eighties that the two most visible and influential teachers for American Buddhists—Thich Nhat Hanh and His Holiness the Dalai Lama—were both celibate monks firmly rooted in monastic tradition. At the same time, however, they both demonstrated masterful, creative responses to the social upheavals and challenges of the late twentieth century, thereby demonstrating the strength, resiliency, and resourcefulness (and perhaps necessity) of the Buddhist monastic tradition.

Thich Nhat Hanh had visited the United States in 1966 at the invitation of the Fellowship for Reconciliation, speaking out against the Vietnam War and calling for a ceasefire and reconciliation. He spoke with politicians such as then–Secretary of Defense Robert McNamara, angry antiwar protesters who told him he should have stayed in Vietnam to fight the imperialists, and fellow religious leaders such as Thomas Merton and Martin Luther King, Jr., who subsequently nominated him for the Nobel Peace Prize. Both the South and North Vietnamese governments, however, announced that he would be arrested if he returned to his country, and he went into exile in France. From there he risked his life more than once to help the boat people by picking them up at sea—until the Singapore government deported him, and Thailand, Malaysia, and Indonesia denied him entry. Since then he has lived and worked with other Vietnamese refugees at Plum Village, a community in France.

During the eighties, Thich Nhat Hanh made a number of visits to North America, offering retreats for Vietnam veterans, artists, environmentalists, psychotherapists, peace activists, and children, as well as for the large Vietnamese immigrant community. He emphasized mindfulness of breathing in an especially positive, life-affirming way. "If you breathe in and out and realize that you are alive, capable of touching the sunshine, the trees, your eyes and so on, it is a wonderful thing. If you keep practicing like that, you water the seeds of joy, peace and life within yourself." He also delighted in finding ways to apply mindfulness to the speed of American life—to the demands of the telephone and the frustrations of driving in cities, for example. So he added telephone meditation, instructing students to use the bell of the telephone as a bell of mindfulness. "When the phone rings," he said, "stop and become aware of your breathing for two or three breaths. Then pick it up." When driving, he suggested using the red light in the same way: "The next time you see a red light, smile to it, sit back, enjoy your breathing in and out."

During a retreat for psychotherapists, he suggested that "Buddhism *and* psychotherapy can come together and learn from each other." But he challenged the "superstition that every time you get angry, you must express your anger. The Buddhist attitude is to take care of your anger," he said. "We don't suppress it. We don't run away from it. We just breathe and hold our anger in our arms with utmost tenderness." He also urged psychotherapists to develop their own practice of joy and peace and to address the "roots of sickness in nature, the environment, society and family."

During a retreat at Mount Madonna, California, he said that "Buddhism in America may be mostly lay Buddhism. The family should become a field of practice, and the Buddhist center should be a center for families to come and practice. That does not mean that monastic Buddhism should not exist. But it should exist in a way that has a very close link to other kinds of Buddhism. Democracy, science, and art should contribute as well. We should build Buddhism with the local materials."

A number of those who listened to Thich Nhat Hanh went on to join the Tiep Hien Order, which Thich Nhat Hanh founded in Vietnam as a way to put the tenets of "engaged Buddhism" into practice. In English, it is the Order of Interbeing, a new word for the old notion "that nothing can exist by itself." Adopting the disciplines of the order means living simply, in order to "share one's time, energy and material resources with those who are in need." The first of the sixteen "disciplines" of the order reminds members that "one should not be idolatrous about or bound to any doctrine, any theory, any ideology, including Buddhist ones. Buddhist systems of thought must be guiding means and not absolute truth." Other disciplines were directly related to the practice of engaged Buddhism: "Have the courage to speak out about situations of injustice even when it may threaten your safety. . . . One's religious community should take a clear stand against injustice and should strive to change the situation without engaging in partisan conflict. . . . Do not kill. Do not let others kill. Find whatever means possible to protect life and prevent war."

X

Like Thich Nhat Hanh, the Dalai Lama is also a monk—"a simple Buddhist monk," as he likes to describe himself. But he is, at the same time, the incarnation of Avalokiteshvara, the Bodhisattva of Compassion, the head of the Tibetan government-in-exile, and the recipient of the Nobel Peace Prize for 1989. He had been given the prize, the Nobel Committee emphasized, because in his struggle to free Tibet from Chinese domination he "consistently has opposed the use of violence" and "instead advocated peaceful solutions based upon tolerance and mutual respect. . . . The Dalai Lama has developed his philosophy of peace from a great reverence for all things living and upon the concept of universal responsibility embracing all mankind as well as nature."

The Nobel Peace Prize catapulted the Dalai Lama, already well known among many people, into celebrity status. He received word of the award while attending an ecumenical conference in Newport Beach, California. "As a Buddhist monk, my concern extends to all members of the human family and, indeed, to all sentient beings who suffer," he told the press. "I believe all suffering is caused by ignorance. People inflict pain on others in the selfish pursuit of their own happiness or satisfaction."

Two years later, touring the United States during the Year of Tibet, he charmed thousands of people, many of whom did not consider themselves Buddhists, with his unpretentious simplicity, humility, and what the *New York Times* called his "impish sense of delight." Speaking of the human need for freedom, he observed that "it may be even more than human. I have a cat," he said. "People feed this cat. They pet this cat. They give the cat everything he needs. But every time the window is open just a little, he runs away."

The Dalai Lama spoke with philosophers, theologians, and scientists; he met with Christian and Jewish leaders, business people, and politicians. In Santa Fe, he consulted privately with Hopi and Pueblo elders. In Washington, he addressed congressional leaders in the Rotunda and then met with the President, hoping to persuade the American government to bring pressure to bear on China. He spoke widely on the need to revive basic human values. "We must complement the human rights ideal by developing a widespread practice of universal human responsibility," he said. "This is not a religious matter. It arises from what I call the 'Common Human Religion'—that of love, the will to others' happiness, and compassion, the will to others' freedom from suffering. . . ."

At the same time, he continued to give teachings that brought together American Buddhists of all schools. In Santa Fe, he explained the unity of all four major schools of Tibetan Buddhism at the stupa built by Kalu Rinpoche; in California, he gave advanced teachings on Dzogchen meditation; and in New York City, thousands of people packed Madison Square Garden for the Kalachakra Tantra initiation.

As for the problems that had concerned so many American Buddhists during the eighties, he emphasized that it was important for students to test teachers for five, ten, or even fifteen years. "Part of the blame lies with the student, because too much obedience, devotion, and blind acceptance spoils a teacher," he said. "Part also lies with the spiritual master because he lacks the integrity to be immune to that kind of vulnerability. . . . I recommend never adopting the attitude toward one's spiritual master of seeing his or her every action as divine or noble. This may seem a little bit bold, but if one has a teacher who is not qualified, who is engaging in unsuitable or wrong behavior, then it is appropriate for the student to criticize that behavior."

When a reporter asked him if he had any observations to make about the future of Buddhism in America, His Holiness scratched his head in his characteristic way and seemed momentarily stumped. "Difficult question," he said, and thought some more. "I think that any person is the same human being, and has the same problem," he began, "birth, old age, and internal attachment. As far as the teaching aspect is concerned, it will always remain the same because the origin is the same. But the cultural aspect changes. Now you see Buddhism comes West. Eventually, it will be Western Buddhism. That, I think, is very helpful—that Buddhism become a part of American life."

And so it is becoming. American Buddhism is hammering out its own shape: an emphasis on householder instead of monk, community instead of monastery, and a practice that integrates and makes use of all aspects of life, for all people, women as well as men. But whatever the shape taken, the shining well-worn gold of the Buddha's teaching remains the same: the Four Noble Truths—the fact of suffering, its origin, cessation, and the path—and the practice that puts it all into practice, again and again and again.

SOURCES AND NOTES

My major sources, which do not constitute a complete bibliography, are arranged by chapter and according to subject matter within each chapter, alphabetically by author. In order not to clutter the text with hundreds of notes, I have arranged my citations in order of occurrence.

General Sources

Dumoulin, Heinrich and Moraldo, John. *The Cultural, Political, and Religious Signifigance of Buddhism in the Modern World*. New York: Macmillan, 1976.

Humphreys, Christmas. *Sixty Years of Buddhism in England (1907–1967): a history and a survey*. London: The Buddhist Society, 1968.

Kubose, Gyomay. *American Buddhism. A New Direction*. Chicago: The Dharma House, 1976.

Layman, Emma McCloy. *Buddhism in America*. Chicago: Nelson-Hall, 1976.

Murano, Kuran. *What American Buddhist Pioneers Think*. Los Angeles, 1939.

Prebish, Charles S. *American Buddhism*. Belmont, Ca.: Duxbury Press, 1979.

Notes

Front Matter

Shakyamuni to the goddess Vimalaprabha. *History of Buddhism by Bu-ston. Part II, The History of Buddhism in India and Tibet*. Translated by E. Obermiller. Heidelburg, 1932. Suzuki Research Foundation Reprint Series 5, p. 105.

H.D. Thoreau: ". . . there is an orientalism. . . ." *A Week on the Concord and Merrimack Rivers*. Boston: Houghton and Mifflin Sentry Editions, p. 157.

CHAPTER ONE

Sources

My source for the life of the Buddha was primarily Bu-ston, the twelfth-century Tibetan historian. For the description of the Buddha's enlightenment, however, I have followed the Zen tradition.

The Life of the Buddha

Bu-ston. *History of Buddhism.* Translated from the Tibetan by Dr. E. Obermiller. Heidelberg, 1931.

Miura, Isshu and Sasaki, Ruth Fuller. *Zen Dust.* New York: Harcourt, Brace and World, 1966.

Thomas, Edward J. *The Life of Buddha as Legend and History.* London: Routledge & Kegan Paul, 1927.

Warren, Henry Clark. *Buddhism In Translations: Passages Selected from the Buddhist Sacred Books and Translated from the Original Pali Into English.* Volume 3 of The Harvard Oriental Series. Cambridge: Harvard University Press, 1947.

The Development of Buddhism

Conze, Edward. *Buddhism, Its Essence and Development.* Oxford: Cassirer, 1963.

Conze, Edward. *Buddhist Thought in India.* London: George Allen & Unwin, 1962.

Rahula, Walpola. *What the Buddha Taught.* New York: Grove Press, 1974.

Robinson, Richard. *The Buddhist Religion, An Historical Introduction.* Belmont: Dickenson, 1979.

Sangharakshita, Bhikshu. *A Survey of Buddhism.* Boulder: Shambhala, 1980.

Taranatha. *History of Buddhism in India.* Translated from the Tibetan by Lama Chimpa and Alaka Chattapadhyaya. Simla: Indian Institute of Advanced Study, 1970.

Zurcher, E. *Buddhism. Its Origin and Spread in Words, Maps and Pictures.* New York: St. Martin's Press, 1962.

Notes

I

The Buddha: "Wonder of wonders. . . ." For the Zen tradition of the Buddha's enlightenment in the *Hua-Yen Sutra*, Miura and Sasaki, p. 254.

CHAPTER TWO

Sources

West-East History

Basham, A.L. *The Wonder That Was India*. New York: Grove Press, 1954.

Davids, T.W. Rhys, trans. *The Questions of King Milinda*. New York: Dover Publications, 1963.

Demascene, St. John. *Barlaam and Iosaph*, with an English Translation by the Rev. G.R. Woodward and H. Mattingly. Cambridge: Harvard University Press, 1953.

Grousset, Rene. *In the Footsteps of the Buddha*. London: George Routledge & Sons, 1932.

Ikeda, Daisaku. *Buddhism, The First Millenium*. Translated by Burton Watson. Tokyo-New York: Kodansha International, 1977.

Jacobs, Joseph. *Barlaam and Josaphat, English Lives of Buddha*. London: D. Nutt, 1896.

Kaempfer, Englebert. *The History of Japan*. London, 1727. Extracted in *Cat's Yawn*, The Buddhist Society of America, Vol. I, No. 12 (June 1941).

Kennedy, J. "Buddhist Gnosticism," in *Journal of the Royal Asiatic Society of Great Britain and Ireland*, 1902.

Lang, David Marshall. *The Wisdom of Balahvar; a Christian legend of the Buddha*. New York: Macmillan, 1957.

McNeill, William. *The Rise of the West, A History of the Human Community*. Chicago and London: The University of Chicago Press, 1963.

Rawlinson, H.G. *Intercourse Between India and the Western World From the Earliest Times to the Fall of Rome*. Oxford: Cambridge University Press, 1916. Reprinted by Octagon Books, New York, 1971.

Sansom, George B. *The Western World and Japan*. New York: Vintage Books, 1973.

Tennakoon, Vimalananda. *Buddhism in Ceylon Under the Christian Powers and The Educational and Religious Policy of the British Government in Ceylon 1797–1832*. Colombo: M.D. Gunasena, 1963.

Viereck, Valerie E. *The Lotus and the Word: Key Parallels in the Saddharma-Pundarika Sutra and the Gospel According to John*. Cambridge: Cambridge Buddhist Association, 1972.

Welbon, Guy Richard. *The Buddhist Nirvana and Its Western Interpreters*. Chicago and London: The University of Chicago Press, 1968.

Fu-Sang

Bancroft, H. H. *The Works of Hubert Howe Bancroft*, Volume V: *The Native Races of the Pacific States*, Vol. V: *Primitive History*. San Francisco: The History Company, 1886.

Bruer, Hans. *Columbus Was Chinese, Discoveries and Inventions of the Far East*. New York: Herder and Herder, 1972.

Deguines, M. *Recherches sur les Navigations des Chinois du cote de l'Amerique*. Paris: Memoires de l'Academie des Inscriptions, tom. xvii, 1761.

Hawken, Paul. "Long Before Columbus, The Buddhist Discovery of America." *New Age* (Oct. 1976).

Leland, Charles G. *Fusang or the Discovery of America by Chinese Buddhist Priests in the Fifth Century*. London: Traubner and Co., 1875.

Mertz, Henriette. *Pale Ink: Two Ancient Records of Chinese Exploration in America*. Chicago: Swallow Press, 1972.

Steiner, Saul. *Fusang, The Chinese Who Built America*. New York: Harper & Row, 1979.

Vining, Edward Payson. *An Inglorious Columbus; or, Evidence That Hwui Shan and A Party of Buddhist Monks From Afghanistan Discovered America In the Fifth Century A.D.* New York: Appleton & Co., 1885.

Weight, Harold O. "Rock of the People From the Sea." *Westways* (May 1955).

Notes

I

". . . the cultural anthropologist Tadao Umesao." Ikeda, p. 72.

Mandanis: ". . . trying to explain." Rawlinson, p. 62.

Rene Grousset: "Could the Chinese pilgrims. . . ." Grousset, p. 105.

II

Clement of Alexandra: "Indians who follow the precepts of Boutta. . . ." Rawlinson, p. 29.

Father De Lubac on Basilides: "Although there is an undeniable analogy. . . ." Welbon, p. 9.

Bardesanes: "Both the Brahmins and the Buddhist monks. . . ." Rawlinson, pp. 143–144.

Origen: "In that island. . . ." Ikeda, p. 74.

III

William of Rubuck: "They all listened. . . ." Sansom, p. 39.

Marco Polo: "For a certainty. . . ." Welbon, p. 17.

IV

De Lubec: "A 'monstrous religion. . . .' " Welbon, p. 20.

Noel Alexander: "The secret doctrine of. . . ." Ibid., p. 19.

Sir Emerson Tennent: "There is no page. . . ." Tennakoon, p. xxiv.

A Sinhalese historian: men "were thrown over bridges. . . ." Ibid., p. xxvi.

The Dutch in Ceylon: "They make offerings. . . ." Ibid., p. lxiii.

V

Xavier: "Some are counting. . . ." Sansom, pp. 117–119.

VI

La Loubere: "Nireupan is not a place. . . ." Welbon, pp. 21–22.

Kaempfer: "A person blessed with. . . ." Kaempfer, in *Cat's Yawn*, p. 50.

VII

The Chinese account: "During the reign. . . ." Vining, pp. 262–300.

Bancroft: "Although bearing various names. . . ." Bancroft, p. 23.

CHAPTER THREE

Sources

Asia, America and Europe

Christy, Arthur A. "The Sense of the Past," in *The Asian Legacy and American Life*, ed. Arthur Christy. New York: The John Day Co., 1942.

Leites, Edmund. "Confucianism in Eighteenth-Century England: Natural Morality and Social Reform." *Actes du II Colloque International de Sinologie*. Paris, 1980. Les Belles Lettres, pp. 65–81.

Northrop, F.S.C. *The Meeting of East and West. An Inquiery Concerning World Understanding*. New York: The Macmillan Co., 1950.

Said, Edward. *Orientalism*. New York: Pantheon, 1978.

Schwab, R. *La Renaissance orientale*. Paris: Payot, 1950.

Sir William Jones

Arberry, A.J. *Oriental Essays; portraits of seven scholars*. London: George Allen & Unwin, 1960.

Cannon, Garland. *Oriental Jones. A Biography of Sir William Jones*. Bombay: Council for Cultural Relations, Asia Publishing House, 1964.

Cannon, Garland. "Freedom of the Press and Sir William Jones" in *Journalism Quarterly*, XXXIII (Spring 1956).

Cannon, Garland. "Sir William Jones and Benjamin Franklin" in *Oxford University College Record*, IV (Oct. 1961). Includes four previously unpublished letters from Jones to Franklin.

Franklin, Benjamin. *The Works of Benjamin Franklin*. Edited by Jared Sparks. Boston: Hilliard, Gray & Co., 1927. Volume VIII, pp. 543–547 contains "A Fragment of Polybius."

Jones, Sir William, editor. *Asiatick Researches; transactions of the Society Instituted in Bengal for Inquiering into the History and Antiquities, the Arts, Sciences, and Literature of Asia*. Vol. the First. Calcutta: Manuel Cantopher, 1788.

Meester, Marie, editor. *Oriental Influences in the English Literature of the Nineteenth Century*. Heidelburg: Carl Winters Universtatsbuchhandlung, 1915.

Mukherjee, S. *Sir William Jones: A Study in Eighteenth Century British Attitudes to India*. Cambridge: Cambridge University Press, 1968.

Nehru, Jawaharlal. *The Discovery of India*. New York: John Day Co., 1946.

Pinto, V. Sola. "Sir William Jones and English Literature." *Bulletin of the School of Oriental and African Studies*. University of London, XI. 4 (1946).

Rayapati, Rao J.P. *Early American Interest in Vedanta; Pre-Emersonian Interest in Vedic Literature and Vedantic Philosophy*. New York: Asia Publishing House, 1973.

Teignmouth, Lord. *Memoirs of the Life, Writings, and Correspondence of Sir William Jones*. Vols. I and II of *The Works of Sir William Jones*. London: John Stockdale and John Walker, 1807.

Notes

I

La Morale de Confucius: "Everything herein is solid. . . ." *The Morals of Confucious, A Chinese Philosopher* (Randal Taylor, London, 1691) pp. xi–xii. (Translation of *La Morale de Confucius, Philosophe de la Chine* (Amsterdam, 1688); and Eustace Bludgell: a "Maxim, which ought to be observed. . . ." Eustace Bludgell, *A Letter to Cleomenes*. London: A Moore, 1731, p. 91. Quoted in Leites.

Christian Wolf: praised the Chinese Emperors . . . for "passing over. . . ." Christy, p. 23.

II

Jones: Preface to the grammar of the Persian Language: "Some men never heard. . . ." Quoted in Arberry, p. 79.

Jones to Althorp: he would "accept a noble offer. . . ." Quoted in Cannon (1961), p. 35.

Jones to Franklin: "I have no wish to grow old in England. . . ." Ibid., p. 34.

Jones: "As to my politics. . . ." Cannon (1964), p. 108.

III

Franklin: "I cannot conceive of a match. . . ." Rayapati, pp. 46–47.

Lord Teignmouth: "Had he been an infidel. . . ." Teignmouth, Vol. II, pp. 8–9.

Jones: "I am no Hindu. . . ." (to Earl of Spencer, 4 Sept. 1787). Quoted in Mukerjee, p. 119.

IV

Jones: "At the mid-point" of his voyage . . . when "India lay before us. . . ." *A Discourse on the Institution of a Society, for Inquiering into the History, Civil and Natural, the Antiquities, Arts, Sciences, and Literature of ASIA* by the President. *Asiatick Researches*, Vol. I. Calcutta, 1877.

Halhed: "The Importance of the commerce. . . ." Quoted in Mukerjee, p. 80.

The English: who had prohibited the Indians. . . . Nehru, p. 317.

Jones: "Though not a Brahmin. . . ." Cannon (1964), p. 132.

V

Jones: "Whenever we direct our attention to Hindu literature. . . ." in "On the Literature of the Hindus, from the Sanskrit." *Asiatick Researches*, Vol. I, p. 340.

Jones: The Brahmin Philosophers strolling through "groves and seminaries. . . ." "Third Discourse on the Hindus." *Asiatick Researches*, Vol. I, p. 125.

Jones: "To what shall I compare my literary pursuits. . . ." Quoted in Mukerjee, p. 116.

VI

Jones: "We need say no more of the heterodox writings. . . ." *Asiatick Researches*, Vol. I, p. 354.

Turnour: "During the time we were in the room, I observed. . . ." *Asiatick Researches*, Vol. I, p. 354.

A Contemporary Tibetan account: "Although the visitors were not knowers. . . ." Schuyler Cammann, *Trade Through the Himalayas, The Early British Attempts to Open Tibet*. Princeton: Princeton University Press, 1951.

VII

Jones: "The Sanskrit language, whatever be its antiquity. . . ." "On the Hindus," *Asiatick Researches*, Vol. 1, pp. 422–3.

VII

Jones: "May I find wisdom and goodness. . . ." Quoted in Cannon (1961), p. 43.

Teignmouth: "lying on his bed in a posture of meditation. . . ." Teignmouth, Vol. II, p. 261.

CHAPTER FOUR

Sources

Ames, Van Meter. *Zen and American Thought*. Honolulu: University of Hawaii Press. 1962.

Ando, Shoei. *Zen and American Transcendentalism—An Investigation of One's Self*. Tokyo: The Hokuseido Press, 1970.

Boston and the China Trade. Boston: A Massachusetts Historical Society Picture Book, 1970.

Christy, Arthur A. *The Orient in American Transcendentalism. A Study of Emerson, Thoreau, and Alcott*. New York: Columbia University Press, 1932. Reprinted, Octagon Books, 1972.

Frothingham, Octavius Brooks. *Transcendentalism in New England, A History*. New York: G.P. Putnum, 1876. Philadelphia: University of Pennsylvania Paperback, 1972.

Morison, Samuel Eliot. *Maritime History of Massachusetts, 1783–1860*. Boston: Houghton Mifflin, 1921.

Rayapati, J.P. Rao. *Early Interest in Vedanta. Pre-Emersonian Interest in Vedic Literature and Vedantic Philosophy*. New York: Asia Publishing House, 1973.

Emerson

Carpenter, Fredric Ives. *Emerson and Asia*. New York: Haskell House, 1968.

Emerson, Ralph Waldo. *Emerson's Essays. First and Second Series.* New York: Thomas Y. Crowell, 1926.

Emerson, Ralph Waldo. *Indian Superstition.* Edited with a Dissertation on Emerson's Orientalism at Harvard by Kenneth Walker Cameron. Hanover, New Hampshire: The Friends of Dartmouth Library, 1954.

Emerson, Ralph Waldo. *The Journals and Miscellaneous Notebooks of Ralph Waldo Emerson.* Vol. I, 1819–1822. Edited by William T. Gilman. Cambridge: Harvard University Press, 1960.

Paramananda, Swami. *Emerson and Vedanta.* Boston: The Vedanta Centre, 1918.

Rusk, Ralph L. *The Life of Ralph Waldo Emerson.* New York: Charles Scribner's Sons, 1949.

Thoreau

Krutch, Joseph Wood. *Henry David Thoreau.* New York: Morrow, 1974.

Ricketson, Anna and Walter, eds. *Daniel Ricketson and His Friends.* Boston: Houghton Mifflin, 1902.

Sanborn, F.B. "Thoreau and His English Friends," in *The Atlantic Monthly,* LXXII (Dec. 1893), pp. 741–56.

Thoreau, Henry D., editor, *The Dial,* IV (Jan. 1844), pp. 391–401.

Thoreau, Henry David. *Familiar Letters.* F.E. Sanborn, editor. Boston and New York: Houghton Mifflin, 1894.

Thoreau, H.D. *The Transmigration of the Seven Brahmins. A Translation From the Harivansa of Langlois By Henry David Thoreau,* edited from Manuscript, with an Introduction and Notes by Arthur Christy. New York: William Edwin Rudge, 1932.

Thoreau, H.D. *The Writings of Henry David Thoreau.* Vol. I *A Week On the Concord and Merrimack Rivers.* Vol. II *Walden.* Boston: Houghton Mifflin, 1906.

Whitman

Allen, Gay Wilson. *The Solitary Singer, A Critical Biography of Walt Whitman.* New York: New York University Press, 1967.

Chari, V.K. *Whitman in the Light of Vendantic Mysticism: An Interpretation.* Lincoln: University of Nebraska Press, 1965.

Rajasekharaiah, T.R. *The Roots of Whitman's Grass: Eastern Sources of Walt Whitman's Poetry.* Rutherford, N.J.: Fairleigh Dickenson University Press, 1971.

Whitman, Walt. *The Portable Walt Whitman.* Selected and with Notes by Mark Van Doren. New York: The Viking Press, 1973.

Bronson Alcott

Alcott, Bronson. *The Letters of A. Bronson Alcott,* edited by Richard Herrnstadt. Iowa State University Press, 1969.

Edwin Arnold

Arnold, Edwin. *The Light of Asia, or The Great Renunciation, Being the Life and Teachings of Gautama, Prince of India and Founder of Buddhism.* Boston: Trubner & Co., 1879.

Peiris, William. *Edwin Arnold, A Brief Account of His Life And Contribution to Buddhism*. Kandy: Buddhist Publication Society, 1970.

Wright, Brooks. *Interpreter of Buddhism to the West: Sir Edwin Arnold*. New York: Bookman Association, 1957.

Notes

I

Frederic Tudor and the ice trade: Morison, pp. 279–285.

Thoreau: "Thus it appears that. . . ." *Writings*, II, pp. 328–29.

Emerson: "the ostentatious ritual. . . ." Quoted in Rao, p. 95.

Emerson: "One is apt to lament. . . ." Christy, p. 65.

Emerson: "330 million gods. . . ." to "admiration paid. . . ." in *Journals*, I, 326–7.

Emerson: "The death of a dear. . . ." *Essays*, p. 92.

Aunt Mary: "It is far sadder . . ." to ". . . confused & dark. . . ." Quoted in Rusk, p. 167.

Thoreau: Jones's *Laws* ". . . comes to me. . . ." *Journals*, I, p. 188.

III

Thoreau: "The Preaching of the Buddha." *The Dial*, IV (Jan. 1844), pp. 395–6.

IV

Thoreau: "Sometimes, in a summer morning. . . ." *Writings*, II, pp. 123–124.

Thoreau: "I know that some. . . ." *A Week On the Concord and Merrimack*, p. 68.

Thoreau: "No god ever dies. . . ." Ibid., p. 65.

Thoreau: "Every sacred book. . . ." Ibid., p. 155.

Thoreau: "As we have said. . . ." Ibid., p. 157.

Thoreau: ". . . we are not so much concerned. . . ." Ibid., p. 159.

Thoreau to H.G.O. Blake: ". . . even I am a Yogi." Quoted in Christy, p. 201.

Moncure Conway of Thoreau: "Like the pious yogi. . . ." Ibid., 202.

John Weiss of Thoreau: "His countenance had not a line. . . ." Ibid., p. 233.

V

Emerson of Whitman: "a mixture of the Bhagavad-Gita and the New York Herald." Quoted in Rao, p. 12.

Thoreau to Whitman: "wonderfully like the Orientals." Ibid., p. 13.

Whitman: "My faith is the greatest of faiths. . . ." "Song of Myself" in *The Portable Walt Whitman*, p. 85.

Whitman: *Passage to India*. Ibid., pp. 275–284.

Whitman: "Perhaps indeed the efforts. . . ." *Speciman Days*, Ibid., p. 640.

VI

Emerson and the *Bhagavad Gita*: ". . . he refused, thinking 'it not only some desecretion. . . .' " Rusk, p. 371.

Channing to Alcott: "Poem and Poet should be widely known. . . ." Quoted in Christy, p. 250.

The Reviews of *Light of Asia*: Ibid., pp., 253–258.

Arnold: "His sources were. . . ." Wright, p. 86. Peiris, however, suggests that Arnold read a biography of the Buddha published by the Russian I. J. Schmidt in the *Asiatic Journal*, works by Hodgson, Csoma de Koros, Eugene Burnouf and Franz Anton von Schiefner's translation of Taranatha's *History of Buddhism*, among others.

CHAPTER FIVE

Sources

The Chinese

Barth, Guenther. *Bitter Strength*. Cambridge: Harvard University Press, 1964.

Chinn, Thomas W., editor. *A History of the Chinese in California; A Syllabus*. San Francisco: Chinese Historical Society of America, 1969.

Lancaster, Lewis. "Buddhism in the United States: The Untold and Unfinished Story." *Shambhala Review of Books and Ideas*, Vol. 5, Nos. 1–2 (Winter 1976), pp. 23–25.

Miller, Stuart Creighton. *The Unwelcome Immigrant: The American Image of the Chinese, 1785–1882*. Berkeley and Los Angeles: The University of California Press, 1969.

Steiner, Saul. *Fusang; the Chinese Who Built America*. New York: Harper & Row, 1979.

Sienkiewicz, Henryk. "The Chinese in California As Reported by Henryk Sienkiewicz." Translated with Foreword by Charles Morley. *California Historical Society Quarterly*, Vol. XXXIV, No. 4 (Dec. 1955), pp. 301–316.

Wells, Marianne Kaye. *Chinese Temples in California*. San Francisco: R & E Research Associates Reprints, 1971.

William, George M., Wong, Danial D., Wong, Brenda L. "The Chinese Temples of Northern California" in *The Life, Influence and the Role of the Chinese in the United States 1776–1960*. Proceedings/Papers of the National Conference held at the University of San Francisco July 10–12, 1975. San Francisco: Chinese Historical Society of America, 1975.

The Japanese

Buddhist Churches of America. *75 year History 1899–1974*. Vol. I. Chicago: Buddhist Churches of America, 1974.

Hosokawa, Bill. *Nisei, The Quiet Americans*. New York: William Morrow, 1969.

Hunter, Louise H. *Buddhism In Hawaii; Its Impact on a Yankee Community*. Honolulu: University of Hawaii Press, 1971.

Imamura, Y. *History of the Hongwanji Mission in Hawaii.* Honolulu: The Publishing Bureau of the Hongwanji Mission, 1918.

Ito, Kayo. *Issei, A History of Japanese Immigrants in North America.* Seattle: Japanese Community Services, 1973.

Matsunami, Kodo. *Introducing Buddhism, Jodo Mission Handbook.* Honolulu: Jodo Mission of Hawaii, 1965.

Ogawa, Dennis M., editor. *Kodomo no tame ni: For the sake of the children. The Japanese American Experience in Hawaii.* Honolulu: The University Press of Hawaii, 1965.

Notes

I

The California Courier: "We have never seen. . . ." Quoted in Steiner, pp. 108–109.

Mark Twain: "they proved themselves. . . ." *Roughing It.* Hartford, CT: American Publishing Co., 1872.

Miller: ". . . the first departure. . . ." Miller, p. 3.

Charles Taylor: "So gratifying a scene. . . ." Quoted in Miller, p. 115.

A group of Chinese American historians: "The temple symbolized. . . ." William, et al. p. 294.

The Case of John Eldridge vs. See Yup Co: "The California Supreme Court preserved. . . ." Barth, pp. 123–124.

Sienkowicz: "But we have not yet entered. . . ." Sienkowicz, pp. 303–304.

II

Whitman: "Over the Western seas hither from Niphon. . . ." "A Broadway Pageant," in *Leaves of Grass*, p. 206, N.Y.: New American Library 1980.

Kagahi and history of Hawaii: Hunter, pp. 33–45.

Petition to Hongwanji: ". . . the religion here is dominated. . . ." Ibid., p. 60.

Mr. Saito: "the consul in Seattle. . . ." Buddhist Churches of America, Vol I, p. 46.

"Because of their youth and lack of responsibilities." Ibid., p. 44.

CHAPTER SIX

Sources

Leneman, Leah. "The Hindu Renaissance of the Late Nineteenth Century," in *History Today*, Volume 30 (May 1980).

The Theosophical Movement, 1875–1950. Los Angeles: The Cunningham Press, 1957.

Wilson, Colin. *The Occult, A History.* New York: Random House, 1971.

Madame Blavatsky

Blavatsky, H.P. *Isis Unveiled.* 2 Vols. New York: J.W. Bouton, 1877.

Blavatsky, H.P. *Secret Doctrine*. 2 Vols. London: The Theosophical Publishing Co., 1888.

Murphet, Howard. *When Daylight Comes. A Biography of Helena Petrovna Blavatsky*. Wheaton, Illinois: The Theosophical Publishing House. 1975.

Olcott, Henry Steel. *Inside the Occult. The True Story of Madame H.P. Blavatsky*. (Original title, *Old Diary Leaves*). Philadelphia: Running Press, 1975.

Wachtmeister, Constance. *Reminiscences of H.P. Blavatsky and the Secret Doctrine*. Wheaton, Illinois: The Theosphical Publishing House, 1976.

Williams, Gertrude Marvin. *Madame Blavatsky, Priestess of the Occult*. New York: Knopf, 1946.

Henry Steel Olcott

Elwood, Robert S., Jr. "Colonel Olcott and Madame Blavatsky's Journey to the East," in *Alternative Altars. Unconventional and Eastern Spirituality in America*. Chicago: The University of Chicago Press, 1979.

Malagoda, Kitsiri. *Buddhism in Sinhalese Society—1750–1900. A Study of Religious Revival and Change*. Berkeley: University of California Press, 1976.

Murphet, Howard. *Hammer on the Mountain. The Life of Henry Steel Olcott*. Wheaton, Illinois: The Theosophical Publishing House, 1972.

Olcott, Henry Steel. *The Buddhist Catechism*. Wheaton, Illinois: The Theosophical Publishing House, 1970. Forty-fifth edition.

Olcott, Henry Steel. *Old Diary Leaves*. (6 vols.) Madras: The Theosophical Publishing House, 1928–35.

Anagarika Dharmapala

Sangarakshita, Bhikshu. *Anagarika Dharmapala. A Biographical Sketch*. Kandy: Buddhist Publication Society, 1964. First published in 1952 in the *Maha Bodhi Society Diamond Jubilee*.

Sinnett, A.R. *Esoteric Buddhism*. Boston: Houghton Mifflin, 1884.

Notes

I

The Saturday Review: "one of the most unequivically degrading superstitions. . . ." Quoted in *The Theosophical Movement* (hereafter *TTM*), p. 15.

II

For Olcott's meeting with HPB, see Olcott, *Inside the Occult*, pp. 1–26.

III

Madame Blavatsky: ". . . the mysterious lever of all intellectual forces, the Tree of Knowledge. . . ." Quoted in *TTM*, p. 33.

The Three Objects of the Society: "to form the nucleus. . . ." Ibid., p. 44.

Olcott: ". . . an Oriental clad in white garments. . . ." *Inside the Occult*, pp. 379–381.

Blavatsky and *Isis Unveiled*: "I wrote this last night 'by order'. . . ." and following quotes. Olcott, *Inside the Occult*, pp. 202–219.

IV

Madame Blavatsky: "When we arrived in India. . . ." Quoted in *TTM*, pp. 113–114.

Olcott: "The youth of India will shake off their sloth. . . ." Murphet (1972) pp. 106–107.

Olcott: "When we had finished. . . ." Murphet (1972) p. 135.

Olcott: "Our Buddhism was that. . . ." Ibid., pp. 135–136.

V

Dharmapala: "I have never ceased to love. . . ." Sangarakshita, p. 22.

Dharmapala: "In those days the theosophic atmosphere. . . ." Ibid., p. 27.

VI

Olcott: "The Sinhalese Buddhists have never yet. . . ." Olcott, *The Buddhist Catechism*, p. 1.

The SPR Report: ". . . all the marvelous narratives . . ." and "For her own part. . . ." *TTM*, p. 96.

VII

Thomas Rhys-Davids: "I had heard of his learning as a Pali scholar. . . ." Carolyn Rhys-Davids. *A Manual of Buddhism*. London: The Sheldon Press, 1932, p. 7.

Olcott and the Buddhist flag: "It was a splendid idea. . . ." Olcott, *Old Diary Leaves*, Vol. III, pp. 363–364.

VIII

Olcott in Japan: "We are praying Colonel Olcott. . . ." and following quotes. Murphet (1972), pp. 145–152.

Dharmapala and Japan: "a sovereign star. . . ." and following quotes. Sangarakshita, pp. 37–43.

IX

Soyen Shaku: "My teacher loved. . . ." An autobiographical fragment ("A Rent in the Buddhist Robe.") in Senzaki's uncatalogued papers, Oriental Library, UC Berkeley.

Letters of Soyen Shaku to Kosen: In *Like A Dream, Like A Fantasy: The Zen Writings and Translations of Nyogen Senzaki*. Edited and with an Introduction by Eido Shimano Roshi. Tokyo: Japan Publications, 1978, pp. 91–99.

X

Olcott in Burma: ". . . considering what a marvel. . . ." *Old Diary Leaves*, Vol. III, p. 214.

Olcott: "If I should bring you. . . ." Murphet (1972), p. 151.

XI

Edwin Arnold: "The spot dear, and divine . . ." and "I think there never was an idea. . . ." Peiris, pp. 81–89.

Dharmapala: "Within a mile. . . ." Sangarakshita, p. 46.

Dharmapala: "This night at 12. . . ." Ibid., p. 48.

CHAPTER SEVEN

Sources

Barrows, Rev. John Henry, editor. *The World's Parliament of Religions. An Illustrated and Popular Story of the World's First Parliament of Religions, Held in Chicago in connection with The Columbian Exposition of 1893.* (2 vols.) Chicago: The Parliament Publishing Company, 1893.

Dharmapala, Anagarika. "Mr. H. Dharmapala At the Parliament of Religions, Chicago," in *Journal of the Maha-Bodhi Society*, Vol. II, No. 7, Calcutta (Nov. 1893).

Strauss, C.T. *The Buddha and His Doctrine.* London: William Rider & Son, 1923.

Strauss, C.T. "A Convert to Buddhism," reprinted from *Salt Lake Weekly*, and "Remarkable Religious Researches of C.T. Strauss of New York," in *Journal of the Maha-Bodhi Society*, Vol. II, No. 8, Calcutta (Nov. 1893).

Notes

Barrows: Their work had "opened a new field. . . ." Barrows, Vol. I, p. 191.

Barrows: ". . . and since it is as clear. . . ." Ibid., p. 3.

Barrows: Others said "that Religion as such. . . ." Ibid., p. 4.

The Archbishop of Canterbury: "the Christian religion is the religion. . . ." Ibid., p. 20.

Rev. J. Eitel: "Let me warn you. . . ." Ibid., p. 26.

Rev. T.F. Hawks: "no greater obstacle. . . ." Ibid., p. 56.

Barrows: "Religion, like the white light. . . ." Ibid., p. 3.

Dharmapala: "With his black, curly locks thrown back. . . ." *St. Louis Observor*, Sept. 21, 1893. Barrows, p. 95.

Dharmapala: Opening address. Ibid., pp. 95–96.

Pung Kwang Yu: "Confucianism." Ibid., pp. 374–439.

Z. Noguchi: "The Religion of the World." Ibid., pp. 440–443.

Kinza Hirai: "The Real Position of Japan Toward Christianity." Ibid., pp. 444–450.

Hori Toki: "Buddhism in Japan." Ibid., pp. 543–552.

Prince Chadradat Chudadharn: "Buddhism As It Exists in Siam." Ibid., pp. 645–649.

Banryu Yatsubuchi: "Buddhism." Ibid., pp. 715–723.

Soyen Shaku: "The Law of Cause and Effect, As Taught by Buddha." Barrows, Vol. II, pp. 829–831.

Dharmapala: "The World's Debt to Buddha." Ibid., pp. 862–880.

Dharmapala: "And now history is repeating itself. . . ." Ibid., p. 863.

Zitsuzen Asitsu: "Buddha." Ibid., pp. 1038–1040.

Rev. McFarland and Rev Gordan: "The Christian missioneries took their turn. . . ." Ibid., pp. 1293–1297.

Dharmapala: "Five only! Four hundred and seventy-five millions. . . ." Ibid., p. 1571.

Barrows: "The Parliament has shown that Christianity. . . ." Ibid., p. 1580.

C.T. Strauss: "As the audience was about to go. . . ." *Journal of the Mahabodhi Society*, Vol. II, No. 8 (Nov. 1893), p. 6.

C.T. Strauss: ". . . the first person to be admitted. . . ." Sangarakshita, p. 64.

CHAPTER EIGHT

Sources

Philangi Dasa

Carter, Paul Allen. "The Meeting of East and West," in *The Spiritual Crisis of the Gilded Age*. Dekalb: Northern Illinois University Press, 1971.

Dasa, Philangi, editor. *The Buddhist Ray. A Monthly Magazine Devoted to The Lord Buddha's Enlightenment*. Vol. 1–7, 1888–1894. Santa Cruz.

Dasa, Philangi. *Swedenborg the Buddhist, or the Higher Swedenborgianism Its Secrets and Thibetan Origin*. Los Angeles: The Buddhistic Swedenborgian Brotherhood, 1887.

Anagarika Dharmapala

Dharmapala, Anagarika. Letters to Paul Carus in the Special Collections/Morris Library, Southern Illinois University at Carbondale.

Friis-Holm, Gudrun. "Vesak in the United States," in *The Maha-Bodhi*, (Nov-Dec. 1934).

Sangarakshita, Bhikshu. *Anagarika Dharmapala. A Biographical Sketch*. Kandy: Buddhist Publication Society, 1964.

Paul Carus

Carus, Paul. *Buddhism and Its Christian Critics*. Chicago: Open Court, 1897.

Carus, Paul. "A Buddhist Prelate of California," in *The Open Court*, Vol. XXVI, No. 2 (Feb. 1912).

Carus, Paul. *The Gospel of Buddha*. Chicago: Open Court, 1904.

Carus, Paul. *Karma/Nirvana. Two Buddhist Tales by Paul Carus*. Preface by Leo Tolstoy. La Salle: Open Court, 1973.

Carus Paul. Letters to and from D.T. Suzuki, Anagarika Dharmapala, Soyen Shaku, Zitsuzen Ashitsu and others at the Paul Carus Collection/Morris Library, Southern Illinois University, Carbondale.

Gordan, M.L. "Shall We Welcome Buddhist Missioneries to America?" *Open Court*, XIL (May 1900).

Jackson, C.T. "Meeting of East and West: The Case of Paul Carus." *Journal of Historical Ideas*, 29: 73–92 (Jan. 1968).

Mazziniananda, Swami. *The Order of the Buddhist High Mass*. Chicago: Open Court, 1913.

Sheridan, J.F. *Paul Carus: A Study of the Thought and Work.* Dissertation, University of Illinois, 1957.

Suzuki, D.T. "A Glimpse of Paul Carus." Introduction to *Modern Trends in World Religion*, Joseph Mitsuo Kitagawa, editor. (Paul Carus Memorial Symposium, held September 9–12, 1956, Peru, Illinois.) La Salle: Open Court, 1959.

D.T. Suzuki

Bando, Shojun. "D.T. Suzuki's Life in La Salle," in *The Eastern Buddhist* New Series, II, No. 1 (August 1967).

Dornish, Margaret H. "Aspects of D.T. Suzuki's Early Interpretations of Buddhism and Zen." *Journal, The Blaisdell Institute*, Vol. VI, No. 1 (Oct. 1970).

Farkas, Mary. "Daisetz Teitaro Suzuki 1870–1966," *Zen Notes*, Vol. XVIII, No. 7 (July 1966).

Sargent, Winthrop. "Great Simplicity." Profile of D.T. Suzuki in *The New Yorker*, Aug. 31, 1957, pp. 34–53.

Suzuki, D.T., trans. *Ashvagosha's Discourse on the Awakening of Faith in the Mahayana.* Chicago: Open Court, 1900.

Suzuki, D.T. "Early Memories." *Middle Way*, XXXIX (November 1964). Also in *The Field of Zen*, edited and with a foreward by Christmas Humphreys. New York: Harper and Row, 1970. Prepared from notes taken by Carmen Blacker and Mihoko Okamura when Dr. Suzuki was ninety-five.

Suzuki, D.T. *The Outlines of Mahayana Buddhism.* New York: Schocken Books, 1963.

The First Japanese Missionaries

The Buddhist Churches of America, Vol. I. *75 year History, 1899–1974.* Chicago: Buddhist Churches of America, 1974.

Notes

I

Dasa on the Parliament: the Buddhist brethren . . . who "ungrudgingly shook hands. . . ." *Buddhist Ray*, Vol. VI, Nos. 11–12 (Nov.-Dec. 1893), p. 1.

Dasa on Theosophy: "The truth is that. . . ." *Buddhist Ray*, Vol. V, Nos. 3–4 (March-April 1892), p. 2.

The Santa Cruz Surf: "a gentleman, who. . . ." Ibid., May 1893.

II

Dharmapala: "The true spirit. . . ." Sangarakshita, p. 67.

Dharmapala to Carus: "O ye gods. . . ." Original in Special Collections/Morris Library. Calcutta, April 15, 1896.

Dharmapala to Carus: "They have been taught. . . ." Original in Special Collections/Morris Library. Calcutta, March 31, 1896.

Dharmapala: ". . . these so-called Christians. . . ." Sangarakshita, p. 72.

His biographer: "Several American women. . . ." Ibid.

Dharmapala to Carus: "a triumphant unfurlment. . . ." Original in Special Collections/Morris Library. San Francisco, March 17, 1896.
Professor James: "Take my chair. . . ." Sangarakshita, p. 78.
Mrs. Foster: "Why frettest thou. . . ." *Diamond Jubilee*, pp. 138–139.
Dharmapala: "I would like to be reborn. . . ." Ibid., p. 64.

III

Soyen Shaku to Carus: "This 19th century of ours. . . ." Quoted in Dornish, p. 23.

D.T. Suzuki: "before the publication of *The Gospel of Buddha*. . . ." Suzuki, "A Glimpse of Paul Carus." p. xv.

Soyen Shaku: "The advanced state of modern science . . ." Preface to "A Japanese Translation of *The Gospel of Buddha*," ca. 1900. Original (English translation) in Special Collections. Morris Library.

D.T. Suzuki: "I was busy during. . . ." Suzuki, "Early Memories." pp. 101–108

Soyen Shaku to Carus: "My dear friend and brother, T. Suzuki . . . ." Letter, Feb. 2, 1897. Original in Special Collections/Morris Library.

D. T. Suzuki: "The Chinese are masters. . . ." Suzuki, "Gimpses of Paul Carus." p. xiii.

D.T. Suzuki: "Let us ask whether. . . ." Suzuki, *Outlines of Mahayana Buddhism*, p. 12.

D.T. Suzuki: "that element in religion. . . ." Ibid., p. 23.

D.T. Suzuki: "This greater depth. . . ." Suzuki, "Early Memories." pp. 101–108.

D.T. Suzuki to Soyen Shaku: "Innen are indeed. . . ." Quoted in Bando, p. 145.

IV

Tolstoy to Carus: "I deeply regret. . . ." Undated letter, in Special Collections/ Morris Library.

Ananda Metteya to Carus: "Here I think you forget. . . ." Rangoon, Sept. 5, 1904. Original in Special Collections/Morris Library.

Carus to Metteya: "music could be used. . . ." November 15, 1905. Original in Special Collections/Morris Library.

Rt. Rev. Mazzinianande Swami: "Some probably have the idea. . . ." Sacramento, March 22, 1911. Original in Special Collections/Morris Library.

V

Reverend Honda: "When I discussed. . . ." Buddhist Churches of America, p. 46.

Formal Petition: "For those of us. . . ." Ibid.

Dr. Sonada and Rev. Nishijima: had come "to convert the Japanese and later Americans. . . ." San Francisco Chronicle, Sept. 13, 1899. Quoted by Buddhist Churches of America, p. 47.

Dr. Norman: "In spite of the unfavorable comments. . . ." Ibid., p. 83.

CHAPTER NINE

Sources

Edward Morse

Hickman, Money and Fetchko, Peter. Catalogue for *Japan Day by Day*, An Exhibition in Honor of Edward Sylvestor Morse. Peabody Museum of Salem, 1977. Morse's diary impression, p. 14.

Wayman, Dorothy. *Edward Sylvestor Morse*. Cambridge: Harvard University Press, 1942.

Morse, Edward. *Japan Day by Day*. Boston: Houghton Mifflin, 1917.

Morse, Edward. *Japanese Homes and Their Surroundings*. New York: Dover, 1961.

Ernest Fenollosa

Brooks, Van Wyck. *Fenollosa and His Circle*. New York: E.P. Dutton, 1962.

Chisolm, Lawrence W. *Fenollosa: The Far East and American Culture*. New Haven: Yale University Press, 1963.

Fenollosa, Ernest. *Epochs of Chinese and Japanese Art*. Mary Fenollosa, editor. 2 vols. London: Heinemann, 1912. Revised edition, New York: Stokes, 1921.

Fenollosa, Ernest. *My position in America*. Fenollosa papers, Houghton Library, Harvard University. Dated May 1, 1891.

Fenollosa, Ernest. Pencil notes on Buddhism. Houghton Library, Harvard University.

Fenollosa, Ernest. *Ernest Fenollosa's "Ode on Re-incarnation*." Akiko Murakata, editor. Harvard Library Bulletin, Vol. XXI, No. 1 (January 1973).

Fenollosa, Ernest. *East and West, The Discovery of America and Other Poems*. New York: Crowell, 1893.

Sansom, G.B. *The Western World World and Japan. A Study in the Interaction of European and Asiatic Cultures*. New York: Vintage, 1973.

Whiting, Lilian. "Boston Days." Column in *The Times Democrat* (New Orleans).

Okakura Kakuzo

Horioka, Yasuko. *The Life of Kakuzo, Author of the Book of Tea*. Tokyo: The Hokuseido Press, 1963.

Kakuzo, Okakura. *The Book of Tea*. London & New York: G.P. Putnam's Sons, 1906.

Henry Adams

Adams, Henry. "Buddha and Brahma." (Poem) *The Yale Review*, N.S. Vol. V (October 1915). First written in 1895.

Adams, Henry. *The Education of Henry Adams*. Boston: The Massachusetts Historical Society, 1918.

Adams, Henry. *Letters of Henry Adams*. (1858–1891). Worthington Chauncey Ford, editor. Boston: Houghton Mifflin, 1930.

Adams, Henry. *Letters from Japan*. Donald Richie and Yoshimori Harashima, editors. Tokyo: Kenkyusha Pocket English Series, 1960.

Adams, Henry. *The Life of George Cabot Lodge*. Boston: Houghton Mifflin, 1911.

Adams, Henry. *Mont–Saint–Michel and Chartres*. Boston: Houghton Mifflin, 1933.

Samuels, Ernest. *Henry Adams: The Middle Years*. Cambridge: The Belknap Press of Harvard University Press, 1958.

Tharp, Louise Hall. *Saint–Gaudens and the Gilded Era*. New York: Little Brown & Co, 1969.

William Sturgis Bigelow

Bigelow, W.S. *Buddhism and Immortality. The Ingersoll Lecture 1908*. Boston: Houghton Mifflin, 1908.

Bigelow, W.S. "Certificate of Bodhisattvasila" for W.S. Bigelow (Gesshin) on August 14th, the 21st year of Meiji (1888) in the collection of the Massachusetts Historical Society, Cambridge, Mass.

Bigelow, W.S. *Fragmentary Notes on Buddhism*. Taken Jan. 30 and 31, 1922. Being Dr. Bigelow's answers to questions and also comments on Sakurai Ajari's lectures. Houghton Library, Harvard University.

Murakata, Akiko. *Selected Letters of Dr. William Sturgis Bigelow*. The George Washington University, Ph.D. dissertation, 1971. History, Modern. 71–27, 990.

Lafcadio Hearn

Hearn, Lafcadio. *The Buddhist Writings of Lafcadio Hearn*. Edited with an introduction by Kenneth Rexroth. Santa Barbara: Ross-Erikson Publishers, 1977.

Hearn, Lafcadio. *Gleanings in Budda–Fields. Studies of Hand and Soul in the Far East*. Boston: Houghton Mifflin, 1897.

Ezra Pound and Ernest Fenollosa

Eames, Elizabeth R. "Philip E.B. Jourdain and the Open Court Papers." *ICarbS*, Vol. II, No. 2., Fall, 1975. Southern Illinois University, Carbondale. p. 101.

Fenollosa, Ernest and Pound, Ezra. *The Chinese Written Character As A Medium for Poetry*. First ran in installments in *The Little Review*, September, 1919.

Fenollosa, Ernest and Pound, Ezra. *Certain Noble Plays of Japan*: from the manuscripts of Ernest Fenollosa, chosen and finished by Ezra Pound, with an introduction by William Butler Yeats. Churchtown, Dundrum: The Cuala Press, 1916.

Fenollosa, Ernest and Pound, Ezra. *Noh, or Accomplishment*. London: Macmillan, 1916.

Fletcher, John Gould. "The Orient and Contemporary Poetry." In *The Asian Legacy and American Life*, Arthur Christy, editor. New York: The John Day Co., 1942.

Kenner, Hugh. *The Pound Era*. Berkeley: University of California Press, 1971.

Pound, Ezra. *Cathay*. London: Elkin Matthews, 1915.

Yip, Wai–lim. *Ezra Pound's Cathay*. Princeton: The University of Princeton Press, 1969.

Notes

I

Morse: "Never will these first impressions. . . ." Quoted in Hickman and Fetchko, p. 14.

Inouye: "To Inouye the Hegelian dialectic. . . ." Sansom, p. 485.

Fenollosa: "Despite such superiority. . . ." Quoted in Chisolm, p. 4.

Fenollosa: "I shall never forget. . . ." Quoted in Brooks, pp. 18–19.

Fenollosa to Morse: Fenollosa came to consider his work. . . "just as important at bottom. . . ." Quoted in part in both Brooks and Chisolm, but the most complete text is in Wayman, pp. 289–91.

Morse and Okakura: "Many fine things of Japanese art. . . ." The anecdote was given to Wayman in 1939 by Atomi Gyukushi, then eighty–two, a former student of Fenollosa's.

II

Fenollosa: "In the small vehicle. . . ." Pencil notes on Buddhism, Fenollosa papers, Houghton Library, Harvard University.

III

Adams to Hay: "He got the better of us. .. ." Letter of June 11, 1886. Ford. *Letters of Henry Adams*, p. 366.

Adams: "I myself was a Buddhist. . . ." Quoted in Samuels, 300–301.

Adams: "One feels no impulse to exert. . . ." Ibid., 307.

St. Gaudens: "Adams. Buddha. . . ." Ibid., p. 335.

Adams: "His first step on returning. . . ." Adams, *Education of Henry Adams*, p. 329.

IV

Fenollosa: "Within the coming century. . . ." Fenollosa, *East and West*, p. vi.

Fenollosa: "I must take a broad view. . . ." Typescript, *My position in America*, Fenollosa papers, Houghton Library, Harvard University. Quoted in part in Murakata (1973), p. 52.

Dow: "the pupil learns to draw. . . ." Quoted in Chisolm, p. 184.

Barbara Rose: Fenollosa "was instrumental. . . ." Rose, "O' Keefe's Trail," *New York Review of Books*, March 31, 1977, pp. 30–31.

Lilian Whiting: "we are the heirs of all ages." "The American Buddhist A Figure of Today." in "Boston Days" Dec. 19, 1894.

Lilian Whiting: "Professor Rhys Davids . . . represented the exact opposite. . . ." in "Boston Days," Nov. 13, 1894.

Fenollosa: What Crawford called "Buddhism" was nothing more than "theosophy. . . ." F. to Isabella Gardner, ca. 1894, in Chisolm, p. 104.

Mary Fenollosa: "Life was carried on in a purely Japanese way. . . ." Intro. to *Epochs of Chinese and Japanese Art*.

Lafcadio Hearn: Buddhism, which he believed to "accord with scientific opinion. . . ." Kenneth Rexroth in *The Buddhist Writings of Lafcadio Hearn*, pp. xiii–xiv.

V

Theodore Roosevelt of Bigelow: "But Cabot. . . ." Quoted in Murakata (1971) p. 10.

Henry Adams: "Early in his college years. . . ." Adams, *The Life of George Cabot Lodge*, pp. 47–48.

VI

Fenollosa of *Epochs*: "that single personal life impression. . . ." Epochs, intro. p. xxvi.

Pound: "a treasury to which. . . ." in "The Renaissance," *Literary Essays of Ezra Pound*, edited with an introduction by T.S. Eliot. London: Faber and Faber, 1960, pp. 218, 214, 215.

Pound: "We have here not a bare philological discussion. . . ." Pound, Introduction to *The Chinese Written Character*, p. 3.

Fenollosa: China's history, "her fate and her curse. . . ." Fenollosa *Epochs*, pp. 118–119.

T.S. Eliot: "Translation is valuable by a double power. . . ." in "The Noh and The Image," *Egotist*, iv, August 7, 1907. Quoted, also as conclusion, in Wai–lim Yip, p. 165.

CHAPTER TEN

Sources

Soyen Shaku

Furuta, Shokin. "The Footsteps of A Modern Japanese Zen Master," in *The Modernization of Japan (A Special Edition of The Philosophical Studies of Japan)*, Vol.VIII, 1967.

Senzaki, Nyogen. *Like A Dream, Like A Fantasy: The Zen Writings and Translations of Nyogen Senzaki*. Edited and with an Introduction by Eido Shimano Roshi. Tokyo: Japan Publications, 1978.

Soyen Shaku. Letters and other papers in the Paul Carus Collection, Special Collections/Morris Library, Southern Illinois University at Carbondale.

Soyen Shaku. "Poems by the Late Right Reverend Soyen Shaku, Abbot of Engakuji. Translated by Seiren. *The Eastern Buddhist*, Vol. III (Oct.–Nov.–Dec. 1924), p. 273.

Soyen Shaku. *Sermons of A Buddhist Abott*. Translated and edited by D.T. Suzuki. LaSalle: Open Court, 1906.

Mrs. Alexander Russell

Robbins, Millie. "Mystery At the Seaside," and "A House of Mystery," in "Millie's Column," *San Francisco Chronicle*, May 24, 1963, and Nov. 6, 1968.

Nyogen Senzaki

Reps, Paul (in collaboration with Nyogen Senzaki). *Zen Flesh, Zen Bones. A Collection of Zen and Pre–Zen Writings*. New York: Anchor Books, 1961.

Senzaki, Nyogen (with Ruth McCandless). *Buddhism and Zen*. New York: Philosophical Library 1953.

Senzaki, Nyogen (with Paul Reps). *The Gateless Gate*. Translated from the Chinese. Los Angeles: John Murray, 1934.

Senzaki, Nyogen. *Like A Dream, Like A Fantasy*. (*See above*.)

Senzaki, Nyogen; Soen, Nakagawa; Tai Shimano, Eido. *Namu Dai Bosa: A Transmission of Zen Buddhism to America*. Edited and with an Introduction by Louis Nordstrom. New York: Theatre Arts Books, 1976.

Senzaki, Nyogen. Papers. Catalogued at The Zen Studies Society, New York City, and an uncatalogued collection, mostly duplicates, at the Oriental Library, University of California at Berkeley.

Senzaki, Nyogen. *Sufism and Zen*. Tucson: Ikhwan Press, 1972.

Senzaki, Nyogen and McCandless, Ruth. *The Iron Flute*. Tokyo: Tuttle, 1961.

Senzaki, Nyogen. *Zen Meditation*. Kyoto: Bukkasha, 1936.

Sokatsu Shaku

Sokei-an, "Our Lineage," in *Cat's Yawn*, The Thirteen Numbers Published from 1940 to 1941 by The Buddhist Society of America, now the First Zen Institute of America, Reproduced in Facsimile. New York: The First Zen Institute of America, 1947.

Sokei-an Sasaki

Farkas, Mary. "Sokei-an, 1882–1945," in *Zen Notes*, Vol. V, No. 5 (May 1958).

Huxley, Aldous. "Notes on Zen," in *Vedanta For Modern Man*, Christopher Isherwood, editor. New York: Harper & Brothors, 1945.

Sokei-Ann [sic] Sasaki. *Ananda and Maha-Kasyapa. From the Chinese Version of the Sutras of Buddhism*. Sokei-Ann Sasaki, trans. New York: C.M. Neumann, 1931.

Sokei-an. "The Autobiography: Keynote I," in *Zen Notes*, Vol. XX (Nov.-Dec. 1973).

Sokei-an. "Our Lineage," in *Cat's Yawn*. (*See above*.)

Sokei-an Sasaki and Bodenheim, Maxwell. Translations from the Chinese of Li Po, "I Go to Visit a Semi-God," in *The Little Review*, Vol. IV, No. 7.

Utsubo, Kubotu. "The Man Called Sasaki Shigetsu," in *Tanka Kenkyu*, June-July-August, 1958.

Dwight Goddard

Goddard, Dwight. *A Buddhist Bible*. First edition. Thetford, Vermont, 1932.

Goddard, Dwight. *The Buddha's Golden Path. A Manual of practical Dhyana Buddism*. Santa Barbara, 1931.

Goddard, Dwight and Wai-Tao, Bhikshu. *The Diamond Sutra, A New Translation From the Chinese Text of Kumarajiva*. Santa Barbara, 1935.

Goddard, Dwight. *Fellowship Following Buddha*. Series of 1939. Quarterly. No. 2. Woman in Buddhism. Thetford, Vermont.

Goddard Dwight. *Followers of Buddha. The ideal and rules of an American Buddhist Brotherhood*. Santa Barbara, 1934.

Goddard, Dwight. *The Principles and Practice of Mahayana Buddhism. An Interpretation of Professor Suzuki's Translation of Ashvagosha's Awakening of Faith.* Thetford, Vermont, 1933.

Goddard, Dwight. *Self-Realization of Nobel Wisdom. A Buddhist Scripture Based upon Professor Suzuki's translation of the Lankavatara Sutra.* Edited, Interpreted, and Published by Dwight Goddard. Thetford, Vermont, 1932.

Goddard, Dwight. *The Seventh and Eighth Stages of Buddha's Noble Path with the First Annual Report of the Followers of Buddha, An American Brotherhood.* Santa Barbara, 1935.

Goddard Dwight. *A Simple Method for Practicing the Seventh Stage of the Noble Path.* Thetford, Vermont, 1937.

Goddard, Dwight. *A Vision of Christian and Buddhist Fellowship In the Search for Light and Truth.* Los Gatos, 1924.

Goddard, Dwight, editor. *Zen, A Buddhist Magazine.* Thetford, Vermont, 1931–32.

Starry, David. "Dwight Goddard—The Yankee Buddhist," in *Zen Notes*, Vol. XXVII, No. 7 (July 1980).

Alan Watts

Watts, Alan. *In My Own Way: An Autobiography.* New York: Pantheon, 1972.

Watts, Alan. *The Spirit of Zen.* London: Murray, 1946.

Notes

I

Soyen Shaku: *Enroute to America.* Senzaki papers, University of California at Berkeley.

Mrs. Russell: "It is our desire. . . ." Millie Robbins, Millie's Column, "Mystery at the Seaside," *San Francisco Chronicle*, May 24, 1963, p. 20.

Soyen Shaku: "The daily life of the family. . . ." Quoted in Furuta, p. 81.

Soyen Shaku: "The Fifth Patriarch told a new monk. . . ." "To Mrs. Alexander Russell, the First American Zen Student," in Senzaki, *Like A Dream, Like A Fantasy*, pp. 109–110.

II

Senzaki's first impression of Soyen: "That strange monk. . . ." Nyogen Senzaki, "Commemoration of So-yen Shaku, 1954," Senzaki papers.

Soyen Shaku: "Monk Nyogen tries to live. . . ." Introduction to *A Grass in the Field*, 1901, Quoted in *Zen Notes*, Vol. XX1, No. 5 (May 1974).

Soyen to Senzaki: "This may be better for you than being pampered. . . ." Senzaki, "Commemoration of So-yen Shaku, 1954," Senzaki papers.

Soyen Shaku: "No dust clings. . . ." and following poems. Senzaki papers.

Dr. Barrows: "the goal which made. . . ." Soyen Shaku, "Reply to A Christian Critic." (Letter Written in 1896 to Dr. John H. Barrows). *Sermons Of A Buddhist Abbot*, pp. 121–122.

Soyen Shaku: the practice of *dhyana*. . .was not "trance or self hypnotism. . . ." "Practice of Dhyana," Ibid., p. 156.

III

Soyen to Sokatsu Shaku: "Normally monks live. . . ." *Zen Notes*, Vol. XVIII, No. 12 (Dec. 1971).

Soyen to Sokatsu: "You have acquired. . . ." Sokei-an, "Our Lineage," *Cat's Yawn*, p. 16.

Sokei-an: "Carve me a Buddha. . . ." *Zen Notes*, Vol. XV, No. 6 (June 1968).

Sokei-an: "And so in September. . . ." Sokei-an, *Cat's Yawn*, p. 19.

Ruth Fuller Sasaki: "While his interest in Zen. . . ." *Wind Bell*, Publication of Zen Center (San Francisco), Vol. VIII, Nos. 1–2 (Fall 1969), p. 13.

Sokatsu to Sokei-an: "Your message. . . ." *Cat's Yawn*, p. 23.

V

Sokei-an: "I had a home and a chair. . . ." *Wind Bell*, op. cit., p. 15.

Sokei-an: "holding a lotus. . . ." Ibid., p. 19.

VI

Senzaki: "A Buddhist monk. . . ." in "What Does A Buddhist Monk Want," letter from Heart Mountain, Wyoming, Oct. 15, 1942. Senzaki papers.

Senzaki: "I do not know. . . ." Article in *Kyo-Gaku News*, Tokyo, four installments beginning August 4, 1934. *Zen Notes*, Vol. XXI, No. 2 (Feb. 1974).

VII

Sokei-an and Senzaki: "In this pair. . . ." *Zen Notes*, Vol. XXIII, No 5 (May 1975). "Mister Money Talks."

VIII

Dwight Goddard: "Their method was. . . ." *Followers of Buddha*, p. v.

Huston Smith: "No other collection. . . ." Preface to *Buddhist Bible*, p. vii (20th Edition) Boston: Beacon Press, 1970.

IX

Alan Watts: found Suzuki to be "about the most gentle. . . ." Watts, *In My Own Way*, p. 78.

Ruth Fuller Everett (Sasaki): Her purpose . . . "was simply to see. . . ." *Wind Bell*, Vol. VIII, Nos. 1–2 (Fall 1969), p. 21.

Sokei-an: "Well, at least I have a roof. . . ." Ibid., p. 18.

Ruth Fuller Sasaki: "Sokei-an was a most remarkable teacher. . . ." Ibid.

Mary Farkas: "When I was, in recent years, asked. . . ." *Zen Notes*, Vol. XIII, No. 6 (June 1966).

Watts: Sokei-an "never fidgeted. . . ." Watts, p. 145.

Watts: the Amitabha of the Shin "need not be considered. . . ." Ibid., p. 153.

Watts: "growing realization that Christianity. . . ." Ibid., p. 156.

X

Sokei-an: "It is an unhappy death. . . ." *Wind Bell*, op. cit., p. 17.

XI

Senzaki: "A government must practice. . . ." September 5, 1942. Quoted in Senzaki, et al., *Namu Dai Bosa*, p. 14.

Senzaki: "For forty years I have not seen. . . ." Quoted in *Like A Dream, Like A Fantasy*, p. 41.

CHAPTER ELEVEN

Sources

D.T. Suzuki

D.T. Suzuki Memorial Issue, *The Eastern Buddhist*, N.S., Vol. II, No. 1 (Aug. 1967).

Briggs, William. *Anthology of Zen*. Introduction by William Barrett. New York: Grove Press, 1961.

Sargent, Winthrop. "Profile: Great Simplicity; Dr. Daisetz Teitaro Suzuki." *The New Yorker*, Aug. 31, 1957.

Suzuki, D.T. *An Introduction to Zen Buddhism*. New York: Grove Press, 1964.

Suzuki, D.T. *Essays in Zen Buddhism*. First Series. New York: Grove Press, 1961.

Suzuki, D.T. *Essays in Zen Buddhism*. Second Series. London: Rider & Co., 1958.

Suzuki, D.T. *Essentials of Zen Buddhism: An Anthology of the Writings of Daisetz T. Suzuki*. Edited and with an Introduction by Bernard Phillips. London: Rider & Co., 1962.

Suzuki, D.T. *Manual of Zen Buddhism*. New York: Grove Press, 1960.

Suzuki, D.T. *Mysticism, Christian and Buddhist*. New York: Harper & Row, 1957.

Suzuki, D.T. *Shin Buddhism*. New York: Harper & Row, 1970.

Suzuki, D.T. *Zen Buddhism: Selected Writings of D.T. Suzuki*. Edited by William Barrett. New York: Anchor Books, 1956.

Suzuki, D.T.; Fromm, Erich; DeMartino, Richard. *Zen Buddhism and Psychoanalysis*. New York: Harper & Row, 1960.

John Cage

Cage, John. "The Music of Contingency," an interview in *Zero, Contemporary Buddhist Life and Thought*. Eric Lerner, editor. Vol. III. Los Angeles.

Cage, John. *A Year From Monday. New Lectures and Writings*. Middletown, Conn.: Wesleyan University Press, 1963.

Kostelanitz, Richard. *John Cage, Documentary Monographs in Modern Art*. New York: Praeger, 1970.

Tomkins, Calvin. *The Bride and the Bachelors. Five Masters of the Avant-Garde*. New York: The Viking Press, 1965.

Sogen Asahina

Asahina, Sogan. *Zen*. Translated by Carmen Blacker. The Kawata Press, 1976.

Farkas, Mary. "A Zen Master in Our Midst." *Zen Notes*, Vol. 1, No. 9 (Sept. 1954).

Nyogen Senzaki and Soen Nakagawa
(*See* Chapter Ten).

R.H. Blyth

Aitken, Robert. "Willy-Nilly Zen," typescript. Also personal interview, Maui, Hawaii, Dec. 1978.

Blyth, R.H. *Zen in English Literature and Oriental Classics*. Tokyo: Hokuseido Press, 1942.

"R.H. Blyth." *The Eastern Buddhist*, Vol. 1, No. 1 (Sept. 1965).

Cambridge Buddhist Association

Fujimoto, Rindo. *The Way of Zazen*, with an introduction by Elsie Mitchell. Cambridge, Mass.: Cambridge Buddhist Association, 1969.

Mitchell, Elsie. *Sun Buddha, Moon Buddha, A Zen Quest*. New York-Tokyo: Weatherhill, 1973.

Ruth Fuller Sasaki

Fowler, George B. "September Meeting with Mrs. Sasaki," in *Zen Notes*, Vol. XV, No. 10 (Oct. 1968).

Miura, Isshu and Ruth Fuller Sasaki. *The Zen Koan, Its History and Use in Rinzai Zen*. New York: Harcourt, Brace & World, 1965.

Sasaki, Ruth Fuller. *The First Zen Institute of America in Japan*. Kyoto, 1959.

Sasaki, Ruth Fuller. *Rinzai Zen Study For Foreigners in Japan*. Kyoto: The First Zen Institute of America in Japan, 1960.

Sasaki, Ruth Fuller. *Zen, A Method For Religious Awakening*. Kyoto: The First Zen Institute of America in Japan, 1959.

Sasaki, Ruth Fuller. *Zen, A Religion*. Kyoto: The First Zen Institute of America in Japan, 1958.

Sasaki, Ruth Fuller and Miura, Ishhu. *Zen Dust*. New York: Harcourt, Brace and World, 1966.

Sasaki, Ruth Fuller. Writing on her investiture. *Zen Notes*, Vol. V, No. 7.

Allen Ginsberg

Ginsberg, Allen. *Allen Verbatin; Lectures on Poetry, Politics, Consciousness*. Gordan Ball, editor. New York: McGraw-Hill, 1974.

Ginsberg, Allen. *As Ever, The Collected Correspondence of Allen Ginsberg and Neal Cassady*. Berkeley: Creative Arts Book Co., 1977.

Ginsberg, Allen. *Empty Mirror: Early Poems*. New York: Totem/Corinth, 1961.

Ginsberg, Allen. *Howl, and Other Poems*. San Francisco: City Lights Books, 1959.

Ginsberg, Allen. *Journals, Early Fifties, Early Sixites*. Gordan Ball, editor. New York: Grove Press, 1977.

Tytell, John. *Naked Angels. The Lives and Literature of the Beat Generation*. New York: McGraw-Hill, 1977.

Jack Kerouac

Aronowitz, Alfred. "The Beat Generation," Article X, *New York Post*, March 19, 1959.

Charters, Ann. *Kerouac, A Biography*. San Francisco: Straight Arrow Books, 1973.

Gifford, Barry and Lee, Lawrence. *Jack's Book, An Oral Biography of Jack Kerouac*. New York: St. Martins Press, 1978.

Kerouac, Jack. *Big Sur*. New York: Farrar, Strauss, and Cudhay, 1962.

Kerouac, Jack. *Desolation Angels, A Novel*. New York: Coward-McCann, 1965.

Kerouac, Jack. *The Dharma Bums*. New York: Viking Press, 1959. (*See* Signet paperback for citations.)

Kerouac, Jack. *Mexico City Blues*. New York: Grove Press, 1959.

Kerouac, Jack. *On the Road*. New York: Viking Press, 1959.

Kerouac, Jack. "Paris Review Interview," in *Writers at Work, The Paris Review Interviews*. Fourth Series. George Plimpton, editor. New York: Viking Press, 1974.

Kerouac, Jack. *The Scripture of the Golden Eternity*. New York: Corinth Books, 1971.

Montgomery, John. *Kerouac West Coast, A Bohemian Pilot; Detailed Navigational Instructions*. Palo Alto: Fels & Firn Press, 1976.

Whalen, Philip. "Remembering Jack Kerouac," in *Off the Wall, Interviews with Philip Whalen*. Writing 37. Bolinas: Four Seasons Foundation, 1972.

Snyder, Gary

Snyder, Gary. *Cold Mountain Poems*. First printed in *Evergreen Review*, No. 6, 1958. *Riprap and Cold Mountain Poems*. San Francisco: Four Seasons Foundation, 1976.

Snyder, Gary. *Earth House Hold. Technical Notes & Queries to Fellow Dharma Revolutionaries*. New York: New Directions, 1957.

Snyder, Gary. *Myths and Texts*. New York: The Totem Press, 1960.

Snyder, Gary. *The Real Work: Interviews and Talks 1964–1979*. W.S. McLean, editor. New York: New Directions, 1980.

Lew Welch

Kerouac, Jack; Saijo, Albert; Welch, Lew. *Trip Trap; Haiku Along the Road from San Francisco to New York 1959*. Bolinas: Grey Fox Press, 1973.

Saroyan, Aram. *Genesis Angels, the Saga of Lew Welch and the Beat Generation*. New York: William Morrow & Co., 1979.

Welch, Lew. *I Remain: The Letters of Lew Welch and The Correspondence of His Friends*. Vol. One: 1949–1960; Vol. Two: 1960–1971 Don Allen, editor. Bolinas: Grey Fox Press, 1980.

Alan Watts

Mahoney, Stephen. "The Prevalence of Zen," in *The Nation*, Oct. 1958.

Watts, Alan, "Beat Zen, Square Zen, and Zen," in "Zen Issue" of *Chicago Review*, Vol. 12, No. 2 (Summer 1958). Irving Rosenthal, editor.

Watts, Alan. *Beat Zen, Square Zen, and Zen*. Revised edition. San Francisco: City Lights Books, 1959.

Watts, Alan. *In My Own Way: An Autobiography*. New York: Pantheon, 1972.

Watts, Alan. *The Way of Liberation in Zen Buddhism*. San Francisco: American Academy of Asian Studies, 1955.

Notes

I

Richard DeMartino: remembers Suzuki "sitting on his knees. . . ." DeMartino, "On My First Coming to Meet Dr. D.T. Suzuki," *The Eastern Buddhist*, New Series, Vol. II, No. 1 (Aug. 1967), p. 72.

John Cage: "confused both in my personal life. . . ." Cage, "The Music of Contingency," an interview in *Zero*, Vol. III, pp. 69–70.

D.T. Suzuki: "Kegon is believed. . . ." A.W. Sadler, "In Remembrance of D.T. Suzuki" in *The Eastern Buddhist*, Vol. II, No. 1 (Aug. 1967), p. 198.

II

Asahina Sogen: "A symbol of freedom. . . ." "A Zen Master in Our Midst," *Zen Notes*, Vol. 1, No. 9 (Sept. 1954).

Mary Farkas: "Don't you think we have made. . . ." *Zen Notes*, Vol. X, No. 10 (Oct. 1963).

III

Soen Nakagawa: Soen Nakagawa's First Talk in America. Senzaki, et al., *Namu Dai Bosa*, pp. 127–129.

Robert Aitken: "The world seemed transparent. . . ." Robert Aitken, "Willy-Nilly Zen," in MS and personal interview, Maui, 1977.

Soen Nakagawa: The fact "that all the Sangha in America. . . ." "Letter from Soen on His Inauguration." Senzaki papers.

IV

Thomas Merton: "In meeting him one seemed to meet. . . ." Merton, "D.T. Suzuki: The Man and His Work," *The Eastern Buddhist*, op. cit., p. 4.

D.T. Suzuki: "As I conceive it. . . ." Barrett, p. xx.

Ruth Fuller Sasaki: "Zen had always been credited. . . ." Sasaki, *Rinzai Zen Study For Foreigners in Japan*, p. 2.

D.T. Suzuki: "Psychologists talk a great. . . ." in *Essentials of Zen Buddhism*," pp. 60–61.

Erich Fromm: "*a change of mood began to be apparent*. . . ." "Memories of Dr. Suzuki," *The Eastern Buddhist*, op. cit., p. 88.

V

Fujimoto-roshi: "Both original enlightenment and practice. . . ." Fujimoto, *The Way of Zazen*, p. 9.

Elsie Mitchell: "neither a technique to achieve something. . . ." Ibid., p. xi.

VI

Ruth Fuller Sasaki: "Zen study demands full time. . . ." *The First Zen Institute of America in Japan*, Kyoto, 1959, p. 16.

Ruth Fuller Sasaki: "To know the Zen of the past. . . ." Ibid., p. 6.

VII

Allen Ginsberg: "I had only the faintest idea. . . ." Letter of May 14, 1953. *As Ever*, p. 141.

Jack Kerouac: "I didn't know what to do. . . ." Alfred G. Aronowitz, "The Beat Generation," Article X, *New York Post*, March 19, 1959. p. 22.

Jack Kerouac: "Practicing meditation and realizing. . . ." To Allen Ginsberg, Feb. 10, 1955. Original in Ginsberg Archives/Columbia University Library.

VIII

Jack Kerouac: "giving out little wows and yesses of approval. . . ." *Dharma Bums*, p. 14.

Gary Snyder: "My shock of recognition. . . ." "The *East West* Interview" with Peter Barry Chowka, in *The Real Work*, pp. 93–94.

Gary Snyder: "The convergence that I really found. . . ." Ibid., p. 94.

Gary Snyder: "For those seeking jobs. . . ." Snyder, "Anyone With *Yama-Bushi* Tendencies," *Zen Notes*, Vol. 1, No. 11 (November 1954).

Jack Kerouac: "nothing in it but typical Japhy appurtenances. . . ." *Dharma Bums*, pp. 16–17.

Philip Whalen: "He was incapable of sitting for more. . . ." *Off the Wall*, p. 80.

Alan Watts: Ruth Fuller Sasaki "who entranced. . . ." *In My Own Way*, p. 275.

Jack Kerouac: "Gary Snyder said, 'All right, Kerouac. . . .' " Charters, p. 258.

Jack Kerouac: "Stare into the world before you. . . ." *Scripture of the Golden Eternity*, p. 26.

IX

Goto-roshi and Mrs. Sasaki: See "September Meeting with Mrs. Sasaki," by George B. Fowler, *Zen Notes*, Vol. XV, No. 10 (Oct. 1968).

X

Eido Shimano: remembers "this elderly man. . . ." and following quotes. Senzaki et al., *Namu Dai Bosa*, pp.173–178.

Senzaki: "I imagined that I was going. . . ." Senzaki, "My Last Words," *Like A Dream, Like A Fantasy*, pp. 71–73. Also, letter from Katherine Edson-Mersohon, Senzaki papers.

Lew Welch: "I agree with you about the importance. . . ." *I Remain, The Letters of Lew Welch*, Vol. I, p. 158. To Gary Snyder, April 13, 1959.

Albert Saijo: "The Buddha on the altar. . . ." "A Recollection," in *Trip Trap*, p. 8.

Alan Watts: "it had often been said. . . ." *In My Own Way*, p. 262.

Alan Watts: "the old Chinese masters steeped in Taoism," and following quotes. "Beat Zen, Square Zen, and Zen," pp. 3–11.

Gary Snyder and Oda Roshi: "an especially gentle and quiet man. . . ." *The Real Work*, pp. 97–98.

Jack Kerouac: "I see a vision of a great rucksack revolution. . . ." *The Dharma Bums*, p. 78.

Jack Kerouac: "I rang Mr. Suzuki's door. . . ." *Berkeley Bussei*, 1960. Roy Okamura, editor. Published by the Young Men's Buddhist Association of Berkeley. The meeting is also described in Aronowitz, "The Beat Generation," X, *New York Post*, March 19, 1959.

CHAPTER TWELVE

Sources

Shunryu Suzuki-roshi

Hiestand, Barbara, editor. *Haiku Zendo. Chronicles of Haiku Zendo*, including *Memories of Shunryu Suzuki Roshi*. Los Altos: Haiku Zendo Foundation, 1973.

Needleman, Jacob. "Zen Center," in *The New Religions*. New York: Doubleday, 1970.

Rowley, Peter. *New Gods in America*. New York: David McKay Co., 1971.

Suzuki, Shunryu. *Zen Mind, Beginner's Mind. Informal Talks on Zen meditation and practice*, Trudy Dixon, editor. New York: Weatherhill, 1970.

Wind Bell, San Francisco Zen Center. As cited, but particularly Vol. IX, 1972.

Hakuun Yasutani Roshi

Aitken, Robert. "Yasutani Hakuun Roshi 1885–1973," in *The Eastern Buddhist*, N.S., Vol. VII, No. 1 (May 1974).

Yamada, Koun. "The Stature of Yasutani Hakuun Roshi," in *The Eastern Buddhist*, N.S., Vol. VII, No. 2 (Oct. 1974).

"Yasutani Memorial Issue." *ZCLA* (Zen Center of Los Angeles) *Journal*. Vol. 3, Nos. 3 & 4 (Summer, Fall 1973). Edited by John Daishin Buksbazen.

Philip Kapleau

Kapleau, Philip. "Report From A Zen Monastery, All Is One, One Is None, None Is All." *New York Times Magazine*, March 6, 1966.

Kapleau, Philip. *The Three Pillars of Zen*. New York: Weatherhill, 1965.

Kapleau, Phillip. *Zen: Dawn In the West*. Garden City: Anchor Press, 1979.

Buddhism and The Counterculture

Aitken, Robert. "Discipleship," *Blind Donkey*, Vol. 3, No. 6 (Nov.–Dec. 1977).

"Drugs and Buddhism— A Symposium." (With D.T. Suzuki, Alan Watts, Ray Jordan, Robert Aitken and Richard Leavitt.) *The Eastern Buddhist*, Vol. IV, No. 2, N.S. (Oct.1971).

Graham, Don Aelred. *Conversations: Christian and Buddhist*. New York: Harcourt, Brace, Jovanovich, 1968.

Hanh, Thich Nhat. *The Miracle of Being Awake, a manual on meditation for activists*. Nyack, N.Y.: Fellowship Books, 1975.

Hanh, Thich Nhat. *Vietnam, Lotus in a Sea of Fire: The Buddhist Story*. New York: Hill and Wang, 1967.

Kramer, Jane. *Allen Ginsberg in America*. New York: Random House, 1968.

Leary, Timothy. *The Psychedelic Experience: A Manual Based on the Tibetan Book of the Dead.* Seacaucus, N.J.: Citadel Press, 1976.

Roszak, Theodore. *The Making of a Counter Culture*. Garden City: Anchor Books, 1973.

Snyder, Gary. "Passage to More Than India," in *Earth House Hold.*

Notes

I

Shunryu Suzuki. "Where there is practice. . . ." *Wind Bell*, Vol. VI, Nos. 2–4 (Fall 1967), p. 71, "Sesshin Lecture."

II

Alan Watts: "a circumscribed service center. . . ." *In My Own Way*, pp. 269–268.

A member of the First Zen Institute: "We have a new priest. . . ." *Zen Notes*, Vol. XIX, No. 1 (Jan. 1972). "Shunryu Suzuki Roshi," by Mary Farkas.

Shunryu Suzuki: "My first young person. . . ." Rowly, p. 201.

Shunryu Suzuki: Like most Japanese priests. . . . Biographical material adapted from *Wind Bell*, Volume IX (1972), pp. 7–8.

A student remembered: "Roshi laughed a lot. . . ." Barbara Kaiser, "Memories of Shunryu Suzuki Roshi," *Haiku Zendo*, p. 33.

Shunryu Suzuki: "When a fish swims. . . ." *Wind Bell*, Vol. V, No. 3 (Summer 1968), p. 8.

III

Shunryu Suzuki: "In the beginner's mind. . . ." *Zen Mind, Beginner's Mind*, p. 21.

Shunryu Suzuki: "You think two hundred and fifty precepts. . . ." *Wind Bell*, Vol. V, No. 3 (Summer 1966), p. 8.

Shunryu Suzuki: "He knew he was an obstinate fellow. . . ." *Zen Mind, Beginner's Mind*, p. 45.

Shunryu Suzuki: "Sometimes we bow to dogs. . . ." Ibid., p. 44.

IV

Robert Aitken: "that the Dharma could best. . . ." "Yasutani Hakuun Roshi, 1185-1973" *The Eastern Buddhist*, N.S., Vol. VII, No. 1 (May 1974), pp. 150-152.

Philip Kapleau: he "could often be seen. . . ." *The Three Pillars of Zen*, p. 26.

Yasutani-roshi: "To experience kensho. . . ." Senzaki et al., *Namu Dai Bosa*, p. 184.

Eido Shimano: "That five-day sesshin. . . ." Ibid.

Robert Aitken: "a foundation for, rather than just postponement. . . ." "Yasutani Hakuun Roshi 1185–1973," *The Eastern Buddhist*, N.S., Vol. VII, No. 1 (May 1974), pp. 150–152.

Yasutani-roshi: "It is clear from public records. . . ." Quoted in "The Stature of Yasutani Hakuun Roshi," by Koun Yamada, *The Eastern Buddhist*, N.S., Vol. VII, No. 2 (Oct. 1974), p. 116.

Philip Kapleau: "The fact that they. . . ." *Three Pillars of Zen*, p 25.

Yasutani-roshi: "I was altogether a blind fellow. . . ." Quoted in "The Stature of Yasutani Hakuun Roshi," p. 109.

Yasutani-roshi: "Rinzai and Soto have their respective. . . ." "Reflections on the Book of Equanimity," "Yasutani Roshi Memorial Issue," *ZCLA Journal*, Summer/Fall 1973, pp. 10–11.

Robert Aitken: "he mimed as clearly. . . ." "Yasutani Hakuin Roshi," *Diamond Sangha*, N.S., Vol. 1, No. 2, p. 6.

Tai-Shimano: "We removed our Japanese style. . . ." "White Cloud," by Shitsu Eido Roshi, *ZCLA Journal*, op. cit., p. 51.

Tai Shimano-sensei: "had been pondering a nineteenth century . . ." and the following adapted from "The Way to Dai Bosatsu," by Shimano Eido Roshi, *Namu Dai Bosa*, pp. 191–201.

V

Philip Kapleau: "Zen's not philosophy. . . ." *The Three Pillars of Zen*, p. 209.

Philip Kapleau: "threw (himself) into Mu. . . ." Ibid., p. 227.

Philip Kapleau: "Oh what a battle. . . ." In "What is the Sound of American Zen?" Rick Fields, *New Age*. Nov. 1976.

Yasutani-roshi: the *Heart Sutra* ". . . had evolved. . . ." Kapleau, *Zen Dawn in the West*, p. 269.

VI

Shinzen Young: "A perfect knowledge. . . ." in "Notes on the Translation," *Zero*, Vol. III, p. 17.

Sasaki-roshi: "It was the historical Buddha. . . ." in "On the Nature of Zero," Ibid., p. 11.

VII

Gary Snyder: "unabashedly religious. . . ." Aelred Graham, "LSD and All That," *Conversations: Christian and Buddhist*, p. 83.

Japhy Ryder to Kerouac: "You old son. . . ." in *A Bibliography of Works by Jack Kerouac 1939–1975* (Revised Edition). Compiled by Ann Charters. The Pheonix Bibliographies. New York: The Phoenix Bookshop, 1975, p. 25.

Gary Snyder: "Those who do not have. . . ." in "Passage to More than India," *Earth House Hold*, p. 109.

Yamada Koun: "This isn't form. . . ." Graham, p. 66.

Gary Snyder: "people who have started. . . ." Ibid., p. 62.

Suzuki-roshi: "that the LSD experience. . . ." Suzuki-roshi had added: "But [they] stop making progress after a year or two unless they get beyond the impression of their acid experience." (Baker-roshi, in conversation).

Mary Farkas: asked Suzuki-roshi about the "Zen-drug. . . ." *Zen Notes*, Vol. XIX, No. 1 (Jan. 1972).

D.T. Suzuki: LSD "has reached a point. . . ." in "Drugs and Buddhism—A Symposium." *The Eastern Buddhist*, Vol. IV, No. 2 (Oct. 1971), p. 129.

Ray Jordan: "LSD might be. . . ." in "Psychedelics and Zen: Some Reflections." Ibid., pp. 138, 140.

Alan Watts: much depended on "the mental state. . . ." in "Ordinary Mind is the Way," Ibid., pp. 134–136.

Robert Aitken: "the yogic end of the counterculture. . . ." in "LSD and the New American Zen Student." Ibid., pp. 141–143.

VIII

Robert Aitken: "Suppose the American. . . ." Ibid., p. 142.

Robert Aitken: "If my country calls. . . ." in "Discipleship," *Blind Donkey*, Vol. 3, No. 6 (Nov–Dec. 1977).

Secretary Lodge: "In that part of our family. . . ." Personal interview with Richard Gard, New York City, 1977.

Self-immolation: According to one authority, "it was practiced. . . ." Heinz Bechert and Vu Duy-Tu, "Buddhism in Vietnam," in *The Cultural, Political, and Religious Significance of Buddhism in the Modern World*, H. Dumoulin and J. Moraldo, editors. New York: Macmillan, 1976, p. 192.

Dr. Thien-an: "That was an emergency case. . . ." "An Interview with Thich Thien-an," in *Loka, A Journal From Naropa Institute*, R. Fields, editor. Garden City: Anchor Press/Doubleday, 1975, p. 136.

IX

One participant recalls: "Usually Roshi started off. . . ." Barbara Hiestand, "Chronicles of Haiku Zendo," in *Haiku Zendo*, pp. 11–12.

Shunryu Suzuki: "We pull the weed and bury the plant. . . ." Margo Locke, "Memories of Shunryu Suzuki Roshi," *Haiku Zendo*, p. 25.

Shunryu Suzuki: "Because of your complete practice. . . ." *Wind Bell*, Vol. IX, No. 1 (Winter 1970), p. 3.

X

Tassajara: Encouragement came from many quarters. Quotes from Aitken, Ross, Smith, et al., from "Zen In America, An Unconditioned Response to A Conditioned World." Zen Center Brochure.

Shunryu Suzuki: "the ultimate hair-style." Quoted in "The Way to the Gateless Gate," by Ernie Barry, *Berkeley Barb*, Sept. 29-Oct. 5, 1967.

Wind Bell: "many students left Tassajara feeling. . . ." "Zen Mountain Center Report," *Wind Bell*, Vol. VI, 2–4 (Fall 1967), p. 13.

Kobun Chino: instructed the students to ask "questions. . . ." and following quotes. Ibid., pp. 15–16.

D.T. Suzuki: "Thank you!" in "The Stone Bridge of Joshu," by Akishesa Kondo, *The Eastern Buddhist*, Vol. II, No. 1 (Aug. 1967). p. 36.

XI

Tatsugami-roshi: proposed that the students simply "put locks. . . ." "City Practice," *Wind Bell*, Vol. IX, Nos. 3–4 (Fall/Winter) 1970–71, p. 13.

Shunryu Suzuki: "To have a strong practice. . . ." Ibid., p. 14.

Shunryu Suzuki: not "to give some special idea. . . ." Ibid., p. 9.

Shunryu Suzuki: "I think this is a good example. . . ." Ibid., pp. 10–11.

Chogyam Trungpa: "All his gestures and communications. . . ." "Suzuki Roshi, A Recollection of Buddha, Dharma, and Sangha," in *Garuda*, Spring 1972, p. 45.

Shunryu Suzuki: His wife tried to slow him down, and following. Adapted from *Wind Bell*, Vol. XI (1972), pp. 33–34.

Richard Baker-roshi: "This piece of incense. . . ." Ibid., p. 16.

Wrote one observor: "Suzuki-roshi was helped to his feet. . . ." Denis Lahey in *Wind Bell*, op. cit., pp. 11–13.

CHAPTER THIRTEEN

Sources

Tibetan History

Norbu, Jigme and Turnbull, Colin. *Tibet, An account of the history, the religion and the people of Tibet*. New York: Simon and Schuster, 1968.

Stein, R.A. *Tibetan Civilization*. Stanford: Stanford University Press, 1972.

Snellgrove, David and Richardson, Hugh. *A Cultural History of Tibet*. Boulder: Prajna Press, 1980.

The Dalai Lama

Avedon, John F. *An Interview with the Dalai Lama*. New York: Littlebird Publications, 1979.

The Dalai Lama. *My Land and My People. Memoirs of the Dalai Lama of Tibet*. New York: McGraw-Hill, 1962. Potola Corp., 1977.

Other Refugees

Avedon, John F. "Tibet in Exile: Triumph of a People," in *Geo*, Vol. 3, May 1981.

Desjardins, Arnoud. *The Message of the Tibetans*. London: Stuart & Watkins, 1969.

Chogyam Trungpa

George, James. "Searching for Shambhala," in *Search, Journey on the Inner Path*. Edited by Jean Sulzberger. San Francisco: Harper & Row, 1979.

Trungpa, Chogyam. *Born in Tibet*, as told to Esme Cramer Roberts. Third edition. Boulder: Shambhala, 1977. Prajna Press, 1981.

The Karmapa

Douglas, Nik and White, Meryl. *Karmapa: The Black Hat Lama of Tibet*. London: Luzac & Co., 1976.

Thinley, Karma. *The History of the Sixteen Karmapas of Tibet*. Boulder: Prajna Press, 1980.

Tibetan and Western Scholars

Bharati, Agehananda. *The Tantric Tradition*. Garden City: Anchor/Doubleday, 1970.

Conze, Edward. *Buddhist Studies 1934–1972. Thirty Years Of Buddhist Studies, Further Buddhist Studies*. San Francisco: The Wheelwright Press.

Conze, Edward. *The Memoirs of A Modern Gnostic*, Part I, II. Sherbourne: The Samizdat Publishing Co., 1979.

De Koros, Csoma. *The Life and Teaching of Buddha*. With a biographical memoir by W.W. Hunter. Calcutta: Susil Gupta, 1957.

Dudjom Rinpoche, H.H. Explanation and oral commentary to *The Four-themed Precious Garland* by Long-Ch'en Rab-Jam-pa. (With Beru Khyentze). Dharamsala: Library of Tibetan Works and Archives, 1979.

Evans-Wentz, W.Y. *The Tibetan Book of the Dead*. Psychological Commentary by Dr. C.G. Jung. Oxford: Oxford University Press, 1960.

Guenther, H.V. *The Jewel Ornament of Liberation by sGam.po.pa*. Berkeley: Shambhala, 1971. Prajna Press, 1981.

Lhalungpa, Lobsang. "Taming the Wild Horse": An Interview in *Parabola*, Vol. III, No. 4.

Nyima, Thupten Ngawang. *A Short Account of the Sakyapa Order of Tibetan Buddhism*. Ipoch, Malaysia, 1977.

Snellgrove, D.L. *The Hevajra Tantra, A Critical Study*. London: Oxford University Press, 1959.

Strickmann, Michael. "A Survey of Tibetan Buddhist Studies," in *The Eastern Buddhist*, N.S., Vol. X, No. 1 (May 1977).

Thurman, Robert. "Shambhala and the American Revolution," in *East West Journal*, March 1977.

Wangyal, Geshe. *The Door of Liberation*. New York: Maurice Girodias, 1973.

Pilgrims

Ginsberg, Allen. *Indian Journals*. San Francisco: Dave Haselwood/City Lights, 1970.

Kyger, Joanne. *Indian-Japan Journals*. Bolinas: Tombouctou 1981.

Snyder, Gary. "Now, India," in *Caterpiller 19*, Oct. 1972. Clayton Eshelman, editor.

Thomas Merton

Merton, Thomas. *The Asian Journals of Thomas Merton*. New York: New Directions, 1973.

Merton, Thomas. *Mystics and Zen Masters*. New York: Farrar, Straus, and Giroux. 1967.

Merton, Thomas. *The Way of Chuang Tzu*. New York: New Directions, 1969.

Merton, Thomas. *Zen and the Birds of Appetite*. Philadelphia: New Directions, 1968.

Woodcock, George. *Thomas Merton, Monk and Poet; A Critical Study*. New York: Farrar, Straus and Giroux, 1978.

Notes

I

The Dalai Lama: "Being a refugee is. . . ." Avedon, p. 22.

II

The Dalai Lama: "From a deep point of view. . . ." Ibid., pp. 24–25.

Jane Werner: "There were endless questions. . . ." Personal interview, New York City, 1977.

Chogyam Trungpa: found England "very strange. . . ." *Born in Tibet*, p. 252.

Chogyam Trungpa: both involved "a very precise discipline. . . ." In *An Interview with Chogyam Trungpa, Rinpoche* by Pat Patterson. Los Angeles Institute of Contemporary Art, 1980.

Chogyam Trungpa: "a general sense of inquisitiveness. . . ." Personal interview, Los Angeles, Dec. 1980.

Chogyam Trungpa: Jamgon Kongtrul of Sechen, "a big, jolly. . . ." *Born in Tibet*, p. 51.

Chogyam Trungpa: "a forward step. Nevertheless. . . ." Ibid., pp. 252–253.

III

Csoma de Koros: "The basis of all Tibetan religion. . . ." Quoted in Hunter, p. 9.

Csoma de Koros: "The Literature of Tibet," in *The Life and Teachings of Buddha*, p. 137.

Japanese Buddhists: "pronounced him the first Western Bodhisattva. . . ." William Peiris, *The Western Contribution to Buddhism*, Delhi: Motilal Banarsidass, 1973, p. xxii.

J.B. Pratt: "I have said nothing whatever. . . ." *The Pilgrimage of Buddhism*, p. viii.

Evans-Wentz: "wandering from the palm-wreathed. . . ." *The Tibetan Book of the Dead*, pp. xix-xx.

C.C. Jung: "For years, ever since. . . ." Ibid., xxxvi.

Evans-Wentz: not "in disagreement with. . . ." Ibid., p. 6.

Edward Conze: "must remain relatively barren. . . ." *Thirty Years of Buddhist Studies*, pp. 23–24.

Geshe Wangyal: "I don't know about all that. . . ." and following quotes. Robert Thurman, personal interview, New York City, 1977.

One student recalls: "When you had understood. . . ." Brian Cutillo, personal interview, Los Angeles, 1980.

IV

Gary Snyder: "Allen & Peter asked him. . . ." "*Now, India*," in *Caterpiller, 19*, Oct. 1972, p. 81. See also the account of the same meeting in Joanne Kyger, *India-Japan Journals*.

Dudjom Rinpoche: "If you see anything horrible. . . ." Allen Ginsberg, *India Journals*, p. 4.

Thomas Merton: "If the West continues. . . ." *Mystics and Zen Masters*, quoted in Woodcock, p. 155.

Thomas Merton: He went "as a pilgrim. . . ." *Asian Journals*, p. 312. Met Trungpa, p. 30. With Dalai Lama, pp. 100–102, 112–113, 124–125, referred to at Bangkok, 337–336. With Sonam Kazi, p 82. With Chatral Rinpoche, p. 143. At Polonnaruwa, pp. 233–236. "Marxism and Monastic Perspectives," pp. 239, 340, 343.

The Trappist delegates: "In death Father Louis. . . ." "Letter to Abbot Flavian Burns," *Asian Journals*, p. 346.

Chogyam Trungpa: "For a few days nothing. . . ." *Born in Tibet*, p. 253.

James George: "We had been asking. . . ." From the original MS. For the published version, see *Search*, p. 14.

Chogyam Trungpa: "I went through. . . ." and following. *Born In Tibet*, pp. 254–255.

CHAPTER FOURTEEN

Sources

Tarthang Tulku

Anderson, Walt. *Open Secrets. A Western Guide to Tibetan Buddhism*. New York: The Viking Press, 1979.

Annals of the Nyingma Lineage in America: Volume II, 1975–1977. Published June 1, 1977 as a private document.

Needleman, Jacob. "Tibet in America," in *The New Religions*. Garden City: Doubleday, 1970.

Tarthang Tulku, editor. *Crystal Mirror*, Vols. I-V. Emeryville: Dharma Publishing, 1971–1977.

Tarthang Tulku. *Openness Mind*. Emeryville: Dharma Publishing, 1978.

Tarthang Tulku. *Gesture of Balance*. Emeryville: Dharma Publishing.

Tarthang Tulku. *Reflections of Mind. Western Psychology Meets Tibetan Buddhism*. Emeryville: Dharma Publishing, 1975.

Tarthang Tulku. *Skillful Means*. Emeryville: Dharma Publishing, 1978.

Chogyam Trungpa

Bancroft, Anne. "The Middle Way of Buddhism," in *Twentieth Century Mystics and Sages*. Chicago: Henry Regency, 1976.

Fields, Rick. "How the Swans Came to the Lake. Chogyam Trungpa and His Holiness the Gyalwa Karmapa," in *New Age*, March 1977.

Fields, Rick, editor. *Loka, A Journal From Naropa Institute*. Garden City: Anchor/Doubleday, 1975. *Loka II*, 1976.

Greenfield, Robert. *The Spiritual Supermarket, An Account of Gurus Gone Public in America*. New York: Saturday Review Press/E.P. Dutton, 1975.

Trungpa, Chogyam. *Born in Tibet*, as told to Esme Cramer Roberts. Boulder: Shambhala, 1977. Especially the Epilogue, "Planting the Dharma in the West."

Trungpa, Chogyam. *Cutting Through Spiritual Materialism*. Berkeley: Shambhala, 1973.

Trungpa, Chogyam. *Glimpses of Abhidharma.* Boulder: Prajna Press, 1978.

Trungpa, Chogyam. *Meditation in Action.* Berkeley: Shambhala, 1969.

Trungpa, Chogyam. *The Myth of Freedom and the Way of Meditation.* Boulder: Shambhala, 1976.

Trungpa, Chogyam. "Things Get Very Close When You're Cornered," interview in *The Laughing Man*, No. 2.

Trungpa, Chogyam and Guenther, Herbert. *The Dawn of Tantra.* Boulder: Shambhala, 1975.

The Vajradhatu Sun. (A bimonthly newspaper). Boulder: Vajradhatu Publications.

The Theravadins

Goldstein, Joseph. *The Experience of Insight: A Natural Unfolding.* Santa Cruz: Unity Press, 1976.

Kornfield, Jack. *Living Buddhist Masters.* Santa Cruz: Unity Press, 1976.

Lerner, Eric. *Journey of Insight Meditation, A Personal Experience of the Buddha's Way.* New York: Schocken Books, 1977.

Levine, Stephen. *A Gradual Awakening.* Garden City: Anchor Books, 1979.

Mahasi Sayadaw. *Mahasi Abroad.* (Lectures by Mahasi Sayadaw on his World Missionary Tour 1979). Rangoon, Burma: Mahasi Sasana Yeiktha, 1979.

Mahasi Sayadaw. *Practical Insight Meditation.* San Francisco: Unity Press, 1972.

His Holiness Dudjom Rinpoche

Dudjom Rinpoche. *The Alchemy of Realization, an exposition of the essential teaching for making a meditation retreat according to the Dzogchen tradition*, translated and annotated by Vajranatha (John Reynolds). Kathmandu: Simhanada Publications, 1978.

Dudjom Rinpoche. "Padmasambhava, A Guru for Turbulant Times." Commentary and translation by Sogyal Rinpoche. An interview in *The Shambhala Review of Books and Ideas*, (Winter 1976).

His Holiness the Sixteenth Karmapa

Empowerment, The Visit of His Holiness the 16th Gyalwa Karmapa to the United States. Boulder: Vajradhatu Publications, 1976.

Palmo, Sister. "The Moment You See Him," interview in *The Laughing Man*, No. 2.

Zim, Joshua. "Dharma taking root in the (south) West," in *CoEvolution Quarterly*, Winter Solstice, 1974.

Notes

I

Tarthang Tulku: "Dear Joel, I don't know if. . . ." Quoted in Needleman, p. 172.

Tarthang Tulku: "Americans are only interested. . . ." *Crystal Mirror*, Vol. II (Summer 1972), p. 14.

One student: "Westerners may liken. . . ." Jane Wilhelms, "Bum Nga," *Annals of the Nyingma Lineage in America*, Vol. II, p. 55.

Tarthang Tulku: "Meditation is the essence. . . ." *Crystal Mirror*, Vol. I, p. 73.

Tarthang Tulku: the practice of his sadhana "especially important. . . ." *Crystal Mirror*, Vol. 1, p. 18.

Tarthang Tulku: "Like the characteristically open-minded. . . ." *Annals*, Vol. II, p. 7.

Padmasambhava: "When the iron bird flies, and horses run. . . ." As quoted in *Annals of the Nyingma Lineage in America*, Vol. I, p. 4.

The editors of *Crystal Mirror*: "In establishing the Vajrayana. . . ." *Crystal Mirror*, Vol. I, p. 59.

Tarthang Tulku: "Before I came here. . . ." *Crystal Mirror*, Vol. II, p. 15.

II

Chogyam Trungpa: found "an undisciplined atmosphere. . . ." *Born In Tibet*, p. 257.

Chogyam Trungpa: "deceiving ourselves into thinking. . . ." *Cutting Through Spiritual Materialism*, p. 3.

Chogyam Trungpa: "In order to follow. . . ." *Meditation In Action*.

Chogyam Trungpa: "Some scholars would say that. . . ." *Vajradhatu Seminary Transcripts, Hinayana and Mahayana*. Jackson Hole, Wyoming, 1973.

Chogyam Trungpa: "In order to launch Vajrayana in America. . . ." "Devotion," *Empowerment*, p. 60, and "I hope you'll be able to relate what you have studied. . . ." *Vajradhatu Seminary Transcripts, Vajrayana*. Jackson Hole, 1973, p. 1.

III

The Nyingma Institute: "the transmission of the psychological. . . ." *Annals*, Vol. II, p. 66.

Gay Gaer Luce: "This was not the smoothly staffed. . . ." "Western Psychology Meets Tibetan Buddhism." in *Reflections of Mind*, Tarthang Tulku, editor, pp. 20–21.

Tarthang Tulku: "What is thought? What is the difference. . . ." Ibid., p 21.

Tarthang Tulku: asked them "to sit in a chair. . . ." and following quotes. Ibid., pp. 28–33.

Dr. Luce: "These Tibetan exercises. . . ." Ibid., p. 25.

Tarthang Tulku: "The master, teacher, or therapist. . . ." *Crystal Mirror*, Vol. IV, p. 258.

Agehananda Bharati: "Psychology is bad enough. . . ." in "Guentheriana," *Kailash, A Journal of Himalyan Studies* (Kathmandu, Nepal), Vol. V, No. 2 (1977), p. 198.

Hugh Richardson: "as a true fortress of Tibetan Buddhism. . . ." Ibid., p. 186.

IV

Agehananda Bharati: "Lastly, where can tantra. . . ." In "The Future (if any) of Tantra," *Loka, A Journal From Naropa Institute*, p. 128.

Chogyam Trungpa: "There is a particular philosophy. . . ." In "Sparks," Ibid., p. 18.

V

Joseph Goldstein: "As the practice matures. . . ." and following quotes. Quoted in "The Return of the Elders," by Rick Fields, *New Age*, October 1977.

Mahasi Sayadaw: "It is very difficult to explain. . . ." During a retreat at Yucca Valley, California, May, 1978.

VI

Dudjom Rinpoche: "We could illustrate the different. . . ." Quoted in *The Vajradhatu Sun*. Vol. I, No. 1 (Aug. 1978).

Sogyal Rinpoche: "This particular era. . . ." In "Padmasambhava, A Guru for Turbulent Times, An Interview with His Holiness Dudjom Rinpoche," *Shambhala Review of Books and Ideas*, Vol. 5, Nos. 1 & 2 (Winter 1976), p. 14.

Dudjom Rinpoche: "The uniqueness of Guru Rinpoche's. . . ." Ibid.

VII

Sister Palmo: "It's really wonderful to have. . . ." In "The Moment You See Him, An Interview with the Karmapa's Disciple Sister Palmo," *Laughing Man*, No. 2, p. 51.

The Karmapa: had no message "for Americans. . . ." and following quotes. Quoted in "Black Hat Lama Performs Rite at Hub Arts Center," James Franklin, *The Boston Globe*, December 10, 1976, p. 3.

Chogyam Trungpa: "one of the most revealing. . . ." *Vajradhata Seminary Transcripts*, 1976.

Chogyam Trungpa: "which makes the student persist. . . ." In "Devotion," *Empowerment*.

Ken Green: "The teaching was definitely upgraded. . . ." Quoted in "How the Swans Came to the Lake," op.cit.

VIII

Sarah Harding: "At the beginning. . . ." and following quotes. Personal interview, Los Angeles, Feb. 1981.

IX

Chogyam Trungpa: "a colorful personality. . . ." *Born in Tibet*, p. 258.

Narayana: "During our visit last week. . . ." Quoted in "Ten Years in North America," supplement to *The Vajradhatu Sun*, Vol. II, No. 6 (Aug./Sept. 1980).

Swami Satchitananda: "You'll always be. . . ." and following quotes. "Interview with Ken Green," *The Vajradhatu Sun*, Dec./Jan. 1979.

Chogyam Trungpa: "He is arrogant and humble. . . ." and following quotes. *Born in Tibet*, p. 263.

Osel Tendzin: "It was basically my lack. . . ." Quoted in "Portrait of a Very Modern Buddhist," by Michael Grieg, San Francisco Chronicle, Apr. 8, 1978, p. 12.

Chogyam Trungpa: "I hand you my power. . . ." In "Ten Years in North America," supplement to *The Vajradhatu Sun*.

Sources

The Chinese

Blofeld, John. *Bodhisattva of Compassion. The Mystical Tradition of Kuan Yin*. Boulder: Shambhala, 1978.

Ch'en, Kenneth. *Buddhism In China, A Historical Survey*. Princeton: Princeton University Press, 1964.

Heng Ju, Bhikshu and Heng Yo, Bhikshu. *Three Steps, One Bow*. San Francisco: Ten Thousand Buddhas Press, The Buddhist Text Translation Society, 1977.

Hua, Dhyana Master. *Pure Land & Ch'an Dharma Talks*. Bhiksunis Heng Yin and Heng Ch'ih, trans. San Francisco: Sino-American Buddhist Association, 1974.

Hua, Hsuan. *Records of the Life of the Venerable Master Hsuan Hua*, Vol. I, Part 2. San Francisco: Committee for the Publication of the Venerable Master Hsuan Hua, 1973, 1975.

Kuo Tak. *The Remarkable Events of Dhyana Teacher To-Lun*, Reported by Kuo Tak; Hwa Kwo Che, trans. Published by Tam Kuo Ching.

Welch, Holmes. *The Practice of Chinese Buddhism 1900–1950*. Cambridge: Harvard University Press, 1967.

World Peace Gathering, A miscellany of articles and speeches occasioned by Bhikshu Heng Ju and Bhikshu Heng Yo on their pilgrimage for world peace. Commemorative Edition. San Francisco: Sino-American Buddhist Association, 1975.

The Koreans

Ku San. *Nine Mountains. Dharma Lectures of the Korean Meditation Master Ku San*. Republic of Korea: International Meditation Center, Song Kwang Sa Monastery, 1976.

Kyung-Bo Seo. *A Study of Korean Zen Buddhism Approached Through the Chodangjip*. Temple University, Ph.D. Thesis.

Seung Sahn. *Dropping Ashes on the Buddha. The Teaching of Zen Master Seung Sahn*. Compiled and edited by Stephen Mitchell. New York: Grove Press, 1976.

The Vietnamese

Hanh, Thich Nhat. *Zen Keys*. Garden City: Anchor/Doubleday, 1974.

Thien-an, Thich. *The Zen-Pure Land Union and Modern Vietnamese Buddhism*. Los Angeles: International Buddhist Meditation Center, 1971.

Notes

I

A stranger: "The only way to escape. . . ." *The Remarkable Events of Dhyana Teacher To-Lun*, Reported by Kou Tak, p. 2.

Master Hua: "The noble Yun saw me. . . ." *Records of the Life of Ch'an Master Hsuan Hua*, Part II, p. 31.

Master Hua: "This year the Dharma flower. . . ." *Records of the Life of the Venerable Master Hsuan Hua*, Vol. I, p. xiii.

One student: "like a fairy tale. . . ." Upasaka Kuo Hsien Farrelly in *Pure Land & Ch'an Dharma Talks* by Dhyana Master Hua, p. 22.

Master Hua: "The most important point of recitation. . . ." Ibid., p. 8.

Heng Ju: "there was something. . . ." *Three Steps, One Bow*, p. 5.

Heng Ju: "We were plagued with. . . ." *World Peace Gathering*, p. 63.

Heng Ju: "Bowing a thousand miles. . . ." *World Peace Gathering*, p. 54.

A three-by-five card: "Because people are constantly suffering. . . ." Upasaka Kuo Chou Rounds, *World Peace Gathering*, p. 23.

Master Hua: "Practicing what is difficult. . . ." *Three Steps, One Bow*, p. 22.

Heng Ju: "But just at that moment I looked over. . . ." Ibid., pp. 24–25.

Heng Ju: "Today you all have a chance. . . ." *World Peace Gathering*, p. p. 120.

II

Master Ko Bong: "A monk once asked Jo-ju. . . ." and following quotes. *Dropping Ashes On the Buddha*, pp. 229–231.

An early student: "I think that's why some Americans. . . ." Stephen Mitchell, personal interview, New York City, 1977.

Soen-sa-nim: "I ask you: what is love?" *Dropping Ashes On the Buddha*, p. 232.

Ku San Sunim: "Throughout the length and breadth. . . ." *Nine Mountains*, p. 210.

III

A group of American students: "In Vietnam there are many. . . ." "Biography of the Ven. Dr. Thich Thien-An," pamphlet, *In Memorium*, Los Angeles, 1980.

One student: "a Zen master without a bark." Shinzen Young, interview with Don Farber, Los Angeles, 1981.

One of his students: "I remember going into his room. . . ." and following quotes. Sister Karuna, personal interview with Don Farber, Los Angeles, 1981.

An American monk: "The significance of conducting. . . ." Thich An Tinh, "An Ocean Service for 'The Boat People'." *Lotus In the West*, Vol. 1, No. 7, p. 12.

CHAPTER SIXTEEN

Sources

The Pioneers Revisted and Zen

Aitken, Robert. *A Zen Wave. Basho's Haiku and Zen*. Forward by W.S. Merwin. New York-Tokyo: Weatherhill, 1978.

Baker, Richard. Talk in *The Art of Living in the Cultural Revolution*, Jacob Needleman, editor. San Francisco: Harper & Row, 1978.

Butler, Katy. "The Shadow Side of Buddhist America." *Common Boundary.* Vol. 8, Issue 3 (May-June 1990).

Collcut, Martin. "Epilogue: Problems of Authority in Western Zen." In *Zen Tradition and Transition: A Sourcebook by Contemporary Zen Master and Scholars*, edited by Kenneth Kraft. New York: Grove Press, 1988.

Dalai Lama. *Kindness, Clarity, and Insight.* Ithaca, N.Y.: Snow Lion, 1984.

Dalai Lama. *Ocean of Wisdom: Guidelines for Living.* San Francisco: Harper & Row, 1989.

Eppsteiner, Fred. *The Path of Compassion: Writings on Socially Engaged Buddhism.* Berkeley: Parallax Press, 1988.

Friedman, Lenore. *Meetings with Remarkable Women: Buddhist Teachers in America.* Boston: Shambhala Publications, 1987.

Ingram, Catherine. *In the Footsteps of Gandhi: Conversations with Spiritual Social Activists.* Berkeley: Parallax Press, 1990.

Kornfield, Jack. "Sex Lives of the Gurus" in *Yoga Journal*, July-August 1985, no. 63.

Kornfield, Jack. "Is Buddhism Changing in North America?" In *Buddhist America*, edited by Don Morreale. Santa Fe, N.M.: John Muir Publications, 1988.

Leviton, Richard. "Being Peace with Thich Nhat Hanh." *East West*, January 1990, pp. 57–80.

Mackenzie, Vickie. *The Boy Lama.* San Francisco: Harper & Row, 1988.

Rutter, Peter. *Sex in the Forbidden Zone.* Los Angeles: Jeremy P. Tarcher, 1989.

Thich Nhat Hanh, with Anne Simpkinson. "Seeding the Unconscious: New Views on Buddhism and Psychotherapy." *Common Boundary*, November-December 1989.

Tworkov, Helen. *Zen in America: Profiles of Five Zen Teachers*, San Francisco: North Point Press, 1989.

Notes

I

For the cremation and will of Chogyam Trungpa, Rinpoche, see *The Vajradhatu Sun*, June 1987.

II

For the San Francisco Zen Center, see *Wind Bell*, Vol. XVII, No. 2 (Winter 1983); and *CoEvolution Quarterly*, No. 40 (Winter 1983), "Events Are the Teacher," by Katy Butler, p. 112; Helen Tworkov's profile in *Zen in America*; and "A Zen-America Tale," an interview with Baker-roshi by Keith Thompson in *Esalen Catalog*, Spring 1985.

Norman Fischer: "Teacher-student relationships . . ." in "On Teachers and Students," by Norman Fischer, *Buddhist Peace Fellowship Newsletter*, Spring 1991, p. 21

III

For Maezumi Roshi, see *The Ten Directions*, Vol. VI, No. 1 (Spring 1985).

For Seung Sunim and the Insight Meditation Society, see "The Conspiracy of Silence," in Sandy Boucher's *Turning the Wheel.*

For Osel Tendzin, see *New York Times*, February 21, "Buddhists in U.S. Agonize on AIDS Issue," by Dyan Zaslowsky; *Los Angeles Times*, March 3, 1989, "Buddhist Sect Alarmed by Reports That Leader Kept AIDS a Secret," by John Dart; Katy Butler, "The Shadow Side of Buddhist America," in *Common Boundary* (May-June 1990), pp. 14–22; Stephen T. Butterfield, "When the Teacher Fails," *The Sun*, Issue 162; and *Sangha*, Vol. 1, No. 1 (1990), which includes Rick Field's, "The Most Interesting Question"; and Vol. 1, No. 3 (1990). For Osel Tendzin's death and cremation, see *The Vajradhatu Sun*, Vol. 13, No. 1, October/November 1990.

IV

Peter Rutter: "Sexual violation of trust . . ." in Rutter, *Sex in the Forbidden Zone*, p. 2.

The quote from the Buddha and Yvonne Rand's remark, from "Sex, Power, and Buddha Nature," in *Buddhist Peace Fellowship Newsletter*, Spring 1991, p. 15.

The reference to Zen sickness and the quote from Bodhidharma, "One who thinks only that everything is void but is ignorant of causation falls in everlasting pitch-black hell," is from "Zen Teachers and Sex: A Call for Enlightened Standards," by Bodhin Kjolhede, *Buddhist Peace Fellowship Newsletter*, Spring 1991, p. 19. A sample of responses may also be found in the same issue.

Thich Nhat Hanh's story: quoted by Katy Butler in "Vietnam Vet's Retreat," *Buddhist Peace Fellowship Newsletter*, Summer 1989, p. 28.

V

"A million people in America who call themselves Buddhists . . ." see *The National Survey of Religious Identification*, conducted by the City College of New York Graduate Center between 1989 and 1990.

Gary Snyder: "not as a 'Zen Center' . . ." in "Chan on Turtle Island," a conversation with Gary Snyder, *Inquiring Mind*, Vol. 4, No. 2 (Winter 1988), p. 4.

"A recent anthology . . ." is *Beneath a Single Moon: Buddhism in Contemporary American Poetry*, edited by Kent Johnson and Craig Paulenich. Boston: Shambhala Publications, 1991.

VI

Denison: "We are not women . . ." in Lenore Friedman, *Meetings With Remarkable Women*, p. 139.

Karuna Dharma: "I've had women try . . ." in Friedman, p. 207.

Sandy Boucher: "At first we communicated . . ." in Boucher, *Turning the Wheel*, pp. 385–386.

VII

Jack Kornfield: "It will take a great deal of courage . . ." in *Buddhist America*, edited by Don Morreale, p. xviii. "There were major areas . . ." in *Inquiring Mind*, Vol. 5, No. 1 (Summer 1988), p. 10.

VIII

Thich Nhat Hanh: "Many people have taken action . . ." in Ingram, *In the Footsteps of Gandhi*, p. 95. "A tiny bud of a smile . . ." in Richard Leviton, "Being Peace with Thich Nhat Hanh, *East West*, January 1990, pp. 58–59; "People might be used to distinguishing . . ." ibid., p. 80.

Bernard Tetsugen Glassman-sensei: "will pick up Western tendencies . . ." in "Livelihood," by Adam Gropnik, *Buddhist Peace Fellowship Newsletter*, Summer 1989, p. 19. (Reprinted from *The New Yorker*, May 22, 1989). See also "Greyston Family Inn," by Sandra Jishu Holmes, *Buddhist Peace Fellowship Newsletter*, Summer 1990, and "The Greyston Network: Serving the Homeless," by Mitchell Mitsujo Zucker, *The Ten Directions*, Vol. XI, No. 2 (Fall-Winter, 1990).

Issan Dorsey: "The doors of Hartford Street . . ." quoted by Tensho David Schneider in "Issan Dorsey Climbs the Mountain Seat," *The Vajradhatu Sun*, April-May 1990, p. 4.

IX

Thich Nhat Hanh: "If you breathe in and out . . . ," transcript from talk at Veteran's Retreat, Omega Institute, June 1991. "Buddhism and psychotherapy . . ." in "Seeding the Unconscious: New Views on Buddhism and Psychoterapy by Thich Nhat Hanh and Anne Simpkinson, *Common Boundary*, Vol. 7, Issue 6 (November-December 1989), p. 14. "The Buddhist attitude . . ." ibid., p. 19. "Buddhism in America . . ." in Ingram, *In the Footsteps of Gandhi*, p. 93.

X

"Dalai Lama Wins Nobel Peace Prize," by Sheila Rule, *New York Times*, October 6, 1989, p. A6.

Dalai Lama: "As a Buddhist monk . . . ," Dalai Lama on the acceptance of the Nobel Prize for Peace (December 10, 1989, Oslo, Norway), in *Ocean of Wisdom*, p. x. "It may be more than human . . ." in "Prophet of Middle Way," by Dennis Hevesi, *New York Times*, October 6, 1989, p. A6. "We must complement . . . ," remarks on accepting the Raul Wallenberg Congressional Human Rights Award, June 1989, in *Buddhist Peace Fellowship Newsletter*, Fall 1989, p. 4. "Part of the blame . . . ," at a conference in Newport Beach California, 1989; quoted by Katy Butler in "The Shadow of Buddhist America," *Common Boundary* (May-June 1990), p. 19. "Difficult question . . ." in *The Vajradhatu Sun*, Vol. 7, No. 2 (December 1984–January 1985), "Diplomat of Compassion," by Rick Fields, p. 4.

INDEX

This is a select index that includes names of people, organizations, and a few places.